Alan Rogers

2005

Britain
& Ireland

Quality camping & caravanning parks

INSPECTED CAMPSITES & SELECTED

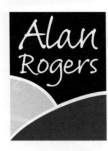

Compiled by: Alan Rogers Guides Ltd

Designed by: Paul Effenberg, Vine Design Ltd

Maps created by Customised Mapping (01769 560101)
contain background data provided by GisDATA Ltd
Maps are © Alan Rogers Guides and Gis DATA Ltd 2004

Published by: Alan Rogers Guides Ltd,
Spelmonden Old Oast, Goudhurst, Kent TN17 1HE
www.alanrogers.com Tel: 01580 214000

British Library Cataloguing-in-Publication Data:
A catalogue record for this book is available from the
British Library.

ISBN: 0-9545271-1-9

Printed in Great Britain by The Westdale Press Limited

CONTENTS

the Alan Rogers
approach

IT IS NEARLY 40 YEARS SINCE ALAN ROGERS PUBLISHED THE FIRST CAMPSITE GUIDE THAT BORE HIS NAME. SINCE THEN THE RANGE HAS EXPANDED TO SIX TITLES WITH GUIDES TO ITALY AND SPAIN & PORTUGAL ADDED IN 2004, AND A NEW GUIDE TO CENTRAL EUROPE AND CROATIA FOR THIS YEAR. WHAT'S MORE, ALAN ROGERS GUIDES ARE FAST BECOMING A FORCE TO BE RECKONED WITH IN HOLLAND TOO: ALL SIX TITLES ARE ALSO AVAILABLE IN THE NETHERLANDS, STOCKED BY WELL OVER 90% OF ALL DUTCH BOOKSHOPS.

There are over 5,000 camping and caravanning parks in Britain and Ireland of varying quality: this guide contains impartially written reports on almost 500, including some of the very finest, each being individually inspected and selected. All the usual maps and indexes are also included, designed to help you find the choice of park that's right for you. We hope you enjoy happy and safe travels – and some pleasurable 'armchair touring' in the meantime!

INDEPENDENT AND HONEST

Whilst the content and scope of the Alan Rogers guides have expanded considerably since the early editions, our selection of campsites still employs exactly the same philosophy and criteria as defined by Alan Rogers in 1988.

'warts and all'

Firstly, and most importantly, our selection is based entirely on our own rigorous and independent inspection and selection process. Campsites cannot buy their way into our guides – indeed the extensive Report which is written by us, not by the site owner, is provided free of charge so we are free to say what we think and to provide an honest, 'warts and all' description. This is written in plain English and without the use of confusing icons or symbols.

" ...the campsites included in this book have been chosen entirely on merit, and no payment of any sort is made by them for their inclusion."
Alan Rogers, 1968

INSPECTED SINCE 1968 & SELECTED

A question of quality

The criteria we use when inspecting and selecting parks are numerous, but the most important by far is the question of good quality. People want different things from their choice of campsite so we try to include a range of campsite 'styles' to cater for a wide variety of preferences: from those seeking a small peaceful campsite in the heart of the countryside, to visitors looking for an 'all singing, all dancing' park in a popular seaside resort. Those with more specific interests, such as sporting facilities, cultural events or historical attractions, are also catered for.

The size of the park, whether it's part of a chain or privately owned, makes no difference in terms of it being required to meet our exacting standards in respect of its quality and it being 'fit for purpose'. In other words, irrespective of the size of the park, or the number of facilities it offers, the essentials (the welcome, the pitches, the sanitary facilities, the cleanliness and the general maintenance) must all be of a high standard.

Expert opinions

We rely on our dedicated team of Site Assessors, all of whom are experienced campers, caravanners or motorcaravanners, to visit and recommend parks. Each year they travel some 100,000 miles around Europe inspecting new campsites and re-inspecting the older ones. Our thanks are due to them for their enthusiastic efforts, their diligence and integrity and their commitment to the philosophy of the Alan Rogers Guides.

We also appreciate the feedback we receive from many of our readers and we always make a point of following up complaints, suggestions or recommendations for possible new parks. Of course we get a few grumbles too – but it really is a few, and those we do receive usually arrive at the end of the high season and relate mainly to overcrowding or to poor maintenance during the peak school holiday period.

Please bear in mind that although we are interested to hear about any complaints we have no contractual relationship with the campsites featured in our guides and are therefore not in a position to intervene in any dispute between a reader and a campsite. If you have a complaint about a campsite featured in our guides the first step should be to take the matter up with the site owner or manager whilst on the campsite.

Widely regarded as the 'Bible' by site owners and readers alike, there is no better guide when it comes to forming an independent view of a campsite's quality. When you need to be confident in your choice of campsite, you need the Alan Rogers Guide.

- ✔ Parks only included on merit
- ✔ Parks cannot pay to be included
- ✔ Independently inspected, rigorously assessed
- ✔ Impartial reviews
- ✔ 36 years of expertise

Written in plain English, our guides are exceptionally easy to use, although a few words of explanation may be helpful. For England we have used official Tourist Board Regions and the counties within them. For Wales, Scotland and Ireland (North and South) we use the counties.

Indexes

Our three indexes allow you to find parks by their number and name, by region and park name, or by the town or village where the park is situated. See also the handy Quick Reference sections at the back.

Campsite Maps

The maps at the back relate to the geographical areas and will help you identify the approximate position of each campsite. The colour of the campsite name indicates whether it is open all year or not.

Tourist Board area

The Reports – *Example of an entry*

Number **Park name**

Postal Address (including county)

A description of the park in which we try to give an idea its general features – its size, its situation, its strengths and its weaknesses. This column should provide a picture of the park itself with reference to the facilities that are provided and if they impact on its appearance or character. We include details on pitch numbers, electricity (with amperage), hardstandings etc. in this section as pitch design, planning and terracing affects the park's overall appearance. Similarly we include reference to pitches used for caravan holiday homes, chalets, and the like. Importantly at the end of this column we indicate if there are any restrictions, e.g. no tents, no children, naturist sites.

Facilities	Directions
Lists more specific information on the park's facilities, as well as certain off site attractions and activities.	Separated from the main text in order that they may be read and assimilated more easily by a navigator en-route. Bear in mind that road improvement schemes can result in some road numbers being altered. Websites like **www.mappy.com** and others give detailed route plans.

At a glance

Welcome & Ambience	✓✓✓✓✓	Location	✓✓✓✓✓
Quality of Pitches	✓✓✓✓✓	Range of Facilities	✓✓✓✓

Our inspectors grade each site out of five, giving a unique indication of certain key criteria that may be important when making your decision.

Charges 2005

Reservations

Including contact details

Open

Park opening dates.

Facilities

Toilet blocks: We assume that toilet blocks will be equipped with British style WCs, washbasins with hot and cold water and hot showers with dividers or curtains, and will have all necessary shelves, hooks, plugs and mirrors. We also assume that there will be an identified chemical toilet disposal point, and that the campsite will provide water and waste water drainage points and bin areas. If not the case, we comment. We mention certain features that some readers find important: washbasins in cubicles, facilities for babies, facilities for those with disabilities and motorcaravan service points. Readers with disabilities are advised to contact the park of their choice to ensure that facilities are appropriate to their needs.

Shop: Basic or fully supplied, and opening dates.

Bars, restaurants, takeaway facilities and entertainment: We try hard to supply opening and closing dates (if other than the campsite opening dates) and to identify if there are discos or other noisy entertainment.

Children's play areas: Fenced and with safety surface (e.g. sand, bark or pea-gravel).

Swimming pools: If particularly special, we cover in detail in the first column but reference is always included in the second column. Opening dates, charges and levels of supervision are provided where we have been notified.

Leisure facilities: For example, playing fields, bicycle hire, organised activities and entertainment.

Dogs: If dogs are not accepted or restrictions apply, we state it here. Check the quick reference list at the back of the guide.

Off site: This briefly covers leisure facilities, tourist attractions, restaurants, etc nearby.

At a glance: All Alan Rogers parks have been inspected and selected – they must meet stringent quality criteria. A campsite may have all the boxes ticked when it comes to listing facilities but if it's not inherently a 'good park' then it will not be in the guide.

These 'at a glance' ratings are a unique indication of certain key criteria that may be important when making your decision. Quite deliberately they are subjective and, modesty aside, are based on our inspectors' own expert opinions at the time of their inspection.

General Information

Charges: These are the latest provided to us by the parks. In those few cases where 2004 or 2005 prices are not given, we try to give a general guide.

Opening dates: Are those advised to us during the early autumn of the previous year – parks can, and sometimes do, alter these dates before the start of the following season, often for good reasons. If you intend to visit shortly after a published opening date, or shortly before the closing date, it is wise to check that it will actually be open at the time required. Similarly some parks operate a restricted service during the low season, only opening some of their facilities (e.g. swimming pools) during the main season; where we know about this, and have the relevant dates, we indicate it – again if you are at all doubtful it is wise to check.

Special Pitches: We note an ever increasing number of 'special' pitches under a variety of fancy names (for example, Executive, Panorama, Super). These provide a range of extra facilities such as waste water disposal, TV and phone connections, hardstanding, patios, etc. and they are often booked up well in advance. Readers interested in such pitches should contact the park concerned to check exactly what is provided. People with disabilities are also advised to telephone before turning up to ensure that facilities are appropriate to their particular needs. Special thanks are due to Chris and Gerry Bullock for continuing their work in advising on the facilities provided by parks for visitors with disabilities.

Whether you're an 'old hand' in terms of camping and caravanning or are contemplating your first trip, a regular reader of our Guides or a new 'convert', we wish you well in your travels and hope we have been able to help in some way. We are, of course, also out and about ourselves, visiting parks, talking to owners and readers, and generally checking on standards and new developments.

We wish all our readers thoroughly enjoyable Camping and Caravanning in 2005 – favoured by good weather of course!

The West Country is a diverse region of beautiful sandy beaches, steep craggy cliffs, desolate moors and rolling green hills. Home of clotted cream teas, it also boasts a range of historical and modern attractions, including the celebrated Eden Project.

The South West is comprised of:
Isles of Scilly, Cornwall, Devon, Somerset, Bath, Bristol, South Gloucestershire, Wiltshire and Dorset.

With its dramatic cliffs, pounded by the Atlantic ocean, and beautiful coastline boasting warm waters, soft sandy beaches and small seaside towns, Cornwall is one of England's most popular holiday destinations. The coast is also a surfers paradise, while inland the wild and rugged Bodmin Moors dominate the landscape. In Devon, the Dartmoor National Park has sweeping moorland and granite tors where wild ponies roam freely. Much of the countryside is gentle rolling green fields, dotted with pretty thatched cottages. The coastline around Torbay is known as the English Riviera which, due to its temperate climate, allows palm trees to grow. Stretching across West Dorset is the fossil-ridden Jurassic Coast. It is also home to Chesil Beach, Lyme Regis and Weymouth, which comes alive in summer when regular entertainments, including a carnival and firework displays, are held along the seafront. Famous for its cider and cheese, Somerset is good walking country, with plenty of walking trails in the Exmoor National Park, which also straddles Devon. Wiltshire's natural attractions include the Marlborough Downs, Savernake Forest and the River Avon. It also boasts one of the most famous prehistoric sites in the world, the ancient stone circles of Stonehenge.

Did you know?

Chesil Beach is an 18 mile stretch of fortress-like walls of pebbles, formed 12,000 years ago

There are numerous white horses carved into the landscape across the South West

The Jurassic Coast is a Natural World Heritage Site stretching 95 miles from Exmouth to Swanage

Cornish pasties originated as portable lunches for tin miners, fishermen and farmers to take to work

The Black Death entered England through the port in Weymouth in 1348

Britain's oldest complete skeleton, Cheddar Man, was buried in Gough's Cave 9,000 years ago

At 404 feet Salisbury Cathedral has the tallest medieval spire in the world

Rabbits are considered bad luck on Portland, even the word is taboo

Places of interest

Bath: World Heritage Site full of Roman and Georgian architecture, elegant streets such as the Circle and Royal Crescent, Roman baths

Bristol: steeped in maritime history with the world's first great Ocean Liner; Brunel's Clifton Suspension bridge; range of museums and art galleries

Cornwall: seaside town of St Ives; Land's End; Eden Project; Penzance and St Michael's Mount

Devon: popular seaside resorts of Torquay, Paignton and Brixham; cities of Exeter and Plymouth

Somerset: Weston-Super-Mare; Wells Cathedral; Cheddar Gorge and Wookey Hole caves

West Dorset: Dorchester, home of Thomas Hardy; Isle of Portland; Abbotsbury village, with swannery

Wiltshire: Salisbury; Glastonbury; Longleat manor house and safari park

tip

BETWEEN SEPT-NOV, SOMERSET TOWNS AND VILLAGES COME ALIVE WITH FIREWORKS, STREET ENTERTAINMENT AND COLOURFUL FLOATS AS THE ILLUMINATED CARNIVALS TAKE PLACE.

WIN A FUN FILLED HOLIDAY FOR FOUR!

Families or couples looking for superb camping and touring in the West Country need look no further than the Woolacombe Bay Holiday Parcs in North Devon. Family owned and run, these four award winning parcs are situated in idyllic National Trust surroundings with stunning sea views, close to 3 miles of blue flag beach. They offer tree lined camping parcs, grass and hard standing pitches, sauna, steam room and individual showers plus electric hook-ups, laundry facilities and on-site shops for all your requirements.

In addition to the camping and touring facilities you can choose from luxury lodges, apartments and holiday homes in superb settings. With a selection of bars and restaurants on site you can eat out and have fun every night whilst the free entertainment can only add to your holiday.

Each of the four parcs has its own unique atmosphere.

The Golden Coast Parc offers a lively holiday with lots to see and do. The superb accommodation is complemented by many FREE facilities and guarantees a holiday to remember.

The Woolacombe Bay Parc is set in an area of outstanding natural beauty overlooking the sea. Its holiday homes and stunning campsite are perfect for a quieter holiday with all the facilities you could want.

Twitchen Holiday Parc offers superb camping, touring and holiday homes in delightful National Trust surroundings and is perfect for a relaxing holiday.

Whilst Easewell Parc specialises in camping and touring in stunning surroundings, complemented by its very own golf club.

Choose the parc to suit your requirements then enjoy all the facilities including:
- 10 PIN BOWLING • Golf • Crèche
- 17th Century Inn • Restaurants
- Indoor Bowls

Plus Free:
- 10 Pools • Water Slides • Health Suite
- Nightly Entertainment • Tennis
- Kid's Indoor and Outdoor Play Areas and of course the ever popular 'Billy Beachball Children's Club'.

Win a Holiday for four people by entering our PRIZE DRAW.

Q: How many fun filled Holiday Parcs are there at Woolacombe Bay Holiday Parcs?

Answers on a postcard please to:
Alan Rogers Competition, Woolacombe Bay Holiday Parcs, Woolacombe, North Devon EX34 7HW

Be sure to include your name and address.
Closing date: June 30th 2005

So much to see
So much to do

WOOLACOMBE BAY

Telephone:
01271 870 343
for a brochure or visit www.woolacombe.com
for full details of all the parcs and our latest offers.

LUNDY ISLAND

Lundy lies in the Bristol Channel, about 11 miles from the coast of North Devon.

Three miles long and half a mile wide, this granite crop rises 400 feet above sea level and is a place of outstanding natural beauty, with tremendous views of England, Wales and the Atlantic.

An Island of contrasts, Lundy has dramatic rugged terrain on its west side, but more sheltered aspects to the east means a gentler coastline, with grassy slopes, trees and many types of wild flower, including the rare Lundy cabbage.

Lundy is never crowded, even in the height of summer. In a place of wide spaces and big skies, without roads, cars or pollution, simply walking is a profound pleasure. Lundy has a milder climate than the mainland, with more sunshine and less rain.

Lundy has a tempestuous history. It was a notorious pirate lair and to control the island Henry III built the castle in 1244. In the 16th Century, as shipping increased, piracy flourished again even though the Elizabethan Admiral, Sir Richard Grenville, owned the island. During the civil war Lundy held out for the king long after support from the mainland had surrendered and later, in a particularly infamous period, convicts worked the island. In the 19th century it became respectable at last. The Reverend Hudson Heaven built the church and Lundy became the Kingdom of Heaven.

Today only a few people live on the island. Lundy is financed and administered by the Landmark Trust, an independent charity that acquires and restores buildings, so that visitors have the opportunity to visit often remote and beautiful places such as Lundy.

People return time and again to the simple pleasure that Lundy affords.

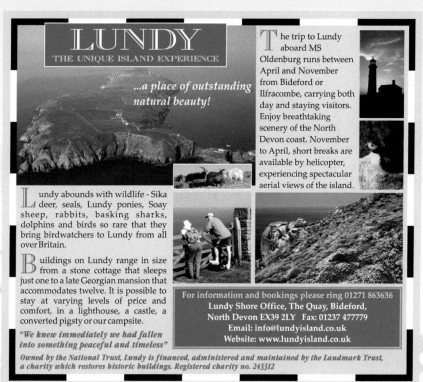

UK0470 Little Trevarrack Tourist Park

Laity Lane, Carbis Bay, St Ives TR26 3HW (Cornwall)

This traditional Cornish park covers 16 acres, with views from the top of the site across St Ives bay towards Hayle and the surrounding countryside. It is now being updated by Neil Osborne, son of the owners of Polmanter Park. There are 233 pitches, in four open fields (the top ones with gentle slopes), 168 with 16A electricity. Bushes have been planted which will in time form hedging to provide individual type pitches. Developments for 2005 include a new entrance, reception, play area and games room and there are plans to add caravan holiday homes. Carbis Bay is less than a mile and in high season a bus runs hourly into St Ives (10.00-23.30 hrs). This is a developing park which will provide a quiet, peaceful base from which to explore St Ives and the southern tip of Cornwall.

Facilities

The large, central toilet block is modern and well equipped. Dishwashing sinks under cover. New baby room. Laundry. Games room. Play area and play field. Putting. No kites allowed. Off site: Supermarket, fish and chips and pasta restaurants nearby. Fishing 1 mile. Golf and riding 2 miles.

Open

1 May - 17 September.

At a glance

Welcome & Ambience	✓✓✓✓	Location	✓✓✓✓
Quality of Pitches	✓✓✓✓	Range of Facilities	✓✓✓

Directions

Follow signs for St Ives and take A3074 at Carbis Bay. Site is signed on left opposite junction to Carbis Bay beach. Follow road for 150 yds, cross small crossroads and site is 250 m. on right. O.S.GR: SW52737

Charges 2004

Per unit incl. 2 persons	£ 8.50 - £ 14.00
child (3-15 yrs)	£ 1.75 - £ 2.50
electricity	£ 2.50
dog (max. 2)	free - £ 1.50

Reservations

Made with deposit of £25 per week booked.
Tel: 01736 797580. Email: littletrevarrack@hotmail.com

UK0030 Ayr Holiday Park

Higher Ayr, St Ives TR26 1EJ (Cornwall)

On first arrival Ayr Park seems to be all caravan holiday homes, but behind them, with marvellous views over St Ives Bay and Porthmeor beach, is a series of naturally sloping fields providing 40 touring pitches. Level, hard-core, terraced areas and hardstandings provide places for motorcaravans and caravans, 23 serviced and 40 with electricity (16A) on grass. An extra field for tents is open in July and August. This is a popular park with St Ives centre and supermarkets within easy walking distance, as is the new Tate Gallery. There is direct access to the coastal footpath.

Facilities

A new toilet block will be in place for 2005 (under construction when we visited). Motorcaravan point. Games room with pool table and TV, hot drinks and snack machines. Adventure play area and football field. One dog per pitch, up to medium size, is permitted but contact the park as dogs are not allowed on St Ives beaches in high season. Off site: Spa shop nearby.

Open

All year.

At a glance

Welcome & Ambience	✓✓✓✓	Location	✓✓✓✓✓
Quality of Pitches	✓✓✓✓	Range of Facilities	✓✓✓✓

Directions

After leaving the A30 turn left on A3074 at miniroundabout following signs for St Ives for heavy vehicles (not town centre). In 2 miles join B3311 and then B3306 about 1 mile from St Ives (octagonal building on left). Turn left at mini-roundabout and park is 600 yds at Ayr Terrace. O.S.GR: SW515388.

Charges 2004

Per adult	£ 2.50 - £ 4.25
child (5-16 yrs)	£ 1.20 - £ 2.00
pitch	£ 6.00 - £ 16.50

Reservations

Made with £35 deposit. Tel: 01736 795855.
Email: recept@ayrholidaypark.co.uk

UK0040 Trevalgan Holiday Farm

Trevalgan Farm, St Ives TR26 3BJ (Cornwall)

Trevalgan is now owned by the same family that own Ayr Holiday Park. We understand that it will be run on very much the same lines as it has been, although electricity points, etc. will be increased. It is a quiet, traditional style of park, located on the cliffs 1.5 miles west of bustling St Ives. There are 120 clearly marked pitches (at least 43 with 16A electricity) in two level fields edged by Cornish stone walls - it could be a little exposed on a windy day. The park is very popular with walkers with direct access to the coastal path. It is a 45 minutes walk to St Ives. A member of the Countryside Discovery group.

Facilities

A purpose built toilet block has curtained washbasins, plus a baby room, laundry and washing up, and even a hot drinks machine. Small shop (1/6-15/9). Takeaway (July/Aug), popular for breakfast or suppers. Gas available. Games field, play area and crazy golf. Games room in a barn with table tennis, pool and a comfortable upstairs TV room. Off site: Fishing 3 miles, bicycle hire 8 miles, riding and golf within 2 miles. In July/Aug. bus service once a day from the park to St Ives (10 am. returning at 5 pm).

At a glance

Welcome & Ambience	✓✓✓✓	Location	✓✓✓✓
Quality of Pitches	✓✓✓	Range of Facilities	✓✓✓

Directions

Approach site down a narrow Cornish lane from the B3306 St Ives - Lands End road. O.S.GR: SW490400.

Charges 2004

Per unit incl. 2 persons, electricity	£ 10.00 - £ 18.50
child (5-16 yrs)	£ 1.20 - £ 2.00
dog	£ 1.00

Reservations

Contact park. Tel: 01736 796433.
Email: trevalgan@aol.com

Open

Easter - 30 September.

UK0050 Polmanter Tourist Park

Halestown, St Ives TR26 3LX (Cornwall)

Polmanter is a good example of a sympathetic conversion of a farm from agricultural to leisure use and the Osborne family have developed the park well to provide an attractively laid out environment. The converted farm buildings provide a cosy bar lounge overlooking the heated swimming pool, toddler's pool and sunbathing area and good value meals are served. There is a family area with high chairs and a conservatory between the bar and the pool provides extra space for families (open all day, with a hot drinks machine). Occasional entertainment is organised in season. The 240 touring pitches (no caravan holiday homes) are well spaced in several fields with growing, but established, shrubs and hedges giving individual large pitch areas and connecting tarmac roads. There are 16 hardstandings, 190 electric hook-ups (16A) and 80 deluxe pitches with electricity, water and waste water. It is a busy park with a happy atmosphere within 1.5 miles of St Ives - a footpath leads from the park (20 minutes downhill) or there is a bus service from the park in high season (hourly, 10 am. - midnight). The park gates are closed midnight - 6.30 am. with outside parking. A member of the Best of British group.

Facilities

The toilet blocks vary - as the park has grown, so extra blocks have been added. All can be heated and still incorporate the ideas of the first block, which include a wall cupboard for clothes in each shower to keep them dry. A new block is planned for 2005 to include facilities for diabled visitors. Two family shower rooms (more planned). Baby room. Dishwashing sinks and good laundry provision. Motorcaravan service point. Well stocked shop (shop and pool Whitsun - mid Sept). Bar with food and family area (Easter, then Whitsun - mid Sept). Takeaway. Swimming pool. Tennis (charged). Minigolf. Play areas. Sports field. Games room with pool tables, table tennis and games machines. Off site: Golf 1 mile, fishing, riding, bicycle hire and boat launching within 2 miles. Indoor pool at St Ives. Dogs are banned from St. Ives beaches in high season.

At a glance

Welcome & Ambience	✓✓✓✓✓	Location	✓✓✓✓✓
Quality of Pitches	✓✓✓✓✓	Range of Facilities	✓✓✓✓✓

Directions

Take A3074 to St Ives from the A30 and then first left at a mini-roundabout taking 'Holiday Route' (B3311) to St Ives (Halestown). At T-junction turn right for Halestown, right again at the Halestown Inn then first left. O.S.GR: SW509392.

Charges 2004

Per unit incl. 2 persons, awning	£ 10.00 - £ 17.00
incl. mains services	£ 13.50 - £ 21.00
extra adult	£ 2.50 - £ 5.00
child (3-15 yrs)	£ 2.00 - £ 4.00
dog	free - £ 1.50
Camping Cheques accepted.	

Reservations

Made with £30 deposit. Contact site for details of min. stays. Tel: 01736 795640.
Email: reception@polmanter.com

Open

Easter - 31 October (full facilities to 10 Sept).

UK0070 Gwendreath Silver Sands Holiday Park

Kennack Sands, Ruan Minor, Helston TR12 7LZ (Cornwall)

Under new ownership, Silver Sands is a small, peaceful 'away-from-it-all' park in a remote part of the Lizard peninsula, the most southerly part of mainland Britain and an area of outstanding natural beauty. The park is only reached after passing Culdrose Naval Base and the Goonhilly Earth Station down a single track road. Silver Sands is tucked away behind two other holiday home parks (possible noise in season). A half mile footpath leads down through a small valley to the twin beaches of Kennack Sands (one is dog-free) divided by a small headland. This is generally an unspoilt walking area with the coastal path passing through and under the care of English Nature. The park itself has 14 caravan holiday homes, along with 36 touring pitches of which 20 have 5A electrical hook-ups. The pitches are large, attractively situated and divided into individual bays by growing flowering shrubs and bushes. The adjoining tent field has similar pitches (4 with electricity) where the shrubs are growing (some pitches are slightly sloping). A member of the Countryside Discovery group.

Facilities

The toilet block has been completely refurbished to provide modern facilities. En-suite room for disabled visitors, doubling as a family room. Some play equipment. An undeveloped three-acre field can be used for walking, kite flying, etc. Off site: Shop and restaurant 20 yards on the next park, pub within walking distance. Fishing 1 mile. Bicycle hire 5 miles. Boat launching 2 or 7 miles. Riding 5 miles. Golf 6 miles.

Open

Easter - mid September.

At a glance

Welcome & Ambience	✓✓✓✓✓	Location	✓✓✓✓
Quality of Pitches	✓✓✓✓	Range of Facilities	✓✓✓

Directions

From Helston take A3038 Lizard road. After Culdrose turn left on B3293 passing Goonhilly after 4 miles. At next crossroads turn right (Kennack Sands), continue for 1.5 miles then left to Gwendreath on single track road - site is 1 mile. O.S.GR: SW732170.

Charges 2004

Per unit incl. 2 persons, electricity	£ 11.00 - £ 16.50
child (3-13 yrs)	£ 1.10 - £ 1.80
dog	£ 1.10 - £ 1.80
Reductions for some bookings. No credit cards.	

Reservations

Made with 25% deposit, min. £30; balance on arrival. Tel: 01326 290631.
Email: enquiries@silversandsholidaypark.co.uk

13

UK0490 Mullion Holiday Park

Helston TR12 7LJ (Cornwall)

For those who enjoy plenty of entertainment, both social and active in a holiday environment, Mullion would be a good choice. This holiday park is situated on the Lizard peninsula with its sandy beaches and coves. It has all the trimmings - indoor and outdoor pools, super play areas, clubs, bars and a wide range of nightly entertainment. Recent developments include a new look 'Stargate Club' and a 'village square' with a bandstand. These amenities form the core of the park and are well organised and managed. The touring area past the holiday homes has a more relaxed atmosphere and is set on natural heathland with clumps of bramble and gorse which provide breaks and recesses making for a more informal layout. Linked by a circular gravel road, all 160 pitches are numbered, 10 with hardstanding and 105 with electricity (16A). Land drainage could be a problem if there is heavy continuous rain. A resident warden is now based at the entrance to the touring section. Eurotents for hire. There is much to see in the area including Goonhilly Satellite Station and Flambards Village, the theme park, Lizard Point and Lands End.

Facilities

A central modern toilet block is fully equipped and includes a baby unit and bath. It is supplemented with additional 'portacabin' style facilities for high season. Dishwashing sinks under cover, two laundry sinks and two washing machines. Large launderette in main complex. Freezer pack service. Large supermarket with off licence. Pub with family room, restaurant and takeaway (half board or breakfast options). Stargate Club with live shows and cabarets, big screen satellite TV. Excellent outdoor play areas (fenced). Toddlers' soft play area. Amusement arcade, bowling alley. Heated outdoor pool and paddling pool (26/5-8/9). Heated indoor fun pool with slide, both supervised. Sauna and solarium. Crazy golf, pitch and putt. Barbecue.

At a glance

Welcome & Ambience	✓✓✓✓	Location	✓✓✓✓
Quality of Pitches	✓✓✓	Range of Facilities	✓✓✓✓✓

Directions

From Helston take A3083 for The Lizard and continue for 7 miles. Site on left immediately after the right turning for Mullion. O.S.GR: SW698185.

Charges 2005

Per pitch	£ 12.50 - £ 23.50
electricity	£ 3.00
serviced pitch	£ 17.00 - £ 28.50
awning	£ 5.00
dog (one only)	£ 5.00

Half board or breakfast options available.

Reservations

Contact site. High season and Spr. B.H. bookings must be Sat. - Sat. Tel: 0870 4445344.
Email: touring@weststarholidays.co.uk

Open

22 May - 11 September.

See advertisement on page 101

UK0015 Rose Hill Touring Park

Porthtowan, Truro TR4 8AR (Cornwall)

The road down to Porthtowan takes you past tall chimneys, stark on the skyline, evocative of the Cornwall mining era. Porthtowan itself is a super little Cornish holiday village offering one of the UK's premier surfing beaches (with 'Blue Flag' status). Cafes, bars, surf schools - it has it all, but the park itself, situated back from the village and hidden from it, is something else again. It has a sheltered situation in a quite steep, wooded valley of broad leaf trees edged with natural vegetation that encourages wild life. We understand, for example, that the garlic mustard plant attracts the orange tipped butterfly and a tawny owl nests every year overlooking the park. The 50 grass pitches, terraced where necessary, are neatly cut and just fit in, with car space allocated where necessary. All pitches have 10/16A electricity and 8 have hardstanding. The village and beach are within easy walking distance (4 minutes) and should meet all your needs. It is wiser to leave your car on site. If you want to go further, St Austell with the Eden Project, Falmouth with the Maritime Museum and St Ives with the Tate Gallery are all nearby. In fact, Lands End is only 28 miles. The site is family run, very comfortable and well maintained in a delightful environment - good for families or couples, not suitable for huge twin axle caravans.

Facilities

Modern heated toilet block with coded access, very well equipped with some en-suite units. Facilities for disabled people but some up and down walking. Wet suit wash, also useful to wash sand off! Covered dishwashing sinks. Fully equipped laundry, sink useful as baby bath. Telephone – mobile phones do not work on site or in the village. Small licensed shop (some camping equipment; limited hours out of season). Crusty bread and croissants baked to order. Dogs not accepted July/Aug (dogs are not allowed on the beach Easter Sunday - 1 Oct). Off site: Large play area in village.

At a glance

Welcome & Ambience	✓✓✓✓✓	Location	✓✓✓✓✓
Quality of Pitches	✓✓✓✓	Range of Facilities	✓✓✓✓

Directions

From Chiverton Cross roundabout on A30 (near Redruth) take exit for St Agnes (B3277) and follow for about 1 mile. Turn left for Porthtowan, passing Beach Road (which goes into the village), and continue up hill to site 100 yds on left. O.S.GR: SW693472

Charges 2004

Per unit incl. 2 persons and car	£ 10.90 - £ 16.90
child (over 2 yrs)	£ 2.30
electricity	£ 2.50
dog (excl. July/Aug)	£ 1.80

Caravans not taken 16 July - 4 Sept.

Reservations

Made with deposit (£5 per day). Tel: 01209 890802.
Email: reception@rosehillcamping.co.uk

Open

1 April - 26 September.

UK0060 River Valley Country Park

Relubbus, Penzance TR20 9ER (Cornwall)

River Valley is a quiet park in the natural environment of a pleasant river valley. Run by Brian and Eileen Molson, it provides 150 large, well spaced touring pitches in small meadows or natural clearings. Most are clearly defined with shrubs, hedges or trees which have been planted to supplement where needed and in the more open areas to edge the pitch space thus giving your own individual area. Most pitches have electrical connections (15A) and hardstanding, with special sections for families, couples and tents. There are now 60 caravan holiday homes and log cabins, some privately owned, in more or less separate areas, beside the river at the far end of the park or on the hillside at the back. There is no playground, but tame ducks on the river will entertain. A fence separates the park from the river and there is a pleasant walk for 2.5 miles alongside it. St Michael's Mount is only 3 miles and can be reached by footpath. Much of the valley is a protected nature reserve and the park encourages wildlife by not using weed killers and by leaving parts uncut - badgers, foxes, herons, kingfishers and glow-worms are regular visitors. A member of the Best of British group.

Facilities

Three good quality, carefully maintained toilet blocks are well placed for all pitches. Two male and two female family shower rooms are in the block at the far end. Some private cabins for ladies and make-up room with hair dryers. Separate laundry facilities and baby bath. Covered dishwashing sinks. Motorcaravan service point. Shop. Dogs are not accepted from 2005. Off site: Bicycle hire 5 miles, riding or golf 3 miles.

Open

23 March - 31 October and Christmas.

Directions

From A30 at St Michaels Mount roundabout, take A394 towards Helston. At next roundabout take B3280 to Relubbus. In approx. 3 miles in village turn left just over a small bridge. O.S.GR: SW566320.

Charges 2004

Per unit incl. 2 adults	£ 7.00 - £ 12.00
incl. electricity	£ 8.50 - £ 13.50
extra person	£ 1.50 - £ 3.25
awning/pup tent	£ 1.00
dog	£ 1.50

Reservations

Any period with deposit (£20). Tel: 01736 763398. Email: rivervally@surfbay.dircon.co.uk

At a glance

Welcome & Ambience	✓✓✓✓✓	Location	✓✓✓✓✓
Quality of Pitches	✓✓✓✓✓	Range of Facilities	✓✓✓✓

UK0480 Boscrege Caravan Park

Ashton, Helston TR13 9TG (Cornwall)

A pretty little site hidden deep in the countryside, Boscrege will suit those who want a quiet peaceful base for their Cornish holiday. The main large touring field nestles at the foot of Tregonning Hill with its striking hill top cross, and has neatly cut grass with a gentle slope from the top. The pitches are generously spaced around the edge, backing on to hedging leaving plenty of room in the centre. Three small, attractive paddock areas, two with holiday homes (26), the other for tourers, complete the total provision of 51 pitches, 28 with 10A electricity. It is popular with couples and families with young children.

Facilities

The traditional style toilet block is fully equipped including a smaller basin for children (M/F). Dishwashing sinks, laundry sink, washing machine and dryer and microwave. Reception keeps emergency supplies (nearest shop at Godolphin). Two play areas for smaller children and central ball area. Amusement machines and pool table. TV room. Off site: Godolphin House and garden.

Open

Easter/1 April - 31 October.

Directions

From Helston take A394 for Penzance. At top of Sithney Common Hill turn right just before garage on B3302 (Hayle) road. Pass General Stores on left and take next left (Carleen/Godolphin). Continue to Godolphin village and turn left signed Ashton. Go up hill bearing left at top until camp signs where sharp left and straight on into lane to site. O.S.GR: 593305.

Charges 2004

Per unit	£ 6.50 - £ 13.50
electricity	£ 2.50

Reservations

Made with deposit (£35 p/week. Tel: 01736 762231. Email: enquiries@caravanparkcornwall.com

At a glance

Welcome & Ambience	✓✓✓✓	Location	✓✓✓✓
Quality of Pitches	✓✓✓	Range of Facilities	✓✓✓

UK0180 Carnon Downs Caravan & Camping Park

Carnon Downs, Truro TR3 6JJ (Cornwall)

Carnon Downs is an excellent all year park run personally and enthusiastically by Simon Valence, a very forward thinking owner. This is a thoughtfully laid out, level park with attractive hedging and flowering shrubs providing some pleasant bays for caravans. Gravel roads connect 120 pitches, 100 with electricity (10/15A) and 55 with hardstanding. Of these 29 are fully serviced, with 16 new ones being exceptionally large. Tent pitches, some with electricity, are well spaced around the outside of three level fields, the centre of one for goal posts and adventure-type play equipment, and one containing the mobile home used as reception. Here you will receive a warm welcome, a neatly presented layout plan of the park and a touring information pack including comprehensive details on walks and cycle paths leading from the park. Some of the park's amenities are to be found in the round-house next to the TV and information room. The round-house used to house the donkeys that turned the mill which once operated on the site! Although one side of the park is next to the A39 road, it is well screened with a band of mature woodland so noise should be minimal. This quiet, quality family park is well situated to explore the tip of Cornwall. A member of the Best of British group.

Facilities

An excellent modern, heated block provides 12 en-suite units and dishwashing. Two other well maintained toilet blocks can also be heated and provide good facilities, including some washbasins in cubicles and showers (unisex). Three very good family bath/shower rooms, one suitable for use by disabled people or families. Mother and toddler room (heated), including two baby sinks and full sized bath. Two laundries with freezers. Motorcaravan service point (ask at reception). Gas, newspapers and caravan accessories. General room with TV, library, table tennis and tourist information. Recycling centre. Caravan storage. Off site: 'Brewsters' pub 100 yds. Fishing 3 miles. Riding or bicycle hire 2 miles. Golf 1 mile. Walks direct from site.

At a glance

| Welcome & Ambience | ✓✓✓✓✓ | Location | ✓✓✓✓✓ |
| Quality of Pitches | ✓✓✓✓✓ | Range of Facilities | ✓✓✓ |

Directions

From Truro take A39 Falmouth road. After 3 miles, park entrance is directly off the Carnon Downs roundabout. O.S.GR: SW805406.

Charges 2004

Per unit incl. 2 persons, electricity	£ 12.00 - £ 17.50
extra adult	£ 2.00
child (5-14 yrs)	£ 1.70
all service hardstanding	£ 2.00

Reservations

Made with £20 deposit p/week. Tel: 01872 862283. Email: info@carnon-downs-caravanpark.co.uk

Open

All year.

UK0110 Calloose Caravan Park

Leedstown, Hayle TR27 5ET (Cornwall)

A family touring park, Calloose is quietly situated in an inland valley, covering 12 acres. It is about four miles from Hayle with an extra half a mile to the beaches beyond, nine to St. Ives on the north coast and six to Helston and Praa Sands on the south. Attractively landscaped with almost a tropical feel, but the terrain is dry and mainly flat with two slightly raised areas on terraces where 17 caravan holiday homes are located. There are 120 touring pitches (96 with 10A electricity, 8 with water and 28 with gravel hardstanding). Close together with individual markers, the pitches are mostly arranged round the perimeter with some free space in the middle. A heated swimming pool and separate paddling pool are neatly landscaped with a sunbathing terrace and access for disabled people. A large recreation block with a themed bar and a family room serving bar meals. Entertainment is organised each evening in the main season, including weekly barbecues in peak season. All public areas have wheelchair access. A popular park, booking is essential. The park is now opening for Christmas and the New Year.

Facilities

Both toilet blocks are well kept, providing washbasins in cubicles, a family shower room, baby room, en-suite unit for disabled visitors, dishwashing sinks under cover. Laundry room and first aid room. Well stocked shop and off-licence (including gas). Swimming pool (40 x 20 ft. open mid-May to mid-Sept). Bar with bar meals (daily in high season, slightly restricted in early season). Takeaway (mid-May - late Sept). TV lounge, pool table, games room with skittle alley and arcade machines. All-weather tennis court. Crazy golf (floodlit). Table tennis. Adventure playground. Sun lounger and mountain bike hire. Four acres of recreation fields include dog exercise fields, a full size football pitch and mountain bike scramble track. Off site: Village with shops, pubs, etc. within walking distance. Golf 4 miles, fishing 2 miles, riding 5 miles.

At a glance

| Welcome & Ambience | ✓✓✓✓ | Location | ✓✓✓✓✓ |
| Quality of Pitches | ✓✓✓✓ | Range of Facilities | ✓✓✓✓✓ |

Directions

From crossroads of B3280 and B3302 in Leedstown take the B3302 towards Hayle. First right, then left on 0.5 miles access road to park. O.S.GR: SW599353.

Charges 2004

Per unit incl. 2 persons	£ 9.00 - £ 15.00
extra person (over 3 yrs)	£ 1.00 - £ 3.00
electricity (10A)	£ 3.00
'super' pitch plus	£ 2.00
pup tent (max 1.8 x1.2m)	£ 1.00 - £ 2.00
dog	£ 1.00 - £ 2.50

Reservations

Made with £20 deposit per pitch, balance on arrival. Tel: 01736 850431.

Open

1 April - early November, plus Xmas and New Year.

UK0010 Chacewater Park

Cox Hill, Chacewater, Truro TR4 8LY (Cornwall)

For those who want to be away from the hectic coastal resorts and to take advantage of the peace and quiet of an 'adults only' park, this will be an excellent value-for-money choice. Chacewater has a pleasant rural situation and the site is run with care and attention by Richard Peterken and his daughters Debbie and Mandy. It provides 100 level touring pitches, all with electricity (10A) and 80 with hardstanding, in two large field areas (slight slope) edged with trees or in small bays formed by hedges. There are 29 serviced pitches (electricity, water, drainage and sewage) and an area for dog owners. The modern reception is not at the entrance but through the park to one side in a pleasant courtyard area.

Facilities
The main toilet block provides well equipped showers and two en-suite units. Dishwashing sinks under cover. Laundry room. Second fully equipped block near reception providing roomy showers open direct to outside. Gas supplies. Icepack service. Only adults are accepted (over 30 yrs). One dog only (by arrangement). Off site: Golf, riding and bicycle hire, all within 3 miles. Cornish tramways/railway coast to coast trail to walk or cycle nearby.

Open
1 May - 30 September.

At a glance
Welcome & Ambience	✓✓✓✓	Location	✓✓✓✓
Quality of Pitches	✓✓✓✓✓	Range of Facilities	✓✓✓

Directions
Approach either from the A390 road or from the A30. Park is 0.5 miles west of the village - follow signs. O.S.GR: SW742439.

Charges 2004
Per unit incl. 2 persons from	£ 9.95 - £ 12.95
extra person	£ 4.00
dog (one only)	£ 1.00

Weekly rates for pre- booked pitches. Discounts for senior citizens. Weekly rates for pre- booked pitches.

Reservations
Made with £15 deposit per week or part week, balance on arrival. Tel: 01209 820762.
Email: chacepark@aol.com

UK0130 Liskey Holiday Park

Greenbottom, Truro TR4 8QN (Cornwall)

Liskey is a quiet, family run park, pleasantly landscaped with rockery plants and well manicured grass - first impressions of loving care are carried all through the park. The main, slightly sloping camping area is beautifully landscaped with trees, shrubs and heathers and the level, well spaced pitches have good views across the countryside. The 79 touring pitches have 10A electricity and 12 are fully serviced with level hardstanding and a gravel area for awnings. There are also 23 caravan holiday homes in a semi-separate area and a few seasonal places. There is a feeling of spaciousness, mainly because the enthusiastic new owners do not try to fit in too many units. Breathable groundsheets are welcome on the grassy pitches. A pub with good food and real ale is only 600 yards away and buses to Truro pass the gate. Liskey is a good place for the family that can amuse itself without the need for discos and gaming machines.

Facilities
The central, very clean and well maintained toilet block can be heated and is supplemented by a small good second block. Some washbasins are in cubicles. Family bathroom (50p). Well equipped laundry room and dishwashing sinks under cover. Motorcaravan service facilities. Shop for basics at reception, plus excellent maps. Adventure playground. Volleyball and basketball nets. Table tennis, games field and mini fun golf course. Winter caravan storage. Off site: Coarse fishing 400 yards, bicycle hire 3 miles, riding 2 miles, golf 1 mile. Within 5 miles are beaches and facilities for tennis and boat launching. Truro supermarkets 3 miles.

At a glance
Welcome & Ambience	✓✓✓✓✓	Location	✓✓✓✓
Quality of Pitches	✓✓✓✓✓	Range of Facilities	✓✓✓

Directions
From the A30 take A390 to Truro. At next roundabout turn right (Threemilestone), then at mini-roundabout, right again towards Chacewater. Park is 600 yds on right past small business unit. O.S.GR: SW772452.

Charges 2004
Per unit incl. 2 persons, electricity	£ 11.00 - £ 14.00
extra person (over 3 yrs)	£ 2.00
serviced pitch	£ 1.50

Reservations
Made with £3 deposit per night booked or payment in full if less than 5 days. Tel: 01872 560274.
Email: enquiries@liskeyholidaypark.co.uk

Open
Mid-March - end October.

17

UK0120 Silverbow Park

Goonhavern, Truro TR4 9NX (Cornwall)

Silverbow has been developed by the Taylor family over many years and they are justifiably proud of their efforts. It is a select and spacious park seeking to encourage couples and quiet families with young children (no teenagers over 12). The Taylors believe Silverbow is a way of life and staying is an experience – they have certainly created a relaxed and tranquil atmosphere. Hard work, planting and landscaping has provided a beautiful environment set in 21 acres. There are 90 tourist pitches which are all of good size and include 69 'super' pitches in a newly developed area, with electricity, water and drainaway, which are even larger. Many are on a slight slope with some attractive views. There are also 15 park-owned, high quality leisure homes. Much free space is not used for camping, including an excellent sports area with two all-weather tennis courts (free coaching in season), two outdoor badminton courts, as well as wild meadow and wooded areas ideal for walks. A natural area with ponds has been created to encourage wildlife (Silverbow was the first in Cornwall to gain the coveted '5-year Bellamy Gold' award for conservation). The park is 2.5 miles from the long sandy beach at Perranporth (30 minutes walk away from traffic) and 6 miles from Newquay.

Facilities

Three good toilet blocks include private cabins for each sex, four family shower/toilet rooms, two accessible for wheelchairs, and a bath on payment. Enclosed dishwashing sinks. Laundry room. Motorcaravan services. Recycling bins. Free freezer service. Shop (mid May-mid Sept). Attractive, kidney shaped, heated swimming pool and small paddling pool (mid-May - mid-Sept) sheltered by high surrounding garden walls. Games room with pool table, table tennis and tourist information. Adventure playground and general play field. Tennis and badminton courts. Short mat bowls. Mountain biking from the park (but no bikes on site). Off site: Gliding, riding and fishing nearby. Concessionary green fees available at Perranporth golf club. Pub within walking distance.

At a glance

Welcome & Ambience	✓✓✓✓✓	Location	✓✓✓✓✓
Quality of Pitches	✓✓✓✓	Range of Facilities	✓✓✓✓

Directions

Entrance is directly off the main A3075 road 0.5 miles south of Goonhavern. O.S.GR: SW781531.

Charges 2004

Per unit incl. 2 adults	£ 7.00 - £ 16.00
extra adult under 50 yrs	£ 3.00 - £ 6.00
extra child (2-12 yrs) or adult 50+	£ 2.50 - £ 4.50
full service pitch incl. electricity	£ 3.00
dog	free - £ 1.50

Children over 12 yrs with or without parents not accepted. Discounts available.

Reservations

Made with £20 p/week deposit (Sat. - Sat. only 17/7-21/8). Tel: 01872 572347.

Open

4 May - 28 September.

UK0510 Summer Valley Touring Park

Shortlanesend, Truro TR4 9DW (Cornwall)

Approached down a short single track road from the Truro - Perranporth road this is a quiet and mature, but very pleasant, small rural park. South-facing, the park consists of a large well kept grass area with reception and facilities to one side. A tarmac road circles this and mature trees edge the site providing shelter but still allowing rural views. Caravans go on the central area which slopes gently and is divided down the centre with more mature trees and shrubs. The pitches around the perimeter are semi-divided by shrubs and used more for tents. There is provision for 60 units of all types, 45 with electricity (10/16A). The owners live on site and provide a warm welcome. A Countryside Discovery site.

Facilities
A good quality, solid toilet block is well maintained with ladies to the left and men to the right, plus unisex showers. Some washbasins in cabins and one shower/toilet en-suite per sex. Dishwashing and laundry sinks are in the same building. Laundry facilities. Reception/licensed shop (basics) with freezer pack service (reduced hours out of main season). Gas supplies. Small play area. Off site: Village within walking distance with post office and pub. Fishing 2.5 miles. Golf 3 miles. Riding 5 miles. Bicycle hire 2.5 miles. Beach 6 miles (dogs are allowed away from the village end).

At a glance
Welcome & Ambience	✓✓✓✓	Location	✓✓✓✓✓
Quality of Pitches	✓✓✓✓	Range of Facilities	✓✓✓✓

Directions
From Truro take B3284 north, signed Perranporth for 2.5 miles. Site is signed on left just through the village of Shortlanesend. O.S.GR: SW 800479.

Charges 2004
Per unit incl. 2 adults, electricity	£ 9.50 - £ 12.00
child (3-16 yrs)	£ 1.00
dog	£ 0.25

Reservations
Made with deposit (£25 per week); balance on arrival. Tel: 01872 277878. Email: sv@summervalley.co.uk

Open
1 April - 31 October.

UK0090 Trethem Mill Touring Park

St Just-in-Roseland, St Mawes, Truro TR2 5JF (Cornwall)

St Mawes is a very popular, pretty village on the Roseland peninsula, which is itself an 'area of outstanding natural beauty'. Only three miles away, Trethem Mill is well placed for sailing, walking the coastal path around the peninsula, visiting the gardens of Trelissick or Heligan, or simply lazing on the nearby beaches. The Akeroyd family are proud of their park and work hard to keep it really well maintained. Trethem is 'strictly touring' with 84 pitches, 50 with 16A electricity and several classified as all-weather. The pitches are large, most on slightly sloping ground, with the lower field more level and sheltered. All are individual or in bays, divided by hedging (some still growing) giving your own area. Generally there is a good spacious feel, with a tarmac circular access road and careful landscaping (it is a mass of colour in season). The area around reception is particularly pretty where a small watermill has been built amongst the flowers - the sound of gently flowing water is very relaxing. Trethem Mill aims to attract couples and families looking for peace and tranquillity, without a bar and on site entertainment.

Facilities
The central toilet block is of a very high standard and kept spotlessly clean. Heated in cooler weather, it is well equipped. A room for disabled visitors doubles as a family room. Laundry and dishwashing sinks. Reception/shop, only small but well stocked and licensed. Freezer for ice packs (free). Motorcaravan services. Games room. Well equipped, fenced adventure playground (closed at 9 pm). Large field used as a recreation and ball game area. Extra field for dog walking. Off site: Fishing 1.5 miles. Boat launching 2 miles. Bicycle hire 4 miles. Golf 6 miles. Riding 8 miles.

At a glance
Welcome & Ambience	✓✓✓✓✓	Location	✓✓✓✓✓
Quality of Pitches	✓✓✓✓✓	Range of Facilities	✓✓✓

Directions
From Tregony follow A3078 to St Mawes. About 2 miles after passing through Trewithian, watch for caravan and camping sign. O.S.GR: SW863264.

Charges 2004
Per unit incl. 2 persons	£ 9.00 - £ 12.00
with electricity	£ 11.00 - £ 14.00
extra person	£ 2.50 - £ 3.50

Reservations
Made with £30 deposit. Tel: 01872 580504. Email: reception@trethem.com

Open
1 April - 13 October.

19

UK0140 Penrose Farm Touring Park

Goonhavern, Truro TR4 9QF (Cornwall)

Penrose Farm is a quality, family park for tourers only, with a quiet comfortable atmosphere on the edge of the village of Goonhavern. The park is level and sheltered, with the pitches spread over five fields with flower beds and bushes set amongst them. These colourful flowers and those at the entrance give the park a neat and well cared for feel. The enthusiastic owners, Alan and Sharman, take pride in the pitches and facilities they provide and enjoy getting to know their customers, many of whom return each year. Children have a well kept adventure playground and an indoor animal centre with guinea pigs, rabbits, chickens, fish, terrapins and birds to admire. There are 75 pitches with 16A electricity and 8 pitches with hardstanding (6 with electricity) and some seasonal places. Alan ensures that each unit has plenty of space and does not feel overcrowded. It is only a short walk to the village and its popular pub, and buses to Newquay stop in the village. The superb beach at Perranporth is only 2.5 miles. To retain the quiet family image, there are no plans for bars or entertainment and only couples and families are admitted.

Facilities

The fully equipped toilet block is well maintained and includes four excellent family rooms containing an adjustable shower, washbasin, WC and hairdryer. One of these is accessible for wheelchairs. Well equipped laundry. Dishwashing sinks. Small shop (Easter, then May - Sept). Adventure playground. Caravan storage. Bicycle hire arranged. Off site: Fishing or riding 0.5 miles, golf 1 mile.

Open

1 April - 31 October

At a glance

Welcome & Ambience	✓✓✓✓✓	Location	✓✓✓✓✓
Quality of Pitches	✓✓✓✓✓	Range of Facilities	✓✓✓✓

Directions

Take A30 from Exeter past Bodmin and Indian Queens. Just after wind farm take B3285 to Perranporth. Park is on the left as you enter Goonhavern village. O.S.GR: SW790535.

Charges 2004

Per unit incl. 2 persons	£ 9.00 - £ 13.50
extra person (5 yrs and over)	£ 3.00 - £ 3.50
electricity (16A)	£ 2.70 - £ 3.00
dog	free - £ 2.00
Less 50p for over 60s if booked.	

Reservations

Made with £30 deposit. Tel: 01872 573185.

Penrose Farm

- Quiet family park - no club/bar
- Families & couples only
- Award winning private superloos
- Animal Centre
- Adventure play area
- Just over 2 miles from Perranporth beach
- Good spacing
- Level & sheltered

From £8 per night (except Peak Season) for ALAN ROGERS readers

Goonhavern, Nr Truro, Cornwall Tr4 9QF

Tel: 01872 573 185 www.penrosefarm.co.uk

UK0450 Pennance Mill Farm Chalet & Camping Park

Maenporth, Falmouth TR11 5HJ (Cornwall)

Pennance Mill Farm has been in the hands of the Jewell family for three generations and is listed as a typical Cornish farmstead in an Area of Outstanding Natural Beauty and you can enjoy the woodland walk with 200 year old beech trees. In the high season country games and barbecue evenings are organised in keeping with the relaxed and friendly atmosphere generated by the owners. The camping area is in three sheltered south-facing and fairly level fields with rural views and providing for 75 pitches (40 with 16A electricity and 3 hardstandings). Caravans are accepted but this is not a site for those who like neat manicured lawns and flower beds. An old mill wheel reminds one of the site's origins and you book in at the farmhouse. Continuing on past the site you come to the sandy beach at Maenporth.

Facilities

The two toilet blocks are fully equipped. The first near the entrance is the original one but it is well kept with good hot water, washing machine, dryer, laundry and dishwashing sinks. The block in the top meadow is more modern, heated and includes dishwashing sinks. Small farm shop. Gas available. Small play meadow with new play equipment. Table tennis. Off site: New Maritime Museum. Tennis courts, golf course and pitch and putt within walking distance. Coastal footpath to the Helford River.

At a glance

Welcome & Ambience	✓✓✓✓	Location	✓✓✓✓
Quality of Pitches	✓✓✓	Range of Facilities	✓✓✓

Directions

From Truro, follow signs for Falmouth on A39. At first roundabout pass Asda then right at next roundabout signed Maenporth. Follow camping signs for 1.5 miles and down the hill to site. O.S.GR: SW789307.

Charges 2005

Per adult	£ 3.00 - £ 4.00
child (over 3 yrs)	£ 1.00 - £ 1.50
pitch	£ 4.00 - £ 6.00

Reservations

Contact park. Tel: 01326 317431.

Open

Easter - November.

UK0160 Newperran Holiday Park

Rejerrah, Newquay TR8 5QJ (Cornwall)

This is a large, level park in rural Cornish countryside. Being on high ground makes it quite open but also gives excellent views of the coast and surrounding district. The owners, Keith and Christine Brewer, have plans to improve and develop the site in the next few years adding caravan holiday homes and have already added a new pub, shop and reception. Newperran is only 2.5 miles from Perranporth beach, but there is a free heated swimming pool on site and a range of facilities. It has a licensed bar and restaurant open every evening, more in high season. The traditional layout of the park provides a number of flat, well drained, hedged meadows divided into over 250 individual pitches. Some fields have larger and reservable spaces with more free space in the middle. There are 160 electrical connections (10A) including 15 'all-service' pitches. This is a park with plenty of space and activites for families.

Facilities

Toilet facilities comprise four clean blocks, two heated. Most washbasins are in cabins, there are two bathrooms, baby room with sink and changing mat, hairdressing room and a unit for disabled visitors. Dishwashing sinks. Launderette. Good self-service licensed shop. Licensed bar and restaurant with takeaway (both B.Hs and main season, as required in low season). Outdoor heated swimming pool with paddling pool (Whitsun - Sept). TV room. Adventure playground and separate toddlers play area. Games room with table tennis, pool tables and games machines. TV room. Crazy golf. Off site: Riding or golf 2 miles. Fishing 1 mile. Goonhavern village within walking distance with pubs and post office.

At a glance

Welcome & Ambience	✓✓✓✓	Location	✓✓✓✓
Quality of Pitches	✓✓✓✓	Range of Facilities	✓✓✓✓

Directions

Turn off A3075 to west at camping sign 7 miles south of Newquay and just north of Goonhavern village. O.S.GR: SW794546.

Charges 2004

Per adult	£ 3.95 - £ 6.50
child (3-16 yrs)	£ 2.50 - £ 3.95
pitch incl. electricity	£ 2.75
serviced pitch plus	£ 6.25
dog	£ 1.00 - £ 1.50

Reservations

Advised in high season; made with £25 p/w deposit and £2.50 fee. Tel: 0845 1668407.
Email: holidays@newperran.co.uk

Open

Easter - October.

Peaceful family holiday park, renowned for its spacious, flat perimeter pitching, with breathtaking open countryside and sea views.

Call Keith or Christine Brewer for a Free Colour Brochure

- Modern heated toilet blocks
- free showers • bathrooms
- baby rooms • disabled facilities • launderette
- premium all-service pitches
- shop/off licence
- cafe/bar • entertainments
- TV room • games room
- crazy golf • aviary
- adventure playground
- toddlers play area
- outdoor heated swimming pool with sunbathing terraces

Luxury Holiday Units for Hire

Rallies Welcome

Rejerrah, Newquay,
Cornwall TR8 5QJ
Tel: 0845 1668407 (local rate)
Fax: 01872 571254
www.newperran.co.uk

 ▶ ▶ ▶

UK0200 Newquay Holiday Park

Newquay TR8 4HS (Cornwall)

Part of the Parkdean Group, Newquay Holiday Park lies peacefully on a terraced hillside only just outside the town, 2 miles from the beaches and town centre. Its main feature is an attractively laid out group of three heated swimming pools with a giant water slide (lifeguards in attendance) and surrounding 'green' sunbathing areas overlooked by a terrace for cool drinks. With a large proportion of caravan holiday homes (for let), there are still 212 marked pitches for touring units in a series of hedged fields, some sloping. Some fields are just for caravans, others are for tents. Most pitches are individual ones marked out by lines on ground but with nothing between them. Electricity points (16A) are provided for caravans and tents, plus 10 special 'star' pitches with hardstanding, water and drainage. Family entertainment is provided each night with live music, discos etc. in the site's Fiesta Club which also has a bar, TV lounge and games room with pool and snooker tables (all open when the site is open). A bus service runs to Newquay from the main road at the site entrance.

Facilities

Two good-sized, modern toilet blocks include a unit for disabled visitors and baby bath. An extra block is opened for the main season when facilities may be under pressure. Covered dishwashing sinks. Launderette. Well stocked self-service shop (gas available at reception). Bar/lounge with Sky TV. New café/restaurant with all day food also 'pub grub' in evenings (all season good value). Outdoor pool complex with slide (and lifeguards). Pitch and putt and crazy golf. Playground for little ones and adventure play area for older children. Children's club. Recreation field for football and volleyball. Amusement arcade. Pool tables. Dogs or other pets are not accepted.

At a glance

Welcome & Ambience	✓✓✓✓	Location	✓✓✓✓
Quality of Pitches	✓✓✓✓	Range of Facilities	✓✓✓✓✓

Directions

Park is east of Newquay on A3059 road 1 mile east of junction with A3058. O.S.GR: SW853626.

Charges 2004

Per unit incl. 4 persons	£ 7.00 - £ 23.00
with services	£ 9.00 - £ 28.00
extra person	
(over 3 yrs; max.4 people)	free - £ 2.00
awning	free - £ 2.00

Reservations

Advised for peak season and made with deposit; contact park for details. Tel: 01637 871111. Email: enquiries@parkdean.com

Open

Easter - October.

UK0310 Trekenning Tourist Park

St Columb Major, Newquay TR8 4JF (Cornwall)

Trekenning's new owners are working hard to develop a popular park with a range of good facilities. Easy access just off the A39 roundabout at St Columb Major leads to a large sloping field with neatly cut grass and all the facilities tucked into the top corner. There are 75 pitches, 68 with 10A electricity. Some have been levelled, others are tucked away at a lower level shaded by tall trees. A well hidden tent field with just a water point is edged by a wooded small stream. The star of the show is undoubtedly the kidney shaped pool and paddling pool which are in a garden-like setting with gazebos and sun loungers surrounded by lawn and overlooked by the patio bar at the top - lovely for summer evenings. The 'olde worlde' upstairs bar is a cosy feature for cooler times with a useful 'eatery' underneath. Entertainment is provided every night in the main season (for example, singers, quiz nights, Connect-4 nights, discos on Fridays). The A39 runs parallel to one side of the site, so there may be road noise.

Facilities

Two toilet blocks, one providing normal showers and vanity style washbasins, the other with two en-suite bathrooms (50p) and six large family showers, well refurbished. Laundry room. Covered dishwashing sinks. Shop for basics. Free freezer service. Play area. Outdoor pool with poolside bar(Whitsun - end Aug). Games room with table tennis and pool and some amusement machines. Characterful bar with curries, etc. served. New takeaway including breakfasts (B.Hs and July/Aug). Off site: Fishing 1 mile. Riding and golf 2 miles. Bicycle hire 6 miles.

At a glance

Welcome & Ambience	✓✓✓✓	Location	✓✓✓✓
Quality of Pitches	✓✓✓✓	Range of Facilities	✓✓✓✓✓

Directions

Take A3059 turning to Newquay from St Columb Major then turn immediately left; park is signed (this was the old road). O.S.GR: SW907625.

Charges 2004

Per adult	£ 4.00 - £ 6.00
child (3-15 yrs)	£ 1.50 - £ 4.00
electricity	£ 3.50
dog	£ 2.00

Reservations

Made with deposit (£20) and fee (£2). Tel: 01637 880462. Email: enquiries@trekenning.co.uk

Open

All year.

UK0170 Trevella Caravan & Camping Park

Crantock, Newquay TR8 5EW (Cornwall)

One of the best known and respected of Cornish parks with its colourful flower-beds and driveway (a regular winner of a 'Newquay in Bloom' award), Trevella is also one of the first to fill up and has a longer season than most. Well organised, the pitches are in a number of adjoining meadows, most of which are on a slight slope. Of the 250 pitches for touring units (any type), some 200 can be reserved and these are marked, individual ones. Over 200 pitches have electricity (10A), with 59 'premium' serviced pitches (with hardstanding, electricity and TV hook-ups, water, waste water, sewage). Trevella is essentially a quiet family touring park with the accent on orderliness and cleanliness; on-site evening activities are limited. Access is free to three fishing lakes, two on site (permits from reception); with some fishing instruction and wildlife talks for youngsters in season. There is a pleasant walk around the lakes, a protected nature reserve, and it is also possible to walk to Crantock beach but check the tides first. A member of the Best of British group.

Facilities

Kept very clean, three blocks provide sufficient coverage with individual washbasins in private cabins for ladies, hair-dressing room and baby room. Launderette. Well stocked supermarket and heated outdoor pool (both Easter - October). Freezer pack service. 'Nicky's Kitchen' offers hot dishes and snacks to take away or eat there, open late. Games room with pool tables and table tennis. Separate TV room. Crazy golf, large adventure playground, separate play and sports area and pets corner. Fishing. Off site: Shuttle bus service to Newquay in high season. Nearest beach is 0.5 miles on foot, 1 mile by car and Newquay is 2 miles. Pubs and restaurants at Crantock, 1 mile. Riding 1 mile, golf 3 miles.

At a glance

Welcome & Ambience	✓✓✓✓✓	Location	✓✓✓✓✓
Quality of Pitches	✓✓✓✓	Range of Facilities	✓✓✓✓

Directions

To avoid Newquay leave A30 or A392 at Indian Queens, straight over crossroads with A39 and A3058, left at A3075 junction and first right at camp sign. O.S.GR: SW802598.

Charges 2004

Per adult	£ 3.40 - £ 6.00
child (3-16 yrs)	£ 1.95 - £ 4.00
pitch incl. electricity	£ 2.75
with services	£ 6.00
dog	£ 0.70 - £ 1.30
Families and couples only.	

Reservations

Made with £20 deposit and £2 booking fee (16/7-27/8: Fri/Fri or Sat/Sat only) Tel: 01637 830308. Email: trevellapark@aol.com

Open

Easter - 31 October.

UK0530 Trethiggey Touring Park

Quintrell Downs, Newquay TR8 4LG (Cornwall)

Trethiggey is a garden-like park with a ten month season, set some three miles back from the busy Newquay beaches and night life. The 157 pitches are in sharp contrast to some of the large, open fields of some of the bigger sites, broken up by trees, shrubs and plants to provide a pleasant 'green' atmos-phere. With natural areas including a small wildlife pond and fishing lakes to enjoy, conservation is high on the agenda. There are 32 hardstandings and 94 numbered pitches have electricity (6/12A) with 12 caravan holiday homes interspersed amongst the touring pitches and a tent field open in main season. Some level pitches are formally arranged with others more informal on gently sloping grass. Facilities keep the informal touch with reception alongside the Trethiggey Trading Post which provides basic supplies, an off licence and a small library. A snack bar with covered eating area operates in the school holidays for breakfasts and simple evening meals, curries etc. with children catered for.

Facilities

The traditional style toilet block can be heated and is fully equipped, including an 'easy access' toilet/washbasin for disabled people, baby room, wetsuit washing point, laundry and dishwashing sinks. New toilet block (virtually complete when we visited) near the tent area provides en-suite toilet/washbasins, showers, unit for disabled people and a laundry room to increase facilities for high season. Games room with TV, 2 amusement machines and a pool table. Shop. Snack bar/takeaway. Play area and recreation field. Coarse fishing. Gates locked at midnight. Off site: All the delights of Newquay within 3 miles with nightly minibus service (book in shop). Pub within walking distance.

At a glance

Welcome & Ambience	✓✓✓✓	Location	✓✓✓✓
Quality of Pitches	✓✓✓✓	Range of Facilities	✓✓✓✓

Directions

Site is a few hundred yards south of roundabout where A393 crosses the A3058 at Quintrell Downs (beside the A3058). O.S. GR: SW846596.

Charges 2004

Per adult	£ 3.60 - £ 6.00
child (5-15 yrs)	free - £ 2.95
car	free - £ 1.00
pitch incl. electricity	£ 2.50
dog	£ 1.80 - £ 2.00
Min. stay 3 nights at B.Hs.	

Reservations

Made with £15 deposit per pitch, per week. Tel: 01637 877672.

Open

2 March - 2 January.

UK0210 Hendra Holiday Park

Newquay TR8 4NY (Cornwall)

Hendra is a long-established holiday park for the family that likes to be entertained, as the entertainment programme here is very comprehensive. There are comedians, show bands, cabaret, dancing, bingo, discos, plus entertainment and clubs for children. The 700 pitches are on various well mown, slightly sloping grass fields with country views and mature trees, some more sheltered than others. There are tarmac roads and lighting and 200 pitches have electricity (16A). Some landscaped hardstanding 'super' pitches have individual water, electricity, light, sewer drainage and satellite TV connections (dogs are not accepted on these pitches). There are caravan holiday homes for hire but they are separate from the tourers. The entrance and reception are very attractive with a mass of well tended flower beds which, along with the other facilities, form an attractive, village-like centre to the park. The 'star of the show' at Hendra is the Oasis complex consisting of an indoor fun pool with flumes, river rapids and beach. It is open to the public - really a mini water-park. The outdoor heated pool with grass sunbathing area is free to campers and activities are well catered for with a range of amenities. The park is only 1.5 miles from Newquay and its fabulous surfing beaches and a bus to the town passes the gate. Hendra welcomes families and couples.

Facilities

Three modern toilet blocks are fully equipped, including some facilities for babies and disabled visitors. Large launderette. Motorcaravan services. Gas supplies. Well stocked shop. Bars and restaurants, open all season (limited hours in early season), breakfast included. Pizzeria (main season only). Takeaway. Outdoor pool. Indoor pool complex (£2.20 per family group, max. 4 persons, under 5s free; timed sessions if busy). Various play areas including one for soft play. Tennis. Minigolf. Bowling. Off site: Fishing or riding 1 mile. Bicycle hire or golf 2 miles. Beach 1.5 miles.

Open

23 March - 31 October

At a glance

Welcome & Ambience	✓✓✓✓	Location	✓✓✓✓
Quality of Pitches	✓✓✓✓	Range of Facilities	✓✓✓✓✓

Directions

Park is on left side of A392 Indian Queens - Newquay road at Newquay side of Quintrell Downs. O.S.GR: SW833601.

Charges 2004

Per adult	£ 3.65 - £ 6.25
child (3-14 yrs)	free - £ 3.99
vehicle	£ 1.15
hardstanding pitch (electricity, water and drainage)	£ 3.95
'super' pitch (incl. chemical disposal, TV point, hardstanding, no dogs)	£ 8.50
dog	£ 3.00

Reservations

Made with deposit (£ 30) and fee (£3). Tel: 01637 875778. Email: enquiries@hendra-holidays.com

UK0220 Trevornick Holiday Park

Holywell Bay, Newquay TR8 5PW (Cornwall)

Trevornick, once a working farm, is now a modern, busy and well run family touring park providing a very wide range of amenities close to one of Cornwall's finest beaches. A modern reception with welcoming staff sets the tone for your holiday. The park is well managed with facilities and standards constantly monitored. It has grown to provide caravanners and campers (no holiday caravans but 68 very well equipped 'Eurotents') with 450 large grass pitches (350 with 10A electricity and 55 fully serviced) on five level fields and two terraced areas. There are few trees, but some good views. Providing 'all singing, all dancing' facilities for fun packed family holidays, the farm buildings now provide the setting for the Farm Club. Furnished in keeping, it has a bar and food, children's rooms and a cafeteria 'De Caff' with terrace and takeaway, plus much entertainment from bingo, quizzes to shows, discos and cabaret. The rest of the development provides a pool complex, an 18 hole golf course, with a small, quiet club house offering bar meals and lovely views out to sea and three fishing lakes. Next door is the Holywell Bay 'fun' park (reduced rates) and the sandy beach is five minutes by car. An innovative idea is the 'Hire shop' where it is possible rent anything you might have forgotten from sheets, a fridge, travel cot, etc. to a camera or a wet suit to catch the famous Cornish surf!

Facilities

Five toilet blocks of a standard modern design provide coin-operated showers (20p), a family shower room, two bathrooms (50p), baby bath, dishwashing, laundry facilities, and provision for disabled visitors. Well stocked shop with bread made on site (both from late May). Hire shop. Bars (with TV), restaurant, cafe and takeaway. Entertainment (nightly in season). Impressive pool complex with outdoor pool, paddling pool, sunbathing decks, solarium, sauna and massage chair. Super Fort Knox style adventure playground, crazy golf, Kiddies Club and indoor adventure play area (supervised for 2-8 yr olds at a small charge). Amusement arcade and bowling alley. Teenage meeting room. 18-hole pitch and putt with golf pro shop. Bicycle hire. Coarse fishing with three lakes. Dogs are accepted in one field only. Off site: Boat launching 4 miles, riding within 1 mile.

At a glance

Welcome & Ambience	✓✓✓✓✓	Location	✓✓✓✓✓
Quality of Pitches	✓✓✓✓	Range of Facilities	✓✓✓✓✓

Directions

From A3075 approach to Newquay - Perranporth road, turn towards Cubert and Holywell Bay. Continue through Cubert to park on the right. O.S.GR: SW776586.

Charges 2004

Per adult	£ 4.30 - £ 7.50
child (4-14 yrs)	£ 1.10 - £ 5.35
electricity	£ 3.50
'super' pitch incl. electricity	£ 7.50
dog	£ 2.00

Families and couples only. Many special discounts.

Reservations

Made with £ 30 deposit per week (Sat. to Sat. only July/Aug). Tel: 01637 830531. Email: bookings@trevornick.co.uk

Open

Easter - mid-September.

UK0150 Sea View International

Boswinger, Gorran Haven, St Austell PL26 6LL (Cornwall)

Sea View is one of the best examples of a well cared for, quality park and this is reflected in the number of awards it has won in the last 20 years. The enthusiastic new owners Mr and Mrs Royden are continually improving the park with the aim of providing quality camping for the discerning camper. Although somewhat exposed, the park is colourful with flower beds and flowering shrubs and has well manicured grass of exceptional quality. The area around the pool is particularly attractive, with sunbathing areas with free sun-beds on tiled terraces surrounded by flowers creating private little areas, all with magnificent views of the sea and the distant headland. An attractive covered, flowered walkway, created with hanging baskets, connects the two excellent toilet facilities which are topped by a handsome clock tower. There are no bars, restaurant or evening entertainment which seems to be the main reason many return year after year - booking for July/Aug. is advisable. Reception has a free ice machine and coffee - a nice touch. Many of the 163 large, level pitches have views, all have 16A electricity and 43 are fully serviced, including 12 hardstandings suitable for large motorhomes. There are 38 caravan holiday homes for hire in a separate area. Anyone not restricted by school holidays will find May and June a particularly good time to visit. The area is full of places to visit, not forgetting the safe beaches, one of which is only a half mile walk from the park. A member of the Best of British group.

Facilities

The toilet blocks are excellent - centrally positioned, well maintained, with good quality fittings and central heating. Large showers, baby baths, facilities for disabled visitors (two showers and WCs), and a hairdressing area, plus bathrooms (on payment). Smart dishwashing area with two small kitchens (one with a microwave, one with a mini-grill and hob) and a well equipped laundry. Motorcaravan service point with car wash. Shop and off-licence with gas (June-end Sept). Takeaway (Whit-mid Sept). Swimming pool open all season, heated end May-mid Sept. Large playing field - tennis, volleyball, badminton, football, putting green, table tennis, crazy golf, petanque, play area for under-7s, and adventure playground. Games room. Bicycle hire. Field for dog walks. Off site: Fishing 0.5 miles, boat launching 2 miles, riding 1 mile, golf 9 miles.

At a glance

Welcome & Ambience	✓✓✓	Location	✓✓✓✓✓
Quality of Pitches	✓✓✓✓✓	Range of Facilities	✓✓✓✓

Directions

From St Austell take B3273 towards Mevagissey; 1 mile before Mevagissey village turn right at Gorran and camp sign and continue towards Gorran for 5 miles. Fork right at sign and follow signs to park. O.S.GR: SW991412.

Charges 2004

Per unit incl. 2 persons, electricity	£ 12.00 - £ 25.00
incl. water and drainage	£ 12.00 - £ 27.00
extra adult	£ 2.00 - £ 5.00
child (5-14 yrs)	£ 2.00 - £ 4.00
dog (limited breeds and numbers)	£ 2.00

Reservations

Min 7 nights, w/e - w/e, 19/7-30/8. other times, any length, with £30 deposit and £2 fee. Tel: 01726 843425. Email: holidays@seaviewinternational.com

Open

1 April - 3 October.

UK0315 White Acres Holiday Park

White Acres Country Park, White Cross, Newquay TR8 4LW (Cornwall)

White Acres is an impressive park in a rural setting, inland from Newquay and is part of the Parkdean Group. The main emphasis here is on holiday homes and lodges which are well spaced around the park. A very popular and attractive feature, 15 coarse fishing lakes, complete with tackle shop, are in a woodland setting at the bottom of the site. This facility is also open to the public. There is provision for 40 touring units near the lakes, mostly on grass and level with 16A electricity, some hardstandings and 25 with water and drainage. There are some sloping tent pitches. The extensive facilities are arranged around the entrance with a leisure complex including indoor heated pool, sauna, jacuzzi, gym and an on-site beautician. A comprehensive entertainment programme caters for all the family with daytime clubs for under fives, 5-10 year olds and for teenagers. Ten pin bowling is an added attraction. This is a well organised park with lots going on to suit all ages. Should you tire of all that is on offer the popular resort of Newquay with its surfing beaches is five miles down the road and the Eden project is nearby.

Facilities

Two modern toilet blocks offer roomy shower cubicles which include washbasins, 2 baby rooms, unit for disabled visitors. Dishwashing sinks and launderette. Shop. Restaurant, pizzeria and takeaway. Range of bars. Coffee shop. Indoor swimming pool with lifeguards. Sauna, spa, gym, and sun beds. Beautician and hair stylist. Play areas, 'Fun factory' and inflatable jungle run. Amusement arcade. Crazy golf. Football pitch. Evening entertainment with bingo, cabaret, disco, quizzes and competitions.

At a glance

Welcome & Ambience	✓✓✓✓✓	Location	✓✓✓✓✓
Quality of Pitches	✓✓✓✓	Range of Facilities	✓✓✓✓✓

Directions

From A30 or A39 take A392 Newquay road and after about 1 mile park is on right. O.S.GR: SW889597.

Charges 2004

Per unit incl. 4 persons	£ 8.50 - £ 28.00
incl. electricity	£ 12.50 - £ 32.00
extra person	£ 3.50 - £ 5.00
serviced pitch, plus	£ 2.00
dog	£ 3.00

Reservations

Made with £25 deposit or full amount if less. Tel: 0845 4580065. Email: enquiries@whiteacres.co.uk

Open

March - October.

UK0460 Croft Farm Holiday Park

Luxulyan, Bodmin PL30 5EQ (Cornwall)

This secluded park is just one mile from the Eden Project. Croft Farm was once part of a larger site and you pass some of the residential homes on the way in. Mature trees and shrubs edge most of the site, except for an open top field. A number of mobile homes are on site, some privately owned and some for hire by the site, along with two holiday cottages. In the top field with good views, there are 30 individual pitches with new hedges planted. The original mature area provides a further 27 pitches (with 10A electricity for the majority), 15 with hardstanding and 5 of these fully serviced. The park has won a Bellamy Gold award and it is the first time we have seen recycling complete with compost unit. The one mile woodland trail is also part of the conservation effort and takes you through the rest of the park's natural areas which are indeed left very natural!

Facilities

Heated toilet block of older design but neatly updated to provide showers with a plastic door instead of a curtain and plenty of room to change, a baby room, an en-suite washbasin and toilet for ladies, and a new family bathroom. Three dishwashing sinks under cover, one laundry sink with spin dryer. Two new toilets and washbasins in top field. 'Field kitchen' with sinks in the top field. Reception takes newspaper orders and keeps basic necessities such as milk. Grass area with adventure type play equipment and goal net. Games room with pool table and amusement machines. Tourist information. Eden tickets sold. Off site: Fishing 1 mile. Golf or riding 3 miles. Village pubs under a mile and the Eden project on the doorstep.

At a glance

Welcome & Ambience	✓✓✓✓	Location	✓✓✓✓
Quality of Pitches	✓✓✓✓	Range of Facilities	✓✓✓

Directions

From A391 Bodmin - St Austell road follow directions for the Eden project. When you come to the entrance of the project continue straight on for approx. 1 mile, and site is on the left side of this road in the direction of Luxulyan. O.S.GR: SX045588.

Charges 2004

Per unit incl. 2 adults	£ 9.00 - £ 13.00
extra adult	£ 2.00
child (5-15 yrs)	£ 1.20

Reservations

Made with £20 deposit p/week or £3 p/night for shorter visits. Tel: 01726 850228. Email: lynpick@ukonline.co.uk

Open

21 March - 21 January.

UK0250 Pentewan Sands Holiday Park

Pentewan, St Austell PL26 6BT (Cornwall)

Pentewan Sands is a popular, well managed family park with an ideal position right beside a wide sandy private beach. A busy, 32 acre holiday park with lots going on, there are 501 touring pitches, 401 with electricity, and 120 caravan holiday homes for hire. The good-sized pitches are on level grass with nothing between them, and are marked and numbered by frontage stones, mostly in rows adjoining access roads. A good sized free heated pool with a paddling pool is beside the 'Beach Club'. This contains a restaurant, two bars upstairs and a further one downstairs opening on to the pool area, open all day and serving good value food in season. A full entertainment programme, beach activities, water sports and a children's club are organised, and a small water sports centre is on the beach. The adjoining sailing club offers scuba diving, windsurfing courses, etc. to campers. Jet-skis are not permitted and 4WD vehicles are not allowed on the beach. The Pentewan Valley Trail, a six mile route for cycling or walking follows the old carriageway to Mevagissey with its throngs of tourists (two miles by the main road). The park and the beach have been owned by the Tremayne family for 60 years.

Facilities

The four main toilet blocks serve their purpose, receiving heavy use in peak season but have individual cleaners. Two bathrooms and a baby room, plus facilities for disabled people. Well equipped laundry room and dishwashing sinks. Motorcaravan service point. Large, self-service shop with off licence (from Easter but hours may be limited). Bistro and fast food (Whit - mid-Sept). Bars, bar meals. Entertainment programme. Swimming pools (supervised and open Whit - mid Sept). Adventure playground. Games room with arcade games. Tennis courts (one full size, one compact). Bicycle hire. Slipway and boat launching (Whit - mid Sept). Freezer service for ice packs, battery charging service. Gas available. Security barrier at entrance. Caravan and boat storage. Dogs are not accepted. Off site: Riding or golf 2 miles.

At a glance

Welcome & Ambience	✓✓✓✓	Location	✓✓✓✓✓
Quality of Pitches	✓✓✓	Range of Facilities	✓✓✓✓✓

Directions

From St Austell ring road take B3273 for Mevagissey. Park is 3.5 miles, where the road meets the sea. O.S.GR: SX018468.

Charges 2004

Per unit incl. 2 adults, electricity	£ 9.95 - £ 24.15
extra adult	£ 1.75 - £ 4.55
child (3-15 yrs)	£ 1.00 - £ 3.35
extra small tent, boat or car	£ 1.65 - £ 2.30

Sea front pitch plus 10-20%.
Camping Cheques accepted.

Reservations

Made Sat - Sat or Wed - Wed with deposit (£35-£75, acc. to season), £6.50 booking fee and compulsory cancellation insurance (£5-10). Tel: 01726 843485. Email: info@pentewan.co.uk

Open

5 April- 31 October.

UK0410 Heligan Woods Caravan Park

St Ewe, St Austell PL26 6EL (Cornwall)

A peaceful park in a mature garden setting, Heligan Woods is now owned by the Tremayne family of Pentewan Sands. We are happy to feature this park to complement the Pentewan site with its busy beach life and many activities. Part of this park's boundary actually edges The Lost Gardens of Heligan (although nothing can be seen), and at some time the land must have been part of the Gardens. One can enjoy the mature trees and flowering shrubs here which have been further landscaped to provide an attractive situation for a number of holiday homes, some privately owned. These face out over a part of the 'Lost Valley' of Heligan fame and are interspersed with touring pitches, with some below on sloping grass and others in a more level situation amongst trees and shrubs. In all, there are 100 good sized touring pitches, 80 with 16A electricity. The many facilities of Pentewan Sands are open to Heligan Woods visitors. There is access to the Pentewan Trail to walk or cycle into Mevagissey or Pentewan.

Facilities

A modern toilet block is heated, fully equipped and well kept, including a unisex room with bath and small size bath. Dishwashing sinks under cover, a laundry room with two washing machines, two dryers, two irons and boards, but no hand washing sink. Small shop with good takeaway (fish and chip style; peak season only). Adventure playground. Off site: Riding 4 miles, golf 5 miles. Lost Gardens of Heligan next door to site.

Open

3 May - 26 September.

At a glance

Welcome & Ambience	✓✓✓✓	Location	✓✓✓✓
Quality of Pitches	✓✓✓✓	Range of Facilities	✓✓✓

Directions

From St Austell ring road take B3273 for Mevagissey. After 3.5 miles, pass Pentewan Sands, continue up hill and turn right following site signs. Park is on left just before reaching Heligan Gardens. O.S.GR: SW999464.

Charges 2004

Per unit incl. 2 adults and electricity	£ 9.35 - £ 21.45
extra adult	£ 2.10 - £ 3.75
child (3-15 yrs)	£ 1.00 - £ 2.70
extra tent, car or boat	£ 1.55 - £ 1.95

Reservations

Made with deposit (£35-£75, acc. to season); write to Pentewan Sands (no. 0250). Tel: 01726 842714. Email: info@pentewan.co.uk

29

UK0290 Carlyon Bay Caravan & Camping Park

Bethesda, Carlyon Bay, St Austell PL25 3RE (Cornwall)

Tranquil open meadows edged by mature woodland, well cared for by the Taylor family, provide a beautiful holiday setting with a busy Blue Flag beach five minutes walk from the top gate at this park. The original farm buildings have been converted and added to, providing an attractive centre to the park, also home for the owners, with a certain individuality of design which is very pleasing, particularly in the impressively tiled toilet blocks which are of excellent quality and design. The 180 pitches in five areas are spacious and allow for a family meadow, a dog free meadow, and an area for couples, etc. All are on flat, terraced or gently sloping grass with flowers and shrubs in some areas. The 104 pitches with electricity (5/10A) are marked. The attractive kidney shaped, heated pool with paddling pool, is walled and paved for sunbathing. Socially the park provides entertainment in high season for families but those who wish for more can choose between the Cornish Leisure World complex on the beach, with its pool, bars and discos, or the social club near the entrance to the park. The coastal footpath passes near.

Facilities

Three modern toilet blocks provide a mix of facilities from vanity style washbasins to en-suite toilets and basins, comfortable, roomy, pre-set showers with divider, shelf, etc, facilities for hair-care and make-up and thoughtful provision for babies. Dishwashing sinks under cover at all blocks. Fully equipped laundry room (hot water metered). TV lounge, crazy golf, table tennis and pool table. Swimming pool (Easter - Sept). Two play areas, one adventure type. Modern reception with a good little shop and takeaway (May-mid Sept). Eden Project tickets available. Off site: Buses to St Austell and Fowey run from the entrance. Golf course.

Directions

From Plymouth on A390, pass Lostwithiel and 1 mile after St Blazey, turn left at roundabout beside Britannia Inn. After 400 yds turn right on a concrete road and right again at site sign. O.S.GR: SX053526.

Charges 2004

Per unit incl. 2 persons	£ 8.00 - £ 22.00
extra person	£ 2.00 - £ 4.00
electricity	£ 2.00 - £ 2.50

Reservations

Made with £30 deposit and £2 fee. Tel: 01726 812735. Email: holidays@carlyonbay.net

Open

April - October.

At a glance

Welcome & Ambience	✓✓✓✓✓	Location	✓✓✓✓✓
Quality of Pitches	✓✓✓✓	Range of Facilities	✓✓✓✓

Carlyon Bay CARAVAN & CAMPING PARK

AA CAMPSITE OF THE YEAR 1999 - SOUTH WEST
- Award winning family park 2km from Eden Project
- Set in over 30 acres of meadows and mature woodlands
- Up to 180 touring pitches (no statics)
- Footpath to large sandy beach
- Close to championship Golf Course
- Heated Swimming & paddling pool
- Ben's Play World for kids nearby
- Pool, table-tennis and crazy-golf

For colour brochure **call: 01726 812735**
St Austell, Cornwall
www.carlyonbay.net   e-mail:holidays@carlyonbay.net

UK0155 Tregarton Park

Gorran, Mevagissey, St Austell PL26 6NF (Cornwall)

Run by the welcoming Hicks family, Tregarton Park itself dates back to the 16th century. The twelve acre caravan park is made up of three meadows, with good views of the rural surroundings. The 125 pitches, all with electric hook ups (10A), are of generous size with most separated by either hedges or fencing; some are gently sloping. The large heated outdoor pool is surrounded by decked terraces, with tables and chairs where one can relax. An adventure playground is in one of the meadows where there are also goal posts and an all-weather tennis court. Close to the small harbour town of Gorran and 2.5 miles from Mevagissey, with several beaches close by, this is an ideal site for those who do not want lots of entertainment, but would enjoy the option of various activities available nearby.

Facilities

Traditionally designed toilet block provides showers, open style washbasins and toilets. Laundry room and enclosed dishwashing area. Well stocked shop with camping supplies and off-licence. Takeaway. Gas supplies. Heated swimming and paddling pools. Dog exercise meadow. Playground. Facilities open Whitsun - mid Sept. Off site: Beaches 2 miles.

Open

1 April - 30 September.

At a glance

Welcome & Ambience	✓✓✓✓	Location	✓✓✓✓
Quality of Pitches	✓✓✓✓	Range of Facilities	✓✓✓✓

Directions

Leave St Austell going south on B3273 through London Apprentice and Pentewen. Follow site signs and turn right at crossroads at top of hill (Gorran Haven). Don't go into Mevagissey. O.S.GR: SW989435.

Charges 2005

Per unit incl. 2 persons, electricity	£ 4.95 - £ 19.50
extra person (over 4 yrs)	£ 2.00 - £ 3.00

Reservations

Made with deposit (£4 per night booked) and £1 fee. Tel: 0845 10 80 113. Email: reception@tregarton.co.uk

UK0190 Polruan Holidays Camping & Caravanning

Polruan-by-Fowey PL23 1QH (Cornwall)

Polruan is a rural site in an elevated position not far from Fowey in an area of Outstanding Natural Beauty 200 metres from the Coastal path. With 47 touring pitches and 11 holiday homes to let, this is a very pleasant little site. The holiday homes are arranged in a neat circle, with a central area for some tourers, including 7 pitches with gravel hardstanding and electricity, one fully serviced. The remaining touring pitches are in an adjacent field with 8 electricity hook-ups, which is part level for motorcaravans and part on a gentle slope with tree views. There are marvellous sea views, but it could be a little exposed when the wind blows off the sea. A raised picnic area, with a table provided, gives more views right across the estuary to Fowey. This is a nice little park in a popular tourist area, within walking distance (downhill all the way, and vice-versa!) of the village, where there are various hostelries and a passenger ferry to Fowey. A member of the Countryside Discovery group.

Facilities

The small sanitary block of older design has been added to, providing modern controllable showers and includes a laundry sink plus a washing machine - in the ladies'. New dishwashing sinks. Motorcaravan service facilities. Range of recycling bins. Reception (with a small terrace) doubles as a small shop for basics and gas, with drinks machine and provides a freezer for ice packs, tourist information and bus timetables (for Looe, etc). Sloping field area for children's play with swings. Off site: Riding or bicycle hire 3 miles, fishing 0.5 miles, golf 10 miles.

At a glance

Welcome & Ambience	✓✓✓✓	Location	✓✓✓✓✓
Quality of Pitches	✓✓✓	Range of Facilities	✓✓✓

Directions

From the main A390 road at East Taphouse take B3359 towards Looe. After 5 miles fork right signed Bodinnick and ferry. Watch for signs for Polruan and site to left. Follow carefully along narrow Cornish lanes to site on right just before village. O.S.GR: SX133509.

Charges 2004

Per unit incl. 2 persons, electricity	£ 9.00 - £ 13.00
extra person	£ 2.00

No credit cards.

Reservations

Advised for July/Aug. and made with £30 deposit.
Tel: 01726 870263. Email: polholiday@aol.com

Open

Easter - 10 October.

UK0280 Powderham Castle Tourist Park

Lanlivery, Lostwithiel PL30 5BU (Cornwall)

This is a most pleasant, peaceful touring park with plenty of sheltered green space and a natural, uncommercialised atmosphere. This has been enhanced by careful planting of trees and shrubs to form a series of linked paddocks with a small unfenced stream running through. The nearest beach at Par is some 4 miles. The park has 38 private caravan holiday homes in a separate field and 75 numbered touring pitches spread round the perimeter of the paddocks, each with 10-15 pitches. All have electricity connections (5/10A) and 7 have hardstanding (awning groundsheets must be lifted alternate days). There are 'adult only' sections for tents and touring caravans. For children, a large, well equipped activity play area with a super range of adventure type equipment on grass is in one of the hedged paddocks with a fenced paddling pool. Indoor tennis courts (Bodmin) and a swimming pool are near. The village pub is within walking distance and there are several good local restaurants. The Eden Project is very close.

Facilities

The single central toilet block is good but is quite a walk from some pitches. Hot showers are on payment, with curtained cubicles in the ladies' and a family washroom with shower, basin, WC, etc. Separate dishwashing area with five sinks. Fully equipped laundry room. Motorcaravan service point. Gas supplies. Play area. Torch useful. Off site: Fresh water fishing 1.5 miles or sea fishing 3 miles. Bicycle hire 4 miles. Riding 2 miles. Golf 1.5 miles.

Open

Easter/1 April - 31 October.

At a glance

Welcome & Ambience	✓✓✓✓	Location	✓✓✓✓
Quality of Pitches	✓✓✓✓	Range of Facilities	✓✓✓

Directions

Park approach road leads off A390 road 1.5 miles southwest of Lostwithiel. Follow white or brown camping signs. No other approach is advised. O.S.GR: SX083592.

Charges 2004

Per unit incl. 2 persons, electricity	£ 9.50 - £ 16.00
extra adult	£ 2.00 - £ 3.00
child (3-16 yrs)	£ 0.60 - £ 1.50

No single sex groups (excl. bona fide organisations). No credit cards.

Reservations

Made with £20 deposit. Tel: 01208 872277.

31

UK0400 Trelay Farmpark

Pelynt, Looe PL13 2JX (Cornwall)

Situated a little back from the coast, just over three miles from Looe and Polperro in a rural situation, this is a real gem of a park. Neat, tidy and quiet, there is no farm adjacent. On your right as you drive in, and quite attractively arranged amongst herbaceous shrubs, are caravan holiday homes (15 privately owned, some let by the park). The touring area is behind and slightly above, on level to gently sloping, neatly cut grass. An oval hard-core road connects the good sized, numbered pitches that border the site and back onto hedges, the majority with rural views. There are 43 pitches with electricity hook-ups, with a further 12 pitches for tents, etc. Outside the main season the central area is kept free for ball games. You will receive a good welcome from the enthusiastic owners, Heather and Graham Veale and their family, who live in the chalet bungalow near the entrance where the small reception is located.

Facilities	Directions
Excellent chalet-type toilet block, purpose built, heated, well equipped and maintained, with some semi-private washbasins. En-suite unit with ramp for disabled visitors (key from reception); it includes a baby bath. Two dishwashing sinks and a laundry sink. Washing machine and dryer. Gas supplies. Free fridge/freezer. Tourist inform ation including map sales and loan. Off site: Village with pub and shops within 0.5 miles. 'Coastal Hoppa' bus from the gate on Thursdays. The Eden Project is 10 miles west.	From A390 Lostwithiel road take B3359 south at Middle or East Taphouse towards Looe and Polperro. Site is signed 0.5 miles past Pelynt on the left. From Looe take A387 towards Polperro and after 2 miles turn right onto B3359 towards Pelynt. Site is signed 1 mile on right. O.S.GR: SX210545.

Open

1 April - end October.

Charges 2004

Per unit incl. 2 persons	£ 7.00 - £ 10.50
extra person over 5 yrs	£ 2.50
child (under 5 yrs)	£ 1.00
electricity	£ 2.00
dog	£ 0.70

No credit cards.

At a glance

Welcome & Ambience	✓✓✓✓	Location	✓✓✓✓
Quality of Pitches	✓✓✓✓	Range of Facilities	✓✓✓

Reservations

Advised for July/Aug. Tel: 01503 220900.
Email: stay@trelay.co.uk

UK0350 Whitsand Bay Holiday Park

Millbrook, Torpoint PL10 1JZ (Cornwall)

A major development programme is taking place at Whitsand Bay over the next three years commencing in the Autumn of 2004. The aim is to provide an 'all year round' holiday park to meet the growing needs of visitors to this amazing area. The sinking of HMS Scylla in the bay which has provided Europe's first artifical reef has kick started this development. However, the unique situation of this park, its marvellous views and its history as a 19th century hilltop fort (home to the coastal gun battery) which gave it its Ancient Monument Status made it a front runner for development. Now, in conjunction with English Heritage and with the co-operation of other interested bodies, work is planned to restore the gun emplacements, tunnels and ammunition rooms with the redevelopment and landscaping of the site with indigenous plants to blend with the environment. Sixty-eight wood lodges will be sited on the present touring pitches by 2006 which will benefit from the amazing views. New fully serviced, individually hedged pitches will be created inside the monument around the gun batteries. The café, bar and restaurant will be rebuilt or refurbished and the pool upgraded. In the owner's words, 'a low density, high quality development'. Most of the work will be carried out in low season. Most of the existing touring pitches will remain for 2005 along with the toilet facilities, the heated pool, bar, café and shop. Entertainment will continue to be provided. A steep 200 ft. cliff path provides access to Whitsand Bay (unsuitable for small children or the infirm).

Facilities	Directions
The two toilet blocks are acceptable. Each block has a dishwashing sink under cover. Laundry room. Well stocked shop. Café open all day in season, with takeaway. Barbecue area. Bars with entertainment in high season. Indoor, heated pool and paddling pool, sauna and sun bed. Adventure play area, multi-sport court, amusement arcade and table tennis. 'Kids Club'. Off site: New diving centre close by. Fishing 0.5 miles, boat slipway 2 miles, golf 2 miles. Riding 5 miles.	Take the Torpoint ferry and on disembarking follow A374 Liskeard road for 3 miles. At village of Antony fork left for Millbrook (B3274) and continue for 2 miles to T-junction. Turn left for Whitsand Bay, then almost immediately right following narrow road overlooking the bay for a further 2 miles. Park is on the left - watch for sign. O.S.GR: SX417506.

Open

All year.

Charges 2004

Per unit incl. up to 6 persons	£ 8.00 - £ 19.00
electricity (16A)	£ 2.00
dog	£ 1.00

Woodland mini-pitches for cyclists or walkers less 50%. Club membership incl.

At a glance

Welcome & Ambience	✓✓✓✓	Location	✓✓✓✓✓
Quality of Pitches	✓✓✓✓	Range of Facilities	✓✓✓✓✓

Reservations

Made with £10 deposit p/week. Tel: 01752 822597.
Email: rob@whitsandbayholidays.co.uk

UK0320 Polborder House Caravan & Camping Park

Bucklawren Road, St Martins by Looe PL13 1QR (Cornwall)

Polborder House may appeal to those who prefer a quiet, well kept little family site to the larger ones with many on-site activities. With good countryside views, up to 31 touring units can be accommodated on well tended grass. Pitches are marked with hedging between pairs of pitches to give privacy and there are 28 electrical connections (10A). A number of hardstandings and 10 serviced pitches have been added recently. The owners live on the park. Polborder is well situated with Seaton only 2 miles, Looe 2.5 and the nearest beach a 20-25 minutes walk from a gate in the corner of the park. A 'Hoppa' bus calls at the site Mondays to Thursdays from mid June to mid September. This is a good area for walking with links to the coastal path through Duchy woodland.

Facilities

The sanitary block (key entry) is well kept, of ample size and provides hot showers, a baby room, fully equipped laundry room, and three covered sinks outside for dishwashing. En-suite toilet unit for disabled visitors has a ramped approach. Rubbish is recycled. Motorcaravan service facilities. Shop (all season) for gas and basics, including off licence and some camping accessories. Toddler's play area. Hut with tourist information. Off site: Fishing, golf and boat launching within 2 miles, riding 8 miles. Restaurant 500 m.

Open

29 March - 2 November.

At a glance

Welcome & Ambience	✓✓✓✓	Location	✓✓✓✓
Quality of Pitches	✓✓✓✓	Range of Facilities	✓✓✓

Directions

Park is less than a mile south of the B3253. Turn off 2 miles east of Looe and follow signs to park and Monkey Sanctuary at junctions; care is needed with narrow road. O.S.GR: SX283555.

Charges 2004

Per unit incl. 2 persons	£ 8.00 - £ 11.00
extra person	£ 3.50 - £ 4.00
child (5-16 yrs)	£ 1.00 - £ 1.50
electricity	£ 1.85
dog	£ 0.75
Less 10% for senior citizens if booked over 7 nights.	

Reservations

Any period, £20 deposit (non-refundable). Tel: 01503 240265. Email: rlf.polborder@virgin.net

UK0440 Dolbeare Caravan & Camping Park

St Ive Road, Landrake, Saltash PL12 5AF (Cornwall)

Mark and John are proud of their small, but well kept park. It is in a rural setting (but very easily accessible from the main A38) and consists of a large rectangular field of neat grass edged with trees and sloping slightly at the top, connected by a gravel road. Caravans and motorcaravans go mainly around the edge, with most of the terraced pitches having hardstanding. Tents tend to go in the central area where there is also play equipment and water and refuse points. All 60 pitches are numbered and of comfortable size, 53 with electricity (16A). An extra field doubles as a rally and games field and part is set aside for a dog exercise area. At reception, leaflets are provided on 'Where to Eat', 'Where to Walk', and 'Suggestions for what to do' with a good supply of tourist information and maps. Dog kennels nearby can provide day care from £3.50, but the drawback is that there could be some noise depending on season and wind direction. This is a very usefully situated park said to be 20 minutes from everywhere - Plymouth, beaches, National Trust properties, Dartmoor and Bodmin Moor, etc.

Facilities

The bright, cheerful and well kept heated toilet block to one side of the field is fully equipped. Covered dishwashing sinks. Laundry next to reception. Motorcaravan services. Reception doubles as a small shop for basics including gas (limited hours out of main season). Park has arranged discounts at the St Mellion Golf and Country Club for golf and leisure facilities. Site barrier (card system with £5 deposit, £1 fee). Off site: Fishing 3 miles. Golf 5.5 miles.

Open

All year.

At a glance

Welcome & Ambience	✓✓✓✓✓	Location	✓✓✓✓
Quality of Pitches	✓✓✓✓✓	Range of Facilities	✓✓✓

Directions

After crossing the Tamar Bridge into Cornwall, continue on A38 for a further 4 miles. In Landrake village turn right following signs and site is 0.75 miles on the right. O.S.GR: SX366616.

Charges 2005

Per unit incl. 2 adults and car	£ 9.00 - £ 15.00
extra adult	£ 2.50
child (5-16 yrs)	£ 1.50
awning	£ 1.00
No credit cards	

Reservations

Made with £10 deposit. Tel: 01752 851332. Email: dolbeare@btopenworld.com

Need a **POWR Product?**

SEE PAGE 294

UK0430 Trerethern Touring Park

Padstow PL28 8LE (Cornwall)

Trerethern is a traditional park made up of wide open fields, although some hedging is gradually developing in places despite the rabbits and the elements. There is room for 300 units but only 100 are taken so there is plenty of open space and the views across Bodmin Moor and the estuary are marvellous. The grass is neatly cut and the pitches mostly level, although there is a gentle slope in parts. Electricity (10A) is available on 64 pitches, there are ten water points and nine hardstanding places for motorcaravans, seven of these with electricity plus an emptying point (the site can accommodate 32-34 ft motorhomes). The 'Kernow' pitches have private facilities. The owners live on site and, along with site wardens, ensure a well run and orderly park. Padstow is a mile away either by footpath through the fields (20-30 minutes) downhill or for bicycles by the road. A bus service passes (the site is a request stop) and reception holds timetables. Rick Stein's restaurant or bistro may tempt you - if you can get a reservation!

Facilities
Two toilet blocks are simple but clean and tidy, with two washbasins in cabins in the smaller better block (closed at night). A toilet with washbasin and ramp access is provided at the back of the main block at the far side of the park. A unique feature is the six individual en-suite washrooms for use with the 'Kernow' pitches. For private use, these have a key (with deposit) and are part of the smaller block. Dishwashing sinks. Laundry facilities with two washing machines, spin dryer, tumble dryer and iron. Reception/shop for gas and basic supplies. Play area. Off site: Nearest beach at Padstow, others are within 5 miles. Access to the Camel Trail cycle route. Riding or fishing 2 miles, golf 5 miles.

At a glance
| Welcome & Ambience | ✓✓✓✓ | Location | ✓✓✓✓ |
| Quality of Pitches | ✓✓✓ | Range of Facilities | ✓✓✓ |

Directions
Park is signed from the A389, SSW of Padstow. Follow unmade road, then into park. O.S.GR: SW912739.

Charges 2004
Per adult	£ 2.75 - £ 3.75
child (under 15 yrs)	£ 1.75 - £ 1.75
pitch	£ 4.00 - £ 5.00
electricity	£ 2.50 - £ 2.75
'Kernow' pitch incl. electricity plus	£ 6.00 - £ 7.50
dog	£ 0.50 - £ 0.50

No credit cards.

Reservations
Made with deposit (£15 p/week). Tel: 01841 532061. Email: camping.trerethern@btinternet.com

Open
Easter/1 April - 7 October.

UK0500 Trewince Farm Holiday Park

St Issey, Wadebridge PL27 7RL (Cornwall)

This well established and popular park four miles from Padstow has been developed around a dairy farm with magnificent countryside views. Careful attention has been made to the development of the park, maintaining trees and adding flowering shrubs and plants. There are 35 caravan holiday homes discreetly terraced, some privately owned, some to let. Two touring areas on higher ground provide both hardstanding and level grass pitches with a sheltered tent area. Over half of the 120 touring pitches have electricity (10A) and 34 have water and drainage. The park's main feature is an excellent sheltered, walled and heated swimming pool with paddling pool, and paved sunbathing area. Farm rides and pasty suppers in the barn are organised in the high season.

Facilities
Two fully equipped, well maintained toilet blocks include washbasins in cabins, hair care rooms, dishwashing under cover and laundry rooms. Also children's room with bath (20p) and facilities for disabled visitors. Well stocked shop (all season) by reception. Fish and chip van calls twice weekly, a butcher once a week. Swimming pool. Play area. Games room. Crazy golf. Off site: Pubs and restaurants in nearby village of St Issey. Camel Trail nearby for walking or cycling (goes to Padstow).

Open
23 March - 31 October.

At a glance
| Welcome & Ambience | ✓✓✓✓ | Location | ✓✓✓✓ |
| Quality of Pitches | ✓✓✓✓ | Range of Facilities | ✓✓✓✓ |

Directions
From Wadebridge follow A39 towards St Columb and pick up the A389 for Padstow. Site signed on left in 2 miles. Follow for short distance to park entrance on right. O.S. GR: SW937715.

Charges 2004
Per unit incl. 2 persons	£ 8.00 - £ 13.00
incl. electricity	£ 9.75 - £ 14.50
hardstanding, drainage, electricity	£ 10.25 - £ 15.00
extra adult	£ 3.20
child (3-15 yrs)	£ 1.60 - £ 2.65
dog	£ 1.10

Reservations
Made with £40 p/week deposit (non-refundable); balance on arrival. Tel: 01208 812830.

UK0355 Saint Minver Holiday Park

St Minver, Near Rock, Wadebridge PL27 6RR (Cornwall)

This holiday village, part of the Parkdean Group, is based in the grounds of a former manor house near the well known Cornish coastal resorts of Rock and Padstow. There are over 200 privately owned caravan holiday homes which merge into landscape, with a further 145 for rent. A sloping grass touring field provides 120 pitches, 70 with 16A electricity, with toilet facilities based in the far corner and rural views across the fields. A central village area, providing reception and most of the facilities including an indoor swimming pool with waterslide, is the hub of the site. The manor house itself is home to a bar/bistro and all the entertainment with cabaret, live music, disco and quiz nights. A children's club ensures there is something for everyone. A footpath through the woods takes you to the village of St Minver. You can take the passenger ferry from Rock to Padstow with its harbour where Rick Stein has his cookery school and restaurants. The Camel Trail is nearby for cycling enthusiasts. The nearby beach at Rock and Daymar beach are renowned for swimming, windsurfing and sailing.

Facilities

A fully equipped toilet block is supplemented at peak times by an older block. Baby bath. En-suite unit for disabled people. Dishwashing sinks. Launderette. Shop. Bar, restaurant and takeaway. Indoor pool with lifeguards. Indoor soft play area and outdoor play area. Crazy golf. All amenities open when site is open. Sports programme with aqua-aerobics and scuba diving and laser clay pigeon shooting (high season only). Entertainment programme.

At a glance

Welcome & Ambience	✓✓✓✓	Location	✓✓✓✓
Quality of Pitches	✓✓✓	Range of Facilities	✓✓✓✓✓

Directions

From Wadebridge take B3314 for Port Isaac. Follow for 3 miles then turn left for Rock and park is 250 yds on right. O.S.GR: SW965768.

Charges 2004

Per unit incl. 4 persons	£ 7.00 - £ 23.00
extra person	free - £ 2.00
awning, pup tent	free - £ 2.00
dog	£ 2.00 - £ 2.50

Reservations

Made with £25 deposit or full amount if less.
Tel: 01208 862305. Email: enquiries@newquay.com

Open

Mid March - October.

UK0306 Ruthern Valley Holidays

Ruthernbridge, Bodmin PL30 5LU (Cornwall)

This is a little gem of a site set in 7.5 acres of woodland, tucked away in a peaceful little valley not far from Bodmin. The park was landscaped over 30 years ago with an amazing range of trees and shrubs now all carefully tended by its present owners, Tim and Eileen Zair. This lends itself to the informal layout of the level touring pitches and the self catering accommodation. Wooden chalet/bungalows (12) and caravan holiday homes (6) blend into the natural wooded environment. There are 16 touring pitches informally spaced but numbered in the main, tree-lined field, 6 with electricity, and a further 13 in smaller fields and alcove areas amongst the woods with a small stream meandering through and alive with bluebells when we visited. A very good adventure-type play area is set away from the pitches, and a small, basic toilet block and a little shop complete the provision. This is a site for relaxing with time to enjoy the simpler pastimes of walking or birdwatching. Over 40 species of bird have been recorded.

Facilities

The small toilet block provides everything necessary including a shower each per sex plus washing machines, dryer, laundry sink and dishwashing sinks (H&C). The shop with basic provisions shares with reception (reduced hours in low season). Barbecue hire. Play area with excellent equipment including five-a-side goal posts. Dogs are not accepted in the touring areas during July/Aug. Off site: Nearest pub 3-4 miles. Riding 2 miles. Bicycle hire at Wadebridge or Padstow.

Open

April - October.

At a glance

Welcome & Ambience	✓✓✓✓✓	Location	✓✓✓✓✓
Quality of Pitches	✓✓✓	Range of Facilities	✓✓✓

Directions

Approaching Bodmin from A30 or A38 turn right at the first mini roundabout and proceed anti-clockwise round the inner ring road. Go straight over double mini-roundabout, leaving Bodmin on A389/A391 towards St Austell. Ignore first Nanstallon and Ruthernbridge sign, after 1.5 miles, at top of hill, turn right. At Nanstallon village sign (0.75 miles), turn left then filter left. Continue for 1 mile dropping down into Ruthernbridge. Turn left immediately before bridge. Site is on left in 300 yards. O.S.GR: SX012668.

Charges 2004

Per unit incl. 2 persons	£ 8.00 - £ 10.00
with electricity	£ 10.00 - £ 12.00
extra person over 4 yrs	£ 1.50 - £ 2.00
pet (low season only)	£ 1.00

Reservations

Made with deposit (min £25 or full fee). Tel: 01208 831395. Email: holiday@ruthernvalley.fsnet.co.uk

UK0230 Glenmorris Park

Longstone Road, St Mabyn PL30 3BY (Cornwall)

The beaches of north Cornwall and the wilds of Bodmin Moor are all an easy drive from Glenmorris Park. The park is being gradually improved and carefully maintained by its young owners and it provides a spacious and relaxed atmosphere. There are 80 level pitches, 60 with 16A electricity, on well drained and well mown grass with 20 hardstandings. There are some caravan holiday homes to let. A nice, sheltered outdoor pool is an added attraction. There is no bar although the local village inn has a good reputation for food. The Camel Trail is two miles, providing a means to cycle or walk all the way to Bodmin, Wadebridge or Padstow. Bodmin and Wadebridge are only five or six miles for supermarket shopping.

Facilities

The fully equipped modern toilet block includes one en-suite unit per sex. Dishwashing sinks and laundry. Heated outdoor swimming pool and paddling pool (late May - early Sept), surrounded by a sheltered, paved and grass sunbathing areas. Good, fenced adventure play area with bark safety base. Tiny tots play area. Games room for teenagers. Caravan storage. Off site: Fishing, riding or golf 3 miles, bicycle hire 5 miles.

Open

Easter - 31 October.

At a glance

Welcome & Ambience	✓✓✓✓	Location	✓✓✓✓
Quality of Pitches	✓✓✓	Range of Facilities	✓✓✓✓

Directions

From Bodmin or Wadebridge on A389, take B3266 north signed Camelford. At village of Longstone turn left signed St Mabyn and brown camping sign. Site is 400 yds. on right. Ignore all other signs to St Mabyn. O.S.GR: SX053732.

Charges 2004

Per adult	£ 3.50 - £ 4.75
child (3-15 yrs)	£ 1.00
electricity (16A)	£ 2.00 - £ 2.25
dog	£ 1.00
Weekly rate available.	

Reservations

Made with deposit (£10 per week per unit). Tel: 01208 841677. Email: info@glenmorris.co.uk

UK0300 The Colliford Tavern Campsite

Colliford Lake, St Neot, Liskeard PL14 6PZ (Cornwall)

Colliford Tavern must be unique, quietly situated high on Bodmin Moor near Colliford Lake but hidden and protected by tall pines with a camping area and a tavern. The Cooper family run the free house with home cooked food and ale in an old world atmosphere complete with a 90-year-old well and en-suite accommodation. There is a bar, dining room, a family room with outside terrace, garden, water wheel and a good, fenced play area with a Wendy House The tavern is open to campers and caravanners and the general public. The camping area is quiet and simple and has been kept very natural with short grass (helped by the rabbits) and sheltered from the moor by tall pines. The main field provides 40 fairly level pitches with 19 electric hook-ups (16A) and 6 hardstandings backing on to the pine trees. Reception is in the tavern building. The site gate is closed at night but there is a 24 hour bell. Ideally situated for Colliford Lake and the Moor be it for walking, fly fishing (permits available) or birdwatching, the park is also suitable for excursions to both the north or south coast.

Facilities

The pine-fitted, heated toilet block is fully equipped and includes a baby room and unit for disabled people (no shower), laundry sink and two washing up sinks. Service wash and tumble dry (Monday to Friday). Restaurant and bar. Play area. Some occasional family entertainment. Tickets available for the Eden Project (20-30 minutes by car). Barbecues permitted with prior permission.

Open

Easter - end September.

At a glance

Welcome & Ambience	✓✓✓✓	Location	✓✓✓✓
Quality of Pitches	✓✓✓	Range of Facilities	✓✓✓

Directions

On the A30 travelling south, pass Jamaica Inn and site is signed a further 1-1.5 miles on the left. Follow for 0.5 miles to Colliford Lake Park. O.S.GR: SX168730.

Charges 2004

Per unit incl. 2 adults	£ 10.00
extra person (over 12 yrs)	£ 3.00
electricity	£ 3.00
child (5-12 yrs)	£ 1.50

Reservations

Advised for high season and made with £10 deposit, plus £5 for electric hook-up. Tel: 01208 821335. Email: info@colliford-tavern.co.uk

Killarney Springs

Set in 66 acres of beautiful Cornish countryside, Killarney Springs offers a unique day out for all the family. It has the perfect combination of all-action rides and simple pleasurable activities.

For those happy to get wet, try the White Water Rapids - the ultimate in water slides; or how about the steep North Ridge toboggan run? Bumper Boats* are perfect to splash around in, whilst the Supakarts* offer yet another thrill! The whole family can enjoy a cruise around the Island of Willow Creek, visiting and feeding the animals, or maybe a gentle row on the lake is more to your liking?

After all that activity, lunch can be served indoors or out in the licensed restaurant, or maybe a quick bite in the burger bar. Then on to work off all that food with a game of basketball or swingball, a round of golf, or just a leisurely stroll along the Nature Trail. The kids can try the assault course or enjoy the experience of The Power House indoor area, with its slides, chutes and ball-parks; whilst the youngest members of the family can play to their heart's content in the well-equipped under-6s area and the sand pit. And remember, we also cater for birthday parties and special events!

Killarney Springs changed hands at the beginning of last season and consequently has undergone extensive re-development. The new owners have worked tirelessly through the winter up-grading the existing attractions and for 2005 have installed, amongst other things, thrilling new rides to add to your enjoyment. For the first time entertainment will go on into the evening and will include concerts and firework displays.

The Park caters for all size of vans, so if you plan a day out, wish to stay just one night or an extended visit, telephone now on 01288 331475 to book in and prepare for a truly memorable visit to Killarney Springs Family Leisure Park.

*The Bumper Boats and Go-karts are the only chargeable rides on the park.

Killarney Springs
FAMILY LEISURE PARK

Unique Family Fun on dry land...

- North Ridge Toboggan Run
- The Power House with twin twister and drop slides
- Play Town - soft play and ball pits for under 6s
- F1 & F2 Supakarts and Race Track

...or on water

- White Water Rapids - 3 of the fastest and longest water rides in the country
- Bumper Boats • Boating Lake
- Family Favourite Willow Creek Boat Ride where you can feed the animals

OVER 20 ACTIVITIES

Morwenstow, Bude, North Cornwall. Follow the brown tourist signs on the A39. Admission costs £6.95 - £8.50 per person. Under 3s and disabled FREE.

Call us for more information on: 01288 331 475

UK0360 Lakefield Caravan Park

Lower Pendavey Farm, Camelford PL32 9TX (Cornwall)

Lakefield is a small, simple touring park on what was a working farm. Now the main focus is on the BHS approved equestrian centre. With only 30 pitches, it is no surprise that the owners, Maureen and Dennis Perring, know all the campers. The well-spaced pitches backing onto hedges and with 24 electric hook-ups (16A) are in view of the small lake (fenced) and its inhabitants. The white-washed shop/reception, converted from one of the old barns and including a picture gallery, is open all day and all season which impressed us for such a small site. It incorporates a tea room offering cream teas. A dozen colourful picnic tables are dotted about the site. Children will love the animals and 'Wabbit World'. With over 30 horses, from Shetlands to thoroughbreds, the riding school is very much part of the site, offering lessons and hacks with qualified supervision and instruction. You can even bring your own horse. Nearby, Tintagel, Boscastle, Bodmin Moor and numerous beaches wait to be explored.

Facilities	Directions
The refurbished toilet block is simple but adequate. Washing machine and dryer in the ladies'. Dishwashing sink and a laundry sink outside but under cover. No facilities for disabled visitors. Shop and tea room. Gas supplies. Torches may be useful. Off site: Fishing (sea 4 miles, coarse 5 miles). Golf 2 miles.	Follow B3266 north from Camelford. Park access is directly from this road on the left just before the turning for Tintagel, clearly signed. O.S.GR: SX097852.

Open

1 April - 31 October.

Charges 2004

Per unit incl. 2 adults	£ 6.00 - £ 10.00
extra adult or child (5 yrs and over)	£ 1.00
electricity	£ 2.00

No credit cards.

Reservations

Made with £ 30 deposit per week. Tel: 01840 213279. Email: lakefield@pendavey.fsnet.co.uk

At a glance

Welcome & Ambience	✓✓✓✓	Location	✓✓✓
Quality of Pitches	✓✓✓	Range of Facilities	✓✓✓

UK0380 Wooda Farm Park

Poughill, Bude EX23 9HJ (Cornwall)

Wooda Farm is spacious and well organised, with some nice touches. A quality, family run park, it is part of a working farm, under two miles from the sandy, surfing beaches of Bude. In peaceful farmland with plenty of open spaces (and some up and down walking), there are marvellous views of sea and countryside. The 200 large pitches are spread over four meadows on level or gently sloping grass. There are 139 with electricity connections (10A), 61 plus with hardstanding and 21 grass, hedged 'premium' pitches (electricity, water, waste water) linked by tarmac roads. A late arrivals area has electricity. A few friendly farm animals welcome assistance at feeding time! Tractor and trailer rides, archery and clay pigeon shooting with tuition are provided according to season and demand, likewise barn dances, plus woodland (to find the pixies) and orchard walks and excellent coarse fishing. There is much to do in the area with Tintagel and Clovelly nearby. A member of the Best of British group.

Facilities	Directions
Three well maintained toilet blocks, one heated, include a unit suitable for disabled people, two baby rooms and five en-suite family bathrooms (coded access). Dishwashing sinks under cover. Two laundry rooms. Motorcaravan service point. Shop with off-licence. Attractive courtyard bar with meals and pleasant restaurant. Play area with plenty of room for ball games, 9 hole 'fun' golf course (clubs provided). Games room with TV, table tennis and pool. Coarse fishing. Certain breeds of dogs not accepted. Caravan storage. Off site: Village inn 5 minutes walk.	Park is north of Bude at Poughill; turn off A39 on north side of Stratton on minor road for Coombe Valley, following camp signs at junctions. O.S.GR: SS225080.

Charges 2004

Per unit incl. 2 adults, electricity	£ 10.50 - £ 15.50

Camping Cheques accepted.

Reservations

Made with £20 p/week deposit Tel: 01288 352069. Email: enquiries@wooda.co.uk

Open

1 April - October.

At a glance

Welcome & Ambience	✓✓✓✓✓	Location	✓✓✓✓✓
Quality of Pitches	✓✓✓✓✓	Range of Facilities	✓✓✓✓

38

UK0690 Stowford Farm Meadows

Berry Down, Combe Martin, Ilfracombe EX34 0PW (Devon)

Stowford Farm is set in 500 acres of the rolling North Devon countryside, available for recreation and walking, yet within easy reach of five local beaches. The touring park and its facilities have been developed in the fields and farm buildings surrounding the attractive old farmhouse and provide a village like centre with a comfortable spacious feel. There are 710 pitches (including 238 used by seasonal units) on five slightly sloping meadows separated by Devon hedges of beech and ash. Unseparated, the numbered and marked pitches are accessed by tarmac or hard-core roads, most have electricity (10/16A) and there are well placed water points. The Old Stable Bars, refurbished to a high standard offers entertainment in high season including barn dances, discos, karaoke and other musical evenings. Children will also be entertained by the indoor heated pool and under cover mini-zoo (Petorama) where they can handle many sorts of animals (on payment). In low season some facilities may only open for limited hours. Stowford provides plenty to keep families occupied without leaving the park, including woodland walks and horse riding from the park's own stables. This is a friendly family, countryside base for exploring the North Devon coast and Exmoor.

Facilities

Five identical toilet blocks, each looked after by resident wardens, are fully equipped and provide good, functional facilities, each block with laundry facilities and dishwashing sinks under cover. The newest block (in field 5) has under-floor heating and includes facilities for disabled visitors. Extra good facilities for disabled visitors and private family washrooms are beside reception. Well stocked shop (with holiday goods and gas). Good value takeaway with restaurant area. Bars and entertainment in season. Swimming pool (22 x 10 m; heated Easter - Oct) at a small charge (£1.25). Riding. 18-hole pitch and putt. Crazy golf. Bicycle hire. 'Kiddies kar' track (all charged). Games room. Large play area. Games and activities organised in high season. ATM. Dogs welcome in three sections (max. 2 per pitch). Summer parking and winter caravan storage. Caravan workshop, sales accessories and repair centre. Off site: Fishing and boat launching 4 miles.

At a glance

Welcome & Ambience	✓✓✓✓	Location	✓✓✓✓
Quality of Pitches	✓✓✓✓	Range of Facilities	✓✓✓✓✓

Directions

From Barnstaple take A39 towards Lynton. After 1 mile turn left on B3230. Turn right at garage on A3123 and park is 1.5 miles on the right. O.S.GR: SS565438.

Charges 2004

Per unit and car incl. 2 persons	£ 7.50 - £ 20.00
extra person	free - £ 3.00
child (5-12 yrs)	free - £ 2.00
awning with groundsheet	£ 2.00 - £ 3.00
dog	£ 1.00 - £ 2.00

Low and mid season discounts for over 50s.

Reservations

Any length, deposit £2 per night, £12 per week, £20 per fortnight. Balance due 28 days before arrival. Tel: 01271 882476. Email: enquiries@stowford.co.uk

Open

Easter - end October.

39

UK1070 Woolacombe Bay Holiday Village

Sandy Lane, Woolacombe EX34 7AH (Devon)

Woolacombe Bay, and its sister site Golden Coast nearby, are well known holiday parks providing a range of holiday accommodation from caravan holiday homes to chalets and apartments, with many on site amenities including pools, restaurants and bars, and providing a wide range of entertainment. A camping section at the Woolacombe Bay park caters for tents and trailer tents only, so touring visitors can enjoy all the activities and entertainment of both parks. Partly terraced out of the hillside and partly on the hill top with some existing pine trees but with many more trees planted for landscaping, the site has magnificent views out across the bay. Marked and numbered pitches have been provided on grass for 146 tents, 94 with electricity (10/16A). All should be level, having been terraced where necessary and they are connected by gravel roads. Some up and down walking is needed for the toilet block. A bus service (small charge) runs between the two parks, the third and fourth parks in the group (Twitchen Parc and Easewell Farm) and the beach during the main season, although there is a footpath to the beach from the site. The three larger parks have varied entertainment programmes and children's clubs and Woolacombe Bay also boasts a health spa and beauty suite.

Facilities

A super central toilet block has excellent facilities, including en-suite shower and washrooms and separate toilets, baby facilities, and also a sauna and steam room - unusual but nice. Separate dishwashing and laundry rooms. Two units for disabled visitors. Supermarket. Bars, restaurant and entertainment. Indoor (heated) and outdoor pools with flumes and slides. Sauna and gym. Tennis courts. ATM. Dogs are welcome at Woolacombe Bay but not at Golden Coast. Off site: Fishing or riding 1 mile. Beach 1 mile.

At a glance

Welcome & Ambience	✓✓✓✓	Location	✓✓✓✓
Quality of Pitches	✓✓✓✓	Range of Facilities	✓✓✓✓✓

Directions

Take A361 Barnstaple - Ilfracombe road through Braunton. Turn left at Mullacott Cross roundabout towards Woolacombe then right towards Mortehoe. Now follow the camping signs by turning left and park is on the left. O.S.GR: SS469443.

Charges 2004

Per adult	£ 4.50 - £ 13.00
child (5-15 yrs)	£ 2.25 - £ 6.50
dog	£ 1.50

Reservations

Advised for peak season; contact park Tel: 01271 870343. Email: goodtimes@woolacombe.com

Open

11 May - 21 September (camping).

UK0730 Twitchen Parc

Mortehoe, Woolacombe EX34 7ES (Devon)

Set in the grounds of an attractive Edwardian country house, Twitchen Parc is now under the same ownership as Woolacombe Bay. Its main concern lies in holiday caravans and flats, although it also provides marked pitches for tourers at the top of the park, with some views over the rolling hills to the sea. With a more recently developed touring field, they include 155 pitches with 16A electricity, many with tarmac hardstanding (not always level), mostly arranged around oval access roads in hedged areas. Further non-electric pitches are behind in two open, unmarked fields which are sloping (blocks are thoughtfully provided, stored in neat wooden boxes next to water points). A smart, modern entertainment complex incorporates a licensed club and family lounge with snacks, a restaurant, teenage disco room, cartoon lounge, outdoor pool and smart indoor pool complex. Twitchen is very popular for families with children. If they become bored, there are always the excellent beaches nearby with a footpath down to the sea. All the facilities of Golden Coast and Woolacombe Bay Parcs and Easewell Farm are free to visitors at Twitchen, with a bus (small charge) running regularly between the four parks and to the beach.

Facilities

There are two toilet blocks. The latest should be ready for 2005 with en-suite washrooms and a sauna and steam room. Dishwashing and laundry facilities at each block plus a good modern launderette at the central complex. Motorcaravan service point. Shop and takeaway. Club, bars, restaurant and entertainment for adults and children, day and evening. Creche for children (charge). Outdoor pool (heated mid-May - mid-Sept). Attractive indoor pool with sauna, paddling pool, fountain and a viewing area. Putting green. Games rooms for table tennis, pool, snooker and arcade games. Good adventure play area. ATM. American motorhomes are accepted (up to 30 ft). Off site: Beach 1 mile. Golf 1 mile. Fishing, riding and bicycle hire 2 miles.

At a glance

Welcome & Ambience	✓✓✓✓	Location	✓✓✓✓
Quality of Pitches	✓✓✓✓	Range of Facilities	✓✓✓✓✓

Directions

From Barnstaple take A361 towards Ilfracombe and through Braunton. Turn left at Mullacott Cross roundabout towards Woolacombe and then right towards Mortehoe. Park is on the left before village. O.S.GR: SS465451.

Charges 2004

Per caravan or motorcaravan	£ 14.00 - £ 30.00
with services	£ 19.00 - £ 34.00
tent - adult	£ 4.50 - £ 13.00
tent - child (5-15 yrs)	£ 2.25 - £ 6.50
dog	£ 1.50
Special offers available.	

Reservations

Made with deposit (£2 per pitch per night). Tel: 01271 870343. Email: goodtimes@woolacombe-bay.com

Open

1 April/Easter- end October.

UK0720 Easewell Farm Holiday Parc

Mortehoe, Woolacombe EX34 7EH (Devon)

Near to the sandy beaches of Woolacombe, Easewell Farm is now part of the Woolacombe Bay Holiday Parc group who own the Woolacombe Bay, Golden Coast and Twitchen parks. A shuttle bus runs between the four parks and to the beach (tickets £1 per person per holiday). This is a traditional style touring park which during the day is a hive of activity, but the nights are quiet and peaceful. The largest of the camping fields is sloping with superb views across the headland to the sea. Two smaller fields are terraced and one area has hardstandings. Together they provide 250 pitches, 90 with electricity connections (15A) and 20 also with TV and water connections. The shop is well stocked (gas available), there is a takeaway and restaurant and an attractive bar with patio overlooking a small duck pond. The park has its own very well maintained nine hole golf course which is popular and has reduced fees for campers. One of the huge redundant farm buildings has been put to excellent use: divided into three areas, it provides table tennis and pool, a skittle alley and two lanes of flat green bowling with changing rooms. Walks to the local village and along the coastal path are easy from the site and a bus to Ilfracombe and Barnstaple stops 100 yards from the entrance.

Facilities

The central toilet block has been regularly upgraded and can be heated. Two washbasins in the ladies have hoses for hair washing, controllable showers (no dividers). Small area with baby bath facilities. Dishwashing sinks under cover. Laundry. These facilities are arranged around the farmhouse area and include a very well equipped unit for disabled people with everything in one large room including a hairdryer. Motorcaravan service point. Shop. Bar. Golf. Small heated indoor swimming pool is well used, as are games and TV rooms. Fenced play area with bark base. Indoor skittle alley, bowls, and table tennis. In high season only one dog per pitch is allowed. Off site: Fishing or riding 1 mile, bicycle hire 3 miles. Tarka Trail for walking and riding. Boat trips to Lundy Island.

Directions

From Barnstaple, take A361 Ilfracombe road through Braunton. Turn left at Mullacott Cross roundabout on B3343 to Woolacombe, turning right after 2-3 miles to Mortehoe. Park is on right before village. O.S.GR: SS465455.

Charges 2004

Per caravan or motorcaravan	£ 14.00 - £ 30.00
tent - adult	£ 4.50 - £ 13.00

Reservations

Made with £2 deposit per night booked. Tel: 01271 870225. Email: goodtimes@woolacombe.com

Open

Easter - 30 September.

At a glance

Welcome & Ambience	✓✓✓✓	Location	✓✓✓✓
Quality of Pitches	✓✓✓✓	Range of Facilities	✓✓✓

UK1075 Golden Coast Holiday Village

Station Road, Woolacombe EX34 7HW (Devon)

The Golden Coast is part of the Woolacombe Bay Holiday Parcs group that includes Woolacombe Bay, Twitchen Parc and the recently acquired Easewell Farm. It comprises predominantly brick-built holiday accommodation, however, there are two small camping areas providing 93 pitches, 18 of which are fully serviced. The toilet block is adequate rather than good, and was quite clean when we visited. Campers can enjoy an extensive program of entertainment for children and adults, and qualified nursery nurses run a crèche. A shuttle bus runs between the four parks and to the beach several times a day (£1 per person per holiday). A visit to the Old Mill Inn should not be missed; it serves bar meals, and has an excellent beer garden with adventure play area for the children. The range of amenities and facilities at this large park will suit families looking for a lively holiday filled with entertainment and activities.

Facilities

A new building provides good facilities including good showers. One washing machine and a dryer in the ladies' section. Dishwashing sinks inside. Large, well stocked supermarket, boutique and beauty salon. Indoor and outdoor swimming pools, outdoor flume, sauna and solarium. Bar, club, Old Mill Inn, restaurant and takeaway. Floodlit tennis court. Adventure playgrounds. Snooker. Games room. Soft play area and crèche. 9-hole golf course. Indoor and outdoor bowls, ten-pin bowling. Fishing. Woodland walks. Off site: Woolacombe beach is about 2 miles, and for walkers there is the coastal path. Amenities at sister parks available to all visitors.

Directions

From Barnstaple, take A361 (signed Braunton and Ilfracombe). Turn left on B3343 (signed Woolacombe) and follow the road towards the town. The park is on the left near the top of the hill. O.S.GR: SS480435.

Charges 2004

Per caravan or motorcaravan	£ 14.00 - £ 30.00
with services	£ 19.00 - £ 34.00
tent - per adult	£ 4.50 - £ 13.00
tent - per child (5-15 yrs)	£ 2.25 - £ 6.50

Reservations

Made with £2 deposit per pitch per night. Tel: 01271 870343. Email: goodtimes@woolacombe.com

Open

12 February - 2 January.

At a glance

Welcome & Ambience	✓✓✓✓	Location	✓✓✓✓
Quality of Pitches	✓✓✓	Range of Facilities	✓✓✓✓✓

UK0735 Woolacombe Sands Holiday Park

Beach Road, Woolacombe EX34 7AF (Devon)

With sea views and within walking distance of Woolacombe's lovely sandy beach, this family park has been terraced out of the valley side as you drop down into the village. Apart from its smart entrance, it has been left natural. The pond and stream at the bottom are almost hidden with gated access to the National Trust fields across the valley. The 200 terraced level grass pitches all with 10A electricity are accessed by gravel roads with some good up and down walking needed to the toilet blocks (probably not the best environment for disabled people). Some 50 mobile homes and 14 bungalows are in the more central area, and tents tend to be placed on the bottom terraces. The park boasts both indoor and outdoor pools (accessed by code) with a full time attendant. Evenings see Woolly Bear emerge from his 'shack' to entertain children, with adult family entertainment later. A good plus factor is the fact that all facilities open when the site opens. A useful path leads from the site to the beach via the car park and the walk is said to take 15 minutes.

Facilities

Four basic toilet blocks with good hot water are spread amongst the terraces. The newer shower block has separate toilets opposite. Shop (open 07.00 - 22.00). Self service food bar providing good value meals and breakfast (main season and BHs). Two bars and entertainment area. Indoor and outdoor pools both with paddling pool areas. Fenced play area on bark with plenty of equipment'. Ball area with nets. Crazy golf. 'Kingpin' bowling. Off site: Beach 15 mins walk. Riding next door. Golf 0.5 miles. Fishing: (fresh water) 0.5 miles.

At a glance

Welcome & Ambience	✓✓✓✓	Location	✓✓✓✓
Quality of Pitches	✓✓✓	Range of Facilities	✓✓✓✓✓

Directions

Follow A361 from Barnstaple through Braunton towards Ilfracombe. At Mullacott Cross roundabout turn left for Woolacombe (B3343). Site clearly signed on left as you go down the hill into the village. O.S.GR: SS468436.

Charges 2004

Per unit incl. 6 persons (max. 4 adults) and electricity	£ 12.50 - £ 32.50
dog	£ 5.00

Reservations

Advised for peak season and made with deposit (£30 per pitch/week. Tel: 01271 870569.

Open

1 April - 1 November.

NORTH DEVON & CORNWALL

Time to sample the delights of The Milky Way. One of Devon's Top Attractions!

The North Devon Coast's largest all weather attraction just gets better. Rain or shine, you can be sure to have a great day, with huge undercover facilities and 18 acres of outdoor fun. Experience the Clone Zone Alien Encounter, Europe's first interactive alien adventure featuring a suspended coaster; and the not to be missed Time Warp indoor adventure play areas with massive slides - built for adults as well as children.

The little ones are taken care of too - Toddler Town and Fantasy Farm are perfect with dedicated under 5s play provisions. Come and pilot the Droid Destroyer's Dodgem Cars with special sessions allocated for parents and small children.

Prepare to be thrilled with the live shows including the North Devon Bird of Prey Centre's spellbinding twice daily displays; and the highly entertaining Ferret Racing - with the world's first flying ferret!

Also available, the sports hall with laser target shooting, golf and archery, Lybarn railway, Lost in Space maze, pets corner where you can feed and cuddle the baby lambs and goats.

Open every day 10.30am - 6.00pm throughout the summer.

UK1150 Ruda Holiday Park

Parkdean Holidays, Croyde Bay, Croyde EX33 1NY (Devon)

Ruda Holiday Park is the latest addition to Parkdean Holidays, now comprising 12 parks in Scotland, Wales and southwest England. Ruda is right beside a Blue Flag beach and provides 313 camping and touring pitches in two distinct areas. A large camping area divided into four sections is reserved for tent campers and motorcaravans (there are some electricity hook-ups around the perimeter and it is served by two toilet blocks that are aging but clean). Touring caravan and motorcaravan pitches, all with electricity connections (13A), are in a separate field across the road and have direct access to the beach. Here, the toilet facilities are modern with coded entry to stop day visitors using them. A central complex (well away from the camping fields) houses a supermarket, laundry, food outlets, and all of the entertainment clubs and bars. The Cascade Tropical Pool, a fun pool with flume and water features is supervised at all times (children under five must wear arm bands which are provided free of charge). A large adventure play area, a tennis court and a sports field are also a short distance from the camping fields so that visitors are not disturbed. There's plenty of walking on the sand dunes and around the park, and Croyde Bay is renowned for surfing.

Facilities

Two blocks in the camping fields provide toilets, showers with preset controls, and communal washbasins; these are aging but were clean at the time of visit. A separate bathroom with toilet has a door wide enough for wheelchairs (key from reception), however there are no aids for visitors with disabilities. A third, modern building provides all facilities in the touring field. Dishwashing sinks under cover. Laundry with washing machines, dryers and irons. Bar, restaurant, snack bar and takeaway. Amusement arcade. Cascade Tropical pool. Adventure playground. Tennis court. Sports field. Fishing lake. Supermarket, boutique and hire centre. Surfing equipment for hire. Direct access to sheltered beach. Caravan holiday homes and lodges for hire. Off site: Surfing, Trip to Lundy Island.

Directions

From Barnstaple, take A361 signed Braunton and Ilfracombe. At Braunton, take sharp left (narrow road) towards Croyde (signed) and follow the road all the way to the beach. Entrance to Ruda is on the right. O.S.GR: SS561331.

Charges 2004

Per pitch	£ 7.00 - £ 22.00
pitch with services	£ 10.00 - £ 34.00
Prices are for pitch and up to 4 persons;	
max. 8 persons per pitch.	

Reservations

Made with £25 deposit or full amount if less. Tel: 01271 890477. Email: enquires@ruda.co.uk

Open

March - November.

At a glance

Welcome & Ambience	✓✓✓✓	Location	✓✓✓✓✓
Quality of Pitches	✓✓✓✓	Range of Facilities	✓✓✓✓✓

UK1140 Lobb Fields Caravan & Camping Park

Saunton Road, Braunton EX33 1EB (Devon)

Braunton village, Saunton Sands, the famous Tarka Trail for cycling, Baggy Point for walking, the biosphere at Braunton Burrows (one of only 13 similar special reserves in the country), Marwood Gardens, and wind surfing and water skiing on the Taw estuary are just some of the many attractions within a short distance of Lobb Fields. If you just want to sit and relax, then the pitches at the park offer views of the Taw estuary and Saunton, as well as magnificent sunsets. Lobb Fields has two camping areas providing 180 pitches on sloping grass, with a few hardstandings. Twelve pitches are reserved for seasonal caravans, and 61 have 16A electricity hook-ups. A third field is open for campers for 28 days only in high season. The pitches are marked and grass roads lead to the amenities. As the two toilet blocks are at the very bottom or very top of the fields, some up and down walking is inevitable. A small play area with wooden adventure equipment is located in the lower field. Managers, Robert and Diana Gleed, assisted by Bruce and Maureen Reeves, offer their guests a friendly welcome and are pleased to give information about the area. Lobbs Fields may be close to many holiday activities, but it is also a peaceful retreat for those wanting a quiet holiday.

Facilities

Two elderly toilet blocks (one in each field) have all the usual facilities. Baby room (upper block only). Laundry. Dishwashing sinks under cover. Cleaning and maintenance can be variable. The lower block can be heated and has good facilities for disabled visitors in a recently built unit. Hair dryers and irons available from reception (£5 returnable deposit). Adventure play area. Off site: Nearest shops less than a mile.

Open

28 March - 26 October.

Directions

Take A361 Barnstaple to Braunton road, then B3231 (signed Croyde) to Braunton. Park is 1 mile from Braunton on the right - take care through Braunton as roads are quite narrow and busy. O.S.GR: SS474370.

Charges 2004

Per unit incl. 2 persons	£ 6.50 - £ 14.00
incl. electricity	£ 7.50 - £ 16.50
extra person	£ 1.00
dog	£ 1.00

Reservations

£10 deposit for each week, non refundable - min. stay 3 nights during B.Hs. Tel: 01271 812090. Email: lobbfields@compuserve.com

At a glance

Welcome & Ambience	✓✓✓✓	Location	✓✓✓✓
Quality of Pitches	✓✓✓	Range of Facilities	✓✓✓

UK0710 Hidden Valley Touring & Camping Park

West Down, Ilfracombe EX34 8NU (Devon)

The owners, Martin and Dawn Fletcher, run this aptly named award-winning, family park to high standards. In a sheltered valley setting between Barnstaple and Ilfracombe beside a small stream and lake (with ducks), it is most attractive and is also convenient for several resorts, beaches and the surrounding countryside. The original part of the park offers some 74 level pitches of good size on three sheltered terraces. All have hardstanding, electricity hook-ups (16A) and free TV connections (leads for hire), with a water point between each pitch. Kingfisher Meadow, a little way from the main facilities and reached by a tarmac road, provides a further 60 pitches entirely on grass (so suitable for campers with tents), all with electricity, water, waste water and TV hook-ups. Two good adventure play areas have wooden equipment and safe bark surfaces (one near a fast flowing stream). There is a small shop with off-licence, takeaway, a lounge bar and a good value, family restaurant serving a range of home cooked meals in attractive surroundings, plus a games room. Essentially this is a park for those seeking good quality facilities in very attractive, natural surroundings, without too many man-made distractions - apart from some traffic noise during day time. It provides a relaxed setting with woodland walks direct from the site.

Facilities

Two modern toilet blocks (one for each area, one heated) are tiled and have non-slip floors. Some washbasins in cubicles, some en-suite with toilets in the Kingfisher Meadow block. Bathroom (tokens). Baby room. Laundry facilities including washing machine, dryer and iron. Dishwashing sinks under cover. Complete facilities for people with disabilities. Supplementary clean 'portacabin' style facilities in the original area. Motorcaravan service facilities. Gas supplies. Shop, bar and takeaway. Good restaurant open to the public (weekends only out of season). Play areas. Up to two dogs are accepted (otherwise by prior arrangement). Caravan storage. Off site: Fishing and golf 2 miles. Bicycle hire 4 miles. Riding 5 miles. Beach 5 miles.

At a glance

Welcome & Ambience	✓✓✓✓	Location	✓✓✓✓
Quality of Pitches	✓✓✓✓	Range of Facilities	✓✓✓✓

Directions

Park is on A361 Barnstaple - Ilfracombe road, 3.5 miles after Braunton. O.S.GR: SS499408.

Charges 2004

Per unit incl. 2 persons	£ 6.00 - £ 15.00
with services	£ 9.50 - £ 17.50
extra adult	£ 1.50 - £ 2.50
child (5-15 yrs)	£ 1.00 - £ 1.75
dog	free - £ 0.50

Discounts for over 50s.

Reservations

Essential in high season and accepted with deposit (low season £20, high £35). Tel: 01271 813837. Email: relax@hiddenvalleypark.com

Open

All year.

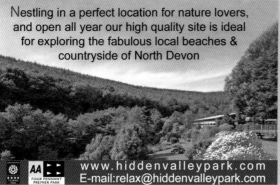

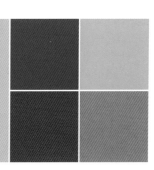

UK1120 Napps Touring Holiday Park

Old Coast Road, Berrynarbor, Ilfracombe EX34 9SW (Devon)

Set in an idyllic location in North Devon, this popular, family-run site offers peace and quiet on site, with plenty to see and do off site. A path just outside the gates leads down to a private beach with safe bathing; although it is only 200 yards to the gate, there are 200 steps down to the beach so it is not suitable for wheelchair users. Combe Martin and Ilfracombe beaches are also close by. The local pub (300 yards down the lane) offers snacks, a beer garden, restaurant and entertainment. The 170 touring pitches, most with views of Watermouth Bay, are terraced and spacious, 60 are serviced with electricity, water tap and waste point, and a further 70 have a 10A hook-up. An outdoor heated swimming pool with shallow section for children is unsupervised, but there is a terrace with table and chairs for non-swimmers to watch or enjoy a light meal from the snack bar. In high season, a ceramics studio is organised for older children; they choose a piece of pottery and paint it themselves, then it's glazed and fired for them. Light entertainment is organised during the high season. All the services are at the bottom of the site and it can be quite a climb back up, especially to the terraces and tent area.

Facilities

The modern toilet block includes open plan washbasins. Laundry. Dishwashing. Licensed shop. Gas supplies. Bar with light entertainment during high season. Takeaway. Heated outdoor pool with paddling pool and small toddlers' slide. Tennis. Ceramic studio. Games room. Adventure play area and 5-a-side football pitch. Caravan storage. Off site: Beach and fishing 200 yds. Golf and boat launching 1.5 miles. Bicycle hire and riding 5 miles. Coombe Martin 1.5 miles. Ilfracombe 3.5 miles.

Open

Easter - end-November.

At a glance

Welcome & Ambience	✓✓✓✓	Location	✓✓✓✓✓
Quality of Pitches	✓✓✓✓	Range of Facilities	✓✓✓✓

Directions

Leave M5 at junction 27, take A361 to South Molton and then A399 to Combe Martin. Site is 1.5 miles west of Combe Martin on the A399 (signed). O.S.GR: SS559475.

Charges 2004

Per unit incl. 2 persons	£ 6.00 - £ 14.00
incl. electricity	£ 8.00 - £ 17.00
extra person over 5 yrs	free - £ 2.00
awning	free - £ 2.00
dog	free - £ 2.00

Reservations

Made with £30 deposit per week or part week (non-refundable). Tel: 01271 882557. Email: info@napps.fsnet.co.uk

UK0700 Greenacres Touring Caravan Park

Bratton Fleming, Barnstaple EX31 4SG (Devon)

A neat, compact, rural park on the edge of Exmoor, Greenacres is managed and run alongside, but separately from, the working farm owned by the family. Drive through the farm access to the park (clearly signed) - you will need to go back and call at the house to book in. No tents are taken. The site has 30 very large, well drained pitches (all with 16A electric hook-ups) with connecting gravel paths to the road - in theory you can get to your unit without stepping on the grass. The top area is level, the lower part next to the beech woods is semi-terraced to provide six hardstandings and some hedged places. There are marvellous views outside the beech hedge that shelters the site. To the west of Exmoor, the park is very suitable for the coast at Ilfracombe and Combe Martin, or for exploring the moor. The family has opened up a woodland walk through newly planted trees and across the fields to a secluded valley picnic area beside a stream to take advantage of the marvellous views and surroundings. The West Country cycle way passes within a mile of the park and the area is the setting for the classic novel, 'Lorna Doone'.

Facilities

The toilet block, kept very clean and tidy, is in the centre of the horseshoe layout with showers (1M, 1F) on payment (20p). Units for disabled visitors (and general use in peak times). Laundry room, with sink, spin dryer, iron and board, and dishwashing room. Washing lines provided. Gas supplies. Tourist information kiosk. Area for children with football and volleyball nets and swings, separated by a Devon bank from the 2 acre dog exercise field. Recycling centre. Off site: Pubs, restaurants and takeaways within 3 mile radius. Fishing 3 miles. Riding 6 miles. Golf 12 miles.

At a glance

Welcome & Ambience	✓✓✓✓	Location	✓✓✓✓
Quality of Pitches	✓✓✓✓✓	Range of Facilities	✓✓✓

Directions

From North Devon link road (M5, exit 27) turn north at South Molton onto A399. Continue for 9 miles, past turning for Exmoor Steam Centre and on to Stowford Cross. Turn left towards Exmoor Zoological Park and Greenacres is on the left. O.S.GR: SS660404.

Charges 2004

Per unit incl. 2 persons	£ 5.25 - £ 8.50
incl. electricity	£ 6.75 - £ 10.00
extra person (over 7 yrs)	£ 1.25 - £ 1.75
dog	free

No credit cards.

Reservations

Made with £5 deposit. Tel: 01598 763334.

Open

Easter/1 April - 31 October.

UK0750 Minnows Touring Caravan Park

Sampford Peverell EX16 7EN (Devon)

Minnows is an attractive, neat small park with views across the Devon countryside, separated from the Grand Western canal by hedging. Easily accessible from the M5, it is suitable as an ideal touring centre for Devon and Somerset, for cycling or walking, or simply for breaking a long journey. A small, neat park, open for nine months of the year, it provides 45 level pitches all with 16A electricity. Of these, 34 are all weather (grass and gravel). A further 3.5 acres have been added to the park providing space for more and larger pitches, a tent area, a playground and a large field for ball games. The village of Sampford Peverell, with pub and farm shop, is only a half mile walk via the towpath, with Tiverton 7.5 miles. In fact, there are 12 miles of level walking on the towpath or one can take a trip on a horse-drawn barge. The site is on Sustran cycle route 3. Fishing permits are available from reception. A Caravan Club affiliated site, non-members are also very welcome. There could be some road noise from the adjacent A361.

Facilities

The heated toilet block is clean and comfortable with all modern facilities and constant hot water. Facilities for disabled visitors and babies. Covered dishwashing sinks. Laundry with washing machine, dryer and ironing. Motorcaravan service point. Gas supplies. Newspaper delivery arranged. Excellent tourist information. Play area. Bicycle hire (delivery to site). American RVs accepted (up to 38 ft), advance booking necessary. All year caravan storage. Site gates closed 9 pm. and locked 11 pm.- 7.30 am. Off site: Boat slipway 400 yds. Golf driving range near, full course 4 miles. Riding 6 miles.

At a glance

| Welcome & Ambience | ✓✓✓✓ | Location | ✓✓✓✓ |
| Quality of Pitches | ✓✓✓✓✓ | Range of Facilities | ✓✓✓ |

Directions

From M5 exit 27 take A361 signed Tiverton. After 600 yds take first exit signed Sampford Peverell. After 200 yds turn right at roundabout and cross bridge over A361 to second roundabout. Go straight on and park is ahead. From North Devon on A361 go to M5 exit 27 and return back up A361. O.S.GR: ST042148.

Charges 2004

Per adult	£ 3.30 - £ 6.80
child (5-16 yrs)	£ 1.10 - £ 1.60
pitch	£ 3.25 - £ 4.75

Senior citizen discounts.Credit cards £10 or more.

Reservations

Made with £10 deposit. Tel: 01884 821770.

Open

7 March - 14 November.

UK1060 Yeatheridge Farm Caravan Park

East Worlington, Crediton EX17 4TN (Devon)

Yeatheridge is a friendly, family park with riding, fishing lakes, and indoor pools. Based on a 200-acre farm, 9 acres have been developed over many years into an attractive touring park. Around the site there are views of the local hills and Dartmoor away to the south, and Exmoor lies to the north. You can explore three woodland walks ranging from 1 to 2.5 miles and the banks of the River Dalch. There are two deep coarse fishing lakes (bring your own rod), the top one offering family fishing and the lower one for serious fishing (age 14 or over and free of charge). Horse riding is available on site (best to bring your own hat) with hour-long and park rides available. The ponies and goats are also popular with adults and children alike. The touring area is very neat and tidy with a spacious feel to it as units are sited around the perimeter or back onto hedges, leaving open central areas. The 85 numbered, grass pitches are flat, gently sloping or on terraces and are sufficiently large, 80 with electricity connections (10A). Seasonal tourers take up 25 pitches and in addition there are 4 caravan holiday homes. The owners, Geoff and Liz, are constantly upgrading the park (recently opening a new reception and amenity building) and they try very hard to make everyone feel at home.

Facilities

Two toilet blocks provide family rooms, washbasins in cubicles, showers and facilities for babies. En-suite room for disabled visitors. Dishwashing (hot water 10p) and laundry. Shop. Bar, restaurant and snack bar (hours vary acc. to season). Unsupervised indoor pools, toddlers' pool and water slide open daily, 10 am - 8 pm. Fenced play area with fort for under 10s (parental supervision). Football field. TV room. Pool table, table tennis and skittles. Fishing. Riding.

Open

22 March - 29 September.

At a glance

| Welcome & Ambience | ✓✓✓✓ | Location | ✓✓✓✓ |
| Quality of Pitches | ✓✓✓✓ | Range of Facilities | ✓✓✓✓✓ |

Directions

Park is off B3042 Witheridge - Chawleigh (not in East Worlington). From M5 take exit 27 A361 to Tiverton. Turn left on A396 for 0.5 miles then right on B3137 almost to Witheridge. Take B3042 for 3 miles to site, signed on concrete road on left. O.S.GR: SS770114.

Charges 2004

Per unit incl. 2 persons	£ 7.00 - £ 11.00
extra person over 4 yrs	£ 1.20 - £ 2.00
electricity	£ 1.20
dog (first two)	£ 0.50 - £ 1.00

Reservations

Advised for Bank and school holidays and made with £35 deposit. Tel: 01884 860330. Email: yeatheridge@talk21.com

49

UK1050 Springfield Holiday Park

Tedburn Road, Tedburn St Mary, Exeter EX6 6EW (Devon)

Quietly situated to explore both Dartmoor and Exmoor, yet easily accessible, Springfield has room for 88 units on its 9 acres, mainly on level, grass terraces with views across the Devon countryside. Sixty pitches have 10A electricity. There are 32 seasonal units and 24 caravan holiday homes which are to be found at the lower part of the park. The reception/shop is on the right as you drop down into the park and gravel access roads radiate out from here along the terraces and link up at the bottom where there's a family 'terrace bar' with a grass terrace making the most of the rural views. Good value meals are served to eat in or takeaway, even cream teas and the odd musical evening. A small play area with wooden equipment is located in the sports field which becomes the overflow camping area when required. Martin and Eileen Johnson, the owners, are keen to help everyone enjoy their stay and can provide plenty of local information on Dartmoor walks and where to find the best fishing lakes, etc. A new bridge on the A30 provides much easier access to the site and to Dartmoor.

Facilities

The two toilet blocks are of older design with pre-set showers (20p external meter), a family bathroom and baby changing facilities. Washing up and laundry sinks (H&C), three washing machines and two dryers. Facilities could be stretched in high season. Well stocked licensed shop featuring local produce. Gas supplies. Terraced bar with bar meals or takeaway (open Easter, then May - Sept evenings and Sunday lunch). Small heated swimming pool, naturally sheltered (unsupervised). Play area and games room with skittle alley. Off site: Fishing 6 miles, bicycle hire 8 miles, riding 10 miles, golf 2 miles.

At a glance

Welcome & Ambience	✓✓✓✓✓	Location	✓✓✓✓
Quality of Pitches	✓✓✓	Range of Facilities	✓✓✓✓

Directions

From M5 junction 31 take A30 towards Okehampton. Take third exit from the A30 (Woodleigh junction) and follow signs over bridge to park. O.S.GR: SX788936.

Charges guide

Per caravan, trailer tent or motorcaravan	£ 8.00 - £ 10.00
family tent (acc to season/size)	£ 10.00 - £ 12.00
extra person (over 3 yrs)	£ 1.50
electricity	£ 1.80
walker or cyclist (1 person and tent)	£ 5.00 - £ 6.00

Reservations

Made with deposit (£25 per unit per week or £5 per night with electricity, £2 per night without). Tel: 01647 24242. Email: springhol@aol.com

Open

15 March - 15 November.

UK0760 Barley Meadow Camping & Caravan Park

Crockernwell, Exeter EX6 6NR (Devon)

This peaceful little park is located on the northern edge of Dartmoor with easy access from the A30. It is sheltered from the weather by good hedging and, although not always visible from the pitches, there are open views across the moorland to the south. The site would be a suitable base for visiting Exeter, Okehampton and Plymouth, hiking over the moors, or just enjoying the local area. The Two Moors Way for walkers is only 400 yards from the site. The 40 pitches are mostly on level grass, well spaced, with 13 hardstandings (some taken by seasonal units), and 27 electric hook-ups (10/16A). The resident owners can provide packed lunches and cream teas to order.

Facilities

The single heated toilet block is well maintained and provides all facilities including a well equipped room for disabled campers and babies. Laundry. Small shop for basic groceries, small camping items and gas. Games room with pool table and TV. Playground. Small library and information chalet. Only small American RVs (up to 30 ft.) accepted. Off site: Fishing 1 mile (river) or 2 miles (lake). Golf 2.5 miles. Riding 2 miles. Nearby is Castle Drogo, the youngest castle in the U.K. At Fingle Bridge there are walks and an Inn. Further afield is Canonteign Falls, home of Englands highest waterfall. Okehampton 15 mins.

Open

15 March - 15 November.

At a glance

Welcome & Ambience	✓✓✓✓	Location	✓✓✓✓✓
Quality of Pitches	✓✓✓✓	Range of Facilities	✓✓✓

Directions

From M5 exit 31, take A30 towards Okehampton. After 10 miles turn left towards Cheriton Bishop. After 0.5 miles pass through village, and continue for 1 mile towards Crockernwell, and site entrance is on your left. From the west on A30, at the 'Merry Roundabout' at Whiddon Down, take first left towards Cheriton Bishop. Continue for 2 miles and site entrance is on right. O.S.GR: SH742924.

Charges 2004

Per unit incl. 2 persons	£ 7.50 - £ 9.00
incl. electricity	£ 9.50 - £ 11.00
extra adult	£ 2.00
child (1-14 yrs0	£ 1.50
dog	£ 0.50

Reservations

Advised for peak season and B.Hs. Tel: 01647 281629. Email: angela.waldron1@btopenworld.com

UK0790 Harford Bridge Park

Peter Tavy, Tavistock PL19 9LS (Devon)

Harford Bridge has an interesting history - it was the Wheal Union tin mine until 1850, then used as a farm campsite from 1930 and taken over by the Royal Engineers in 1939. It is now a quiet, rural, mature park inside the Dartmoor National Park. It is bounded by the River Tavy on one side and the lane from the main road to the village of Peter Tavy on the other, with Harford Bridge, a classic granite moorland bridge, at the corner. With 16.5 acres, the park provides 120 touring pitches well spaced on a level grassy meadow with some shade from mature trees and others recently planted; 40 pitches have electricity and 5 have 'multi-services'. Out of season or by advance booking you may get one of the delightful spots bordering the river (no electricity). Some holiday caravans and chalets are neatly landscaped in their own area. A central grassy area is left free for games which is also used by the town band, village fete, etc. While the river (unfenced) will inevitably mesmerise youngsters, a super central adventure play area on a hilly knoll will claim them. In early summer there are chicks to watch (Mr Williamson's hobby) and the ducks are a feature. With its own and the local history, plus its situation, this is a super place.

Facilities

The single toilet block is older in style but fully equipped and well kept. Facilities for disabled visitors double for babies. Good launderette and drying room. Freezer. Motorcaravan service point. Games room with table tennis. TV room. Play area. Tennis court (free). Two communal barbecue areas. Fly fishing (licence, £3 p/day, £10 p/week). Off site: Bicycle hire, riding and golf, all within 2.5 miles.

Open

Late March - early November (all year for holiday homes).

At a glance

Welcome & Ambience	✓✓✓✓✓	Location		✓✓✓✓✓
Quality of Pitches		✓✓✓✓	Range of Facilities	✓✓✓

Directions

Two miles north of Tavistock, off A386 Tavistock - Okehampton road, take the road to Peter Tavy. O.S.GR: SX504768.

Charges 2004

Per unit incl. 2 persons	£ 7.25 - £ 12.50
with electricity	£ 10.25 - £ 14.50
with services	£ 10.75 - £ 16.00
extra adult	£ 3.00 - £ 3.50
child	£ 1.90

Reservations

Made for any length with first night's fees. Tel: 01822 810349. Email: enquiry@harfordbridge.co.uk

HARFORD BRIDGE HOLIDAY PARK

Peter Tavy, Tavistock, Devon PL19 9LS
Tel: 01822 810349 Fax: 01822 810028
Email: enquiry@harfordbridge.co.uk
Website: www.harfordbridge.co.uk

ROSE AWARD
HOLIDAY PARK

- Level sheltered park set in Dartmoor beside the River Tavy, with beautiful views of Cox Tor
- Riverside camping and other level spacious pitches - Open end Mar to Nov
- Self-catering luxury caravan holiday homes - Open all year
- Children's play area, tennis and table tennis, fly-fishing, dog exercise field
- Nearby pony-trekking and golf • Bellamy Gold and Rose Award

Just 2 miles from Tavistock off A386 Okehampton Road, take Peter Tavy turn

UK0805 Woodovis Park

Woodovis House, Gulworthy, Tavistock PL19 8NY (Devon)

Woodovis Park nestles in a sheltered wooded position covering 14 acres, by the edge of the Tamar Valley on the border of Devon and Cornwall. John and Dorothy Lewis run Woodovis Park, helped by their very welcoming staff. There are 50 good sized pitches, 42 with 10/16A electricity and 16 with hardstanding. Split over two fields, most are on level, neat grass, some are gently sloping. Landscaped in between are 35 caravan holiday homes, 14 for hire. The area is sheltered by thick hedges and woodland but in places you can see across the valley to Cornwall. An indoor heated pool with spa pool and sauna are a welcome attraction, as are the freshly baked croissants or bread ordered the night before at reception. The approach is down a tree lined lane with passing places. This is a peaceful spot with some nice touches.

Facilities

A purpose built, modern toilet block is fully equipped. One washbasin in cabin for ladies. Bathroom (coin operated) could be used by disabled people or for babies. Toilet for disabled visitors at the pool. Dishwashing sinks. Fully equipped laundry. Shop for basics with off licence. Indoor heated swimming pool (no swimming alone). Good games room including pool table. Fenced play area. Minigolf. Off site: Pub within walking distance. Fishing 1.5 miles. Golf, riding and bicycle hire 3 miles. Tavistock 4 miles.

At a glance

Welcome & Ambience	✓✓✓✓✓	Location		✓✓✓✓✓
Quality of Pitches		✓✓✓✓	Range of Facilities	✓✓✓✓

Directions

From Tavistock take A390 for Liskeard. After 3 miles right at Gulworthy crossroads (Chipshop, Lammerton) to park in 1 mile on the left. O.S.GR: SX431743.

Charges 2004

Per person (over 5 yrs)	£ 3.50
pitch incl. electricity	£ 6.00 - £ 10.00

Reservations

Made with deposit of £10 at time of booking. Tel: 01822 832968. Email: info@woodovis.com

Open

1 April/Easter - 1 November.

UK0802 Langstone Manor Holiday Park

Moortown, Tavistock PL19 9JZ (Devon)

Situated on the southwest edge of Dartmoor, this holiday park has been developed in the grounds of the old Langstone Manor house. The pitches are tucked into various garden areas with mature trees and flowering shrubs, or in the walled garden area with views over the moor. In all there are 42 level grass pitches which vary in size (20 with 10A electricity). You pass through a number of holiday caravans on the way to reception and the touring pitches where you will also find some holiday cottages and flats for rent. The 'pièce de resistance' is the unexpected traditional bar and restaurant in the Manor House, complete with a terrace that catches the evening sun. Open in high season and on demand in low season it has an open fire (if needed). Approaching over a short section of the moor, you realise how well Langstone Manor is situated to explore Dartmoor by foot, by car or on bike. The market town of Tavistock is 3 miles away and there is a wealth of National Trust Houses and Gardens to visit nearby.

Facilities

The toilet block is set to one side of the walled garden area, fully equipped and well maintained. Showers on payment (20p tokens from reception or bar). Fully equipped laundry room and covered dishwashing facilities. Changing mat for babies in the ladies. Basic supplies kept in reception. Bar /restaurant. Play area. Off site: Leisure centre and pool 2 miles. Golf 1 mile. Fishing 2 miles. Bicycle hire 3 miles.

Open

20 March - 29 October.

At a glance

Welcome & Ambience	✓✓✓✓	Location	✓✓✓✓✓
Quality of Pitches	✓✓✓✓	Range of Facilities	✓✓✓✓

Directions

From Tavistock take B3357 Princetown road. After about 2 miles turn right at crossroads (site signed). Pass over cattle grid onto the moor and follow site signs, leaving the moor to shortly find site on right. O.S.GR: SX524738.

Charges 2004

Per unit incl. 2 persons	£ 7.00 - £ 9.00
electricity and water	£ 2.00
child	£ 1.00 - £ 2.00

Reservations

Made with deposit (£10 p/week). Tel: 01822 613371. Email: web@langstone-manor.co.uk

UK0800 Higher Longford Caravan Park

Moorshop, Tavistock PL19 9LQ (Devon)

This attractive well organised, family run park is situated within the Dartmoor National Park boundaries with views up to the higher slopes of the moor. A neat, sheltered field provides 40 level pitches arranged on each side of a circular access road, with three smaller touring areas for a further 12 units, a small terraced camping field with good views and a seasonal camping field for a further 40. Facilities include 65 electrical hook-ups, several multi-serviced pitches and an area of hardstanding for motorcaravans in poor weather. Privately owned residential homes are in a separate, adjacent area and some attractive converted cottages form a courtyard area with the farmhouse, reception and bar. Within the 14th century farmhouse is a small licensed shop with gas and some fresh farm produce. It adjoins a pleasant, cosy campers' lounge with a pool table and TV which is open all day. Takeaway meals are offered. Higher Longford is an ideal centre for touring Dartmoor, either by car, on foot, or astride a local pony (riding stables nearby). Plymouth and the Channel ferries are a 30 minute drive, Tavistock is 3 miles, with a good market and Goose Fair in October.

Facilities

A super new toilet block provides excellent full en-suite facilities (amongst the best we have seen) plus extra toilets and washbasins. Full laundry facilities. Indoor dishwashing sinks. Motorcaravan services. Ice block swap service. Shop and takeaway (hours limited in winter). Campers' lounge with pool and TV. Large recreation field with adventure play area in centre. Caravan storage. Off site: Game or coarse fishing 3 miles, Tavistock golf course 1 mile. Bicycle hire and riding 3 miles.

At a glance

Welcome & Ambience	✓✓✓✓✓	Location	✓✓✓✓✓
Quality of Pitches	✓✓✓✓✓	Range of Facilities	✓✓✓✓

Directions

Park is clearly signed from B3357 Princetown road, 2 miles from Tavistock. O.S.GR: SX520747.

Charges 2004

Per unit incl. 2 adults, electricity	£ 12.00 - £ 13.00
tent pitch incl. 2 adults	£ 10.00 - £ 11.00
extra adult	£ 2.50
child	£ 1.50

Reservations

Made with £10 deposit. Tel: 01822 613360. Email: stay@higherlongford.co.uk

Open

All year.

UK0840 Woodlands Leisure Park

Blackawton, Totnes TQ9 7DQ (Devon)

Woodlands is a pleasant surprise - from the road you have no idea of just what is hidden away deep in the Devon countryside. To achieve this, there has been sympathetic development of farm and woodland to provide a leisure centre, open to the public and with a range of activities and entertainment appealing to all ages, plus a touring caravan park. Children (and many energetic parents too!) will thoroughly enjoy a huge variety of imaginative adventure play equipment, amazing water toboggan runs, the new 'Rock and Roll Tug Boat', the 'Woodlands Chuffer' and much more, hidden amongst the trees. Those more peacefully inclined can follow woodland walks around the attractive ponds. The 'Empire of the Sea Dragon' indoor play centre provides marvellous wet weather facilities comprising five floors of play areas and amazing slides. With a two night stay, campers on the touring park are admitted free of charge to the leisure park. The camping and caravan site overlooks the woodland and the leisure park, taking 320 units on three sloping, grassy fields, the original terraced one maturing nicely. One of the others has been fully terraced to provide groups of four to eight flat, very spacious pitches (90% with 10A electricity hook-ups and a shared water tap, drain and rubbish bin). The newest field has 120 pitches (with electricity) designed with a more open feel to provide space for larger groups or rallies. A popular park, early reservation is advisable.

Facilities

Three modern, heated toilet blocks, well maintained and kept very clean, include private bathrooms (coin-operated, 20p) and 16 family shower cubicles. Two laundry rooms, dishwashing areas and freezer for ice packs. Baby changing facilities. The leisure park café, with terrace, provides good value meals and a takeaway service for campers. Café opening hours and the adjoining gift shop (with gas and a few basic food supplies) vary according to season and demand. TV and games room. Dogs are accepted on the campsite but not in the leisure park (kennels available). Caravan storage Off site: The charming town of Dartmouth and the South Hams beaches are near. Fishing 3 miles. Golf 0.5 miles. Riding 5 miles. Beach 4 miles.

At a glance

Welcome & Ambience	✓✓✓✓	Location	✓✓✓✓
Quality of Pitches	✓✓✓✓✓	Range of Facilities	✓✓✓✓✓

Directions

From A38 at Buckfastleigh, take A384 to Totnes. Before town centre turn right on A381 Kingsbridge road. After Halwell turn left at Totnes Cross garage, on A3122 to Dartmouth. Park is on the right after 2.5 miles. O.S.GR: SX813521.

Charges 2004

Per unit incl. 2 persons	£ 10.50 - £ 18.50
extra person over 2 yrs	£ 5.50
electricity	£ 2.50
dog (contact site first)	£ 2.50

Free entry to leisure park for stays 2 nights or more.

Reservations

Accepted for min. 3 nights with £35 deposit (July/Aug. min. 7 days, £50 deposit). Bal. 21 days before arrival. Tel: 01803 712598. Email: fun@woodlandspark.com

Open

Easter - 1 November.

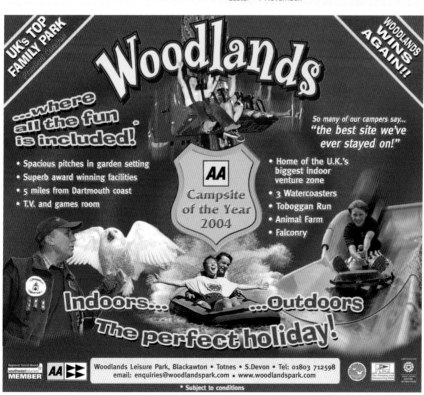

UK0820 Moor View Touring Park

California Cross, Modbury PL21 0SG (Devon)

Moor View has a gently sloping position with terraced, individual, fairly level grass pitches with marvellous views across to the Dartmoor Tors. It provides 68 pitches of varying size, connected by hard-core roads. All have 10A electricity, 33 are on hardstanding, with water and drainage on 13. Bushes and shrubs on the lower terraces are growing well, giving the park a more mature feel. A two acre field provides space for the odd rally. The amenities have been designed in one block near the entrance, not too far from the furthest pitches. The block includes a shop cum reception stocking fresh local produce and some camping accessories. Burgh Island and Bigbury Bay are nearby, Dartmoor is within striking distance. This is a park in a lovely corner of Devon, with enthusiastic new owners, Edward and Liz Corwood. A member of the Countryside Discovery group and now an adult only park.

Facilities

Traditional style, heated toilet facilities have access from a courtyard area and are kept clean, providing all necessary facilities including a laundry room and sink, and covered dishwashing sinks. Shop. Takeaway in season (to order, 6.30-7.30 pm). TV room. Off site: Golf 5 miles, riding and fishing 6 miles. A local country pub is within walking distance, the small town of Modbury is 3 miles.

Open

15 March - 15 November.

At a glance

Welcome & Ambience	✓✓✓✓	Location	✓✓✓✓
Quality of Pitches	✓✓✓	Range of Facilities	✓✓✓✓

Directions

On the A38 from Exeter, pass exit for A385 (Totnes) and continue for a further 2 miles. Just past Woodpecker Inn leave the A38 at Wrangaton Cross, signed Ermington, Modbury and Yealmpton. Turn left and follow straight on at crossroads (Kitterford Cross) signed Modbury, Loddiswell, Kingsbridge for 3 miles to California Cross. Leave garage on left and follow towards Modbury (B3207). Park is 0.5 miles on left. O.S.GR: SX705533.

Charges 2005

Per couple incl. electricity, hardstanding, water and drainage	£ 6.50 - £ 12.95
premier pitch	£ 1.00

Reservations

Made with £10 deposit. Tel: 01548 821485. Email: info@moorviewtouringpark.co.uk

UK0830 Slapton Sands Camping & Caravanning Club Site

Middle Grounds, Slapton, Kingsbridge TQ7 2QW (Devon)

Slapton is a charming village with tiny lanes and cottages, a shop and two historic pubs, one dominated by the ruined tower of an old monastery. The village (unsuitable for camping traffic) is about half a mile inland from the shingle beach of Slapton Sands and the fresh water Ley which is administered as a nature reserve by the Field Studies Council. The Camping and Caravanning Club site is situated on the road which leads from the Sands, on a well kept meadow overlooking the bay - the sea views are panoramic from most areas of the site, with shelter provided by some large bushes and the surrounding hedge. There are 115 grass pitches, some with a slight slope, and electrical connections (16A) are available for 46 (including 10 with hardstanding). Motorcaravans, trailer tents and tents are accepted without problems but the planners will only permit 8 caravan pitches which are kept for club members. This area was used for rehearsals for the WW2 Normandy landings, when the whole population was evacuated - there are memorials which include a tank in the village of Torcross. The quaint port of Dartmouth is 7 miles, Kingsbridge 8 miles and a variety of beaches and coves around the beautiful South Hams coastline are within easy reach.

Facilities

The modern toilet block is central, can be heated and is kept very clean, with washbasins in private cabins. Useful parent and child room and separate unit for disabled visitors (with key). Dishwashing facilities, laundry sinks, washing machine and dryer (and outside lines). Motorcaravan service point. Reception has a small library, gas and freezer for ice blocks. Small play area. Off site: Riding 0.5 miles. The Field Studies Centre arranges guided walks and short study courses on a wide variety of interests and can issue fishing permits for the Ley (perch and pike, of legendary size, in the summer months). Beach fishing is also popular.

Open

March - October.

At a glance

Welcome & Ambience	✓✓✓✓	Location	✓✓✓✓
Quality of Pitches	✓✓✓✓	Range of Facilities	✓✓✓✓

Directions

From A38 Exeter - Plymouth road, take A384 to Totnes. Just before town, turn right on A381 to Kingsbridge, then A379 through Stokenham and Torcross to Slapton Sands. Half way along the beach road turn left to Slapton village and site is 200 yds on right. Note: Avoid the very narrow Five Mile Lane from the A381 which is signed Slapton (just after a filling station) 6 miles from Kingsbridge. O.S.GR: SX825450.

Charges 2005

Per adult	£ 4.30 - £ 6.40
child (6-18 yrs)	£ 1.90
non-member pitch fee	£ 5.00

Reservations

Necessary and made with deposit; contact site or Central Reservations 0870 243 3331. Site tel: 01548 580538.

UK0850 Galmpton Park

Greenway Road, Galmpton, Brixham TQ5 0EP (Devon)

Within a few miles of the lively amenities of Torbay, Galmpton Park lies peacefully just outside the village of Galmpton, overlooking the beautiful Dart estuary just upstream of Dartmouth and Kingswear. This is a family park with some 120 pitches (60 marked for caravans) arranged on a wide sweep of grassy, terraced meadow, each pitch with its own wonderful view of the river. Situated on the hillside, some parts have quite a slope, but there are flatter areas (the owners will advise and assist). There are 90 electrical connections (10A) and 19 pitches have water and drainage. There is a separate tent field. Galmpton is a quiet and simple park (with the gates closed 11.15 pm - 7.30 am) in a most picturesque setting, within easy reach of all the attractions of South Devon. A member of the Countryside Discovery group.

Facilities

A central, substantial looking toilet block provides clean facilities including three washbasins in cabins, a very attractive under 5s bathroom (key), baby unit and hair care areas. Dishwashing room also with washing machine, dryer, iron and ironing board. Reception/shop sells a range of basics including gas. Bread to order. Good adventure play equipment. Dogs (max. 2 per unit) accepted at the owner's discretion and not mid-July and Aug. Motorhomes over 21 ft. not accepted. Off site: Local pub is 5 minutes walk.

Open

Easter - 30 September.

At a glance

Welcome & Ambience	✓✓✓	Location	✓✓✓✓✓
Quality of Pitches	✓✓✓✓	Range of Facilities	✓✓✓

Directions

Take A380 Paignton ring road towards Brixham until junction with the Paignton - Brixham coast road. Turn right towards Brixham, then second right into Manor Vale Road. Continue through the village, past the school and site is 500 yds on the right. O.S.GR: SX885558.

Charges 2004

Per unit incl. 2 persons and awning	£ 7.90 - £ 14.10
de-luxe pitch plus	£ 11.30 - £ 16.20
extra adult	£ 2.50
child (5-16 yrs)	£ 1.20

Various discounts available.

Reservations

Made with £20 deposit p/week booked.
Tel: 01803 842066.
Email: galmptontouringpark@hotmail.com

UK1130 Hoburne Torbay

Goodrington, Paignton TQ4 7JP (Devon)

Situated to the south of central Paignton, with a short, signed walk to the sea and some sea views of Torbay, this Hoburne-owned park's major interest is a complex of 504 holiday homes (135 to let) which totally dominate the higher of the two touring sites. However, there are 137 touring pitches (no tents) in two sections, each with a resident warden. One, probably the quieter of the two, is on flat grass by the entrance. The other is on higher ground, through the holiday homes at the top of the park with the sites large shop and café (with bakery) close by. It is on a gentle slope with some views. Pitches are of reasonable size, though with some variation, and all have 10A electricity. For those who like entertainment, the central club complex is the parks best feature, with a good sized heated outdoor pool (80 x 40 ft). and a super indoor pool with views across the bay, complete with flume, sauna and steam room. The clubhouse has a large club lounge with dance floor, a separate bar/restaurant (with views of Torbay). Entertainment is organised for adults and children from Spr. B.H to end Sept. and at Easter.

Facilities

Three toilet blocks, two of modern design in lower touring field, third block is of older design at the top touring field. Large launderette. Dishwashing area. Recycling bins. Motorcaravan service point. Well stocked shop. Gas available. Club room. Restaurant/bar. Takeaway. Café. Heated outdoor pool. Indoor pool with flume and fountain, sauna and steam room (all free). Mini two lane bowling alley. Pool and snooker tables. Amusement arcade. TV room showing cartoons. Crazy golf. Adventure playground. Indoor soft adventure play area. Daily children's entertainment. Reception is busy but efficient. Up to 30 American motorhomes accepted (25 ft. max). No dogs or other pets are accepted.

At a glance

Welcome & Ambience	✓✓✓✓	Location	✓✓✓✓
Quality of Pitches	✓✓✓✓	Range of Facilities	✓✓✓✓✓

Directions

Park is signed from the outer Paignton ring road. Look for left turn into Goodrington Road, then left into Grange Road. O.S.GR: SX890585.

Charges 2004

Per unit incl. up to 6 persons	£ 10.00 - £ 25.00

Reservations

Advised for high season. Made for 1-6 nights with payment in full, for 7 nights or over with £50 deposit p/week. Min. 7 days in high season.
Tel: 01803 558010.
Email: enquiriestorbay@hoburne.com

Open

14 February - 15 January excl. 2 weeks at Xmas.

UK0870 Beverley Park Holiday Centre

Goodrington Road, Paignton TQ4 7JE (Devon)

Beverley Park is a quality holiday centre, attractively landscaped, with marvellous views over Torbay. The pools, a large dance hall, bars and entertainment, are all run in an efficient and orderly manner. The park has 195 caravan holiday homes and 23 lodges, mainly around the central complex. There are 189 touring pitches in the lower areas of the park, all reasonably sheltered, some with views across the bay and some on slightly sloping ground. All pitches can take awnings and have 16A electricity (15 m. cable), 38 have hardstanding and 21 are fully serviced. Tents are accepted and a limited number of tent pitches have electrical connections. The park has a long season and reservations are essential for caravans. Entertainment is organised at Easter and from early May in the Starlight Cabaret bar. There are indoor and outdoor pools, each one heated and supervised. The Oasis fitness centre provides a steam room, jacuzzi, sun-bed and an excellent fitness room. The park is in the heart of residential Torbay, with views across the bay to Brixham and Torquay, and sandy beaches less than a mile away. This popular park has lots to offer and is well maintained and run. A member of the Best of British group.

Facilities

Good toilet blocks adjacent to the pitches, well maintained and heated, include roomy showers, some with washbasins en-suite. Baths on payment. Unit for disabled visitors. Facilities for babies. Laundry. Gas supplies. Motorcaravan service point. Large general shop (21/3-31/10). Restaurant, bars and takeaway (all Easter, then 30/5-26/10, and Autumn half-term). Swimming pools. Fitness centre. Tennis court. Crazy golf. Playground. Nature trail. Amusement centre with pool, table tennis and amusement machines. Soft play area. Dogs are not accepted. Off site: Regular minibus service to Paignton (timetable at reception) or normal services from outside the park. Fishing, bicycle hire, riding and golf all within 2 miles.

At a glance

Welcome & Ambience	✓✓✓✓✓	Location	✓✓✓✓
Quality of Pitches	✓✓✓✓✓	Range of Facilities	✓✓✓✓✓

Directions

Park is south of Paignton in Goodrington Road between A379 coast road and B3203 ring road and is well signed on both. O.S.GR: SX882584.

Charges 2004

Per serviced pitch	
incl. 2 persons and electricity	£ 11.00 - £ 21.50
incl. mains services and awning	£ 11.00 - £ 23.50
tent pitch incl. 2 persons	£ 7.00 - £ 19.50
extra adult	£ 4.50
child (4-14 yrs)	£ 3.00
awning or pup tent	£ 3.00
Max. 6 persons per reservation.	

Reservations

Made with £25 deposit (7, 14 or 21 days 17/7-3/9, min. 2 nights all other times); balance payable more than 28 days before arrival. Tel: 01803 661978. Email: info@beverley-holidays.co.uk

Open

16 February - 30 November.

UK0860 Whitehill Country Park

Stoke Road, Paignton TQ4 7PF (Devon)

Whitehill Country Park is beautifully situated in rolling Devon countryside, just 2.5 miles from the nearest beaches. Extending over 40 acres, a definite sense of space characterises this park and ten acres of ancient woodland are available for walks and attract a great deal of wildlife. Whitehill is a friendly park with 329 large grassy pitches which are located in separate fields around the site with evocative names, such as Nine Acres, Sweethill and Coombe Meadow. Most pitches have electrical connections (16A). Around 60 pitches are used for caravan holiday homes. The park boasts an attractive swimming pool (max. depth 1.3 m.) with a children's paddling pool alongside, as well as a good range of other leisure facilities, notably The Hayloft bar (with satellite TV), a café and a well-stocked shop.

Facilities

Two well maintained sanitary blocks include private, individual washing facilities for ladies. Ample laundry facilities. Gas supplies. Shop. Bar. Café (29/5-4/9). Swimming and paddling pools (heated 29/5-4/9). Three play areas. Dogs and other pets are not accepted. Off site: Paignton 2.5 miles. Beach 3 miles. Fishing, golf and riding 2 miles. Torquay, Dartmoor, Quay West Aqua Park. Bus stop at site entrance.

Open

15 May - 2 October.

At a glance

Welcome & Ambience	✓✓✓✓	Location	✓✓✓✓✓
Quality of Pitches	✓✓✓✓	Range of Facilities	✓✓✓✓

Directions

Turn left at The Parkers Arms off the A385 Paignton to Totnes road, signed Stoke Gabriel. Site is 1 mile along this road. O.S.GR: SX857587.

Charges 2004

Per unit incl. 2 persons and elecricity	£ 13.50
tent pitch (no electricity)	£ 11.50
extra person	£ 2.50
child (4-14 yrs)	£ 1.50
awning or pup tent	£ 2.00

Reservations

Contact site. Tel: 01803 782338.
Email: info@whitehillfarm.co.uk

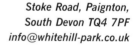

UK0845 Hillhead Caravan Club Holiday Park

Hillhead, Brixham TQ5 0HH (Devon)

Hillhead is a fully refurbished Caravan Club site set in 22 acres of beautiful Devon countryside. Originally developed in the 1960s within what is now a coastal protection area two miles from Brixham, the park has benefited from a £3 million redevelopment. Unusually for a Caravan Club site, it offers a full entertainment programme in peak season. Hillhead comprises 243 pitches, most with electrical hook-ups and many with fine views. Amenities are to a uniformly high standard, notably the main complex based around an attractive courtyard, and housing a shop, bar, games room and restaurant. The children's play area is outstanding with a range of imaginative items including a large wooden fort. Hillhead is rightly proud of its strong commitment to sound environmental practice, with a plan to promote species diversity and the encouragement of good practice by site workers and visitors alike.

Facilities

The two sanitary blocks are new and maintained to a high standard. Each block includes 3 special private family bathrooms (key from reception) and facilities for disabled visitors. Laundry facilities. Motorcaravan service point. Shop. Bar and restaurant. Swimming pool (heated May - Sept) with children's pool adjacent. Large play area. Skateboard ramp. Games room. TV. Entertainment in season. Games field. Dog walking area. Off site: Nearest beach and coastal path 2 miles. Bus stop at site entrance. River Dart boat trips. Paignton, Torquay and Brixham. Golf (18 holes) and riding 2 miles. Bicycle hire 2.5 miles.

At a glance

Welcome & Ambience	✓✓✓✓	Location	✓✓✓✓
Quality of Pitches	✓✓✓✓	Range of Facilities	✓✓✓✓✓

Directions

Site is well signed from A379 Paignton - Dartmouth road and is located on the B3205 (Slappers Hill Road). Entrance is on the left after 400 yards. O.S.GR: SX904534.

Charges 2004

Per unit incl. 2 persons, electricity	£ 12.00 - £ 17.00
extra adult	£ 4.00 - £ 5.00
child	£ 1.50 - £ 3.00

Reservations

Required for peak season - contact site.
Tel: 01803 853204.
Email: enquiries@caravanclub.co.uk

Open

30 April - 31 October.

UK0880 Dornafield

Two Mile Oak, Newton Abbot TQ12 6DD (Devon)

The entrance to Dornafield leads into the charming old courtyard of a 14th Century farmhouse giving a mellow feeling that is complemented by the warm welcome from the Dewhirst family. The reception, shop, tourist information/ecology room have been sympathetically converted from farm outbuildings, with the games room from the old milking parlour, complete with stalls. Having booked in, continue down the lane (overlooked by a tree covered bank and alive with wild flowers) to the Buttermeadow, a tranquil valley providing 75 individual, numbered pitches on flat grass, separated by grassy ridges and in some places, wild rose hedges. You pass the walled Orchard area, secluded and cosy for tents. Or take the road up the hill to Blackrock Copse with large luxury pitches with all facilities including a chemical disposal point for each pitch and TV connections, very cleverly concealed and 61 with hardstanding. Electricity points are 10A. Whilst having been carefully designed, the environment remains natural. Both Buttermeadow and Blackrock have super, well maintained woodland adventure play areas. Dornafield is a member of the Caravan Club's 'managed under contract' scheme, with both members and non-members made welcome. Dornafield's rural situation is delightful and, being away from the coast and without any evening activities, it is a haven for those seeking a quiet, restful holiday. A park that is well worth consideration.

Facilities

Both modern toilet blocks are excellent and heated, with some washbasins in cubicles and comfortable roomy showers, but the new block up the hill could be said to be 'state of the art' with under-floor heating and a heat recovery system. Both blocks have facilities for disabled visitors and babies, laundry rooms and covered washing up areas. Shop, Gas supplies. All-weather hard tennis court. Games room with table tennis. Play areas. All year caravan storage. Off site: Local inn 0.5 miles. Fishing 2.5 miles. Golf 1 mile.

At a glance

Welcome & Ambience	✓✓✓✓✓	Location	✓✓✓✓✓
Quality of Pitches	✓✓✓✓✓	Range of Facilities	✓✓✓

Directions

Park is northwest of A381 Newton Abbot - Totnes road. Leave A381 at Two Mile Oak Inn, opposite garage, and turn left at crossroads after about half a mile. Entrance is on the right. O.S.GR: SX848683.

Charges 2004

Per unit incl. 2 adults, electricity	£ 10.50 - £ 18.00
incl. mains services	£ 11.50 - £ 19.00
extra adult	£ 3.30 - £ 5.00
child (5-16 yrs)	£ 1.10 - £ 1.60
dog	£ 1.00

Reservations

Any length, £10 p.w. low season, £30 p/week high season. Tel: 01803 812732.
Email: enquiries@dornafield.com

Open

13 March - 31 October.

UK0910 Ross Park

Park Hill Farm, Ipplepen, Newton Abbot TQ12 5TT (Devon)

Ross Park has to be seen to appreciate the amazing floral displays with their dramatic colours, that are a feature of the park. These are complemented by the use of a wide variety of shrubs which form hedging for most of the 110 pitches to provide your own special plot, very much as on the continent. Many pitches have wonderful views over the surrounding countryside and for those who prefer the more open style, one small area has been left unhedged. The owners, Mark and Helen Lowe, continue to strive to provide quality facilities and maintain standards, and this is reflected in the awards they have won. The New Barn which provides a comfortable lounge, a mezzanine bar with bar snacks and a restaurant with extra seating in the conservatory which is home to some exotic and colourful plants. The touring area is divided into bays or groups by hedging and shrubs and provides 110 pitches all with electricity (16A). Some 82 of these have a hardened surface, some made larger with a further gravel area. An orchard area alive with daffodils in the spring and a conservation area with information on wild flowers and butterflies, and with extended views, completes these environmentally considered amenities. Barn dances are organised on Sundays in high season. A well cared for park worthy of consideration.

Facilities

Six well equipped, heated en-suite units, one with baby facilities, one suitable for disabled people. Further separate shower, washbasin and toilet facilities. Extra heated block with toilets, washbasins in cabins and hair-care centre. Fully equipped laundry room. Utility room with dishwashing, freezer and battery charging. Dog shower. Motorcaravan services. Recycling. Licenced shop. Gas supplies. Bar, bar snacks and restaurant (all April - end Oct, plus Christmas and New Year). Games room. Bowling and croquet greens. Large well equipped adventure playground. Caravan storage. Off site: Dainton Park 18 hole golf course adjacent. Fishing 3 miles. Riding 1 mile.

At a glance

Welcome & Ambience	✓✓✓✓✓	Location	✓✓✓✓
Quality of Pitches	✓✓✓✓✓	Range of Facilities	✓✓✓✓

Directions

From A381 Newton Abbot - Totnes road, park is signed towards Woodland at Park Hill crossroads and Jet filling station. O.S.GR: SX845671.

Charges 2004

Per unit incl. 2 persons	£ 9.75 - £ 15.75
incl. electricity	£ 10.75 - £ 16.75
extra adult	£ 3.25 - £ 5.00
child (4-16 yrs)	£ 1.50

Christmas packages available. No credit cards.

Reservations

Made with £20 deposit. Tel: 01803 812983. Email: enquiries@rossparkcaravanpark.co.uk

Open

All year excl. January and first two weeks of Feb.

ROSS PARK

Ross Park offers peace and tranquility, beautifully landscaped gardens to relax in, centrally heated shower block, a restaurant with tropical conservatory, snooker, croquet, table tennis, children's play area and dog walks are situated in a conservation area which forms part of our spacious 20 acre park. 18 hole golf course opposite. **FREE COLOUR BROCHURE**

AWARD-WINNING PARK

TEL/FAX: 01803 812983
enquiries@rossparkcaravanpark.co.uk
www.rossparkcaravanpark.co.uk

ROSS PARK, PARK HILL FARM, IPPLEPEN, NEWTON ABBOT, DEVON TQ12 5TT

UK0930 Ashburton Caravan Park

Waterleat, Ashburton TQ13 7HU (Devon)

For tents and motorcaravans only, Ashburton Park's four acres nestle in a hidden valley below Dartmoor, bordered by mature woodland. The Ashburn stream with rocky pools, evenly divides and screens holiday homes from the camping area. Sheltered and south facing, the park is a tranquil retreat, although for the energetic a half mile steep uphill walk brings you to the moor. There are 35 level or gently sloping pitches, 8 with electricity (16A), on either side of a tarmac road that culminates in a small field area.

Facilities

First class toilet block with washbasins in cabins for ladies. Toilet and washbasin for disabled visitors. Washing machine, dryer, and iron. Gas, freezer service, maps and walks and daily weather report. Dogs (limited breeds only). Torches useful. Off site: Shops, etc. at Ashburton, a pleasant riverside walk away. Bicycle hire 1 mile, riding and golf 3 miles.

At a glance

Welcome & Ambience	✓✓✓✓	Location	✓✓✓✓✓
Quality of Pitches	✓✓✓✓	Range of Facilities	✓✓✓

Directions

In centre of Ashburton turn northwest into North Street. Bear right before bridge following signs for 'Waterleat' 1.5 miles to park. O.S.GR: SX752721.

Charges 2004

Per unit incl. 2 persons	£ 8.50 - £ 13.00

No credit cards.

Reservations

Made for min. 3 nights with £15 deposit. Tel: 01364 652552. Email: info@ashburtoncaravanpark.co.uk

Open

Easter - mid October.

UK0950 River Dart Adventures

Holne Park, Newton Abbot TQ13 7NP (Devon)

The park is marketed as 'River Dart Adventures', where campsite and adventure experiences are enjoyed by old and young from all over Europe. Once part of a Victorian estate with mature woodland on the edge of Dartmoor in the beautiful Dart valley, the park and its activities are now open to the general public on payment. It features a variety of unusual adventure play equipment (eg. a giant spider's web) arranged amongst and below the trees, 'Lilliput Land' for toddlers, Jungle Fun, and woodland streams and a lake with raft for swimming and inflatables, fly fishing and marked nature and forest trails - all free to campers except fishing. It does become busy at weekends and school holidays with supervised activities for 7 year olds and upwards, such as caving, canoeing or climbing paid for with 'Dare Devil' tokens (£1 per token, obtainable from any outlet on the park). The camping and caravanning area is in the more open parkland overlooking the woods and is mainly on a slight slope with some shade from mature trees. There are 185 individual pitches of very reasonable size, marked by lines on the grass, some slightly sloping, with 105 electrical connections (10/16A) and 12 hardstandings.

Facilities

Two wooden toilet blocks, one quite smart, the older a little tired, can both be heated. Washbasins in cubicles, baby facilities, laundry and dishwashing, freezer, en-suite unit for disabled visitors (access by key), family bathroom and drying room. Motorcaravan service point. Shop (all season). Restaurant, bar (all season) and takeaway (20/7-31/8). Large TV and games room. Indoor climbing room (some of these open all year for the activities on offer). Small, heated swimming pool (all season). Tennis. Max. two dogs per pitch. American motorhomes only accepted in dry periods (no hardstandings). Off site: Bicycle hire or riding 4 miles. Golf 6 miles.

Open

1 April - 30 September.

At a glance

Welcome & Ambience	✓✓✓✓	Location	✓✓✓✓✓
Quality of Pitches	✓✓✓✓	Range of Facilities	✓✓✓✓✓

Directions

Signed from the A38 at Peartree junction, park is about 1 mile west of Ashburton, on the road to Two Bridges. Disregard advisory signs stating 'no caravans' as access to the park is prior to narrow bridge. O.S.GR: SX734701.

Charges 2004

Per unit incl. 2 persons	£ 9.50 - £ 16.50
extra person (over 3 yrs)	£ 4.00 - £ 6.00
electricity	£ 2.00
dog (max. 2)	£ 2.00

Camping Cheques accepted.

Reservations

Advised for high season and made with £10 deposit per pitch (additional high season deposit £30 for 7 nights or less, £40 for longer). Balance due 21 days before arrival. All deposits non-returnable.
Tel: 01364 652511. Email: enquiries@riverdart.co.uk

61

UK0960 Parkers Farm Holiday Park

Higher Mead Farm, Ashburton, Newton Abbot TQ13 7LJ (Devon)

Well situated with fine views towards Dartmoor, Parker's Farm is a modern touring site on a working farm. Close inspection reveals a unique chance to experience Devon country life at first hand, with pigs, sheep, goats, calves and rabbits, etc. in pens to feed and touch or the milking to get involved with. In addition the Parker family have added a family bar which provides entertainment during the season (quiz night, bingo, guitar player) and fills the gap created by the closure of the local pub. Farm walks are tremendously popular and take place four evenings a week in high season, on request at other times. The 100 touring pitches, with electricity (12A), are set directly above the farm buildings on terraces giving broad, flat groups of pitches, all with good views across the valley (to the A38 which may give some road noise). Hardstandings are available. Young trees and hedges are maturing nicely on the lower terraces. Parker's Farm will suit those who don't seek the sophisticated amenities of more developed parks and a warm welcome awaits - in the words of one camper, 'You come here and feel you belong'.

Facilities

Two modern and clean shower and toilet blocks provide good facilities with two family shower rooms, baby bathroom, en-suite room for disabled visitors, dishwashing and laundry. Small shop (Whitsun - mid Sept). Restaurant, comfortable bar with family room (Whitsun - mid Sept.) and entertainment. Games room with table tennis, pool and amusement machines. Indoor play and TV area. Large outdoor play area. Trampolines. Caravan storage. Rallies welcome. American motorhomes accepted by prior arrangement. Off site: Bicycle hire 5 miles. Golf 4 miles. Riding 5 miles.

At a glance

Welcome & Ambience	✓✓✓✓✓	Location	✓✓✓✓
Quality of Pitches	✓✓✓✓	Range of Facilities	✓✓✓✓

Directions

From Exeter on A38, 26 miles from Plymouth, turn left at Alston Cross signed 'Woodland Denbury'. Site is 400 yards. O.S.GR: SX757702.

Charges 2004

Per unit incl. 2 persons	£ 5.50 - £ 11.00
incl. electricity	£ 7.50 - £ 12.50
extra person	£ 1.70
child (3-15 yrs)	£ 1.50
dog	£ 1.00

Reservations

Made with £10 deposit. Tel: 01364 652598. Email: parkersfarm@bt.com

Open

Easter - 31 October.

UK0980 Lemonford Caravan Park

Bickington, Newton Abbot TQ12 6JR (Devon)

Lemonford is a well run, neat and tidy site for all ages and families on the southern edge of the National Park, some three miles from both Ashburton and Newton Abbot. It has the look and atmosphere of the 'cultivated' caravan park, close to the main road, yet set in a sheltered, peaceful dip bordered by the pretty River Lemon. Well mown grass and smart, trimmed hedges create the tranquil, attractive atmosphere the owners work hard to maintain. There are 85 pitches (45 used as seasonal pitches) on level grass and grouped in four areas according to whether they are to be used by families, couples or individuals. Most pitches have 10A electricity, about 55 have hardstanding. The park is well located for excursions and two good pubs are within walking distance, one along the banks of the river.

Facilities

Two modern toilet blocks, one new, can be heated and provide some private cabins, a ladies' bathroom (£1 payment) and a family bathroom. The new block has facilities for disabled visitors. Dishwashing area under cover. Laundry facilities. Shop. Gas supplies. Freezer service. Play area. Putting green. No commercial vehicles are accepted. Off site: Fishing 4 miles, riding and bicycle hire 3 miles, golf 2 miles. Leisure pool in Newton Abbot.

Open

End March - 31 October.

At a glance

Welcome & Ambience	✓✓✓✓✓	Location	✓✓✓✓
Quality of Pitches	✓✓✓✓✓	Range of Facilities	✓✓✓✓

Directions

Travelling from Exeter, turn off A38 Plymouth road at A382 (Drumbridges) exit signed Newton Abbot, Bovey Tracey, Mortonhampstead. At roundabout take third exit to Bickington. Continue for 1 mile to Toby Jug Inn in the village and park is on left at the bottom of the hill. From Plymouth, take A383 (Goodstone) exit, cross A38 and take first left to Bickington to site on right. O.S.GR: SX793723.

Charges 2004

Per unit incl. 2 persons	£ 7.00 - £ 11.00
extra person	£ 2.00
child (3-15 yrs)	£ 1.50
electricity	£ 2.00
dog	£ 1.00

Special low season offers. No credit cards.

Reservations

Advised for July/Aug. and made with £20 deposit (min. 3 nights July/Aug). Tel: 01626 821242. Email: mark@lemonford.co.uk

UK0940 Holmans Wood Holiday Park

Harcombe Cross, Chudleigh TQ13 0DZ (Devon)

Close to the main A38 Exeter - Plymouth road, with easy access, this attractive, neat park makes a sheltered base for touring south Devon and Dartmoor. The hedged park is arranged on well kept grass surrounding a shallow depression, the floor of which makes a safe, grassy play area for children. Many attractive trees are growing and the park is decorated with flowers. In two main areas and accessed by tarmac roads, there are 125 level pitches (including a number of seasonal pitches) and 25 mobile homes. There are 100 pitches with electrical hook-ups (10A) and 70 with hardstanding, electricity, water and drainage. A picturesque eight acre meadow is provided for tents. Adventure play equipment is provided for children, with badminton and tennis nets and an extra meadow for recreation. There may be some traffic noise on pitches to the west of the park. This is a pleasant, well run park and with no other on-site amenities would suit couples or families who prefer a peaceful stay.

Facilities

The single, good quality toilet block includes facilities for babies and disabled visitors, a dishwashing room and a laundry room. Children's play area. Caravan storage. Off site: Pub/restaurant nearby in Chudleigh village. The beach or Dartmoor are 7 miles and Haldon Forest for walks is 2 miles. Sunday market at Exeter Racecourse (2 miles). Fishing 1 mile, golf or riding 4 miles.

Open

Mid-March - end October.

At a glance

Welcome & Ambience	✓✓✓	Location	✓✓✓✓
Quality of Pitches	✓✓✓✓	Range of Facilities	✓✓✓

Directions

From Exeter on A38 Plymouth road, 0.5 miles after the racecourse and just after a garage, take Chudleigh exit (signed). Park is immediately on the left. From Plymouth turn off A38 for Chudleigh/Teign Valley, then right for Chudleigh. Continue through the town and park is 1 mile. O.S.GR: SX882811.

Charges 2004

Per unit incl. 2 persons, awning and electricity	£ 10.00 - £ 14.00
de-luxe pitch	£ 11.00 - £ 15.00
extra adult	£ 1.95 - £ 2.50
child (4-14 yrs)	£ 1.60 - £ 1.80
dog	£ 1.50

Reservations

Any length, £30 deposit per week. Tel: 01626 853785. Email: enquiries@holmanswood.co.uk

UK1090 Peppermint Park

Warren Road, Dawlish Warren, Dawlish EX7 0PQ (Devon)

First impressions of this extensive family run park are perhaps somewhat formal. However, this is quickly dispelled by the friendly reception staff, abundant flowers and the way the level, terraced pitches have been laid out on the slightly sloping ground. There are 250 pitches, ranging in size, each with electricity (10A), with at least another 60 hook-ups available for tent campers. Tarmac roads thread through the site giving easy access to all areas, each pitch being marked and numbered. Visitors to Peppermint Park out of season can use the full facilities at the adjacent sister site (Golden Sands), which include a large indoor pool. Peppermint Park's own pool complex includes a water slide in the larger pool. Nightly entertainment is staged in the Peppermint Club in high season and at Golden Sands at other times. This site's 'jewel in the crown' is the walking distance (700 yds) to the large, safe beaches of Dawlish Warren and its associated pleasure complex - ideal for families. For others, there is the adjacent coastal footpath or the city of Exeter (7 miles) with its cathedral, museums and historic Quay complex. A passenger ferry operates from Starcross (2 miles) across the estuary to Exmouth during high season. Dawlish Warren nature reserve is adjacent and includes an 18 hole links golf course.

Facilities

The two modern sanitary blocks are kept in spotless condition and can be heated. Two units (WC, washbasin and shower) are provided for disabled visitors. Fully equipped mother and baby room. Laundry (washing machines, dryers and free irons) and dishwashing. Shop with gas. Restaurant, bar and takeaway (28/5-10/9). Entertainment. Swimming pool (28/5 - Sept). Playground on a hill. Field for ball games. Small coarse fishing lake (£2.50 for adult day ticket). Off site: Golf at Dawlish Warren (links course), 9-hole course at Starcross.

Open

15 April - 28 October.

At a glance

Welcome & Ambience	✓✓✓✓	Location	✓✓✓✓
Quality of Pitches	✓✓✓✓	Range of Facilities	✓✓✓✓✓

Directions

Leave M5 at junction 30 and take A379 Dawlish road. After passing through Starcross (7 miles) turn left to Dawlish Warren just before Dawlish. Continue for 1.5 miles down hill and park is on left in 300 yards. O.S.GR: SX978788.

Charges 2004

Per unit incl. 2 persons, electricity	£ 10.00 - £ 16.00
awning or gazebo	£ 1.50 - £ 3.00
extra adult	£ 1.30 - £ 3.00
child (2-13 yrs)	£ 1.10 - £ 3.00
dog	£ 1.10 - £ 5.00

Reservations

Made with £15 deposit (Sat. - Sat. only 24 July - 28 Aug). Tel: 01626 863436. Email: info@peppermintpark.co.uk

ONE OF DAWLISH WARREN'S BEST KEPT SECRETS

THE NEAREST TOURING & CAMPING PARK TO THE BEACH

Peppermint Park Only 680 Metres from the beach!

A family-owned park just 680 metres level walk from Dawlish Warren's famous stretch of golden sands and dunes. A green oasis surrounded with gentle grassy slopes, mature trees, hedges and flowers. Individually marked pitches for touring caravans, motorhomes and campers.

- **FREE** Nightly Family Entertainment - Licensed Club & Bar
- **FREE** Heated Swimming Pool and Water Chute
- Electric hook-ups
- Coarse Fishing • Children's Club & Play Area
- Holiday Homes at Peppermint Paddocks
- Holiday Homes & Lodges for sale
- **SPECIAL OFFER** - £2.00 Off Service Pitch per night in Low & Mid season. (Advance bookings only. Min 3 nights).
- Festival of Country & Western Music 17-24 September
- Over 40's PEPP-UP Week - 4-11 June FREE Entertainment

DAWLISH WARREN'S ONLY ETC ★★★★ TOURING PARK

PEPPERMINT PARK • WARREN ROAD DAWLISH WARREN • SOUTH DEVON EX7 0PQ

AA DE LUXE PARK

LISTED

FREE BROCHURE: tel: 01626 863436 • fax: 01626 866482 www.peppermintpark.co.uk e-mail info@peppermintpark.co.uk

UK0970 Cofton Country Holidays

Starcross, Dawlish EX6 8RP (Devon)

About 1.5 miles from a sandy beach at Dawlish Warren this popular, family site takes over 400 touring units on a variety of fields and meadows with beautiful country views. Although not individually marked, there is never a feeling of overcrowding. The smaller, more mature fields, including a pleasant old orchard for tents only, are well terraced. While there are terraces on most of the slopes of the larger, more open fields, there are still some quite steep gradients to climb. There are some 300 electrical connections (10A) and a few hardstandings. One area has 66 park-owned, holiday homes. A well designed, central complex overlooking the pool and decorated with flowers and hanging baskets, houses reception, a shop and off-licence and a bar lounge, the 'Cofton Swan', where bar meals are usually available (all Easter - 30 Sept). A family room and bar are on the first floor of this building and there is an outdoor terrace and some light entertainment in season. The adjacent supervised kidney-shaped heated pool with paddling pool and slide, has lots of grassy space for sunbathing. Coarse fishing is possible in three lakes on the park and there is a woodland trail towards Dawlish Warren.

Facilities

Toilet facilities comprise four blocks, one on each side of the road dividing the park for the touring pitches and the third near the holiday home area. The newest, at the top of the larger fields is first rate, with laundry and facilities for disabled visitors and babies. Hair dryers. Dishwashing facilities under cover. In addition three 'portacabin' style units with basic toilet facilities are provided for the peak season. Two launderettes. Gas available. Ice pack hire. Bar lounge. Shop. Fish and chip shop - breakfast possible. Swimming pool (overall length 100 ft. open Spr. B.H - mid Sept). Games room (busy in high season). Adventure playground in the woods overlooking the pools and two other well equipped play areas. Pony rides in high season. Coarse fishing (from £16.50 per rod for 7 days, discount for senior citizens outside July). Winter caravan storage. Off site: Golf 3 miles. Beach 1.5 miles. Woodland walks/pub 0.5 miles.

At a glance

Welcome & Ambience ✓✓✓✓✓ Location ✓✓✓✓
Quality of Pitches ✓✓✓✓✓ Range of Facilities ✓✓✓✓✓

Directions

Access to the park is off the A379 road 3 miles north of Dawlish, just after Cockwood harbour village. O.S.GR: SX965797.

Charges 2004

Per unit incl. 2 persons	£ 7.50 - £ 13.50
incl. electricity	£ 9.00 - £ 18.50
extra adult	£ 1.60 - £ 2.90
child (2-13 yrs)	£ 1.40 - £ 2.70

Small low season discount for Senior Citizens. Camping Cheques accepted.

Reservations

Made for min. 3 nights, 4 nights in peak season with £20 deposit. Tel: 01626 890111. Email: info@coftonholidays.co.uk

Open

Easter - 27 October.

UK1010 Lady's Mile Touring & Camping Park

Dawlish EX7 0LX (Devon)

Lady's Mile is a popular, large family touring park that caters well for children. It has extensive grassy fields (with some trees for shade), in addition to the main, landscaped camping area which is arranged in broad terraces. There are 486 pitches, mostly marked by lines but with nothing between them, and most with electricity (10A). It is a 20 minute walk to a good sandy beach at Dawlish Warren and 10 minutes to Dawlish beach, but the park also has a good sized, free outdoor swimming pool with 200 ft. plus slide, paddling pool and a paved surround, plus a super heated indoor pool (20 x 10 m.) with 100 ft. flume and separate paddling pool (both with lifeguards). A large and attractive bar complex has a family area overlooking the indoor pool and an entertainment programme. Below is a spacious games room including pool tables and video games, and a new separate disco and bar. A sloping recreation field is ideal for kite flying and the large fenced adventure playground has a safe, sand surface. A nine hole golf course is on site (free but with small charge for hire of clubs) and a multi-sports pitch. The park is popular over a long season, with reservation necessary for high season.

Facilities

Four toilet blocks of various ages and styles, but of a good standard, are well spaced around the main areas of the park with an additional shower block. Facilities for disabled people. Four family bathrooms (50p). Dishwashing sinks under cover. Two launderettes. Mini-market. Fish and chip takeaway (both Easter - mid Sept). Bars. Indoor (Easter - Oct) and outdoor (May - Sept) pools. Adventure play area. Games room. Golf (9 hole). Ball area with nets. Tarmac area at reception for late arrivals. Winter caravan storage. Off site: Riding and bicycle hire 1 mile. Fishing 3 miles.

At a glance

Welcome & Ambience	✓✓✓✓	Location	✓✓✓✓
Quality of Pitches	✓✓✓✓	Range of Facilities	✓✓✓✓✓

Directions

Park is 1 mile north of Dawlish with access off the A379 (Exeter - Teignmouth) road. O.S.GR: SX969778.

Charges 2004

Per unit incl. 2 adults	£ 10.50 - £ 18.00
extra person over 2 yrs	£ 9.00 - £ 15.00
extra child's tent	£ 1.50 - £ 3.00
electricity	free - £ 1.00
dog	£ 1.50 - £ 3.00

Low season special offers and discount for OAPs.

Reservations

Made for Sat to Sat only in peak seasons, with £15 deposit. Tel: 01626 863411. Email: info@ladysmile.co.uk

Open

13 March - 31 October.

UK1100 Webbers Caravan & Camping Park

Castle Lane, Woodbury, Exeter EX5 1EA (Devon)

Set in a lovely location in East Devon, with rural views, this family run park has developed over 20 years to one that can boast spacious, modern facilities, yet still retain its relaxed, rural atmosphere. The 115 marked, grass pitches are large, with the majority level and a few gently sloping. Some of the higher pitches have marvellous views across the Exe river valley. There are 100 electricity connections (10/16A). The park is surrounded by fields and visitors can watch the wildlife and grazing sheep from a fenced walk around the park perimeter. Within the park is a 'pets paddock' with a friendly donkey, Shetland pony and goats. A short drive takes you to the two miles of glorious sand at Exmouth or the delightful pebble beach at Budleigh Salterton. Woodbury Common for excellent heathland walks is just over a mile away, whilst for a little city life, Exeter is also nearby. A member of the Countryside Discovery group.

Facilities

There are two modern toilet blocks, the newest (completed in 2002) a light and airy building with 4 family shower rooms, a bathroom (£1) and a unit for disabled visitors (WC, shower and washbasin). Dishwashing and laundry facilities. Unusual in terms of number, are seven chemical disposal points, located at each water point (and adequately separated). Motorcaravan service point. Small shop at reception for essentials. Ice pack service. Gas supplies. Play area and games field. All year caravan storage. Off site: Woodbury village within walking distance with excellent pub/restaurant, post office, etc. Exeter 6 miles. Fishing or golf (Woodbury Park Golf Club) 1 mile. Riding 4 miles. Bicycle hire or boat launching 5 miles.

At a glance

Welcome & Ambience	✓✓✓✓✓	Location	✓✓✓✓
Quality of Pitches	✓✓✓✓	Range of Facilities	✓✓✓

Directions

From M5 exit 30 take A3052 (Sidmouth) for 5 miles and turn right at Halfway Inn. From A30, Daisymount exit, take B3180 for 3 miles to Halfway Inn and go straight across at crossroads. All routes then follow B3180 (Budleigh Salterton/Exmouth). After 2 miles turn right into lane (signed Woodbury, golf and caravan parks). Follow downhill for 1 mile. Park on left just before Woodbury village. O.S.GR: SY017874.

Charges 2004

Per pitch incl. 2 persons	£ 11.00 - £ 15.00
extra person (over 2 yrs)	£ 2.00
pup tent	£ 4.00

Reservations

Essential for peak periods and made with £20 deposit. Tel: 01395 232276. Email: reception@webberspark.co.uk

Open

Easter - 29 September.

UK1110 Salcombe Regis Camping & Caravan Park

Salcombe Regis, Sidmouth EX10 0JH (Devon)

0n the edge of Salcombe Regis village, 1.5 miles from Sidmouth and less than a mile from the sea. Salcombe Regis Park covers 16 acres of land. It is surrounded by farmland with views of the combe and the sea beyond. The focal point of the main camping area is a large 'village green' where the play area and pitch and putt are located. The reception and pitches are arranged around the green, all connected by a tarmac road. The 110 pitches are level and have their own water supply, with 98 electricity hook-ups (16A). A 25 minute walk across fields takes you to a small secluded beach, although the walk there is fairly steep - we are told there are 129 steps that take you down to the beach! There are many footpaths and coastal walks nearby, protected by the National Trust and with views of Sidmouth and Weston Mouth. Sidmouth town, originally a small fishing town but now a seaside resort, is host to the annual International Folk Festival, where for one week in summer the town is filled with folk artists from all over the world.

Facilities

The traditional style toilet block is kept spotlessly clean by the resident wardens and includes a bathroom for families and disabled visitors. Licensed shop at reception for basic supplies and local produce. Dishwashing area under cover. Laundry room with washing machines, dryers and ironing board. Motorcaravan service point. Play area. Pitch and putt. Caravan storage. Off site: Fishing, bicycle hire and golf 1.5 miles. Riding 3 miles. Sidmouth and beach 1.5 miles.

Open

Easter - 28 October.

At a glance

Welcome & Ambience	✓✓✓✓	Location	✓✓✓✓
Quality of Pitches	✓✓✓✓	Range of Facilities	✓✓✓

Directions

Park is well signed on the A3052 Exeter - Lyme Regis road. From the east, take first left after Donkey Sanctuary. From the west proceed up the hill out of Sidford. Do not take first road signed Salcombe Regis, but take the next right at top of hill. Follow road round to site on left after golf range. O.S.GR: SY149892.

Charges 2004

Per unit incl. 2 persons	£ 7.85 - £ 12.85
extra person	£ 3.10
child (5-15 yrs)	£ 1.85
electricity	£ 2.60

Reservations

Made with £20 p/week deposit. Book 7 nights, get 1 free. Tel: 01395 514303. Email: info@salcombe-regis.co.uk

Fancy a
trip to France?
turn to the directory and look for Portsmouth Port

UK1020 Oakdown Touring & Holiday Home Park

Weston, Sidmouth EX10 0PH (Devon)

Developed by the Franks family over the past 30 years, attention to detail at this award winning park is evident as soon as you arrive. With easy access and beautiful floral displays, you are welcomed by a friendly member of the Oakdown team. With a spacious feel, the 100 level touring pitches are arranged in landscaped bays, screened by a growing range of trees and shrubs and linked by a circular road. All have 16A electricity, most have hardstanding and many have water and a drain. In separate areas there are 16 caravan holiday homes for rent and Oak Grove, a neat area containing 46 privately owned holiday homes. It is the attention to all things natural and the encouragement of wildlife that makes Oakdown special. Waste water is dealt with by a Victorian style reed bed which has encouraged more birds and a hide has been established. Surrounded by wild flowers (many named - there are 152 different varieties on the park), a trail leads through the fields to the nearby Donkey Sanctuary. The latest addition is a nine-hole, par 3 Approach golf course, together with a lake, dew pond and wild flower areas. Recent improvements to the amenities make this park an excellent choice for visitors with disabilities. A Best of British Group member.

Facilities

The solid central toilet block provides good, fully equipped, heated sanitary facilities, all well maintained. One private cabin for ladies. Two unisex family bathrooms (bath, shower, toilet, washbasin and coin operated entry), double as useful units for disabled people. Dishwashing sinks. Laundry facilities plus free freezer and microwave. Motorcaravan service point. Recycling point (glass, paper, cans). Fax service. TV room. Good, grass based play area with adventure style equipment and play castle. Fishing. Golf. No cycling, skate-boarding or kite flying is permitted. Certain breeds of dog not accepted. Site has closed circuit TV and secure, alarmed caravan storage. Off site: Riding 6 miles. Golf 2 miles. Beach 2 miles.

At a glance

Welcome & Ambience	✓✓✓✓✓	Location	✓✓✓✓✓
Quality of Pitches	✓✓✓✓✓	Range of Facilities	✓✓✓✓

Directions

Turn south off the A3052 (Exeter - Lyme Regis) road between Sidford and Colyford, 2.5 miles east of the A375 junction and park is on left. O.S.GR: SY167902.

Charges 2004

Per pitch incl. 2 persons	£ 8.90 - £ 13.25
with electricity	£ 11.75 - £ 16.10
incl. mains services	£ 16.70 - £ 21.30
extra person (5 yrs and over)	£ 1.90
dog	£ 1.20
awning	£ 1.10 - £ 1.90

Less 70p for senior citizens in low season.

Reservations

Made with £20 p/w deposit, min. 3 days at B.Hs. and Sidmouth Folk Festival week. Tel: 01297 680387. Email: enquiries@oakdown.co.uk

Open

26 March - 31 October.

UK1000 Forest Glade Holiday Park

Cullompton EX15 2DT (Devon)

Forest Glade, owned and run by the Wellard family, is set in the Blackdown Hills (designated an area of outstanding natural beauty), deep in mid-Devon away from the hectic life on the coast. A sheltered site set amongst woodland with extensive walking without using your car, there are 80 level touring pitches, 68 of which have 16A electricity connections, 4 have full services and 24 have hardstanding. There is a small heated, covered pool with a paddling pool and patio area outside, and a large games room (up a flight of steps, so not suitable for visitors with disabilities). The surrounding forest makes this a dog lover's paradise (dogs are accepted). Touring caravans must book in advance and the easiest route for them will be explained then (telephone bookings accepted). Although set in the country, the beaches of East Devon are a fairly easy drive away.

Facilities

There is one main toilet block, heated in cold weather, with some washbasins in cubicles, and washing up sinks. Separate suite for visitors with disabilities. Laundry with washing machines and dryers, ironing facilities and a stool. New baby room. Extra facilities of 'portacabin' style with toilets, washbasins and showers are at the swimming pool for swimmers' use. Drain for motorcaravan waste water tanks. The shop (all season) is quite well stocked including gas and locally made bread and pastries with a takeaway (open evenings except Sunday). Microwave for tent campers in kitchenette. Adventure playground. Games room with table tennis, video games and two pool tables. Swimming pool (free). Sauna. All weather tennis court. Separate area for ball games. Caravan storage. Off site: Fishing or riding 1.5 miles, golf 6 miles. Beach 17 miles.

At a glance

Welcome & Ambience	✓✓✓✓	Location	✓✓✓✓
Quality of Pitches	✓✓✓✓	Range of Facilities	✓✓✓✓

Directions

Park is 5.5 miles from M5 exit 28. Take A373 for 3 miles, turning left at camp sign towards Sheldon. Park is on left after approx. 2.5 miles. This access is not suitable for touring caravans owing to a steep hill - phone the park for alternative route details. O.S.GR: ST101073.

Charges 2004

Per unit incl. 2 adults, electricity incl. mains services and awning	£ 10.95 - £ 14.95 £ 11.95 - £ 15.95
extra adult	£ 2.20
student (10 yrs-end of study)	£ 2.20
child (5-9 yrs)	£ 1.10

Reservations

Any length with deposit of £5 p/day or £30 p/week, (£20 for B.H. w/ends). Essential for B.Hs and school holidays. Tel: 01404 841381.
Email: enquiries@forest-glade.co.uk

Open

Mid March - end October.

South West England

69

UK1380 Hoburne Blue Anchor

Blue Anchor Bay, Minehead TA24 6JT (Somerset)

Although mainly a holiday park, with almost 300 caravan holiday homes, Blue Anchor nevertheless offers good facilities for 103 touring units. Trailer tents are accepted but not other tents (other than pup tents with a touring booking). Virtually in a separate touring area, the level pitches all have 16A electricity and hardstanding for cars and motorcaravans (with caravans going on the adjacent grass). A feature of the park is a good sized, irregularly shaped indoor swimming pool with an area for small children, complete with a mushroom shaped fountain. With views of the sea from the pool, it is heated and supervised. Although not actually within the park itself, there are restaurants and takeaways within easy walking distance. The park's situation, directly across the small road from the beach, is unusual and gives some beautiful views across the Bristol Channel to South Wales. Dunster Castle, Exmoor, the Quantocks and Minehead are close and the West Somerset Steam Railway runs along one side of the park. Part of the Hoburne Group.

Facilities

Toilet facilities provide large, free hot showers (with push-button), dishwashing and laundry sinks under cover, and a fully equipped launderette in a single, modern block serving just the touring area. Indoor heated swimming pool (free). Excellent adventure-style play area in a copse. Note: an unfenced river runs along one boundary of the park. Crazy golf. Small supermarket/shop with coffee shop (open 8 am - 9 pm in high season, less at other times). American motorhomes accepted (max. 36 ft). Dogs are not accepted. Off site: Beach 100 yds. Riding and bicycle hire 5 miles. Golf 6 miles.

At a glance

Welcome & Ambience	✓✓✓✓	Location	✓✓✓✓✓
Quality of Pitches	✓✓✓✓	Range of Facilities	✓✓✓

Directions

From M5 exit 25, take A358 signed Minehead. After 12 miles turn left onto A39 at Williton. After 4 miles turn right onto B3191 at Carhampton signed Blue Anchor. Park is 1.5 miles on right. O.S.GR: ST024535.

Charges 2004

Per unit incl. up to 6 persons, electricity and awning	£ 9.00 - £ 18.50

Weekend breaks available.

Reservations

For stays of 1-6 days, payment required in full at time of booking; for 7 nights or more £50 deposit. Min. bookings at B.Hs. Tel: 01643 821360. Email: enquiries@hoburne.com

Open

1 March - 31 October.

UK1370 Burrowhayes Farm Caravan & Camping Site

West Luccombe, Porlock, Minehead TA24 8HT (Somerset)

This delightful park with riding stables on site, is on the edge of Exmoor. The stone packhorse bridge over Horner Water beside the farm entrance sets the tone of the park, which the Dascombe family have created over the last thirty years having previously farmed the land. The farm buildings have been converted into riding stables with escorted rides available (from 7 April). Touring and tent pitches are on partly sloping field with marvelous views or a flatter location in the clearing by the river, while 20 caravan holiday homes are in a separate area. Electricity is available (10A), although some long leads may be needed. With walking, birdwatching, plenty of wild life to observe, pretty Exmoor villages and Lorna Doone country nearby there is much to do. Children can ride, play in the stream or explore the woods at the top of the site. Limited trout fishing is available in Horner Water (NT permit) alongside the park.

Facilities

A new heated toilet block provides controllable hot showers, one washbasin cubicle for each sex, hairdressing and shaving areas. In the reception and stable block area are a laundry room, unit for disabled visitors and babies, and an indoor dishwashing room. A second older block is opened in high season with extra WCs and washbasins. Motorcaravan service point. Well stocked shop doubles with reception (from 22/3). Off site: Beach 2 miles. Fishing 2 miles. Bicycle hire 5 miles. Golf 6 miles. Minehead 5 miles. Local pub 20 minutes walk.

At a glance

Welcome & Ambience	✓✓✓✓	Location	✓✓✓✓✓
Quality of Pitches	✓✓✓✓	Range of Facilities	✓✓✓✓

Directions

From A39, 5 miles west of Minehead, take first left past Allerford to Horner and West Luccombe. Site is on right after 400 yards. O.S.GR: SS899461.

Charges 2004

Per unit incl. 1 or 2 persons	£ 7.00 - £ 10.00
extra person	£ 2.00 - £ 3.00
child (3-15 yrs)	£ 1.00 - £ 1.50
dog	free
electricity	£ 2.00

Reservations

Made with deposit (£10 per week or part week, per pitch). Tel: 01643 862463. Email: info@burrowhayes.co.uk

Open

15 March - 31 October.

UK1360 Halse Farm Touring Caravan & Camping Park

Winsford, Minehead TA24 7JL (Somerset)

A truly rural park with beautiful, moorland views, you may be lucky enough to glimpse red deer across the valley or be able to see ponies and foals grazing outside the main gate on one of the highest points on Exmoor. Two open, neatly cut fields (level at the top) back onto traditional hedging and slope gently to the middle and bottom where wild flowers predominate. One field provides electricity points (10A) and is used for motorcaravans and caravans, the other is for tents. There is no reception - you leave your unit by the toilet block and walk down to the farm kitchen to book in. The pretty village of Winsford is one mile (footpath from farm) with a post office, shop, pub and restaurant. Mrs Brown has encapsulated maps available (at a small cost) detailing six walks of varying distances, starting and finishing at the farm. Also available is a list of the wild birds, flowers, etc. to be found on the site. A member of the Countryside Discovery group.

Facilities

The central toilet block is of good quality and heated. Well equipped and maintained, it includes a toilet, washbasin and shower for visitors with disabilities, washing machine, dryer and iron, and tourist information. Gas is available at the farm. Play equipment. Well behaved dogs are accepted (free). Off site: Fishing 4 miles, bicycle hire 5 miles, riding 2 miles. Tarr Steps and Barle Valley 3 miles. Winsford village 1 mile.

Open

18 March - 1 November.

At a glance

Welcome & Ambience	✓✓✓	Location	✓✓✓✓
Quality of Pitches	✓✓✓	Range of Facilities	✓✓✓

Directions

Turn off A396 Tiverton - Minehead road for Winsford (site signed). In Winsford village turn left in front of the Royal Oak (not over ford) and keep on uphill for 1 mile (go slowly round sharp bend at the bottom). Cross cattle grid onto moor and turn immediately left to farm. Caravans should avoid Dulverton - keep to the A396 from Bridgetown (signed). O.S.GR: SS898342.

Charges 2005

Per unit incl. 2 adults	£ 8.50 - £ 10.50
with electricity	£ 10.50 - £ 12.30

Less 10% for 7 days paid in advance 10 days before arrival.

Reservations

Advised for July/Aug. and made with £10 deposit. Tel: 01643 851259. Email: enquiries@halsefarm.co.uk

UK1306 Mill Farm Caravan & Camping Park

Fiddington, Bridgwater TA5 1JQ (Somerset)

On the edge of the village of Fiddington, in a countryside location at the foot of the Quantock Hills, Mill Farm is just 7 miles from Bridgwater and 4 miles from the sea. This is an extensive and popular family holiday site with three main fields, each taking 50-60 units with a toilet block, a playground and a plentiful supply of water points. Extra fields are opened for the peak season allowing a total capacity of around 300 units. There are 200 electricity connections (10A). The site has a large swimming pool complex with indoor and outdoor pools, free to campers. There is a licensed riding school, rowing boats on the little lake and organised daytime activities in high season, including treasure hunts, relay races and games tournaments. A well stocked mini-market provides all the usual items. American motorhomes are not accepted, motorcyclists at the management's discretion. Mill Farm is a good family holiday base, very much children orientated with a wide range of activities to keep them happy.

Facilities

Three toilet blocks include facilities for disabled visitors (Radar key), one washbasin in cubicle for each sex, bathrooms (on payment) baby changing rooms and dishwashing rooms. These blocks do come under pressure in peak seasons and a fourth is opened to cater for the 'overflow' fields. Launderette. Mini-market (all year). Large club room with bar, takeaway (weekends and peak seasons), games room with pool, table tennis and air hockey etc. and family entertainment (high season). Heated indoor pool with whirlpool and paddling pool (Easter-10/11) and two outdoor pools with giant waterslide (15/5-15/9). Both pools unsupervised, but monitored by CCTV and have panic alarm facilities. Pony riding and trekking, canoe hire, and trampolining (charged). Off site: Beach 4 miles. Fishing 4 miles. Golf 3 miles. Bridgwater has the Somerset Brick and Tile Museum (free admission), and the Carnival in early November.

At a glance

Welcome & Ambience	✓✓✓✓	Location	✓✓✓✓
Quality of Pitches	✓✓✓	Range of Facilities	✓✓✓✓

Directions

From M5 exit 23 or 24, turn west and pass through Bridgwater and continue on the A39. After 6 miles turn right towards Fiddington. Continue through narrow lane with passing places for 1 mile to site entrance. Park where instructed on the long entry driveway, and report to reception. O.S.GR: ST217407.

Charges 2004

Per unit incl. 2 persons, awning	£ 11.00 - £ 15.00
incl. electricity	£ 13.00 - £ 17.00
extra adult	£ 2.00
child	£ 1.00
dog	£ 1.00

Reservations

Essential for peak season and B.Hs. Tel: 01278 732286.

Open

All year.

UK1590 Exe Valley Caravan Site

Bridgetown, Dulverton TA22 9JR (Somerset)

Occupying a prime position in a wooded valley alongside the River Exe, Exe Valley Caravan Site is ideally situated for visiting the Doone Valley, Tarr Steps, Dulverton and many other beautiful venues in the area. Fly fishing along the River Exe is possible from the site or at Wimbleball Reservoir just over four miles away. Travellers find this part of Somerset is a haven for walkers, cycling, horse riding, pony trekking, or as a place to just sit and relax. Owned and managed by Paul and Christine Matthews, this is a four acre 'adult only' campsite with 30 large pitches (mostly grass but some hardstandings at the top end), all of which have 16A electricity and TV hook-ups. The reception is part of a small shop. The owners live in the adjacent old mill, complete with water wheel, which they hope to restore to working order. They also hope to install CCTV so campers may watch the bat colony in the loft from a screen in the shop.

Facilities

The refurbished toilet block houses the usual facilities and an en-suite room for disabled visitors (quite short steep ramp to enter). Excellent laundry with domestic washing and drying machines, plus a microwave (free). Small shop with basic provisions. Gas supplies. Free fly fishing. This is an adult-only park. Off site: Riding 6 miles. Golf 14 miles. Pub at Bridgetown. Winsford village has a general stores, pub and tea rooms.

Open

1 March - 30 October.

At a glance

Welcome & Ambience	✓✓✓	Location	✓✓✓✓	
Quality of Pitches	✓✓✓✓	Range of Facilities	✓✓✓	

Directions

Bridgetown is roughly midway between Dunster and Tiverton on the A396. As you enter Bridgetown from Tiverton, look for site sign and turn left in minor road; the site is 100 yards on the right. O.S.GR: SS923332.

Charges 2004

Per unit incl. 2 adults	£ 7.50 - £ 12.50
extra adult	£ 2.00
electricity (16A) and TV hook-up	£ 2.50
awning	£ 1.00
dog	free

Reservations

Made for any length with £5 deposit.
Tel: 01643 851432.

UK1520 Waterrow Touring Park

Wiveliscombe, Taunton TA4 2AZ (Somerset)

Beside the River Tone in a pretty part of South Somerset, Tony and Anne Taylor have enthusiastically developed Waterrow into a charming, landscaped touring park for adults only. Nestling in a little sheltered valley, it is very peaceful and possible for an overnight stop (just over 30 minutes from M5) or ideal as a base for exploring nearby Exmoor and the Brendon Hills. There are 45 touring pitches, 27 of which are on level hardstandings, including 4 with full services. The remainder are on flat or gently sloping grass with little shade as yet but bushes and trees are maturing. All have electricity (16A), spring and mains water are available and TV aerial points have been installed (your own lead is required, sometimes quite long). A small area has been set aside for tent campers. Converted barns have been put to good use, providing local tourist information, a small library, nature and conservation notes and diary and a visual record of the park's development. Further down the park, below the touring area, wide steps lead to a private nature reserve where you can find the recently constructed Otter Holt, go fly fishing for wild brown trout, take a riverside walk or just relax and watch the birds. This 'adult only' site is open all year.

Facilities

A modern, clean 'portacabin' style toilet unit, well fitted out and with heating, provides WCs and washbasins, some in curtained cubicles. New heated shower block. Facilities for disabled people (key). Dishwashing. Washing machine and dryer. Limited provisions are available in reception. Order jacket potatoes before lunchtime for the evening for just 60p. The Taylors will 'dog sit' if you are visiting somewhere your pet is not allowed (£5 per day). Water colour and drawing holidays and photography workshops arranged at certain times. Caravan storage with 'store and stay' system. Site is not suitable for American motorhomes. Off site: Golf and fishing 7 miles. Bicycle hire 10 miles. Riding 12 miles. The Rock Inn is a short walk and provides good value meals and real ales. Wiveliscombe 3 miles.

At a glance

Welcome & Ambience	✓✓✓✓✓	Location	✓✓✓✓✓	
Quality of Pitches	✓✓✓✓✓	Range of Facilities	✓✓✓✓	

Directions

From M5 exit 25 take A358 (signed Minehead) round Taunton for 4 miles, then at Staplegrove onto the B3227 for 11.5 miles to Wiveliscombe where straight over at lights to Waterrow (still on B3227). Park is on left shortly after the Rock Inn. O.S.GR: ST052250.

Charges 2004

Per unit incl. 2 persons (adults only, 18 years and over)	£ 10.50 - £ 15.00
extra adult	£ 4.00

Reservations

Advised for B.Hs. and high season and made with £20 deposit. Tel: 01984 623464.

Open

All year.

UK1350 Quantock Orchard Caravan Park

Crowcombe, Taunton TA4 4AW (Somerset)

The old adage 'small is beautiful' certainly fits Quantock Orchard, nestling at the foot of the Quantocks in quiet countryside, yet close to many of the attractions of the area. Attractively developed, mature apple trees, recently planted trees, shrubs and pretty flower beds with a nice use of heathers, make a very pleasant environment and the clock tower on the sanitary block adds interest. With access from gravel roads, there are 55 touring pitches, part separated by growing shrubs and hedging, of which 20 are for tents. Of various sizes, all touring pitches have 10A electricity hook ups, 20 have hard-standing, 4 have TV hook-up and 5 are fully serviced (two extra large, with patio and barbecue). Only 'air-flo' style groundsheets are permitted on grass pitches. A leisure suite provides a sauna, steam room, jacuzzi, mini-gym and conservatory rest area (this facility is open to the public; visitor membership optional with a range of tariffs; children must be accompanied). It is complemented by the outdoor heated swimming pool, which is walled with paved sunbathing surrounds.

Facilities

The central, heated sanitary block is very well maintained. Some washbasins in cubicles for ladies, excellent family bathroom and separate mother and baby room. Good dishwashing provision, microwave, and laundry facilities. Drain for motorcaravan waste water tanks. Well stocked licensed shop includes camping accessories. Mountain bike hire (some with buggies for children). Fish and chip van visits (twice weekly in summer). Swimming pool (40 x 20 ft. and open May - Sept). Leisure suite. Games room, Sky TV. Fenced safe-based play area. Caravan storage Oct. - March. Off site: The Carew Arms serving meals is within walking distance in the mellow village of Crowcombe.

At a glance

Welcome & Ambience	✓✓✓✓	Location	✓✓✓✓
Quality of Pitches	✓✓✓✓	Range of Facilities	✓✓✓✓

Directions

Park is west off A358 road (Taunton - Minehead), about 1 mile south of Crowcombe village. O.S.GR: ST140363.

Charges 2004

Per unit incl. 2 adults, electricity	£ 10.95 - £ 15.95
tent pitch and car incl. 2 adults	£ 7.95 - £ 12.95
extra adult	£ 3.49
child (3-15 yrs)	£ 1.49 - £ 2.49
backpacker or cyclist	£ 3.95 - £ 5.95

Reservations

Made with £20 per week deposit, per booking (non-returnable). Tel: 01984 618618. Email: qocp@flaxpool.freeserve.co.uk

Open

All year.

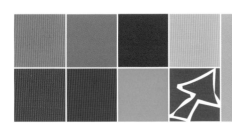

Have you
forgotten something?

see the Alan Rogers
Directory ON PAGE 294

UK1575 Holiday Resort Unity

Coast Road, Brean Sands TA8 2RB (Somerset)

Holiday Resort Unity offers everything for everyone, from young children to the 'young at heart'. Apart from the extensive on-site amusements and entertainment programme, campers can also use the swimming pools, funfair and other leisure pursuits at the adjoining Brean Leisure Centre (owned by the same family), some free of charge and others by paying a small fee. Access to the five-mile stretch of sandy beach is via a footpath opposite the site entrance. Fishing (with a licence) is permitted from Unity Lake in the Yellow Field. RJ's is a club with bars, food and nightly entertainment for the whole family. Sarah's Pantry offers takeaway or sit-down meals (including the Sunday roast), while fish and chips are available at Porkers Bar. Three large touring fields provide pitches that are flat and open, mostly grass but some on concrete hardstandings (motorcaravans up to 30 ft can be accommodated). Most pitches have 16A electricity hook-ups. A separate warden looks after each camping field. Ready equipped tents and a substantial number of caravan holiday homes are available for rent.

Facilities

Four toilet blocks provide ample showers. Some toilets and washbasins have been adapted for people with disabilities (key). Dishwashing and hair care rooms, well-equipped laundries. Motorcaravan service point. Recycling. Well stocked shop. Gas exchange. RJ's Club, Sarah's Pantry and Porkers Bar. Large adventure play area. Cyber Zone (high season; £1 for 10 mins). Gym, Sally's sun beds. Monday market, Sunday car boot sales. All facilities open during high season, most open during mid season, and most at weekends in low season. Torches advised. Off site: Walking access from park to Brean leisure Centre (swimming pool, funfair etc); horse riding, cycling, cinema, walks, golf all within walking distance. Bus to Weston Super Mare and Cheddar Gorge stops at gates. Beach 100 m.

At a glance

Welcome & Ambience	✓✓✓	Location	✓✓✓✓
Quality of Pitches	✓✓✓	Range of Facilities	✓✓✓✓✓

Directions

From M5, exit 22, follow signs for Burnham on Sea (B3140), Berrow and Brean. Holiday Resort Unity is on right along the main street of Brean, well signed. Take care as road through Berrow and Brean is rather narrow. O.S.GR: ST290539.

Charges 2004

Per unit incl. 4 persons	£ 6.00 - £ 22.00
serviced pitch	£ 8.00 - £ 26.00
with hardstanding	£ 10.00 - £ 30.00

Price includes entertainment/swimming & Piglet Club. Credit cards accepted £2 charge.

Reservations

Made with deposit; contact park. Tel: 01278 751235. Email: rjh@hru.co.uk

Open

14 February - 25 November.

UK1570 Northam Farm Touring Caravan Park

Brean Sands, Burnham-on-Sea TA8 2SE (Somerset)

Brean has been a popular holiday destination for decades and many large campsites have evolved. Northam Farm is one of them; it is a large family park with good facilities and an ongoing programme of improvements. Of the 850 pitches, 400 are for seasonal units and these are separated from the four tourist fields. Visitors are always shown to their pitch and sited. Pitches are large so you won't feel cramped and 154 have block paved hardstanding. There are two play areas for youngsters, a sports field with mobiliser swing, football, bicycle track, and cricket pitch for teenagers, and fishing on the lake for adults. The owners and staff are happy to help visitors enjoy their stay. About 500 yards down the road is The Seagull, also owned by Northam Farm. Here you'll find an excellent restaurant, bar and nightly live entertainment, even in low season. Visitors can book a free bus to Cheddar, famous for its gorge and caves. Alternatively, just down the road is Brean Leisure Park with its pool, funfair, golf and much more.

Facilities

Five good toilet blocks, well maintained and within reasonable distance of all pitches, provide ample toilets and washbasins (mostly open plan). Four blocks have large showers (20p). Bathrooms (£1), baby room, hair washing and drying, and slatted bench seats. Rooms for visitors with disabilities (opened by key). Dishwashing. New laundry. Dog shower. Licensed shop. Snack bar/takeaway. Free entry to live entertainment at The Seagull. Games room. Two play areas. Sports field. Fishing lake. Caravan repairs, servicing and storage. Dogs are not accepted in one field.

At a glance

Welcome & Ambience	✓✓✓✓	Location	✓✓✓✓
Quality of Pitches	✓✓✓✓✓	Range of Facilities	✓✓✓✓

Directions

Leave M5 at junction 22 and follow the signs to Burnham-on-Sea, Berrow and then Brean. Continue through Brean and Northam Farm is on the right, half a mile past Brean Leisure Park. O.S.GR: ST297556.

Charges 2004

Per unit incl. 2 persons	£ 5.00 - £ 16.75
extra adult	£ 1.00 - £ 1.50
child	£ 0.75 - £ 1.00

Reservations

Made with deposit to cover two night's fees. Tel: 01278 751244. Email: enquiries@northamfarm.demon.co.uk

Open

March - October.

74

UK1580 Warren Farm Touring Park

Warren Road, Brean Sands, Burnham-on-Sea TA8 2RP (Somerset)

Warren Farm is a popular venue for family campers who want the beach, fun and entertainment. With over 1,000 pitches, the park is divided into several fields, with touring and seasonal pitches kept well apart; Sunnyside, part of Warren Farm, is about 200 yards further down the road and has its own warden. Access roads are wide and all the 565 touring pitches are grassy and level, with 16A electric hook-ups. There are no hardstandings so motorhomes may have difficulties in extremely wet weather. Play equipment, each piece on a rubberised surface, is located in a line through the centre of the camping fields - ranch-style wooden fences break up the fields and couples usually park around the perimeter overlooking fields and views of the Mendip Hills. A fabulous Play Barn incorporates an indoor play centre, bowling alley, bouncy tractor, ball pit, large-screen television, and electronic games. Warren Farm's Beachcomber Inn offers a variety of facilities including a bar, restaurant (with excellent food), Pirate's Cove for youngsters, and cabaret room for live entertainment. With its on-site fishing, direct access to the beach, sports field and walks, this is a holiday park that caters for everyone.

Facilities

Several toilet blocks of varying styles provide WCs, showers (on payment) and mostly communal washbasins. Facilities vary depending on which block you are using. Showers are of adequate size - only one block with no dividers; the newest building in field 5 has larger ones. Facilities for disabled visitors in the block in field 5 (plus pitches which may be reserved nearby). Three laundries. Supermarket, snack bar and takeaway (opening times vary). Chinese takeaway at Sunnyside. Fish bar. Beachcomber Inn. Play equipment for toddlers. Play barn. Sports field. Fishing lake. Two 'no dogs' fields. Off site: Burnham-on-Sea, Weston-super-Mare, Cheddar, Wells and Glastonbury are all close by. Golf and riding 1.5 miles.

At a glance

Welcome & Ambience	✓✓✓✓	Location	✓✓✓✓✓
Quality of Pitches	✓✓✓✓	Range of Facilities	✓✓✓✓

Directions

Leave M5 at junction 22 and follow the B3140 to Burnham-on-Sea, then to Berrow and Brean. Continue through Brean and Warren Farm is on the right about 1.5 miles past Brean Leisure Park. O.S.GR: ST297564.

Charges 2004

Per unit incl. 2 persons	£ 6.00 - £ 12.00
extra person over 3 yrs	£ 1.00
electricity (16A)	£ 2.00

Reservations

Made with deposit equal to two night's stay. Tel: 01278 751227.
Email: enquiries@warren-farm.co.uk

Open

28 March - 13 October.

UK1480 Home Farm Holiday Park & Country Club

Edithmead, Burnham-on-Sea TA9 4HD (Somerset)

Home Farm is neatly and attractively laid out covering 44 acres, and is convenient for those using the M5. The 780 level pitches (including 180 privately owned holiday homes) laid out on level mown grass are all clearly marked, accessed by tarmac roads and divided into various sections, for example an area for those with pets. Including 183 pitches with hardstanding, there are 20 serviced pitches for RVs and motorcaravans with water and grey water drainage. Electrical connections (10A) are available everywhere with plenty of water points in all the sections, but one central refuse area. A large, modern pool with paved surrounds and a paddling section is neatly walled and overlooked by a pool-side terraced café and takeaway. There is a well equipped playground. early evening children's entertainment, plus amusement machines and pool tables for those interested. The club house (with free membership) is a feature of the site providing carvery meals, a range of entertainment, a function room, adult-only room, wide screen TV, an attractive conservatory and outside barbecue area. In all, it is an excellent provision and Burnham-on-Sea is only a mile away – there is a footpath from the site crossing the railway line. With Berrow Sands and Brean Down there is over seven miles of beach to choose from! There is some road and rail noise but this quietens at night. Tents are not accepted.

Facilities

Two main, refurbished toilet blocks are heated and well situated for touring areas. Hot showers in one block are larger, but minus dividers. Bathrooms (key with £5 deposit). Baby changing room. Dishwashing facilities under cover and a well equipped laundry room. Facilities for disabled visitors. Dog shower. Shop with groceries, camping accessories and camping gaz. Bar. Restaurants, takeaway (open BHs, weekends and high season). Swimming pool (May-Sept, lifeguard w/ends, B.Hs and school holidays). Play area. ATM. Security patrols at night. Barrier card (£2). Off site: Boat launching 1 mile. Golf 2 miles. Riding 3 miles. Beach 3 miles.

At a glance

Welcome & Ambience	✓✓✓✓	Location	✓✓✓
Quality of Pitches	✓✓✓✓	Range of Facilities	✓✓✓✓

Directions

Home Farm is 400 yards from M5 junction 22 and the A38. It is signed from the B3140 into Burnham-on-Sea. O.S.GR: ST328493.

Charges 2004

Per pitch incl. 2 persons,	
electricity and awning	£ 7.00 - £ 18.50
extra person	£ 3.00 - £ 5.00
child (4-17 yrs)	£ 1.50 - £ 4.00
hardstanding	£ 2.50 - £ 4.00
dog	£ 1.00 - £ 2.00
Club membership free. Special breaks available.	

Reservations

Contact park for details Tel: 01278 788888.
Email: office@homefarmholidaypark.co.uk

Open

10 February - 6 January.

UK1530 Slimeridge Farm Touring Park

Links Road, Uphill, Weston-super-Mare BS23 4XY (Somerset)

This small touring site is next to the beach in Uphill village at the southern end of Weston Bay. There are 56 pitches (24 taken on seasonal lets), on level grass with electricity (16A) available, separated from the beach by stone walling. The view across the bay is quite something, with Brean Down and Steep Holm Island standing out. However it is worth noting that, because of its close proximity to the beach, the site could be affected by the tide in extreme adverse winter weather conditions. A circular tarmac road connects the marked and numbered pitches (allocated by the wardens) which include eight hardstandings for motorcaravans. Arrive betweeon 11.00 and 17.00 hrs only. Weston-super-Mare with all its leisure activities and entertainment is 2 miles, Cheddar Gorge, Wooky Hole and Glastonbury are within easy driving distance.

Facilities

A modern toilet block with electronic code entry system is well equipped and includes en-suite shower facilities that are also provided for disabled visitors. Laundry room and dishwashing sinks. Chemical disposal unit also used for waste water. Off site: Post office, general stores and pubs within close walking distance. Golf (golfers have right of way to cross the park as the golf course is split by the site).

Open

1 March - 30 October.

At a glance

Welcome & Ambience	✓✓✓	Location	✓✓✓✓✓
Quality of Pitches	✓✓✓	Range of Facilities	✓✓✓

Directions

Site is south of Weston-super-Mare. From A370 follow sign for Uphill village and sands. O.S.GR: 312588.

Charges 2004

Per unit incl. 2 adults, electricity and awning	£ 10.00 - £ 20.00
extra adult	£ 1.50 - £ 3.00
child (4-9 yrs)	£ 1.00 - £ 2.50
dog	£ 0.50 - £ 1.00

Min. stay 2 nights at B.Hs. No credit cards.

Reservations

Made with deposit of £5 p/night; no refunds given.
Tel: 01934 641641.
Email: homefarmholidaypark@compuserve.com

UK1440 Baltic Wharf Caravan Club Site

Cumberland Road, Bristol BS1 6XG (Somerset)

This excellent, city centre site is operated by the Caravan Club. In Bristol's re-developed dockland, it is well laid out and maintained with access via a lockable gate to the Baltic Wharf dockside. It is screened from the road by a high wall with a boatyard on one side and residential apartments on the other, and is well designed with a good use of trees. The view across the dock towards Clifton village and Bristol is unique and you can even glimpse the suspension bridge. The 58 pitches are accessed by a circular tarmac road, the central 9 on grass (not used in the winter), the rest on stone chippings and ideal for all year round use (steel pegs are sold at reception). All are supplied with 16A electricity. It is a 30 minute walk to the city centre, a daily ferry runs throughout the year or there's a regular bus service (not Sundays). An extra ferry runs from the SS Great Britain to Templemeads. TV reception is poor but a booster is available. This is a well serviced situation and a very popular site so advance booking is necessary. Arrive between 12 noon and 8 pm. Space for large units and RVs is very limited and there is no space for trailers, boats, etc.

Facilities

The toilet block provides good clean facilities including controllable showers and washbasins in cubicles (heated in winter). Good facilities for disabled visitors, plus toilets for the walking disabled and showers in the main block. Dishwashing under cover. Fully equipped laundry room. Motorcaravan service point. Tourist information room. Dogs are welcome but there is no dog walk. Wardens live on the site. Off site: Fishing (licences from Harbour Master's office).

Open

All year.

At a glance

Welcome & Ambience	✓✓✓✓	Location	✓✓✓✓✓
Quality of Pitches	✓✓✓✓✓	Range of Facilities	✓✓✓

Directions

Easiest access is to follow signs for the 'Historic Harbour' and SS Great Britain. Site is just west of the SS Great Britain, on the right behind a high wall - look carefully for the club sign (no brown signs to follow). O.S.GR: ST574721.

Charges 2004

Per adult	£ 4.00 - £ 5.00
child (5-16 yrs)	£ 1.00 - £ 1.80
pitch incl. electricity (non-member)	£ 9.00 - £ 12.00

Reservations

Essential at all times and made with £10 deposit; contact the Wardens with SAE for confirmation.
Tel: 0117 926 8030.

SOUTH WEST ATTRACTIONS

Bristol Zoo Gardens

There's so much to experience at Bristol Zoo Gardens, with over 300 species of wildlife in beautiful gardens, your day will certainly be packed full of fun, facts, and fantastic animals. Bristol Zoo Gardens have won 'Zoo of the Year 2004' voted by the readers of the Good Britain Guide.

Bristol Zoo Gardens is dedicated to conservation and involved in international breeding programmes, so watch out for new baby animals throughout the Zoo. As a charity, we use any money we receive to uphold our mission to care for and protect animals and plants.

Visit 'Zona Bristol', the Brazilian exhibit at Bristol Zoo Gardens, to experience first hand the species found in the threatened coastal rainforests of Brazil. A winding wooden walkway will lead you past stunning birds, dainty agouti, grazing tapirs, and the world's largest living rodent - the capybara.

Award winning 'Seal & Penguin Coasts' with fantastic underwater viewing is a must for all visitors to the Zoo. Come face to face with penguins and seals in their natural element. With its exceptional views, landscaped beaches, cliffs and amazing shipwreck, this is most exciting animal exhibit in the South West and totally unique in Europe.

Other favourites include Bug World, Twilight World, the Monkey House, the Reptile House and the children's play area. The Gardens are also very popular at any time of the year with plenty of benches for visitors to relax in a wonderful environment.

There's plenty of hands-on fun in the Activity Centre with face painting, badge making, brass rubbing, touch table items and the very popular animal encounters where you might get the chance to meet a spider or touch a snake!

Opening Hours: Open daily from 9.00am until 5.30pm in summer (4.30pm in winter). Closed Christmas Day.

Entrance Prices: Adult £9.50, children (3-14) £6.00, concession £8.50, under 3s FREE. NEW family ticket (2 adults & 2 children) £28.00.

For further information visit www.bristolzoo.org.uk or call 0117 973 8951.

UK1430 Mendip Heights Camping & Caravan Park

Priddy, Wells BA5 3BP (Somerset)

Historic Priddy is the highest village in the Mendips and is famed for its annual Sheep Fair in August. Nearby are extensive Roman lead-workings, Bronze Age burial mounds, the Priddy Circle and access to Swildons Hole, one of the popular cave systems in the Mendips. This well kept, family run park is half a mile from the village with tranquil views across the Mendip fields, characterised by dry stone walling. It has a simple charm with field margins left natural to encourage wildlife and nest boxes in the mature trees edging the three fields which comprise the site. These provide space for 92 units on mostly level short grass with 21 electric hook-ups (9 at 10A, 12 at 16A), 8 with hardstanding and 10 seasonal pitches. The only marked pitches are those with electric hook-up, so visitors can site themselves where they like. A range of activities can be arranged covering canoeing, abseiling, archery, caving, mountain biking and others, with equipment provided. The park is also on the Padstow-Bristol Sustran Route 3. Many tourist attractions are within a 20 mile radius. A member of the Countryside Discovery group.

Facilities

The refurbished toilet block with all facilities is bright, cheerful and heated. Two family rooms (one with high and low toilet and shower). Dishwashing and laundry facilities. The reception/shop doubles as the village shop and is therefore open all season selling groceries, Calor gas, etc. with an off licence and tourist information. Wendy house, swings and table tennis for children. Torches useful. Off site: Two traditional village pubs with very different characters stand by the village green within walking distance (0.5 miles). Fishing 6 miles, riding 2 miles.

Open

1 March - mid-November.

At a glance

Welcome & Ambience	✓✓✓✓	Location	✓✓✓✓
Quality of Pitches	✓✓✓	Range of Facilities	✓✓✓

Directions

From M5 exit 21 take A371 to Banwell. Turn left on A368, right on B3134 and right on B3135. After 2 miles turn left at camp sign. From M4 westbound exit 18, A46 to Bath, then A4 towards Bristol. Take A39 for Wells and right at Green Ore traffic lights on B3135; after 5 miles turn left at camp sign. From Shepton Mallet, follow A37 north to junction of B3135 and turn left. Continue on B3135 to traffic lights at Green Ore. Straight on and after 5 miles turn left at camp sign. O.S.GR: ST522518.

Charges 2004

Per adult	£ 4.00 - £ 6.00
child (4-16 yrs)	£ 2.00
pitch with services incl. electricity	£ 2.50
dog	£ 0.50

Reservations

Made with £15 deposit (min. 3 nights for electricity at B.Hs.). Tel: 01749 870241.
Email: enquiries@mendipheights.co.uk

UK1550 Bucklegrove Caravan & Camping Park

Wells Road, Rodney Stoke, Cheddar BS27 3UZ (Somerset)

Bucklegrove is set right in the heart of Somerset on the southern slopes of the Mendip Hills and close to the tourist attractions of Cheddar Gorge, Wookey Hole, and Wells. The 125 touring pitches are split between two fields joined by a woodland walk. The top slightly undulating field is more suitable for tents and caravans, while the lower field with some short hardstandings is a little more level and would be suitable for caravans and smaller motorhomes. The play area (for under 14s) includes a fort, swings and obstacle course. Campers also have a games room and a heated indoor swimming pool (adult only sessions 10.00 - 11.00 daily). Adjoining the pool is a licensed bar with terrace providing simple bar menus and low-key entertainment mainly during high season or depending on the number of campers on site.

Facilities

Two bright and cheerful toilet blocks house all the usual amenities including some washbasins in cubicles and some spacious showers. The larger, heated block near reception also provides bathrooms (50p) with baby changing facilities, and a room for visitors with disabilities. Dishwashing and laundry rooms. Freezer for ice packs. Well stocked shop. Indoor swimming pool and paddling pool with terrace bar. Games room with pool table, video and electronic games. Play area. Dogs are accepted in low season only. Off site: Riding 2 miles. Golf 3 miles. Fishing 5 miles. Beach at Weston-Super-Mare 12 miles. Wookey Hole 2 miles, Wells Cathedral 4 miles, Cheddar 7 miles. A bus to Wells and Cheddar stops at the park entrance.

At a glance

Welcome & Ambience	✓✓✓✓	Location	✓✓✓✓
Quality of Pitches	✓✓✓✓	Range of Facilities	✓✓✓✓

Directions

Take A371 Wells to Cheddar road. Park is on right about 1 mile past Westbury village. Take care as the road between Wells and Cheddar is rather narrow through some of the villages. O.S.GR: ST490496.

Charges 2005

Per unit incl. 2 persons, electricity	£ 5.00 - £ 17.50
pup tent	£ 0.50 - £ 1.50
extra adult	£ 2.00
child (4-14 yrs)	£ 0.50 - £ 1.50
dog (off peak only)	£ 1.00

Reservations

Special offers are available at certain times of the year if booking in advance. Tel: 01749 870261.
Email: info@bucklegrove.co.uk

Open

1 March - 31 December.

UK1510 Bath Chew Valley Caravan Park

Ham Lane, Bishop Sutton BS39 5TZ (Somerset)

A small and secluded garden site for adults only, Chew Valley has been developed with much tender love and care by Ray and Val Belton. The result is that caravans are sited on neat lawns amongst colourful beds of flowers and the cars are tucked away on the car park, providing a tranquil and restful atmosphere. The warden will assist you in placing your caravan. Groundsheets are not permitted on the grass in order to protect it. There are neat hardstandings on 14 pitches and, again to protect the grass, motorcaravans must always use them. This park will particularly appeal to garden lovers; a very nice touch is the small nursery 'Gone to Pot' where you can purchase some of the plants found on-site. Chew Valley lake is a walk of about half a mile with trout fishing available and Blagdon lake is popular for birdwatching. There are several circular walks in the area - visitors may borrow the route plans and a walking stick from reception. Bristol and Bath are within an easy distance and Cheddar Gorge or Longleat make excellent days out. A Best of British group member.

Facilities
The heated toilet block (it has a 'home from home' feel), provides washbasins in cubicles and all the other fittings that make life comfortable. Two separate en-suite units. Useful utility room for dish or hand washing with a spin drier, together with a washing machine and tumble drier for service washes only. Motorcaravan service point. Off site: The village is 100 yds up the road with a useful general store, newsagent, two pubs and a post office. Supermarkets are within 15 minutes drive. Fishing 1 mile. Golf 4 miles. Riding 8 miles. Beach 15 miles.

At a glance
Welcome & Ambience	✓✓✓✓✓	Location	✓✓✓✓
Quality of Pitches	✓✓✓✓✓	Range of Facilities	✓✓✓

Directions
From Bath direction on A368 turn right opposite the Red Lion pub in Bishop Sutton. Road appears a little narrow but continue past small track to the left (50 yds) for a further 50 yds. Park entrance appears on your left with neat, clear entrance. O.S.GR: ST584599.

Charges 2005
Per adult	£ 4.00
pitch incl. electricity, awning and pets	£ 8.00
serviced pitch	£ 10.00

Reservations
Contact park. Tel: 01275 332127.
Email: enquiries@bathchewvalley.co.uk

Open
All year.

UK1460 Newton Mill Camping Park

Newton Road, Bath BA2 9JF (Somerset)

In a peaceful valley and semi-rural position, relatively close to the historic city of Bath and with direct access to the local cycle track network, Newton Mill should make a good base from which to explore the area. The site has been created around an old mill, the bar and restaurant now occupying part of the original building, and there is a modern timber chalet style reception building with a small, well stocked shop. The restaurant (lunches/evenings all year) serves speciality meals including ostrich and lobster, and breakfasts are available (weekends Easter-October, daily in summer). The tent meadow is in an elevated position, or alternatively you may prefer the paddock, a small field alongside the steam which is a car free zone with a separate parking area. The site accepts 105 tents and also has 90 caravan pitches (with 30 long stay) which are located at the other end of the valley. All of these have hardstandings, with electricity (10A) and satellite TV hook-ups. This end of the park is closest to the main Bristol - London railway line, not visually obtrusive but occasional rail noise may be noticeable.

Facilities
Two new heated toilet blocks provide excellent modern facilities with some washbasins in cubicles, free hot showers, bathrooms (on payment), baby rooms, dishwashing rooms and a good suite for disabled campers. Launderette. Basic motorcaravan service point. Shop, bar, restaurant with garden seating area. Play area. Boules court. Fishing. Off site: Bus service into Bath runs from Twerton village which is a 10 minute walk. Nearby Bristol & Bath Railway Path (a traffic free cycle way) links to the West Bath Riverside Path, and the Kennet and Avon towpath.

Open
All year.

At a glance
Welcome & Ambience	✓✓✓✓	Location	✓✓✓✓
Quality of Pitches	✓✓✓✓	Range of Facilities	✓✓✓✓

Directions
Site is 3 miles west of Bath, about 1 mile southeast of the roundabout where the A4 meets the A39. From north take M4 exit 19, turn onto M32 and almost immediately take A4174 (Avon ring road) for 7.5 miles to the A4. Turn left towards Bath, after 5 miles at second roundabout, take second exit signed Newton St Loe, pass Globe public house to site on your left after about 1 mile. O.S.GR:ST713647.

Charges 2004
Per adult	£ 4.00 - £ 5.00
child (3-17 yrs)	£ 1.50
pitch incl. car	£ 2.00 - £ 6.00
dog	£ 0.50

Reservations
Advised for peak season and B.Hs. Tel: 01225 333909.
Email: newtonmill@hotmail.com

79

UK1450 Bath Marina & Caravan Park

Brassmill Lane, Bath BA1 3JT (Somerset)

British Waterways have taken the lease for the Bath Marina and Caravan Park. Conveniently located alongside the Bath to Bristol cycle path, the site is within walking distance of the city and a park-and-ride facility. There are 88 pitches of varying sizes pleasantly interspersed with grass, flowering trees and bushes; every pitch has a concrete hardstanding with a 16A electricity connection. Two wooden cabins provide clean facilities and amenities (accessed with a security code). Television reception is poor so future development will include an aerial and connections to every pitch. There is no shop (except postcards, some basic camping equipment and gas exchange), however visitors can order newspapers, milk, and bread at the reception to be delivered to their pitches the next morning. Meals are available at the Boathouse Inn, just a two-minute walk along the river path.

Facilities

Two fan-heated buildings provide toilets, washbasins (with privacy curtain in ladies), showers and hairdryers. Some toilets have been modified for use by visitors with disabilities. Dishwashing sinks under cover. Large laundry. Recycling bins. Gas exchange. Drain for motorcaravan waste water. Tourist information. Children's play park adjacent to park. Boat launching (free) from Marina. Off site: Bath 2 miles, Bristol 8 miles, Bristol-Bath cycle path.

Open

All year.

At a glance

Welcome & Ambience	✓✓✓✓	Location	✓✓✓✓
Quality of Pitches	✓✓✓✓	Range of Facilities	✓✓✓

Directions

Park is off the A4 Bristol to Bath road. From Bristol, stay on the A4 towards Bath, at roundabout (junction with A39) continue for 1.3miles (keep left as the road forks), cross the river and turn right just past the garage into Brassmill Lane and park is 100 yards on the right. O.S. GR: ST720655.

Charges 2004

Per pitch all inclusive	£ 15.00

Reservations

Advised for B.Hs. and school holidays and made with £15 deposit. Tel: 01225 424301. Email: arthur.currie@bwml.co.uk

Bath Marina and Caravan Park

Open All Year

Riverside tranquillity and great access to beautiful Bath, including the Roman Baths & Royal Crescent. All just a 10 minute bus ride or a 30 minute river walk away - we offer great value in a great location.

Open all year. Up to 80 pitches available. Every pitch has hard standing & electrical hook up. Heated Toilet & shower blocks. On site laundry facility.

For more information & bookings call

01225 424301

Bath Caravan Park, Brassmill Lane, Bath BA1 3JT
F: 01225 424301, E: arthur.currie@bwml.co.uk
www.bwml.co.uk

UK1490 Greenacres Camping

Barrow Lane, North Wootton, Shepton Mallet BA4 4HL (Somerset)

Greenacres is a rural site in Somerset countryside for tents, trailer tents and small motorcaravans only. Hidden away below the Mendips and almost at the start of the 'Levels', it is a simple green site - a true haven of peace and quiet. The grass is neatly trimmed over the 4.5 acres and hedged with mature trees, though there is a view of Glastonbury Tor in one direction and of Barrow Hill in the other. All of the 30 pitches are around the perimeter of the park, leaving a central area safe for children to play. At the narrower neck end, 5 pitches have electricity hook-ups (16A) and are ideal for those without children or birdwatchers. Wild life abounds. A speciality of the park is the 'Turf Rider' that tows the cart used to give children an evening ride. You can cycle into both Wells and Glastonbury using Sustran Route 3.

Facilities

The central wooden toilet block is simple but perfectly acceptable and kept clean. Hot showers are accessed from the outside. Two dishwashing sinks, two laundry sinks (H&C) and a spin dryer, with and iron, board and hairdryer available from the park office. Play equipment, badminton net and play house. The office is across the lane at the owner's bungalow. Here are fridges and freezers (free), a library, tourist information and bicycle hire. Batteries may be charged or borrowed. Dogs are not accepted. Off site: In North Wootton itself (under 1 mile) large pub/restaurant and a vineyard. Fishing and riding nearby.

At a glance

Welcome & Ambience	✓✓✓✓	Location	✓✓✓✓
Quality of Pitches	✓✓✓✓	Range of Facilities	✓✓✓

Directions

From A39 (Glastonbury - Wells) turn east at Brownes Garden Centre and follow camping signs. From A361 Glastonbury - Shepton Mallet road follow camp signs from Pilton or Steanbow. O.S.GR: ST553416.

Charges 2005

Per adult	£ 6.00
child (4-16 yrs)	£ 2.00
electricity	£ 2.00
No credit cards.	

Reservations

Made with £2 deposit. Tel: 01749 890497.

Open

March - October.

UK1540 Batcombe Vale Campsite

Batcombe Vale, Shepton Mallet BA4 6BW (Somerset)

Set in a secluded valley with fields gently rising around it, contented cows grazing with watchful buzzards cruising above and views across the distant hills, this is a very special place. Home to Donald and Mary Sage, Batcombe Vale House is a mellow, attractive building covered with wisteria, to one side of the valley overlooking the lakes and the 'wilder' landscape. Trees and shrubs have been skilfully placed to enhance the natural environment providing a range of colour and shape. Designated an 'area of outstanding natural beauty', there are 120 acres around the valley where you are welcome to wander and picnic in the fields - a haven for wild flowers, birds and butterflies. For those who fish, two of the lakes have carp and tench up to 18lbs but you must have a current licence. Descending slowly down the narrow entrance drive you see the pitches, attractively set and terraced where necessary, in an oval with the lakes below. The grass is left natural around the 32 pitches (20 have 10A electricity) and paths mown where needed. If you tire of the views and the fishing there is a range of circular walks from the site or you can potter about in one of the four small rowing boats. There are many places to visit nearby, from Glastonbury with the Tor, to Cheddar Gorge and the Caves.

Facilities

The small rustic toilet block covered in honeysuckle meets all needs, including a freezer and dishwashing sinks. Groundsheet awnings must be lifted daily. Fishing. Caravan storage. Coarse fishing (up to 20 lbs) adults £3 p/day (child £1.50). One dog per pitch is welcome (no dangerous breeds). Off site: Golf, riding and bicycle hire 5 miles. Bruton (for shops, etc.) is 2 miles. Launderettes at Shepton or Frome.

Open

Easter - September.

At a glance

Welcome & Ambience	✓✓✓✓✓	Location	✓✓✓✓✓
Quality of Pitches	✓✓✓✓	Range of Facilities	✓✓✓

Directions

Bruton is south of Shepton Mallet and Frome and north of Wincanton where the A359 intersects the B3081. About 2 miles north of Bruton on B3081 turn on bend (site signed) into narrow lane. Turn left at T-junction and follow signs to site 500 yds on left. Access drive is steep. O.S.GR: ST684376.

Charges 2004

Per unit incl. 2 adults	£ 12.00
extra adult	£ 3.50
child (4-18 yrs)	£ 1.00 - £ 2.50
electricity	£ 2.00
dog	£ 1.00

No commercial vehicles or motorcycle 'packs' - family groups only.

Reservations

Contact park for details. Tel: 01749 830246.
Email: DonaldSage@compuserve.com

UK1390 The Old Oaks Touring Park

Wick Farm, Wick, Glastonbury BA6 8JS (Somerset)

The Old Oaks, an 'adults only' park, is tucked below and hidden from the 'Tor', in a lovely secluded setting with views across to the Mendips. There are 40 extra large pitches in a series of paddocks, all with 10A electricity, 18 with hardstanding and 4 fully serviced (including sewage). Mainly backing on to hedges, they are attractively arranged and interspersed with shrubs and flowers in a circular development or terraced with increasing views. A quiet orchard area or a separated hedged paddock for camping and a larger field with chemical disposal facilities complete the provision. Mature trees and hedging combine with the mellow farm buildings to give a sense of timelessness, tranquillity and peace. Whether you fish or not, the pond which is well stocked with carp, roach and tench is worth a visit not only for its view of the Tor, but also to see the ducks and the chickens on your way. There is parking for disabled visitors within 25 yards of the pond. In an area steeped in history and legend, this is a very well equipped and maintained park which should meet the needs of the discerning camper or caravanner. Only adults are accepted (18 yrs and over). A member of the Best of British group.

Facilities

The heated toilet block, converted from the old stables, is of excellent quality and well equipped. Neatly paved outside, it has digital security locks (a public footpath from the Tor passes through the farm). Some washbasins are in cubicles. Two en-suite rooms and a bathroom (50p). Disabled visitors have two rooms, one with a toilet and basin, the other with a shower, toilet and basin. Fully equipped laundry room. Dishwashing under cover. Motorcaravan service facilities. Two recycling points. Freezer for ice packs (free). Useful dog wash. Shop for basics and local bread in the main season and an off licence (limited hours). Bicycle hire (together with hire of helmets and panniers). Games room. Fishing. Off site: Riding 5 miles and golf 6 miles. Market day is Tuesday.

At a glance

Welcome & Ambience	✓✓✓✓✓	Location	✓✓✓✓✓
Quality of Pitches	✓✓✓✓✓	Range of Facilities	✓✓✓✓

Directions

Park is north off A361 Shepton Mallet - Glastonbury road, 2 miles from Glastonbury. Take unclassified road signed Wick for approx. 1 mile and the park is on the left. O.S.GR: ST521394.

Charges 2005

Per unit with 2 persons	£ 9.00 - £ 13.00
with electricity (10A)	£ 11.00 - £ 15.00
awning with breathing groundsheet	£ 1.00
dog	£ 1.00

Reservations

Advised for high season and made with £15 non-refundable deposit Tel: 01458 831437.
Email: info@theoldoaks.co.uk

Open

1 March - 31 October.

UK1400 The Isle of Avalon Touring Caravan Park

Godney Road, Glastonbury BA6 9AF (Somerset)

This modern park is under new ownership. It has a friendly atmosphere and is only a short walk from the centre of Glastonbury. Developed on flat, grassy ground, the park has been landscaped, part with trees and shrubs, part open, to provide 70 individual pitches. Well spaced and connected by hard roads, they have hardstanding with adjacent grass for awning and electricity points (5/10A). A further 50 tent spaces are on the adjoining field, the top corner being left clear as a play area. Water and refuse points are well distributed around and attractively surrounded by trees and shrubs. All visitors are personally seen to their pitches. A well stocked shop with takeaway and some camping accessories and reception with gas and tourist information is at the entrance.

Facilities

The single, tiled toilet block is comfortable, spacious and can be heated. Some washbasins in cubicles for women and excellent units for disabled visitors (plus ramps to the shop and reception). Large laundry room and dishwashing area. Motorcaravan point. Shop and takeaway. Bicycle hire. Dogs are accepted but by prior arrangement only on tent pitches. American motorhomes welcome. Winter caravan storage. Off site: Riding or golf 2 miles, fishing 200 yds.

At a glance

Welcome & Ambience	✓✓✓✓	Location	✓✓✓✓
Quality of Pitches	✓✓✓✓	Range of Facilities	✓✓✓✓

Directions

Park is on west side of the town bypass (A39), just off B3151 (Wedmore Road) with good signs from the bypass. O.S.GR: ST494397.

Charges 2004

Per person	£ 1.50 - £ 2.00
pitch	£ 5.00 - £ 6.00
incl. electricity	£ 7.00 - £ 8.00

Reservations

Any length with £10 deposit. Tel: 01458 833618.

Open

All year.

UK1420 Southfork Caravan Park

Parrett Works, Martock TA12 6AE (Somerset)

Don't be put off by the address which is historic - this was once a 17th century flax mill. Michael and Nancy Bradley now own and run this excellent, modern, well drained site just outside the lovely village of Martock. With 30 touring pitches on grass with a gravel access road (21 with 10A electrical hook-ups), it is an orderly, quiet park on two acres of flat, tree lined meadow near the River Parrett. All the expected facilities are close to the entrance and as the owners live on the premises, the park is open all year. Most things are available, including an NCC approved caravan repairs/servicing centre. Despite the rural setting, the A303 trunk road is just five minutes away. This area of South Somerset contains so much of interest, including the Fleet Air Arm Museum, Haynes Motor Museum and Cricket St Thomas Wildlife.

Facilities

The heated well maintained toilet block is fully equipped and includes some washbasins in cabins. Laundry room with washing machine and dryer, plus dishwashing sink. Shop and limited off licence. Play area. Off site: Fishing (with licences). Golf 5 miles. Bicycle hire 8 miles. Riding 10 miles.

Open

All year.

At a glance

Welcome & Ambience	✓✓✓✓	Location	✓✓✓✓
Quality of Pitches	✓✓✓✓	Range of Facilities	✓✓✓✓

Directions

From A303 between Ilchester and Ilminster take signs for South Petherton or Martock; park is mid-way between the two villages. O.S.GR: ST446187.

Charges 2004

Per unit incl. 2 persons	£ 8.00 - £ 11.00
extra person over 5yrs	£ 1.50
electricity (10A)	£ 2.25 - £ 3.00

Reservations

Made with £10 deposit. Tel: 01935 825661.
Email: southfork.caravans@virgin.net

UK1500 Long Hazel International Caravan & Camping Park

High Street, Sparkford, Yeovil BA22 7JH (Somerset)

Pamela and Alan Walton are really enthusiastic about their neat, small park in the Somerset village of Sparkford where they will make you most welcome. With level grass, attractive beech hedging, silver birches and many newly planted trees, the park has a comfortable feel. It provides 75 touring pitches for all types of units, 50 with electrical hook-ups (16A), 40 pitches with hardstanding, some extra long, and the entrance has been widened for easier access. There is a post office/shop in the village selling bread baked on the premises and the village inn provides good food. The park edges the A303 bypass; although it is well hedged, there could be road noise at times in some areas.

Facilities

The well equipped heated toilet block is kept immaculate. Well planned en-suite facilities for disabled visitors. Washing machine and dryer. Motorcaravan point. Gas. Recycling. Central recreation area providing play equipment. American style motorhomes accepted. Off site: Mini-market 400 yards. Riding or fishing 8 miles. Golf 5 miles.

At a glance

Welcome & Ambience	✓✓✓✓	Location	✓✓✓✓
Quality of Pitches	✓✓✓✓	Range of Facilities	✓✓✓

Directions

From Yeovil direction on A303 turn into Sparkford. Park is on left 100 yds before Inn. O.S.GR: ST604263.

Charges 2004

Per unit incl. 2 persons, electricity	£ 12.00 - £ 14.00

No credit cards.

Reservations

Contact park. Tel: 01963 440002.
Email: longhazelpark@hotmail.com

Open

16 February - 16 January.

UK1630 Brokerswood Country Park

Brokerswood, Westbury BA13 4EH (Wiltshire)

This countryside campsite is located in an 80 acre country park, with ancient broadleaf woodland, plenty of marked walks, a woodland railway which also runs 'Santa Specials' (bookings taken from 1 Aug). The gift shop has a special Christmas theme from the end of October. The park also has adventure playgrounds and play trails amongst its many activities for the family. Most are free for campers, except for the train. Fishing in the lake is available, ask at reception. Cycling in the park is forbidden. The campsite has 65 pitches arranged around an open meadow area, served by a circular gravel roadway, with low level site lighting. There are 25 hardstanding pitches, and 30 electric hook-ups (10A). Although recently laid-out, the site is maturing well. In the interest of environmental conservation it has its own biological waste management system. There are also recycling bins for glass, paper and metal cans. American RVs and other large units should use the coach entrance (phone the site before arrival).

Facilities

A recently constructed, well insulated and heated, timber clad building provides the usual facilities including large, controllable hot showers. Fully equipped suite for disabled people with ramped approach and alarm. Covered dishwashing sinks, but no laundry. Motorcaravan services. Gas available. Milk, bread, newspapers to order from reception/shop. Broadleaf Café serving meals and refreshments all day. Entry barrier (key code). Off site: Golf 6 miles. Pub with excellent meals (800 yds). Nearest shops at Dilton Marsh and Westbury. Longleat 6 miles. Bath 12 miles.

At a glance

Welcome & Ambience	✓✓✓✓	Location	✓✓✓✓✓
Quality of Pitches	✓✓✓✓	Range of Facilities	✓✓✓✓

Directions

From Trowbridge take A361 south for 2 miles, turning left (east) at Southwick, and follow signs to Country Park. O.S.GR: ST840524.

Charges 2004

Per pitch	£ 8.00 - £ 19.00
incl. electricity	£ 9.00 - £ 17.00
cyclists and walkers (2 persons)	£ 7.00

Reservations

Made with non-refundable deposit; contact site. Tel: 01373 822238. Email: woodland.park@virgin.net

Open

All year.

UK1690 Longleat Caravan Club Site

Warminster BA12 7NL (Wiltshire)

What a magnificent situation in which to find a caravan park, amidst all the wonders of the Longleat Estate including the Elizabethan House, gardens designed by Capability Brown and the Safari Park. Visitors can roam the woodlands and enjoy the views, watch the wildlife and marvel at the azaleas, bluebells, etc. according to the season or listen to the occupants of the Safari Park. The site itself, well managed by Club wardens, is set in 10 acres of lightly wooded, level grassland within walking distance of the house and gardens. There are 165 generous pitches (101 with hardstanding and 64 on grass), all with 16A electricity connections. Water points and re-cycling bins are neatly walled with low night lighting. Two new buildings provide immaculate facilities. Tents are not accepted (except trailer tents).

Facilities

Two heated toilet blocks provide washbasins in cubicles, controllable showers and a vanity section with hairdryers. Baby/toddler room. Suite for disabled visitors. Laundry and dishwashing. Family room with DVD player. Two motorcaravan service points. Play area. Office stocks basic food items and gas, papers can be ordered (manned 9 am - 6 pm). Fish and chip van calls. Late arrivals area. Off site: Longleat House and its attractions. Frome 7 miles.

Open

31 March - 30 October.

At a glance

Welcome & Ambience	✓✓✓✓✓	Location	✓✓✓✓✓
Quality of Pitches	✓✓✓✓✓	Range of Facilities	✓✓✓✓✓

Directions

The main entrance to Longleat which caravans must use is signed from A362 Frome - Warminster road near to where it joins the A36 Warminster bypass. Turn into the estate and follow Longleat House route through tolls for 2 miles then Club signs for 1 mile. There are shorter ways to leave. O.S.GR: ST806434

Charges 2004

Per adult	£ 4.00 - £ 5.00
child (5-16 yrs)	£ 1.10 - £ 1.80
pitch incl. electricity (non-member)	£ 9.00 - £ 12.00

Reservations

Advisable for B.Hs. and school holidays and made with £5 deposit. Tel: 01985 844663.

83

UK1660 Piccadilly Caravan Park

Folly Lane West, Lacock, Chippenham SN15 2LP (Wiltshire)

Piccadilly Caravan Park is set in open countryside close to several attractions in northern Wessex, notably Longleat, Bath, Salisbury Plain, Stourhead, and Lacock itself. It is a small, quiet family owned park that is kept neat and tidy. Landscaped shrubs and trees are maturing, giving the impression of three separate areas. There are 40 well spaced, clearly marked pitches, 12 of which have hardstanding. Electrical connections (10A) are available on 34 pitches. Lacock Abbey was once the home of Henry Fox-Talbot, pioneer of photography, and there is now a museum in the village. A bus service runs from Lacock village to Chippenham (entry to the Chippenham museum and Heritage centre is free of charge).

Facilities

The one toilet block is well maintained and equipped, should be adequate in size for peak periods and can be heated in cool weather. Dishwashing area. Laundry room with baby changing facilities. Ice pack service. Small, bark-based playground and a large, grass ball play area. Limited gas supplies. Papers can be ordered. Off site: Fishing 1 mile, bicycle hire 6 miles, riding 4 miles, golf 3 miles.

Open

Easter/1 April - October.

At a glance

| Welcome & Ambience | ✓✓✓✓ | Location | ✓✓✓✓ |
| Quality of Pitches | ✓✓✓✓ | Range of Facilities | ✓✓✓ |

Directions

Park is signed west off A350 Chippenham - Melksham road (turning to Gastard with caravan symbol) by Lacock village. 300 yds. to park. O.S.GR: ST911683.

Charges 2004

Per unit incl. 2 persons	£ 10.00
extra person over 5 yrs	£ 1.00
electricity	£ 2.00
No credit cards.	

Reservations

Any length; deposit of 1 nights fee.
Tel: 01249 730260. Email: piccadillylacock@aol.com

Open Apr to Oct

Piccadilly Caravan Park

- Set in open countryside close to several attractions
- Small quiet family owned park kept neat and tidy
- Electrical connections on 34 pitches
- 40 well spaced, clearly marked pitches
- Bark-based playground and large grass play area
- Well maintained toilet block
- Laundry room

01249 730260

piccadillylacock@aol.com
www.caravancampingsites.co.uk/wiltshire/piccadilly.htm

Folly Lane West
Lacock, Chippenham
Wiltshire SN15 2LP

RAC APPOINTED

AA

UK1680 Plough Lane Caravan Site

Plough Lane, Kington Langley, Chippenham SN15 5PS (Wiltshire)

Catering for adults only, this is a good example of a well designed, quality, modern touring site. The 50 pitches (all for touring units) are attractively laid out over four acres, access roads are gravel and the borders are stocked with well established shrubs and trees. The pitches are half grass, half hardstanding and all have electricity (16A). Eight pitches are fully serviced. The site entrance has a barrier system for security. This site is an ideal base for visiting Bath, Westonbirt Arboretum, Abbey House and Gardens at Malmesbury and the many attractive villages of north Wiltshire and south Gloucestershire.

Facilities

The sanitary building is heated, spacious, light and airy, and has all the usual facilities including some washbasins in cubicles, with a hairdressing area for ladies. Separate en-suite room for disabled visitors with ramp access. Dishwashing sinks under cover. Fully equipped laundry with two further dishwashing sinks. Max. 2 dogs per unit, a gravel dog walking path is provided. This park is for adults only (over 18 yrs). Barrier card deposit £10. Off site: Local facilities include a supermarket, two public houses, and two garages - both stocking Calor and Camping Gaz. Golf less than 1 mile.

At a glance

| Welcome & Ambience | ✓✓✓✓ | Location | ✓✓✓✓ |
| Quality of Pitches | ✓✓✓✓ | Range of Facilities | ✓✓✓ |

Directions

From M4 exit 17 turn south on A350 for 2 miles, then left at traffic lights (site signed). From Chippenham head north on A350 (towards M4), approaching traffic lights (signed for site and Kington Langley) you need the right hand lane. O.S.GR: ST914764.

Charges 2004

Per unit incl. 2 adults and electricity	£ 12.00
incl. services	£ 14.00
extra adult (max. 2 extra)	£ 3.00
No credit cards.	

Reservations

Made with £ 12 deposit. Tel: 01249 750795.
Email: ploughlane@lineone.net

Open

Mid March - mid October.

UK1700 Devizes Camping & Caravanning Club Site

Spout Lane, Seend, Melksham SN12 6RN (Wiltshire)

First opened in 1998, this site occupies a level field with gravel roads and centrally located facilities. It is also adjacent to the Kennet and Avon Canal (opened in 1810 and recently extensively restored) and the towpath now provides a traffic-free route passing the Caen Hill flight of 29 locks into Devizes (4 miles). In the other direction the towpath runs towards Melksham (also 4 miles). There are 50 hardstanding and 45 grass pitches, 77 with electricity (16A). The Millennium Wood on the site contains more than 1,000 trees. The site is central for visiting many places of interest including the stone circles at Stonehenge and Avebury. A more unusual outing is to Sandridge Farm, renowned for its speciality bacons, hams and sausages. The farm shop is open daily, May to Sept. and visitors can see the pigs and piglets (admission free - wellies advisable). The Vale of Pewsey cycle route can be accessed from the canal towpath to the east of Devizes, and runs for 41 miles between Great Bedwyn and Corsham.

Facilities

The modern, heated toilet block provides spacious hot showers, washbasins in cubicles, laundry, dishwashing room, and a baby room. Facilities for disabled visitors are in a suite (with alarm system) by reception. Motorcaravan services (in the late arrivals area). Small playground. Reception opens 09.00-10.00 and 16.00-17.30, and stocks basic foods and drinks, snacks and gas supplies, fishing licences and local tourist information.

Open

All year.

At a glance

Welcome & Ambience	✓✓✓✓	Location	✓✓✓✓
Quality of Pitches	✓✓✓✓	Range of Facilities	✓✓✓

Directions

From Devizes take A361 westbound, and 0.5 miles before Seend village, take A365 towards Melksham. Cross the canal bridge, take next left by 'Three Magpies' and the site entrance is on your right. Approaching from the M4 junction 17, use A350 to Melksham and A365 to the site. O.S.GR: ST950620.

Charges 2005

Per adult	£ 5.55 - £ 6.40
child	£ 1.90
pitch fee (non-members)	£ 5.00

Reservations

Advised for B.Hs. and peak season; contact site or Central Reservations 0870 243 3331. Site tel: 01380 828839.

UK1640 Greenhill Farm Camping & Caravan Park

New Road, Landford, Salisbury SP5 2AZ (Wiltshire)

Located on the northern edge of the New Forest, this is an attractive, uncommercialised, hide-away for adults only (over 18 yrs), set around two small lakes, one of which is reserved for coarse fishing. The 100 level pitches, 35 hardstanding (the rest on grass), come complete with 16A electric hook-ups, and are attractively spread around the 14 acre site. An area for tents is in a separate hill-top meadow with views over the nearby forest. There is also a separate area set aside for pets. Several local pubs serving meals are close by and a bus stop outside the site entrance provides services to Salisbury or Southampton. Local attractions include Paultons Park, Breamore House, Downton Moot and the New Forest.

Facilities

Portacabin-type units of varying ages located around the site perimeter provide basic facilities and can be heated when necessary. Showers are free, but a token is issued with a refundable £1 deposit. No dedicated facilities for disabled persons. Laundry with washing machine and dryer. Gas supplies. Milk, eggs, gifts, maps etc. stocked. Tourist information from public telephone. Coarse fishing lake (£3 per rod per day). Torches useful. One vehicle only per camping unit (others to remain in car park). American motorhomes not accepted. Off site: Landford village (15 minute walk) has a bakery, post office, off licence and general stores. Golf 3 miles.

At a glance

Welcome & Ambience	✓✓✓✓	Location	✓✓✓✓✓
Quality of Pitches	✓✓✓✓	Range of Facilities	✓✓✓

Directions

From M27 exit 2 take A36 north towards Salisbury for about 6 miles. Pass through West Wellow and after passing a B.P. garage on left, take next left into New Road, and continue for under 1 mile to site entrance on left. O.S.GR: SU264184.

Charges 2005

Per unit incl. 2 persons, awning and electricity	£ 11.00
tent incl. 2 persons	£ 10.00
extra person	£ 3.00

Reservations

Advised for B.Hs; contact park. Tel: 01794 324117.

Open

All year.

UK1650 Coombe Touring Park

Coombe Nurseries, Race Plain, Netherhampton, Salisbury SP2 8PN (Wiltshire)

A true touring park with outstanding views over the Chalke Valley, Coombe is adjacent to Salisbury race-course. There are 100 spacious pitches all on level, well mown grass, 50 with electric hook-ups (10A). The tent pitches are generally around the outer perimeter. Many pitches are individual and sheltered by hedging, with picnic tables provided on many. Reception also has a small shop, there are supermarkets in Salisbury (4.5 miles), and pubs in Netherhampton and Coombe Bissett (2 miles) both serving meals.

Facilities

A well built and recently re-fitted, centrally heated sanitary unit, provides an ample supply of WCs, spacious press button showers, washbasins in cubicles for the ladies, and a family room (with bath) has facilities for disabled persons, babies and toddlers. Dishwashing room. Laundry with washing machines, dryers and ironing stations. Small shop (May-September). Open grass play area. Gas available. Off site: Nearby attractions include Wilton House, Wilton Carpet Factory and the Wilton Shopping Village, Salisbury Cathedral, Stonehenge. Golf 400 yards. Riding and tennis in Wilton 2.5 miles. Indoor pool, leisure centre and cinema in Salisbury 4.5 miles.

Open

All year.

At a glance

Welcome & Ambience	✓✓✓✓	Location	✓✓✓✓
Quality of Pitches	✓✓✓✓	Range of Facilities	✓✓✓

Directions

From A36 two miles west of Salisbury (just east of Wilton roundabout), turn south on A3094 towards Netherhampton and Harnham. After 0.5 miles on sharp left hand bend, turn right to Stratford Tony and Racecourse (site signed). Continue to top of hill by racecourse entrance, and turn left (signed) on narrow lane behind racecourse for 700 yards to site entrance. O.S.GR: SU098282.

Charges 2004

Per unit incl. 2 persons	£ 10.00
extra adult	£ 3.00
child (3-17 yrs)	£ 1.00 - £ 2.00
electricity	£ 1.50
dog	£ 0.20

Low season package (30 Sept - Easter) £8.00 incl.
No credit cards.

Reservations

Advisable for B.Hs and July/August.
Tel: 01722 328451.

UK1670 Alderbury Caravan & Camping Park

Southampton Road, Whaddon, Salisbury SP5 3HB (Wiltshire)

At the southern end of Alderbury/Whaddon village, this small touring park is conveniently located for visiting Salisbury and the New Forest. Situated on level ground, there is a gravel access road to the 39 numbered pitches; 26 with electricity (16A) and 12 on hardstanding. The park has some mature trees for shade, as well as younger trees, shrubs and flowers. More recently a small playground has been added. The village shop and post office, a pub serving meals and a bus stop are within easy level walking distance of the entrance. There are bus services to Salisbury, Southampton and Romsey. The country lanes around the area are good for cycling and walking. Salisbury Museum, the Cathedral and its Close are all well worth a visit. There is some road noise, most noticeable at the far end of the park.

Facilities

The central toilet block is practical, clean and well maintained. Showers in cubicles with curtain, separate unit for disabled visitors, dishwashing sink, freezer, washing machine and microwave also in a separate room. Gas supplies. American motorhomes accepted by prior arrange-ment. Off site: Fishing 1 mile, bicycle hire 3 miles, riding 2 miles, golf 5 miles.

Open

All year.

At a glance

Welcome & Ambience	✓✓✓	Location	✓✓✓✓
Quality of Pitches	✓✓✓✓	Range of Facilities	✓✓✓

Directions

From Salisbury take A36 towards Southampton and, after 3 miles (at far end of the dual-carriageway), turn left (Alderbury and Whaddon), then right, over bridge, and left for park entrance. From Southampton on A36 towards Salisbury, continue past A27 (Romsey) junction and over Pepperbox Hill. At end of a downhill straight, left on slip road marked Alderbury, park is signed. O.S.GR: SU198263.

Charges 2004

Per unit incl. 2 adults	£ 8.50 - £ 10.50
with 16A electricity	£ 11.00 - £ 13.00
extra adult	£ 2.00 - £ 2.50
child (under 14 yrs)	£ 1.00 - £ 1.50
awning	£ 1.25 - £ 2.00

No credit cards.

Reservations

Contact park for details. Tel: 01722 710125.
Email: alderbury@aol.com

UK1760 Wood Farm Caravan Park

Axminster Road, Charmouth DT6 6BT (Dorset)

Wood Farm is an excellent, family run park, maintained to high standards and with an indoor swimming pool. Situated on the western side of Charmouth beside the A35 (some road noise may be expected) but only a mile or two from Lyme Regis and its beaches. This area is now part of England's first natural World Heritage site, 'The Jurassic Coast'. Wood Farm it is part of the Caravan Club's 'managed under contract' scheme (non-members are also very welcome). On sloping, well landscaped ground, it has splendid rural views across the Marshwood Vale. There are 200 pitches for touring units of which 180 are neat, level all-weather pitches with hardstanding, electricity (10A) and TV connections, and provision for awnings. Some are divided by neat, box-like leylandii hedging, some are terraced. Water and waste water hook-ups are also available. One grassy terraced field takes about 25 tents and there are 80 caravan holiday homes in separate areas. Wood Farm makes excellent provision for disabled visitors, although there is considerable up and down walking due to the terrain. A member of the Best of British group.

Facilities

Four modern, well equipped toilet blocks can be heated and include some washbasins in cubicles, en-suite family rooms, 3 with showers and 1 with bath (charged). Excellent facilities for disabled people including low sinks for wheelchair access both for laundry and dishwashing. Baby care unit. Two laundry rooms. Covered dishwashing sinks. Motor-caravan service point. Shop by reception. Fish and chip van opens 2-4 times a week (acc. to season). Good heated indoor pool (27 x 54 ft; £1.50 per session, under 3s free). Recreation hall with two pool tables and family games area with table tennis, TV, 'soft play' and table football. Internet access. Bridge club. Outdoor draughts. Outdoor tennis court. Play field. Two coarse fishing ponds (carp, rudd, roach, tench, perch) adjacent - day and weekly tickets (rod licence required, also available from park). Dog walk area Off site: Golf 1 mile. Riding 4 miles. Beaches and shops 1 and 2 miles.

At a glance

Welcome & Ambience	✓✓✓✓	Location	✓✓✓✓
Quality of Pitches	✓✓✓✓✓	Range of Facilities	✓✓✓✓

Directions

Park is 0.5 miles west of Charmouth village with access near roundabout at junction of A35 with A3052 (Lyme Regis) road. O.S.GR: SY356940.

Charges 2004

Per adult	£ 3.50 - £ 5.00
child (5-16 yrs)	£ 1.50 - £ 1.75
pitch incl. 10A electricity, awning	£ 4.50 - £ 8.00
incl. water and drainage	£ 7.50 - £ 11.00
pup tent, dog, extra car	£ 1.00

Special senior citizens low season discounts.

Reservations

Made with £30 deposit (non-returnable), min. 5 nights in high season, 3 nights other times.
Tel: 01297 560697. Email: holidays@woodfarm.co.uk

Open

1 April - 31 October.

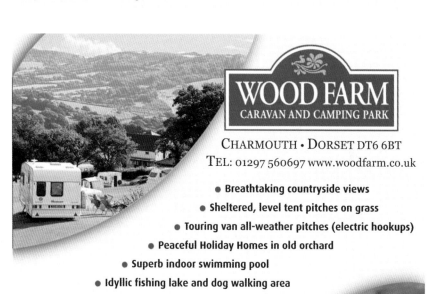

UK1730 Monkton Wyld Farm Caravan Park

Monkton Wyld Farm, Charmouth DT6 6DB (Dorset)

Opened in 1991 by Simon and Joanna Kewley, Monkton Wylde is maturing nicely. Planting of flowering shrubs and trees continues (hydrangea and lavender) making an attractive, peaceful park, and a woodland walk has been created in 80 acres of the beautiful countryside surrounding the park. An abundance of mature trees around the perimeter provides shade and plenty of space between the 60 pitches gives a feeling of spaciousness. Most pitches have 16A electricity and around 35 have hardstanding. On site facilities are limited but an area at the top of the park has been turned into a play area, with a good space for ball games, a climbing frame, trampoline, etc. A separate site has been developed next to the existing park for the Camping and Caravanning Club (open to non-members), managed by wardens. Bread, milk, groceries and papers may be obtained from here in the main season (09.00-19.00 hrs).

Facilities

The modern, well maintained toilet block has a fully equipped family room with baby changing facilities and that can also be accessed by wheelchairs. Individual showers with folding screen are very spacious. Small laundry with washing machine and dryer. Washing up is under cover. Gas supplies. Play area. Caravan storage. Gate locked at 11 pm. Off site: Fishing or riding 2 miles, bicycle hire, golf and boat launching 3 miles. Shops and local pubs are within a mile's walking distance and Charmouth and Lyme Regis are only 3 miles (buses leave from just along the road to both towns).

Open

30 March - 28 October.

At a glance

Welcome & Ambience	✓✓✓✓	Location	✓✓✓✓
Quality of Pitches	✓✓✓✓	Range of Facilities	✓✓✓

Directions

Park is signed on A35 between Charmouth and Axminster, approx. 2.5 miles west of Charmouth. Turn right at Greenway Head (B3165 signed Marshwood) and park is 600 yds on the left past the Club site. Don't go to Monkton Wylde hamlet - the road is very steep. O.S.GR: SY329966.

Charges 2004

Per unit incl. 2 adults	£ 7.60 - £ 13.00
extra adult	£ 2.50
child (5-16 yrs)	£ 0.60 - £ 1.60
electricity	£ 2.40
pup tent	£ 1.00
dog	£ 1.10

Reservations

Made with deposit of £5 per night booked.
Tel: 01297 34525.
Email: holidays@monktonwyld.co.uk

UK1770 Binghams Farm Touring Park

Melplash, Bridport DT6 3TT (Dorset)

Binghams is a small, purpose built park, for adults only. In a pleasant, rural situation two miles from the market town of Bridport, with views seaward towards West Bay and inland across Beaminster Downs and Pilsdon Hill, it is open all year. The park provides an area of individual pitches with 10A electricity and over 40 hardstandings, nicely landscaped with shrubs and trees growing between the pitches, plus an open sloping field overlooking the valley with 20 electrical hook-ups. The entrance to the park is neatly tarmaced and a cottage has been converted into two flats to let. A path is provided to the river which links with the main footpaths for Bridport (20 minutes) or local hostelries. A limited bus service runs on the main road. The Brit Valley is an unspoilt area of West Dorset with an ancient heritage and coastal West Bay is only a couple of miles.

Facilities

The original farm buildings have been sympathetically converted to provide reception, a good heated toilet block and the other amenities: The toilet block, with under floor heating for winter use, provides well fitted, tiled, curtained showers, hairdryers, a separate, fully equipped room for the less able with ramped access and a laundry room. The former games room has been converted into five luxury shower rooms with washbasins (four with a toilet as well). Dishwashing under cover. Restaurant serving home cooked food at weekends and daily except Thurs. in high season. Gas available. Adults only. Off site: Sea fishing and golf 3 miles.

At a glance

Welcome & Ambience	✓✓✓✓	Location	✓✓✓✓
Quality of Pitches	✓✓✓✓	Range of Facilities	✓✓✓✓

Directions

At main roundabout on A35 road, on east side of Bridport, take A3066 towards Beaminster. Watch for site entrance after approx. 2 miles on the left. O.S.GR: SY482963.

Charges 2004

Per pitch incl. 2 persons and electricity (10A)	£ 13.30 - £ 16.30
extra adult	£ 4.00
awning	£ 1.50
dog	£ 1.50

Reservations

Made with £25 non-returnable deposit per week or part. Tel: 01308 488234.
Email: enquiries@binghamsfarm.co.uk

Open

March - November, Xmas and New Year.

UK1810 Newlands Caravan Park

Charmouth DT6 6RB (Dorset)

Newlands is well situated on the Jurassic Coast, the first natural world heritage site in England. A family owned park, it is run with care and enthusiasm, occupying a prominent position beside the road into Charmouth village with rural views southwards to the hills across the valley. The terrain is terraced in two fields to provide over 200 well spaced places for touring units, some for seasonal units and over 80 for caravan holiday homes (some for hire). The mainly sloping tent field also has super views towards the sea and Lyme Regis. Electricity (10A) is provided on 160 pitches and 30 have hardstanding, water and drainage. Five special 'Millennium' pitches have a washing machine and dryer for individual use. Other accommodation includes smart pine lodges, apartments and motel rooms. All the facilities are located in a modern building to one side of the wide tarmac entrance. The club bar opens each evening and lunch times to suit. Family entertainment includes a children's club during school holidays with Dino Dan dinosaur. The indoor pool and an adjacent outdoor pool are walled, paved and sheltered. A large play area in the field below the tent field is open dawn to dusk. This is a comfortable site for families with the beach and village within easy walking distance, with some evening and family activity.

Facilities

Two modern, heated toilet blocks provide roomy showers and adjoining covered dishwashing areas and laundry rooms. Well stocked shop (March-Nov). Licensed club bar (limited hours Nov-March). Restaurant (open evenings 6-9 pm. March-Nov plus Xmas/New Year) including takeaway. Outdoor heated pool (supervised in high season; the entrance is key coded). Indoor pool and jacuzzi (small charge, open all year, limited hours Nov-March). Nine-pin bowling alley for hire at £5 per half hour. Play area.
Off site: Beach 0.5 miles. Fishing 1 mile. Riding 3 miles. Golf 2 miles. Charmouth is known for its fossil finds and its connection with Jane Austen

At a glance

Welcome & Ambience	✓✓✓✓✓	Location	✓✓✓✓
Quality of Pitches	✓✓✓✓	Range of Facilities	✓✓✓✓✓

Directions

Approaching from Bridport leave the A35 at first sign for Charmouth at start of the bypass and site almost directly on your left. O.S.GR: SY373935.

Charges 2004

Per unit incl. up to 6 persons	
and awning	£ 10.00 - £ 20.00
incl. electricity	£ 13.00 - £ 22.00
dog (max. 2)	£ 1.00 - £ 3.00
serviced pitch	£ 12.00 - £ 28.00
extra pup tent	£ 4.00

Only one van or tent per pitch.
Camping Cheques accepted.

Reservations

Made with £30 deposit per week. Tel: 01297 560259.
Email: enq@newlandsholidays.co.uk

Open

All year.

UK1740 Golden Cap Holiday Park

West Dorset Leisure Holidays, Eype, Bridport DT6 6AR (Dorset)

Golden Cap, named after the adjacent high cliff (the highest in southern England) which overlooks Lyme Bay, is only 150 metres from a shingle beach at Seatown and is surrounded by National Trust countryside and the Heritage Coastline. The park is arranged over several fields on the valley floor, sloping gently down towards the sea. It is in two main areas, having once been two parks, each separated into fields with marvellous views around and providing 108 touring pitches. All have electricity and 29 also have hardstanding with drainaway and gravel awning area. An extra sloping tent area is used for peak season (torch useful), although it is a five minute walk from here to the toilet blocks and shop. There are 219 caravan holiday homes in their own areas. A coarse fishing lake has recently been opened and the heated indoor pool at Highlands End (under the same ownership, 3 miles away) is open for campers at Golden Cap on payment. Beaches are nearby, sea fishing, boat launching, riding or fossil hunting are possible in the area, plus good walks including access to the coastal path. A well run park and a member of the Best of British group.

Facilities

The modern toilet block is of good quality with spacious shower cubicles (some with toilet and washbasin). Facilities for visitors with disabilities. Baby room. Two other smaller blocks around the park. Laundry room. Motorcaravan service point. Useful and well stocked shop (8 am - 6 pm, or 9 pm in high season). Gas supplies. Small play area. Fishing lake (day tickets from shop). American motorhomes are not accepted. Off site: Pub with food service close. Golf 2 miles. Beach 150 yds.

Open

20 March - 1 November.

At a glance

Welcome & Ambience	✓✓✓✓	Location	✓✓✓✓
Quality of Pitches	✓✓✓✓	Range of Facilities	✓✓✓✓

Directions

Turn off A35 road at Chideock (a bigger village with shops and restaurants) 3 miles west of Bridport, at sign to Seatown opposite church. Park is less than 1 mile down narrow lane. O.S.GR: SY423919.

Charges 2004

Per unit incl. 2 persons, awning and electricity	£ 10.75 - £ 16.50
extra adult	£ 3.25 - £ 3.50
child (4-17 yrs)	£ 1.75 - £ 2.00
all service pitch plus	£ 1.75
pitch with sea view plus	£ 3.00

Reservations

Essential in high season and made with £20 deposit (min. 4 days in high season). For information or booking contact: West Dorset Leisure Holidays, Eype, Bridport, Dorset DT6 6AR. Tel: 01308 422139. Email: holidays@wdlh.co.uk

UK1750 Highlands End Holiday Park

West Dorset Leisure Holidays, Eype, Bridport DT6 6AR (Dorset)

On slightly sloping ground with superb open views, both coastal and inland, Highlands End is quietly situated on the Dorset Heritage Coastline. With access to the coastal path, a path in front of the park runs along the cliff top and then leads down to a shingle beach a little further along. It is a good quality park with 180 caravan holiday homes, mostly privately owned, and 195 touring pitches in two areas nearest to the sea – one has to travel through the holiday homes to reach them. All have electricity and 45 also offer water, drainage, hardstanding and a gravel awning area. A further area is used for tents in high season. A modern, attractive building houses a lounge bar, good value restaurant with takeaway facility, family room and games room with some musical evenings in high season. The park's amenities also include an excellent, air-conditioned indoor heated pool, a tennis court and pitch and putt (all charged). The owners have a long term interest in the fire brigade and an historic fire engine (1936 Leyland Pump Escape) along with memorabilia make an interesting display in the bar. The park was used to film scenes for Nick Berry's TV series based on nearby West Bay harbour. A well run park and a member of the Best of British group.

Facilities

Two well maintained toilet blocks near the touring sections can be heated. Some washbasins in cubicles with toilets, large, roomy showers. Covered dishwashing sinks and a dishwashing room. En-suite facilities for disabled visitors. Baby care room. Laundry room. Motorcaravan service point. Well stocked shop (opening times vary), including gas supplies. Bar, restaurant and takeaway (evenings and Sunday lunch). Tennis. Indoor pool (20 x 9 m; £2 per session, £1 for children), sauna/steam room. Games room. 9-hole pitch and putt. Two adventure play areas. Large sloping field for ball games. Off site: Golf 2 miles. Fishing 3 miles. Beach 0.5 miles.

Open

20 March - 1 November.

At a glance

Welcome & Ambience	✓✓✓✓	Location	✓✓✓✓✓
Quality of Pitches	✓✓✓✓✓	Range of Facilities	✓✓✓✓✓

Directions

Follow Bridport bypass on A35 around the town and park is signed to south (Eype turning), down narrow lane. There is a new exit road. O.S.GR: SY452914.

Charges 2004

Per unit incl. 2 persons, awning and electricity	£ 10.75 - £ 16.50
all services and hardstanding plus	£ 1.75
extra adult	£ 3.25 - £ 3.50
child (4-17 yrs.)	£ 1.75 - £ 2.00
dog	£ 1.75 - £ 2.00

Reservations

Essential in high season and made with £20 deposit (min. 4 days in high season). Contact West Dorset Leisure Holidays, Eype, nr. Bridport, Dorset DT6 6AR Tel: 01308 422139. Email: holidays@wdlh.co.uk

---

UK1800 East Fleet Farm Touring Park

Chickerell, Weymouth DT3 4DW (Dorset)

East Fleet Farm has a marvellous situation on part level, part gently sloping meadows leading to the shores of the Fleet, with views across to the famous Chesil Bank with the sea beyond. Part of the World Heritage Jurassic Coast, the Fleet is a lagoon renowned for its wildlife and popular with bird watchers. The park itself has been developed within the confines of a 300-acre organic working dairy and arable farm and is maturing nicely as bushes and trees grow. The 270 pitches are a comfortable size so there is no feeling of crowding. Of these, 200 are level and marked with 10A electric hook-ups, 25 also having hardstanding. The terraced bar with views over the Fleet, (open from Easter to Sept. with meals), was converted from the barn, and features original beams and brick work. The busy resort of Weymouth with its safe bathing beaches and many watersports facilities is only 3 miles away (bicycle hire and boat launching possible). In peak season a bus runs three times a day from the top of the lane (about half a mile) and Abbotsbury Swannery and Gardens are nearby.

Facilities

Fully equipped, central toilet facilities are in a natural stone block. Dishwashing under cover (H&C). Laundry room including self-contained unit for disabled people and two family shower rooms (charged). Extra new toilets and a family bathroom are beside the bar. Motorcaravan service point. Reception plus shop with basic groceries, bread, papers and gas, etc. opens longer in high season (bar and shop Easter - Sept). Games room with pool table. Fenced play area (remember, elsewhere this is a working farm). Off site: Riding or golf 2 miles. Access to the Fleet and coastal path.

Open

15 March - 15 January.

At a glance

Welcome & Ambience	✓✓✓✓	Location	✓✓✓✓✓
Quality of Pitches	✓✓✓✓	Range of Facilities	✓✓✓✓

Directions

Park is signed from B3157 Weymouth - Bridport road, approx. 3 miles west of Weymouth. The narrow approach road, which has been widened with tarmac and plenty of passing places, is by the army camp on the southern side of the B3157. O.S.GR: SY639798.

Charges 2004

Per unit incl. 2 persons	£ 5.50 - £ 13.50
incl. electricity	£ 7.50 - £ 16.00
extra adult	£ 0.50 - £ 3.00
child (5-12 years)	£ 0.25 - £ 0.50
awning	£ 2.00
dog	£ 0.25 - £ 1.00
Senior citizen discount in June (10%).	

Reservations

Write with £20 deposit. Tel: 01305 785768. Email: enquiries@eastfleet.co.uk

UK1780 Freshwater Beach Holiday Park

Burton Bradstock, Bridport DT6 4PT (Dorset)

Family run parks for families with direct access to a beach are rare in Britain and this one has the added advantage of being in beautiful coastal countryside in West Dorset. The site is next to the sea and a beach of fine pebbles, sheltered from the wind by pebble banks. The River Bride edges the park and joins the sea here. Approached by a fairly steep access road, the park itself is on level, open ground. The 500 plus touring pitches, 400 with 10A electricity, are on an open, undulating grass field connected by tarmac or hard-core roads. Caravan pitches (10 x 11 m.) are marked and evenly spaced in lines. Some tent pitches are in the main field, with others well spaced on a newly terraced extra field. In separate areas there are 270 caravan holiday homes, with 40 for hire. This lively holiday park has an extensive range of facilities which include an outdoor pool, a good value licensed restaurant and three bars with an evening entertainment programme in season. Daytime entertainment caters for all ages - don't miss the donkey derby! Footpaths lead to the thatched village of Burton Bradstock or West Bay. The overall impression is of a large, busy holiday park with a friendly reception and happy atmosphere.

Facilities

Toilet facilities are in two refurbished blocks, plus another with washbasins and toilets only. A third luxurious block was added in the tent field for 2004. In all, it is a good provision for a busy beach park. The main blocks have facilities for disabled people (Radar key), and a baby care room (key system). Laundry and dishwashing sinks cope well at peak times. Launderette. Bars with entertainment. Licensed restaurant (weekends only in late season; closed Mondays all season). Good value supermarket and takeaway. Heated and supervised outdoor swimming and paddling pools (15/5-30/10) with lessons available. New indoor games room with pool table, music, TV and soft drinks bar. Adventure play area. Pony trekking (stables on site). Off site: Golf course adjacent. Fishing possible from Chesil Bank. Abbotsbury Sub-Tropical Gardens and Swannery 17 miles.

At a glance

Welcome & Ambience	✓✓✓✓✓	Location	✓✓✓✓✓
Quality of Pitches	✓✓✓✓	Range of Facilities	✓✓✓✓✓

Directions

Park is immediately west of the village of Burton Bradstock, on the Weymouth - Bridport coast road (B3157). O.S.GR: SY980898.

Charges 2004

Per unit incl. up to 6 persons, car and awning	£ 8.00 - £ 26.00
extra person, car or boat	£ 2.00
electricity	£ 2.00
small tent incl. 2 persons (no car)	£ 4.00 - £ 15.00
dog	£ 2.50

Single sex groups not admitted.

Reservations

Made for min. 1 week with £20 deposit p/week, plus £1 fee. Short break reservations available - ring for details. Tel: 01308 897317.
Email: enquiries@freshwaterbeach.co.uk

Open

Mid March - mid November.

Rich in maritime heritage and historical attractions, the Southern region comprises tranquil English countryside boasting picture-postcard villages, ancient cities and towns, formidable castles and grand stately homes, coupled with a beautiful coastline and lively seaside resorts.

This region includes:
East Dorset, Hampshire, Isle of Wight, Oxfordshire, Berkshire and Buckinghamshire

The south coast is a popular holiday destination for those looking for a beach holiday. Seaside resorts include Lulworth, Swanage, and Bournemouth, with its seven miles of golden sand. Also along this coastal stretch is Durdle Door, a natural arch that has been cut by the sea, and Europe's largest natural harbour at Poole Bay. Nearby, the Isle of Purbeck is not actually an island, but a promontory of low hills and heathland that juts out below Poole Harbour. Across the water is the Isle of Wight, easily reached via a short ferry trip across the Solent. Rural Southern England comprises green rolling hills and scenic wooded valleys, with numerous walking and bridle paths passing through picturesque villages with quintessential English pubs. The New Forest, well known for its wild roaming ponies, is a distinctive, peaceful retreat. The River Thames weaves its way through the Thames basin and Chilterns area, passing charming riverside villages, castles, stately homes and beautiful countryside, including that around Oxford. This city of dreaming spires has lovely scenic walks, old university buildings to explore, plus a huge selection of restaurants, pubs and shops. Along the river you can go punting, hire a little rowing boat, or take one of the many river-boat trips available.

Did you know?

The Cerne Giant is thought to have represented a pagan god dating back to pre 13th century

Gosport is home to one of the worlds largest sundials covering 40 metres

T.E Lawrence 'Lawrence of Arabia' was a fellow of All Souls College in Oxford and lived in Dorset

Remains of more than 20 different species of dinosaur have been recovered on the Isle of Wight

The annual Olney Pancake Race in Bucks has been running since around 1445

Author Charles Dickens was born in Portsmouth, the house where he was born is now a museum

Windsurfing was invented on Hayling Island by Peter Chilvers in 1958

Places of interest

East Dorset: Monkey World in Wareham; village of Cerne Abbas, with Cerne Giant

Hampshire: historic Winchester; Portsmouth, home of the Mary Rose; Southampton maritime museum

Isle of Wight: Cowes; Sandown with Dinosaur Isle; Shipwreck Centre in Ryde; Smuggling Museum in Ventnor; Carisbrooke Castle in Newport

Oxfordshire: Blenheim Palace; Didcot Railway Centre; historic market town of Chipping Norton

Berkshire: Windsor, with Legoland, Windsor Castle; Reading

Buckinghamshire: Bletchley Park near Milton Keynes; county town of Aylesbury; Beaconsfield, once home to Enid Blyton, and now housing the world's first model village

tip

WINCHESTER HAT FAIR IS BRITAIN'S LONGEST RUNNING FESTIVAL OF STREET THEATRE. A MIX OF CIRCUS, CRAFT STALLS AND WORLD MUSIC, THIS FREE 3-DAY EVENT TAKES PLACE IN JULY.

UK2010 Sandyholme Holiday Park

Moreton Road, Owermoigne, Dorchester DT2 8HZ (Dorset)

A peaceful haven in Thomas Hardy country, Sandyholme provides 52 holiday homes (privately owned or to hire) and 30 numbered pitches for touring units (with 10A electricity) on level, short grass fields with one corner lightly wooded. The next door field is operated by the local farmer on a 28 day licence and can be used for tents or rallies. The Holme Club (free membership) is a pleasant provision, open every evening at B.Hs. during April and May, then mid-July to mid Sept. It has a cosy bar and patio, and a good bar meal menu. An unusual feature is a rather special duck pond with an amazing variety of ducks from all over the world with a pleasant walk and seats around the edge (an electric fence keeps the foxes at bay!) There are walks and cycling direct from the site or in Puddletown and Wareham Forests, or along the coastal path. Lulworth Cove, Durdle Door and Weymouth, with its sandy beach, are all near at hand.

Facilities

A modern, fully equipped toilet block includes some washbasins in cubicles. En-suite facilities for disabled visitors doubles as a family room with baby changing facilities. Laundry room. Room for dishwashing. Shop/reception stocks all basic necessities including papers and gas. Bar and bar meals (open peak times with takeaway service). Good, fenced, safe-based adventure play area. Games room with pool table and amusement machines. Off site: Bicycle hire and golf 5 miles. Riding 6 miles. Beach 6 miles.

Open

Easter/1April - 31 October.

At a glance

Welcome & Ambience	✓✓✓✓	Location	✓✓✓✓
Quality of Pitches	✓✓✓✓	Range of Facilities	✓✓✓✓

Directions

On A352 Dorchester - Wareham road going west, watch for short dual carriageway section before Weymouth - Osmington roundabout. Turn north through Owermoigne village and park is on the left (clearly signed) after approx. 400 yards. O.S.GR: SY768863.

Charges 2004

Per pitch incl. 2 persons	£ 8.00 - £ 12.75
with services	£ 10.50 - £ 15.00
extra adult	£ 2.00
child (3-17 yrs)	£ 1.25
dog	£ 1.15

Reservations

Made with £20 deposit (non-refundable); include SAE for receipt. Tel: 01305 852677.
Email: smeatons@sandyholme.co.uk

UK2090 Whitemead Caravan Park

East Burton Road, Wool BH20 6HG (Dorset)

The Church family continue to make improvements to this attractive little park which is within walking distance of the village of Wool, between Dorchester and Wareham. Very natural and with open views over the Frome Valley water meadows, it provides 95 numbered pitches on flat grass sloping gently north and is orchard-like in parts. The pitches are well spaced and mostly back onto hedges or fences. There are 76 electrical connections for touring units (10A) and no caravan holiday homes. The park is 4.5 miles from the nearest beach at Lulworth and is handily placed for many attractions in this part of Dorset (train services and limited bus service close). There may be some rail noise.

Facilities

The traditional but comfortably sized toilet block includes a baby room, dishwashing and laundry sinks, washing machine, and tumble dryer. Smart reception cum shop (limited hours) with off licence, gas supplies and information room/library. Takeaway with breakfasts at weekends (low season Tues, Fri and Sunday, otherwise all 15/03-31/10). Games room with pool table and darts. Playground. Caravan storage. Off site: The Ship Inn is 300 m. Riding, fishing and golf 3 miles. Bicycle hire 2 miles.

Open

15 March - 31 October.

At a glance

Welcome & Ambience	✓✓✓✓	Location	✓✓✓✓
Quality of Pitches	✓✓✓	Range of Facilities	✓✓✓

Directions

Turn off main A352 on eastern edge of Wool, just north of level crossing, onto East Burton road. Site is 300 m. on right. O.S.GR: SY841871

Charges 2004

Per person (over 5 yrs)	£ 1.25
pitch	£ 4.70 - £ 9.00
with services	£ 6.70 - £ 11.00
awning	£ 0.50 - £ 1.50
dog	£ 0.50 - £ 1.00
No credit cards.	

Reservations

Made with £15 deposit, min. 3 nights at B.Hs.
Tel: 01929 462241. Email: whitemeadcp@aol.com

For all your **camping and touring needs**

TURN TO PAGE 294 for details

UK2070 The Inside Park

Touring Caravan & Camping Park, Blandford Forum DT11 9AD (Dorset)

The Inside Park is set in the grounds of an 18th century country house that burned down in 1941. Family owned and carefully managed alongside a dairy and arable farm, this is a must for those interested in local history or arboriculture and it is a haven for wildlife and birds. The reception/toilet block and games room block are respectively the coach house and stables of the old house. The nine acre camping field, a little distant, lies in a sheltered, gently sloping dry valley containing superb tree specimens - notably cedars, with walnuts in one part - and a dog graveyard dating back to the early 1700s under a large Cedar of Lebanon. In total there are 125 spacious pitches, 90 with electricity (10A) and some in wooded glades. The six acres adjoining are the old pleasure gardens of the house. No vehicle access to the park is allowed after 10.30 pm. (there is a separate late arrivals area and car park). Extensive walks are marked through the farm (guide available in the shop).

Facilities

The toilet block provides some washbasins in cubicles, comfortably sized showers and facilities for disabled visitors or mothers and babies. Dishwashing sinks. Laundry room. Recycling bins. Shop with basics, gas and camping provisions (limited opening in low season). Mobile fish and chips twice weekly. Spacious games room with pool tables, table tennis, etc. Safe based adventure play area. Day kennelling facilities for dogs. Mountain bike course. Winter caravan storage. Off site: Blandford leisure and swimming centre (temporary membership possible) 2 miles. Fishing and riding 2 miles, golf 3 miles.

Open

Easter - 31 October.

At a glance

Welcome & Ambience	✓✓✓✓	Location	✓✓✓✓
Quality of Pitches	✓✓✓✓	Range of Facilities	✓✓✓

Directions

Park is about 2 miles southwest of Blandford and is signed from roundabout junction of A354 and A350 roads. If approaching from the Shaftesbury direction, do not go into Blandford but follow the bypass to the last roundabout and follow camp signs. O.S.GR: ST864045.

Charges 2004

Per adult	£ 2.85 - £ 3.45
child (5-16 years)	free - £ 1.25
pitch	£ 3.95 - £ 5.95
electricity	£ 2.50 - £ 2.50
dog	£ 0.60 - £ 1.00

Reservations

Essential for B.Hs and high season; made with £10 deposit (min. 4 nights 14/7-2/9). Tel: 01258 453719. Email: inspark@aol.com

www.alanrogers.com for latest campsite news

UK2050 Rowlands Wait Touring Park

Rye Hill, Bere Regis BH20 7LP (Dorset)

Rowlands Wait is in an Area of Outstanding Natural Beauty (AONB). The top of the park, edged by mature woods (full of bluebells in spring) is a haven for tents (and squirrels) with marvellous views and provides 30 places in three descending fields. The rest of the park is a little more formal – and nearer to the central toilet block. Most pitches back on to hedging or trees and they are generally level. There are 71 pitches in total with 18 seasonal pitches. Many walks are possible from the park with information provided on wildlife. It is possible to walk into the village of Bere Regis. The new owners Robert and Stevie Cargill are keen to welcome nature lovers who enjoy bird watching, walking and cycling. The park is a member of the Countryside Discovery group. The park is open in winter by arrangement.

Facilities

The purpose built toilet block is well equipped, including free hot showers. Laundry room. Covered dishwashing area. Recycling bins. Shop (high season) providing milk, papers and basic essentials and a freezer for ice packs. Play area for little ones with miniature assault course and castle is well placed near reception. Games room with pool table, table tennis and table football behind the toilet block. Crazy golf. Bicycle hire. Torch useful. Rallies are welcome. Off site: The village, a 10 minute walk, has shops, two pubs, etc. plus a bus service for Dorchester and Poole. Fishing 5 miles, golf 3 miles, riding 9 miles.

At a glance

Welcome & Ambience	✓✓✓✓	Location	✓✓✓✓✓
Quality of Pitches	✓✓✓✓	Range of Facilities	✓✓✓

Directions

Park is south of Bere Regis, just off the road to Wool, well signed from A35/A31 roundabout. O.S.GR: SY842933.

Charges 2004

Per unit incl. 2 persons	£ 7.50 - £ 10.50
extra adult	£ 2.50 - £ 3.00
child (under 16)	£ 1.20 - £ 1.50
awning, pup tent	free - £ 1.50
dog	£ 1.00 - £ 2.00

Reservations

Made with £15 deposit per week. Tel: 01929 472727. Email: ar@rowlandswait.co.uk

Open

16 March - 31 October, and winter by arrangement.

UK2020 Ulwell Cottage Caravan Park

Ulwell, Swanage BH19 3DG (Dorset)

Nestling under the Purbeck Hills in this unique corner of Dorset on the edge of Swanage, Ulwell Cottage is a family run holiday park with an indoor pool and wide range of facilities. A good proportion of the park is taken by caravan holiday homes (140), but an attractive, undulating area accessed by tarmac roads is given over to 77 numbered touring pitches. There are 68 electricity hook-ups (16A) and 18 hardstandings, 8 of which are serviced. The mixture of level and sloping pitches, interspersed with trees and shrubs, is quite pretty. The colourful entrance area is home to the Village Inn with a courtyard adjoining the heated, supervised indoor pool complex (both open all year and open to the public) and modern reception. The hill above the touring area, Nine Barrow Down, is a Site of Special Scientific Interest for butterflies overlooking Round Down. It is possible to walk to Corfe Castle this way. With Brownsea Island, Studland Bay, Corfe village and the Swanage Railway, Ulwell Cottage makes a marvellous centre for holidays.

Facilities

The modern, cheerful toilet block can be heated and includes a unit for disabled visitors. Supplemented by an older block in the holiday home section. Both are well equipped. Laundry room and baby sinks in the lower block. Dishwashing under cover. Well stocked shop with gas (Easter - mid Sept). Bar snacks and restaurant meals with family room. Indoor pool with lifeguard (times vary acc. to season). Playing fields and play areas. Off site: Bicycle hire or riding 2 miles. Fishing and golf 1 mile. Beach 1 mile.

Open

1 March - 7 January.

At a glance

Welcome & Ambience	✓✓✓✓	Location	✓✓✓✓✓
Quality of Pitches	✓✓✓✓	Range of Facilities	✓✓✓✓✓

Directions

From A351 Wareham - Swanage road, turn on B3351 Studland road just before Corfe Castle, follow signs to right for Swanage and drop down to Ulwell. O.S.GR: SZ019809.

Charges 2004

Per unit incl. up to 6 persons	£ 14.25 - £ 30.00
full services with hardstanding	£ 16.00 - £ 32.00
extra tent, car or boat	£ 2.00
Less £2 for two persons only, less £1 for three persons.	

Reservations

Made with 25% deposit (min. £20); balance 2 weeks prior to holiday. Tel: 01929 422823. Email: enq@ulwellcottagepark.co.uk

UK2030 Wareham Forest Tourist Park

North Trigon, Wareham BH20 7NZ (Dorset)

This peacefully located, spacious park in an unspoilt corner of Dorset is now under the enthusiastic ownership of Tony and Sarah Birch (some may know them from their days at Carnon Downs in Cornwall). They plan to improve the management of various aspects of the park, including the outdoor pool which is a popular feature, and are looking forward to making other improvements whilst keeping in tune with the natural forest environment. There is a choice of formal pitching, with or without hardstanding, for caravans or natural pitches for tents in pine wood or open field. Drainage appears satisfactory. There is space for 200 units, all pitches with electrical connections (16A) and 102 with hardstanding. There are 8 luxury pitches on hardstanding with water, drainage, TV aerial, dustbin and light (available 1/3-31/10 only). It is possible to walk straight into the forest and the park is well situated to explore the Dorset coast and Thomas Hardy country. The park's setting in Wareham Forest makes it a very popular venue and it can become very busy in high season.

Facilities

Two well maintained toilet blocks are of a good standard with some washbasins in cubicles for ladies. The block used in the winter months is centrally heated. Facilities for disabled people. Well equipped laundry rooms and deep sinks for washing up. Motorcaravan service point. Small licensed shop with gas (limited hours). Cafeteria (main season). Open-air swimming pool (60 x 20 ft), heated from Spring B.H. to early Sept. Large adventure play area. Entrance closed 11 pm. - 7 am. Resident wardens on site. Caravan storage facilities. Off site: Fishing 5 miles, bicycle hire or golf 3 miles, riding 8 miles.

Open

All year.

At a glance

Welcome & Ambience	✓✓✓✓✓	Location	✓✓✓✓✓
Quality of Pitches	✓✓✓✓	Range of Facilities	✓✓✓✓

Directions

Park is north of Wareham between Wareham and Bere Regis, located off the A35 road. O.S.GR: SY899903.

Charges 2004

Per adult	£ 1.50 - £ 3.00
child 2-14 yrs	£ 1.00 - £ 2.00
standard pitch	£ 5.50 - £ 8.00
serviced pitch	£ 8.00 - £ 10.00
'superior' pitch	£ 10.00 - £ 12.00
dog, extra tent, awning, boat	£ 0.60 - £ 1.50

Couples and families only.

Reservations

Made with £25 non-returnable deposit and £2 admin. fee, balance 28 days before arrival. Tel: 01929 551393. Email: holiday@wareham-forest.co.uk

For further details and free coloured brochure write or phone:
Tel/Fax: (01929) 551393.
Tony and Sarah Birch, Wareham Forest Tourist Park, North Trigon, Wareham, Dorset BH20 7NZ.
www.wareham-forest.co.uk
email: holiday@wareham-forest.co.uk
Credit cards accepted.

UK2150 Woolsbridge Manor Farm Caravan Park

Three Legged Cross, Wimborne BH21 6RA (Dorset)

Adjacent to the Moors Valley Country Park, this family run site is conveniently close to the holiday resort and beaches of Bournemouth and Poole, and the ancient market town of Wimborne Minster. The 7-acre camping meadow has 60 large level pitches, 45 with 10A electricity hook-ups, arranged on either side of a central tarmac road with a modern, centrally located toilet block. A nice touch here are the bicycle racks outside. Reception has a well stocked shop and a good selection of tourist information, again there are cycle racks outside. The site is part of a working beef cattle farm, so parents should be aware of moving farm machinery and tractors. A cycleway/footpath crosses the fields to the Country Park – very safe for children – where amenities include coarse fishing, golf, steam railway, bicycle hire, a tea room and a country shop.

Facilities

The neat, white, modern toilet block is well maintained and has ample facilities. Two newly built family rooms each with shower, WC, basin, handrails and ramped access provide for disabled people, babies and toddlers. Washing machine, dryer and ironing facilities. Covered dishwashing sinks. Shop. Gas available. Playground. Fishing. Recycling of aluminium cans. American RVs accepted, advance booking appreciated. Torches useful. Caravan storage. Off site: Old Barn Farm inn and restaurant 400 yds. Riding, golf and bicycle hire 0.5 miles.

Open

Easter - 31 October.

At a glance

Welcome & Ambience	✓✓✓✓	Location	✓✓✓✓
Quality of Pitches	✓✓✓✓	Range of Facilities	✓✓✓

Directions

From Ringwood take A31 southwest towards the large Ashley Heath roundabout, avoid underpass and take left hand slip road up to roundabout, and turn right on unclassified road signed Three Legged Cross, Ashley Heath, Horton and Moors Valley Country Park. Follow signs to Country Park (2 miles), pass the park entrance on right, continue for another 400 yards to campsite entrance (well signed on right). O.S.GR: SZ099052.

Charges 2004

Per unit incl. 2 persons, electricity	£ 10.00 - £ 15.00
extra adult	£ 3.00 - £ 3.50
child (under 16 yrs)	£ 2.00 - £ 2.50
awning or extra car	£ 1.25
dog	£ 1.00 - £ 1.25

Reservations

Advised for B.Hs and July/Aug. Made with deposit of 50% of total fees. Tel: 01202 826369. Email: woolsbridge@btconnect.com

UK2080 Merley Court Touring Park

Merley, Wimborne BH21 3AA (Dorset)

Merley Court celebrated its 20th anniversary during 2003 and is a credit to the Wright family. All aspects of this well planned, attractively landscaped park are constantly maintained to the highest of standards. The historic walled garden dating back to the 18th century provides ideal surroundings for a pleasant stroll or a family picnic with the opportunity to play croquet, crazy golf, boules, volleyball, short tennis or basketball. Tarmac roads connect 160 touring pitches (all with 16A electricity) on neat lawns or one of the many hardstandings. This provision includes 18 neat all-service pitches with water, waste disposal and satellite TV. The entire park is interspersed with a variety of shrubs, plants and the odd ornamental urn. Some attractive tent pitches are to be found in a small wooded valley. A well-furnished club complex provides a lounge bar where meals are available, snack bar, takeaway, large games room with pool tables and a family room leading onto a spacious sheltered patio. This in turn leads to the paved walled swimming pool area. There are woodland walks (including dog walks) directly from the site connecting to the disused railway line where nature has returned with an abundance of wild flowers, which in turn leads to Delph woods with designated nature trails. A member of the Best of British group.

Facilities

Three heated toilet blocks, two with showers, are of good quality. Separate facilities for disabled visitors and babies. Dishwashing and laundry facilities. Motorcaravan service point. Shop with caravan accessories and gas. Café and takeaway. Bar with food (limited hours in low and mid season). Outdoor pool (30 x 20 ft) with children's section open mid May - Sept. Tennis court. Table tennis. Play areas. Games room with pool tables. Tourist information. Conference/meeting venue in the Leisure Garden Orangery. Dogs are not accepted in high season (14/7-31/8). Barrier card £5 deposit. Off site: Fishing, riding and golf all within 5 miles. Poole 5 miles, Bournmouth 8 miles. Tower Park leisure and entertainment centre is nearby, Kingston Lacy House, Knoll Gardens, Brownsea Island and the Moors Valley Country Park are also near.

At a glance

Welcome & Ambience	✓✓✓✓✓	Location	✓✓✓✓✓
Quality of Pitches	✓✓✓✓✓	Range of Facilities	✓✓✓✓✓

Directions

Site clearly signed at the junction of A31 and A349 roads (roundabout) on the Wimborne bypass. O.S.GR: ST008984.

Charges 2004

Per standard pitch incl. 2 persons and electricity	£ 10.50 - £ 15.50
all service pitch	£ 13.50 - £ 18.50
extra adult	£ 3.50
child (3-13 yrs)	£ 2.50
dog (outside 19/7-29/8)	£ 1.00

No extra pup tent as well as awning.

Reservations

Made with deposit (£40 p/w). Tel: 01202 881488. Email: holidays@merley-court.co.uk

Open

All year excl. 8 January - 28 February.

UK2060 Wilksworth Farm Caravan Park

Cranborne Road, Wimborne BH21 4HW (Dorset)

Wilksworth Farm is a spacious, quiet park and is well suited for families, with a heated outdoor pool. It has a lovely rural situation just outside Wimborne and around 10 miles from the beaches between Poole and Bournemouth. With its duck pond at the entrance, it is well designed on good quality ground with fairly level grass and some views. It takes 65 caravans (awning groundsheets up in daytime) and 25 tents mainly on grass with a gravel hardstanding area. All pitches have electrical connections, 10 also have water and drainage. There are some 77 privately owned caravan holiday homes in a separate area. Facilities are in attractively converted farm barns designed to be in keeping with the listed buildings. The heated swimming pool and a tennis court are on the far side of the touring area.

Facilities

The central, refurbished toilet block has under-floor heating, a family bathroom, shower/bath for children and baby changing. Facilities for disabled visitors. Dishwashing sinks under cover. Laundry room. New reception and shop (basics only, Easter - 30 Sept). Gas supplies. Freezer for ice packs. Attractive coffee shop serving simple meals and takeaway service (weekends and B.Hs. only outside the main season). Heated 40 x 20 ft. swimming pool (unsupervised, but fenced and gated, open May - Sept) with small children's pool. Football ground. Adventure play area. BMX track, golf practice net. Two tennis courts, one full and one short size. Games room with table tennis, pool, some games machines. Winter caravan storage. Off site: Golf, fishing and riding 3 miles. Wimborne town centre 1 mile.

At a glance

Welcome & Ambience	✓✓✓✓	Location	✓✓✓✓
Quality of Pitches	✓✓✓✓	Range of Facilities	✓✓✓✓

Directions

Park is 1 mile north of Wimborne, west off the B3078 road to Cranborne. O.S.GR: SU010019.

Charges 2004

Per pitch incl. 2 adults	£ 8.00 - £ 18.00
extra adult	£ 2.00
child (3-16 yrs)	free - £ 1.00
full services	£ 1.00
dog	£ 1.00
No credit cards.	

Reservations

Advised for July/Aug. and B.Hs. Made with £20 per week deposit; balance more than 28 days beforehand (min. 5 days at B.Hs). Tel: 01202 885467.
Email: rayandwendy@wilksworthfarmcaravanpark.co.uk

Open

1 March - 30 October.

Wilksworth Farm *Caravan Park*

"I knew that one day as a Phantom Caravanner I would come across a real gem of a park & this one is a diamond. Hidden away in deepest Dorset, this superb park is so family orientated." The Phantom, April 1997

01202 885467
www.wilksworthfarmcaravanpark.co.uk
rayandwendy@wilksworthfarmcaravanpark.co.uk
CRANBORNE ROAD • WIMBORNE • DORSET • BH21 4HW

UK2180 Beacon Hill Touring Park

Blandford Road North, Poole BH16 6AB (Dorset)

Beacon Hill is located in a marvellous, natural environment of partly wooded heathland, with areas of designated habitation for protected species such as sand lizards and the Dartford Warbler. Wildlife ponds encourage dragonflies and other species (fishing is possible). Conservation is obviously important in such a special area but one can ramble at will over the 30 acres. Grassy open spaces provide 170 touring pitches, 120 with 16A electricity, on sandy grass which is sometimes uneven. The undulating land and the trees allows for areas to be allocated for varying needs, e.g. young families near to the play area, families with teenagers close to the games room or those with dogs near the dog walking area. The park provides a range of facilities with something for everyone and is well situated for beaches and Poole.

Facilities

Two fully equipped toilet blocks include facilities for disabled people. Laundry facilities. Dishwashing sinks. Well stocked shop. Coffee bar and takeaway (main season). Bar (on demand in low season). Heated swimming pool. Tennis court. Adventure play areas. Games room. Fishing. Off site: Brownsea Island, Studland beach. Poole 3 miles.

Open

Easter/16 April - end September.

At a glance

Welcome & Ambience	✓✓✓	Location	✓✓✓✓
Quality of Pitches	✓✓✓	Range of Facilities	✓✓✓✓

Directions

Park is approx. 3 miles north of Poole, 400 yards north of the junction of the A35 and A350 towards Blandford. O.S.GR: SY977945.

Charges 2004

Per adult	£ 3.50 - £ 5.50
child (under 16 yrs)	£ 2.50
pitch	£ 3.00 - £ 18.00
electricity	£ 0.50
dog	£ 1.50

Reservations

Made with £20 non-refundable deposit per pitch; balance 21 days before arrival. Tel: 01202 631631.

UK2100 Sandford Caravan Park

Holton Heath, Poole BH16 6JZ (Dorset)

Sandford Park is an 'all singing, all dancing' park with a wide range of facilities near the popular coastal areas of Dorset. It has a large permanent section with 248 static holiday homes and lodges. However, the touring section in an attractive secluded area and can accommodate around 500 units of any type, mainly on distinctive individual pitches, on level grass with mature evergreen hedging, or in a more open style area broken up by shrubs all with 10A electrical connections. Early booking is advisable. Sandford is a large, very busy holiday park with a wide range of entertainment. The clubhouse (free membership) is spacious with dance floor, bar and seating area, and caters for different tastes and age groups. There is also a large air-conditioned ballroom for entertainment and dancing. Both are open over a long season. There is a variety of bars, restaurants (book in busy periods) and simple hot meals, breakfasts and takeaway elsewhere in peak season. The heated outdoor swimming pool (25 m. long, open May-Oct. and supervised) and a very large play pool with a sandy beach, ideal for children, are attractively situated with a snack bar, terraced area and go-kart track. There is also an impressive, heated and supervised indoor pool.

Facilities

The main toilet block in the touring area also provides facilities for disabled visitors and a baby room. A new block was added for 2004. Large launderette. Ladies' hairdresser. Bars, restaurants. TV lounges. Outdoor swimming pool (May-Sept) and indoor pool. Large supermarket and other shops, including well stocked camping accessory shop (all peak season only). Soft indoor play area (April - Oct and Christmas, supervised). Playground. Two tennis courts. New multi-sports court. Table tennis. Two short mat bowling greens (outdoor). Crazy golf. Mountain bike hire. Riding lessons available at stables on site. Dogs or pets are only permitted in the touring section in low or mid season (phone site to advise). Off site: Beach 9 miles. Golf 3 miles.

At a glance

Welcome & Ambience ✓✓✓✓ Location ✓✓✓✓
Quality of Pitches ✓✓✓✓ Range of Facilities ✓✓✓✓✓

Directions

Park is just west off A351 (Wareham - Poole) road at Holton Heath. O.S.GR: SY940913.

Charges 2004

Per pitch	£ 12.50 - £ 23.50
incl. electricity	£ 15.50 - £ 26.50
serviced pitch	£ 17.00 - £ 28.50
dog (1 only, after 2 Sept)	£ 5.00

Reservations

Early booking advisable (min. 3 days).
Tel: 0870 0667793.
Email: touring@weststarholidays.co.uk

Open

February - January.

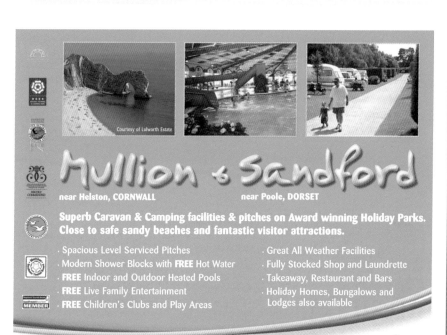

UK2110 Pear Tree Touring Park

Organford Road, Holton Heath, Poole BH16 6LA (Dorset)

Pear Tree is a neat, well cared for park welcoming families with young children and couples only. The new management has done much work to improve the landscaping of the park. Set in 7.5 acres, with mature trees and views across to Wareham Forest, there are 120 grass pitches with 10A electricity, 50 with full services (water, waste water and electricity) of which 26 have hardstanding. Only breathable groundsheets are permitted for awnings. The tent area is a tranquil secluded spot with many mature trees. Reception, tourist information and a small shop supplying milk, bread, gas and other basics is at the park entrance where the gates (with key) are closed at dusk, although latecomers are admitted. A large, hedged play field is at the top of the park with swings, climbing frame, trampolines and ball games area, all for younger children. A bus stops outside for Wareham (2.5 miles) or Poole (5 miles).

Facilities

The main heated toilet block (opened by key) has been refurbished and provides some washbasins in cubicles. Baby changing unit and two WCs for disabled visitors. Separate small block near the tent area. All is kept spotlessly clean. Motorcaravan service point. Shop (basics only). Play area. All year caravan storage. Off site: The Clay Pipe Inn is just 500 m. Bicycle hire and fishing 0.5 miles. Golf 2.5 miles. Riding 5 miles.

Open

Easter - early October.

At a glance

Welcome & Ambience ✓✓✓✓✓ Location ✓✓✓✓
Quality of Pitches ✓✓✓✓✓ Range of Facilities ✓✓✓✓

Directions

Park is just west off A351 (Wareham - Poole) road at Holton Heat. O.S.GR: SY940915.

Charges 2004

Per unit incl. 2 persons, electricity
and awning £ 11.50 - £ 16.00
incl. services £ 13.50 - £ 18.00
extra adult £ 3.00
Security key deposit £10 (refundable).

Reservations

Made with £40 deposit (min. 5 nights in high season). Tel: 01202 622434. Email: info@visitpeartree.co.uk

Pear Tree TOURING PARK
- Quiet, well landscaped, country park with grass grounds and good hard road for access
- Young children's play area
- Shop, laundry & baby changing facilities
- Dogs on leads welcome
- Low season discounts
- Ideally situated for Poole, Bournemouth, Swanage and the New Forest

✆ +44(0)1202 622434
✉ info@visitpeartree.co.uk 🖰 www.visitpeartree.co.uk

A 7 acre Holiday Park set in wooded surroundings some 8 miles from Bournemouth and ideally situated for the New Forest. This family Park is secluded and caters for discerning holidaymakers

- Large, level, well drained Pitches
- Licensed Clubhouse
- Shop and Off Licence
- Take Away Food Bar / Bar Meals
- Electricity Hook-ups
- Launderette
- Games Room
- Children's Playground
- Pre-bookable Pitches
- Horse Riding, Fishing & Sailing nearby
- Plus Winter Storage

HEATED SWIMMING POOL
(01202) 873302

For a relaxing holiday, come to Shamba Holiday Park. Telephone now for our brochure and booking form.
Shamba Holiday Park, 230 Ringwood Road, St. Leonards, Ringwood, Hants BH24 2SB

UK2130 Grove Farm Meadow Holiday Park

Meadowbank Holidays, Stour Way, Christchurch BH23 2PQ (Dorset)

Grove Farm Meadow is a quiet, traditional park with caravan holiday homes and a small provision for touring caravans. The grass flood bank which separates the River Stour from this park provides an attractive pathway. The river bank has been kept natural and is well populated by a range of ducks and a resident swan family and early in the season they parade their young through the park. It is also popular with bird watchers. There are just under 200 caravan holiday homes (117 privately owned, 75 for hire), regularly sited in rows. For touring units 41 level grass pitches, all with 15A electricity, are clearly numbered, backing on to fencing or hedging and accessed by tarmac roads. Some are fully serviced (with hardstanding, shingle base for awnings and chemical disposal point), the other grass pitches sharing service points. The impressive modern reception has a good collection of tourist information. The Littledown Centre, said to be the south coast's premier leisure facility is nearby. Bournemouth is 10 minutes by car, Christchurch 5.

Facilities

The well kept toilet block provides a bathroom for each sex (50p). Separate toilet and washbasin with ramped access for disabled visitors. Baby room. Dishwashing sinks, together with spin dryer, iron and board and washing lines provided. Launderette near reception. Well stocked shop (limited hours in low season). Games room with pool table and video games. Adventure play area beside the river bank. Fishing (permits from reception). No dogs or other pets are accepted. Off site: Boat launching 4 miles. Golf nearby. St Catherine's nature reserve.

Open

1 March - 31 October.

At a glance

Welcome & Ambience	✓✓✓✓	Location	✓✓✓✓
Quality of Pitches	✓✓✓✓✓	Range of Facilities	✓✓✓

Directions

From A388 Ringwood - Bournemouth road take B3073 for Christchurch. Turn right at the first roundabout and Stour Way is the third road on the right. O.S.GR: SZ136946.

Charges 2004

Per luxury pitch incl. 2 persons and electricity	£ 13.00 - £ 25.00
large pitch	£ 10.50 - £ 21.00
standard pitch (no awnings)	£ 7.00 - £ 16.00
extra person over 5 yrs	£ 1.00 - £ 2.00
extra car or boat	£ 1.00 - £ 2.00

Reservations

Made for Sat-Sat or Sun-Sun in high season, min. 3 nights at other times, with £30 deposit. Contact Meadowbank Holidays at above address. Tel: 01202 483597. Email: enquiries@meadowbank-holidays.co.uk

UK2340 Shamba Holiday Park

Ringwood Road, St Leonards, Ringwood BH24 2SB (Hampshire)

The Gray family have been gradually upgrading Shamba over the last few years and it is developing into a comfortable, friendly park. There are some seasonal pitches. Most of the amenities are good and as the owners have a young family themselves, they seem to be aware of their needs and cater for them. The Grays live on site and have managed to create a relaxed, pleasant atmosphere. Bournemouth with its beaches is 8 miles, Ringwood 2.5 miles and the Moors Valley Country Park 1 mile. The site is near the A31 so there could be some road noise. The access road is rather rough, but persevere and you will find a pleasant site.

Facilities

The showers are in a separate heated block. The rest of the provision is adequate if a little dated, although it is kept clean and includes a small toilet and washbasin for children, and a belfast sink for a baby bath. Covered dishwashing sinks. Laundry sink, two washing machines and two dryers. Improvements to these facilities are planned. Well stocked shop. Cosy bar offering bar snacks, takeaway and a small family room, heated and with a pool table. Large play area. Games room with video games and table football. Small heated outdoor fenced pool. Dogs are accepted but there is no dog walk. Off site: Riding stables and a fishing lake 500 yds.

At a glance

Welcome & Ambience	✓✓✓✓	Location	✓✓✓
Quality of Pitches	✓✓✓	Range of Facilities	✓✓✓✓

Directions

Site is signed directly off the A31 Ringwood - Wimborne road, 400 yds. down a small lane. Approaching from the east, after passing Little Chef, you will need to go round the next roundabout back on yourself, then immediately left down lane. O.S.GR: SU104026.

Charges 2004

Per pitch incl. 2 persons, electricity	£ 11.00 - £ 15.50
extra person	£ 2.00 - £ 3.50
child (6-11 yrs)	£ 1.00 - £ 2.50
dog	£ 1.00 - £ 2.00
Camping Cheques accepted.	

Reservations

Made with non-returnable deposit of £25 Tel: 01202 873302. Email: holidays@shamba.co.uk

Open

1 March - 31 October.

UK2350 Red Shoot Camping Park

Linwood, Ringwood BH24 3QT (Hampshire)

Red Shoot is set on three acres of open, slightly sloping, level grass-land, in the heart of the New Forest. A rural retreat with panoramic views of the surrounding countryside and forest, it is very popular in high season. There are around 130 good sized pitches, 45 with electrical hook-ups (10A), served by a circular gravel road. There is no site lighting so a torch would be useful. Only breathable groundsheets are permitted. The adjacent Red Shoot Inn (under separate ownership) serves hot or cold meals and brews its own real ales - Forest Gold and Tom's Tipple. There are ample opportunities for walking, cycling and naturalist pursuits, and nearby Ringwood has a market on Wednesday. Local attractions include water-sports at the New Forest Water Park near Ringwood, a Doll Museum in Fordingbridge, cider making in Burley, and Breamore House just north of Fordingbridge.

Facilities

The sanitary facilities are fairly modern, well maintained and practical, but not luxurious. Dishwashing sinks under cover. Laundry plus baby bath facility. Good unit for disabled visitors. Very well stocked shop provides fresh and frozen foods, camping equipment and gas, wine and beer, toys and gifts plus maps and guides. Fenced adventure style playground. Mountain bike hire.

Open

1 March - 31 October.

At a glance

Welcome & Ambience	✓✓✓	Location	✓✓✓✓✓
Quality of Pitches	✓✓✓	Range of Facilities	✓✓✓

Directions

From A338 about 1.75 miles north of Ringwood, turn east (signed Linwood and Moyles Court). Follow signs, over a staggered cross-roads, and continue straight on for another 1.75 miles to Red Shoot Inn. O.S.GR: SU188095

Charges 2004

Per adult	£ 5.20
child (0-14 yrs)	£ 1.30 - £ 3.20
pitch	free - £ 2.00
electricity	£ 3.10
dog	£ 0.95

Reservations

Advised for w/ends, B.Hs and peak season (school holidays) and made with £18 deposit per week or part week. Tel: 01425 473789. Email: enquiries@redshoot-campingpark.com

Red Shoot Camping Park

Set in the heart of the New Forest and close to Bournemouth and Ringwood, this is a first class family-run park. Excellent facilities, cycle hire service, children's play area and adjacent to Red Shoot Inn. See our website for full details and saving discounts.

www.redshoot-campingpark.co.uk 01425 473789

UK2360 Hill Cottage Farm Caravan Park

Sandleheath Road, Alderholt, Fordingbridge SP6 3EG (Hampshire)

First opened in 2000, this is a newly constructed, modern site set in 47 acres of beautiful countryside on the Dorset and Hampshire border. The 32 pitches, all on hardstandings with electric hook-ups (16A) are arranged around a circular gravel roadway. Secluded and sheltered, they have views across the surrounding countryside. A field alongside the camping area is used for tents and rallies, and has space for ball games and a small playground. Also on site are a tennis court and a lake for coarse fishing, and there are many woodland walks in the area. Overall this site is more suitable for adults and small children - it is not really designed for active teenagers.

Facilities

A large modern barn-style building provides excellent heated facilities, including covered dishwashing sinks, a laundry room with washing machines and dryers, plus facilities for disabled people and babies - in all, a very generous provision. The first floor has a games room with a full size snooker table, two pool tables and a darts board, plus a separate function room. Motorcaravan services. Playground. Off site: The village centre with pub, church, Post Office and store is a 20 minute woodland walk. Local attractions include Rockbourne Roman Villa, Cranborne Chase, The Dolls Museum at Fordingbridge, Salisbury, and Ringwood with its Wednesday market.

At a glance

Welcome & Ambience	✓✓✓✓	Location	✓✓✓✓
Quality of Pitches	✓✓✓✓	Range of Facilities	✓✓✓

Directions

From Fordingbridge take B3078 westwards for 2 miles to Alderholt. On entering the village, at left hand bend, turn right towards Sandleheath (site signed) and site entrance is about 300 yards on the left. O.S.GR: SU120130.

Charges 2004

Per unit incl. 2 adults, electricity	£ 11.00 - £ 16.00
extra adult	£ 2.50
child	£ 1.50 - £ 2.00
dog	£ 1.50

Reservations

Made with minimum £20 deposit. Advised for B.Hs and peak season. Tel: 01425 650513.

Open

All year (ring first in low season).

UK2290 Sandy Balls Holiday Centre

Godshill, Fordingbridge SP6 2JZ (Hampshire)

Sandy Balls, probably one of the best known and one of the oldest 'camp sites' in the UK, sits high above the sweep of the Avon River amongst woodland which is protected as a nature reserve. The history and development of the park, and how it came to get its name is interesting and it deserves the entry it has maintained in these guides for over 30 years. A very well run and progressive park set within 120 acres and open all year, it covers an extensive area in a series of fields or woodland. This provides 131 lodges and caravan holiday homes (many for rent), some tent areas with unmarked pitches, and 233 serviced pitches for touring units separated by hedging wih part-hardstanding, part-grass (10/16A electricity and TV connection). In winter only 50 pitches are available. The central village area with all the amenities is designed to blend with the forest surroundings and provides all round family entertainment. It includes a large indoor pool and a solar heated outdoor pool both with lifeguards and free at all times (in high season, sessions may be timed). In all there are 120 acres of woodland to explore with a woodland leisure trail where wild animals and birds can be observed in their natural surroundings. The thatched giftshop is must for children! The New Forest is close at hand, together with Paultons Park and Beaulieu.

Facilities

Three modern toilet blocks have under-floor heating and washbasin cubicles. One 'portacabin' style unit remains as an overflow in the tent field (28 day). One block has a bath in each section (M&F). Toilets for disabled visitors and baby facilities. Excellent launderette plus washing machines in all blocks. Motorcaravan services. Recycling stations - look for the green coloured sheds. Supermarket with bakery. Takeaway. Restaurants, bars and family room. Pizzeria. Wide screen TV and entertainment (high season). Indoor pool (66 x 30 ft). Outdoor pool (25/5-30/8). Well equipped fitness gym, jacuzzi, steam room, toning tables, sauna and solarium and dance studios. Games room. Adventure playground and play areas. Soft play area. Clay modelling tuition and story telling. River fishing on permit. Riding stables. Bicycle hire. Archery, orienteering and hot air balloon rides. Dogs only allowed on certain fields. Off site: Golf 6 miles. Beach 20 miles.

At a glance

Welcome & Ambience	✓✓✓✓✓	Location	✓✓✓✓✓
Quality of Pitches	✓✓✓✓✓	Range of Facilities	✓✓✓✓✓

Directions

Park is northwest off B3078 (Fordingbridge - Cadnam) just west of Godshill village, and about 1.5 miles east of Fordingbridge. O.S.GR: SU168147.

Charges 2004

Per pitch	£ 12.75 - £ 18.50
adult	free - £ 3.50
young adult (12-17 yrs)	free - £ 2.00
child (3-11 yrs)	free - £ 1.50
dog	free - £ 2.00

Reservations

Made with deposit and compulsory cancellation insurance. Tel: 01425 653042.
Email: post@sandy-balls.co.uk

Open

All year.

UK2280 Lytton Lawn Touring Park

Lymore Lane, Milford-on-Sea SO41 0TX (Hampshire)

Lytton Lawn is the touring arm of Shorefield Country Park, a holiday home park and leisure centre. Situated 2.5 miles from Shorefield itself, campers and caravanners staying at Lytton Lawn are entitled to free membership of the Leisure Club there. The comprehensive facilities at Shorefield are of a very good standard and are mostly free (extra charges are made for certain activities). They comprise a very attractive indoor pool (20 m. heated), solarium, sauna, spa bath and steam room, dance studios and two all weather tennis courts, open all year with fully trained attendants. There are outdoor pools, crazy golf (Easter - Sept) restaurant facilities including a bistro (Easter - 2 Nov) and a range of entertainment and activity programmes, fitness classes and treatments, all well managed and organised. Lytton Lawn provides 136 marked pitches, including 53 'premier' pitches (hardstanding, 16A electricity, pitch light, water and waste water outlet) in a hedged area of natural grass. This section, with its heated toilet block, is open for a longer season. The rest of the pitches, all with electrical connections (tenters note), are in the adjoining, but separate, gently sloping field, edged with mature trees and hedges and with a further toilet block. Access roads are either tarmac or gravel. The New Forest, Isle of Wight, Bournemouth, Southampton and the beach at Milford on Sea are near.

Facilities
Two purpose built, modern toilet blocks are tiled and well fitted. Dishwashing, washing machine and dryer in each block. Baby changing facilities in one block and facilities for disabled visitors (Radar key). Simple shop (Easter - end Oct), with a supermarket and takeaway (main season) at Shorefield. Small fenced play area and hedged field with goal posts. Only one dog per pitch is accepted.
Off site: Village pub 10 minutes walk. Golf, riding, coarse fishing (all within 3 miles), sailing, windsurfing and boat launching facilities (1.5 miles).

Open
All year except 4 Jan - 9 Feb.

At a glance
Welcome & Ambience ✓✓✓✓ Location ✓✓✓✓✓
Quality of Pitches ✓✓✓✓✓ Range of Facilities ✓✓✓

Directions
From M27 follow signs for Lyndhurst and Lymington on A337. Continue towards New Milton and Lytton Lawn is signed at Everton; Shorefield is signed at Downton. O.S.GR: SZ293937.

Charges 2004
Per 'premier' pitch incl. all persons, electricity, water, drainage and TV connection	£ 10.00 - £ 29.00
standard pitch incl. electricity	£ 9.00 - £ 27.00
pup tent or awning free, both together	£ 4.00
dog (1 only)	£ 1.50 - £ 3.00
Less 40% Mon - Thurs in certain periods.
Minimum weekly charge at busy times.

Reservations
Made with deposit and cancellation insurance - contact Shorefield Holidays Ltd, Shorefield Road, Milford on Sea, nr. Lymington, Hampshire SO41 0LH. Tel: 01590 648331. Email: holidays@shorefield.co.uk

UK2270 Oakdene Forest Park

St Leonards, Ringwood BH24 2RZ (Hampshire)

Set in 55 acres of park and woodland, with direct access to the Avon Forest and near the New Forest, Oakdene provides caravan holiday homes to let or over 200 pitches for all types of unit. These include 'premier' pitches with hardstanding, electric hook-up (10A), water, drainage and pitch light (no tents on these pitches), and some grass pitches with or without electricity mostly in the Meadow area. The Leisure and Country Club (free membership) provides a bar, buffet and a range of entertainment. Super new additions are an indoor pool with a flume, sauna, spa bath and gym and a walled outdoor pool with paddling pool. Oakdene is now under the same ownership as Shorefield Country Park at Milford on Sea and massive investment is being carried out (as can be seen by the pool and gym complex) and the second phase of development (started November 2002) covers a new reception, coffee shop, offices, restaurant, ballroom, supermarket and bars. The aim is to provide the quality, standard and range of facilities and entertainment found at Shorefield and Lytton Lawn (no. 2280).

Facilities
The new fully equipped, purpose built toilet block includes some washbasins in cabins, but 'portacabin' style facilities remain for the Meadow area. Launderette and dishwashing sinks. Shop. Indoor and outdoor pools. Gym. Table tennis and pool table Crazy golf, compact bowling. Amusment arcade. Play area. Free Squirrel's Kids Club. Bicycle hire.
Off site: Forest Pines Riding Centre (10% reduction). Forest walks.

Open
All year except January.

At a glance
Welcome & Ambience ✓✓✓✓ Location ✓✓✓✓
Quality of Pitches ✓✓✓ Range of Facilities ✓✓✓✓

Directions
Park access leads off the main A31 westbound carriageway about 2.5 miles west of Ringwood. O.S.GR: SU101016.

Charges 2004
Per pitch incl. electricity and water	£ 10.00 - £ 29.00
standard pitch incl. electricity	£ 8.00 - £ 27.00
Min. stays at B.Hs.

Reservations
Bookings are handled by Shorefield Country Parks, Shorefield Road, Milford on Sea, nr Lymington, Hampshire SO41 0LH. Tel: 01590 648331. Email: holidays@shorefield.co.uk

Open
All year except January.

UK2250 Hoburne Bashley

Sway Road, New Milton BH25 5QR (Hampshire)

This is an attractive, well run park with many holiday homes (380), but it also has a very sizeable tourist section and can take 300 touring units. However, tents, trailer tents and pup tents are not accepted. Spread over three flat meadows the numbered touring pitches are large, divided by hedging or low fencing, and include 20 'super' pitches. These are of mixed grass and hardstanding with electricity. Set in pleasant park-like surroundings not far from beaches, Bournemouth and the New Forest, the site has a good clubhouse with excellent facilities. This overlooks an 18 m. circular outdoor swimming pool and 18 m. paddling pool, a sensible size and fun with its geysers, clown and beach effect. An impressive indoor pool complex houses a water flume, sauna, solarium, spa bath and steam room, which are all well supervised by lifeguards. The club facilities are comprehensive, with a ballroom, large lounges and bars, and a wide range of entertainment from cabaret, talent shows, bingo, quizzes and competitions to discos (Spring B.H. to mid-Sept. Children's entertainment covers sports and games for the teens and Sammy the Seahorse club for under 12s. The Hungry Woodcutter provides simple hot food and takeaway all day. A popular park with lots going on, Bashley is part of the Hoburne group.

Facilities
Three well constructed toilet blocks, one central to each area, are fully tiled with modern fittings in cheerful yellow and blue with washbasins in cabins. Showers are pre-set (no dividers, but shower heads are set fairly low). Baby changing facilities. Covered washing-up sinks. Launderette. Clubhouse with bars, restaurant and takeaway. 10 pin Bowling Alley. TV room. Video arcade and games room with snooker tables, plus two pool tables, table tennis and darts in other rooms. Children's club. Shop (mid-May - end Sept). Indoor pool. Outdoor pools (heated mid-May - mid-Sept). Crazy golf. Golf course (9 hole, par 3). Tennis courts (3). Adventure play area. Soft ball play area. Only one dog or pet permitted per unit. American motorhomes accepted. Off site: Fishing or riding 1 mile. Mudeford beach 8 miles.

At a glance
Welcome & Ambience ✓✓✓✓✓ Location ✓✓✓✓✓
Quality of Pitches ✓✓✓✓✓ Range of Facilities ✓✓✓✓✓

Directions
Park is on the B3055 about 400 yards east of the crossroads with the B3058 in Bashley village. O.S.GR: SZ246969.

Charges 2005
Per unit incl.up to 6 persons and electricity	£ 10.50 - £ 35.00
multi-service pitch	£ 13.00 - £ 37.00
2 car pitch	£ 13.00 - £ 37.00
pet (1 only)	£ 2.00

Weekend breaks available.

Reservations
Necessary for peak season and made for any length: £50 p/w deposit, balance 6 weeks before arrival. Tel: 01425 612340. Email: enquiries@hoburne.co.uk

Open
28 March - 2 January.

UK2300 Ashurst Caravan & Camping Site

The Forestry Commission, Lyndhurst Road, Ashurst SO4 2AA (Hampshire)

An attractive Forestry Commission site on the fringe of the New Forest, Ashurst is set in a mixture of oak woodland and grass heathland which is open to the grazing animals of the Forest. Smaller than the Hollands Wood site (23 acres), it provides 280 pitches, 180 of which have been gravelled to provide semi-hardstanding; otherwise you pitch where you like, applying the 20 ft. rule on ground that can be uneven. There are no electricity connections. Some noise must be expected from the adjacent railway line - the station is just five minutes walk away. Reception is run by the very helpful site managers who provide a freezer pack service, charging service for mobile phones and batteries and sell various camping accessories. Charcoal and disposable barbecues are for sale (but barbecues are not permitted in dry weather). There is a late arrivals area and separate car-parking area for those arriving or returning after the gate has closed (22.30 hrs).

Facilities
The single central toilet block has been refurbished and provides everything necessary, including hairdryers, a well equipped unit for visitors with disabilities (key required) and a good laundry room. It could be under pressure when the site is full in the main season. Motorcaravan service point. Bread and milk to order. Dogs are not accepted. A torch is useful. Off site: A local garage sells gas. Nearby pub by footpath across an adjacent field. Shops and local buses within a five minute walk. Guided forest walks are organised during the main season. Golf 4 miles.

Open
March - September.

At a glance
Welcome & Ambience ✓✓✓✓ Location ✓✓✓✓
Quality of Pitches ✓✓✓ Range of Facilities ✓✓✓

Directions
Site is 2 miles east of Lyndhurst, set back from the A35 Southampton - Bournemouth road, 5 miles southwest of Southampton. O.S.GR: SU334099.

Charges 2004
Per unit incl. up to 4 persons	£ 6.90 - £ 14.70
extra person (over 5 yrs)	£ 1.20
extra car, gazebo or pup tent	£ 4.40

Less 20% all year for disabled guests and outside 7/7-28/8 for senior citizens.

Reservations
Necessary for B.Hs and peak times (min. 2 nights or 3 nights at B.Hs) with £30 deposit. Contact (at all times): Forest Holidays, Forestry Commission, 231 Corstorphine Road, Edinburgh EH12 7AT. Tel: 0131 3146505. Email: fe.holidays@forestry.gov.uk

UK2310 Hollands Wood Caravan & Camping Site

The Forestry Commission, Lyndhurst Road, Brockenhurst SO43 7QH (Hampshire)

Hollands Wood is a large, spacious 168-acre secluded site in a natural woodland setting (mainly oak), in the heart of the New Forest, with an abundance of wildlife, including the famous New Forest ponies. The site is arranged informally with 600 level unmarked pitches but it is stipulated that there must be at least 20 feet between each unit. There are no electrical connections and possible traffic noise from the A337 which runs alongside one boundary. One area of the site is designated a dog free zone. The site is only about half a mile from Brockenhurst village where there are shops for supplies and gas, etc, plus trains and buses. Reception offers a freezer pack service and sells batteries, maps and guides. Barbecues are not permitted in dry weather. The site can get very busy and we include the smaller Ashurst site as an alternative.

Facilities

Two large utilitarian toilet blocks (and a third smaller, older one) are full equipped if somewhat basic. Facilities for disabled people and baby changing surfaces. Two laundry rooms with washing machines and dryers. These facilities are under pressure at peak times. Motorcaravan service point. Bread and milk to order. Night security with the barrier closed 22.30 - 07.30 hrs (overnight area). Torches essential. Off site: Bicycle hire and riding 2 miles. Golf 3 miles.

Open

26 March - 27 September.

At a glance

Welcome & Ambience	✓✓✓✓	Location	✓✓✓✓
Quality of Pitches	✓✓✓	Range of Facilities	✓✓✓

Directions

Site entrance is on east side of A337 Lyndhurst - Lymington road, half a mile north of Brockenhurst. O.S.GR: SU303038.

Charges 2004

Per unit incl. up to 4 persons	£ 7.70 - £ 15.70
extra person (over 5 yrs)	£ 1.30
extra car, gazebo or pup tent	£ 4.60

Less 20% all year for disabled guests and outside 7/7-28/8 for senior citizens.

Reservations

Necessary for B.Hs and peak times (min. 3 nights with £30 deposit). Contact (at all times): Forest Holidays, Forestry Commission, 231 Corstorphine Road, Edinburgh EH12 7AT. Tel: 0131 3146505

UK2320 Chichester Camping & Caravanning Club Site

Main Road, Southbourne PO10 8JH (Hampshire)

This small, neat site is just to the west of Chichester and north of Bosham harbour. Formerly an orchard, it is rectangular in shape with 58 pitches on flat, well mown lawns on either side of gravel roads. All pitches have 16A electricity, 42 with level hardstanding. Although the A27 bypass takes most of the through traffic, the site is by the main A259 road so there may be some traffic noise in some parts (not busy at night). Opposite the park are orchards through which paths lead to the seashore. Unfortunately there is no overnight area for late arrivals; the gates are shut between 11 pm. and 7 am. with no parking outside. Nearby are Bignor Roman villa, Apuldram Roses and the Weald and Downland open-air museum.

Facilities

The well designed, brick built toilet block is of first class quality. Fully tiled and heated in cool weather, with facilities for people with disabilities (access by key). Washing machines and dryers. Gas supplies. No ball games permitted on the park. Dogs can be walked in the lane opposite the entrance. Off site: Shops, restaurants and pubs within easy walking distance in the nearby village and the park is on a main bus route. Chichester has a leisure centre and market day is Wednesday. Excellent caravan shop nearby. Bicycle hire 1 mile. Fishing or golf 5 miles, riding 6 miles.

At a glance

Welcome & Ambience	✓✓✓✓	Location	✓✓✓✓
Quality of Pitches	✓✓✓✓	Range of Facilities	✓✓✓

Directions

Park is on main A259 Chichester - Havant road at Southbourne, 750 yards west of Chichester Caravans. O.S.GR: SU774056.

Charges 2005

Per adult	£ 5.55 - £ 7.40
child (6-18 yrs)	£ 1.90
non-member pitch fee	£ 5.00

Reservations

Necessary and made with deposit; contact site or Central Reservations 0870 243 3331. Tel: 01243 373202.

Open

February - November.

UK2530 Waverley Park Holiday Centre

Old Road, East Cowes PO32 6AW (Isle of Wight)

This pleasant small family owned and run site is set in the grounds of an old country house with magnificent views over the Solent and just five minutes from the Cowes ferry terminal. The 45 touring pitches are in short rows, back to back on sloping grassland, whilst tents are pitched on the lower half nearer to the promenade and sea. To one side of the site is an area housing 75 private and rental holiday homes. Motorcaravans will need some levelling blocks, and there are only 28 electric hook-ups (10A) at present. The newly rebuilt sanitary unit is at the top of the site, and at the bottom of the site a gate leads onto the promenade which provides good walks, and the pebble beach which is popular with sailors, windsurfers, etc. The site is an ideal vantage point for Cowes Week, and has good views of the ocean liners sailing in and out of Southampton.

Facilities

A high quality, recently rebuilt unit provides the usual facilities, including some spacious cubicles with washbasins en-suite. Laundry facilities. Dishwashing room. Good suite for disabled people with a baby changing deck. Basic chemical disposal point in the static area. Small well stocked shop. Heated outdoor pool and paddling pool with sun terrace. Club with restaurant and bar serving good value meals, plus family entertainment in season (all Whitsun - early Sept). Small adventure style playground. Games room. Nine hole putting green. Boats accepted by prior arrangement - public slipway nearby. Off site: Tennis courts close to lower end of site, key available, ask at reception. Public slipway. Cowes, with its shops and services is within walking distance. A chain ferry operates between East and West Cowes across the Medina River and there is a bus stop outside the site entrance.

At a glance

Welcome & Ambience	✓✓✓✓	Location	✓✓✓✓✓
Quality of Pitches	✓✓✓✓	Range of Facilities	✓✓✓✓

Directions

Immediately after leaving Southampton - Cowes ferry, take first left, then right into Old Road, and park entrance is 300 yds on left. O.S.GR: SZ505958.

Charges 2004

Per adult	£ 4.00 - £ 6.00
child (5-13 yrs)	£ 2.00 - £ 3.00
pitch incl. free electricity	£ 2.50
dog	£ 0.50 - £ 1.20

Min. fee in high season £11, excl. electricity.

Reservations

Essential for B.Hs, peak season and Cowes Week (1st week August). Made with deposit (25%). Tel: 01983 293452. Email: sue@waverley-park.co.uk

Open

29 March - 30 September (statics all year).

UK2510 Whitecliff Bay Holiday Park

Hillway, Whitecliff Bay, Bembridge PO35 5PL (Isle of Wight)

Whitecliff Bay is a very large complex divided by a lane, with a holiday home and chalet park on the right hand side, and a touring site on the left hand side. The large touring site is on a sloping hillside with commanding views over the surrounding countryside. The 429 pitches are spread over three fields, the top and second fields are terraced, but field three (the only one in which dogs are permitted in low season only) is quite level. Half of the pitches have electric hook-ups (10A), and there are around 44 gravel hardstandings, 12 in the top field, the remainder in lowest field. There are only 13 individual hedged multi-serviced pitches available, so book early. Three toilet blocks serve the site and are situated to one side. On the opposite side of the lane, in the holiday home and chalet park, you will find all the main entertainment and leisure facilities. These include The Culver Club with its bar, dance floor, stage and a full programme of evening entertainment and shows in season. On the cliff above the beach is the pub and restaurant, a heated outdoor pool with a large paved surround and indoor facilities including a funpool with jacuzzi, small gym, a soft playzone (under 8 yrs), and a snack bar.

Facilities

Three sanitary units, one on the lower part of the site. The other two are fairly close together, not far from reception and both of these have been refitted to a good standard, and provide showers (on payment), and a suite (with shower) for disabled people. A second suite with a hip bath/shower is at the lower block with a similar facility to serve as a baby/family room. (this block due for refurbishment). Laundry with ironing. Small mini-market. Motorcaravan services. Playground. At the holiday home park: Launderette, hairdresser and second larger shop. The Culver Club with bar and evening entertainment. Several snack bars, takeaways. Swimming pool (Whitsun - end Aug). Indoor funpool with jacuzzi, sauna and sunbed, small gym, soft playzone (under 8 yrs), and a snack-bar. Both pools are supervised. Most facilities open March - Oct. Dogs only accepted in lower field outside 20/7-31/8. Off site: Close to the outdoor pool a very steep path leads down to a sandy beach. Normal bus service weekdays, site runs a courtesy mini-bus at weekends to Bembridge and Sandown. Golf 5 miles. Bicycle hire 4 miles. Riding 2 miles.

At a glance

Welcome & Ambience	✓✓✓✓	Location	✓✓✓✓✓
Quality of Pitches	✓✓✓✓	Range of Facilities	✓✓✓✓✓

Directions

Bembridge is at the eastern end of the island. From the A3055 between Ryde and Sandown, turn east at Brading on B3395 for approx. 2 miles passing the Airfield and Propeller Club, fork right (site signed). Follow signs to site, first entry on right is static area, touring entrance is on left shortly after. O.S.GR: SZ635865.

Charges 2004

Per pitch incl. 2 persons	£ 8.00 - £ 14.00
incl. electricity	£ 10.80 - £ 17.30
incl. full services	£ 13.30 - £ 20.70
extra adult	£ 3.50 - £ 5.40
child (5-13 yrs)	£ 2.60 - £ 3.60
dog (excl. 18/7-4/9)	£ 1.00

Reservations

Made with deposit of £40 per week (£80 if special offer package). Tel: 01983 872671. Email: holiday@whitecliff-bay.com

Open

22 March - 26 October.

UK2450 The Orchards Holiday Caravan Park

Newbridge, Yarmouth, Isle of Wight PO41 0TS (Isle of Wight)

In a village situation in the quieter western part of the island, The Orchards is a busy and lively family holiday park combining 63 caravan holiday homes (in a separate area) with a neat touring area. A good place from which to explore, the beaches and Yarmouth are only four miles away. There are 175 marked touring pitches, arranged on gently sloping meadow, broken up by apple trees, mature hedges and fences. All have electricity and 84 have hardstanding, including 10 new 'all service' pitches with landscaping all around. The large reception provides useful tourist information. A meeting room (up to 50 persons) is suitable for small rallies. Golfing and walking holidays are arranged. Part of the Caravan Club`s 'managed under contract' scheme, non-members are also very welcome. The park is a member of the Best of British group.

Facilities

Three toilet blocks of varying age and size should together be an ample provision. A few washbasins are in private cabins. Baths on payment. The latest block, a smart mobile unit, provides en-suite facilities (shower, WC and basin). Facilities for disabled visitors (a hardstanding pitch close by can be reserved). Full laundry facilities. Motorcaravan service point. Ice pack and battery charging services. Gas supplies. Well stocked shop and takeaway service (mid-March - Oct, limited opening at quiet times). Indoor and outdoor heated pools. Football pitch. Multi-court. Exercise stations. Pool, table tennis, TV and amusements rooms (no evening entertainment on site). Coarse fishing (no closed season). Off site: Bicycle hire, boat launching 4 miles, riding 1 mile. Membership available for village social club. Small discount at Freshwater golf course (4 miles) - ask at reception.

At a glance

Welcome & Ambience	✓✓✓✓	Location	✓✓✓✓
Quality of Pitches	✓✓✓✓	Range of Facilities	✓✓✓✓

Directions

Park is in Newbridge village, signed north from B3401 (Yarmouth - Newport) road. O.S.GR: SZ411878.

Charges 2004

Per unit incl. 2 adults and electricity	£ 11.00 - £ 15.30
extra adult	£ 4.50 - £ 6.50
child	£ 1.50 - £ 4.50
dog	£ 3.00

No pitch fee for hikers or cyclists. Packages incl. ferry travel available - ring park for best deal.
Camping Cheques accepted.

Reservations

Made for min. 5 days with £30 p/wk deposit.
Tel: 01983 531331.
Email: info@orchards-holiday-park.co.uk

Open

All year except 3 January - 15 February.

Have you **forgotten something?**

see the Alan Rogers Directory ON PAGE 294

UK2470 Southland Camping Park

Newchurch, Sandown, Isle of Wight PO36 0LZ (Isle of Wight)

Southland was opened in 1981 in the grounds of a former nursery and it has matured nicely with many attractive shrubs and trees. In the peaceful country setting of the Arreton valley, it is a sheltered and well run park with 120 large, level pitches backing on to and separated by hedging. Comfortable and spacious, all have electricity (10/16A) and some water points. Two acres of land have been acquired recently and a nature area is being developed overlooking the countryside at the back of the site (no dogs). Nearby Arreton and Newchurch have craft shops and in August there is the National Garlic Festival. Sandown and Shanklin are 3 miles, the beach at Lake, 2.5 miles. A member of the Countryside Discovery group.

Facilities

The excellent toilet block is well maintained - the ladies' is modern, with washbasins in spacious cubicles, low level washbasins for children, three en-suite basin and shower cubicles, and a hairdressing area. Bathroom (on payment), baby room, a good unit for disabled people, and two family shower rooms also suitable for disabled visitors. Laundry and dishwashing sinks. Motorcaravan service point. Shop (4/4-30/9). Fenced play area. Only raised barbecues are permitted. More than one dog per pitch by prior arrangement only. Off site: Fishing 1 mile, riding 2 miles, bicycle hire or golf 3 miles. Main bus route stops at the top of the road, two pubs are within walking distance and there is access to walks and bridleways.

At a glance

Welcome & Ambience	✓✓✓✓✓	Location	✓✓✓✓✓
Quality of Pitches	✓✓✓✓✓	Range of Facilities	✓✓✓

Directions

Park is signed from A3055/6 Newport-Sandown road, southeast of Arreton. O.S.GR: SZ558848.

Charges 2005

Per adult	£ 5.00 - £ 7.30
child (3-15 yrs)	£ 1.85 - £ 3.80
dog	£ 1.10

Electricity incl. Packages incl. ferry travel available. Special low season offers.

Reservations

Made for any length with £30 deposit per pitch, per week (or part week). Tel: 01983 865385. Email: info@southland.co.uk

Open

Easter - end September.

UK2520 Thorness Bay Holiday Park

Thorness Bay, Cowes PO31 8NJ (Isle of Wight)

Spread over a large area of rural down and woodland that slopes down to the beach at Thorness Bay, this is a large site with more than 500 holiday homes. The touring site has around 90 marked pitches, most with electricity (16A) including 27 multi-serviced pitches on gravel hardstandings with electricity, water, drain and TV points. These and some grass pitches are on newly created terraces served by tarmac roads. The remainder are on sloping open grassland either divided by ranch style rails or in an open tent area, and all have views of the surrounding countryside. The main activity centre is located in the holiday home area, a short walk from the touring site. Outdoor sporting activities on-site include a multi-court, soccer, archery, and fencing. The indoor pool provides snorkelling, scuba diving and adult only swimming sessions. There is evening entertainment for all the family, with some 'big name' stars and a variety of supporting events. Children will be entertained by an adventure playground, Sparkys Krew Club (5-11 yrs) and for older children the 'Mix' (12-16 yrs) has a variety of challenging activities. 'Day Camp Action' is for 7-16 year olds (extra charge, only run during school holidays) with high ropes, abseiling, climbing tower and quad bikes.

Facilities

Several 'portacabin' style buildings provide the usual showers, WCs, and open washbasins. Separate units contain a suite for disabled persons (note: very steep short ramp, impractical for wheelchairs) and dishwashing sinks. Tower Diner and bar which also serves breakfasts. Indoor playroom for small children. Shop. Launderette. ATM machine. Takeaway. Games arcade. Indoor fun pool, with lifeguards. Regatta View showbar with entertainment programme including cabarets. Large adventure playground. Multi-sports court. Off site: The beach is easily accessed from the main entertainment complex. All the attractions of the Island are within easy day-trip distances. Golf 4 miles.

Open

2 April - 29 October.

At a glance

Welcome & Ambience	✓✓✓	Location	✓✓✓✓
Quality of Pitches	✓✓✓✓	Range of Facilities	✓✓✓✓

Directions

Thorness Bay is southwest of Cowes. From East Cowes ferry terminal follow signs to Newport. From centre follow A3054 towards Yarmouth. Continue for about 2.5 miles to crossroads, turning right (north) to Thorness Bay. After about 2 miles, on a sharp right bend, turn left where site is signed. After 400 yds. entrance on right leads to parking area and reception in main building. O.S.GR: SZ452926.

Charges 2004

Per pitch incl. up to 6 persons	£ 3.00 - £ 24.00
hardstanding pitch	£ 4.00
dog	free - £ 3.00

Reservations

Essential for B.Hs and peak season. Made with deposit of £5 per pitch per night for less than 7 nights, or £35 per pitch per week. Tel: 01983 523109.

UK2475 Lower Hyde Holiday Park

Landguard Road, Shanklin PO37 7LL (Isle of Wight)

This site is located on the edge of Shanklin within walking distance of shops and services and only 1.5 miles from the beach. Lower Hyde is a large holiday park complex with around 200 rental and 114 privately owned holiday homes. The separate touring area has 115 well spaced and numbered pitches, 85 with electric hook-ups (16A) of which 26 are multi-service with hardstanding, water, drain, electricity and TV hook-up. The touring area has recently been redeveloped, and is now in an elevated position with some good views over the surrounding countryside. There are good surfaced roads, low level site lighting, toilet and shower facilities in modern 'portacabin' style units, a late arrivals area, and a permanent warden. Outdoor sporting activities on-site include a multi-court, soccer, archery, fencing and tennis. The small indoor pool and spa pool and outdoor fun pool provide snorkelling, scuba diving and adult only swimming sessions. There is evening entertainment for all the family, with some 'big name' stars and a variety of supporting events. For children there is an adventure playground, Sparkys Krew Club (5-11 yrs), and for older children the 'Mix' (12-16 yrs) has a variety of challenging activities. 'Day Camp Action' is for 7-16 year olds, (extra charge, only run during school holidays) with high ropes, abseiling, climbing tower and quad bikes.

Facilities

A group of several modern 'portacabin' style units standing on a new concrete base currently provide all services, although a permanent building is in the planning stage. Current provision is adequate and well looked after, providing some good showers, open washbasins, dishwashing sinks, and an easily accessible suite for disabled campers. Launderette near reception. Shop. Takeaway. Hudson's bar and diner. Squires celebrity showbar. Games arcade. Indoor and outdoor pool complex with lifeguards. Adventure playground. Sparkys Krew Club, the Mix for teenagers. ATM. Off site: Fishing and boat launching 1.5 miles. Golf 2.5 miles. Riding and bicycle hire 5 miles.

Open

2 April -29 October.

At a glance

Welcome & Ambience	✓✓✓✓	Location	✓✓✓✓
Quality of Pitches	✓✓✓✓	Range of Facilities	✓✓✓✓

Directions

From East Cowes ferry terminal take A3021 for about 2.5 miles to roundabout and turn right on A3054 to Newport. From Newport take A3020 towards Sandown and Shanklin. After 1.5 miles (at Blackwater) continue straight on joining A3056 to Sandown. Keep on this road until you pass Safeway on the left, and shortly afterwards, turn right into Whitecross Lane (signed Landguard Camping). Keep straight on, past Landguard and site is on right after 1 mile. O.S.GR: SZ576817.

Charges 2004

per unit incl. up to 6 persons	£ 3.00 - £ 25.00
hardstanding pitch	£ 4.00
dog	free - £ 3.00

Reservations

Essential for B.Hs and peak season. Made with deposit of £5 per pitch per night for less than 7 nights, or £35 per pitch per week. Tel: 01983 866131.

UK2500 Heathfield Farm Camping

Heathfield Road, Freshwater PO40 9SH (Isle of Wight)

Heathfield is a pleasant contrast to many of the other sites on the Isle of Wight, in that it is a 'no frills' sort of place, very popular with tenters, cyclists and small camper vans. Despite its name, it is no longer a working farm. A large, open meadow provides 60 large, level pitches, 30 with electricity (10A). Two small fenced areas provide traffic free zones for backpackers and cyclists' tents. A play field for ball games also has two picnic tables and two barbecues provided. There is no shop as you are only eight minutes walk from the centre of Freshwater. The site overlooks Colwell Bay and across the Solent towards Milford-on-Sea and Hurst Castle. It is ideal for visiting attractions on the western side of the island including Totland and Freshwater Bays, The Needles and Old Battery, Compton Down, and Mottistone Manor Garden. The Military road which runs from Freshwater Bay to St Catherine's Point gives spectacular coastal views.

Facilities

The main toilet unit is housed in a modern, ingeniously customised, 'portacabin' type unit including one washbasin cubicle for ladies and a baby room. Showers are slightly different in that they have two pushbutton controls, one for pre-mixed hot water, the other for cold only (provided at the special request of some of the regular customers). A second similar unit has WCs and washbasins in cubicles, plus facilities for disabled visitors. Laundry with washing machine and dryer, ironing facilities and dishwashing sinks. Recycling bins. Motorcaravan service point. Gaz and ice pack service. Play field. No commercial vehicles are accepted. Gate locked 22.30-07.00 hrs.

At a glance

Welcome & Ambience	✓✓✓✓	Location	✓✓✓✓
Quality of Pitches	✓✓✓✓	Range of Facilities	✓✓✓

Directions

From A3054 north of Totland and Colwell turn into Heathfield Road where site is signed. Site entrance is on right after a short distance. O.S.GR: SZ336879.

Charges 2004

Per adult	£ 4.00 - £ 4.50
child (3-15 yrs)	£ 1.50 - £ 2.00
pitch	£ 0.50
with electricity	£ 2.00 - £ 3.00

Min pitch fee July/Aug £ 8.00 - £ 12.00 (no fee for backpacker pitches). Booking supplement for one night £2.00. No credit cards.

Reservations

Advisable for B.Hs and peak season; made with £15 deposit. Tel: 01983 756756. Email: web@heathfieldcamping.co.uk

Open

1 May - 30 September.

UK2610 Bo Peep Caravan Park

Aynho Road, Adderbury, Banbury OX17 3NP (Oxfordshire)

Set amongst 85 acres of farmland and woodland, there is an air of spacious informality about this peaceful, friendly park and it blends perfectly with the surrounding views. Part of the Caravan Club's 'managed under contract' scheme, non-members are also very welcome. All of the 112 numbered, pitches are large, have 16A electricity and, with the exception of eight that slope gently, are otherwise quite level. Gravel roads connect the various areas, such as Poppy Field, The Paddocks and The Warren, with reasonable shelter provided by hedges and trees. Pitches are mostly grassy and set around the perimeters, leaving central areas free for a liberal sprinkling of picnic tables. A separate 4 acre field is reserved for tents and 28 seasonal units occupy the hardstandings and some other pitches. Children are welcome but there is no play area. A network of circular walks around the site, including the pleasant river walk, has wide, well-kept paths and is being continually extended and developed; even bench seats and waste bins are provided. Dogs are also welcome on these walks. A 15 acre field is available for recreation use.

Facilities

The original toilet block has been supplemented by a larger, purpose-built unit, all clean and heated. Large showers with changing space, hairdryers. Dishwashing sinks under cover. Laundry rooms. Motorcaravan service point. Low level lighting. Small shop with off licence, gas and basic supplies. Information centre (with maps, leaflets, sample menus from local pubs, etc). Fishing (apply to office). Caravan storage. Caravan cleaning area. Off site: Golf course next door. Banbury is just 3 miles, the famous Blenheim Palace 6 miles. Great day trips to Stratford upon Avon, Warwick and its castle and even Silverstone can be entertained from this base.

At a glance

Welcome & Ambience	✓✓✓✓	Location	✓✓✓✓
Quality of Pitches	✓✓✓✓	Range of Facilities	✓✓✓✓

Directions

Adderbury village is on the A4260 Banbury - Oxford road. At traffic lights in Adderbury turn on B4100 signed Aynho; park is clearly signed, 0.5 miles on the right (0.5 mile drive). O.S.GR: SP482355.

Charges 2004

Per adult	£ 3.50 - £ 4.75
child (over 5 yrs)	£ 2.00
pitch (non member)	£ 1.00 - £ 6.50
electricity	free
tent camper per adult	£ 4.50 - £ 4.75
tent camper per child	£ 2.00

No credit cards.

Reservations

Advised and made with £10 deposit. Tel: 01295 810605. Email: warden@bo-peep.co.uk

Open

16 March - 1 November.

UK2600 Barnstones Caravan & Camping Park

Great Bourton, Banbury OX17 1QU (Oxfordshire)

Three miles from Banbury and open all year round, this small, neat park provides an excellent point from which to explore the Cotswolds, Oxford and Stratford-upon-Avon. The 49 level pitches all have gravel hardstanding with a grass area for awnings (no groundsheets are allowed) and 10A electricity; 20 of these are fully serviced. Shrubs, flowers and an oval tarmac road convey a tidy impression throughout and the low level lighting is subtle but effective. A 36 pitch rally field (with 10A hookups) is near the main road, so some traffic noise is to be expected. New arrivals should report to the warden's caravan at the park entrance. The church in Great Bourton (250 m.) has a most unusual lych gate and there is a canal-side walk to Banbury (3 miles).

Facilities

The upgraded toilet block is small, but it can be heated and is quite adequate for the number of people it serves. Adjustable, unisex showers. Separate dishwashing and laundry rooms. Gas supplies. Small, fenced play area (grass and bark chipping base) adjacent to the entrance road. American motorhomes accepted by prior arrangement. Off site: Nearest shop 1 mile, supermarket 3 miles, pub 150 yds. Fishing, bicycle hire, golf and riding, all within 3 miles.

Open

All year.

At a glance

Welcome & Ambience	✓✓✓✓	Location	✓✓✓✓
Quality of Pitches	✓✓✓✓	Range of Facilities	✓✓✓

Directions

From M40 take exit 11 for Banbury. Turn off following signs for Chipping Norton, straight on at two small roundabouts. At third roundabout turn right on A423 signed Southam and in 2.5 miles turn right signed Great Bourton. Site entrance is 100 yds on right. O.S.GR: SP454454.

Charges 2004

Per unit incl. 2 persons, electricity	£ 7.50 - £ 9.50
extra person	£ 1.50
child (5-12 yrs)	£ 1.00
awning	£ 0.50 - £ 1.00
1 man tent	£ 3.50

OAPs less 50p per night. No credit cards.

Reservations

Contact park. Tel: 01295 750289.

UK2620 Wysdom Touring Park

The Bungalow, Burford School, Burford OX18 4JG (Oxfordshire)

You'll have to go a long way before you find anything else remotely like this site! The land is owned by Burford School and the enterprising caretaker and his wife, caravanners themselves, suggested that they create this wonderful place to raise money for the school (hence cheques payable to Burford School). It is really like putting your caravan or motorcaravan (tents are not accepted) into their own private garden. The 25 pitches (6 seasonal) are separated by hedges, all have electricity (16A) and a picnic table and some have their own tap. When we visited, the site was a true riot of colour. This is a lovely location for exploring the Cotswolds - Burford calls itself the 'Gateway to the Cotswolds'. The turn into the site off the school drive is narrow and the site is not therefore considered suitable for large motorhomes. It is also best to avoid school pick-up and drop-off when the drive can be congested. This is now an 'Adults Only' park.

Facilities

The small sanitary building offers all you need although, whilst it meets statistical requirements, with only one shower per sex (20p token) there may be a queue at times. Dogs permitted (max 2 per pitch). Off site: Burford is yards away with its famous shop lined hill full of antique shops, old coaching inns and all those 'interesting' shops it is so much fun rooting about in. Burford Golf Club is next door and you can walk from your caravan to the first tee.

At a glance

Welcome & Ambience	✓✓✓	Location	✓✓✓✓
Quality of Pitches	✓✓✓✓	Range of Facilities	✓✓

Directions

From roundabout on A40 at Burford, take A361 and site is a few yards on the right signed Burford School. Once in school drive watch for narrow entrance to site on right in about 100 yards. O.S.GR: SP250115.

Charges 2004

Per unit incl. 2 adults and electricity	£ 8.00 - £ 9.00
extra adult	£ 1.50
dog (max. 2)	free

No credit cards.

Reservations

Contact park. Tel: 01993 823207.

Open

All year.

UK2580 Cotswold View Caravan & Camping Park

Enstone Road, Charlbury OX7 3JH (Oxfordshire)

On the edge of the Cotswolds and surrounded by fine views, this well-run family site offers a warm welcome. It successfully combines a working farm, touring site and self catering country cottages. Wide gravel or tarmac roads ensure easy access to the 132 pitches (all with 10A electricity) in the 10-acre touring area. Part of this area has been carefully developed more recently to a high standard and will naturally take some time to mature. The small reception also serves as a licensed shop selling freshly baked bread, home-made cakes and eggs from their own hens. Farmhouse breakfasts (ordered the night before) are served in the farmhouse itself with B&B also offered. The farm's animals (sheep, hens, pigs, rabbits, ducks, goats, ponies and a donkey) add great interest to one's stay. Well defined and maintained trails around the enclosures enable the animals to be safely observed, whilst additional trails and woodland plantations provide more walking opportunities, particularly for dogs which can be allowed off the lead. Convenient for touring the Cotswolds, there is also a good train service for day trips to London.

Facilities

Two well maintained toilet blocks provide excellent facilities including washbasins in cubicles, showers with ample changing space, two family rooms, baths (50p), hairdryers, central heating and even soft piped music! Both blocks have good units for disabled people. Baby changing facilities, laundry room, freezers for ice packs and dishwashing sinks under cover. Motorcaravan service point. Shop. Children have a two sheltered grass areas in which to play and a games room with table tennis, pool table and football table. Hard tennis court. Latest addition is an under 5s fenced, rubber surfaced play area. Outdoor chess. Bicycle hire. Skittle alley is for hire. American motorhomes accepted. Security barrier system (£5 deposit). Off site: Fishing 1 mile, riding 10 miles, golf 7 miles.

At a glance

Welcome & Ambience	✓✓✓✓	Location	✓✓✓✓✓
Quality of Pitches	✓✓✓✓	Range of Facilities	✓✓✓✓

Directions

From A44 Oxford - Stratford-on-Avon road, take B4022 to Charlbury, just south of Enstone. Park is 2 miles on left. O.S.GR: SP365210.

Charges 2004

Per unit incl. 2 persons, electricity	£ 12.00 - £ 15.00
extra adult	£ 2.00
child (6-16 yrs)	£ 1.50
dog	free

Reservations

Advisable for B.Hs and peak season. Tel: 01608 810314. Email: bookings@cotswoldview.f9.co.uk

Open

Easter - 31 October.

UK2570 Lincoln Farm Park

High Street, Standlake, Witney OX29 7RH (Oxfordshire)

From its immaculately tended grounds and quality facilities, to the efficient and friendly staff, this park is a credit to its owner. Situated in a small, quiet village, it is well set back and screened by mature trees, with wide gravel roads, hedged enclosures, attractive brick pathways and good lighting. All 90 numbered, level touring pitches are generously sized and have electrical connections (10/16A), 75 with gravel hardstanding and adjacent grass for awnings, and 22 are fully serviced (fresh and waste water, electricity and satellite TV). Gazebos or extra tents are not permitted on pitches. Although only a relatively small site its leisure facilities are quite outstanding. The indoor leisure centre boasts two heated pools plus a toddlers' pool, spa pools, saunas, steam room, sun bed and a fitness suite. Charges for all of these are modest, and outside of the open sessions everything can be hired privately by the hour. Oxford and the Cotswolds are conveniently close. A member of the Best of British group.

Facilities

The two heated toilet blocks are of notable design and quality, well maintained and exceptionally clean, with showers (sensibly sized and designed), and washbasins in cubicles. A well equipped, separate unit for disabled people is adjacent to a specially reserved pitch with direct access. Two family bathrooms (incorporating baby bath and changing facilities). Each block also contains a laundry room, dishwashing sinks under cover (more throughout the site), freezers, fridges and microwaves. Motorcaravan service point. Shop (basic supplies). Information kiosk. Outdoor chess/draughts, putting green and sizeable adventure play area (bark chipping and rubber base). Indoor swimming pools. Up to two dogs are welcome with allocated walks. Off site: Fishing (lake and river) 300 yds - 5 miles, riding centre and water sports nearby.

At a glance

Welcome & Ambience	✓✓✓✓	Location	✓✓✓✓
Quality of Pitches	✓✓✓✓✓	Range of Facilities	✓✓✓✓✓

Directions

Take A415 Witney - Abingdon road and turn into Standlake High Street by garage; park is 300 yds on the right. O.S.GR: SP396029.

Charges 2004

Per unit incl. 2 persons	£ 7.95 - £ 14.95
electricity	£ 2.50 - £ 2.75
extra adult	£ 2.25
child (5-14 yrs)	£ 1.50
dog	£ 1.00
Low season offers.	

Reservations

Made with £15 non-returnable deposit. Tel: 01865 300239. Email: info@lincolnfarm.touristnet.uk.com

Open

1 February - mid November.

UK2750 Highclere Farm Country Touring Park

Newbarn Lane, Seer Green, Beaconsfield HP9 2QZ (Buckinghamshire)

Only 25 miles from London and 10 miles from Legoland and Windsor, this is a peaceful park that backs onto fields and woodland. Originally developed around a working chicken farm, there are also sheep, geese and a pot-bellied pig with horses and stabling to provide that country feel. There are 60 level grass pitches, most with 10A electricity and gravel hardstanding, the rest being reserved for tents. The atmosphere is friendly, but informal, with reception doubling as a small shop that can supply all types and sizes of fresh laid eggs. A fenced play area and a footpath are at the top of the park. A bus service to Uxbridge passes the site, London is 35 minutes by train, whilst Windsor Castle and Thorpe Park are also within easy reach. A member of the Countryside Discovery group.

Facilities
The new toilet and shower block is fuly equipped and can be heated. Large showers (20p). Unit with toilet and washbasin for disabled people. New launderette. Shop. New play area. Off site: Golf 0.5 miles. Riding 2 miles. Bicycle hire 3 miles. Fishing 8 miles.

Open
All year except February.

At a glance
Welcome & Ambience	✓✓✓✓	Location	✓✓✓✓
Quality of Pitches	✓✓✓✓	Range of Facilities	✓✓✓

Directions
From M40 take exit 2, then follow A40 towards London. Take first left for Seer Green, then follow site signs. O.S.GR: SU977927.

Charges 2004
Per unit	£ 12.00 - £ 16.00
tent	£ 10.00 - £ 18.00
extra pup tent	£ 1.00
awning, dog or extra car	free
electricity	£ 2.00

Reservations
Contact park. Tel: 01494 874505.
Email: highclerepark@aol.com

For all your **camping and touring** needs TURN TO PAGE 294 for details

UK2700 Hurley Riverside Park

Hurley, Maidenhead SL6 5NE (Berkshire)

On the banks of the river Thames, not far from Henley-on-Thames, you will find the picturesque village of Hurley where some buildings date back to 1086. Just outside the village is Hurley Riverside Park. You can enjoy walks along the banks of the Thames or visit the various pubs and restaurants in the village for a good meal and a pint. Nearby Windsor has its famous castle or for younger members of the family, Windsor is the home of Legoland. At Henley you can watch the regatta. Alternatively, you can just relax in the peaceful settings of the site. The touring area is flat and separated into smaller fields, with the pitches arranged around the outside edges of each field and the centre left free, the park has a very spacious feel. There are 138 pitches with 10A electricity including 14 fully serviced. Even some of the tent pitches have hook-up points. A very popular park, there is also a large rally field.

Facilities
Three wooden clad toilet blocks (raised on legs) include showers (a little cramped) and facilities for disabled visitors. Laundry. Dishwashing. Motorcaravan service point. Shop. Re-cycling point. Off site: Golf, riding 3 miles. Bicycle hire 4 miles. Legoland at Windsor.

Open
1 March - 31 October.

At a glance
Welcome & Ambience	✓✓✓✓	Location	✓✓✓✓✓
Quality of Pitches	✓✓✓✓	Range of Facilities	✓✓✓

Directions
From M4 exit 8/9 take A404M and after 3 miles take A4130 signed Henley. Go down steep hill and Hurley village is signed on the right - ignore this turning and take next right (site signed from here). O.S.GR: SU825838.

Charges 2004
Per unit incl. 2 persons	£ 8.00 - £ 15.25
extra adult	£ 1.50
child (5-17 yrs)	free - £ 1.50
electricity (10A)	£ 0.75
multi-services	£ 1.75
dog	£ 1.00

Reservations
Made for min. 2 nights (3 nights at B.Hs.); contact park. Tel: 01628 823501.
Email: info@hurleyriversidepark.co.uk

117

UK2690 Wellington Country Park

Riseley, Reading RG7 1SP (Berkshire)

Wellington Country Park is open to all on payment of an entry fee (entry for campers included in pitch fee) and many visit it for a day out. It contains a boating and fishing lake, a large adventure playground and other activities for children, nature trails, deer park, crazy golf, miniature railway and animal farm. The camping site is situated in a wood within the 350 acre park. It has 73 pitches, 18 with hardstanding and 56 with electricity hook-ups (10A). Some 'Premium' pitches are larger and have barbecues and picnic tables. There are several individual pitches and some small groups all within woodland clearings which gives a very rustic and casual feel to this site. It is a very pleasant setting and once the Country Park closes at 5.30 pm. all is very quiet. You must make advance arrangements if you plan to arrive after 5.30 pm when the main park reception centre closes.

Facilities

The toilet block has been refitted to provide comfortable facilities including washbasins in cubicles and well equipped showers with good dry areas. Dishwashing sinks, and ample laundry. Shop stocks basics (from 1/5). Gas supplies. Fishing. Family events. Torch useful. Off site: Riding nearby. Legoland and Windsor 30 minutes drive.

Open

Mid-February - November.

At a glance

Welcome & Ambience	✓✓✓✓	Location	✓✓✓✓✓
Quality of Pitches	✓✓✓✓	Range of Facilities	✓✓✓

Directions

Park is signed at Riseley, off A32/A33 road between Reading and Basingstoke, and from M4. It is 4 miles south of M4 exit 11 and 7 miles north of M3 exit 5. O.S.GR: SU727628.

Charges 2005

Per unit incl. up to 2 adults	
and 2 children	£ 10.00 - £ 20.75
extra adult	£ 2.00
child	£ 1.50
electricity	£ 1.75
dog	free

Reservations

Made with £16 non-returnable deposit (min 2 nights June, July or Aug. or 3 nights at B.Hs).
Tel: 01189 326444.
Email: info@wellington-country-park.co.uk

WELLINGTON
COUNTRY PARK

Wellington Country Park, Riseley, Reading, RG7 1SP
For further information please call: 0118 932 6444
Email: info@wellington-country-park.co.uk
www.wellington-country-park.co.uk

Land of 1066, the South East is brimming with historical sights as castles, stately homes and cathedrals abound. It also boasts miles of footpaths and cycle routes through some of the best landscapes in England, passing chalk downland, wooded valleys and dramatic white-faced cliffs.

The South East is comprised of:
East Sussex, West Sussex, Surrey and Kent

The chalk countryside of golden downland in Sussex offers many opportunities for an active holiday, from walking and cycling to more adventurous pursuits such as rock climbing or ballooning. Once an ancient forest, much of the Weald is now taken up with farmland, but some areas still remain, including Ashdown Forest, a walker's paradise with stunning views of the High Weald and South Downs. The many rivers of the county have cut their way through gaps in the chalk landscape, ending spectacularly in white cliffs on the coast. Here you will find the regency resorts of Bognor Regis and Brighton, with its Royal Pavilion, famous pier and quirky shops. Often referred to as the 'Garden of England', Kent is a richly fertile region flourishing with hop fields, fruit orchards and flowers. It is also home to the world renowned Canterbury Cathedral, several splendid castles, hidden towns, and quaint villages with oast houses. Surrey too boasts a rich heritage with numerous stately homes and National Trust sites plus large areas of ancient woodland. With a network of rivers, an enjoyable way to explore the beautiful countryside is by boat, stopping off at a riverside pub – or two!

Did you know?

Hastings is home to Britain's first Norman castle, built by William the Conqueror

Some of England's finest writers have found inspiration from living in Sussex – Rudyard Kipling, Sir Arthur Conan Doyle and A.A.Milne

Bexhill housed one of the country's first cinemas and was the first to permit 'risqué' mixed sea bathing

The world famous Mclaren F1 racing team has its base in Woking

Runnymede takes its name from the meadow where the Magna Carta, the great charter of English liberties, was sealed by King John in 1215

Places of interest

East Sussex: Runnymede; Thorpe Park in Chertsey; Bexhill; historical towns of Hastings and St Leonards

West Sussex: Eastbourne; Chichester; Bognor Regis; Arundel, with castle; Littlehampton

Surrey: Guildford castle and cathedral; Mole Valley; Royal Horticultural Society's gardens at Wisley; Chessington World of Adventures; Dorking, a renowned centre for antiques

Kent: Leeds Castle and gardens, the oldest stately home in the country; Canterbury, a designated World Heritage Site; Dover, with museum and castle; traditional seaside resort of Folkstone; Hever Castle in Sevenoaks; market town of Maidstone; Isle of Thanet incorporating Margate, Broadstairs and Ramsgate

tip

CHICHESTER FESTIVITIES HAS OVER 200 EVENTS PACKED INTO A BUMPER FESTIVAL OF 16 DAYS, TAKING PLACE IN NUMEROUS VENUES THROUGHOUT THE CITY IN JULY.

UK2810 Chertsey Camping & Caravanning Club Site

Bridge Road, Chertsey KT16 8JX (Surrey)

This long-established site (1926) is splendidly located on the banks of the River Thames, only a few minutes walk from the shops and amenities of Chertsey. A flagship site for the Club, it was totally redeveloped for 2004 at a cost of over £1 million pounds. There are 200 pitches including 50 new serviced pitches with hardstanding and 16A electricity and 15 'super service' pitches which have TV aerial points, water and waste drainage. The work included a new road system, heated toilet blocks with family bathroom and disabled facilities, recreation hall and much more. There has been extensive landscaping and the existing Thames creek has been extended to flow through the site with marshland areas to support the local wildlife environment. When possible energy saving devices have been used. Squirrels, rabbits and ducks abound and trees and plants create a pretty site with views across the water and towards Chertsey bridge. Unfortunately there is some road noise and, depending on flight paths, aircraft noise. The rail station for London is at Chertsey or Weybridge. Fishing is possible and canoeing can be arranged (Chertsey is the main base of the Club's canoe section). The river can flood but the site has a well established warning system and will not allow camping near the river when floods are expected.

Facilities

The well equipped toilet blocks can be heated and include washbasins in cabins, family bathroom and facilities for disabled visitors. Hairdryers. Laundry. Dishwashing area. Motorcaravan service point. Well stocked shop for essentials and gas (8-11 am. and 4-6 pm). Recreation hall. Play area on bark. Fishing (adults £1.20, NRA licence needed). Short dog walk areas. Caravan storage. Torches are necessary.

Open

All year.

At a glance

Welcome & Ambience	✓✓✓✓	Location	✓✓✓✓✓
Quality of Pitches	✓✓✓✓	Range of Facilities	✓✓✓

Directions

Suggested: from M25 use junction 11. Turn left at roundabout on A317 towards Shepperton and continue to second set of traffic lights. Turn right then almost immediately left watching for green Club camp sign just before Chertsey bridge; the opening is narrow. O.S.GR: TQ052667.

Charges 2005

Per adult	£ 5.60 - £ 7.80
child (6-18 yrs)	£ 1.90
non-member pitch fee	£ 5.00

Reservations

Necessary and made with deposit; contact site or Central Reservations 0870 243 3331.
Tel: 01932 562405.

UK2820 Horsley Camping & Caravanning Club Site

Ockham Road North, East Horsley KT24 6PE (Surrey)

London and all the sights are only 40 minutes away by train, yet Horsley is a delightful, quiet unspoilt site with a good duck and goose population on its part lily covered lake (unfenced). It provides 135 pitches, of which 70 have 16A electrical connections and 42 are all weather pitches (most with electricity). Seventeen pitches are around the bank of the lake, the rest further back in three hedged, grass fields with mostly level ground but with some slope in places. There is a range of mature trees and a woodland dog walk area (may be muddy). The soil is clay based so rain tends to settle - sluice gates remove extra water from the lake area when the rain is heavy. A recreation hall with table tennis (bats to hire) is sometimes used for bingo. Basic provisions, gas and books are kept in reception and resident managers will make you comfortable. Guildford and the R.H.S. gardens at Wisley are close by.

Facilities

Two purpose built, heated toilet blocks with good design and fittings, with some washbasins in cabins, a Belfast sink and parent and child room with vanity style basin, toilet and wide surface area. Dishwashing sinks, laundry room and new drying areas. Well designed facilities for disabled people. Papers and milk can be ordered the day before at reception. Play area. Fishing is possible from May (£3.30 per day, NRA licence required). Off site: Shops and the station are 1 mile. Pubs 1.5 - 2 miles. Golf 1.5 miles. Riding 2 miles.

Open

March - October.

At a glance

Welcome & Ambience	✓✓✓✓	Location	✓✓✓✓
Quality of Pitches	✓✓✓✓	Range of Facilities	✓✓✓

Directions

From M25 junction 10, in the direction of Guildford, after 0.5 miles take first left B2039 to Ockham and East Horsley, continuing through Ockham towards East Horsley. After 2 miles start to watch for brown site sign - not east to see - and site is on right in 2.5 miles. O.S.GR: TQ083552.

Charges 2005

Per adult	£ 4.30 - £ 7.40
child (6-18 yrs)	£ 1.90
non-member pitch fee	£ 5.00

Reservations

Necessary and made with deposit; contact site or Central Reservations 0870 243 3331.
Tel: 01483 283273.

UK2890 White Rose Touring Park

Mill Lane, Wick, Littlehampton BN17 7PH (West Sussex)

Situated about midway between the imposing castle at Arundel and the beaches of Littlehampton, White Rose makes an excellent base from which to enjoy the many attractions of this popular district. Watersports centres, race courses, beaches, historical and cultural interests, downland walks and the resorts of Bognor and Brighton are within easy reach. There are 124 pitches for tourists, 88 with electricity (10/16A). The flat grassy meadow is surrounded by trees and divided into two areas. The first part has individually hedged pitches, as on the continent, on either side of concrete access roads, with electricity hook-ups and shared water/waste water connections. The second area includes 14 'super' pitches (each having electricity, fresh and waste water and sewage connections, TV aerial socket and night light), further full sized pitches with no electricity, plus a few special pitches for small tents and small motorcaravans. A busy road runs along one side of the park and road noise could be disturbing in the early mornings during the week to a few pitches.

Facilities

The central toilet block is heated and fully equipped, with two rooms for disabled people, one with shower, the other with WC and basin (key from reception). Reception has a few basic supplies and gas. Central play area for children. Trailed boats by prior arrangement only. Off site: Supermarket 400 yds. Fishing, boat launching, bicycle hire, riding and golf within 2 miles.

Open

All year excl. 14 December - 15 March.

At a glance

Welcome & Ambience	✓✓✓	Location	✓✓✓
Quality of Pitches	✓✓✓✓	Range of Facilities	✓✓✓

Directions

Take A284 Littlehampton road from A27 just to the east of Arundel station (ignore campsite behind the pub at this junction) and park is signed along on the left. O.S.GR: TQ026041.

Charges 2004

Per unit incl. up to 2 people and electricity	£ 14.00 - £ 16.00
pitch with no services	£ 12.00
full service pitch	£ 16.00 - £ 17.00
extra person over 4 yrs	£ 2.00

Reductions for 1 week or 1 month outside 10 July - 31 Aug.

Reservations

Made with deposit of 1 nights fee p/week reserved. Tel: 01903 716176.
Email: snowdondavid@hotmail.com

UK2950 Washington Caravan & Camping Park

Old London Road, Washington RH20 4AJ (West Sussex)

Washington is an unusual campsite with superb equestrian facilities and a bias towards tenting families. It provides only 21 hardstanding pitches for caravans or motorcaravans, and a large gently sloping grassy field with enough space for 80 tents. The 23 electric hook-ups (16A) are on slot meters (50p). Security is good, but unobtrusive. There is some road noise from the A24. There is an excellent equestrian centre adjacent to the campsite, including an Olympic standard floodlit arena, a small children's pony arena, stabling and paddock facilities. There are excellent riding opportunities on the bridle paths of the South Downs Way. Local attractions (all with free admission, check opening times) include Highdown Chalk Gardens at Worthing, Nutbourne Vineyard near Pulborough, and Steyning Museum.

Facilities

A heated chalet style building houses sanitary facilities of an excellent standard, including spacious shower rooms (on payment) and indoor dishwashing and laundry facilities. No on-site shop but eggs, bread, butter and milk can be obtained from the reception office. Drinks machine and freezer. Off site: Eating out options include the local pub and a nearby restaurant.

Open

All year.

At a glance

Welcome & Ambience	✓✓✓	Location	✓✓✓
Quality of Pitches	✓✓✓	Range of Facilities	✓✓✓

Directions

Site entrance is just east of the junction of A24 and A283 at Washington, 6 miles north of Worthing. O.S.GR: TQ122134.

Charges 2005

Per caravan or motorcaravan incl. 2 persons	£ 12.00
extra person	£ 3.00

Weekly terms acc. to time of year.

Reservations

Contact site for details. Tel: 01903 892869.
Email: washcamp@amserve.com

UK2940 Honeybridge Park

Honeybridge Lane, Dial Post, Horsham RH13 8NX (West Sussex)

Honeybridge's owners, Jeff and Val Burrows, continue to develop this 15 acre park which now has 200 pitches, including 40 with gravel hardstanding and the majority with electric hook-ups (16A). Some pitches are individually hedged places, others are on slightly sloping grass, well spaced and in single rows. The reception building houses a small shop, and the park provides a discount voucher pack for local attractions. A large wooden, adventure-style playground is provided for children on an area of grass well away from the pitches, and simple family entertainment is organised on special occasions. A recent addition is a games room with darts, table tennis and free use of many board games. There's also a TV and the room houses extensive tourist information and maps. This site is ideally situated for visiting the South Downs with its many attractive villages.

Facilities
The original toilet unit can be heated in cool weather and provides all modern facilities including some washbasins in cubicles. Unit for disabled persons. Dishwashing and laundry sinks, washing machine and dryer. A new block should now be open, offering extra facilities including a new laundry, meeting room, family bathroom plus more facilities for disabled persons. Fridge and patio heater hire. Motorcaravan service point. Play area. Games room. Security barrier (card access) is locked 11 pm - 7 am. Off site: Pub in nearby Ashurst. Billingshurst and Horsham both 8 miles. Fishing 1 mile, golf or riding 10 miles.

At a glance
Welcome & Ambience	✓✓✓✓	Location	✓✓✓✓✓
Quality of Pitches	✓✓✓✓	Range of Facilities	✓✓✓✓

Directions
Two miles south of the junction of A24 and A272 at Dial Post, turn east by Old Barn Nurseries. Follow signs to site (0.5 miles approx). O.S.GR: TQ153183.

Charges 2004
Per adult	£ 3.50 - £ 4.50
child (5-14 yrs)	£ 1.75
pitch	£ 5.50 - £ 9.50

Senior citizen discounts. Barrier Pass (£10 deposit).

Reservations
Made with £10 p/night deposit. Tel: 01403 710923. Email: enquiries@honeybridgepark.co.uk

Open
All year.

Spacious 15 acre park adjacent to woodlands. Ideal touring base. Highest standards maintained, EHU's hard standing and grass pitches. Heated amenity blocks, disabled facilities, licensed shop, gas, take away, children's play area. Seasonal pitches. Dogs welcome. Open all year.

Follow brown international signs from A24 Horsham-Worthing trunk road by Old Barn Nursery

Honeybridge Lane, Dial Post, Nr Horsham, West Sussex RH13 8NX
Tel/Fax: 01403 710923 Email: enquires@honeybridgepark.co.uk Website: www.honeybridgepark.co.uk

UK2930 Sheepcote Valley Caravan Club Site

East Brighton Park, Brighton BN2 5TS (East Sussex)

The Caravan Club's Sheepcote Valley Site is a first class base from which to enjoy the many attractions both in the town and this area of the south coast. The site occupies a quiet situation in an almost fully enclosed valley in the South Downs, a mile north of the interesting Marina which has a superstore and good variety of shops and restaurants. A wide tarmac road winds its way through the site, with pitches on either side, leading to terraces with grass pitches on the lower slopes of the valley. With a total of 275 pitches, 170 have electricity (16A), 86 have hardstanding and 11 have water, drainage and TV sockets. Three grass terraces are for tents and these have parking nearby. Although there are a number of trees, many are young so do not yet provide shade. Flower beds add to the attractiveness of the site.

Facilities
Two well built, brick, heated sanitary blocks have excellent facilities including all washbasins in private cabins. In the main season a third timber clad building provides additional services near the tent places. Well equipped room for wheel chair users, another one for walking disabled. Two baby rooms. Laundry. Motorcaravan service point. Gas available. Play area with safety base. Internet terminal.

Open
All year.

At a glance
Welcome & Ambience	✓✓✓✓	Location	✓✓✓✓
Quality of Pitches	✓✓✓✓	Range of Facilities	✓✓✓

Directions
Site is in eastern Brighton, signed from A259 coast road. At Palace Pier roundabout take A259 towards Newhaven for 1.25 miles, join dual carriageway and after 100 yards left (Arundel Road), then right into Wilson Avenue. After 100 yards, turn right into East Brighton Park. Site is 0.5 miles. O.S.GR: TQ341043.

Charges 2004
Per adult	£ 4.00 - £ 5.00
child (5-16 yrs)	£ 1.10 - £ 1.80
pitch incl. electricity (non-member)	£ 9.00 - £ 12.00

Reservations
Made with £5 deposit. Tel: 01273 626546.

UK2900 Horam Manor Touring Park

Horam, Heathfield TN21 0YD (East Sussex)

In the heart of the Sussex countryside, this rural touring park is part of (but under separate management from) Horam Manor which has a farm museum, nature trail and the well known Merrydown Winery. The 90 pitches, 54 with electrical connections, are on two open meadows joined by a tarmac/gravel access road. The field nearer reception has an undulating surface, the second field is flatter but slopes - levelling blocks are needed for motorcaravans. Pitches are of generous size, those with electricity being numbered and marked. Both areas are ringed with a variety of mainly tall trees. The whole park, back from the main Eastbourne to Tunbridge Wells road, is a haven of peace and tranquillity. The site has no shop but the village is close, with supermarkets in Heathfield (3 miles). Two inns are within walking distance and the Lakeside cafe at the Farm Centre serves drinks and snacks (9.30 am. - 5 pm). The Craft Centre to the side of the site has some interesting exhibits, farm machinery and riding stables. The nature trail (with free access for campers) has walks ranging from 30 to 90 mimutes in length (written guide available). Fishing is possible in 10 lakes on the estate (adults £4).

Facilities

The modern, well built toilet block (unheated) is fully equipped and is said to be cleaned four times daily. There are some curtained cubicles now. Family room (access by key from reception) with shower, washbasin and toilet, suitable also for disabled visitors. Laundry and washing up sinks. Washing machine. Gas available. Play area. Up to two dogs per unit are accepted. Off site: Tennis (small fee) 200 yds. Golf within 1 mile.

Open

1 March - 31 October.

At a glance

Welcome & Ambience	✓✓✓✓	Location	✓✓✓✓
Quality of Pitches	✓✓✓✓	Range of Facilities	✓✓✓

Directions

Entry to the park is signed at the recreation ground at southern edge of Horam village. O.S.GR: TQ577169.

Charges 2004

Per unit incl. 2 adults, 2 children under 18)	£ 12.50
extra adult	£ 3.50
extra child	£ 1.15
electricity	£ 1.95 - £ 2.45
extended awning	£ 2.50
dog (max 2)	free

No credit cards.

Reservations

Contact park. Tel: 01435 813662.
Email: camp@horam-manor.co.uk

UK2920 Bay View Caravan & Camping Park

Old Martello Road, Pevensey Bay BN24 6DX (East Sussex)

The Adams family have developed this friendly beach-side park with care over the last few years, a fact which is obvious as soon as you arrive and see the tidy state of everything. There are 5.5 acres of flat grass divided into two separate areas and surrounded by a low bank and newly planted trees, which give shelter if it's windy. Careful use of fencing adds to the attractiveness, whilst also keeping the rabbits off the flowers. The 79 pitches (80 sq.m, 54 with 10/16A electricity and 10 with hardstanding) are neatly marked out by numbered posts, while five caravan holiday homes for hire are at the back of the park. Visitors can enjoy all the attractions of Sussex as well as swimming, fishing, windsurfing and sailing. It is an ideal site for a family beach holiday. A newly developed cycle/walking path leads to Pevensey Bay and Eastbourne. A marina complex is under construction nearby.

Facilities

The toilet facilities are housed in two superior 'portacabin' style buildings which are kept very clean and are heated when necessary. Showers on payment (20p). Laundry room with washing machine, dryer, spin dryer, iron and board, plus tourist information. Motorcaravan service point. Well stocked, good value shop (open long hours as the owners live next to it). Gas available. Popular, well made and fenced play area with bark surface and adventure equipment (10 years and under). Winter caravan storage. Off site: Indoor swimming pool 1 mile. Golf 2 miles.

Open

4 April - 5 October.

At a glance

Welcome & Ambience	✓✓✓✓✓	Location	✓✓✓✓
Quality of Pitches	✓✓✓✓	Range of Facilities	✓✓✓

Directions

Park is about 1 mile west of Pevensey Bay and 2 miles east of Eastbourne, off the A259 Pevensey Bay road. O.S.GR: TQ648028.

Charges 2004

Per unit incl. 1or 2 persons and electricity	£ 12.40 - £ 14.25
2 person tent	£ 9.40 - £ 10.90
extra adult	£ 2.40 - £ 2.85
child (2-16 yrs)	£ 1.70 - £ 2.00
dog	£ 0.70 - £ 1.10

Couples and families only. No commercial vehicles, large vans or pick-ups. No credit cards

Reservations

Made with deposit (£25). Tel: 01323 768688.
Email: holidays@bay-view.co.uk

UK2960 Crazy Lane Tourist Caravan Park

Crazy Lane, Sedlescombe, Battle TN33 0QT (East Sussex)

Formerly known as Whydown Farm, this peaceful, traditional style, two acre park has just 36 pitches arranged on grassy terraces, all with electric hook-ups (5/10A) and 4 with hardstanding. It may be best to phone to make sure space is available before travelling long distances. Set in the heart of '1066 country' with its historical links, other local attractions include the very pretty village of Sedlescombe, two steam railways, an organic vineyard, Rye with its quaint cobbled streets and of course Battle itself. This is an ideal park for couples.

Facilities
The tiny but well maintained sanitary unit has recently been refurbished. It includes controllable hot showers (on payment), laundry facilities with washing machine and dryer, dishwashing sinks and a suite for disabled visitors. Shop at reception.

Open
March - October.

At a glance
Welcome & Ambience	✓✓✓✓✓	Location	✓✓✓✓
Quality of Pitches	✓✓✓✓	Range of Facilities	✓✓✓

Directions
From A21, 100 yards south of junction with B2244 (to Sedlescombe) turn into Crazy Lane, where site is signed. O.S.GR: TQ782170.

Charges 2004
Per unit incl. 2 adults, electricity	£ 13.00 - £ 16.00
tent pitch incl. 2 adults	£ 11.00 - £ 13.50
extra person over 12 yrs	£ 1.50
No credit cards.	

Reservations
Contact site for details. Tel:01424 870147
Email: info@crazylane.co.uk

UK2965 Brakes Coppice Park

Forewood Lane, Crowhurst, Battle TN33 9AB (East Sussex)

Brakes Coppice Park is a small and secluded site set in woodland just a mile away from historic Battle. Reached by a winding private track, it is well sign-posted to prevent visitors taking a wrong turn to the nearby farm of the same name. The site has 30 grassy pitches, 21 with 6 amp electricity, in a gently sloping field. Some pitches are available in a second field at the back of the site, where there is also a small fishing lake. As well as fishing visitors can enjoy walking in the surrounding woods and there is a simple wooden swing and a seesaw in the main field for younger children. The reception building at the site entrance also doubles as the shop and is well stocked with basic essentials. A wealth of information about the attractions of 1066 country can also be found here.

Facilities
The single toilet block is basic but clean with coin operated showers. Laundry room with washing machine, dryer, iron and board. Dishwashing sinks with hot water are outside but under cover. Shop. Gas available. Fishing permits from reception. Off site: Pubs and shops in Crowhurst and Battle.

Open
1 March - 31 October.

At a glance
Welcome & Ambience	✓✓✓✓✓	Location	✓✓✓✓
Quality of Pitches	✓✓✓	Range of Facilities	✓✓✓

Directions
From Battle take A2100 towards Hastings for 2 miles. Turn right on Telham Lane (Crowhurst). Continue into Foreword Lane and turn left on track shortly after sign for Crowhurst village. O.S.GR: TQ764131.

Charges 2004
Per pitch with 2 adults	£ 9.00 - £ 11.50
child (5-15 yrs)	£ 0.50
dog	£ 0.25

Reservations
Made with deposit, telephone site for details.
Tel: 01424 830322. Email: brakesco@btinternet.com

UK3120 Gate House Wood Touring Park

Ford Lane, Wrotham Heath, Sevenoaks TN15 7SD (Kent)

This sheltered park, which opened for its first season in '98, has been created in a former quarry where all the pitches are on well drained grass. A spacious paved entrance with a new reception building and well stocked shop, leads on to the park itself. The 60 pitches are level and open with a few small trees, two brick built barbecue units, and 40 electric hook-ups (10A). A playground has swings, seesaw and a slide, all set on a safety base, and the entire site is enclosed by grassy banks on three sides, with a wild flower walk around the top.

Facilities
Comprehensive toilet facilities are smart and well maintained. Well equipped family room, which is also designed for disabled people. Laundry and dishwashing room at one end of the heated building. No dogs or other pets. Caravans/motorcaravans greater than 25' overall or commercial vehicles not accepted. Off site: Within walking distance are three pubs and a good Cantonese restaurant.

Open
1 April - end October.

At a glance
Welcome & Ambience	✓✓✓✓	Location	✓✓✓
Quality of Pitches	✓✓✓	Range of Facilities	✓✓✓

Directions
From M26 junction 2a, take A20 eastwards towards Wrotham Heath and Maidstone. Just past junction with A25, opposite the Royal Oak pub, turn left into Ford Lane to park on left. O.S.GR: TQ630580.

Charges 2004
Per unit incl. 2 adults	£ 9.00 - £ 11.50
with electricity	£ 11.00 - £ 13.50
No credit cards.	

Reservations
Made with deposit (£5 for 3 days, £10 over 3 days or £10 p/week for longer stays). Tel: 01732 843062.
Email: liane_allsop@gatehousewood.freeserve.co.

UK2975 ShearBarn Holiday Park

Barley Lane, Hastings TN35 5DX (East Sussex)

If you wish to enjoy the lively town of Hastings, with its pubs and amusements, then ShearBarn may well be for you. It is situated on top of a hill on the eastern edge of Hastings with attractive views over the bay and a wooded valley as you approach the park. There are two distinct areas and you arrive at the holiday home park first where you will find the reception. Close by is Barney's Bar complex with a restaurant and amusement arcade upstairs and a pleasant bar area downstairs with real ale and entertainment in high season. Also here are a launderette, shop and a good children's play area with seating for parents. Further up the hill and through a barrier (card entry), you come to the touring section. This consists of open grass areas with around 140 pitches marked by stones. Some are reasonably flat, others sloping, and 100 have electrical connections with water points around. There is a separate, large area for tents at the top of the park where a torch might be useful.

Facilities

The first sanitary building (accessible by card), just inside the touring area, has undergone some modernization and is the best of the three main units. The others are in need of refurbishment. There is a small unit for the tent area in addition to its main one. Chemical disposal points are outside the entrance to the first block and at the back of the other two. Dishwashing rooms. Barney's Bar serves meals and takeaways all season (weekends only outside peak times). Amusement arcade. Shop. Launderette. Off site: There are walks right from the park, with public footpaths running through it and the beach is about 15 minutes walk down the hill. Public transport is roughly 0.25 miles away. Golf and fishing are both within 2 miles.

At a glance

Welcome & Ambience	✓✓✓✓	Location	✓✓✓
Quality of Pitches	✓✓✓	Range of Facilities	✓✓✓

Directions

Follow the A21 to Hastings and signs to the seafront then turn left. Follow the road round to the Stables Theatre then right onto Harold Road. Turn right again into Gurth Road and up the hill into Barley Lane. The park is well signed.

Charges 2004

Per unit	£ 14.00 - £ 16.00
incl. electricity	£ 18.00 - £ 20.00
2-person tent	£ 9.00 - £ 11.00
large tent	£ 12.00 - £ 18.00
dog	£ 2.00
Deposit for touring field access card (£5).	

Reservations

Reservations are advised for peak times with a deposit of £10 per week or part week. Tel: 01424 423583. Email: enquiries@haulfryn.co.uk

Open

1 April - 31 October.

UK3030 Tanner Farm Touring Caravan & Camping Park

Goudhurst Road, Marden TN12 9ND (Kent)

Tanner Farm is a top class, quality park, developed as part of a family working farm in the heart of the Weald of Kent. It is surrounded by orchards, oast houses, lovely countryside and delightful small villages and the owners are much concerned with conserving the natural beauty of the environment. Visitors are welcome to walk around the farm and see the Shire horses and other animals. The park extends over 15 acres, most of which is level and part a gentle slope. The grass meadowland has been semi-landscaped by planting saplings, etc. which units back onto, as the owners don't wish to regiment pitches into rows. Places are numbered but not marked, allowing plenty of space between units which, with large open areas, gives a pleasant, comfortable atmosphere. There are 100 pitches, all with 16A electricity, 26 with hardstanding, 20 with water tap and 1 with waste water point also. The farm drive links the park with the B2079 and a group of refurbished oast houses (listed heritage buildings) with a duck pond in front, along with rare pigs, pygmy goats, lambs, etc. make a focal point. The park is a member of the Caravan Club's Associated Site scheme although non-members are also very welcome.

Facilities

Two heated, well cared for sanitary units include some washbasins in private cubicles in both units. Purpose built facilities for disabled visitors. A bathroom (£1 token) and baby facilities have been added in the newer block (this block is not opened Nov - Easter). Small launderette. Dishwashing sinks. Motorcaravan service point. Small shop/reception (opening hours and stock limited in winter) and reception. Gas supplies. Small children's play area. Fishing on site (on payment). Torches may be useful. Caravan storage all year. Off site: Riding and golf within 6 miles, leisure centres and sailing facilities near and good shopping facilities at Maidstone and Tunbridge Wells. Many National Trust attractions in the area (Sissinghurst, Scotney Castle, Bodiam Castle).

At a glance

Welcome & Ambience	✓✓✓	Location	✓✓✓✓✓
Quality of Pitches	✓✓✓✓✓	Range of Facilities	✓✓✓✓

Directions

Park is 2.5 miles south of Marden on B2079 towards Goudhurst. O.S.GR: TQ732417.

Charges 2004

Per unit incl. electriciry	£ 4.00 - £ 7.00
all service pitch (extra charge)	£ 2.00
adult	£ 3.30 - £ 4.80
child (5-16 yrs)	£ 1.10 - £ 1.60
tent pitch	£ 3.00
Only one car per pitch permitted.	

Reservations

Essential for high season and B.Hs, recommended for other times. Made with deposit £10. A popular park, early reservation is advised. Tel: 01622 832399. Email: enquiries@tannerfarmpark.co.uk

Open

All year.

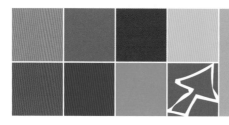

Planning your
next short break?

don't forget to see our directory
ON PAGE 294

UK3050 Pine Lodge Touring Park

Ashford Road, Hollingbourne, Maidstone ME17 1XH (Kent)

Set in the heart of Kent, near Leeds Castle and central for the historical and scenic attractions of this county, this park is under new ownership. On a slight slope, the rectangular field is surrounded by rolling hills, farmland and trees. A tarmac, one-way road circles the site with pitches set against hedges around the perimeter and around a figure of eight in the centre with picnic areas. Trees have been planted for decoration and shade. Of the 88 pitches, all have electricity (16A), 35 have hardstanding and 2 are serviced. It is a useful park near the main London - Folkestone - Dover M20 and access from the A20 road is wide, but there may be background traffic noise. The park is very convenient for events staged at Leeds Castle and is a useful overnight stop between London and the Channel ports.

Facilities

Good sanitary facilities at the entrance to the park include metered showers (20p coin), laundry and washing up facilities, plus a shower and toilet room for disabled visitors. Motorcaravan services. Basic supplies and gas are available from reception plus tourist information. Small play area. Dogs are not accepted. Off site: Golf 0.5 mile. Local shops 1 mile (Bearsted) or 3.5 miles (Maidstone). Riding 2 miles. Fishing 5 miles.

Open

All year.

At a glance

Welcome & Ambience	✓✓✓✓	Location	✓✓✓
Quality of Pitches	✓✓✓✓	Range of Facilities	✓✓✓

Directions

From M20 junction 8, at A20 roundabout, turn towards Bearsted and Maidstone and park is about 0.5 miles on the left. O.S.GR: TQ808548.

Charges 2004

Per unit incl. 2 adults, electricity	£ 12.25 - £ 14.25
extra adult	£ 4.00
child (3-14 yrs)	£ 1.00
awning or extra tent	£ 1.00
Less 10% for 7 nights or more.	

Reservations

Recommended for bank holidays and special events, contact park. Tel: 01622 730018.
Email: booking@pinelodgetouringpark.co.uk

Pine Lodge — We are open all year round for Touring and Camping
01622 730018
Ashford Road Hollingbourne Kent ME17 1XH
for more information visit: www.pinelodgetouringpark.co.uk

UK3040 Broadhembury Caravan & Camping Park

Steeds Lane, Kingsnorth, Ashford TN26 1NQ (Kent)

In quiet countryside just outside Ashford, near to Folkestone and the ferries, this well landscaped, sheltered park takes 65 touring units of any type, plus 25 caravan holiday homes (5 for hire). All pitches are on level, neatly cut grass backing onto hedges, 50 have electrical connections (10A), 4 are fully serviced and have 16A electricity, 8 have double hardstanding plus a grass area for an awning. The park is friendly and popular and often becomes full in the main season, with a good proportion of continental visitors, so reservation is advisable. Security arrangements are excellent - the gates are closed at 11 pm. in high season with coded entry. For those who would like a trip to France, the new International Railway Terminal is at Ashford (Paris in 2 hours) - take your passport. A member of the Best of British group.

Facilities

The single small well equipped toilet block is kept very clean, and can be heated in cool weather. Alongside is a new campers' kitchen, fully enclosed with dishwashing sinks, plus a microwave, fridge and freezer, all free of charge. Small laundry room. Motorcaravan service point. Well stocked shop and comprehensive tourist information. TV and pool room, games room with table tennis. Two children's playgrounds (grass or wood-chip bases) and a play field away from the touring area. Dog exercise field - up to two dogs per pitch are accepted. Off site: Fishing 500 m, bicycle hire or riding 2 miles and golf 1 mile.

Open

All year.

At a glance

Welcome & Ambience	✓✓✓✓✓	Location	✓✓✓✓
Quality of Pitches	✓✓✓✓	Range of Facilities	✓✓✓✓

Directions

From M20 junction 10 take A2070. After 2 miles follow sign for Kingsnorth. Turn left at second crossroads in Kingsnorth village. O.S.GR: TR010382.

Charges 2004

Per unit incl. 2 persons	£ 12.00 - £ 16.00
extra adult	£ 3.00
child (5-16 yrs)	£ 2.00
electricity (10A)	free
'super' pitch supplement	£ 4.00 - £ 8.00
Less 10% outside July/Aug. for bookings of 7 nights or more.	

Reservations

Essential for B.Hs and peak season and made with £5 per night deposit (min. 3 nights at Easter or Spr. B.H). Balance 21 days before arrival for B.Hs, on arrival at other times. Tel: 01233 620859.
Email: enquiries@broadhembury.co.uk

127

UK3130 Sandwich Leisure Park

Woodnesborough Road, Sandwich CT13 0AA (Kent)

A pleasant well kept site, with modern facilities, this park is in one of England's historic old Cinque ports and within walking distance of all its attractions, shops and services. From the entrance barrier by reception, you drive through the area of privately owned holiday homes, to reach the main touring field which has 99 pitches, all on grass with electric hook-ups (10A). There are 18 multi-service pitches with electricity, TV, water and waste water drain, nine of which have hardstandings. A second field is being developed for more tourist pitches, and should be ready for the 2003 season. A railway runs along one side of the site and there is a little rail noise at times during the day but it is quiet at night. The site is well lit at night and all roads are well surfaced. Children will love the large, fenced adventure playground with its tube slides etc. which is on a bark surface, and in the mobile home park area the more adventurous will find the aerial rope-way.

Facilities

Stylish new sanitary building (completed in 2001) provides washbasins in cubicles, controllable hot showers, plus a room which can be heated with some family suites and a full suite for disabled people (radar key). Dishwashing sinks under cover at each end of the building. Laundry in reception building with washing machines, dryers, spin dryer and ironing facility. Adventure playground. Note; skateboarding, rollerblading, skating, scooters and cycling are not permitted on site. Off site: Supermarket 5 minutes walk from the site entrance. Sandwich has a market on Thursdays. In and around the town are a folk museum, Roman fort, nature reserve, swing bridge, the old gaol, weavers, a sports and leisure centre and further afield is the Dreamland Fun Park. Fishing 3 miles, golf and beach 2 miles.

At a glance

Welcome & Ambience	✓✓✓✓	Location	✓✓✓✓
Quality of Pitches	✓✓✓✓	Range of Facilities	✓✓✓✓

Directions

Sandwich is mid-way between Ramsgate and Deal, with access from the A256. The town's streets are narrow and there is a one-way system in operation. Follow the brown campsite signs from anywhere in the town centre, the site is to the west of town, just after a railway level crossing. O.S.GR: TR 330575.

Charges 2004

Per pitch incl. all persons	£ 11.30 - £ 14.00
electricity	£ 1.70
multi-service pitch, plus	£ 4.70
awning	£ 1.00
one man tent	£ 5.50 - £ 8.00

Reservations

Advisable for BHs and peak season.
Tel: 01304 612681.
Email: info@coastandcountryleisure.com

Open

1 March - 31 October.

UK3070 Canterbury Camping & Caravanning Club Site

Bekesbourne Lane, Canterbury CT3 4AB (Kent)

Situated just off the A257 Sandwich road, about 1.5 miles from the centre of Canterbury, this site is an ideal base for exploring Canterbury and the north Kent coast, as well as being a good stop-over to and from the Dover ferries, and the Folkestone Channel Tunnel terminal. There are 200 pitches, 86 with electric hook-ups (10/16A) and, except at the very height of the season, you are likely to find a pitch, although not necessarily with electricity. Most of the pitches are on well kept grass with hundreds of saplings planted, but there are also 21 pitches with hardstanding. Some pitches do slope so blocks are advised. A good sized overnight area for late arrivals can be reached even when the barriers are down. The site is adjacent to Bekepond nature reserve and within walking distance of Howletts Zoo. Although the busy A257 is close, there is minimal noise from the traffic. Note: power lines cross the site.

Facilities

Two modern toilet blocks, the main one with a laundry room, a room for dishwashing, an outside vegetable preparation area, and recycling bins. Motorcaravan service point. Reception stocks a small range of essential foods, milk and gas. Excellent tourist information room. Children's play area with equipment on bark chippings. Off site: Golf adjacent, bicycle hire 2 miles.

Open

All year.

At a glance

Welcome & Ambience	✓✓✓✓✓	Location	✓✓✓✓
Quality of Pitches	✓✓✓✓	Range of Facilities	✓✓✓

Directions

From A2 take Canterbury exit and follow signs for Sandwich - A257. After passing Howe military barracks turn right into Bekesbourne Lane opposite golf course. O.S.GR: TR172577.

Charges 2005

Per adult	£ 4.30 - £ 6.40
child (6-18 yrs)	£ 1.90
non- member pitch fee	£ 5.00

Reservations

Necessary and made with deposit; contact site or Central Reservations 0870 243 3331.
Tel: 01227 463216.

UK3090 Black Horse Farm Caravan Club Site

385 Canterbury Road, Densole, Folkestone CT18 7BG (Kent)

This neat, tidy and attractive six-acre park, owned by the Caravan Club, is situated amidst farming country in the village of Densole on the Downs just 4 miles north of Folkestone, 8 northeast of Dover and 11 south of Canterbury. This makes it ideal for a night stop travelling to or from the continent via the Channel Ports or the Tunnel, or as a base for visiting the many attractions of this part of southeast England. Accessed directly from the A260, the tarmac entrance road leads past reception towards the top field which has gravel hardstanding pitches with a grass area for awnings (possibly some road noise), past hedging to the smaller middle area with 8 hardstandings, then to the large bottom field which has been redeveloped to give 140 large pitches, all with electricity (16A). A late arrivals area and pitches for 'one-nighters' are located in the top field. Opposite the entrance is a general store and newsagent and within 100 m, a pub and filling station.

Facilities

The carefully thought out and well constructed toilet blocks, one below reception and the other at the far end of the site, have washbasins in private cabins with curtains, good sized shower compartments, a baby room and facilities for disabled visitors, laundry and washing-up facilities, all well heated in cool weather. Motorcaravan service point. Gas supplies. Play area. Caravan storage. Off site: Riding 1 mile, golf or fishing 5 miles.

At a glance

Welcome & Ambience	✓✓✓✓	Location	✓✓✓✓
Quality of Pitches	✓✓✓✓	Range of Facilities	✓✓✓

Directions

Directly by the A260 Folkestone-Canterbury road, 2 miles north of junction with A20. Follow signs for Canterbury. O.S.GR: TR211418.

Charges 2004

Per adult	£ 3.30 - £ 4.80
child (5-16 yrs)	£ 1.10 - £ 1.60
pitch incl. electricity (non-member)	£ 8.00 - £ 11.00

Reservations

Advised at all times - contact the Warden.
Tel: 01303 892665.

Open

All year.

UK3060 Yew Tree Park

Stone Street, Petham, Canterbury CT4 5PL (Kent)

Yew Tree Park is a small, quiet site located in the heart of the Kent countryside overlooking the Chartham Downs. Just 5 miles south of Canterbury and 8 miles north of the M20, it is ideally placed either to explore the delights of the ancient city or the many attractions of eastern and coastal Kent. Its nearness to the Channel ports also makes it useful for a night stop on the way to, or on return from, the continent. If catching a late evening ferry you may remain on site after 12 noon for a small payment. With some caravan holiday homes, the site also has 45 pitches for tourers and tents. The 20 with electricity (10A) are marked on mainly level grass either side of the entrance road, the remainder unmarked on a rather attractive, sloping area, left natural with trees and bushes creating cosy little recesses in which to pitch. This neat and tidy park that resident proprietors, Derek and Dee Zanders, have created makes an excellent base away from the hurly-burly of life where you can enjoy the rural scenery and also have the opportunity for walking, riding, visiting local places of interest or for cross-Channel excursions.

Facilities

Two brick-built sanitary blocks (one for each sex) can be heated. Washbasins with warm water from a single tap, and four showers (on payment). Extra toilets on the edge of the camping area. Recently added is a toilet/shower room for families or disabled visitors. Laundry and dishwashing sinks, plus a washing machine, dryer and iron. Gas supplies. Outdoor swimming pool (60 x 30 ft. open June-Sept). Torches may be useful. Dogs are not accepted. Off site: Riding 4 miles, golf 6 miles. Bicycle hire 5 miles. The County cricket ground is 4 miles.

Open

Easter - early October.

At a glance

Welcome & Ambience	✓✓✓	Location	✓✓✓✓
Quality of Pitches	✓✓✓✓	Range of Facilities	✓✓✓

Directions

Park is on B2068 Canterbury-Folkestone road. From south, take exit 11 from the M20. From Canterbury, ignore signs to Petham and Waltham on B2068 and continue towards Folkestone. From either direction, turn into road beside the Chequers Inn, turn left into park and follow road to owners' house/reception. O.S.GR: TR138507.

Charges 2004

Per unit incl. 2 adults	£ 10.00 - £ 14.00
extra adult	£ 2.00 - £ 3.00
child (2-16 yrs)	£ 1.00 - £ 2.00
electricity (deposit required)	£ 2.00 - £ 2.20

Reservations

Made with deposit of £5 per night.
Tel: 01227 700306. Email: info@yewtreepark.com

UK3095 Little Satmar Holiday Park

Winehouse Lane, Capel-le-Ferne, Nr. Folkestone CT18 7JF (Kent)

Capel-le-Ferne is a relatively little known seaside town mid-way between Dover and Folkestone. Little Satmar is a quiet site a short walk from the delightful cliff top paths which run between these towns and which offer fine views across the English Channel. The site is a member of the Keat Farm group and is located about a mile from the village. There are 61 touring pitches, 51 of which have electricity (10A). The pitches generally have a sunny, open setting, a few with rather more shade. Around 78 extra pitches are taken up with mobile homes or chalets, but these are generally in a separate part of the site.

Facilities

Two toilet blocks (one in a 'Portakabin' style unit) are modern and kept very clean and the main block has now been fitted with heating. Washing and drying machines. Shop (with gas). Play area. For more than 1 dog per unit, contact park. Off site: Port Lympne Zoo, seafront funpark nearby.

Open

1 March - 31 October.

At a glance

Welcome & Ambience	✓✓✓✓✓	Location	✓✓✓✓
Quality of Pitches	✓✓✓✓	Range of Facilities	✓✓✓

Directions

Leave A20 Dover - Folkestone road at Capel-le-Ferne exit and follow signs to the village. Site is clearly signed to right afer approx. 0.75 miles. O.S GR: TR256393.

Charges 2004

Per pitch incl. 2 adults	£ 10.00 - £ 12.50
incl. electricity	£ 12.50 - £ 15.00
extra adult	£ 2.50 - £ 3.00
child (5-16 yrs)	£ 1.50 - £ 2.00

Reservations

Advised for high season. Tel: 01303 251188. Email: info@keatfarm.co.uk

UK3110 Quex Caravan Park

Park Road, Birchington CT7 0BL (Kent)

Although there are a fair number of privately owned holiday homes at Quex, they do not intrude on the touring area which is in a sheltered glade under tall trees. There are 60 touring pitches with 48 electric hook-ups (16A). This park does not accept tents. Local attractions include Quex House and gardens, the model village and motor museum at Ramsgate, whilst in the seaside resort of Margate you can walk through 1,000 years of history at the Caves, or visit the Hollywood Bowl. Reception can provide you with a map of the local area. A member of the Best of British group.

Facilities

The central sanitary unit is in a heated chalet style building with all the usual facilities. Dishwashing sinks under cover. Laundry room with sink, washing machine and dryer. Well stocked shop. More than one dog per pitch is accepted by prior arrangement only. Off site: Supermarkets close by. Fishing, golf or riding 3 miles.

Open

7 March - 7 November.

At a glance

Welcome & Ambience	✓✓✓✓	Location	✓✓✓
Quality of Pitches	✓✓✓	Range of Facilities	✓✓✓

Directions

From roundabout at junction of A28 and A299, take A28 east towards Birchington and Margate. At Birchington carry straight on at roundabout by church, then take next right, then right again, and left at mini roundabout. Site is on right in half a mile (well signed). O.S.GR: TR320685.

Charges 2004

Per unit incl. 2 adults	£ 10.00 - £ 12.50
incl. electricity	£ 12.50 - £ 15.00
extra adult	£ 2.50 - £ 3.00
child (5-16 yrs)	£ 1.50 - £ 2.00
dog	£ 1.00

Less 10% for 4 nights booked (and paid for on arrival).

Reservations

Contact site for details. Tel: 01843 841273. Email: info@keatfarm.co.uk

UK3100 Hawthorn Farm Caravan & Camping Site

Martin Mill, Dover CT15 5LA (Kent)

Hawthorn Farm is a large, relaxed park close to Dover. Set in 27 acres, it is an extensive park taking 224 touring units of any type on several large meadows which could accommodate far more, plus 170 privately owned caravan holiday homes in their own areas. Campers not requiring electricity choose their own spot, most staying near the two toilet blocks leaving the farthest fields to those liking solitude. There are 120 pitches with electricity (10/16A), 46 of which are large pitches separated by hedges, the remainder in glades either side of tarmac roads. A well run, relaxed park with plenty of room, mature hedging and trees make an attractive environment. A torch would be useful. Being only 4 miles from Dover docks, it is a very useful park for those using the ferries and is popular with continental visitors. Close to the sea at St Margaret's Bay, it is a fairly quiet situation apart from some rail noise (no trains 23.30 - 05.30). A member of the Best of British group.

Facilities

The heated toilet blocks are well equipped and of good quality, including a WC for disabled visitors and a baby room. Dishwashing and laundry sinks. Launderette. Motorcaravan services. Breakfast and other snacks are served at the shop (all season) and a pub is nearby. Gates close at 8 pm. (10 pm. in July and August) - £10 deposit for card. Caravan storage. Off site: Riding 0.5 miles, golf 3 miles, bicycle hire, fishing and boat launching 4 miles.

Open

1 March - 31 October.

At a glance

Welcome & Ambience	✓✓✓✓✓	Location	✓✓✓
Quality of Pitches	✓✓✓✓	Range of Facilities	✓✓✓

Directions

Park is north of the A258 road (Dover - Deal), with signs to park and Martin Mill where you turn off about 4 miles from Dover. O.S.GR: TR341464.

Charges 2004

Per unit incl. 2 persons	£ 10.00 - £ 12.50
incl. electricity	£ 12.50 - £ 15.00
extra adult	£ 2.50 - £ 3.00

Less 10% for 4 nights booked (and paid for on arrival).

Reservations

Made with deposit (£5 per night, max. £20)
Tel: 01304 852658. Email: info@keatfarm.co.uk

(131)

The largest city in Europe, covering over 600 square miles, London is jam packed with hundreds of magnificent museums, impressive art galleries, historic buildings and monuments, beautiful parks, bustling shopping centres and markets; it really has something to offer everyone.

We have chosen five parks which have easy access to central London, including one in Hertfordshire

Despite its size, London is relatively easy to explore, largely thanks to the efficient underground service. Buses are also very useful and allow you to see the famous sights as you travel, in particular, the open-top tourist buses which ply the streets offer a good introduction to the city. Among London's many landmarks are the Tower of London, Trafalgar Square, Piccadilly Circus, Buckingham Palace, Big Ben and the Houses of Parliament, to name but a few! Running through the heart of London is the River Thames, dividing north and south; over the years many attractions, restaurants and chic bars have appeared along its banks. Being one of the most multicultural cities in the world, there is a huge choice of restaurants offering a diverse variety of cuisine; food markets are dotted all around the capital. Shopping is another major feature of the city, from the famous Harrods store and Harvey Nichols, to commercial Oxford Street and the street markets of Camden town and Portobello Road. If all the crowds become too much then head to one of London's beautiful parks such as St James' Park next to Buckingham Palace, or Hyde Park, where you can take a boat trip along the Serpentine.

Did you know?

One in eight of the UK population live in London and over 200 languages are spoken

The London Underground dates back to 1863 when the first underground railway was opened, from Paddington to Farringdon Street. Today, 150,000 people an hour enter the Tube network

Founded in 1753 the British Museum is the oldest public museum in the world

With 345 steps to the top, the Monument marks the start of the Great Fire of London

London has over 18,000 Licensed Taxis

At over 900 years old, the Tower of London has been a palace, prison, treasury, arsenal and even a zoo. It is now home to the Crown Jewels, which have been housed there since the 14th century

Places of interest

London Eye: world's highest observation wheel, reaching 450 feet. With 32 capsules, carrying 25 passengers in each, it offers breathtaking views

Madame Tussaud's: huge collection of wax figures

Tate Modern: contemporary art gallery housed in a transformed Bankside Power Station

Victoria & Albert Museum: decorative art and design from around the world

Kew Gardens: beautiful botanical gardens, with over 40,000 varieties of plants

London Dungeon: a grisly house of horrors

Hampton Court Palace: one the best palaces in Britain, with maze

British Museum: houses a treasure trove of objects from all over the globe

A MONTH OF LIVE PERFORMANCES, THE EALING SUMMER FESTIVAL INCLUDES COMEDY AND JAZZ FESTIVALS, AN INTERNATIONAL FOOD FAIR, CLASSICAL CONCERTS AND CHILDREN'S SHOWS.

UK3260 Abbey Wood Caravan Club Site

Federation Road, Abbey Wood, London SE2 0LS (London)

Previously run on a lease, the Caravan Club have now been able to buy this strategically situated site and its surrounding woodland. An ambitious redevelopment project is now complete. A secure fence around the perimeter of the site linked to close circuit TV cameras protects the site and re-landscaping left in place the mature trees which gave this site its park like atmosphere. There are 105 level caravan pitches all with 16A electricity and TV aerial connections. Of these, 62 have hardstandings. An additional 42 pitches are provided in high season for motorcaravans and a camping area can accommodate many tents. With a new reception, accommodation for wardens and a late arrivals area, this is a very good provision for a site with easy access to central London. A train service runs every 15 minutes from Abbey Wood station (5 minutes walk) to either Charing Cross or Cannon Street.

Facilities

Three modern, fully equipped toilet blocks, two with under-floor heating, one designed to be open all year, include washbasins in cubicles, baby/toddler washroom, laundry equipment and dishwashing sinks. No facilities for disabled visitors. Motorcaravan service point. Gas. Bread, milk and cold drinks available from reception in high season. Play area. Good travel and information centre (08.30-11.00 hrs) can provide tickets for travel and tourist attractions. Off site: Golf 4 miles. Sports centre at Crook Log, 1 mile.

Reservations

Essential for Easter, Spring B.H. July/Aug with £5 deposit. Tel: 0208 311 7708.

Open

All year.

At a glance

Welcome & Ambience	✓✓✓✓	Location	✓✓✓✓✓
Quality of Pitches	✓✓✓✓✓	Range of Facilities	✓✓✓

Directions

From east on M2/A2 or from central London: on A2 turn off at A221 junction (third exit off the A2) into Danson Road (signed Bexleyheath, Welling and Sidcup). Follow sign Bexleyheath to Crook Log (A207 junction); at traffic lights turn right and immediately left into Brampton Road. In 1.5 miles at traffic lights turn left into Bostal Road (A206); in 0.75 miles at traffic lights turn right into Basildon Road (B213). In 300 yds turn right into McLeod Road, in about 0.5 miles at roundabout turn right into Knee Hill; in 100 yds turn right (second right) into Federation Road. Site on left in 50 yds. From M25, north, west or south approach: leave at junction 2 onto A2 (signed London), then as above. Note: route is well signed with International caravan and camping signs. O.S.GR: TQ472785.

Charges 2004

Per adult	£ 4.00 - £ 5.00
child (5-16 yrs)	£ 1.10 - £ 1.80
pitch incl. electricity (non-member)	£ 9.00 - £ 12.00
Tent campers - apply to site.	

UK3270 Crystal Palace Caravan Club Site

Crystal Palace Parade, London SE19 1UF (London)

The Caravan Club's site at Crystal Palace in south London provides easy access to the city centre and all its many attractions. A pleasant and efficiently run site, it is arranged in terraces overlooking the ruins of the old Crystal Palace, its park and National Sports Centre. It is surprisingly quiet given its location (with the exception of police sirens and over-flying aircraft). In peak season advance booking is always necessary. Most pitches are on gravel hardstanding, so it is particularly useful for out of season stays. There are places for 84 caravans or motorcaravans, all with electricity (16A). Tents are placed on the site's well mown lawns near reception. In summer an overflow area across the approach road (with portacabin style facilities) takes further tents or small motorcaravans. The Crystal Palace park is extensive and provides open spaces for strolls or picnics and plenty of activities for children. The Sports Centre has two swimming pools, tennis and squash courts and gym facilities, with national events in a variety of sports to watch at certain times. The park and the Sports Centre are due for substantial redevelopment and when this begins access will obviously be restricted. An area at the site entrance should be used for arrivals after 10.30 pm.

Facilities

The single toilet block can be heated in cool weather with curtained washbasins for ladies. Facilities for disabled visitors. Laundry room. The block is kept locked and new arrivals are given a key (without deposit). Washing up sinks and neat rubbish bins are outside, under cover. Motorcaravan service facilities. Gas available. Off site: Shops, pubs, etc. 400 yards. Many buses stop outside the site, including services to central London.

Open

All year.

Reservations

Essential at all times and made with £5 deposit - contact site. Tel: 020 8778 7155.

At a glance

Welcome & Ambience	✓✓✓✓	Location	✓✓✓✓
Quality of Pitches	✓✓✓✓✓	Range of Facilities	✓✓✓

Directions

On A205 South Circular road travelling east, pass Dulwich College and golf course on right, turn right at traffic lights (Harvester pub on left). Within 400 yards, at traffic lights, turn right into Sydenham Hill. In 350 yds at roundabout turn left (still Sydenham Hill). Site entrance is 1 mile opposite mini-roundabouts. Travelling west on A205 South Circular, immediately after passing under Catford railway bridge, keep left onto A212 signed Crystal Palace. After 2.75 miles, site entrance is on left at top of Westwood Hill. O.S.GR: TQ341724.

Charges 2004

Per adult	£ 4.00 - £ 5.00
child (5-16 yrs)	£ 1.10 - £ 1.80
pitch incl. electricity (non-member)	£ 9.00 - £ 12.00
Tent campers - apply to site.	

UK3230 Lee Valley Camping & Caravanning Park

Meridian Way, Edmonton, London N9 0AS (London)

Certainly one of the only sites in this guide with a multiplex cinema just outside the gate, you are greeted here by an attractive entrance with flower displays. The site offers 165 spacious level pitches, with hardstandings and 110 with electricity. The pitches are well laid out around a large field and there is a tent area just behind two grassy mounds. The grass and gardens are well trimmed and kept very tidy. There is a small kitchen facility and eating area with TV, for tent campers. The site also offers hook-up points for tents. The cinema complex incorporates a popular restaurant and bar, and from here you can hop on a bus to Edmonton Green or Ponders End station from where there is a regular service into central London (journey time around 40 minutes). The friendly site managers have detailed information about the various Travel Card schemes available. Alternatively, historic Waltham Abbey, Epping Forest and the 1,000 acre River Lee Country Park are all within easy access. This is a popular site, very well looked after and kept clean and tidy by site managers, this is a peaceful stop within easy reach of the city.

Facilities
Two modern, heated toilet blocks include spacious showers and two large en-suite units for disabled people. All facilities are accessed by combination locks. Dishwashing. Laundry. Motorcaravan service point. Kitchen. Shop. Play area. Table tennis, tennis and badminton. Tents for hire. Off site: Cinema, restaurant and bar at entrance. Supermarket 0.5 miles. Fishing 0.5 miles. Golf adjacent. Riding 4 miles.

Open
All year except Christmas, Boxing and New Year's Day.

At a glance
Welcome & Ambience	✓✓✓✓✓	Location	✓✓✓✓✓
Quality of Pitches	✓✓✓✓	Range of Facilities	✓✓✓

Directions
From M25 take exit 25 and follow signs for the city. At the first set of traffic lights turn left, signposted to Freezywater. Continue straight for approximately 6 miles. Follow signs for Lee Valley Leisure Complex. After roundabout with flags, turn left at second set of traffic lights onto the complex. O.S.GR: TQ357940.

Charges 2004
Per adult	£ 6.00
child	£ 2.50
electricity	£ 2.50
dog	£ 1.50

Reservations
Contact site. Tel: 020 8803 6900. Email: leisurecentre@leevalleypark.org.uk

UK3250 Lee Valley Campsite

Sewardstone Road, Chingford, London E4 7RA (London)

This attractive site provides an excellent base from which to visit London, having both easy access to the M25 and excellent public transport links into the centre of London. Close to Epping Forest in the heart of the Lee Valley, this site is on a hillside overlooking the King George reservoir in a very pleasant and relaxed setting. Like its sister sites, it is understandably very popular with foreign tourers. With capacity for 200 units of all types the site is mostly level, with several bush sheltered avenues and plenty of trees throughout. There are 20 pitches with tarmac hardstanding and 100 with electricity (10A). Current redevelopment work will include a kitchen area for tent campers. Just outside the gate is the bus stop (reception have full details of good value Travel Card schemes). The bus (no. 215) will take you to Walthamstow Central Underground station from where a frequent service runs to central London. Alternatively you can park at South Woodford or Chingford stations and use the train for London visits. Staff are very pleasant and helpful.

Facilities
Three blocks offer good facilities (one is heated in low season), all recently totally refurbished. Good en-suite room for disabled visitors, dishwashing, laundry. Motorcaravan service point. Well stocked shop. Gas available. Children's playground. Off site: Waltham Abbey 3 miles, shops 1 mile. Fishing 500 yards. River Lee Country Park nearby. 9 hole golf 1 mile, 18 hole golf 3 miles. Riding 1 mile.

Open
Easter - 27 October.

At a glance
Welcome & Ambience	✓✓✓✓	Location	✓✓✓✓
Quality of Pitches	✓✓✓✓	Range of Facilities	✓✓✓

Directions
From M25 exit 26 (site signed) take A112 to Chingford and site is on right in 3 miles. From A10 take A110 signed Chingford. After passing between reservoirs, at next traffic lights turn left on A112. Site is on left after 1 mile (just over brow of hill). O.S. GR: TQ378970.

Charges 2004
Per adult	£ 5.95
child (under 16 yrs)	£ 2.65
electricity	£ 2.30
dog	£ 1.50
Min charge £8.60 per unit/night	

Reservations
Any length up to 14 days with £5 deposit. Tel: 020 8529 5689. Email: scs@leevalleypark.org.uk

UK3210 Lee Valley Caravan Park

Essex Road, Dobbs Weir, Hoddesdon EN11 0AS (Hertfordshire)

Right on the banks of the River Lee and with easy acces to the 1,000 acre River Lee Country Park, this site offers a large open touring field which is very level. Pitches are well spaced around the outer edge of the field, with a tent area in the centre, with an additional small tent field on the river bank for the keen angler. Of the 100 touring pitches, 36 have 10A electricity. There is a private mobile home area adjacent. Although the site has very few trees, those that are there give some shade and the perimeter trees are tall enough to keep out any noise from the nearby industrial area. The managers work hard to keep the site clean and tidy and they have planted some very attractive tubs and pots around the site. Just outside the site and across the road is the Weir with a large picnic area and even a pub - at weekends and holiday times this spot can get very busy.

Facilities

The large toilet block is old but has been refurbished to provide clean and tidy facilities (all key access). Excellent en-suite disabled room. Dishwashing, laundry, drying area. Motorcaravan service point. Shop with camping accessories and sweets. Snack bar (weekends only). Play area. Barbecue area. Fishing. Twin axle caravans are not accepted. Off site: Hoddesdon 1.5 miles, supermarket 1 mile. Swimming pool 2 miles. Pub and restaurant 100 yards. Cycling and walking from the site. RSPB Rye Meads Nature Reserve. Nearest station is at Broxbourne (10 minutes by car) with frequent fast trains to central London. Hatfield House and Hertford are both within easy access.

Open

1 March - 31 October.

At a glance

Welcome & Ambience	✓✓✓✓	Location	✓✓✓✓
Quality of Pitches	✓✓✓✓	Range of Facilities	✓✓✓

Directions

Take exit 25 from M25 and then north on A10 for 4 miles; take the Hoddesdon exit, turn left at second roundabout following signs for Dobbs Weir and park is on the right within 1 mile. O.S.GR: TL383082.

Charges 2004

Per adult	£ 5.80
child (3-16 yrs)	£ 2.30
electricity	£ 2.50
dog	£ 1.50

Min charge £7.90 (but not appled to backpackers). Checking out time 5 pm.

Reservations

Only necessary for electric pitches and made with £5 deposit - write to park for reservation form. (For information contact PO Box 88, Enfield, Middlesex. Tel: 01992 462090. Email: caravanpark@leevalleypark.org.uk

The East of England is a perfect mix of soft and gentle countryside, ancient cities, historical towns, and storybook villages. Its coastline is largely untouched and studded with nature reserves, ideal for bird-watching, while the traditional beach resorts offer old-fashioned seaside fun.

This region includes the counties of Essex, Suffolk, Norfolk, Cambridgeshire, Hertfordshire and Bedfordshire

Bedfordshire and Hertfordshire are the smallest counties in the region, with peaceful canals, undulating countryside with chalk downs, and some of the greatest stately homes in the country. Essex is full of quaint villages with a smattering of old towns and traditional seasides resorts, including Colchester and Southend-on-Sea. The river Cam winds its way through Cambridgeshire; punting along the river in Cambridge is a good way to relax and take in the many famous university buildings that dominate the waterfront along the 'Backs'. Further along the river is the ancient cathedral city of Ely, once an island before the Fen drainage. The flat Fenland has a network of rivers and canals, ideal for narrow-boat trips, as are the Norfolk Broads. Norfolk itself is very flat, sparsely populated and tranquil, popular with walkers and cyclists, while the numerous nature reserves attract a variety of wildlife. It also has a beautiful coastline; the seaside towns of Great Yarmouth and Hunstanton are major draws. This unspoilt coastline stretches into Suffolk, 'Constable Country'. Full of space, with picturesque villages set amongst lush green countryside, dotted with timbered cottages and ruined abbeys, the county is home to Newmarket, the horse racing capital of the world.

Did you know?

Newmarket has been recognised as the Headquarters of Racing for over 300 years

The highest point of the East of England is the Dunstable Downs at 244 metres (801 feet)

Colchester is Britain's oldest recorded town with Europe's largest Norman Castle keep

The artist John Constable was born in 1776 in the village of East Bergholt. Nearby Flatford Mill, was portrayed in his most famous scene 'The Haywain'

Peterhouse is the first Cambridge college, founded in 1284 by the Bishop of Ely

Epping Forest was the haunt of the renowned highwayman, Dick Turpin

Places of interest

Essex: Clacton-on-Sea; Walton-on-the-Naze, with nature reserve; Colchester, Epping; Chelmsford

Suffolk: Ipswich; Felixstowe; Lowestoft; Bury St Edmonds; village of Clare with country park

Norfolk: Norwich, seaside resort of Cromer; old fishing village of Sheringham, Sandringham Palace near King's Lynn; Banham Zoo

Cambridgeshire: King's College and Chapel in Cambridge plus Fitzwilliam Museum; Peterborough; Imperial War Museum in Duxford; Huntingdon; Wildfowl & Wetland Trust near Wisbech

Hertfordshire: St Albans; stately homes and gardens of Knebworth House and Hatfield House

Bedfordshire: Bedford, Woburn with Abbey and safari park; Whipsnade Wild Animal Park; Shuttleworth Collection near Biggleswade

tip

NOW IN ITS 40TH YEAR THE CAMBRIDGE FOLK FESTIVAL (END OF JULY) CELEBRATES THE BEST OF FOLK MUSIC, ATTRACTING A MIX OF NEW AND WORLD-RENOWNED ARTISTS.

UK3290 Fen Farm Caravan & Camping Site

East Mersea, Colchester CO5 8UA (Essex)

Tents were first pitched at Fen Farm in 1929 and since then the park has 'grown rather than developed' - something of which owners Raph and Wenda Lord are proud. There are two areas for touring units, both with sea views. The smaller field, reached through an area containing over 80 caravan holiday homes, and a larger, more spacious area which will have a new toilet block for 2005 (when we visited 'portacabin' style facilities were in use). The original block in the smaller field provides good facilities. In all there are 45 pitches, all with electricity connections. The site provides facilities for launching boats from the seashore and it is popular with water skiers. There are also many opportunities for walking, either inland or along the beach.

Facilities

New facilities are being built for 'Travers Field' pitches ('portacabin' style sanitary unit at present). Older facilities in the Heron Bay area are clean, tidy and well cared for, although the building is quite old. Facilities for disabled visitors. Recycling. Play area. Basic supplies provided by a visiting van from the local shop, daily in high season, weekends in low season. Gas supplies. Caravan and boat storage. Off site: Village shop and post office 1.5 miles.

At a glance

| Welcome & Ambience | ✓✓✓✓ | Location | ✓✓✓✓ |
| Quality of Pitches | ✓✓✓ | Range of Facilities | ✓✓✓ |

Directions

From Colchester, take B1025 to Mersea Island. Cross causeway bridge and fork left to East Mersea. Follow for 2.75 miles to site. O.S.GR: TM058144.

Charges 2004

| Per unit | £ 13.00 - £ 15.00 |

No credit cards.

Reservations

Not normally necessary, but contact park.
Tel: 01206 383275. Email: fenfarm@talk21.com

Open

1 March - 31 October.

UK3300 Homestead Lake Park

Thorpe Road, Weeley, Clacton-on-Sea CO16 9JN (Essex)

This well laid out, 25 acre park was opened in 2002. It is hidden from the road at the rear of Homestead Caravans sales areas and workshops in the countryside of the Tendring district, at Weeley near Clacton. It offers 25 fully serviced pitches overlooking a fishing lake. The park makes an ideal spot to stay either for fishing or a relaxing weekend, or as a base for touring this part of Essex. A special area has been added to allow wheelchair users to fish. You could even arrange for your caravan to be serviced or repairs to be made while you stay. Homestead also have a large accessories superstore. Breakfast is recommended at the café as a start to your day.

Facilities

The toilet block offers clean and spacious facilities including an en-suite unit for disabled visitors. Shop. Coffee shop and snack bar. Fishing lake. Woodland walks. Caravan sales, workshops and accessory shop.

Open

1 March - 31 October.

At a glance

| Welcome & Ambience | ✓✓✓ | Location | ✓✓✓✓✓ |
| Quality of Pitches | ✓✓✓✓ | Range of Facilities | ✓✓✓✓ |

Directions

From Colchester take A120, then A133 signed Clacton. At roundabout, turn left on B1033 into Weeley. Site and showrooms are on left just past council offices. O.S GR: TM149225.

Charges 2004

| Pitch incl. 2 persons and electricity | £ 12.00 - £ 15.00 |
| extra person | £ 1.00 |

Reservations

Contact site. Tel: 01255 833492.
Email: lakepark@homesteadcaravans.co.uk

UK3315 Orwell Meadows Leisure Park

Priory Lane, Ipswich IP10 0JS (Suffolk)

This popular, family park is set on the edge of the Orwell Country Park near Ipswich with its many miles of walks and the famous Orwell Bridge with views of the Suffolk countryside. The park is run by David and Jane Miles and offers an ideal spot for a family holiday with an outdoor swimming pool and a good clubhouse with a bar, restaurant and a shop. Spacious pitches are around the edges of several separate meadows (surrounded on three sides by earth banks), all offering 16A electricity hook-ups. There is lots to see and do in the area, from towns such as Ipswich and Colchester to unspoilt villages such as Framlingham (with its castle) and Aldeburgh, plus the rest of Constable country.

Facilities

The modern toilet block includes clean and spacious showers. It is kept to a very high standard. En-suite facilities for disabled visitors. Dishwashing area. Well stocked shop. Bar and restaurant. Outdoor pool. Play area. TV/family room. Torches useful.

Open

March - January.

At a glance

| Welcome & Ambience | ✓✓✓✓✓ | Location | ✓✓✓✓✓ |
| Quality of Pitches | ✓✓✓✓ | Range of Facilities | ✓✓✓✓ |

Directions

From A14 Ipswich bypass take Nacton/Ipswich exit and follow signs for Orwell Country Park (narrow lane). Cross single track bridge over the A14 to site entrance 20 yards on left. Follow signs past house/reception up hill and walk back to reception. O.S.GR: TM190408.

Charges 2004

Per unit incl. 2 persons	£ 11.00 - £ 12.50
incl. electricity	£ 13.00 - £ 16.50
extra person	£ 3.50 - £ 5.00

Reservations

Essential for high season. Tel: 01473 726666.

UK3310 Low House Touring Caravan Centre

Foxhall, Ipswich IP10 0AU (Suffolk)

Set in a sheltered 3.5 acres, this site has 30 level, grass pitches and an abundance of shrubs and flowers. In two sections, you drive through the rally field) to reach the more secluded garden area. There are 90 different varieties of trees with an ornamental tree walk leading around the edge of the park. All the pitches have electrical connections (most 16A, but some 10A) and they back onto trees that provide plenty of shade and the opportunity to observe a range of wildlife. The rally field has a more open aspect, but is still well sheltered and tranquil. The enthusiastic owner, John Booth, lives on site and is assisted by wardens with reception in a mobile office near the entrance. A good bus service to Ipswich stops just outside the site. Low House lies between Felixstowe (8 miles) and Ipswich (5 miles) and would be a useful stopover for the Felixstowe port or Harwich.

Facilities

The modern, heated sanitary block is spotlessly clean with hot showers (50p). Chemical disposal facilities. Dishwashing sink. No on-site provisions but a supermarket is 2 miles (towards Ipswich). Frozen goods can be stored. Calor gas is available. Small, secure play area. Pets area with rabbit and ornamental fowl. Torches recommended. Off site: Pub in Bucklesham village (1.5 miles) and other good pubs nearby. Golf 2 miles.

Open

All year.

At a glance

Welcome & Ambience	✓✓✓✓	Location	✓✓✓✓
Quality of Pitches	✓✓✓	Range of Facilities	✓✓✓✓

Directions

Turn off A14 (was A45) Ipswich ring road (south) via slip road onto A1156 (signed Ipswich East). Follow road over bridge crossing over the A45 and almost immediately turn right (no sign). After 0.5 miles turn right again (signed Bucklesham) and site is on left after 400 yards. O.S.GR: TM225423.

Charges 2004

Per unit incl. 2 adults and children	£ 9.00 - £ 10.00
extra adult	£ 2.00
child (5-15 yrs)	£ 1.00
awning	free

No large commercial vehicles. No credit cards.

Reservations

Advanced booking advised - phone any time.
Tel: 01473 659437.
Email: low.house@btopenworld.com

UK3330 Moat Barn Touring Caravan Park

Dallinghoo Road, Bredfield, Woodbridge IP13 6BD (Suffolk)

Mike Allen opened this small, new touring park in April 2000. Family run, it provides just 25 level pitches, all with electricity hook-ups (10A). As yet, the hedges have not matured, but the pitches are spacious and the park provides a tranquil environment making it a very pleasant place to use as a base. Walkers and cyclists will enjoy this location - the park is on the Suffolk Heritage Cycle Route, and also the Hull - Harwich National Cycle Route. Moat Barn also offers bed and breakfast.

Facilities

The well equipped sanitary block can be heated. A separate unit houses a dishwashing sink. Laundry and shop planned. Motorcaravan service point.

Open

April - October.

At a glance

Welcome & Ambience	✓✓✓✓✓	Location	✓✓✓✓✓
Quality of Pitches	✓✓✓✓	Range of Facilities	✓✓✓✓

Directions

From Ipswich on A12 to Lowestoft, after Hasketon roundabout take first left signed Bredfield. At village pump turn right and follow road past pub and church. Continue through S-bends and, after 200 yards, site is on left, just after farm buildings. From Lowestoft, turn right to Bredfield just before Hasketon roundabout, then as above. O.S.GR: TM 270537.

Charges 2004

Per unit incl. 2 adults and electricity	£ 12.00
extra person or car	£ 1.00

Reservations

Advised, especially for B.Hs and made with £10 deposit. Tel: 01473 737 520.

UK3340 Polstead Touring Park

Holt Road, Polstead, Colchester CO6 5BZ (Suffolk)

This lovely 30-pitch touring park in the peaceful Suffolk countryside (in the heart of 'Constable Country') is an ideal base from which to explore many places of interest. These include Flatford Mill, the scene for Constable's famous painting, Sudbury (the birthplace of Gainsborough), Long Melford with its Hall and Colchester, Britain's oldest town. The very neat and well cared for park offers really good facilities, its 30 level pitches all having electricity. Well established hedges separate the pitches and 25 have gravel hardstanding. There is little on-site to occupy younger visitors.

Facilities
The toilet block offers large spacious showers. Facilities for disabled visitors are provided in both men's and ladies' rooms (showers large enough for wheelchair access). Enclosed dishwashing area. Laundry. Reception sells basic supplies. Rally field. Caravan storage. Off site: Fishing and golf nearby. Pub serving food, 3 minutes walk.

Open
All year.

At a glance
Welcome & Ambience	✓✓✓✓	Location	✓✓✓✓✓
Quality of Pitches	✓✓✓✓	Range of Facilities	✓✓✓✓

Directions
From A1071 Hadleigh - Sudbury road, just past the 'Brewers Arms' public house, turn left just before a water tower towards Polstead; park is 250 yards on the right. O.S.GR: TL985403.

Charges 2004
Per adult	£ 3.00 - £ 3.50
child (4-16 yrs)	£ 1.50 - £ 2.00
pitch	£ 2.00 - £ 4.00
dog	£ 0.50

No credit cards.

Reservations
Made with £10 deposit. Tel: 01787 211969.

UK3350 Church Farm Holiday Park

Church Farm Road, Aldeburgh IP15 5DW (Suffolk)

This area of the Suffolk coast has always been a popular destination for visitors, with properties such as beach huts at Southwold fetching prices the same as terrace houses further inland. The coast with its shingle beaches is a haven for birds and other wildlife. The town of Aldeburgh is only 15 minutes walk from this site where one can find good food and drink and many gift and food shops. The famous Church Farm is mainly a site for caravan holiday homes but the large front field is used for touring units, with 85 pitches all offering full services including 16A electricity. Many pitches are surrounded by young hedges giving shelter and creating a sun trap. Reception is decorated with an array of potted plants and flowers to welcome visitors. Tents are not accepted.

Facilities
The single toilet block has spacious cubicles with free showers and adequate hot water at washbasins. Laundry room. Good unit for disabled people. Gas supplies. Off site: Beach 5 minutes walk. Shops, pubs, etc. 15 minutes walk.

Open
Easter - 31 October.

At a glance
Welcome & Ambience	✓✓✓✓	Location	✓✓✓✓✓
Quality of Pitches	✓✓✓✓	Range of Facilities	✓✓✓✓

Directions
On arrival at Aldeburgh, site is signed at roundabout in the direction of Thorpeness. Where road meets seafront, site is on left. From town centre follow road along seafront to site on left at end of town. O.S.GR: TM465572.

Charges 2004
Per pitch	£ 12.00 - £ 14.00
with services	£ 16.00 - £ 18.00

Reservations
Contact site. Tel: 01728 453433.

UK3370 Kessingland Beach Holiday Park

Lowestoft NR33 7RN (Suffolk)

Close to the most easterly point in the UK, this park offers all you need for that total family holiday experience. If you so wish you need never leave Kessingland Beach until your holiday ends. Children will be kept busy with swimming and games of all description, there is evening entertainment for all ages and a selection of bars and restaurants. Although mainly a park for static caravan holiday homes, there is a good touring area here with quite spacious pitching. Electricity hook-ups are available. The toilet block is old but it is kept in good condition and was remarkably clean and tidy at the time of our visit (August). The block is due to be re-built. If you do venture further afield, there is lots to see and do here on the Suffolk coast.

Facilities
The toilet block is old but is well maintained and cleaned (new block winter 2004). Dishwashing and laundry. Bars, restaurants and entertainment complex. Indoor and outdoor swimming pools. Play area. Shop. Tennis courts. Crazy golf. Amusements. Bicycle hire. Off site: Beach and sea fishing 100 yds. Golf and riding 3 miles.

Open
April - 19 September.

At a glance
Welcome & Ambience	✓✓✓✓	Location	✓✓✓✓✓
Quality of Pitches	✓✓✓	Range of Facilities	✓✓✓✓

Directions
From roundabout on A12 near Lowestoft signed Kessingland, follow road through village. At beach take sharp right then follow road to end into site (narrow road). O.S.GR: TM535859.

Charges 2004
Per unit	£ 9.00 - £ 22.00
dog	free - £ 3.00

Reservations
Essential high season and made with deposit (£5 per night). Tel: 01502 740636.

UK3390 The Dower House Touring Park

Thetford Forest, East Harling NR16 2SE (Norfolk)

Set on 20 acres in the heart of of Britain's largest forest on the Suffolk and Norfolk borders, the Dower House provides quiet woodland walks and cycle ways, with an abundance of wildlife. David and Karen Bushell, owners for many years, continue to upgrade the facilities without compromising the park's natural features. There are now 120 really large pitches with electricity available (10A), Most are level, although given the forest location there are a few tree roots. A fourth field provides 60 pitches for tents. Six pitches for visitors with mobility problems are linked by a path to the main facilities. The Dower House, as well as being the owners' home, houses a pleasant bar that also serves bar food (weekends only in low season) and a takeaway. A pleasant patio area is used for occasional entertainment at weekends and there is a small swimming pool. A torch is necessary as there is no site lighting other than at the facilities.

Facilities

Two toilet blocks - a small, refurbished one near the entrance, and a larger one with a baby room. A separate building houses the showers (5 for each sex and 20p) and a unit for disabled people. Dishwashing room, including a lower sink for children or disabled people. Laundry room with washing machine and dryer. Separate licensed shop doubling as reception and open daily in the season, on request at other times. Gas supplies. Information room. TV and quiet rooms (no games machines). A smallish swimming pool (only 1.1 m. deep, late May - early Sept), with a paddling pool alongside, is near the house. Caravan storage. Off site: Fishing nearby (1.5 miles). Snetterton motor racing circuit and Sunday market (2-3 miles).

Open

15 March - 29 September.

At a glance

Welcome & Ambience	✓✓✓✓✓	Location	✓✓✓✓✓
Quality of Pitches	✓✓✓✓	Range of Facilities	✓✓✓✓✓

Directions

From A11 (Thetford - Norwich) road, 7 miles from Thetford, turn right on B1111 towards East Harling. Turn right at church and right at T junction; park is on right. From A1066 Thetford-Diss road take left fork signed East Harling. Ignore signs for Forestry Commission site and park is next on left. Follow long drive (unmade road) for approx. 1 mile - keep speed down. O.S GR: TL969853.

Charges 2004

Per unit incl. 2 persons	£ 10.00 - £ 15.95
with electricity	£ 12.60 - £ 18.75
extra adult	£ 0.75 - £ 2.25
child (4-17 yrs)	£ 0.50 - £ 1.00
No charge for awnings or dogs.	

Reservations

Accepted by phone; deposit of £10 required for electricity. Tel: 01953 717314.
Email: info@dowerhouse.co.uk

UK3530 Welcome Holiday Centre

Butt Lane, Burgh Castle, Great Yarmouth NR31 9PY (Norfolk)

The Welcome Holiday Centre is Peter Liffen's other park, located just a short stroll from Liffens Holiday Park (UK3510). Set in over 20 acres in a rural location, the park is surrounded by trees. There are relaxing walks in the local countryside and plenty on the park to provide an ideal family holiday. There is an indoor pool, a solarium and a fully equipped gymnasium, plus good fishing lakes nearby for adults. Children will be entertained by the indoor splash pool, the play area and lots of open space for running about. In addition, the facilites of the sister park, including an outdoor pool, are available to those staying here. The level touring pitches behind the main complex are sheltered by high hedging whilst the other area is more open and slightly hilly in places (blocks recommended). All 80 touring pitches offer 10A electricity hook-ups. There are 40 caravan holiday homes on the park (25 to rent) and 20 seasonal pitches.

Facilities

Two toilet blocks, one modern in the main complex, the other older block at far end of site (recently re-furbished). Facilities for disabled visitors. Dishwashing. Laundry facilities. Motorcaravan service point. Gas supplies. Shop (May - Sept). Bar. Fish and chips and takeaway (May - Sept). Heated indoor pool. Gym. Solarium. Play area. Pool tables. Off site: Fishing 200 m. Bicycle hire 200 m. Golf 3 miles. Riding 8 miles. Beach 3 miles.

Open

1 March - 31 October.

At a glance

Welcome & Ambience	✓✓✓✓✓	Location	✓✓✓✓
Quality of Pitches	✓✓✓✓	Range of Facilities	✓✓✓✓✓

Directions

From Great Yarmouth and Gorleston take A143 signed Beccles. At dual carriageway (Bradwell) turn right signed Burgh Castle, then right again into Butt Lane. Site is 1 mile on right (narrow lane). O.S.GR: TG481040.

Charges 2004

Per unit incl up to 4 persons	£ 10.00 - £ 18.00
incl. electricity	£ 13.00 - £ 19.00
extra person	free - £ 2.00
pup tent	£ 3.00 - £ 5.00
dog (max. 1)	free - £ 2.00

Reservations

Contact park. Tel: 01493 780481.
Email: welcome@liffens.co.uk

UK3510 Liffens Holiday Park

Burgh Castle, Great Yarmouth NR31 9QB (Norfolk)

This popular well established family holiday park is in a semi-rural location, but within easy reach of Great Yarmouth. On site is an area with 109 privately owned caravan holiday homes, plus 35 site owned units for rent. A separate open, grassy area provides around 150 touring pitches, some slightly sloping, with only 100 having electrical hook-ups (16A), plus 2 fully serviced pitches. A large restaurant/bar providing club style entertainment in season and a takeaway service (noon-7 pm) overlooks a heated outdoor swimming pool. Campers can also use the indoor pool and other facilities at Liffens Welcome Holiday Centre close by. The excellent children's playground and a fenced, hard-surfaced multi-court for ball games are far enough from the pitches to preserve peace and quiet. The site also operates a post office/shop which is adjacent to the site, and a regular bus service runs from here to Great Yarmouth. The remains of a Roman fortress border the site.

Facilities

Two sanitary units of differing ages provide clean but fairly standard facilities with a unit for disabled persons, a baby room, and dishwashing sinks. Laundry in a separate older unit. Restaurant, two bars and takeaway. Swimming pool (60 x 30 ft; open 29/5-10/9) with water slide and children Off site: Golf 2 miles, fishing 400 yards.

Open

1 March - 31 October.

At a glance

Welcome & Ambience	✓✓✓✓	Location	✓✓✓✓
Quality of Pitches	✓✓✓	Range of Facilities	✓✓✓✓✓

Directions

From junction of A12 and A143 at roundabout south of Great Yarmouth take Burgh Road westwards, straight over at next roundabout, then second left into Butt lane. Site is on right. Avoid width restricted road closer to Great Yarmouth. O.S.GR: TM490050.

Charges 2004

Per unit incl. 4 persons	£ 10.00 - £ 18.00
incl. electricity	£ 13.00 - £ 19.00
extra person	free - £ 2.00
extra pup tent	£ 3.00 - £ 5.00
awning	free - £ 2.00
dog (1 only)	free - £ 1.50

Special offer breaks available.

Reservations

Essential for high season and made with £20 p/week deposit. Tel: 01493 780357.
Email: liffens@liffens.co.uk

UK3382 Rose Farm Touring Park

Stepshort, Belton, Great Yarmouth NR31 9JS (Norfolk)

This part of Norfolk is well known for its seaside attractions and the campsites which combine caravan holiday homes and touring pitches. Rose Farm caters for another type of camping holiday, offering space with the peace and tranquility that you may not be expecting in this particular area! With nearby attractions such as Fritton Lake Country Park, Pleasure Wood Hills Theme Park and of course Great Yarmouth with its fun fair and amusement arcades, your holiday in Norfolk could be full of busy days. Sue & Tora Myhra are very proud of Rose Farm and what they have achieved in the few years since taking over what was quite a run-down campsite. Spread over eight acres, the park is split into two separate fields. The first is large and open, surrounded by fencing and hedges, with pitches around the edge. It is very spacious with a very good toilet/shower block. The second field is long and narrow with pitching on either side. A new toilet/shower block here offers top quality facilities. Both blocks are immaculate with plant pots in the windows and on shelves giving a nice touch to the facilities.

Facilities

The two excellent blocks offer super facilities. The newer block is in Norwegian style, with a very modern fresh and spacious interior. Showers are good with changing space, washbasins are open or in cubicles. Laundry in the older block along with an iron and ironing board. Facilities for disabled visitors (pitching can be arranged). Adventure playground by reception. Pool table, TV room, library and tourist information. Off site: Shops nearby. Fishing and golf 3 miles. Riding and bicycle hire 4 miles. Beach 5 miles.

At a glance

Welcome & Ambience	✓✓✓✓✓	Location	✓✓✓✓✓
Quality of Pitches	✓✓✓✓	Range of Facilities	✓✓✓✓

Directions

From Great Yarmouth and Gorleston take A143 signed Beccles and Diss. At dual carriageway (Bradwell) take immediate right to Burgh Castle, take next right, site on right in 25 yards. O.S.GR: TG486033.

Charges 2004

Per unit incl. 2 persons	£ 8.00 - £ 10.00
incl. electricity	£ 10.50 - £ 12.50
extra person	£ 1.50
pup tent	£ 1.50

Special offers available. No credit cards.

Reservations

Essential in high season. Tel: 01493 780896.

Open

All year.

UK3490 The Grange Touring Park

Ormesby St Margaret, Great Yarmouth NR29 3QG (Norfolk)

The appealing overall appearance of this family touring site is that of a garden, with many hanging baskets, flower beds, bluebells and daffodils under the trees in spring, and all carefully tended by the resident wardens. The 70 level grassy pitches are arranged around tarmac access roads, 62 with electricity (5A). Next to the campsite is The Grange itself - a free house offering a wide range of meals, beers and real ale, plus children's play equipment (open all year). The site owner also has a holiday campsite at Hemsby (4 miles) with its own wide sandy beach, which guests at The Grange are welcome to use. Local attractions include Caister Castle and Motor Museum, Norfolk Rare Breed Centre, Yarmouth greyhound stadium and ten pin bowling.

Facilities

A modern stylish toilet building is exceptionally well appointed, and spotlessly clean, housing all the usual facilities including a baby changing room in the ladies'. Laundry room with washing machine and dryer. Washing lines are provided at the rear of the building. Gas supplies. Children's swings. Mobile shop calls daily in high season. Off site: Fishing 4 miles, golf 3 miles.

Open

Mid March - end September.

At a glance

Welcome & Ambience	✓✓✓✓	Location	✓✓✓✓
Quality of Pitches	✓✓✓✓	Range of Facilities	✓✓✓

Directions

Site is north of Great Yarmouth and east of Ormesby St Margaret, just south of the roundabout where the B1159 road joins the A149. O.S.GR: TG515140.

Charges 2004

Per unit incl. up to 4 persons	£ 7.00 - £ 12.50
extra adult	£ 2.00
electricity	£ 2.00
awning	£ 3.00

No credit cards.

Reservations

Advisable for B.Hs (min. 3 nights), school holidays and peak season and made with deposit (£10 for under 7 days or £25 per week). Tel: 01493 730306. Email: info@grangetouring.co.uk

UK3485 Clippesby Hall

Clippesby, Great Yarmouth NR29 3BL (Norfolk)

An unusual park in the grounds of a private estate where one can wander at will, Clippesby offers the choice of pitching in shady secluded woodland or on more open parkland with mature colourful trees and shrubs on gently sloping lawns. The 100 pitches are well spaced and clearly numbered (70 have 10A electricity). Hardstanding is available in the car parking area. There is a friendly welcome from the family who live in the single storey Hall and the opportunity to enjoy the mature gardens and facilities. These include a sunken grass tennis court, a small heated pool with mellow flagstone patio area behind the Hall, the timber adventure playground, putting and recreation greens. The Muskett Arms with attractive and comfortable family bar and a sheltered courtyard outside, provides evening meals, music nights and other family entertainment. Remember a torch and wellington boots - the environment is very natural and is deliberately kept that way. Children can roam at will, and in safety, and parents can unwind in this comfortable park, never mind all the attractions of the Broads and Great Yarmouth on your doorstep and only the peacocks to disturb you!

Facilities

Three timbered heated toilet blocks provide washbasins (some cabins) and ten showers in total including two in the Pinewoods block which are large enough to take a family. Hot water for dishwashing is charged (20p) - the park is not on mains services. Washing machine and dryer. Gas. Shop, café and family bar (from Whitsun). Swimming pool. Pony rides for children (6-11 yrs) on the park. Bicycle hire. Dog walk (max. 1 per pitch). Off site: Riding 3 miles. Golf 5 miles. Fishing 2 miles.

Open

Easter - 20 September.

At a glance

Welcome & Ambience	✓✓✓✓✓	Location	✓✓✓✓✓
Quality of Pitches	✓✓✓✓	Range of Facilities	✓✓✓✓

Directions

Park is signed off B1152 road about a mile north of the junction with A1064, 2 miles south of the junction with A419. O.S.GR: TG423145.

Charges 2004

Per unit incl. 2 persons	£ 13.00 - £ 19.50
extra adult	£ 1.50 - £ 2.00
child or student	£ 0.95
dog (max. 1)	£ 1.50 - £ 2.00
electricity	£ 2.00
Camping Cheques accepted.	

Reservations

Advised for peak periods and made with deposit (£20 per week or part week). Tel: 01493 367800. Email: holidays@clippesby.com

UK3470 Breckland Meadows Touring Park

Lynn Road, Swaffham PE37 7PT (Norfolk)

Within walking distance of the historic market town of Swaffham, this is a pleasant little park with enthusiastic owners that would make a good base to explore Norfolk and the local area. The 45 pitches are on fairly level, neat grass, all with electricity (16A), some with hardstanding. There may be some road noise at times but newly planted trees should reduce this as they mature. Adjacent to the site is the Swaefas Way, a seven mile circular walk which links to the better known Peddars Way. Local attractions include Cockley Cley Medieval Iceni Village and Saxon Church, Castle Acre Priory, Oxburgh Hall and the Thursford Collection of steam engines, mechanical organs and Wurlitzer fame. Swaffham (half a mile) has a popular Saturday market.

Facilities

The toilet block has been completely refurbished and is neat, clean and heated when necessary. It provides all the usual facilities, a separate toilet and washbasin unit for disabled visitors, and outside covered washing-up facilities. Gas. Off site: Fishing 5 miles, riding 4 miles, golf 2 miles.

Open

All year, but reservation essential November - Feb.

At a glance

Welcome & Ambience	✓✓✓✓✓	Location	✓✓✓✓
Quality of Pitches	✓✓✓✓	Range of Facilities	✓✓✓

Directions

Park is just west of Swaffham on the old A47, approx. 1 mile from town centre. O.S.GR: TF809094.

Charges 2005

Per unit incl. 2 adults, electricity	£ 10.00 - £ 12.00
extra adult	£ 2.00
child (5-15 yrs)	£ 1.00
awning	£ 1.00
tent	£ 6.00 - £ 7.00

Reservations

Essential for B.Hs and advised for peak season; made with non-refundable £10 deposit. Tel: 01760 721246. Email: info@brecklandmeadows.co.uk

UK3450 Little Haven Caravan & Camping Park

The Street, Erpingham, Norwich NR11 7QD (Norfolk)

Within easy reach of the coast and the Broads, this is an attractive, peaceful little site with good facilities. Only adults are accepted. The 24 grassy pitches, all with electricity (16A), are arranged around the outside of a gravel access road, with a central lawn and decorative pergola, a neat little garden and a seating area. There is no shop, but two pubs serving food and traditional ales are within walking distance. An ideal base for cycling, walking, riding, or just relaxing, the Weavers Way footpath is within half a mile of the site. Also close by is magnificent Blickling Hall with its superb state rooms, gardens and park, or a short drive takes you to the historic market town of Aylsham.

Facilities

The well maintained toilet unit is heated and includes spacious hot showers and two covered dishwashing and laundry sinks. Gas available. Site is unsuitable for American motorhomes. Note: This is an adults only park.

Open

1 March - 31 October.

At a glance

Welcome & Ambience	✓✓✓✓	Location	✓✓✓✓
Quality of Pitches	✓✓✓✓	Range of Facilities	✓✓✓

Directions

From A140 Cromer - Norwich road, going south towards Aylsham and 3 miles south of Roughton, past the Horseshoes pub and Alby crafts, take first turning right signed Erpingham 2 miles (narrow road). Site is 175 yards on right. O.S.GR: TG190320.

Charges 2004

Per unit incl. 2 adults, electricity and awning	£ 10.00 - £ 12.00

No credit cards.

Reservations

Advisable for B.Hs and peak season and made without deposit. Tel: 01263 768959. Email: patl@haven30.fsnet.co.uk

UK3420 Two Mills Touring Park

Yarmouth Road, North Walsham NR28 9NA (Norfolk)

Two Mills is a quiet site for adults only. Set in the bowl of a former quarry, the park is a real sun trap, both secluded and sheltered, with bird song to be heard at all times of the day. Neatly maintained with natural areas, varied trees, wild flowers and birds, the new owners, Barbara and Ray Barnes, want to add their own touches to this popular park. There are 55 level marked pitches for tourers, 48 all weather gravel, including 8 serviced pitches (hardstanding, patio area, water and waste water drainage). All are generously sized and have electricity (10/16A). This is a good centre from which to explore the north Norfolk coast, the Broads or for visiting Norwich. A member of the Best of British group.

Facilities	Directions
Neat, clean central toilet block can be heated and includes some washbasins in cabins, en-suite facilities for disabled people, laundry and dishwashing rooms. Small shop at reception. TV room with tea and coffee facilities. Dogs are accepted by arrangement only. Only adults are accepted. Off site: Hotel/pub 100 yds. Town 20 minutes walk. Fishing or golf 5 miles. Bicycle hire 1.5 miles. The coast is 5 miles.	From A149 Stalham - North Walsham road, watch for caravan sign 1.5 miles before North Walsham (also signed White Horse Common). The road runs parallel to the A149 and site is on right after 1.25 miles. From North Walsham take Old Yarmouth road past hospital, and park is 1 mile. O.S.GR: TG292287.

Open

All year except 2 January - 1 March.

Charges 2004

Per unit incl. 2 adults	£ 10.50 - £ 16.00
'panorama' pitch	£ 13.50 - £ 18.00
extra person	£ 2.50
Senior citizen discounts.	

At a glance

Welcome & Ambience	✓✓✓✓✓	Location	✓✓✓✓✓
Quality of Pitches	✓✓✓✓✓	Range of Facilities	✓✓✓✓

Reservations

Made with £10 deposit (£30 for B.Hs); balance payable on arrival. Tel: 01692 405829. Email: enquiries@twomills.co.uk

UK3500 Woodhill Park

Cromer Road, East Runton, Cromer NR27 9PX (Norfolk)

Woodhill is a seaside site with good views and a traditional atmosphere. It is situated on the cliff top, in a large gently sloping open grassy field, with 300 marked touring pitches. Of these, 175 have electricity (16A) and many have wonderful views over the surrounding countryside. A small number of holiday homes which are located nearer to the cliff edge unfortunately have the best sea views, although perhaps at times a little bracing! Although the site is fenced there is access to the cliff top path (watch young shildren). Nearby attractions include boat trips to see the seals off Blakeney Point, the Shire Horse Centre at West Runton, the North Norfolk Steam Railway, and at Sheringham you can find 'The Splash' fun pool complex with wave machine.

Facilities	Directions
The three sanitary units (the newest part of the reception building) are fully equipped but could be a little short of showers at peak times. Laundry with washing machines and dryer (iron from reception). Fully equipped unit for disabled persons. Well stocked mini-market. Gas exchange. Good, large adventure playground and plenty of space for ball games. Crazy golf. 9 hole golf course adjacent. Off site: Bicycle hire, golf or riding 2 miles. Fishing 1 mile.	Site is beside the A149 coast road between East and West Runton. O.S.GR: TG190420.

Charges 2004

Per pitch with electricity	£ 8.65 - £ 10.35
multi-service pitch	£ 11.45 - £ 13.35
small pitch (no electricity)	£ 5.00 - £ 7.00
adult	£ 1.50
child (4-16 yrs)	£ 1.00
dog	£ 2.00

Open

19 March - 31 October.

At a glance

Welcome & Ambience	✓✓✓✓✓	Location	✓✓✓✓✓
Quality of Pitches	✓✓✓✓	Range of Facilities	✓✓✓✓

Reservations

Accepted for min. 3 nights with £15 p/week non returnable booking fee. Tel: 01263 512242. Email: info@woodhill-park.com

UK3520 Searles Leisure Resort

South Beach, Hunstanton PE36 5BB (Norfolk)

This 'all-in' family holiday park on the North Norfolk coast offers everything you need for that seaside family holiday. With the beach within walking distance, bars and clubs, pools, a golf course, fishing lakes and bowling greens, there should be something to entertain everyone, Although now a major caravan holiday home park, for more than 50 years touring pitches have remained important. Spacious pitches separated by hedges, either fully serviced, with electricity or not, are set in different areas of the park. Being such a large site security is important and 24 hour CCTV operates. The seaside resort of Hunstanton is under a mile away providing all the usual ice creams, buckets and spades. The Royal House of Sandringham with its gardens and parts of the house open to the public is within easy reach. For bird watchers a trip further round the coast brings some excellent spots to see some interesting species.

Facilities

Three large toilet blocks offer clean and tidy facilities with background music. Washbasins in cubicles. En-suite rooms in all blocks for disabled visitors. Baby room. Laundry. Dishwashing facilities on the side of each block. Indoor and outdoor swimming pools. Gym. Tennis. Golf (9 hole course, driving range and putting course). Fishing lake. Bicycle hire. Off site: Nearest beach 200 yards. Hunstanton 0.5 miles.

Open

March - October.

At a glance

Welcome & Ambience	✓✓✓✓	Location	✓✓✓✓✓
Quality of Pitches	✓✓✓✓✓	Range of Facilities	✓✓✓✓✓

Directions

On the A149 from Kings Lynn take Hunstanton exit at roundabout. At next roundabout take second exit then immediate left into site. O.S.GR: TF670401.

Charges 2004

Per tent or tourer pitch	£ 10.00 - £ 23.00
pitch with electricity	£ 12.00 - £ 27.00
fully serviced pitch	£ 13.00 - £ 30.00
awning	£ 2.50
dog	£ 2.00

Reservations

Contact site. Large units by arrangement.
Tel: 01485 534211. Email: bookings@searles.co.uk

UK3400 The Old Brick Kilns Caravan & Camping Park

Little Barney Lane, Barney, Fakenham NR21 0NL (Norfolk)

This tranquil, family run park is under new ownership and further improvements are taking place. The park's development on the site of old brick kilns has resulted in land on varying levels. This provides areas of level, well drained pitches (eg. the Dell, the Orchard) which include some hardstandings. There are 65 pitches, all with electricity (10/16A), including a new area with serviced pitches. Banks around the park and a wide range of trees and shrubs provide shelter and are home for a variety of wildlife. There are garden areas, including a butterfly garden, and a conservation pond is the central feature. Amenities include a large, comfortable bar and restaurant. A friendly, helpful atmosphere prevails and as the park is 8 miles from the coast, it is ideally situated to explore North Norfolk. Member Best of British group.

Facilities

Smart, heated toilet blocks provide very good, clean facilities with washbasins in curtained cubicles. Baby room. Facilities for disabled people (unisex; Radar key). Laundry room. Motorcaravan services. Good shop with gas supplies and gas barbecues for hire. Bar/restaurant (weekends) with patio area outside with barbecue. TV and games room. Table tennis, giant chess and mini library. Bicycle hire. Fenced play area. Fishing. Winter caravan storage. B&B also available. Off site: Riding 6 miles, golf 5 or 8 miles.

Open

All year excl. 7 January - 20 February.

At a glance

Welcome & Ambience	✓✓✓✓✓	Location	✓✓✓✓✓
Quality of Pitches	✓✓✓✓✓	Range of Facilities	✓✓✓✓

Directions

From Fakenham take A148 Cromer road. After 6 miles, at Thurston, fork right on B1354 Melton Constable road. In 300 yds, turn right, signed Barney, and then first left along a narrow country lane with passing places, for 0.75 miles. O.S.GR: TG004332.

Charges 2004

Per pitch incl. 2 persons, electricity	£ 12.50 - £ 14.75
extra adult	£ 2.00
child (4-15 yrs)	£ 1.00 - £ 1.50
child (0-3 yrs)	£ 0.50 - £ 0.75
dog (max 2)	£ 0.75

Reservations

Advised and made with £15 deposit (non-refundable).
Tel: 01328 878305. Email: oldbrickkilns@aol.com

UK3430 Kelling Heath Holiday Park

Weybourne, Holt, Sheringham NR25 7HW (Norfolk)

Not many parks can boast their own railway station and Kelling Heath's own halt on the North Norfolk Steam Railway gives access to shopping in Holt or the beach at Sheringham. Set in 250 acres of woodland and heathland overlooking the north Norfolk coast, this spacious holiday park offers freedom and relaxation with 300 touring pitches, all with electricity (16A) in four different zones. Pitching is good on quite firm, level grass (no hardstanding). Together with 384 caravan holiday homes (36 to let, the rest privately owned), they blend easily into the part-wooded, part-open heath. A wide range of facilities provides activities for all ages. 'The Forge' has an entertainment bar, an adult only bar and a family room, with comprehensive entertainment all season. 'Fitness Express' provides an indoor pool, spa pool, sauna, steam rooms and gym. An adventure playground with assault course is near. The central reception area is attractively paved to provide a 'village store' and an open air bandstand where one can sit and enjoy the atmosphere. The park's natural environment allows for woodland walks, a nature trail and cycling trails, and a small lake for free fishing (permit holders only). Other amenities include two hard tennis courts, a small, outdoor heated fun pool and play areas (some rather hidden from the pitches).

Facilities

Three toilet blocks serve the touring pitches, one heated and with a conservatory providing covered access all year to disabled people, baby room and laundry and laundry sinks. All blocks have a few washbasins in private cubicles, baby baths and, in season, a nappy disposal service. Washing machines and dryers, with irons to hire. Shop. Gas supplies. Bar, restaurant and takeaway. Indoor leisure centre with pool (19 x 9 m), gym, etc. with trained staff (membership on either daily or weekly basis). Outdoor pool (main season). Adventure play area. Tennis. Fishing. Bicycle hire. Entertainment programme. Special environmental 'Acorn Club' for children. Torches useful. Off site: Felbrigg Hall, the Walsingham Shrine and Norfolk Broads nearby.

At a glance

Welcome & Ambience	✓✓✓✓✓	Location	✓✓✓✓
Quality of Pitches	✓✓✓✓	Range of Facilities	✓✓✓✓✓

Directions

On A148 road from Holt to Cromer, after High Kelling, turn left just before Bodham village (international sign) signed Weybourne. Follow road for about 1 mile to park O.S.GR: TG117418.

Charges 2004

Per unit incl. electricity	£ 14.20 - £ 20.50
awning	£ 2.00
dog (max 2)	£ 2.00

Min 7 day stay in high season. No single sex groups.

Reservations

Necessary for July/Aug. on a weekly basis with £30 deposit. Tel: 01263 588181. Email: info@kellingheath.co.uk

Open

1 March - 16 December.

UK3460 The Garden Caravan Site

Barmer Hall, Syderstone, Kings Lynn PE31 8SR (Norfolk)

This imaginative touring site in an enclosed walled garden, has 30 spacious pitches on gently sloping grass in a most attractive setting behind the Hall. Levelling blocks may be needed. There are 30 electrical connections (16A), each with a TV hook-up as reception is variable, possibly due to the high wall and woodland surrounding the site. However, this does mean that the site is peaceful and a little sun-trap, a haven from the busy world. Reception is in a small kiosk (not always manned, so pitch and pay later).

Facilities

Toilet facilities are in a new building (heated when necessary) including extremely spacious hot showers and free hot water. Dishwashing sinks under cover. No shop, but gas, soft drinks and eggs are usually available. Off site: Bicycle hire 4 miles, riding 6 miles, golf 10 miles.

Open

1 March - 1 November.

At a glance

Welcome & Ambience	✓✓✓✓	Location	✓✓✓✓✓
Quality of Pitches	✓✓✓✓	Range of Facilities	✓✓✓

Directions

Six miles west of Fakenham turn off A148 at garage to Docking and Hunstanton on B1454. After 4 miles turn to Barmer Hall (site signed). O.S.GR: TF810330.

Charges 2004

Per adult	£ 5.00 - £ 6.00
electricity	£ 2.00

No credit cards.

Reservations

Advised for B.Hs and peak season. Tel: 01485 578220. Email: nigel@mason96.fsnet.co.uk

UK3440 Gatton Waters Lakeside Touring Site

Hillington, nr Sandringham, Kings Lynn PE31 6BJ (Norfolk)

Developed around two fishing lakes (formerly stone quarries), Gatton Waters has a peaceful, open aspect. Fishermen will delight in pitching at the lakeside, while other pitches are available away from the water at this adult only park. There are 60 level caravan pitches (all with electricity) and 30 tent pitches in quiet and very pleasant surroundings. With all but 25 pitches taken by seasonal units, there is still room for those looking either to fish (day tickets available) or for a quiet base to visit Sandringham or the north Norfolk coast (although reservations are essential). Everything is kept as natural as possible and skylarks, pheasants, ospreys and leverets are to be seen, in addition to the many types of ducks, etc. on the lakes. In general the site retains a natural look but the grass is well trimmed and cared for. The site is now run by the son of the original owners, who are still adamant that their best ever decision was only to take adults - this also seems popular with their visitors. Only people over 18 years are accepted.

Facilities	Directions
Three modern, heated toilet blocks provide good clean facilities including dishwashing. Extra facilities near reception. Bar with open fire - very welcoming and with the attraction of real ales and good food (booking required). Caravan storage. Torches are necessary. Off site: Riding or golf 8 miles. Within easy reach are Sandringham (2.2 miles) and the North Norfolk Coast (8 miles).	From Kings Lynn follow A148 Cromer road. Site is on left just after West Newton turn, but before Sandringham turn and Hillington village. O.S.GR: TF705255.

Charges 2004

Per unit incl. 2 persons, electricity	£ 10.00 - £ 12.00
tent incl. 2 persons	£ 9.00 - £ 10.00
extra person	£ 1.00

Open

Easter - 1 October.

Reservations

Essential and made for min. 3 days at B.Hs.
Tel: 01485 600643. Email: gatton.waters@virgin.net

At a glance

Welcome & Ambience	✓✓✓✓	Location	✓✓✓✓✓
Quality of Pitches	✓✓✓	Range of Facilities	✓✓✓✓

UK3580 Ferry Meadows Caravan Club Site

Ham Lane Farm, Ham Lane, Peterborough PE2 5UU (Cambridgeshire)

Only three miles from Peterborough and closer still to the East of England Showground, Ferry Meadows occupies 30 acres of the much larger Nene Country Park. The meadows, lakes and woodlands provide ample opportunities to sample the numerous facilities on offer. Open all year the site provides 254 pitches - 160 grass pitches on one side of the park and 94 gravel hardstandings on the newer side, just across the road. Privacy, shade and character are assured by the abundance of trees, bushes and all pitches have electricity (16A). Tents are accepted on the grassed section of the site. Families with children may prefer the grass section, from where they can keep a watchful eye on the well-equipped play area. Returning to the Country Park it covers over 500 acres, within which are miles of walks and cycle ways, horse routes, lakes for course fishing, sailing and windsurfing, a wetland nature reserve, archery field, two golf courses and a miniature railway. Well laid out for the disabled visitor, free wheelchair hire is available on request. Also passing within nostalgic earshot and yielding the occasional tempting aroma of bygone eras is the Nene Valley Steam Railway, complete with Thomas the Tank Engine.

Facilities	Directions
Two modern, heated toilet blocks are of the usual good standard, with curtained washbasins and en-suite facilities for disabled visitors. Baby/toddler washroom. Facilities for disabled visitors. Each section has dishwashing sinks under cover, as well as a laundry room. Motorcaravan service point. The office stocks basic provisions. Tourist information room. Play area. Off site: Nearest shops 1.5 miles. Ice and roller skating in Peterborough.	From A1 south, do not turn onto A1139, but turn left at next junction (signed Showground, Chesterton, Alwalton). At T-junction turn left on A605, continue straight at three roundabouts, following signs for Nene Park to site in Ham Lane. O.S.GR: TL151975.

Charges 2004

Per adult	£ 3.30 - £ 4.80
child (5-16 yrs)	£ 1.10 - £ 1.60
pitch incl. electricity (non-member)	£ 8.00 - £ 11.00

Open

All year.

Reservations

Essential for B.Hs, July/Aug and all w/ends.
Tel: 01733 233526.

At a glance

Welcome & Ambience	✓✓✓✓✓	Location	✓✓✓✓
Quality of Pitches	✓✓✓✓	Range of Facilities	✓✓✓✓✓

For more **site inspiration**
see our directory ON PAGE 294

UK3560 Highfield Farm Touring Park

Long Road, Comberton, Cambridge CB3 7DG (Cambridgeshire)

Situated five miles from Cambridge, this eight acre park is set in a delightfully quiet touring location. Family run and very well kept, the welcome is always warm and the facilities of superior quality. Grass and hedges are extremely well cared for - a visitor from over the North Sea described the owner, Brian Chapman, as 'a professor of grass' which gives you some idea of what to expect. Divided into five enclosures by hedges and conifers, there are also shady glades for those who wish to retreat even further; and an enclosure is reserved for those without children. Offering 60 numbered pitches for caravans or motorcaravans, and 60 for tents, pitching is around the outer edges. As a result, the park never looks crowded even when it is fully booked (which is frequently the case). All pitches have 10A electricity, 50 have gravel hardstanding, and most are level. A good dog walk is provided, which can be extended to a pleasant 1.5 mile walk, with seats, around the farm perimeter. A member of the Best of British group.

Facilities

Three heated toilet blocks provide more than adequate coverage and good facilities. The original block provides controllable showers on payment, and an additional set of unisex showers. The other two blocks have some washbasins in cubicles, all outstandingly clean and well maintained. Baby room but no dedicated provision for disabled visitors, although one block has extra wide doors and easy access. Laundry room. Small but very visible play area. Good shop. Motorcaravan service point. Excellent tourist information room. Bicycle hire. Gates closed midnight to 7.30 am. Off site: Fishing 3.5 miles, golf 2 miles. Cambridge 5 miles, Comberton village 0.5 miles.

Open

23 March - 31 October.

At a glance

Welcome & Ambience	✓✓✓✓✓	Location	✓✓✓✓✓
Quality of Pitches	✓✓✓✓	Range of Facilities	✓✓✓✓

Directions

From M11 take exit 12, the A603 towards Sandy. After 0.5 miles turn right on the B1046 to Comberton. Turn right just before the village signed Maddingly (also caravan sign). Site on right at top of hill. O.S GR: TL391571.

Charges 2004

Per unit incl. 2 persons	£ 8.50 - £ 10.00
extra adult	£ 2.00
child (5-16 yrs)	£ 1.50
awning/pup tent	£ 1.00
electricity	£ 2.00
hiker/cyclist and tent	£ 7.00 - £ 7.75

No credit cards.

Reservations

Made for any length with £10 deposit and 50p fee. Tel: 01223 262308. Email: enquiries@highfieldfarmtouringpark.co.uk

A warm welcome awaits you at our popular award winning park with its excellent facilities, set in peaceful farming countryside. It is close to the historic University City of Cambridge, the Imperial War Museum, Duxford and ideally suited for touring East Anglia.

Comberton, Cambridge CB3 7DG Tel/Fax: 01223 262308

www.highfieldfarmtouringpark.co.uk

149

UK3550 Old Manor Caravan Park

Church Road, Grafham, Huntingdon PE28 0BB (Cambridgeshire)

Situated within easy walking distance of Grafham Water, this small but attractive park combines history with a natural charm. The old white cottage (now reception) was once owned by Oliver Cromwell's family, and the grounds formed part of their garden. To this day the horse pond and part of the moat still remain, while the remnants of an old yew hedge provide an intriguing, natural sculpture. With the exception of seven all-weather pitches the remainder of the 80 numbered and generously sized pitches are grass; many with 10A electrical connections and all easily accessed by a good tarmac road. Privacy and shade is provided by varied and plentiful trees and hedges throughout the six acre, level grounds and the park is most carefully maintained. Sailing, fishing, bicycle hire, nature trails and bird watching can be found at nearby Grafham Water - a large reservoir. Cambridge, the Imperial War Musem at Duxford, Woburn Abbey and the Shuttleworth Collection at Old Warden are nearby too.

Facilities
The single, toilet block is thoughtfully planned and always extremely clean. Dishwashing and laundry rooms, plus a free freezer for ice blocks and food storage. Basic provisions are available from reception (1/3-31/10), with the nearest shops being at West Perry or Buckden (5 and 3 miles respectively) Small playground. Large, heated outdoor pool (small extra charge; unsupervised). An overflow field for 25 units operates during June, July and August.

Open
All year.

At a glance
Welcome & Ambience	✓✓✓✓	Location	✓✓✓✓
Quality of Pitches	✓✓✓✓	Range of Facilities	✓✓✓

Directions
Leave A1 at Buckden roundabout and follow B661 towards Grafham Water for about half a mile. Turn right towards the village of Grafham following camping signs. From A14 at Ellington, turn off and follow camping signs. O.S.GR: TL160680.

Charges 2004
Per unit incl. 2 adults, electricity	£ 14.50 - £ 17.50
tent pitch incl. 2 adults	£ 12.50 - £ 15.50
extra adult	£ 3.50 - £ 4.00
child (5-15 yrs)	£ 2.00 - £ 2.25
dog (max 2)	£ 1.00

Reservations
Made with £10 non-returnable deposit (min 3 nights at B.Hs) Tel: 01480 810264. Email: camping@old-manor.co.uk

UK3575 Stroud Hill Park

Fen Road, Pidley PE28 3DE (Cambridgeshire)

Opened in 2003 as an all year round, adult only site Stroud Hill Park is an excellent example of a well designed, modern and high quality park; a credit to its owners, David and Jayne Newman. Developed from existing farmland where David grew up, the park has been landscaped to create a terraced effect and now incorporates a large fishing lake (well stocked with carp, tench, bream, rudd and roach) plus a superb tennis court. The attractive, timber framed barn that dominates the site is all the more impressive when you know that David built most of it; even to the canopy over the open fireplace. There are no half measures here, from the quality of the building itself through to the fittings throughout, everything has been well thought out and it adds up to a gem of new site. The barn is the hub of the site where you will find reception, shop, terrace and bar, while by 2005 a 44 seat restaurant should be well established. There are 54 pitches, of which 44 are hardstanding, all are large and fully serviced with electricity (16A), fresh water and waste water disposal. The hedges and shrubs around the site are young and need time to mature, but an atmosphere and character has quickly developed and already many return regularly, just because it is such a nice site. Affiliated to the Caravan Club, non-members are equally welcome.

Facilities
Toilets and spacious en-suite shower facilities are located in the main building along with a very well equipped room for disabled users. Good size laundry room plus vegetable preparation and dishwashing room, all spotlessly clean throughout. Motorcaravan service point. Small, licensed shop stocks basic provisions, home-made cakes, local produce, gas and camping accessories. Attractive bar and café/restaurant. Fishing (£4 per day). All-weather tennis court. American motorhomes accepted.

At a glance
Welcome & Ambience	✓✓✓✓✓	Location	✓✓✓✓
Quality of Pitches	✓✓✓✓✓	Range of Facilities	✓✓✓✓

Directions
From A1(N) and A1(S) take A14 east. Turn off A14 at the A141, signed March. Follow signs to March until Warboys. At roundabout turn right on B1040 signed Pidley, then first left past church onto Fen road. Site is 1 mile down Fen Road on right. O.S.GR: TL335787.

Charges 2004
Per unit incl 2 adults, electricity	£ 17.50
tent incl. 2 adults	£ 15.00
extra adult	£ 2.50
dog	£ 1.50

Reservations
Advised - contact park. Tel: 01487 740009.

Open
All year.

Spanning central England, from the ancient borders of Wales on the west across to Lincolnshire on the east coast, the Heart of England is rich in glorious rolling countryside, magnificent castles, fine stately houses and beautiful gardens.

The region comprises of Lincolnshire, Rutland, Northamptonshire, Nottinghamshire, West Midlands, Derbyshire, Staffordshire, Leicestershire, Warwickshire, Herefordshire, Worcestershire, Gloucestershire & Shropshire

The charming and diverse countryside of the Heart of England includes: the Lincolnshire Wolds, with the dramatic open landscape of the Fens; the ragged crags, dales and moorland of the Peak District National Park in Derbyshire and Staffordshire; the heathered hilltops of Shropshire; the famous Sherwood Forest, in the heart of Nottinghamshire; and the miles of lush green countryside of Herefordshire, dotted with black and white timber houses. Rutland Water is a mecca for watersports and the whole region offers superb opportunities for walking, cycling and more daring activities such as rock climbing and caving. The Cotswolds to the west of the region is the largest area of Outstanding Natural Beauty in England and Wales. Here you will find many traditional English villages, with charming country pubs and cottage gardens. Another significant feature of the region are the rivers and canals. Passing pretty towns and villages, a large canal network threads its way through the area, weaving through the Lincolnshire Fens, past the waterside bars and restaurants of Birmingham and along to estuaries of the rivers of Severn and Avon.

Did you know?

Herefordshire is one of the largest apple cider producers in the world

The World Toe Wrestling Championship, held every June in Wetton, is a registered international sport

The hollow trunk of the 'Mighty Tree' in Sherwood Forest is reputedly where Robin Hood and his Merry Men hid from the Sheriff of Nottingham

Quite different from the more familiar tart, the Bakewell pudding was first created in the 1860s

Rutland is the smallest county in Britain, measuring just 16 miles by 16 miles

The Peak District contains over 50 reservoirs, including Ladybower reservoir, where the bouncing bomb used in World War II was tested

The recipe for Worcester sauce was brought back from India by a colonial general

Places of interest

Lincolnshire: Belvoir Castle near Grantham

Rutland: market towns of Oakham and Uppingham

Northamptonshire: Silverstone; Althorp House

Nottinghamshire: Nottingham Castle

West Midlands: Birmingham; Cadbury World

Derbyshire: Bakewell; Buxton; Chatsworth House

Staffordshire: Alton Towers; Stoke-on-Trent

Leicestershire: Snibston Discovery Park; Twycross Zoo

Warwickshire: Warwick Castle; Stratford-upon-Avon

Herefordshire: Hereford Cathedral

Worcestershire: West Midland Safari Park

Gloucestershire: Sudeley Castle; Cheltenham

Shropshire: Shrewsbury and Whitchurch

tip

CHELTENHAM HOSTS A NUMBER OF SUMMER FESTIVALS: THE SCIENCE FESTIVAL IS IN JUNE, WHILE THE FRINGE RUNS ALONGSIDE THE INTERNATIONAL FESTIVAL OF MUSIC IN JULY.

UK3760 Tallington Lakes Caravan & Camping

Barholm Road, Tallington, Stamford PE9 4RJ (Lincolnshire)

This large, 160-acre site spreads around a series of lakes that provides for many watersport activities including water-ski (slalom and jump courses), jet-ski, sailing (sailboards and dinghies), and angling. The touring campsite has recently been brought up to date and now has around 120 pitches, of which 106 have electric hook-ups (10A), and 11 are on hardstandings. Major roads are tarmac, with gravel roads around the pitches, but the small hedges and shrubs separating the pitches are new and will need time to mature. The complex also has a good number of permanent holiday homes.

Facilities	Directions
The heated sanitary unit, newly built in 2000, includes facilities for babies, small children and disabled visitors, plus a room with dishwashing sinks. Additional WCs and showers (also used by the water skiers). Motorcaravan service point. Bar and restaurant. Watersports. Fishing. Dry-ski slope, snowboard centre and tennis. Small, well fenced adventure style playground (age 5-12 yrs). Key-card for toilet unit and barrier (£10 deposit).	From A16, midway between Stamford and Market Deeping, just east of the railway crossing at Tallington, turn north into Barholm Road and site entrance is on the right. (site is signed). O.S.GR: TF085090.

Open

1 March - 31 January.

At a glance

| Welcome & Ambience | ✓✓✓ | Location | ✓✓✓✓ |
| Quality of Pitches | ✓✓✓✓ | Range of Facilities | ✓✓✓✓ |

Charges 2004

Per adult	£ 1.50
pitch	£ 6.00
electricity	£ 2.00
awning or pup tent	£ 1.50
dog (max 2 per unit)	£ 1.00

Reservations

Accepted with full payment. Tel: 01778 347000.
Email: info@tallington.com

UK3750 Foreman's Bridge Caravan Park

Sutton St James, Spalding PE12 0HU (Lincolnshire)

Foreman's Bridge is an extremely pleasant and compact park that is under new ownership. It makes an excellent base for exploring the Fens and Spalding, famous for its annual flower festival. Fishing and cycling are popular pastimes in the area, indeed bicycle hire and fishing licences are both available from the site, with fishing possible in the river that runs just past the entrance. Arranged around a large, level and grassy meadow are 40 level pitches, 32 with electricity (10A) and 20 with gravel hardstanding. Fruit trees, flower beds, hanging baskets and planted troughs provide bursts of vibrant colour.

Facilities	Directions
The modern, brick built toilet unit is spacious and kept very clean, providing really large individual shower rooms with seats and washbasins (showers on payment). Dishwashing room. Laundry room with washing machine, dryer and ironing. Recycling. Motorcaravan service points. Basic provisions and gas are kept. Fishing. Bicycle hire. Site barrier (£5 deposit for card). Winter caravan storage. Off site: Nearest shop 2 miles. Riding 8 miles, golf 5 miles.	From A17 Spalding - Kings Lynn road turn south on B1390 at Long Sutton towards Sutton St James for approx. 2 miles. Site entrance is on the left immediately after the bridge. O.S.GR: TF410198.

Open

1 March - 30 November.

At a glance

| Welcome & Ambience | ✓✓✓✓✓ | Location | ✓✓✓✓ |
| Quality of Pitches | ✓✓✓✓ | Range of Facilities | ✓✓✓ |

Charges 2004

Per unit incl. 2 adults	£ 6.50
extra person	£ 1.00 - £ 2.00
electricity	£ 2.00
No credit cards.	

Reservations

Advisable for Flower Festival, B.Hs (min. 3 nights), and peak season; made with £10 deposit.
Tel: 01945 440346.
Email: foremans.bridge@btinternet.com

UK3770 Low Farm Touring Park

Spring Lane, Folkingham, Sleaford NG34 0SJ (Lincolnshire)

This quiet secluded park is a lovely spot to either just relax or to tour the Lincolnshire countryside. Jane and Nigel Stevens are working hard to make this site a pleasant place to stay and have a really well laid out park offering good quality facilities which are very clean and tidy. The site is in the countryside and offers some good views of Lincolnshire, and about 200 yards from the site is the village of Folkingham with good eating and drinking houses and shops. There are some pleasant walks around the village. The site offers 36 touring pitches, 35 of which have electric hook-ups.

Facilities	Directions
Controllable free showers. Dishwashing and laundry sinks. Off site: For larger shops and other interesting places, Sleaford, Bourne and Lincoln are within easy reach.	Site is on main A15 Lincoln - Peterborough road, 2 miles from A52 roundabout junction. From this roundabout follow A15 towards Peterborough and Folkingham is 1.5 miles. Go through village and down hill. At bottom (site sign), take road opposite to your right and site is at end of lane. O.S.GR: TF070333.

Reservations

Contact site. Tel: 01529 497322.

Open

Easter - 31 October.

At a glance

| Welcome & Ambience | ✓✓✓✓ | Location | ✓✓✓✓✓ |
| Quality of Pitches | ✓✓✓ | Range of Facilities | ✓✓✓ |

Charges 2004

Per unit incl. 2 persons	£ 7.50 - £ 9.00
extra person (over 5 yrs)	£ 1.00 - £ 2.00
electricity	£ 1.75 - £ 2.00
No credit cards.	

UK3700 Pilgrims Way Caravan & Camping Park

Church Green Road, Fishtoft, Boston PE21 0QY (Lincolnshire)

In a rural setting, this delightful, family run park is two miles from Boston and its famous church tower. There are 22 individual pitches all with access to electricity (10A) and including 6 with hardstanding. The park's facilities are housed in a good quality conversion at one end of what was once a workshop. Local attractions include the 'Boston stump', the Pilgrim Fathers Memorial and Maud Foster Windmill, all in and around the town. Boston market days are on Wednesdays and Saturdays and the town also has a fine marina, two leisure centres (one with swimming pools), a ten-pin bowling alley and a tennis centre.

Facilities

Heated in low season, the sanitary facilities are thoughtfully planned and exceptionally clean and well maintained. Entry is by keypad and all of the usual facilities are provided, including, dishwashing and laundry sinks, plus an excellent fully equipped unit for disabled persons. Laundry with washing machine and dryer. Gas available. Groundsheets, kite flying and ball games are not allowed. Site is not really suitable for American motorhomes. Dogs accepted by prior arrangement. Off site: Mini-market within 1 mile. Golf, fishing, bicycle hire and riding within 2 miles.

At a glance

Welcome & Ambience	✓✓✓	Location	✓✓✓✓
Quality of Pitches	✓✓✓✓	Range of Facilities	✓✓✓

Directions

From A52, 1 mile east of junction with A16, turn south by the 'Ball House' public house, continuing past the Boston Bowl towards Fishtoft, where the site is on your left. O.S.GR: TF360420.

Charges 2005

Per unit incl. 2 persons	£ 10.00 - £ 12.00

No credit cards.

Reservations

Advised for B.Hs and peak season. Tel: 01205 366646. Email: pilgrimswaylincs@yahoo.com

Open

1 April/Easter - 30 September.

UK3730 Skegness Sands Touring Site

Winthorpe Avenue, Skegness PE25 1QZ (Lincolnshire)

This well organised touring site is actually part of a much larger caravan holiday home park, but it has its own entrance and its own, more intimate character. It is modern and well appointed, adjacent to the promenade and beach. There are 85 pitches, all level and with electricity (16A). Most are grass but there are 40 gravel hardstandings, 4 of which are fully serviced. Site lighting is good, there are regular security patrols and the gates are locked 6 pm - 8 am. The gate to the promenade is kept locked at all times, campers getting a key. The site is a member of the Caravan Club's 'managed under contract' scheme, members and non-members are all very welcome.

Facilities

The good quality, heated sanitary unit includes washbasins in curtained cubicles plus three family bathrooms comprising WC, washbasin and shower and a well equipped room for disabled people. Two dishwashing sinks are outside under cover. Laundry room. Gas supplies on site. Hairdressing salon. Indoor heated swimming pool (end May - 30 Sept; adult £2, child £1.50) located in the 'static' area of the site. Small playground. Off site: Well stocked shop/post office 200 m. Pubs, fast food outlets and a supermarket are all within easy walking distance. 'Hail and ride' bus service to Skegness and Ingoldmells at 200 m.

At a glance

Welcome & Ambience	✓✓✓✓	Location	✓✓✓✓
Quality of Pitches	✓✓✓✓	Range of Facilities	✓✓✓✓

Directions

Site is north of Skegness. From A52 turn opposite 'Garden City' pub into Winthorpe Avenue. Site is on left at far end of road. O.S.GR: TF570640.

Charges 2004

Per adult	£ 3.80 - £ 5.00
child (5-16 yrs)	£ 1.20 - £ 1.70
non-member pitch fee	£ 8.50 - £ 11.00
services incl. electricity	£ 3.00

Reservations

Advised for B.Hs, school holidays and peak season. Tel: 01754 761484.

Open

All year.

UK3650 Cherry Tree Site

Huttoft Road, Sutton-on-Sea LN12 2RU (Lincolnshire)

For adults only, Cherry Tree is a good example of a small, good value touring park. The grass is neatly trimmed and well drained, and is divided by evergreen hedging. Connected by a one-way circular gravel road, there are 60 good sized pitches, all have 10A electricity and some have hardstandings. Buses stop outside hourly, and a shop and pub are within ten minutes walk. It is also possible to walk to the sea (15 minutes). Mablethorpe beach is known for its sand yacht racing and Skegness, with all its popular attractions is just down the road. A very warm welcome awaits from Geoff and Margaret Murray.

Facilities

The brick built toilet block can be heated and is immaculately kept, providing hot showers. Hairdryers. En-suite unit for disabled visitors. Dishwashing and laundry room with washing machine and dryer. Gas. Off site: Tennis and bowls nearby, fishing 1.5 miles, golf 1 mile, riding adjacent.

Open

1 March - 27 October.

At a glance

Welcome & Ambience	✓✓✓✓	Location	✓✓✓✓
Quality of Pitches	✓✓✓✓	Range of Facilities	✓✓✓

Directions

Park is 1.5 miles south of Sutton-on-Sea on A52 coast road to Skegness, with the entrance leading off a lay-by on the left. O.S.GR: TF518828.

Charges 2004

Per unit incl. 2 persons, electricity	£ 9.00 - £ 12.00
extra adult	£ 2.25
dog	£ 0.50

Reservations

Made with £20 deposit. Tel: 01507 441626. Email: murray.cherrytree@virgin.net

153

UK3660 Walesby Woodlands Caravan Park

Walesby, Market Rasen LN8 3UN (Lincolnshire)

Surrounded by mature Forestry Commission woodland, this family owned, small touring park is therefore mainly very peaceful (if the wind is in a certain direction trains may be heard in the distance). The new owners, Paul and Christine Burrows will make you welcome. About 1.5 miles away is the small town of Market Rasen, but further afield and within easy driving distance, are Lincoln, the east coast including Skegness and, of course, the Lincolnshire Wolds. There are 60 well spaced pitches, 52 with 10A electricity, marked out on a single, mainly flat, grassy field divided by a central gravel road and with a double row of trees providing useful visual screening. The Viking Way passes through Walesby and there are many other shorter walks in the forest and surrounding area.

Facilities

The single, heated toilet block (deposit charged for the key) is spacious and ample for the site. It has toilet facilities for disabled people and outside, covered, dishwashing sinks. Laundry room. Small shop with information section (all season). Battery charging. Gas supplies. Play area. No kite flying - overhead wires. Winter caravan storage. Off site: Market Rasen racecourse is 2 miles. Fishing 3 miles, riding 2 miles, golf 1.5 miles.

At a glance

Welcome & Ambience	✓✓✓✓	Location	✓✓✓✓
Quality of Pitches	✓✓✓	Range of Facilities	✓✓✓

Directions

Park is northeast of, and signed from, the main approach roads to Market Rasen. O.S.GR: TF117907

Charges guide

Per unit incl. 2 persons	£ 8.00 - £ 10.00
with electricity	£ 10.00 - £ 12.00
extra person	£ 1.50
child (under 12 yrs)	£ 1.25
awning	£ 1.25 - £ 1.50

Reservations

Any length, with deposit. Tel: 01673 843285. Email: walesbywoodlands@talk21.com

Open

1 March - 31 October.

UK3692 Glen Lodge Touring Park

Glen Lodge, Edlington Moor, Woodhall Spa LN10 6UL (Lincolnshire)

This quiet, modern site is ideal for couples and families who enjoy the rural lifestyle, yet it is only just over a mile from the thriving village of Woodhall Spa. All 35 pitches have hardstanding and 10A electricity hook-ups (one or two appeared to need long leads). Interconnected by shingle roads with some street lighting, the grass and flowerbeds are obviously tended by someone who enjoys gardening. In fact, the whole park has a much loved feel. Places to visit include the Battle of Britain Memorial Flight, Tattershall Castle, Horncastle with its antiques centre and the city of Lincoln.

Facilities

The modern heated toilet block (key-pad access) is spotlessly clean with vanity style washbasins and piped music. Facilities for disabled visitors. Washing machine and dryer.

Open

1 March - 30 November.

At a glance

Welcome & Ambience	✓✓✓✓✓	Location	✓✓✓✓
Quality of Pitches	✓✓✓✓✓	Range of Facilities	✓✓✓✓

Directions

From mini-roundabout in Woodhall Spa turn towards Bardney on B1191 (Stixwold Road) past Petwood Hotel. About 1 mile from roundabout at sharp left bend, turn right. Site is 300 yards on right. O.S.GR: TF189647.

Charges 2004

Per unit incl. 2 adults and electricity	£ 11.00
extra person (over 4 yrs)	£ 1.50

Reservations

Contact site. Tel: 01526 353523.

UK3690 Bainland Country Park

Horncastle Road, Woodhall Spa LN10 6UX (Lincolnshire)

A family park with many amenities, Bainland has 170 spacious, level pitches in hedged bays, linked by circular roads, forming circles and islands. Of these, 51 are 'super' pitches with hardstanding, honeycombed for awning, individual water, drainage and chemical disposal, electricity and TV aerial hook-ups. The remainder of the pitches are either on gravel hardstanding or level grass, all with 16A electricity. The friendly reception is housed in a pleasant Swiss-style building adjacent to the shop. Also here are the heated indoor pool and jacuzzi, overlooked by a bistro and spacious bar area. These also overlook the golf course and outdoor bowls area. An adventure play area has been created in a large hollow with a sand base in addition to crazy golf, croquet, TV and games room and soft play area. For adults there is the 18 hole, par 3 golf course, and a tennis club with a year round floodlit tennis dome with 3-4 courts including badminton (the dome comes off in the summer). Bainland is 1.5 miles from Woodhall Spa, with its old fashioned charm and Dambusters associations, yet deep in the heart of the Lincolnshire Wolds, surrounded by mature trees and with direct access to woods for walking dogs. A member of the Best of British group.

Facilities

Four solid toilet blocks are heated and equipped for all basic necessities. They include a baby room, unisex shower room for families, family bathroom, fully equipped unit for disabled people. Laundry room. Enclosed dishwashing and separate laundry sinks. Motorcaravan service points. Licensed shop (Feb-Dec). Bistro (all year) and bar, both also open to the public. Indoor pool (under 16s must be accompanied by an adult). Golf. Tennis and badminton. Play areas. Leisure activities, including the pool, are individually booked and paid for at reception. Some entertainment in high season. Winter caravan storage. Off site: Fishing 3 miles, riding 6 miles.

At a glance

Welcome & Ambience	✓✓✓✓✓	Location	✓✓✓✓
Quality of Pitches	✓✓✓✓✓	Range of Facilities	✓✓✓✓✓

Directions

Entrance to park is off B1191 Horncastle road just outside Woodhall Spa by derestriction sign. O.S.GR: TF214637.

Charges 2004

Per unit incl. electricity, awning	£ 11.00 - £ 26.00
serviced pitch	£ 16.00 - £ 31.00
pup tent	free - £ 3.00

Special rate for firework display (min. 2 nights, 5/6 Nov). Discounts for senior citizens.

Reservations

Advised and made for any length. Deposit at B.Hs. only (one night's fee). Tel: 01526 352903. Email: bookings@bainland.com

Open

All year (in winter, 'super' pitches only).

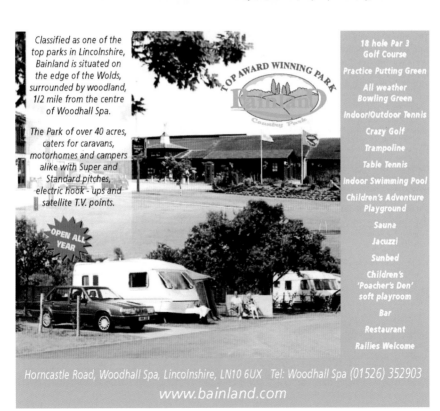

Classified as one of the top parks in Lincolnshire, Bainland is situated on the edge of the Wolds, surrounded by woodland, 1/2 mile from the centre of Woodhall Spa.

The Park of over 40 acres, caters for caravans, motorhomes and campers alike with Super and Standard pitches, electric hook - ups and satellite T.V. points.

OPEN ALL YEAR

TOP AWARD WINNING PARK

18 hole Par 3 Golf Course
Practice Putting Green
All weather Bowling Green
Indoor/Outdoor Tennis
Crazy Golf
Trampoline
Table Tennis
Indoor Swimming Pool
Children's Adventure Playground
Sauna
Jacuzzi
Sunbed
Children's 'Poacher's Den' soft playroom
Bar
Restaurant
Rallies Welcome

Horncastle Road, Woodhall Spa, Lincolnshire, LN10 6UX   Tel: Woodhall Spa (01526) 352903
www.bainland.com

155

UK3950 Orchard Park Touring Park

Marnham Road, Tuxford, Newark NG22 0PY (Nottinghamshire)

This well established family run site has been created in an old fruit orchard in a quiet location. It has 65 pitches, including 34 with hardstanding, 20 of which were occupied by seasonal units at the time of our visit. All pitches have access to electricity (10A). Reception is at the owner's house and at the far end of the park is a picnic area, a grassy area for ball games and a nature walk with wild flowers, birds and butterflies. Local attractions include Sundown Adventureland children's theme park, Laxton Medieval village and Victorian Times, Sherwood Forest parks and Robin Hood Centre.

Facilities

The specially designed toilet unit (with piped music) has the usual facilities including a well equipped room for disabled persons. Laundry with washing machines, dryer and dishwashing sinks. Small shop with basic essentials and gas; more services (some open to 10 pm) are in the village (0.5 miles). Play area. Entrance barrier (£5 deposit for key).

Open

March - October.

At a glance

Welcome & Ambience	✓✓✓✓	Location	✓✓✓✓
Quality of Pitches	✓✓✓	Range of Facilities	✓✓✓

Directions

From the A1 turn onto A6075 towards Lincoln, continue through village to the eastern outskirts, turning right towards High Marnham. Site is on right 0.5 miles after railway bridge (well signed in village). O.S.GR: SK750710.

Charges 2005

Per unit incl. 2 adults	£ 10.00 - £ 11.00
extra adult	£ 1.00
child (4-15 yrs)	£ 0.50
awning or child's pup tent	£ 1.00
extra motorcycle or car	£ 1.00
electricity	£ 1.00

Reservations

Advised for B.Hs (min. 3 nights) with £40 deposit and peak season with £10 deposit. Tel: 01777 870228. Email: info@orchardcaravanpark.co.uk

UK3940 Smeaton's Lakes Touring Caravan Park

Great North Road, South Muskham, Newark-on-Trent NG23 6ED (Nottinghamshire)

This 82-acre site is really ideal for fishermen, with three fishing lakes (coarse, carp and pike) and river fishing on the Trent. Smeaton's Lakes has tarmac access roads and a modern building near the entrance housing reception and the sanitary facilities (quite a walk from some of the pitches). Ground maintenance is good and there are now 130 pitches on grass, 48 with hardstanding (more to come) and 100 with electricity connections (16A). This site is probably the best choice for visiting events at nearby Newark Showground, or Newark town (1 mile) with its castle and various weekly markets. The park is only two minutes from DMG Newark Antique Fairs and Arthur Swallow's Swinderby Antique Fairs. It is also well placed for visiting Southwell Cathedral, Lincoln with its castle and cathedral or Nottingham with its Lace Hall, Castle or Caves and, for people who like to look at motorhomes, Brownhills is close by.

Facilities

Toilet facilities (with keypad access) are heated and include a good unit for disabled people, but no laundry room. Laundry and dishwashing sinks are outside. At busy times these facilities could be stretched. Another shower block has been opened, including facilities for the disabled. Reception keeps gas, soft drinks, dairy produce, etc. and newspapers can be ordered. On site concessions for lake and river fishing. Security cameras and night-time height barrier (about 6 ft). Off site: Bus stop at the end of the entry lane - buses run into Newark every hour until 10 pm.

At a glance

Welcome & Ambience	✓✓✓✓	Location	✓✓✓✓
Quality of Pitches	✓✓✓	Range of Facilities	✓✓✓

Directions

Site lies on A6065 west of the town, south of junction of A616 towards Ollerton (well signed). O.S.GR: SK792558.

Charges 2004

Per unit incl. 2 adults	£ 10.00 - £ 13.50
extra adult	£ 1.50
child (over 5 yrs)	£ 1.00
No credit cards.	

Reservations

Essential for electric hook-ups. Tel: 01636 605088. Email: leslie@smeatonslakes.co.uk

Open

All year.

Need a **POWR Product?**

SEE PAGE 294

UK3920 Riverside Caravan Park

Central Avenue, Worksop S80 1ER (Nottinghamshire)

A town centre touring park, adjacent to the County cricket ground, this excellent site is attractive and surprisingly peaceful. Riverside is within easy walking distance of the town centre pedestrian precinct and shops, and the Chesterfield Canal runs close to its northern side offering delightful tow-path walks or fishing (children would need to be watched). For those who cannot resist the thwack of leather on willow, this site is ideal. Of the 60 marked level pitches, 50 are on gravel hardstanding, some separated by trees and low rails, and all have electric hook-ups (10A). There is excellent site lighting. This is also a good base for exploring Creswell Craggs, Clumber Park, the Dukeries Cycle Trail, and Rufford Mill Craft Centre and Country Park.

Facilities

The modern sanitary unit near reception can be heated and has all the usual facilities, although showers are on payment (20p). No laundry, but a launderette is close by in the town. Off site: Activities locally include squash, flat or crown green bowling, bicycle hire and campers are also very welcome at the cricket ground clubhouse. Worksop provides well for golfers with three courses in the area. One of the town's most interesting buildings, the medieval Priory Gatehouse, is open free of charge. Market days are Wednesday, Friday and Saturday.

At a glance

Welcome & Ambience	✓✓✓✓✓	Location	✓✓✓✓
Quality of Pitches	✓✓✓✓✓	Range of Facilities	✓✓✓

Directions

Easiest approach is from roundabout west of the town (A57) - third roundabout from the A1, junction of A57/A60. Turn into Newcastle Avenue, then left into Stubbing Lane, right into Central Avenue, left into Cricket Ground, follow through to camping site (well signed). O.S.GR: SK580790.

Charges 2004

Per pitch incl. 2 adults, 2 children and electricity	£ 16.15
child (5-13 years)	£ 1.95
extra person	£ 3.75

No credit cards.

Reservations

Advised for B.Hs, peak season and weekends, with £5 deposit. Tel: 01909 474118.

Open

All year.

UK3910 Shardaroba Caravan Park

Silverhill Lane, Teversal, Sutton-in-Ashfield NG17 3JJ (Nottinghamshire)

In a peaceful village location, and yet surprisingly close to the motorway network, this attractive, six acre campsite has 100 pitches in total and takes around 25 seasonal and 75 touring units. Many of the spacious touring pitches are on hardstandings, arranged in well spaced rows surrounded by areas of grass and flower beds. All have electricity hook-ups (10A), and 20 are multi-serviced (electricity, water and waste water). Picnic tables are provided around the site, and the facilities are housed in modern buildings grouped to one side of the site near the entrance. The nearby Carnarvon Arms pub is a short walk away and serves good value meals. A bakery, chip shop and general stores are about a mile away and more comprehensive facilities, including a swimming and fitness complex, are in Mansfield (4 miles). An hourly bus service runs from the pub into the town.

Facilities

Excellent, well equipped, heated sanitary unit includes spacious showers, a family room with facilities for disabled people, and a utility room. Separate laundry has washing machines and dryers. New covered dishwashing sinks. The latest addition is an extra building (also heated) with three full suites (WC, basin, shower) per sex, with more dishwashing sinks under cover to the rear. Drive over motorcaravan service point. Shop with basic essentials. Playground. Bicycle hire. Calor gas. American RVs accepted. Security barrier (£10 deposit for key). Off site: Adjacent to the site is a recently developed country park, with footpaths, cycle and bridleways, and hundreds of newly planted trees - an ideal place for a picnic. Other nearby attractions include Teversal Visitor Centre, Hardwick Hall, The Hardwick Inn (good restaurant), Crich Tramway Museum, Newstead Abbey, and the Pleasley Trails. Golf 800 yds. Riding 200 yds. Fishing 1 mile.

At a glance

Welcome & Ambience	✓✓✓	Location	✓✓✓✓✓
Quality of Pitches	✓✓✓✓	Range of Facilities	✓✓✓✓

Directions

Teversal is central in a triangle formed by M1 junction 28 and junction 29, and Mansfield. Site is signed off B6014 at western end of the village, turning north by the Carnarvon Arms, into Silverhill Lane and site entrance is 300 yds on left. O.S.GR: SK485625.

Charges 2004

Per unit incl. 2 adults	£ 12.00
extra adult	£ 4.00
child (3-14 yrs)	£ 2.00
electricity	£ 2.00
awning	£ 1.00

Reservations

Advisable for B.Hs and July/August. Made with £10 non-refundable deposit Tel: 01623 551838. Email: stay@shardaroba.co.uk

Open

All year.

157

UK3840 Lime Tree Park

Dukes Drive, Buxton SK17 9RP (Derbyshire)

A select park with high quality, modern facilities, Lime Tree is in a convenient, edge of town location that makes a very good base for touring the Peak District. There are 99 pitches including some for seasonal and rental units. The 64 for tourists with 10A electricity (hardstandings available) and an area for tents are on the two upper terraces which have the best views but are slightly more exposed. Below are areas set aside for late arrivals and the caravan holiday homes (most privately owned, some for rent). On site is a small shop for gas and basics, and a recently extended children's playground. Buxton town centre is a comfortable stroll away. A member of the Best of British group.

Facilities

A modern toilet building serves the caravan and motorcaravan area, complete with patio and pergola frontage, whilst the refitted original unit serves the tent area. Both units can be heated and have top quality fittings, including washbasins (some in cubicles), a baby room with the very latest design of baby bath, and a family room with facilities for disabled people. Dishwashing sinks are outside under cover. Laundry room with washing machine and dryer. Motorcaravan service area. Shop. Play area. Games/TV room. Off site: The nearest pub serving food is just around the corner. Fishing, bicycle hire, riding and golf, all within 5 miles. Alton Towers is 22 miles.

At a glance

Welcome & Ambience	✓✓✓✓	Location	✓✓✓✓
Quality of Pitches	✓✓✓✓	Range of Facilities	✓✓✓

Directions

From Buxton take A515 Ashbourne road south. After the hospital on the outskirts of town, turn sharp left into Dukes Drive, go under railway viaduct and site is on the right. O.S.GR: SK069725.

Charges 2004

Per unit incl. 2 adults	£ 12.00 - £ 15.00
extra adult	£ 2.00
child (5-15 yrs)	£ 0.75 - £ 1.00
electricity	£ 2.20
hiker, cyclist or m/cyclist	£ 4.00 - £ 5.00
dog	£ 1.00

Reservations

Made with £10 deposit. Tel: 01298 22988.
Email: limetreebuxton@dukes50.fsnet

Open

1 March - 31 October.

UK3800 Highfields Holiday Caravan Park

Fenny Bentley, Ashbourne DE6 1LE (Derbyshire)

Highfields is set on high, flat ground in the Peak District National Park with marvellous views. Run by the Redfern family, it takes 50 touring units and 50 seasonal vans in open, hedged fields accessed by tarmac roads. There is an area for tents, another for vans with concrete slabs for jockey wheels and an area for adults only. There are 8 hardstandings and 89 electrical connections (16A), with 55 privately owned caravan holiday homes in separate fields. An indoor, heated swimming pool is open all season (restricted times if the park is not very full), with a small charge. Although not supervised at all times, the pool is monitored from reception by closed circuit TV. A room with table and chairs, is available for hire. People frequently venture off the site to enjoy the Peak District - Dovedale and Ilam are only a mile or two's distance by footpath and the Tissington Trail with access to the High Peak Trail passes by the park.

Facilities

The main toilet block is kept locked (deposit for key) and is well maintained. Hot water is metered for laundry and dishwashing, and to the showers. Baby bath. A smaller block is in the far static field and further sanitary facilities are provided adjacent to the rally room. All blocks are heated when necessary. Shop for basics and gas. Good children's playground with new rubber base. Bicycle hire. Swimming pool (90p per session). American motorhomes accepted. Winter caravan storage. Torches are useful. Off site: Pub and restaurant close. Fishing 3 miles, golf 5 miles, riding 2 miles, boat launching 5 miles.

Open

1 March - 31 October.

At a glance

Welcome & Ambience	✓✓✓✓	Location	✓✓✓✓✓
Quality of Pitches	✓✓✓✓	Range of Facilities	✓✓✓✓

Directions

Park is west off A515 Buxton - Ashbourne road, just north of Fenny Bentley village and just south of old railway bridge (take care at sharp turn to site road when approaching from Ashbourne). O.S.GR: SK170510.

Charges guide

Per unit incl. 2 persons	£ 10.00
extra adult	£ 3.50
child (under 17 yrs)	£ 1.00
electricity (16A)	£ 3.00
awning	£ 1.00
dog	£ 1.00

Reservations

Made with payment of one night's fee; min. stay at B.Hs - 3 nights. Tel: 0870 741 8000.

UK3820 Darwin Forest Country Park

Darley Moor, Two Dales, Matlock DE4 5LN (Derbyshire)

Between Matlock and Bakewell, this park, as its name implies, is set amongst 44 acres of mixed woodland close to the Peak District National Park. A large proportion of the park is given over to pine lodges for holiday letting and it is still expanding, but it also provides 50 touring pitches. All with hardstanding and electric hook-up (16A), they are clearly defined with hedging or open fencing in level grass bays amongst the woodland which is home to a variety of birds and wildlife. With an inn and an indoor pool on the park, this is a useful base from which to explore the Peak District.

Facilities

The timberclad toilet block is tiled and well equipped, although WC cubicles are rather small. Washbasins in cabins. Full unit for disabled people. Laundry room and covered washing up area. Small shop. Calor gas. Inn. Heated indoor pool (40 x 20 ft) - charges: adult £1.00 - £2.50, child (4-14 yrs) 50p - £1.50. Adventure play area. Games room. Tennis court, short-tennis. Minigolf. Soft playroom. Off site: Fishing 2 miles, bicycle hire 8 miles, riding 2 miles, golf 4 miles. Alton Towers 40 minutes.

At a glance

Welcome & Ambience	✓✓✓	Location	✓✓✓✓
Quality of Pitches	✓✓✓	Range of Facilities	✓✓✓✓

Directions

Park is best approached via the A632 Chesterfield - Matlock road. North of Matlock take B5057 signed Darley Dale and park is on the right before descending into the village of Two Dales. O.S.GR: SK287633.

Charges 2004

Per unit incl. all persons, electricity £ 13.00 - £ 15.00

Reservations

Advised and made with deposit. Tel: 01629 732428. Email: admin@darwinforest.co.uk

Open

March - October.

UK3850 Rivendale Caravan & Leisure Park

Buxton Road, Alsop-en-le-Dale, Ashbourne DE6 1QU (Derbyshire)

This is an unusual park, recently developed in the bowl of a hill quarry last worked 50 years ago. The steep quarry walls shelter three sides with marvellous views over the Peak National Park countryside to the south. A wide access road passes the renovated stone building which houses reception, a shop, bar and a café/restaurant. It gently climbs to a horseshoe shaped area providing 100 pitches, most of generous size, with 16A electricity. The pitches, a mixture of hardstanding and half grass, half hardstanding, are divided by shrubs which are growing slowly with a further, open, marked grass area accessed by hard core roads. All pitches are within easy reach of the central stone-built toilet block which is in keeping with the environment and thoughtfully provided with under-floor heating. The park covers about 11 acres with further 26 acres belonging to the owners with certain parts suitable for walking - a must to appreciate the Derbyshire countryside with its dry stone walls and wild flowers. The park is almost on the Tissington Trail for walking or off road cycling and linking with the High Peak and Monsal Dale Trail. Other spectacular walks and cycle rides run along the Manifold, Wye and Dove valleys.

Facilities

First rate toilet facilities include some washbasins in cubicles for ladies, and an excellent en-suite room for disabled visitors. Laundry room. Glass and paper recycling bins. Bar (evenings) and café with home-made and local food (open mornings, lunch times and evenings, both with limited opening in low season). Special events monthly and games in main season. Shop (all essentials). Off site: Riding 3 miles, fishing 5 miles, bicycle hire 2.5 miles. Alton Towers 35 minutes drive. Chatsworth House and Gardens, Heights of Abraham and Guillivers Kingdom near.

At a glance

Welcome & Ambience	✓✓✓✓	Location	✓✓✓✓
Quality of Pitches	✓✓✓	Range of Facilities	✓✓✓✓

Directions

Park is about 7 miles north of Ashbourne on the A515 road to Buxton. Pass right turns to Alsop station, village and one other before site is clearly signed to the right a little further on. O.S.GR: SK161566.

Charges 2004

Per pitch incl. 2 adults, electricity	£ 10.80 - £ 13.00
extra adult	£ 2.00
child (4-15yrs)	£ 1.50

Camping Cheques accepted.

Reservations

Made with £10 deposit. Tel: 01335 310311. Email: enquiries@rivendalecaravanpark.co.uk

Open

All year excl. 10 January - 4 February.

Beautiful surroundings in the Peak District National Park. Open all year except 10 Jan – 4 Feb. Ideal for cycling, walking, outdoor and adventure sports. Convenient for Chatsworth, Alton Towers & Dove Dale. Holiday homes for sale.

www.Rivendalecaravanpark.co.uk Tel: +44 (0)1335 310311 or 310441

UK3980 Longnor Wood Caravan & Camping Park

Longnor, nr Buxton SK17 0NG (Derbyshire)

A secluded rural location, deep in the heart of the Peak District, Longnor Wood is an ideal environment for a relaxing break from the outside world. It is a good base for walking, red deer and bird watching (barn owls) and serious cycling - the area is very hilly. There are 47 pitches, of which 14 are taken by holiday homes, the remaining 33 touring pitches are level, some on small terraces, all with 10A electric hookups. Thirrteen are multi-serviced with electricity, water, waste water and TV connections. Twelve are on hardstandings. The tenting area is at the top of the site with wonderful views over the National Park, but you may have a problem with tent pegs as the topsoil can be rather thin in places. A well appointed late arrivals area is at the entrance. Reception has a brochure with the history of the old market town of Longnor (where 'Peak Practice' was filmed) which includes several places worth visiting. This is an adult only park (over 18 yrs).

Facilities

The single heated building has been recently refurbished, and includes cubicles with a toilet and washbasin, spacious showers and has dishwashing sinks under cover and a microwave oven (donations to charity). Laundry with washing machine, dryer and spinner. Reception is licensed and stocks basic requirements. Gas supplies. Putting green, badminton and boules court. Dogs accepted, max. 2 per unit. Site is not suitable for American RVs. Off site: Markets in Buxton (Tues/Sat), Leek (Wed). Sightseeing opportunities include Dovedale and the Manifold Valley, Arbor Low Stone Circle, and Flash, at 1,580 ft. is the highest village in England. Fishing 5 miles, golf 8 miles, riding 8 miles.

At a glance

Welcome & Ambience	✓✓✓✓	Location	✓✓✓✓✓
Quality of Pitches	✓✓✓✓✓	Range of Facilities	✓✓✓

Directions

Longnor village is on the B5053, about 6 miles south of Buxton. Site is west of village (where it is signed) on a minor road (1 mile). Also signed from the A53 between Leek and Buxton, turning opposite the Winking Man public house. O.S.GR: SK072640.

Charges 2004

Per pitch incl. 2 persons, electricity and awning	£ 11.00 - £ 14.50
extra person	£ 1.50

No credit cards.

Reservations

Advisable for weekends, B.Hs and peak season and made with £10 deposit. Tel: 01298 83648. Email: enquiries@longwood.co.uk

Open

1 March - 31 October.

UK3970 Glencote Caravan Park

Station Road, Cheddleton, Leek ST13 7EE (Staffordshire)

At the entrance to the Churnet Valley, three miles south of the market town of Leek, Glencote is a pleasant, family run park of six acres. It has 74 numbered pitches set on flat grass, all with patio style hardstandings, with tarmac access roads. There are 40 pitches for touring units and all have electrical connections (10A) and a dedicated water supply. Pretty flower-beds and trees make a very pleasant environment. An attractive, sunken children's play area, on grass and bark with an abundance of shrubs and flowers, sits alongside the small (fenced) coarse fishing pool, together with a barbecue area with a tented cover. Attractions nearby include a renovated Flint Mill powered by two giant water wheels and Cheddleton railway centre. The Churnet Valley, an Area of Outstanding Natural Beauty is good for walking, the Staffordshire Way is also near. For the more energetic, canoeing, climbing and hang gliding opportunities are close. Alton Towers is 10 miles away.

Facilities

The toilet block is centrally situated and can be heated. Facilities include one private cabin for ladies, a small laundry room, and two dishwashing sinks under cover. Gas supplies. Max. 2 dogs per unit. Security barrier £10 deposit. Off site: In the village of Cheddleton, 0.5 miles away, is a small supermarket and a post office. A variety of inns are within easy walking distance - the Boat Inn beside the canal is very good value. Riding 10 miles, bicycle hire 5 miles, golf 4 miles.

Open

Mid March - end October.

At a glance

Welcome & Ambience	✓✓✓✓	Location	✓✓✓✓
Quality of Pitches	✓✓✓	Range of Facilities	✓✓✓

Directions

Park is signed off A520 Leek - Stone road, 3.5 miles south of Leek on northern edge of Cheddleton Village. O.S.GR: SJ982524.

Charges 2004

Per unit incl. 2 persons	£ 13.50
extra adult	£ 2.50
child (under 16 yrs)	£ 1.50
pup tent or extra car	£ 1.00
electricity (10A)	£ 0.50

For each 7 nights booked, one night pitch fee free. Min. stay of 3 nights at B.Hs.

Reservations

Advised for peak season. Made with deposit (£30 for 4 nights or more, full payment for up to 3 nights). Tel: 01538 360745.

UK4070 Somers Wood Caravan & Camping Park

Somers Road, Meriden CV7 7PL (Warwickshire)

Somers Wood is a useful site near the NEC. However, it is for adults only and does not accept tents. Although near to Birmingham, it is attractively located and edged by pine woods, with views of the adjacent 18 hole golf course (including driving range) and coarse fishing lake; both being available for visitors to use. Log buildings that blend comfortably into their surroundings provide reception, with the owners' home at the entrance and separate sanitary facilities. An oval, gravel road provides access to the 48 large pitches, all on hardstanding with 10A electricity connections. This is a very useful park for those visiting the NEC. For certain shows, such as the National Boat, Caravan and Leisure Show in February, it can be busy, although at other times it is quiet and peaceful. Only adults are accepted.

Facilities	Directions
The central, heated sanitary block is fully equipped. Two dishwashing sinks on the veranda area. Laundry service at reception. Off site: Local shops and restaurant less than 1 mile and visitors also welcome to use the bar and restaurant at the golf club.	From M42 exit 6 (NEC) take A45 towards Coventry. Keep in left lane to roundabout and exit on A452 (Leamington/Meriden). Turn left into Hampton Lane at next roundabout (Stonebridge Golf Centre). Site is signed with golf centre on left. O.S.GR: SP228819.

Open

1 February - 20 December.

Charges 2004

Per pitch incl. 2 persons and electricity £ 16.00

At a glance

Welcome & Ambience	✓✓✓	Location	✓✓✓✓
Quality of Pitches	✓✓✓✓	Range of Facilities	✓✓✓

Reservations

Advised for B.Hs and certain NEC exhibitions; made with deposit of £5 per night booked. Tel: 01676 522978. Email: info@somerswood.co.uk

UK4075 Hollyfast Caravan Park

Wall Hill Road, Allesley, Coventry CV5 9EL (Warwickshire)

Hollyfast is situated in beautiful countryside on the outskirts of Coventry, part of the park being set within a lovely woodland area giving peace and tranquility all year round. Located on the Birmingham side of Coventry, this means a five minute drive into the centre of Coventry and just a ten minute drive to Birmingham's National Exhibition Centre. You will receive a friendly welcome and be directed to a very clean and well spaced site with 35 pitches of varying sizes. A new toilet block provides very clean facilities, along with a laundry room and games room. Rallies are welcome and a club house is provided with a stage, television and kitchen areas for these groups. A motorcaravan sales centre with caravan and motorhome storage, LPG and a children's play area are next to the site.

Facilities	Directions
The modern toilet block provides clean facilities with good sized showers. Toilet and shower for disabled campers. Laundry. Games room. Club house for rallies. Off site: The local area has shops, three pubs (hot and cold food), lovely countryside walks, golf course and horse riding centre. Bus stop 1 mile for Coventry.	From M1/M45 (or M40/A46, or M69/A46) take A45 towards Birmingham. Turn right on A4114 and follow caravan signs. From north take M6 north of Birmingham or M1 north (Nottingham) follow M42 to NEC, then A45 (Coventry) onto A4114 and as above. O.S.GR: SP303831.

Open

All year.

Charges 2004

Per unit incl. 2 persons, electricity	£ 10.00 - £ 14.00
extra adult	£ 2.00
child (5-15 yrs)	£ 1.00

At a glance

Welcome & Ambience	✓✓✓✓	Location	✓✓✓✓
Quality of Pitches	✓✓✓✓	Range of Facilities	✓✓✓

Reservations

Contact site. Tel: 02476 336411.

UK4080 Riverside Caravan Park

Tiddington Road, Tiddington, Stratford-upon-Avon CV37 7AB (Warwickshire)

On the bank of the River Avon, this spacious site has about 250 pitches and about 100 privately owned mobile homes. The 125 touring pitches are on level grass, all with electricity (16A). There is a small shop and café on site serving breakfasts and takeaways. A clubhouse incorporating a bar, restaurant, playground, games room and TV room is on the adjacent Rayford Park which is under the same management. There is a possible flood risk during periods of inclement weather. A river taxi runs to Stratford.

Facilities	Directions
The main toilet unit is bright and comfortable with heating. Spacious pre-set showers, some washbasins in cubicles. Facilities for disabled guests. Utility room with dishwashing and laundry sinks, washing machines and dryers. Slipway and fishing. Courtesy river launch to Stratford. Gas supplies.	From Stratford take B4086 towards Wellesbourne. Site entrance is on left, after one mile, just before Tiddington village. O.S.GR: SP219559.

Charges 2004

Per unit incl. 4 persons	£ 11.00 - £ 18.00
extra person	£ 1.00

Open

1 April - 31 October.

At a glance

Welcome & Ambience	✓✓✓✓	Location	✓✓✓✓
Quality of Pitches	✓✓✓✓	Range of Facilities	✓✓✓

Reservations

Advised for weekends, B.Hs, and peak season and made with £10 deposit. Tel: 01789 292312. Email: info@stratfordcaravans.co.uk

UK4090 Island Meadow Caravan Park

The Mill House, Aston Cantlow B95 6JP (Warwickshire)

This peaceful, traditional, family run site is in a rural location, surrounded by the River Alne and its mill race. A good base for walking, cycling and birdwatching, it has 80 pitches in total, with 56 holiday homes (4 for rent) located around the perimeter. The 24 touring pitches are on the spacious, central grassy area of the site, all have 10A electric hook-ups. Only environmentally friendly groundsheets are permitted. The small shop has an adequate stock of basic requirements and gas supplies, and a good stock of local visitor information. Note: The site is on an island with obvious hazards for small children. There is an excellent playground in the village centre (five minutes walk via footpath across Mill Meadow).

Facilities

Two sanitary units, both heated. The original provides adequate WCs and washbasins for men, and the more modern unit has been provided for women, with a separate access shower unit for the men, and a suite for disabled people on one end. Dishwashing sink. Laundry with washing machine, sink and ironing facility. The millpond and its weir offer good coarse fishing. Off site: The village has its own 'club' (campers welcome) and the local pub serves a good range of meals. Golf 3 miles, riding 4.5 miles, bicycle hire 6 miles. Warwick Castle. Stratford-upon-Avon. Mary Arden's house in Wilmcote is only 1 mile from the site. Buses from village to Alcester and Stratford, including a late night service.

At a glance

Welcome & Ambience	✓✓✓✓	Location	✓✓✓✓
Quality of Pitches	✓✓✓✓	Range of Facilities	✓✓✓

Directions

Site is well signed from the A46 mid-way between Alcester and Stratford-upon-Avon, and also from the A3400 at Wootton Wawen. O.S.GR: SP136598.

Charges 2004

Per unit incl. 2 persons	£ 11.00 - £ 15.00
extra person	£ 1.00
child (5-10 yrs)	£ 0.50
electricity	free - £ 3.00

Gazebos only by prior arrangement.
No credit cards.

Reservations

Advised for B.Hs (3 nights minimum) and July/August. Tel: 01789 488273.
Email: holiday@islandmeadowcaravanpark.co.uk

Open

1 March - 31 October.

UK4040 Clent Hills Camping & Caravanning Club Site

Fieldhouse Lane, Romsley, Halesowen B62 0NH (West Midlands)

Conveniently close to Birmingham and only a couple of miles or so off the M5/M42 intersection, this site is a real surprise in terms of being quiet and peaceful and very pretty with good views. Its only disadvantage is that it is on sloping ground, but the present, very helpful holiday site managers are happy to assist in pitching anyone who has a problem in getting level (mainly motorcaravanners); in fact, there are some level pitches and these are all earmarked for motorcaravans. The 95 pitches are all of a good size, 74 with electrical connections (10/16A) and 17 with hardstanding. The modern reception building with excellent tourist information, arrivals area and larger car parking area are at the entrance. Generally this is a well run and attractive site, very usefully situated.

Facilities

The central sanitary toilet block can be heated and provides the latest facilities, including washbasins in cabins, hairdryers, baby room and a toilet and shower for disabled people. It was spotless when last visited. Washing machine, dryer and ironing facilities. Small play area with rubber safety surface. Gas supplies. Caravan storage. Off site: Riding 1 mile. Fishing 3 miles. Golf 7 miles.

Open

March - November.

At a glance

Welcome & Ambience	✓✓✓✓✓	Location	✓✓✓✓
Quality of Pitches	✓✓✓✓	Range of Facilities	✓✓✓

Directions

From M5 junction 3 take A491, branch right to Romsley on B4551 and watch for site signs in Romsley village by shops. Site is on left. O.S.GR: SO955795.

Charges 2005

Per adult	£ 4.30 - £ 6.40
child (6-18 yrs)	£ 1.90
non-member pitch fee	£ 5.00

Reservations

Necessary and made with deposit; contact site or Central Reservations 0870 243 3331.
Tel: 01562 710015.

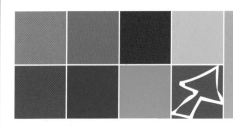

UK4220 Riverside Caravan Park

Little Clevelode (on B4424), Malvern WR13 6PE (Worcestershire)

A traditional, older style site, Riverside at Little Clevelode is set in the picturesque Severn Valley four miles east of Great Malvern, and close to the Malvern Hills. The main touring site is located on high ground above the river near the site entrance, and has around 70 grassy pitches, with a good many seasonal units, but there is usually space for tourists. There are two playgrounds and an area for football and ball games and a tennis hard-court. The lower level of the site near the river has an area for holiday homes and a clubhouse/bar, games room with pool table, electronic machines and TV, a well stocked shop plus a further sanitary unit and a small laundry. No dogs, washing lines, children's cycles, roller skates, skateboards, or scooters are permitted on site.

Facilities

The modernised toilet block serving the touring site provides controllable hot showers, vanity style washbasins and a small dishwashing room. Whilst not luxurious these basic facilities are adequate and kept clean. Shop. Clubhouse/bar (weekends only low season, daily at other times). Off site: Riding and bicycle hire 3 miles. Golf 4 miles.

Open

Easter - 1 November.

At a glance

| Welcome & Ambience | ✓✓✓ | Location | ✓✓✓✓ |
| Quality of Pitches | ✓✓✓✓ | Range of Facilities | ✓✓✓ |

Directions

Little Clevelode is east of Great Malvern on the B4424. From Great Malvern take B4211 east for 2 miles, turning north on B4424 for about 0.5 miles to site. From Worcester (north) take A449 south and fork left on B4424 for 2 miles to site. O.S.GR: SO830460.

Charges 2004

Per unit incl. 2 persons	£ 7.00
extra person (over 4 yrs)	£ 2.00
electricity	£ 2.00

No credit cards.

Reservations

Advised for B.Hs (min. 3 nights) and school holidays and made with one nights pitch fee. Tel: 01684 310475.

UK4180 Ranch Caravan Park

Honeybourne, Evesham WR11 7PR (Worcestershire)

The Vale of Evesham is noted for being a sheltered area growing fruit and other produce from early spring through to late autumn. Ranch lies not far from both Evesham and Broadway in quiet rural surroundings of 50 acres and is also only half an hour's drive from Stratford-on-Avon. A free swimming pool is open and heated from June - September. The park takes 120 touring units - caravans, motorcaravans or trailer tents but not other tents - on flat, partly undulating, hedged meadows with well mown grass and a spacious feel. Pitches are not marked but the staff position units. There are around 100 electrical connections (10A) and 20 hardstandings including 8 fully serviced pitches (electricity, TV, water and sewer connections). There are 169 caravan holiday homes in their own section.

Facilities

Two very well appointed, modern toilet blocks with free showers and heating, make a good provision. Motorcaravan service point. Comfortable clubhouse (weekends only in early and late season) with wide range of good value meals. Entertainment arranged at B.H. weekends and Saturdays in school holidays. Swimming pool (55 x 30 ft; June - Sept). Small games room with TV (incl. Sky), video machines and pool table. Play area. Off site: Fishing 2 miles. Riding close.

Open

1 March - 30 November.

At a glance

| Welcome & Ambience | ✓✓✓✓✓ | Location | ✓✓✓✓✓ |
| Quality of Pitches | ✓✓✓✓ | Range of Facilities | ✓✓✓✓✓ |

Directions

From A46 Evesham take B4035 towards Chipping Campden. After Badsey and Bretforton follow signs for Honeybourne down unclassified road (Ryknild Street, Roman road). Park is through village on left by station. O.S.GR: SP112444.

Charges 2004

Per unit incl. 2 adults, electricity	£ 13.50 - £ 18.00
extra person over 5 yrs	free - £ 2.50
multi-services	£ 2.50
dog	free - £ 2.50

Reservations

Advised for peak weeks and B.Hs. Made with deposit (£5 per night) and essential for B.Hs. (min. 3 days) Tel: 01386 830744. Email: enquiries@ranch.co.uk

163

UK4210 Lickhill Manor Caravan Park

Lower Lickhill Road, Stourport-on-Severn DY13 8RL (Worcestershire)

Lickhill Manor is a well managed touring or holiday site within easy walking distance (15 minutes) of the town centre via a footpath along the River Severn which lies a short distance below the site. There are opportunities for fishing and boating. The touring field has 90 marked, level, grassy pitches accessed via tarmac roads, all with electricity (10/16A). The 124 holiday homes, well screened from the touring area amongst tree lined avenues, are not visually intrusive, and there is a separate rally field (with 50 hook-ups). There is an excellent children's playground and the site has recently created wildlife ponds and planted over 1,000 native trees and shrubs. With its new sanitary block, roads and landscaping and friendly welcoming staff, this park has matured into one of the best in the area. Stourport is a lively bustling town with some splendid public parks, amusements and sports facilities. Kidderminster, the Forestry Commission Visitor Centre at Bewdley, the Severn Valley Railway and West Midland Safari Park are a short drive from the site.

Facilities

A second sanitary building was added in '98 to serve the touring pitches and complement the older unit at the other end of the park. This heated building provides very good, modern facilities including a comprehensively equipped suite for disabled guests which also double as a family washroom with facilities for baby changing. Excellent drive over motorcaravan service point. Recycling bins. Gas supplies. Playground. Off site: Riding 1 mile, bicycle hire 3 miles. Six golf courses within 5 miles. A small parade of shops and the nearest pub are 10 minutes walk.

Open

All year.

At a glance

Welcome & Ambience	✓✓✓✓	Location	✓✓✓✓✓
Quality of Pitches	✓✓✓✓	Range of Facilities	✓✓✓✓

Directions

From centre of Stourport take B4195 northwest towards Bewdley. After 1 mile turn left at crossroads (traffic lights), into Lickhill Road North where site is signed. O.S.GR: SO790730

Charges 2004

Per unit incl. 4 persons, electricity	£ 10.00 - £ 16.00
extra person over 2 yrs	£ 1.00
awning	£ 1.50
2 person tent	£ 9.00
dog	£ 0.50

Weekly rates available. Senior citizen discounts.

Reservations

Advised for B.Hs. and peak season.
Tel: 01299 871041.
Email: excellent@lickhillmanor.co.uk

UK4190 Kingsgreen Caravan Park

Kingsgreen, Berrow, Malvern WR13 6AQ (Worcestershire)

A friendly, comfortable, farm site with views of the Malvern Hills, Kingsgreen has an attractive rural location. An ideal site for adults who like the quiet life, there are no amusements for children. The surrounding countryside is ideal for walking or cycling, and the small, fenced fishing lake on the site is well stocked (£3 per day). There are 45 level, grass and gravel pitches, all with electricity (16A), plus an additional area for tents. Some old orchard trees provide a little shade in parts. The site is 7 miles from the market town of Ledbury with its half timbered buildings and within easy driving distance of Malvern, the Three Counties showground, Cotswolds, Forest of Dean or Tewkesbury with its 12th century Abbey.

Facilities

Modern toilet facilities (key on deposit) provide hot showers (25p token from reception) and a separate unit for disabled people (WC and washbasin). Dishwashing sinks under cover. Laundry room with washing machine, dryer, sink and iron and board (all metered). Gas and barbecue fuels are stocked and a milkman calls daily with milk, eggs, bread, soft drinks, etc. Off site: Nearest shop and pub 1.5 miles. Bicycle hire 2 miles, riding 3 miles, golf 5 miles.

Open

1 March - 31 October.

At a glance

Welcome & Ambience	✓✓✓✓✓	Location	✓✓✓✓
Quality of Pitches	✓✓✓✓	Range of Facilities	✓✓✓

Directions

From M50 junction 2, take A417 towards Gloucester, then first left, where site is signed, also signed the Malverns, back over the motorway. Site is 2 miles from the M50. O.S.GR: SO767338.

Charges 2004

Per unit incl. 2 adults	£ 7.00 - £ 8.00
extra person over 2 yrs	£ 1.00
electricity	£ 1.50
awning	£ 1.00
dog	£ 1.00

No credit cards. VAT not included.

Reservations

Essential for peak season and B.Hs.
Tel: 01531 650272.

UK4110 Tewkesbury Caravan Club Site

Gander Lane, Tewkesbury GL20 5PG (Gloucestershire)

There are two important reasons why the Caravan Club site at Tewkesbury is so popular: firstly, it is within five minutes walk of the town centre and is overlooked by the Norman Abbey, the focal point of the town and secondly, it is a good base for exploring the eastern end of the Cotswolds as well as some of the country's most delightful towns. Covering nine acres, the site has 170 pitches reached by tarmac roads. All are on grass, but some slope so blocks are essential, and all have electric hook-ups (16A). The entrance to the site is locked at night but there is a late arrivals area just outside. A popular site and one of the largest sites operated by the Caravan Club with friendly and helpful wardens.

Facilities
Three toilet blocks, all built and maintained to the Club's high standards. The one in the reception building is without showers. One block has facilities for disabled visitors and two have laundry rooms. Motorcaravan services. Reception sells basic supplies and gas. Off site: Fishing 400 yds, riding 5 miles, golf 1 mile.

Open
April - October.

At a glance

Welcome & Ambience	✓✓✓✓	Location	✓✓✓✓✓
Quality of Pitches	✓✓✓	Range of Facilities	✓✓✓

Directions
From all directions follow signs for town centre and head for the Abbey. Turn by the Abbey into Gander Lane, follow down passing two car parks to site at end of the lane. O.S.GR: SO894324.

Charges 2004

Per adult	£ 3.30 - £ 4.80
child (5-16 yrs)	£ 1.10 - £ 1.60
pitch incl. electricity (non-member)	£ 8.00 - £ 11.00

Reservations
Accepted and are essential for all B.Hs. and June-Aug. Tel: 01684 294035.

UK4140 Winchcombe Camping & Caravanning Club Site

Brooklands Farm, Alderton, Tewkesbury GL20 8NX (Gloucestershire)

This is a popular, quiet site in a rural location, close to the Cotswold attractions. Some pitches surround a small coarse fishing lake, with others in a more recently developed area with open views over the surrounding countryside. There are 80 pitches, 53 with electricity (10A) and 42 with gravel hardstanding. The reception building flanks a small gravel courtyard car park and late arrivals area approached from a tarmac drive. Places to visit include Gloucester Docks and the National Waterways Museum, whilst south of Gloucester are Owlpen Manor near Uley, and the Painswick Rococo Garden.

Facilities
The main, heated sanitary unit, kept very clean and tidy by the wardens, is well equipped. Dishwashing sinks are under cover. To the rear of the site is a small, 'portacabin' style sanitary unit (also heated). Well equipped unit for disabled people. Laundry with washing machine and dryer. Gas supplies. Large games room with bowling alley, table tennis and pool table. Small play area. Off site: Golf 7 miles.

Open
March - January.

At a glance

Welcome & Ambience	✓✓✓✓	Location	✓✓✓✓✓
Quality of Pitches	✓✓✓✓	Range of Facilities	✓✓✓✓

Directions
From M5 exit 9, take A46 Evesham road for 3 miles to Toddington roundabout. Take B4077 towards Stow-on-the-Wold, for a further 3 miles to the site. Ignore signs for Alderton village. O.S.GR: SP 007324.

Charges 2005

Per adult	£ 5.55 - £ 6.40
child (5-16 yrs)	£ 1.90
non-member pitch fee	£ 5.00

Reservations
Advised; contact site or Central Reservations 0870 243 3331. Tel: 01242 620259.

UK4150 Croft Farm Water & Leisure Park

Bredon's Hardwick, Tewkesbury GL20 7EE (Gloucestershire)

Croft Farm is a licensed Watersports Centre with Royal Yachting Association approved tuition available for windsurfing, sailing, kayaking and canoeing. The lakeside campsite has around 96 level pitches, with 80 electric hook-ups (10A), but there are many seasonal units, leaving around 36 pitches for tourists. There are 22 gravel hardstandings but very little shade or shelter. 'Gym & Tonic' is a fully equipped gym with instructors, sun bed and sauna. The 'Playzone' has a soft play area, play structure, bouncy castle table football and a Playstation. Activity holidays for families and groups are also organised. Campers can use their own non-powered boats on the lake with reduced launch fees and there is free fishing.

Facilities
A building (open in summer months) on the far side of the lake, has excellent modern facilities. A heated unit at the back of the gym is always open with laundry and facilities for disabled persons. Gas. Cafe/bar (Fri-Sun low season, daily at other times. Takeaway. Gym. Indoor 'Playzone'. Outdoor playground. River fishing. Key for barrier and toilet block £5 deposit. Off site: Golf 3 miles. Riding 8 miles.

Open
All year, excl. January and February.

At a glance

Welcome & Ambience	✓✓✓✓	Location	✓✓✓✓
Quality of Pitches	✓✓✓✓	Range of Facilities	✓✓✓✓

Directions
Bredons Hardwick is mid-way between Tewkesbury and Bredon on B4080. Site is well signed at western end of village, site entrance opposite 'Cross Keys Inn'. O.S.GR: SO 912353.

Charges 2004

Per unit incl. 2 persons and awning	£ 10.00
extra person (over 3 yrs)	£ 3.00
electricity	£ 2.00

Reservations
Essential for high seasons. Tel: 01684 772321. Email: enquiries@croftfarmleisure.co.uk

165

UK4130 Moreton-in-Marsh Caravan Club Site

Bourton Road, Moreton-in-Marsh GL56 0BT (Gloucestershire)

This excellent, busy, but rural, tree-surrounded site in the heart of the Cotswolds offers most one would hope for from a camping holiday. Only 250 yards from the town, there is plenty of choice for food and pubs. The site has 182 pitches, all with electricity (16A) and TV sockets, 172 with hardstanding. Milk, and ice-cream are available from reception. A large play field provides a climbing frame with bark base and space for football, volleyball, boules and crazy golf. Kite flying is not allowed because of low power cables. Moreton-in-Marsh is famous for its Tuesday street market and is always a busy town, being only a few miles from the pretty villages of Bourton-on-the-Water and Stow-on-the-Wold, just two of the many interesting Cotswold villages worthy of a visit in this lovely area of England. Tents are not accepted.

Facilities

Two toilet blocks offer very good facilities with spacious showers, washbasins in cabins, with facilities in each block for the walking disabled (4 inch step). Excellent en-suite room for disabled visitors in another building, baby room and large laundry. Play area. Boules. Internet access. Off site: Shops, pubs and restaurants 400 yards. Golf 7 miles. Nearby are the Cotswold Falconry Centre, Hidcote Manor Gardens and the Rollright Stones.

Open

All year.

At a glance

Welcome & Ambience	✓✓✓✓	Location	✓✓✓✓✓
Quality of Pitches	✓✓✓✓✓	Range of Facilities	✓✓✓✓

Directions

From Evesham on A44, site on left after Bourton-on-the-Hill village, 150 yards before town sign. From Moreton-in-Marsh take A44 towards Evesham and site is on right, 150 yards past the Wellington museum. O.S.GR: SP200323.

Charges 2004

Per adult	£ 4.00 - £ 4.30
child (5-16 yrs)	£ 1.50
pitch incl. electricity (non-member)	£ 6.50 - £ 10.00

Reservations

Contact site. Tel: 01608 650519.

UK4170 Tudor Caravan & Camping Park

Shepherds Patch, Slimbridge GL2 7BP (Gloucestershire)

This traditional style campsite is adjacent to the Gloucester - Sharpness Canal, and behind the Tudor Arms public house. It has 75 pitches, all with electric hook-ups (16A), and 35 with hardstanding. It is divided into two separate fields, the old orchard for long stay or adults only units, with some concrete wheel track hardstands, and a more open grassy meadow for family touring units. The Wildfowl and Wetlands Centre at Slimbridge, founded in 1946 by artist and naturalist Sir Peter Scott, has an incredible variety of different species which visit each year. This site is an obvious choice if you are at all interested in ornithology, being only 800 yards from the Centre. Other attractions include Berkeley Castle, Frampton with its half timbered buildings and Stroud, famous for alternative medicine, homeopaths, reflexologists, herbalists, acupuncturists, chiropractors and cranial masseurs.

Facilities

The toilet building located to one side of the orchard, provides all the usual facilities including push-button hot showers and it can be heated in cool weather. Dishwashing sinks outside under cover. No facilities for disabled persons. Gas available. Some site lighting but a torch would be useful. Gate locked 22.30 - 07.00. Off site: Meals at the Tudor Arms pub. Shop and cafe in boatyard opposite the site (Easter-Sept), also serves breakfasts. Fishing adjacent. Towpath walks.

Open

All year.

At a glance

Welcome & Ambience	✓✓✓✓	Location	✓✓✓✓✓
Quality of Pitches	✓✓✓✓	Range of Facilities	✓✓✓

Directions

From A38 by the junction with A4135 (Dursley), turn west, signed WWT Wetlands Centre Slimbridge. Continue for 1.5 miles turning left into car park of the Tudor Arms. Site entrance is at rear of car park. O.S.GR: SO728042.

Charges 2004

Per unit incl. 2 persons	£ 8.75
extra adult	£ 1.00
child (under 12 yrs)	£ 0.50
awning	£ 1.50
electricity	£ 2.25 - £ 1.50
dog	£ 0.50

Supplement for B.Hs and school holidays £1. No credit cards.

Reservations

Advisable for B.Hs and July/Aug. Tel: 01453 890483. Email: info@tudorcaravanpark.co.uk

UK4100 Hoburne Cotswold

Broadway Lane, South Cerney, Cirencester GL7 5UQ (Gloucestershire)

Since this park is adjacent to the Cotswold Water Park, those staying will have easy access to the varied watersports there which include sailboarding and water ski-ing. On the park itself there is a lake with pedaloes and canoes for hire. Its wide range of other amenities include an outdoor heated swimming pool and an impressive, large indoor leisure complex. There are 340 well marked touring pitches for any type of unit, all with hardstanding (only fairly level) and a grass surround for awning or tent; 40 are serviced 'super' pitches. Of good size but with nothing between them, all have electricity (some need long leads). There are also 210 holiday units, mainly for letting. The large clubhouse has a big general lounge with giant TV screen, entertainment at times, food service (or food bar in lounge), big games room and a lounge bar which overlooks the outdoor pool and lake with a patio. Part of the Hoburne group.

Facilities

Six toilet blocks, all quite small, but clean and well maintained with pre-set showers and background heating. Baby changing facilities. Basic facilities for disabled visitors are in toilet block 4 and at the clubhouse. The site has heavy weekend trade. Launderette. Supermarket. Indoor leisure complex including pool with flume, spa bath, sauna, steam room (all free) and sun bed (charged). Outdoor pool (open Whitsun - early September; 44 x 22 ft). Clubhouse with bar, food and entertainment. Football field. Tennis courts. Good quality adventure playground with bark base. Crazy golf. Fishing lake (permits from reception). No dogs or pets are accepted.

At a glance

Welcome & Ambience	✓✓✓	Location	✓✓✓✓
Quality of Pitches	✓✓✓✓	Range of Facilities	✓✓✓✓✓

Directions

Three miles southeast of Cirencester on A419, turn west towards Cotswold Water Park at new roundabout on bypass onto B4696. Take second right and follow signs. O.S.GR: SU055957.

Charges 2004

Per pitch incl. max. 6 persons	
and electricity	£ 11.50 - £ 26.50
serviced 'super' pitch	£ 12.50 - £ 28.00

Weekly rates and weekend breaks available.

Reservations

Bookings of 1-6 nights payable in full at time of reservation; caravans with £50 deposit for 1 week. Min. 4 nights booking at B.Hs. Tel: 01285 860216. Email: enquiries@hoburne.co.uk

Open

March - October.

UK4160 Forestry Commission - Christchurch Caravan & Campsite

Bracelands Drive, Christchurch, Coleford GL16 7NN (Gloucestershire)

With 280 unmarked pitches, this 20 acre site is on an undulating, open grassy area in the heart of the Forest of Dean. There are around 60 seasonal units, seven hardstandings, and 95 pitches have electric hook-ups (10A). The reception also houses a well stocked licensed shop (including hot pies and pasties) and has a good selection of tourist information, including a leaflet about the local forest trails (55p). Tenters will appreciate the large pavilion in the centre of the site, a large common room with a wood burning stove (logs supplied), tables and chairs, an ideal retreat if the weather proves inclement. Symonds Yat Rock is within walking distance, with spectacular views over the Wye Valley and also nearby are Clearwell Caves, ancient iron mines and Dean Forest Railway.

Facilities

Four sanitary units, two fairly modern with spacious well equipped showers, some vanity style basins with dividers, plus two much older units with WCs and washbasins only. The central block has a laundry with washing machines and dryers and dishwashing room. Units for disabled people and baby changing in two blocks. Shaded adventure playground on a bark surface. Dogs are not accepted. Off site: Shops and other services in Coleford - 1.5 miles. Ross-on-Wye 8 miles. Fishing 1 mile. Swimming 1 mile. Golf 2 miles. Bicycle hire 3 miles. Riding 10 miles.

Open

21 March - 4 November.

At a glance

Welcome & Ambience	✓✓✓✓	Location	✓✓✓✓✓
Quality of Pitches	✓✓✓✓	Range of Facilities	✓✓✓

Directions

From Monmouth take A4136 east for approx. 5 miles turning north at crossroads at Pike House Inn (site signed), site entrance on left after 0.5 miles. From centre of Coleford take road towards Monmouth, turning right to Symonds Yat and Berry Hill (the site is signed). O.S.GR: SO569129.

Charges 2004

Per unit incl. 2 persons	£ 6.50 - £ 11.80
extra adult	£ 3.00
child (5-14 yrs)	£ 1.80
electricity	£ 2.50 - £ 3.00

Less 20% all year for disabled guests and outside 23/7-31/8 for senior citizens.

Reservations

Necessary for B.H.s and peak times (min 2 nights with £30 deposit). Contact the Forestry Commission, 231 Corstorphine Road, Edinburgh EH12 7AT. Tel: 0131 314 6505.

UK4360 Doward Park Camp Site

Great Doward, Symonds Yat West HR9 6BP (Herefordshire)

Created around 1997 in a disused quarry, this is a very pleasant, peaceful little site, partially terraced, and in a sheltered location. The access roads and the physical proportions of the site make it suitable only for tents, trailer tents and camper vans. A site that is popular with couples and young families, but has nothing to offer teenagers. The 33 pitches are mostly on grass (with 6 hardstandings used by seasonal units when we visited) and there are 8 electric hook-ups (16A) for tourers. This site is totally unsuitable for large units, double axle caravans, and American RVs. Visit King Arthur's Caves, and Seven Sisters Rocks. Walk to Symonds Yat Rock and cross the River Wye on the suspension bridge. In nearby Symonds Yat West you'll find The Amazing Hedge puzzle, and The Splendour of the Orient with gardens, waterfalls, tea-rooms and gift shop.

Facilities

A neat timber clad building provides the usual facilities including hot showers, dishwashing sinks and a freezer for ice packs. Small shop selling basic supplies. Torches are advisable. Off site: Variety of inns at both Symonds Yat West and East all offering meals. Shops and services in Monmouth 4 miles.

Open

1 March - 31 October.

At a glance

Welcome & Ambience	✓✓✓✓	Location	✓✓✓✓✓
Quality of Pitches	✓✓✓✓	Range of Facilities	✓✓✓

Directions

From A40 between Ross-on-Wye and Monmouth, turn for Symonds Yat West, and follow signs for Doward Park and Biblins. Turn into a fairly narrow lane for about 1 mile (passing places) and site entrance is on right, on a sharp left hand bend. O.S.GR: SO548157.

Charges 2004

Per unit incl. 2 persons, electricity	£ 10.00 - £ 12.50
extra person	£ 2.00 - £ 2.50
child (4-15 yrs)	£ 1.00 - £ 1.50
dog	£ 1.00

Reservations

Advised for B.Hs. (min. 3 nights) and made with £10 deposit and S.A.E. Tel: 01600 890438. Email: enquiries@doward-park.co.uk

UK4310 Luck's All Caravan & Camping Park

Mordiford, Hereford HR1 4LP (Herefordshire)

Set in around 17 acres on the bank of the river Wye and benefitting from improvements by the new owners, Luck's All has 80 large, well spaced and level touring pitches, of which 72 have electricity (10/16A) and 25 have hardstanding. The river is open to the site but lifebelts and safety messages are in evidence. Canoes are available for hire - or bring your own - and fishing permits may be obtained from reception. A small, fenced playground and a large grassy area for games are provided for children. The site shop has basic supplies and gas, - a mini-market is within 1.5 miles. Amongst the local places worthy of a visit are the Cider Museum and King Offa Distillery in Hereford, Belmont Abbey and Queenswood Country Park. The park is also a good base for touring the Wye Valley. A member of the Countryside Discovery group.

Facilities

The main sanitary facilities, in a new building, provide showers (20p) and a separate unit for disabled visitors with ramped entrance, WC, washbasin, shower and hand-dryer. Dishwashing sinks. A smaller, older unit near the entrance provides extra facilities for peak periods and a fully equipped laundry room. Shop (basics only). Fishing. Canoeing. Winter caravan storage. Site barrier (2.13 m. height limit) locked 21.00 - 09.00 hrs. Only 'breathable' groundsheets are permitted. Off site: Golf 5 miles, bicycle hire 9 miles.

Open

Easter/1 March- 30 November.

At a glance

Welcome & Ambience	✓✓✓✓	Location	✓✓✓✓
Quality of Pitches	✓✓✓✓	Range of Facilities	✓✓✓

Directions

Between Mordiford and Fownhope, 5 miles southeast of Hereford on B4224, the park is well signed. O.S.GR: SO571355.

Charges 2004

Per unit incl. 2 adults	£ 9.00 - £ 11.50
extra person over 5 yrs	£ 1.00 - £ 2.00
awning	£ 1.25 - £ 2.00
pup tent on same pitch	£ 2.00
small 1 man tent	£ 6.00 - £ 6.75
dog	£ 0.75

Reservations

Essential for B.Hs. and peak season and made with £25 deposit. Tel: 01432 870213.

UK4320 Broadmeadow Caravan & Camping Park

Broadmeadows, Ross-on-Wye HR9 7BH (Herefordshire)

This modern, spacious park, with open views and its own fishing lake, is convenient for the town of Ross-on-Wye. The approach to the site is unusual, but persevere and you will find one of the best laid out, immaculately maintained sites with facilities of the very highest quality. Opened in 1996, it is level and has good lighting. There are 150 large pitches on open grass, and the site is especially good for tents. Each set of four pitches has a service post with water, drain, electricity points (16A) and lighting, and is within view of the clock-tower on one of the heated sanitary buildings. The town centre is within easy walking distance. Although the A40 relief road is at the eastern end of the site, the traffic noise should not be too intrusive (but tenters be aware). This is a good base for touring Herefordshire, the Wye Valley or the Forest of Dean.

Facilities

Two superb modern sanitary buildings are fully equipped, including hairdryers, baby rooms, family bathrooms each with WC, basin and bath, and a comprehensive unit for disabled visitors with alarm and handrails. Dishwashing room and laundry with sinks, washing machine, dryer, iron (tokens from reception), at each building. Basic motorcaravan service point. New entrance barrier and keypad entry system on this and all external doors. Small part-fenced playground. Well fenced fishing lake (coarse fishing £5.50 per day). Off site: Bicycle hire in town, riding 8 miles, golf 3 miles. Supermarket 200 m.

At a glance

Welcome & Ambience	✓✓✓✓	Location	✓✓✓✓
Quality of Pitches	✓✓✓✓	Range of Facilities	✓✓✓

Directions

From A40 relief road turn into Ross at roundabout, take first right into industrial estate, then right in 0.5 miles, before Safeway supermarket, where site is signed. O.S.GR: SO610240.

Charges 2004

Per adult	£ 2.50
child (4-14 yrs)	£ 2.00
pitch	£ 6.00 - £ 10.00
awning or pup tent	£ 1.75
dog	£ 1.00

Reservations

Made with £10 deposit. Tel: 01989 768076. Email: broadm4811@aol.com

Open

Easter/1 April - 30 September.

UK4300 Poston Mill Caravan Park

Peterchurch, Golden Valley HR2 0SF (Herefordshire)

Poston Mill Park is a pleasant, neat park in farmland a mile from Peterchurch in the heart of the Golden Valley. It offers 52 touring pitches set on level grass or hardstanding, including some very pleasant pitches near the River Dore, with mature trees and conifers around the perimeter. All pitches have electricity (10/16A), water and TV connections (leads to hire), and 35 have waste water and sewage outlets. The park covers 33 acres and also has 85 caravan holiday homes and 30 seasonal units. An attractive walk along one side of the park, edging the River Dore (fishing available), follows the line of the old Golden Valley railway and there is a footpath from the site over the fields. Next to the park is 'The Mill' restaurant for lunches, evening meals, takeaway and TV room. Peterchurch village is only one mile. A member of the Best of British group.

Facilities

There is one central sanitary block with a smaller block near the holiday home area. Of reasonably modern construction and fully equipped, they include a unit for disabled people (toilet and basin only) and a baby changing room. Motorcaravan service point. Small, well equipped laundry room housing a campers' fridge and a freezer for ice packs. Gas supplies. Mobile shop calls 10 am. Mondays and Thursdays. Large play area. Pitch and putt. Tennis court. Petanque and croquet. Golf driving range. Football pitch. Games room with snooker and darts. Winter caravan storage. Off site: Riding 3 miles.

At a glance

Welcome & Ambience	✓✓✓✓	Location	✓✓✓✓✓
Quality of Pitches	✓✓✓✓	Range of Facilities	✓✓✓✓

Directions

Park is 1 mile southeast of Peterchurch on the B4348 road. O.S.GR: SO356371.

Charges 2004

Per unit incl. 2 adults, electricity	£ 12.00 - £ 16.00
extra person	£ 2.00
child (4-10 yrs)	£ 1.00
awning	£ 2.00
dog	£ 1.00
Min. charge at B.Hs. 5 nights.	

Reservations

Made with £20 deposit, min. 5 nights for B.Hs. Tel: 01981 550225. Email: enquiries@poston-mill.co.uk

Open

All year.

UK4330 The Millpond Touring Caravans & Camping

Little Tarrington, Hereford HR1 4JA (Herefordshire)

This peaceful little site with its own fishing lake is set in 30 acres of countryside. Opened for the first time in 1997, it only has 30 large pitches on open grassland, all with electricity hook-ups (8A). The large fishing lake (unfenced) is well stocked with a good mix of coarse fish, has facilities for disabled fishermen and offers reduced rates for campers. The large acreage surrounding the campsite has a variety of well-established trees that have been supplemented with many new plantings, and well-mowed paths encourage you to wander and enjoy the many trees, wild flowers, birds and the peaceful surroundings. Site lighting is minimal (local authority regulations) so a torch might be useful, but it is an ideal site for amateur astronomers. A railway track is at the rear of the site, so there may be a little noise at times. The site is just seven miles from Hereford with its cathedral, the fascinating Mappa Mundi and chained library, seven miles from Ledbury and close to the Black & White Village Trail.

Facilities

A modern building houses heated sanitary facilities, laundry and dishwashing sinks, baby changing surface, a unit for disabled persons and a 'common room' with a massive supply of tourist information and walking guides. The site is currently not really suitable for American motorhomes. Off site: The local pub is a 10 minute walk, but there is no shop in the village.

Open

1 March - 31 October.

At a glance

Welcome & Ambience	✓✓✓✓	Location	✓✓✓✓
Quality of Pitches	✓✓✓✓	Range of Facilities	✓✓✓

Directions

Little Tarrington is midway between Hereford and Ledbury. The site is just north of A438 on eastern edge of Tarrington village (signed). O.S.GR: SO627409.

Charges 2005

Per unit incl. 2 adults, awning, electricity and pets	£ 11.50 - £ 13.50
extra person	£ 2.00

Reservations

For 2 nights - payment in full, 3-6 nights - £21, £26 per week. 50% of total for B.Hs. Advised for B.Hs and peak season. Tel: 01432 890243.
Email: enquiries@millpond.co.uk

UK4200 The Boyce Caravan Park

Stanford Bishop, Bringsty, Worcester WR6 5UB (Herefordshire)

The Boyce is a very peaceful park on rolling downland, with distant views of the Malvern Hills. Within its 17 acres are 20 touring pitches (with 10A electrical connections), 150 permanent caravan holiday homes and three chalets for hire. There is a fenced and gated playground for smaller children, plus plenty of open space for ball games (no cycling on the park). The adjacent disused railway line is now the dog walk (dogs accepted by arrangement, no dangerous breeds). Coarse fishing is available across a meadow and the area is rich in wildlife. Nearby Shortwood Farm has Jacob sheep, cider making, sheep shearing and a farm trail. The new reception building offers good tourist information including maps of local walks. Bromyard with its shops and restaurants is 4 miles, and the cathedral cities of Hereford and Worcester are within easy driving distance.

Facilities

The modern toilet unit, built to serve the touring section, can be heated and provides controllable hot showers (10p for 4 mins) and a hairdressing area. Facilities for disabled visitors. Utility room housing dishwashing and laundry sinks, a washing machine, dryer, iron, and a freezer for campers' use. Gas supplies. Off site: Riding 5 miles and several golf courses in the area.

Open

1 March - 31 October.

At a glance

Welcome & Ambience	✓✓✓✓	Location	✓✓✓✓✓
Quality of Pitches	✓✓✓✓	Range of Facilities	✓✓✓✓

Directions

From A44 (Worcester - Leominster), turn on B4220 1 mile east of Bromyard. After 1.5 miles, turn opposite 'Herefordshire House' inn (signed Linley Green), site is 400 yards and signed. O.S.GR: SO696526.

Charges 2005

Per unit incl. 2 adults	£ 10.00
extra person over 5 yrs	£ 1.00
1 person tent	£ 4.00
awning/pup tent	£ 1.50
extra car	£ 1.00

No tent pitches at B.H. weekends.
No credit cards.

Reservations

Made with deposit of one night's fee.
Tel: 01886 884248.
Email: ah.richards@btopenworld.com

UK4345 Townsend Touring & Caravan Park

Townsend Farm, Pembridge, Leominster HR6 9HB (Herefordshire)

Recently created and opened for the first time in 2002, this is a good example of a modern, family run campsite. It provides tarmac roads, good site lighting, well spaced pitches and a drive-over motorcaravan service point, with plenty of open space and a small fishing lake. There are 60 pitches in total, 20 with gravel hardstanding, the remainder on grass, and all have access to multi-service facilities (electricity hook-up 16A, water and waste water drain). Reception is at the Farm Shop by the entrance. This is a real treat as it stocks a wide variety of fresh fruit and vegetables, eggs and has a butchery section with farm produced meats.

Facilities

A modern timber clad building with blown air heating, is accessed through a foyer with a public telephone and tourist information. The building is surrounded by wide decking with ramps giving good access for wheelchairs to all facilities including the dishwashing area, laundry room and chemical disposal point at the rear. Inside are spacious controllable showers, some washbasins in cubicles, a suite for disabled guests, family bathroom and baby changing facilities. Off site: Pembridge is known as the capital of the Black & White Villages and holds its Farmer's Market on the first Saturday of each month. This is a short stroll from the site. Kington 5 miles, Leominster 7 miles. Riding and bicycle hire 0.5 miles. Golf 7 miles.

At a glance

Welcome & Ambience	✓✓✓✓	Location	✓✓✓✓✓
Quality of Pitches	✓✓✓✓	Range of Facilities	✓✓✓✓

Directions

Site is beside the A44, 7 miles west of Leominster. Site is just inside the 30 mph speed limit on the eastern edge of Pembridge village. O.S.GR: SO385580.

Charges 2004

Per unit incl. 2 persons	£ 7.00 - £ 12.00
incl. electricity, water and drainage	£ 9.00 - £ 14.00
extra adult	£ 2.00
child (5-15 yrs)	£ 1.00
awning or pup tent	£ 1.50
dog	£ 1.00

Reservations

Made with £2 per night non-refundable deposit.
Tel: 01544 388527. Email: info@townsend-farm.co.uk

Open

1 March - 18 January.

UK4410 Beaconsfield Farm Caravan Park

Battlefield, Shrewsbury SY4 4AA (Shropshire)

Just north of the historic market town, a drive of half a mile through open fields lead to this purpose-designed park for adults only (21 yrs). It is neatly laid out in a rural situation, with a well stocked trout fishing lake and a small coarse pool forming the main feature. The ground has been levelled and grassed to provide 60 well spaced pitches, 35 are 'de-luxe' hardstanding pitches with 16A electricity connections (with 10A hook-ups to the other pitches). Two further areas accommodate 34 caravan holiday homes. The park is well lit with a circular tarmac access road. A large timber chalet-style building provides reception and a coffee shop that is open during reception hours. Recent additions are the bowling green (use is free and woods may be hired by those without such essential caravanning kit) and the 'Bothy' restaurant. Limousins and pedigree Suffolk sheep graze in neighbouring fields and a 'park and ride' scheme operates nearby for those interested in Shrewsbury and its medieval past, bought to life by the Brother Cadfael novels. This is a top class park, maturing by the year. A member of the Best of British Group.

Facilities

Heated toilet facilities (£2 key deposit) are of excellent quality, with curtained, roomy, pre-set showers and free hairdryers. Excellent unit for disabled visitors. Dishwashing room. Laundry with washing machines, dryers, free irons and boards. Motorcaravan services. Restaurant. Indoor heated swimming pool, available all year, with daily open sessions (£2.50 per person) and to hire privately at other times. Bowling green. Small library. Bicycle hire. Security barrier in operation. Only two dogs per unit are accepted. An adult only park. Off site: Golf 2 miles. Riding 7 miles.

Open

All year.

At a glance

Welcome & Ambience	✓✓✓✓	Location	✓✓✓✓✓
Quality of Pitches	✓✓✓✓✓	Range of Facilities	✓✓✓✓

Directions

Site is north of Shrewsbury and off the A49 Whitchurch road just before the village of Hadnall. Turn opposite the New Inn at brown camping sign towards Astley and park entrance is 400 m. on right. O.S.GR: SJ525195.

Charges 2004

Per grass pitch incl. unit, 2 persons and electricity	£ 13.50 - £ 15.50
hardstanding pitch	£ 15.50 - £ 18.50
extra adult	£ 4.00
awning	£ 1.50
dog (max 2)	£ 0.75

No credit cards. Last arrivals 7 pm. (8 pm. Fridays).

Reservations

Advised for weekends, B.Hs and July/August and made with £20 deposit. Tel: 01939 210370. Email: mail@beaconsfield-farm.co.uk

UK4390 Westbrook Park

Little Hereford, Ludlow SY8 4AU (Shropshire)

A beautifully kept, traditional, quiet touring campsite in a 'working' cider apple orchard, Westbrook Park is bordered on one side by the River Teme and within walking distance of the village and pub. There are 52 level pitches with 10/16A electric hook-ups, some on well mown grass, and 23 on gravel or concrete/gravel all-weather hardstandings with water and waste water drain. Satellite TV hook-ups are available to all pitches (leads for rent). A footpath along the river bank in one direction leads to the Temeside Inn which serves hot meals. There is a pleasant riverside walk and dog walk in the other direction.

Facilities

A modern, timber clad, heated toilet block provides spacious hot showers (20p for 5 mins), washbasins in curtained cubicles, a basic laundry room with washing machine, dryer and dishwashing sinks (hot water 10p). Limited facilities for disabled people (WC and basin) - the current steps need to be replaced with a ramp. Gas supplies. Playground. Fishing (£3 per day). Riverside walks. Caravan 'storage and use'. Gazebos are not permitted. No cycling on the park. Off site: Local attractions include Burford House Gardens, Croft Castle, and the market towns of Tenbury Wells, Leominster, Ludlow. Golf 3 miles. Riding and bicycle hire 5 miles.

At a glance

| Welcome & Ambience | ✓✓✓✓✓ | Location | ✓✓✓✓✓ |
| Quality of Pitches | ✓✓✓✓✓ | Range of Facilities | ✓✓✓ |

Directions

From A49 mid-way between Ludlow and Leominster, turn east at Woofferton on A456 signed Tenbury Wells, Kidderminster. After 2 miles turn right just before bridge over river and the Temeside Inn. Turn left after 150 yds, and park entrance is on your left. O.S.GR: SU547679.

Charges 2004

Per unit incl. 2 adults, electricity	£ 12.00 - £ 16.00
extra person	£ 2.00
child (3-10 yrs)	£ 1.00
dog	£ 1.00

No credit cards.

Reservations

Advised for B.Hs (min. 3 nights) and made with £10 deposit. Tel: 01584 711280.

Open

All year.

UK4400 Stanmore Hall Touring Park

Stourbridge Road, Bridgnorth WV15 6DT (Shropshire)

This good quality park is situated in the former grounds of Stanmore Hall, where the huge lily pond, fine mature trees and beautifully manicured lawns give a mark of quality. There are 135 generously sized pitches, 130 with 16A electricity including 30 hardstanding 'super' pitches with TV connections. A limited number of 'standard' hardstanding pitches are also available, but the majority are on grass. Some pitches are reserved for adult only use (over 18 years). Access and internal roads are tarmac; site lighting is adequate and reassuring. Reception is located within the shop. The adjacent conservatory and patio overlook the lake, accommodating everything from humbler ducks to the resident peacocks who strut proudly around their domain. But there's something else too; this is a peaceful site with personality. Little wonder it needs advance booking and people keep returning to enjoy its atmosphere. Open all year round, there are even groups who spend Christmas and New Year at Stanmore Hall. The Severn Valley is full of interest - Bridgnorth nearby, the Clee Hills and Ironbridge Gorge Museum are just a few suggestions. The site is a member of the Caravan Club's managed under contract scheme but non-members are also very welcome.

Facilities

Access to the centrally heated sanitary block is by key. Facilities are excellent and provide washbasins in cubicles and a room for disabled people (which includes equipment for baby care) demonstrating thoughtful design. Full laundry facilities. Motorcaravan service points. Licensed shop (open all year) is well stocked, including caravan accessories and repair items. Limited, bark based play area. Dogs are limited to two per unit Off site: Fishing at Bridgnorth (1.5 miles). Golf 2 miles. Riding 2 miles.

At a glance

| Welcome & Ambience | ✓✓✓✓ | Location | ✓✓✓✓✓ |
| Quality of Pitches | ✓✓✓✓✓ | Range of Facilities | ✓✓✓✓✓ |

Directions

Site is 1.5 miles from Bridgnorth on the A458 road (signed Stourbridge). O.S.GR: SO744922.

Charges 2004

Per adult	£ 5.45 - £ 5.70
child (5-15 yrs)	£ 1.95
pitch	£ 5.45 - £ 7.20
awning or pup tent	£ 1.25
full services	£ 2.50 - £ 3.00
dog (max. 2)	£ 1.00

Reservations

Advisable and made with £10 deposit. Tel: 01746 761761. Email: stanmore@morris-leisure.co.uk

Open

All year.

UK4420 Severn Gorge Park

Bridgnorth Road, Tweedale, Telford TF7 4JB (Shropshire)

This six acre touring park, in a woodland setting, has 50 pitches, all with electricity (10/16A) and hardstanding (including a few seasonal tourers). A development of park homes has been constructed on one side of the park and a tent area with hardstanding for campers' cars. There could be some road noise from the A442 which runs down one boundary. A barrier is locked at 11.45 pm. but parking and a late arrivals area is outside. The main local attraction has to be the Ironbridge Museums, featuring the Blists Hill Victorian Town, where you can discover and enjoy a working Victorian town. A short distance from the park is the Silkin Way cycle path which runs into Telford town centre or to Ironbridge.

Facilities

The sanitary buildings can be heated and provide comprehensive facilities. Facilities for disabled visitors. Baby room. Dishwashing conservatory leading to an ample laundry (8 am.- 9 pm). Motorcaravan services. Small, limited shop. Gas supplies. Adventure play area. Kite flying is discouraged because of nearby overhead cables. Only two dogs per pitch are accepted. Off site: Two pubs within walking distance, one with a tempting 'Ale and Hearty' menu served until 9 pm. Golf 1 mile, riding 3 miles.

At a glance

Welcome & Ambience	✓✓✓✓	Location	✓✓✓✓✓
Quality of Pitches	✓✓✓✓✓	Range of Facilities	✓✓✓

Directions

From M54 exit 4 follow signs to A442 Kidderminster. Take slip road for Bridgnorth to Brockton roundabout, turn right and pick up park signs. O.S.GR: SJ702051.

Charges 2004

Per unit incl. 2 persons	£ 9.85 - £ 15.75
child (5-15 yrs)	£ 1.25 - £ 1.50
dog (max 2)	£ 1.20

Reservations

Contact park for details. Tel: 01952 684789.
Email: info@severngorgepark.co.uk

Open

All year.

UK4430 Oxon Hall Touring Park

Welshpool Road, Shrewsbury SY3 5FB (Shropshire)

Oxon Hall is a purpose-built park, well situated for visiting Shrewsbury. It is under the same ownership as Stanmore Hall (no. 4400) and has been developed from a green field site by an experienced park operator to a very high standard. The site has matured well and the trees and shrubs now provide some shade and shelter. Of the 120 pitches, half are all weather, full service pitches (fresh and waste water facilities, TV hook-up), the others being either grass or hardstanding. An area is set aside as an 'adult only' section. All pitches have 16A electricity hook-ups. Some extra long hardstandings are provided for American motorhomes. Entry to the park is controlled by electronic barriers. Virtually adjacent to the park is the Oxon 'park and ride' which makes a trip into Shrewsbury some 2 miles away very simple. The Ironbridge Gorge Museum and the mysteries of the Welsh Borders are all easy day trips from this excellent base.

Facilities

Toilet facilities here are first rate with washbasins in cubicles, ample showers, baby room, facilities for disabled visitors, dishwashing room and laundry, all situated at the entrance in a centrally heated building which also houses reception and the shop - perhaps a hike from some of the pitches. Motorcaravan service point. Up to two dogs are welcome per pitch. Deposit for toilet block key £5. Off site: Golf, riding and fishing nearby. Supermarket within walking distance.

At a glance

Welcome & Ambience	✓✓✓✓	Location	✓✓✓✓✓
Quality of Pitches	✓✓✓✓✓	Range of Facilities	✓✓✓

Directions

From junction of A5 and A458, west of Shrewsbury, follow signs for Oxon 'park and ride'. Park is signed just 0.5 miles from junction. O.S.GR: SJ457134.

Charges 2004

Per adult	£ 5.45 - £ 5.70
child (5-15 yrs)	£ 1.95
standard grass pitch	£ 5.45 - £ 7.20
'super pitch' plus	£ 2.50 - £ 3.00
awning or pup tent	£ 1.25

Reservations

Made with £10 deposit. Tel: 01743 340868.
Email: oxon@morris-leisure.co.uk

Open

All year.

UK4440 The Green Caravan Park

Wentnor, Bishops Castle SY9 5EF (Shropshire)

Remotely situated in a pleasant valley in an 'area of outstanding natural beauty' and sandwiched between the Stipperstones and The Long Mynd, the Green would make an ideal base for some serious walking or cycling. The 15 acre site is very natural and is divided into several fields. There are 160 pitches, taking 40 seasonal units, and around 20 holiday homes, with around 100 pitches for tourists (42 with 16A electricity). The main field has some hardstandings. The East Onny is a small, shallow river which runs through the site, much enjoyed by youngsters, who can spend many hours catching minnows. Adults might be more interested in the wildlife with many species of birds, bats and moths to watch out for.

Facilities

One main sanitary block, rather austere in appearance, built into the side of a large barn. However once inside it provides adequate and plentiful facilities with spacious hot showers (on payment), dishwashing and laundry facilities. No dedicated unit for disabled people. Well stocked shop with reception. Playground. Off site: Four pubs, all serving food, within 3 miles (two within walking distance). Trout and coarse fishing 3 miles. Riding 4 miles. Stapely Hill historic trail and standing stone. Trial lessons at local gliding club.

Open

Easter - 31 October.

At a glance

Welcome & Ambience	✓✓✓	Location	✓✓✓✓✓
Quality of Pitches	✓✓✓	Range of Facilities	✓✓✓

Directions

Wentnor is southwest of Shrewsbury, west of Church Stretton. From Shrewsbury take A488 south for 21 miles. At Lydham Heath turn east on A489 for 0.75 miles, then north on minor road (signed Wentnor and campsite). Follow signs for 3 miles to site entrance just after The Inn on the Green. O.S.GR: SO381933.

Charges 2004

Per unit incl. 2 persons	£ 8.00 - £ 9.50
extra adult	£ 2.00
child (3-14 yrs)	£ 1.50
dog	£ 0.50

Reservations

Made with £10 deposit for min 3 or 4 days for B.Hs. Tel: 01588 650605.
Email: info@greencaravanpark.co.uk

UK4380 Fernwood Caravan Park

Lyneal, Ellesmere SY12 0QF (Shropshire)

Fernwood is set in an area known as the Shropshire 'Lake District' – the mere at Ellesmere is the largest of nine meres – and the picturesque Shropshire Union Canal is only a few minutes walk. The park itself is a real oasis of calm and rural tranquillity with its floral landscaping, the setting and the attention to detail, all of a very high standard with planted and natural vegetation blending harmoniously. In addition to 165 caravan holiday homes, used normally only by their owners, the park takes 60 caravans, motorcaravans or trailer tents (but not other tents) in several well cut, grassy enclosures (including 27 seasonal long stay). Some are in light woodland, others in more open, but still relatively sheltered situations. All 60 pitches have electricity (10A). One area is set aside for units with adults only. Siting is carried out by the management and there is always generous spacing, even when the site is full.

Facilities

The small toilet block for tourers has background heating for cooler days and includes some washbasins in cabins and a unit for disabled people, but no dishwashing sinks. Basic motorcaravan services. Laundry room near the shop and adjacent are WCs for ladies and men. Small shop doubling as reception (from 1/4, hours vary). Coarse fishing lake. Forty acres of woodland for walking. Play area on grass.

Open

1 March - 30 November.

At a glance

Welcome & Ambience	✓✓✓✓	Location	✓✓✓✓
Quality of Pitches	✓✓✓✓	Range of Facilities	✓✓✓

Directions

Park is just northeast of Lyneal village, signed southwest off the B5063 Ellesmere - Wem road, about 1.5 miles from junction of the B5063 with the A495. O.S.GR: SJ452338.

Charges 2004

Per unit incl. electricity	£ 13.50 - £ 18.00
awning	free - £ 2.50
extra car	free - £ 1.00

One night free for every 7 booked in advance.

Reservations

Necessary for peak season and B.Hs (min. 3 nights) with deposit of £5 per night. Tel: 01948 710221.
Email: fernwood@caravanpark37.fsnet.co.uk

A beautiful and varied region of rolling hills and undulating moors, Yorkshire has an historic past with a wealth of new attractions. Its landscape has inspired famous authors and been the setting for some of Britain's best-loved television programmes.

The region is divided into North, South, East and West Yorkshire

The major attractions of this region are the parks: the Yorkshire Dales National Park is comprised of 680 square miles of unspoilt countryside with high fells, winding rivers, ancient castles and outstanding views of the surrounding landscapes; the Peak District is noted for its rocky peaks and limestone plateau; while the North York Moors National Park has miles of open, heather covered moorland and pretty villages in its valleys. These areas are ideal places for walking, cycling, horse riding and climbing. Or if you prefer to relax and take in the scenery, the North Yorkshire Moors Railway, starting at Pickering, is one of the many steam railways in the region. On the coast, traditional family resorts like Scarborough, Bridlington and Cleethorpes offer the holidaymaker a wide range of activities. Also by the sea is Kingston Upon Hull, a maritime city with powerful links to Britain's proud seafaring tradition, and the picturesque fishing port of Whitby, once home to Captain James Cook. Elsewhere in the region are the vibrant cities of York, with its wealth of ancient sites including the Minster, Leeds and Sheffield plus the busy market town of Doncaster.

Did you know?

The comedy series Last of the Summer Wine is filmed in the Pennine town of Holmfirth and its surrounding countryside

York is the oldest city in Yorkshire, founded in AD71. The Minster is the largest Gothic Cathedral in Northern Europe

Pontefract has been growing liquorice since medieval times, it is believed that Pontefract cakes were made by the monks for medicinal purposes

The Tan Hill Inn is the highest pub in England at 528 metres above sea level

Dick Turpin, the notorious 17th century highwayman, lived in Pontefract

Rudston, near Bridlington, is said to be the oldest inhabited village in England, named after the Rood-Stone, the mysterious 4000 year old monolith

Places of interest

North: Harrogate; Wensleydale Creamery in Hawes; Jorvik Viking Centre in York; Lightwater Valley Theme Park, near Ripon; Castle Howard near York: Flamingo Land Theme Park and Zoo in Malton; Skipton Castle

South: Hatfield Waterpark near Doncaster; Tropical Butterfly House and Wildlife Centre in Anston; Sheffield Ski Village, Europe's biggest artificial ski resort; Magna science adventure centre in Rotherham

East: Bempton Cliffs RSPB Nature Reserve near Bridlington, England's largest seabird colony; market town of Beverly; Captain Cook Museum in Whitby; Scarborough Millennium

West: Bolling Hall in Bradford; Royal Armouries Museum in Leeds; 'Brontë Country' and village of Haworth; Pontefract

tip

WATCH THE SHEEPDOGS IN ACTION AT THE HARDEN MOSS SHEEPDOG TRIALS IN JUNE OR FOR MORE OUTDOOR FUN VISIT THE KETTLEWELL SCARECROW FESTIVAL IN AUGUST.

(175)

UK4700 Nostell Priory Holiday Park

Nostell, Wakefield WF4 1QD (West Yorkshire)

This tranquil, secluded woodland park is within the estate of Nostell Priory, which is now owned and managed by the National Trust. The site provides 60 touring pitches, all with electrical connections (5A), in a grassy, flat and sheltered area edged with mature trees. There is a hardstanding area suitable for motorcaravans, plus 80 caravan holiday homes in a separate area (5 for hire). Amenities are designed to blend into the environment in rustic wood, including the sanitary block. Nostell Priory itself, with its collection of Chippendale furniture and attractive gardens, is well worth a visit (free passes to the grounds are available from reception for campers). A fishing lake is within the grounds, with golf and watersports locally (details in reception). The park is very well cared for and the natural environment is encouraged so there is an abundance of birds and wildlife. A rally field is adjacent to the site. The Dales, York and the Peak District are all an easy drive away. Buses pass the end of the drive (half a mile long).

Facilities

The toilet block, although older in style, has been refurbished throughout to include some washbasins in cubicles. Accessed by key (£5 deposit), it includes a separate room for dishwashing. Laundry with two washing machines and a dryer (opening times on the door). Gas supplies. Milk and papers can be ordered at reception. Play area (no ball games on site). Fishing. Up to two dogs are accepted. Off site: Nearest shops 2 miles. Golf 5 miles, boat launching 8 miles.

Open

1 April - 30 September.

At a glance

Welcome & Ambience	✓✓✓✓	Location	✓✓✓✓
Quality of Pitches	✓✓✓✓	Range of Facilities	✓✓✓

Directions

Park is off A638 Wakefield - Doncaster road, 5 miles southeast of Wakefield. Follow drive for 0.5 miles keeping rose nursery on left. Approaching from south on A638, the site entrance is almost a mile past entry to the Priory, on the right. O.S.GR: SE394181.

Charges guide

Per unit incl. 2 persons	£ 8.50
with services	£ 10.50
extra person (over 5 yrs)	£ 1.00
dog (max 2)	£ 1.00

Reservations

Advised and made with deposit of one night's charge (non-refundable). No single sex groups or units over 21'6 Tel: 01924 863938.

UK4790 Bronte Caravan Park

off Halifax Road, Keighley BD21 5QF (West Yorkshire)

Bronte Caravan Park is now an 'adult only' site – a peaceful haven set in a 50-acre park with wonderful views. It is hard to believe that you are only 1.5 miles from the busy town of Keighley, as only the rolling hillsides with a village on the opposite side are visible. Ten acres of the land are devoted to the owners' own deer herd. A two acre lake is in a lovely setting with its island, weeping willows and several varieties of waterfowl, not to mention the local heron or kingfisher. It is well stocked to provide sport for both coarse and fly fishermen. The hillside has been terraced and a stream tumbles down into the lake. The River Worth runs alongside the site (well fenced). The level pitches have gravel surfaces and 10A electricity (some are a little small). There are also 25 pitches for tents. The Worth Valley railway, of 'The Railway Children' fame, running alongside the site is a big attraction and one of its smaller stations is only a short walk. Ingrow station with a railway museum and free parking is half a mile. Haworth and its Bronte heritage (2 miles) is a must with the museum, the parsonage where the sisters lived and the moorland walks. Further away at Bradford is the cinema and photography museum and Cliffe castle museum in Keighley is well worth a visit.

Facilities

The well appointed, central toilet block of local stone includes showers on payment and a large room for disabled visitors. Laundry with washing machine, dryer and iron. Dishwashing sinks under cover. This block is quite a walk from some pitches but two 'portacabin' style blocks nearer to the pitches are well equipped with toilets, washbasins and an outside dishwashing sink. Fishing (£3.50 per day). Barrier access (key £10 deposit). Caravan storage. Only two dogs are accepted per pitch. Off site: Supermarkets 1.5 miles. Golf 3 miles.

At a glance

Welcome & Ambience	✓✓✓✓✓	Location	✓✓✓✓
Quality of Pitches	✓✓✓	Range of Facilities	✓✓✓

Directions

Park is south of Keighley off the A629 Keighley - Halifax road, on the right approx. 1.75 miles from Keighley. O.S.GR: SE058385.

Charges 2004

Per unit incl. 2 persons	£ 10.00
extra person over 18 yrs	£ 2.50
electricity	£ 3.00
dog (max. 2)	£ 0.50

Reservations

Made with deposit (£10/20). Tel: 01535 691746. Email: bronte@brontecaravanpark.co.uk

Open

1 April - 31 October.

UK4500 Burton Constable Holiday Park

The Old Lodges, Sproatley HU11 4LN (East Yorkshire)

This park is in the grounds of the stately home of Burton Constable, and consequently the entrance is most impressive - one of the gatehouses acts as reception and tourist information room. The 20-acre campsite is part of the 300 acre park which was landscaped by Capability Brown in the 18th century and with well trimmed grass and hedges, it has a spacious feel. All 200 pitches have 10A electricity, there is a separate field for tents and a large hardstanding area providing electricity, water and drainage for six motorcaravans. All the pitches overlook two small lakes (unfenced), one of which is used for fishing (permits at reception), the other for boating (bring your own, but no engines). Privately owned caravan holiday homes are quite separate and do not intrude. For weekly bookings there is a three day family pass to visit the house and its 30 rooms.

Facilities

Two heated toilet blocks - one older and small with unisex showers, the central newer block including a laundry room with baby changing. Well equipped room for disabled visitors (Radar key). Shop in the mobile home area. Bar with family room and tables outside overlooking the lakes. Good adventure play area. Off site: Sproatley (1 mile) has pubs, a butcher and the occasional bus. Hull 7 miles. Golf 4 miles. Riding 3 miles.

Open

1 March - 31 October.

At a glance

Welcome & Ambience	✓✓✓✓	Location	✓✓✓✓
Quality of Pitches	✓✓✓	Range of Facilities	✓✓✓

Directions

From south via the M62 or Humber Bridge, take A63 into Hull, then follow signs to A165 Bridlington. On eatern outskirts of Hull follow B1238 signed Aldborough. At Sproatley, site is signed to left. From the north and Beverley, take A1035 to Hornsea. At roundabout with A165 (Hull - Bridlington) follow signs to Burton Constable for about 8 miles. Pass the Hall to Sproatley, then follow caravan signs. O.S.GR: TA186357.

Charges 2004

Per unit incl. 2 persons, electricity	£ 11.50 - £ 15.00
tent incl. 2 persons	£ 8.50 - £ 14.50
extra person	£ 1.00
awning	£ 2.00

Reservations

Contact park. Tel: 01964 562508.
Email: info@.burtonconstable.co.uk

UK4640 Goose Wood Caravan Park

Sutton-on-the-Forest, York YO61 1ET (North Yorkshire)

A family owned park in a natural woodland setting, Goose Wood provides a quiet, relaxed atmosphere from which to explore York itself or the surrounding Yorkshire Dales, Wolds or Moors. The park has a well kept air and a rural atmosphere, with 95 well spaced and marked pitches on level grass, all with electricity (16A) and 95 with paved hardstanding and patio pitch. No tents are accepted. For children, there is a 'super plus' adventure playground in the trees at one side of the park and for adults, a small coarse fishing lake and attractive, natural woodland for walking, plus a large scale chess set. The park is popular with families in high season when it can be busy at weekends. A 'park and ride' scheme for York operates from nearby all year, six days a week or there is a local bus every two hours, six days a week. The park is just over a mile from Sutton village and only 7 miles from 'Water World' a water leisure centre with pool, slides, wave machines, etc. A member of the Best of British group.

Facilities

Tiled and heated, the modern toilet block is of excellent quality and well maintained. Bathroom (£1). An additional unit provides shower rooms, WC and washbasins in cubicles and extra dishwashing sinks. Full facilities for disabled visitors and a motorcaravan service point are planned. Laundry room. Small shop (with gas). Fishing lake. Large adventure playground. Games room with pool and TV. Outdoor table tennis. Dogs (max. two per pitch), to be exercised in nearby woodland. No tents are accepted. Off site: Riding or golf 1 mile. Bicycle hire 6 miles. York 6 miles.

At a glance

Welcome & Ambience	✓✓✓✓	Location	✓✓✓✓✓
Quality of Pitches	✓✓✓✓	Range of Facilities	✓✓✓✓

Directions

Park is 6 miles north of York; from the A1237 York outer ring-road take the B1363 for Sutton-on-the-Forest and Stillington, taking the first right after the Haxby and Wigginton junction and follow park signs. O.S.GR: SE595636.

Charges 2004

Per unit incl. 1 or 2 persons	£ 7.50 - £ 14.00
extra person	£ 1.50
awning, extra pup tent (1 only)	£ 1.50
electricity (16A)	£ 2.50

Reservations

Made with £20 deposit (min. 3 nights at B.Hs).
Tel: 01347 810829.
Email: edward@goosewood.fsbusiness.co.uk

Open

All year excl. 15-31 January.

UK4610 Moorside Caravan Park

Lords Moor Lane, Strensall, York YO32 5XJ (North Yorkshire)

Strensall is only a few miles from York, one of England's most attractive cities and Moorside Adult Touring Park will provide a peaceful haven after a day's sightseeing. It will impress you with its pretty fishing lake, masses of flowers and the tranquility (except for the odd passing daytime train). There are 57 marked pitches on neat well trimmed grass, most with electricity (5/10A) and 18 with paved hardstanding. The whole park is very well maintained making it a very pleasant environment. The small lake is well stocked for coarse fishing and the pitches bordering the lake are the most popular. York golf course is almost opposite the site entrance. Children (under 16 years) are not accepted at this park.

Facilities

The purpose built toilet block can be heated and houses immaculately kept facilities with washbasins in cubicles for ladies. One WC is suitable for use by disabled visitors. Fully equipped laundry room. Dishwashing area. Coarse fishing (£2 per day). Caravan storage. Off site: Strensall village with shops and places to eat is less than a mile. Golf 0.5 miles. Riding 3 miles.

Open

March - end October.

At a glance

Welcome & Ambience	✓✓✓✓	Location	✓✓✓✓
Quality of Pitches	✓✓✓✓✓	Range of Facilities	✓✓✓

Directions

From A1237 York outer ring road follow signs for Earswick and Strenshall. At Strenshall follow Flaxton road. Site is on left past signs to Strensall village and York Golf Club. O.S.GR: SE647614.

Charges 2004

Per unit incl. 2 persons	£ 7.50 - £ 11.00
extra person	£ 2.00
hardstanding	£ 0.50
electricity	£ 1.50

No credit cards.

Reservations

Contact park. Tel: 01904 491208.

UK4650 Fangfoss Old Station Caravan Park

Fangfoss, York YO41 5QB (North Yorkshire)

Fangfoss railway station stands on the old York – Beverley line (closed in 1965) and the Station House and its platform give this small, simple site plenty of character. Its rural situation amongst rolling farmland provide peace and tranquility and its owners, a friendly welcome and clean and comfortable facilities. The grassed over track and sidings provide hardstanding and together with the adjacent fairly level grass field, give a total of 75 marked pitches, all with 10A electricity and 19 with hardstanding. York is 8 miles (with 'park and ride'), the Yorkshire Wolds 5 miles. This area will encourage walkers and cyclists.

Facilities

A modern toilet block provides hot showers, vanity style washbasins (two cubicles for ladies). The 'Wendy House', provides covered washing up sinks, a laundry sink and a food preparation bar (useful for tenters). No washing machine but a laundry service is offered. Reception carries food essentials with an off-licence and gas. Some play equipment on grass. Winter caravan storage. Off site: Fishing, bicycle hire, riding and golf within 4 miles.

Open

1 March - 31 December.

At a glance

Welcome & Ambience	✓✓✓✓	Location	✓✓✓
Quality of Pitches	✓✓✓	Range of Facilities	✓✓✓

Directions

From A1079 York - Hull road, follow site signs at Wilberfoss for 1.5 miles (northerly). On A166 York - Bridlington road, park is clearly signed at Stamford Bridge, just after crossing river. O.S.GR: SE748527.

Charges 2004

Per unit incl. 2 persons	£ 8.00 - £ 14.00
incl. electricity	£ 10.00 - £ 16.00
extra person	£ 1.50

No credit cards.

Reservations

Made with £20 deposit. Tel: 01759 380491. Email: info@fangfosspark.co.uk

UK4510 Thorpe Hall Caravan & Camping Site

Rudston, Driffield YO25 4JE (East Yorkshire)

In the grounds of Thorpe Hall, just outside the village of Rudston, this pleasant small touring park is 4.5 miles from the sea at Bridlington. Enthusiastically managed by Jayne Chatterton, it is set on flat grass, largely enclosed by the old kitchen garden wall. The 90 pitches are numbered and well spaced with 78 electrical hook-ups (16A) and TV connections. A separate area takes tents and there are no caravan holiday homes. Information sheets on a range of local walks are provided.

Facilities

The solid, central toilet block can be heated and provides good facilities including washbasins in cabins and a bathroom for disabled visitors and families with young children (deposit for key). Launderette. Covered dishwashing sinks. Small shop with gas, essentials and local produce. Games room. TV room. Coarse fishing lake. Off site: Bicycle hire, golf and boat launching at Bridlington (4.5 miles). Riding 2 miles. Footpath to the village with a shop, post office, garage, a pub serving bar meals and a restaurant, plus a twice weekly bus service to Bridlington.

At a glance

Welcome & Ambience	✓✓✓✓	Location	✓✓✓✓
Quality of Pitches	✓✓✓✓	Range of Facilities	✓✓✓

Directions

Site is by the B1253 road, 4.5 miles from Bridlington, on east side of Rudston. O.S.GR: TA105676.

Charges 2004

Per unit incl. all persons, electricity	£ 9.00 - £ 17.00
tent pitch incl. 2 persons	£ 5.75 - £ 12.00

Less 10% on booked stays of 7 days or over.

Reservations

Made with advance payment (min. 4 nights at Spr. B.H). Tel: 01262 420393. Email: caravansite@thorpehall.co.uk

Open

1 March - 31 October.

UK4780 Lebberston Touring Park

Home Farm, Filey Road, Lebberston, Scarborough YO11 3PE (North Yorkshire)

Lebberston Park is a quiet, spacious touring site, but it takes no tents. It is highly suitable for anyone seeking a quiet relaxing break, such as mature couples or young families. There is no play area and no games room so teenagers may get bored. The only concession to children is a large central area with goal posts. The site itself has a very spacious feel. It is gently sloping and south facing and the views are superb. There are 125 numbered pitches with 75 for touring units. All have 10A electricity and 6 have hardstanding. The circular access road is tarmac, the grass is well manicured and the entrance a mass of flowers. Reception is part of an attractive log cabin, which is also the home of the owners and their young family. The resorts of Filey, Bridlington, Scarborough and Hornsea provide something for everyone, the moors and the Dalby forest are also within a short distance. Because this is such a popular and busy area we feel justified in adding another site, especially one of such quality.

Facilities

Recently upgraded toilet blocks are of high quality, with large shower cubicles and washbasins in cubicles with curtains. Both blocks have dishwashing sinks and one has a family bathroom (20p). Good room for disabled visitors. Laundry with washing machine, dryer, spin dryer, iron and board. A key is supplied for the laundry, bathroom, telephone booth and the disabled room (£10 deposit). Reception sells a few supplies, plus papers, ice cream and gas. Only 'breathable' groundsheets are permitted. Off site: Local pub within walking distance. Each new arrival is given details of parking in Scarborough including a parking disc.

At a glance

Welcome & Ambience	✓✓✓✓	Location	✓✓✓✓
Quality of Pitches	✓✓✓✓	Range of Facilities	✓✓✓

Directions

From A64 Malton - Scarborough road turn right at roundabout (MacDonalds, pub and superstore) signed B1261 Filey. Go through Cayton, Killerby and in 4.5 miles site is signed on right. O.S.GR: TA082823

Charges 2005

Per unit incl. 2 persons, electricity	£ 11.50 - £ 17.00
extra adult	£ 1.50
child (5-14 yrs)	£ 1.00
trailer tent over 8 sq.m.	£ 2.00
full awning	£ 2.00

Reservations

Made with £20 non-refundable deposit.
Tel: 01723 585723.
Email: lebberstontouring@hotmail.com

Open

1 March - 31 October.

UK4590 Jacobs Mount Caravan Park

Stepney Road, Scarborough YO12 5NL. (North Yorkshire)

Situated just two miles from the centre of Scarborough, yet in the heart of the country, Jacobs Mount is well placed to meet many holiday needs. The sea and the sand are the main attractions, but this is also on the doorstep of the North York moors and the Dalby Forest Drive. In addition to caravan holiday homes in separate areas of the park, there are 142 touring pitches, all with electricity. Of these 131 are fully serviced (water, drainage) on well spaced gravel hardstandings. In sunny locations, some pitches have good views. There is a bar with a pleasant lounge (no children), plus a family room and a games and TV room. Bar meals and a quite extensive range of takeaways can be purchased. Footpaths lead into the surrounding woods and buses pass the gates.

Facilities

The heated toilet block is new and of a high standard. Washbasins in cubicles with WCs, large shower cubicles (free) and a family bathroom (metered hot water) and baby changing facilities. Separate unisex cubicles contain WC, washbasin and shower. Motorcaravan service point. Small shop in reception for basic needs. Bar with bar meals and takeaway. Two play areas for different ages. Caravan storage. No gazebo style tents allowed. Up to two dogs per pitch are accepted. Off site: Scarborough centre and beach 2 miles. Golf, fishing or bicycle hire 2 miles. Riding 5 miles.

Open

1 March - 31 October.

At a glance

Welcome & Ambience	✓✓✓✓	Location	✓✓✓✓
Quality of Pitches	✓✓✓✓	Range of Facilities	✓✓✓✓

Directions

Site entrance is on the A170 Pickering - Scarborough road, about 2 miles west of Scarborough (on the right as you start to drop down into the town). O.S.GR: TA021877.

Charges 2004

Per unit incl. 4 persons and electricity (16A)	£ 10.50 - £ 15.00
extra person 3 yrs and over	£ 1.50
awning	£ 2.00
pup tent beside unit	£ 7.00
dog (max 2)	£ 1.00
No single sex parties.	

Reservations

Made with deposit (3 days charge); min. stay at B.Hs 3 nights. Tel: 01723 361178.
Email: jacobsmount@yahoo.co.uk

UK4520 Flower of May Holiday Park

Lebberston Cliff, Scarborough YO11 3NU (North Yorkshire)

Flower of May is a large, family owned park for both touring caravans and caravan holiday homes situated on the cliff tops, 4.5 miles from Scarborough and 2.5 miles from Filey. There is a cliff walk to the beach but it is only suitable for the reasonably active - there is an easier walk down from a car park one mile away. The entrance to the park is very colourful and the reception office is light and airy. The range of leisure facilities grouped around reception, includes an indoor pool with areas for both adults and children, a water flume and a jacuzzi. In the same building are two squash courts, 10 pin bowling, table tennis and amusement machines. The leisure centre is also open to the public (concessionary rates for campers) but during high season is only available to local regulars and the caravanners and campers on the park. The park is licensed for 300 touring units and 184 caravan holiday homes (45 to hire, the remainder privately owned). The touring pitches are pretty level, arranged in wide avenues mainly on grass and divided by shrubs. There are 210 with electricity (5A), including 45 'star pitches' with water and drainage also. Riverside Meadows at Ripon and Rosedale Country Caravan Park near Pickering are under the same ownership as Flower of May.

Facilities

The three toilet blocks, all refurbished in a light and colourful style, are fully tiled with washbasins in both cabins and vanity style, plus baby rooms and facilities for disabled visitors. Well stocked and licensed shop (closes end Sept) near the leisure centre, as is the laundry room. Two modern bar lounges, one for families and one for adults only, with discos in season, a games room with TV, large adventure playground with safety base, and a café plus takeaway fish and chips. Pay and play golf course (£5 a round). Indoor swimming pool. Dog exercise area, but numbers and breeds are limited (one per pitch) and not allowed at all at B.Hs and the six week summer holiday. Skateboard ramps and a basketball court have been added. Off site: The Plough Inn near the park entrance offers a good bar meal. Fishing, boat slipway or riding 2 miles, bicycle hire 4 miles.

At a glance

Welcome & Ambience	✓✓✓✓	Location	✓✓✓✓
Quality of Pitches	✓✓✓✓	Range of Facilities	✓✓✓✓✓

Directions

Park is signed from roundabout at the junction of the A165 and B1261 from where it is 600 yds. O.S.GR: TA088836.

Charges 2004

Per unit incl. up to 4 persons and electricity	£ 12.00 - £ 16.50
tent (no electricity)	£ 9.00 - £ 16.50
extra person (over 3 yrs)	£ 3.00 - £ 6.00
awning	£ 2.50
dog (see above)	£ 1.00

10% discount on pitch fee for weekly bookings. No credit cards.

Reservations

Made for min. 3 days with £20 deposit per week and £1 booking fee (Sat.-Sat. only for Spr. B.H. and 13/7-31/8). Tel: 01723 584311. Email: info@flowerofmay.com

Open

Easter - 31 October.

UK4770 Rosedale Caravan & Camping Park

Rosedale Abbey, Pickering YO18 8SA (North Yorkshire)

In a beautiful location below Rosedale Moor and on the edge of a popular village, this is a campsite that is highly suitable for walkers. The surrounding hillsides are a maze of public footpaths and these and nearby Cropton Forest can all be reached without using your car. The site itself has a wide entrance on the edge of the village and as it is within the National Park, the buildings are in the local stone and in keeping with the area. The site is reasonably level, with 200 pitches, a few with hardstanding and with 28 electricity connections (10A). One field is for tents only, there are some caravan holiday homes (private) and seasonal touring pitches in their own areas, with the remainder for touring caravans and motorcaravans. The majority have superb views of the surrounding hills. In summer the Dales bus runs through the village, connecting several of the popular villages. The 13 mile Rosedale circuit follows the route of the old iron-ore railway, giving magnificent views and reminders of bygone industries. There is a glass blower at the village blacksmith's and the Ryedale Folk Museum at Hutton-le-Hole is 3.5 miles.

Facilities

The toilet blocks still await refurbishment, together with laundry and dishwashing sinks, and do not provide suitable facilities for disabled visitors. Reception provides maps and a small selection of camping accessories, plus gas supplies. Games room with pool and video games. Large play area with space for ball games. Entrance barrier controlled by card (£5 deposit). Off site: The village has a general store with daily papers, a post office, bakery, pubs and a restaurant. Nine 9 hole golf course (set on a picturesque hillside) 200 yards. Riding 0.5 miles. Bicycle hire 1.5 miles.

Open

31 March - 31 October.

At a glance

Welcome & Ambience	✓✓✓✓	Location	✓✓✓✓✓
Quality of Pitches	✓✓✓✓	Range of Facilities	✓✓

Directions

Rosedale is signed from the A170, 2 miles west of Pickering. Site is in the village of Rosedale Abbey, 8 miles north of the A170. O.S.GR: SE725958.

Charges 2004

Per unit incl. electricity and up to 4 persons	£ 12.00 - £ 16.50
tent incl. up to 4 persons	£ 9.00 - £ 13.50
extra person (over 3 yrs)	£ 3.00 - £ 6.00
2-man tent	£ 6.00 - £ 7.00
dog (2 only)	£ 1.00

10% discount on pitch fee for weekly bookings. No credit cards.

Reservations

Contact site. Tel: 01751 417272. Email: rosedale@flowerofmay.com

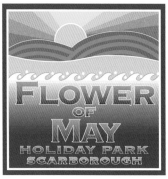

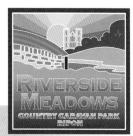

UK4540 St Helens in the Park

Wykeham, Scarborough YO13 9QD (North Yorkshire)

St Helens is a high quality touring park with pleasant views, set within 30 acres of parkland. The 250 mainly level pitches have a spacious feel and the 52 pitches with hardstanding are used by seasonal lets in the summer months, but are available for tourers in winter. Electrical hook-ups (16A) are available on 240 pitches, also in the late arrivals area. Set on a hillside (hence the views), the park's buildings are built in local stone and all is maintained to a high standard. The Downe Arms, a short stroll away, is known for its good food and it occasionally runs family discos in high season. Scarborough is only 5 miles with its beaches and summer shows and buses pass the site gates.

Facilities

Four heated toilet blocks are well equipped and maintained, three having been extended and refurbished. Some washbasins in cabins and baby baths. The new unit for disabled visitors is of a very high standard. All four blocks have dishwashing sinks under cover. Good laundry room. Well stocked shop with snacks and takeaway, and new restaurant (31/3-31/10). Adventure playground set on bark is part of a three acre area set aside for children with goal posts and a mountain bike track. Bicycle hire. Small games room with pool table and amusement machines. Caravan storage. Off site: Nearby Wykeham Lakes offer fishing (trout and coarse), scuba diving, windsurfing and sailing (in your own boat), 1 mile. Golf or riding 2 miles.

At a glance

Welcome & Ambience	✓✓✓✓	Location	✓✓✓✓
Quality of Pitches	✓✓✓✓	Range of Facilities	✓✓✓✓

Directions

Park access road leads off the A170 (Pickering - Scarborough) road in Wykeham village 2 miles west of junction with B1262. O.S.GR: SE963835.

Charges 2004

Per unit incl. 2 persons	£ 9.26 - £ 11.65
electricity	£ 2.40
extra person (over 3 yrs)	£ 1.00
awning	£ 1.70 - £ 2.00
dog	£ 1.00

Reservations

Made with £20 deposit (min. 4 nights for Spr. and Aug. B.Hs). Tel: 01723 862771. Email: caravans@wykeham.co.uk

Open

All year excl. 15 January - 13 February.

St Helens in the Park

250 Spacious pitches set in 30 acres of parkland.

Adventure playground, excellent shop,
games room & amusements
Nearby there is excellent fishing, diving,
windsurfing & sailing

Tel: 01723 862771

UK4740 Jasmine Park

Cross Lane, Snainton, Scarborough YO13 9BE (North Yorkshire)

This is an area of North Yorkshire that is very popular, so although we have other parks nearby, we feel there is room for another. Jasmine is a very attractive, quiet, well manicured park with owners who go to much trouble to produce masses of plants to give a very colourful entrance. Set in the Vale of Pickering, the park is level, well drained and protected by a coniferous hedge. The 106 pitches (54 for touring units) are on grass, with electricity connections (10A) for all caravans and some tents. There is no play equipment for children, although a field is provided for football, etc. Masses of tourist information is provided in a log cabin and the owners are only too happy to advise. The market town of Pickering and the seaside town of Scarborough are both 8 miles. Many local attractions are within easy reach, including Castle Howard, Dalby Forest, Sledmere House, Nunington Hall, Goathland (the setting for ITV's 'Heartbeat') and the North York Moors Railway. Some privately owned log cabins and seasonal tourers are also on the site. This is an award-winning, peaceful park for a restful holiday. A member of the Countryside Discovery group.

Facilities

The toilet block has been refurbished to a high standard and is kept very clean. It includes a large room for families or disabled visitors containing a bath, shower, WC and washbasin (access by key). Laundry room with dishwashing sinks, washing machine, dryer and iron (hot water metered). Motorcaravan service point. Licensed shop selling essentials and gas. Dogs are welcome but there is no dog walk. Off site: Riding 2 miles. Golf driving range 2 miles. Fishing 5 miles.

Open

1 March - 31 December.

At a glance

Welcome & Ambience	✓✓✓✓	Location	✓✓✓✓
Quality of Pitches	✓✓✓✓	Range of Facilities	✓✓✓

Directions

Snainton is on the A170 Pickering - Scarborough road and park is signed at eastern end of the village. Follow Brakers Lane to park on left in 1 mile. O.S.GR: SE928813.

Charges 2004

Per unit incl. 2 persons	£ 9.00 - £ 14.00
with electricity	£ 11.00 - £ 16.00
extra adult	£ 1.50
child (5-14 yrs)	£ 1.00
awning or tent over 150 sq ft	£ 2.00
Min. stay at Easter 4 nights, other B.Hs 3 nights.	

Reservations

Made with £10 deposit and S.A.E. Tel: 01723 859240. Email: info@jasminepark.co.uk

UK4530 Northcliffe Holiday Park

Bottoms Lane, High Hawsker, Whitby YO22 4LL (North Yorkshire)

Northcliffe is a high quality family park with splendid sea views, set within the North Yorkshire Moors National Park. As well as touring units, it caters for 170 caravan holiday homes, although they are entirely separate. The modern park is well planned and attractive, the very friendly owners keeping everything neat and tidy. The toilet facilities are especially good. The 32 touring pitches are of a good size, 30 with electrical hook-up (10A), and 16 fully serviced. Many trees and flowering bushes have been planted to provide wind breaks. The park is situated on the Heritage Coast and one can walk the Cleveland Way into Whitby or to Robin Hood's Bay. Available at reception are leaflets on walks and countryside notes (75p) produced by the park. Whitby and Scarborough with their sandy beaches are within easy reach as are the moors. York is about an hour away. A member of the Best of British group.

Facilities

The toilet block is heated in early and late seasons and uses a coded number pad entry system. Some washbasins are in cabins. Good facilities for babies and for disabled visitors. Dishwashing room. Well equipped laundry. Well stocked shop (with gas) incorporating an attractive tea-room with range of reasonably priced food to eat in or takeaway (8 am - 8 pm in high season, mornings and evenings in low season). Two fenced play areas have good quality fittings and safety bases. Grass area for games. Indoor room with pool table and amusement machines. Dogs are not accepted. Off site: Bicycle hire 0.5 miles. Fishing 4 miles. Riding 5 miles. Golf 4 or 6 miles.

Open

15 March - 31 October.

At a glance

Welcome & Ambience	✓✓✓✓	Location	✓✓✓✓
Quality of Pitches	✓✓✓✓	Range of Facilities	✓✓✓✓

Directions

From the A171 (Scarborough) road, 3 miles south of Whitby turn left on B1447 signed High Hawsker and Robin Hood's Bay. Go through Hawsker village and continue on Robin Hood's Bay road. At top of hill turn left onto private road - go on 0.5 miles towards sea. O.S.GR: NZ936080.

Charges 2004

Per unit incl. 2 persons, electricity	£ 12.00 - £ 14.00
incl. mains services and awning	£ 14.00 - £ 20.00
extra adult	£ 3.00 - £ 4.00
child (under 16 yrs)	£ 1.50 - £ 2.00
Less 10% if 7 nights booked.	

Reservations

Made with deposit and fee, min. 2-6 nights acc. to pitch type and season. Tel: 01947 880477. Email: enquiries@northcliffe-seaview.com

UK4550 Cayton Village Caravan Park

Mill Lane, Cayton Bay, Scarborough YO11 3NN (North Yorkshire)

Cayton Village Caravan Park can only be described as a gem. Just three miles from the hustle and bustle of Scarborough, it is a peaceful, attractive haven. Originally just a flat field with caravans around the perimeter, years of hard work, a lot of time and even more expense has produced a park which is very pleasing to the eye and of which the owner, Carol, can be justly proud. The entrance is a mass of flowers. The late arrivals area here has electrical hook-ups, very handy as the gates are locked at night and anyone leaving early is also expected to use it, so as not to disturb others. The 200 pitches, of which 160 are for touring units, are numbered and everyone is taken to their pitch. There are 170 with electricity, 39 'super' pitches and 51 with hardstanding. A short walk across a field takes you to Cayton Village which has a popular pub providing excellent meals, a shop/post office and a church, and Cayton Bay is half a mile. The North York Moors are a short distance away, as is the Forestry Commission's Dalby Forest Drive with its scenic drive, mountain bike trails and way-marked walks.

Facilities

Three toilet blocks (key code locks) can be heated and have high quality tiling and fittings. Some showers are pre-set, others controllable. Two family shower rooms, family bathroom and baby changing facilities. Reception and shop, both open 8.30 am. to 8 pm. The shop's comprehensive range includes gas and caravan spares. Adventure playground with safety surface. Superb dog walk (an enormous well mown field, floodlit at night). Caravan storage. Off site: Fishing and bicycle hire 0.5 miles, riding 4 miles, golf 3 miles. Regular bus service from the village to Scarborough or Filey.

Open

1 March - 4 January.

At a glance

Welcome & Ambience	✓✓✓✓	Location	✓✓✓✓
Quality of Pitches	✓✓✓	Range of Facilities	✓✓✓

Directions

From A64 Malton - Scarborough road turn right at roundabout (with MacDonald's and pub) signed B1261 Filey. Follow signs for Cayton, in Cayton Village take second left after Blacksmiths Arms down Mill Lane (at brown caravan sign) and park is 200 yds. From roundabout to park is 2.25 miles. From A165 turn inland at Cayton Bay traffic lights and park is 0.5 miles on right. O.S.GR: TA057837.

Charges 2005

Per unit incl. 2 persons, electricity	£ 11.00 - £ 16.00
'super' pitch with hardstanding	£ 17.00 - £ 22.00
tent pitch	£ 10.00 - £ 15.00
extra person (over 3 yrs)	£ 1.00
awning	£ 2.00
dog	£ 1.00
Special offers available.	

Reservations

Advised and made for min. 3 nights (4 at B.Hs) with £20 deposit. Tel: 01723 583171. Email: info@caytontouring.co.uk

UK4620 Upper Carr Chalet & Touring Park

Upper Carr Lane, Malton Road, Pickering YO18 7JP (North Yorkshire)

With a central location in the Vale of Pickering, Upper Carr is well placed for the many attractions the area has to offer. The park is surrounded by a high, well trimmed hedge which protects it from the wind and deadens the road noise. There are colourful gardens and a pets corner where children can feed unusual breeds of poultry. Quiet and well maintained, Upper Carr's six acres provide 80 level pitches, 75 with 10A electricity and some with hardstanding. Seasonal units use 25 pitches. The picturesque village of Thornton Dale can be reached on foot or by cycle along the Upper Carr nature trail. A member of the Countryside Discovery group.

Facilities

The heated toilet blocks are a little dated (in 'portacabin' style) but all are kept very clean and well decorated. Showers are charged for. Baby changing facilities. Separate room with WC and washbasin for disabled visitors. Dishwashing sinks outside, but under cover. Laundry room. Motorcaravan service point. Small shop in reception supplies basic needs and gas. Good play area. Bicycle hire. Nature trail. Off site: Pub 100 yards. Golf (9 hole) or tennis adjacent to park. Riding 6 miles. Fishing 5 miles. Swimming pool 1.5 miles. Bus service passes entrance.

At a glance

Welcome & Ambience	✓✓✓✓	Location	✓✓✓
Quality of Pitches	✓✓✓	Range of Facilities	✓✓✓

Directions

Travelling on the Pickering - Malton A169 road, park is on the left about 1.5 miles south of Pickering. O.S.GR: SE804815.

Charges 2004

Per unit incl. 2 persons	£ 8.00 - £ 15.50
extra person (over 3 yrs)	£ 1.00
awning or child's pup tent	£ 1.50
extra large tent, plus	£ 1.50
electricity	£ 2.00

Reservations

Made with £15 deposit. Tel: 01751 473115. Email: harker@uppercarr.demon.co.uk

Open

1 March - 31 October.

UK4570 Forestry Commission - Spiers House Caravan & Camp Site

Cropton Forest, Cropton, Pickering YO18 8ES (North Yorkshire)

The Spiers House site, run by the Forestry Commission, is set in a sunny clearing in the middle of Cropton Forest. It is an ideal location for a cycling or walking holiday without having to move your car. The site buildings, built in local stone, are set around a central courtyard with a pedestrian archway leading to the pitches. The welcoming reception also incorporates a well stocked shop. Sloping fields provide for 150 pitches, which include 74 with 10A electricity and 19 with hardstanding. The Moors bus calls at the site every Sunday from 1 May - 1 Sept. and daily in the high season (21 July - 1 Sept) making journeys to Rosedale or beyond and Pickering possible. Reception provides leaflets for way-marked walks in the forest and orienteering.

Facilities

The tiled toilet block is spacious, if a little Spartan, with open plan washbasins and roomy, pre-set showers. Unit for disabled campers (WC and washbasin only). Dishwashing sinks under cover with free hot water, laundry room with washing machine, dryer and sinks (hot water charged). Well stocked shop. Large adventure playground and games field set under tall pines. Raised barbecues are permitted. Off site: Pub with home-brewed beer 1 mile. Riding 5 miles. Fishing 7 miles. Golf 12 miles.

Open

26 March - 27 September.

At a glance

Welcome & Ambience	✓✓✓✓	Location	✓✓✓✓✓
Quality of Pitches	✓✓✓✓	Range of Facilities	✓✓✓

Directions

From Pickering take A170 westwards towards Helmsley for about 2 miles. Just after delimited speed sign, take unnumbered road to the right signed Cropton and Rosedale. After 4 miles site is signed to the right into the forest (do not go into Cropton village). O.S.GR: SE758918.

Charges 2004

Per unit incl. 2 persons	£ 7.40 - £ 11.20
extra person over 5 yrs	£ 1.70
electricity	£ 2.50
awning or extra car	£ 3.00

Prices are higher at weekends. Less 20% all year for disabled guests and outside 7/7-28/8 for senior citizens.

Reservations

Necessary for B.Hs and peak times; made for min. 3 nights with £30 deposit. Contact site when open, otherwise Forest Holidays on 0131 314 6505. Tel: 01751 417591.

UK4775 Cote Ghyll Caravan & Camping Park

Osmotherley, Northallerton DL6 3AH (North Yorkshire)

Jon and Helen Hill are working hard to bring their newly acquired park up to a good standard, and already their efforts are evident. The site is set on a secluded hillside with the higher pitches terraced and the lower ones on a level grassy area, bordered by the small Cod Beck stream. Of the 80 pitches, 18 are used for caravan holiday homes, 30 are seasonal pitches, and 50 are for tourers. Most have 10A electricity hook ups. A simple site, Cote Ghyll is highly suited for lovers of peace and quiet, for bird watching or for more energetic hobbies such as cycling and walking. On the western edge of the North York Moors, cycle paths and footpaths lead almost from the site entrance and the three main long distance footpaths, the Lyke Wake walk, the Cleveland Way and the Coast to Coast, all pass close by. A 10 minute stroll takes you to the pretty and popular Osmotherley village, where there is a post office and general store, tea rooms and three pubs selling reasonably priced meals.

Facilities

The newly refurbished, heated toilet block provides free power showers, vanity style washbasins and hairdryers and dishwashing. An older block, due for refurbishment, has clean but very dated facilities. Laundry room with washing machine, dryer, iron and board. Reception sells gas and basic supplies. New play area on forest bark. Caravan storage. Off site: Shop and pubs 10 minutes walk. Fishing 1 mile. Golf 8 miles. Mount Grace Priory 4 miles. Swimming pool and leisure centre 6 miles.

Open

1 March - 31 October.

At a glance

Welcome & Ambience	✓✓✓✓✓	Location	✓✓✓✓✓
Quality of Pitches	✓✓✓✓	Range of Facilities	✓✓✓

Directions

Osmotherley is east of the A19. Leave the A19 at A684 exit signed Northallerton and Osmotherely. Go to Osmotherley and site is at the northern end of the village, well signed. O.S.GR: SE460983.

Charges 2004

Per unit incl. 2 persons	£ 10.00 - £ 12.50
with electricity	£ 12.00 - £ 14.50
walkers or cyclists (2 persons)	£ 4.50 - £ 5.50
extra person	£ 1.50
child under 10 yrs (max. 4)	free
awning	£ 1.20 - £ 1.50

Reservations

Made with £15-£20 deposit per pitch.
Tel: 01609 883425. Email: hills@coteghyll.com

UK4560 Golden Square Caravan & Camping Park

Oswaldkirk, York YO62 5YQ (North Yorkshire)

Golden Square is a popular, high quality, family owned touring park. Mr and Mrs Armstrong are local farmers who have worked hard to turn an old quarry into a very attractive caravan park with a number of level bays that have superb views over the Vale of Pickering. The 130 pitches are not separated but they do have markers set into the ground and mainly back on to grass banks. In very dry weather the ground can be hard, steel pegs would be needed (even in wet weather the park is well drained). All pitches have electrical connections (10A), 24 have drainage and 6 are 'deluxe' pitches (with waste water, sewage, electricity, water and TV aerial connection). The licensed shop is very well stocked, selling home-made fresh bread and cakes, dairy produce, fresh vegetables and groceries, newspapers, gas and gifts. Visitors may have membership of the Ampleforth College sports centre, with its indoor pool, tennis and gym, etc. The area abounds with footpaths and three well known long distance footpaths are near. Dog owners are well catered for with two or three enormous fields for exercising alongside the park.

Facilities

Two heated well cared for toilet blocks are of excellent quality, with some washbasins in private cabins. Showers are pre-set and metered (token) and a bathroom (token) also houses baby changing facilities. Both ladies and men have full facilities for disabled visitors. Dishwashing sinks under cover. Laundry with washing machines, dryers, spin dryer and iron and board. Motorcaravan service point. Tourist information room also houses a microwave and an extra iron and board. Shop. Two excellent play areas allow tiny tots to be kept separate from older children. Games field and a barn with table tennis and pool table. Bicycle hire. All year caravan storage. Off site: Riding 2 miles, golf 3 miles, fishing 5 miles. Outdoor pool at Helmsley, sports centre at Ampleforth, both have shops and pubs with food.

At a glance

Welcome & Ambience	✓✓✓✓✓	Location	✓✓✓✓✓
Quality of Pitches	✓✓✓✓	Range of Facilities	✓✓✓✓

Directions

From York take B1363 to Helmsley. At Oswaldkirk Bank Top turn left on B1257 to Helmsley. Take second left turn signed Ampleforth to site. O.S.GR: SE605797.

Charges 2004

Per unit incl. 2 persons	£ 9.00 - £ 13.00
incl. electricity	£ 11.00 - £ 15.00
incl. full services and awning	£ 18.50 - £ 23.50
extra person (10 yrs or over)	£ 2.00
awning	£ 1.50 - £ 2.00
hikers and bikers, per person	£ 4.25 - £ 4.75
No credit cards.	

Reservations

Essential for B.Hs and made with £10 deposit (£20 for B.Hs). Tel: 01439 788269. Email: barbara@goldensquarecaravanpark.com

Open

1 March - 31 October.

UK4690 Constable Burton Hall Caravan Park

Constable Burton Hall, Leyburn DL8 5LJ (North Yorkshire)

This tranquil park is in beautiful Wensleydale and the emphasis is on peace and quiet, the wardens working to provide a relaxing environment. Being in the grounds of the Hall, it has a spacious, park-like feel. On part level, part sloping, well trimmed grass, the 120 pitches (40 for touring units) are of a good size and all have electricity (10A). There are no pitches for tents. Ideally placed for visiting the Northern Dales, the gardens of the Hall are open to the public, with a collection of maples and terraced gardens developed by Mrs Vida Burton. There is no shop but nearby Leyburn will provide all your needs. Opposite the entrance is the Wyvill Arms for bar meals. Ball games are not permitted and there is no play area.

Facilities	Directions
Two toilet blocks built of local stone and blending in with the local surroundings, have been refurbished recently, are well tiled, kept immaculately clean, and can be heated. New facility for disabled visitors and baby room. The former deer barn has been adapted for use as a laundry room and extra washrooms with basins for both men and women. Gas supplies. Off site: Fishing, riding or golf within 4 miles.	Park is by the A684 between Bedale and Leyburn, 0.5 miles from the village of Constable Burton on the Leyburn side. O.S.GR: SE152907.

	Charges 2004	
	Per unit incl. 2 persons, electricity	£ 10.25 - £ 13.00
	extra adult	£ 2.50
Open	child (5-16 yrs)	£ 1.25
Late March - 31 October.	awning	£ 2.00
	No commercial vehicles. No credit cards.	

At a glance				Reservations	
Welcome & Ambience	✓✓✓✓	Location	✓✓✓✓	Made with deposit (£20 for B.Hs. £5 other times).	
Quality of Pitches	✓✓✓✓	Range of Facilities	✓✓✓	Tel: 01677 450428.	

UK4580 Foxholme Touring Caravan & Camping Park

Harome, Helmsley YO62 5JG (North Yorkshire)

Foxholme is an unusual park with only 60 pitches for caravans and a small field for a few tents. Nearly all the pitches are individual ones in clearings in the quite dense coniferous plantation. The trees give much shade and quite a lot of privacy (manoeuvring may be difficult on some of the pitches). All pitches have electricity (6A, a few need long leads) and six places have hardstanding. Some picnic tables are provided. There are 30 pitches for tourers, the remainder being taken by seasonal units. The site is managed by a warden, with reception usually open 9 am. - 9 pm. (6 days). Very basic provisions are kept. The park is set in quiet countryside and would be a good base for touring, being within striking distance of the moors, the coast and York. There are no on site activities but campers may use the indoor pool at the Pheasant Hotel in Harome. There is lighting, but a torch would be useful.

Facilities	Directions
The toilet block is of good quality, built in local stone, with all washbasins in private cubicles, a bathroom (£3), laundry room with washing machine and sinks and a washing up room. Two further small blocks provide WCs only in other parts of the park. Motorcaravan service point. Caravan storage. Off site: The nearest shops are at Helmsley and Kirkbymoorside, both about 4 miles away, where there is also bicycle hire. Riding and golf also 4 miles.	Turn south off the A170 between villages of Beadlam (to west) and Nawton (to east) at sign to Ryedale School, then 1 mile to park on left (pass another park on right). From east ignore first sign at turn before Nawton. From west turn right 400 yards east of Helmsley, signed Harome, turn left at church, go through village and follow signs. O.S.GR: SE661831.

	Charges 2005	
Open	Per unit incl. 2 persons and electricity	£ 12.00
Easter - 31 October.	extra adult	£ 2.00
	child	£ 1.00
At a glance	No credit cards.	

At a glance				Reservations	
Welcome & Ambience	✓✓✓	Location	✓✓✓	Made for any dates with £20 deposit.	
Quality of Pitches	✓✓✓	Range of Facilities	✓✓✓	Tel: 01439 771696.	

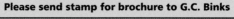

UK4670 Wood Nook Caravan Park

Skirethorns, Threshfield, Skipton BD23 5NU (North Yorkshire)

Wood Nook is a family run park in the heart of Wharfedale, part of the Yorkshire Dales National Park. The access road is narrow for a short distance, but you will find it is well worth this slight rural inconvenience as the site includes six acres of woodland with quite rare flora and wildlife. Reception is in the farmhouse, as is the small shop. The gently sloping fields have gravel roads and provide 25 pitches with gravel hardstanding. All have electricity (10A, long leads may be required) and there are water and chemical disposal points. There is also room for 24 tents and the park has some caravan holiday homes to let. The Thompson family are very friendly, trying always to have time for a chat, although Wood Nook is still a working farm producing beef cattle. New arrivals are usually met with coffee and cakes. The park itself adjoins the fells, with direct access from the top of the site. A visit to the nearby village of Grassington is a must, with its cobbled main street and quaint gift shops. All in all, this is a peaceful park from which to explore the Yorkshire Dales.

Facilities

Farm buildings have been converted to provide modern, neat sanitary facilities which can be heated, are well maintained and kept very clean (opened by key). Washbasins in cubicles for ladies. Roomy showers (in another building) are coin operated. Fully equipped laundry with clothes lines. Dishwashing sinks under cover. Motorcaravan service points. Licensed shop for basics and a range of gifts (from Easter). Gas supplies. Small, attractive play area on top of a small hill. American motorhomes are taken by prior arrangement. Off site: Fishing or bicycle hire 2 miles, riding 3 miles, golf 9 miles. Good range of bar food available locally. Leisure centre with pool nearby.

At a glance

Welcome & Ambience	✓✓✓✓	Location	✓✓✓✓✓
Quality of Pitches	✓✓✓✓	Range of Facilities	✓✓✓✓

Directions

From Skipton take B6265 to Threshfield, then B6160. After 50 yds turn left into Skirethorns Lane and follow signs for 600 yds, up narrow lane then 300 yds. O.S.GR: SD974641.

Charges 2004

Per adult	£ 2.50
child (5-15 yrs)	£ 1.00
young adult (16-17 yrs) as part of family unit	£ 1.50
caravan or motorcaravan incl. electricity	£ 7.00
tent and car	£ 6.00
awning	£ 1.00
Payment also accepted in Euros.	

Reservations

Necessary for high season and B.Hs with £10 deposit. Tel: 01756 752412. Email: enquiries@woodnook.net

Open

1 March - 31 October.

UK4750 Howgill Lodge Caravan & Camping Park

Barden, Skipton BD23 6DJ (North Yorkshire)

Howgill Lodge is a traditional family site, set in the heart of the Dales. Arranged on a sloping hillside, the terraced pitches have fantastic views. It is a small park catering for the needs of walkers, tourers and the people who like to just relax. The whole area is a haven for both experienced walkers or the casual rambler, without having to move your car. All the pitches at the upper part of the park are on hardstanding and have electricity connections (10A), the lower ones are mainly on grass (30 in total). Picnic tables and chairs are provided. Reception also houses a small shop which sells most of the basics including fresh foods. Pretty villages abound in the area, all with attractive inns and nearby Embsay has the Dales Railway with steam trains. This very pleasant park, with clean facilities, has a very relaxing feel to it. A member of the Countryside Discovery group.

Facilities

Heated toilet facilities are at the entrance, close to reception, with dishwashing sinks outside, under cover. Showers are large and adjustable (on payment). Fully equipped laundry room with washing machine, dryer and iron and four unisex showers also here. Outdoor washing lines are provided. Two small blocks housing WCs are lower down the site for the convenience of tent campers. Shop. No children's play area. Fishing licences are available from reception. B&B is available. Off site: Skipton, an agricultural market town, is 8 miles and the well known Bolton Abbey, with its beautiful riverside walks is 3 miles.

Open

1 April - 31 October.

At a glance

Welcome & Ambience	✓✓✓✓✓	Location	✓✓✓✓✓
Quality of Pitches	✓✓✓✓	Range of Facilities	✓✓✓✓

Directions

Turn off A59 Skipton - Harrogate road at roundabout onto B6160 Bolton Abbey, Burnsall road. Three miles past Bolton Abbey at Barden Towers, bear right signed Appletreewick and Pateley Bridge. This road is fairly narrow for 1.25 miles (with passing places). Park is signed on right at phone box. O.S.GR: SE065593.

Charges 2004

Per unit, 2 persons and electricity	£ 12.50
per family unit with electricity	£ 15.00
awning	£ 1.50
hiker	£ 4.00
tent with car and 2 persons	£ 11.00

Reservations

Made with £15 deposit. Tel: 01756 720655. Email: info@howgill-lodge.co.uk

(187)

UK4720 Knight Stainforth Hall Caravan & Camping Park

Little Stainforth, Settle BD24 0DP (North Yorkshire)

This traditional park is located in the heart of the Yorkshire Dales, the whole area a paradise for hill-walking, fishing and pot-holing and with outstanding scenery. The camping area is on slightly sloping grass, sheltered by mature woodland in a very attractive setting. There are 100 touring pitches, 50 with electricity (10A) and 10 with hardstanding. A separate area contains 60 privately owned caravan holiday homes. Buildings near the farmhouse provide reception, a games/TV room and a shop (for basics). A gate leads from the bottom of the camping field giving access to the river bank where the Ribble bubbles over small waterfalls and rocks and whirls around deep pools where campers swim in warm weather. This is not fenced and children should be supervised, although it is a super location for a family picnic. Fishing permits and licences are available from reception and one can fish for trout (or salmon when available). Settle is only 2 miles away, as is Giggleswick and its well known school. Train buffs will want to travel on the Settle - Carlisle railway over the famous Ribblehead Viaduct. The magic of the Dales National Park is on the doorstep and just off the A65 to the west of Settle at Felzor is the Dales Falconry and Conservation Centre.

Facilities	Directions
A new building provides all new facilities including some washbasins in cubicles. Dishwashing sinks. Laundry room with washing machine and dryers. Shop. Games/TV room. New play area with safety base. Fishing. Bicycle hire. Security barrier at entrance; deposit for key to toilet block and barrier £10. Off site: Riding or golf 3 miles.	From Settle town centre, drive west towards Giggleswick. Ignore turning marked Stainforth and Horton, and after 200 yards turn right into Stackhouse Lane (signed Knight Stainforth). After 2 miles turn right at crossroads. O.S.GR: SD815671.

Open

1 March - 31 October.

At a glance

Welcome & Ambience	✓✓✓✓	Location	✓✓✓✓✓
Quality of Pitches	✓✓✓✓	Range of Facilities	✓✓✓

Charges 2004

Per unit incl. 2 adults	£ 10.00
with electricity	£ 12.00
extra adult	£ 2.50
child (5-16 yrs)	£ 1.50

Min. stay at B.Hs 3 nights. Special offers.

Reservations

Made with £10 deposit. Tel: 01729 822200. Email: info@knightstainforth.co.uk

Knight Stainforth Hall
Caravan & Camping

...located in the heart of the Yorkshire Dales
01729 822200 www.knightstainforth.co.uk

UK4760 Riverside Meadows Country Caravan Park

Ure Bank Top, Ripon HG4 1JD (North Yorkshire)

Riverside Meadows has a new name and new owners who have lots of experience in the caravan park world. All the facilities are being upgraded and brought up to their demanding standards. This is a rural park, although the approach to it belies that fact. The short approach from the main road passes a row of houses and a factory, but once they are passed, the park opens up before you and you are once again back in the countryside. There are plenty of caravan holiday homes but they are, on the whole, quite separate from the 64 touring pitches. These pitches, practically all with electrical hook-ups, are mainly on gently sloping grass with just a few hardstandings. A meadow separates the park from the River Ure, a favourite place for strolling and fishing (licences available). There is lots to see and do on and off the park for both families and couples.

Facilities	Directions
The new, tiled toilet block includes a baby room, dishwashing room, a fully fitted shower room for disabled visitors and laundry facilities. New shop, reception, bar with snacks and games room. Well equipped new play area. Off site: Golf course within a mile. The delightful market town (city) of Ripon with its ancient cathedral is only 15 minutes walk.	At the most northern roundabout on the Ripon bypass (A61), turn onto the A6108 signed Ripon, Masham and Leyburn. Go straight on at mini-roundabout and park is signed on right. O.S.GR: SE317727.

Open

Easter - 31 October.

At a glance

Welcome & Ambience	✓✓✓✓	Location	✓✓✓
Quality of Pitches	✓✓✓✓	Range of Facilities	✓✓✓✓

Charges 2004

Per unit incl. up to 4 persons and electricity	£ 12.00 - £ 16.50
tent incl. up to 4 persons	£ 9.00 - £ 13.50
extra person (over 3 yrs)	£ 3.00 - £ 6.00
dog (max 2)	£ 1.00

No credit cards.

Reservations

Made for min. 3 nights with £20 per week deposit. Tel: 01765 602964. Email: riverside@flowerofmay.com

UK4660 Woodhouse Farm Caravan & Camping Park

Winksley, Ripon HG4 3PG (North Yorkshire)

This secluded family park on a former working farm, is only six miles from Ripon and about four miles from the World Heritage site of Fountains Abbey. It is a very rural park with a spacious feel and various pitching areas tucked away in woodland areas or around the edges of hedged fields with the centres left clear for children. There are hard roads and most of the 160 pitches have 16A electricity. There are 56 acres in total, 17.5 devoted to the site and 20 acres of woodland for walks, etc. with a good area where dogs can run free. The 2.5 acre fishing lake (day tickets from reception) is a big attraction and provides a pleasant area for picnics or walks. The tastefully developed bar (daily) and restaurant (weekends only) offers reasonably priced menus. Woodhouse Farm has a quiet, secluded location from which many excursions can be made – the Yorkshire Dales of Nidderdale, Wharfedale, Wensleydale and Swaledale are all within easy reach. As in most parts of the Dales, the peace is occasionally disturbed by passing jets, but happily not very often.

Facilities

The clean, functional toilet block nearer the pitches has been upgraded and includes heating, roomy showers (20p) and some washbasins in cabins. Covered dishwashing sinks. Two bathrooms and facilities for disabled visitors are planned for 2004. Extra facilities are in the farm buildings along with a well equipped laundry, reception and shop. Gas supplies. Motorcaravan services. New bar (daily) and restaurant (weekends). Games room, table tennis, pool table and TV. Play equipment around the park. Fishing. Mountain bike hire. Caravan storage. Deposit for amenity block key £10. Off site: Many attractive villages with inns supplying food and drinks. The small historic city of Ripon has a beautiful cathedral. Riding 3 miles, golf 6 miles.

At a glance

Welcome & Ambience	✓✓✓✓	Location	✓✓✓✓✓
Quality of Pitches	✓✓✓✓	Range of Facilities	✓✓✓✓

Directions

From Ripon take Fountains Abbey - Pateley Bridge road (B6265). After approx. 3.5 miles turn right to Grantley and then follow campsite signs for further 1-2 miles. O.S.GR: SE241715.

Charges 2004

Per unit incl. 2 persons	£ 8.50 - £ 11.00
with electricity	£ 10.50 - £ 13.00
small tent incl. 2 persons	£ 8.00 - £ 10.00
extra person (over 5 yrs)	£ 0.50 - £ 1.50
awning, pup tent	£ 2.00
dog	£ 0.50

Reservations

Made with £10 deposit. Tel: 01765 658309.
Email: woodhouse.farm@talk21.com

Open

1 March - 31 October.

Woodhouse Farm & Country Park

- Fishing
- Restaurant/Bar
- Laundrette
- Licensed shop
- Games Room
- Dogs Welcome
- Easy access to Ripon, Fountains Abbey, Brimham Rocks

Set in glorious tranquil woodland and meadows with its own private coarse fishing lake. The ideal base for exploring the spectacular countryside of North Yorkshire

Winksley, Ripon, North Yorkshire, HG4 3PG
woodhouse.farm@talk21.com
AA ➤➤ 01765 658309 www.woodhousewinksley.com

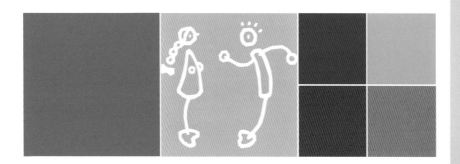

UK4710 Rudding Holiday Park

Follifoot, Harrogate HG3 1JH (North Yorkshire)

The extensive part wooded, part open grounds of Rudding Park are very attractive, peaceful and well laid out. One camping area is sloping but terraces provide level pitches and further pitches are in the very sheltered old walled garden. All 91 touring pitches have electricity (10/16A) and 20 'super pitches' are fully serviced. Further pitches are let on a seasonal basis and a separate area contains 96 owner occupied caravan holiday homes and pine chalets. On the outer edge of the park is an 18 hole golf course and driving range, together with the 'The Deer House', a bar and restaurant open twice daily during B.Hs and school holidays, otherwise only at weekends. Tennis, markets, pubs and restaurants are within a few miles, and the majestic City of York is less than an hour away. This is an attractive park with something for all the family.

Facilities

Two tiled, well maintained toilet blocks are of a good standard (one completely refurbished), with central heating, some washbasins in cabins, a baby room and bathroom. Fully equipped laundry room at each block. Disabled people have well appointed facilities. Motorcaravan service point. Large, well stocked shop (all season, sometimes limited hours). Gas supplies. Restaurant and bar. Heated outdoor swimming and paddling pools with sunbathing areas (Spr.B.H.- early Sept), supervised at all times (extra charge). Adventure playground. Football pitch, games room and minigolf. Golf. Off site: Buses pass the gate hourly to Harrogate and Knaresborough. Fishing 2 miles, riding 1 mile.

At a glance

Welcome & Ambience	✓✓✓✓	Location	✓✓✓✓
Quality of Pitches	✓✓✓✓	Range of Facilities	✓✓✓✓✓

Directions

Park is 3 miles south of Harrogate clearly signed between the A658 and A661 roads. O.S.GR: SE333528.

Charges 2004

Per pitch	£ 11.50 - £ 17.00
with electricity	£ 14.00 - £ 19.50
'supersite' incl. awning, electricity	£ 18.50 - £ 27.00
awning	£ 1.00 - £ 2.00
tent per adult	£ 3.75 - £ 5.50
child (5-16 yrs)	£ 2.00 - £ 3.00

Special offers - contact park.

Reservations

Made with full advance payment (essential for B.H. w/ends). Tel: 01423 870439.
Email: holiday-park@ruddingpark.com

Open

1 March - 31 January.

UK4630 Ripley Caravan Park

Ripley, Harrogate HG3 3AU (North Yorkshire)

Peter and Valerie House are the resident owners of Ripley Park, an 18 acre grass caravan park with an indoor heated pool. Accommodating 100 touring units and 40 caravan holiday homes on fairly level grass, undulating in parts, there are 130 electricity connections (10A) and 20 hardstandings. Connected by a circular gravel road, some pitches are marked, others carefully spaced (allowing the grass to recover). Recent developments include the planting of 2,000 trees and these are developing well to provide individual areas and shelter. A small pond (lake) with ducks provides an attractive feature. The park is situated at the gateway to the Yorkshire Dales National Park and almost midway between the spa town of Harrogate and historic Knaresborough. The village of Ripley, dominated by its castle, is within walking distance.

Facilities

The central, attractively designed toilet block provides washbasins in curtained cubicles, a baby bath and a separate unit with a shower for disabled people. It can be heated and has been extended to provide extra, smart facilities. Small laundry. Dishwashing sinks under cover. Motorcaravan service point. Recycling bins. Shop with gas (limited hours in low seasons). Games room with TV. Nursery playroom. Adventure play equipment and football area. Heated indoor pool (50p per person) and sauna. Up to two dogs per unit are welcome unless by prior arrangement. Winter caravan storage. Off site: Fishing, riding or golf 3 miles. Bus service 150 yds.

At a glance

Welcome & Ambience	✓✓✓✓✓	Location	✓✓✓✓✓
Quality of Pitches	✓✓✓✓	Range of Facilities	✓✓✓✓

Directions

About 4 miles north of Harrogate, site access is 150 yds. down the B6165 Knaresborough road from its roundabout junction with the A61. O.S.GR: SE291601.

Charges 2004

Per unit incl. 2 adults	£ 7.50 - £ 11.00
with electricity	£ 9.50 - £ 12.00
extra adult	£ 2.00
child (5-16 yrs)	£ 1.00
water and drainage	£ 2.50
awning, child's pup tent or extra car	£ 1.00 - £ 1.50
small tent incl. 2 persons, no vehicle	£ 6.00 - £ 7.00

Reservations

Made with £10 deposit, min. 3 nights at B.Hs.
Tel: 01423 770050.

Open

Easter - 31 October.

The northwest region boasts a wealth of industrial heritage with undiscovered countryside, the vibrant cities of Manchester and Liverpool, the seaside resorts of Blackpool and Morecambe Bay, plus miles of glorious coastline, home to a wide variety of bird species.

This region includes:
Cheshire, Lancashire, Merseyside, Greater Manchester and the High Peaks of Derbyshire

The miles of beautiful, North West countryside offers endless opportunities for recreation. For the more active, the peaceful plains of Cheshire are a walker's haven with endless trails to choose from. Lancashire is also good walking country, with way marked paths passing through the outstanding forest of Bowland, which affords marvellous views over the Lake District in Cumbria and the Yorkshire Dales. Birdwatchers are catered for too, with the coast offering some of the best bird spotting activitiy in the country, most notably along the Sefton coast and around the Wirral Peninsula. The region's cities also have their own charm. Manchester, with its fabulous shopping centres and vibrant nightlife, boasts a rich Victorian heritage; the maritime city of Liverpool has more museums and galleries than any other UK city outside London; Lancaster features fine Georgian buildings and an imposing Norman castle; while Chester is renowned for its medieval architecture and shopping galleries. And offering good, old-fashioned seaside fun is Blackpool. England's most popular seaside resort is packed full of lively entertainment and attractions, such as the white knuckle rides at the pleasure beach, amusement games on the pier and the observation decks in the world-famous Tower.

Did you know?

The first public gallery to open in England was in Liverpool in 1877

Lancaster Castle is infamous as host to the Pendle Witch trials in 1612

The first passenger railway station was built in Manchester

Houghton Tower is where King James 1 knighted a loin of beef in 1617 – hence the name Sirloin

To date 300 bird species have been recorded within the boundaries of Sefton

Chester has the most complete set of city walls in Britain

Opened in 1894, the Blackpool Tower was copied from the Eiffel Tower; the height to the top of the flagpole is 518 feet 9 inches

Places of interest

Cheshire: Tatton Park in Knutsford; Chester Cathedral and Zoo; Cheshire Military Museum; Lyme Park stately home in Macclesfield; Beeston Castle; Boat Museum at Ellesmere Port

Lancashire: Williamson Park, Castle and Leisure Park in Lancaster; Camelot Theme Park; Museum of Football in Preston; Morecambe Bay; Hoghton Tower and National Museum of Football in Preston

Merseyside: Liverpool Football Club Museum and Tour Centre; The Beatles Story Museum; Speke Hall Garden and Estate; The Wirral Country Park; Williamson Tunnels Heritage Centre

Greater Manchester: Imperial War Museum North; Manchester United Football Club Museum; The Lowry; Corgi Heritage Centre in Rochdale; Stockport Air Raid Shelter

tip

LANCASTER'S ANNUAL GEORGIAN FESTIVAL FAIR TAKES PLACE IN AUGUST, FEATURING BRITAIN'S WACKIEST RACE, THE NATIONAL SEDAN CHAIR CARRYING CHAMPIONSHIPS.

UK5230 Chester Southerly Caravan Park

Balderton Lane, Marlston-cum-Lache, Chester CH4 9LF (Cheshire)

This is a well managed friendly campsite within three miles of the city of Chester. It is easily accessible from the Chester Southerly bypass and convenient for the new ferry terminal at Mostyn. It enjoys a quiet countryside environment and the 90 pitches, mostly on hardstanding for touring outfits, are spaciously spread in bays around this mature site. Pitches are marked, numbered and level with 10A electricity connections. To the left of the card operated security barrier stands reception which incorporates a small shop selling basic food items. Chester is one of England's most historic cities and this site makes a convenient base for spending time discovering its famous rows, walls, gates and towers. There are many other touring possibilities from here such as the North Wales Coast, the Dee valley, Cheshire Plain, etc.

Facilities	Directions
A single toilet block (key system), whilst not ultra modern is brightly decorated, kept clean and can be heated. Open style washbasins; facilities for people with disabilities (washbasin and WC), laundry room with sinks, washing machine and dryer and dishwashing area. Motorcaravan service point. Shop. Adventure type play area. Off site: City centre 3 miles.	Park is on Dodleston - Kinnerton turn off from A483 and is signed from the junction of A55 and A483 roads. O.S.GR: SJ385624.

Charges 2004	
Per unit incl. 2 persons and electricity	£ 14.00

Reservations

Contact site. Tel: 01244 671308.

Open

Easter - end October.

At a glance

Welcome & Ambience	✓✓✓✓	Location	✓✓✓✓
Quality of Pitches	✓✓✓	Range of Facilities	✓✓✓

UK5240 Lamb Cottage Caravan Park

Dalefords Lane, Whitegate, Northwich CW8 2BN (Cheshire)

This quiet, family run 'adult only' park is set in the midst of the lovely Vale Royal area of Cheshire. New owners, Mike and Lynn Howard are making great improvements wth a complete redevelopment of the touring section and new toilet and shower facilities. The entrance road is flanked by 22 privately owned residential caravan holiday homes which are not unduly obtrusive, and a second area beyond has 28 newly landscaped seasonal caravan pitches. Beyond this again is the new touring area which now has 34 large pitches, all with 16A electric hook-ups. There are 10 grass pitches, and 24 on gravel hardstandings, which are multi-serviced with electricity, water and waste water drain. Only 'breathable' groundsheets are permitted and tents and motorcycles are not accepted. Nearby are Delamere Forest with its walking and mountain biking trails, Whitegate Way walking trail, Oulton Park Motor Racing Circuit, castles at Peckforton and Beeston, and the city of Chester, which is 12 miles.

Facilities	Directions
Toilet and shower facilities are housed in a new custom built 'park home' style unit which includes washbasins in cubicles and facilities for disabled guests. Dishwashing area. Laudry room. Recycling of glass and paper. Calor gas stocked. Fenced dog walk (max. 2 dogs per unit permitted). Off site: Pub serving food and convenience store under 1 mile, supermarket 3 miles. Golf 2 miles. Fishing 3 miles. Riding 1.5 miles. Bicycle hire 4 miles.	From M6 exit 19 take A556 towards Chester. After about 12 miles turn left at traffic lights (signed Winsford and Whitegate) into Dalefords Lane. Continue for about 1 mile and site entrance is on right between white house and bungalow. O.S.GR: SJ614693.

Charges 2005	
Per pitch incl. 2 persons, electricity	£ 15.00 - £ 17.00
extra adult	£ 5.00

Reservations

Essential for peak season and B.Hs.
Tel: 01606 882302. Email: lynn@lccp.fsworld.co.uk

Open

1 March - 31 October.

At a glance

Welcome & Ambience	✓✓✓✓	Location	✓✓✓✓
Quality of Pitches	✓✓✓✓	Range of Facilities	✓✓✓

For all your **camping and touring needs**

TURN TO PAGE 294 for details

UK5250 Capesthorne Hall Touring Caravan Park

Macclesfield SK11 9JY (Cheshire)

The approach to this site is impressive as you enter the main gates, pass the gatekeeper's cottage and proceed carefully up the drive (mind the speed bumps) through the parkland almost to the front door of this imposing stately home. The campsite is set on a five acre meadow to the right of the Hall and with only 30 pitches, everyone has plenty of space arranged around a series of small fenced copses. All have access to electric hook-ups (10A, long leads may be necessary) and most are on grass – there are just two hardstandings. The park, lakes, gardens and woodland walks extend to over 100 acres and caravanners have free access to these between 7am and 7pm. The Hall, Butler's Pantry and Grounds are open to the public on Wednesday, Sunday and Bank Holiday afternoons. A range of events are also held in the park adjacent to the campsite during the year. These include Craft Fairs, horse shows, open air theatre and opera. Wedding receptions are also staged. Site lighting is minimal so torches are useful and only 'breathable' groundsheets are permitted. Tents or trailer tents are not accepted.

Facilities

Toilet facilities are in some of the Hall's outbuildings around a courtyard to the side of the campsite. Only the ladies section is heated but they provide one huge shower room per sex, with free controllable hot water, and a generous supply of WCs and washbasins. Tiny laundry and dishwashing room. All are naturally in a very traditional period style but are very clean. Basic drive over drain for motorcaravans, neatly marked with a cone! Off site: Jodrell Bank and Gawsworth Hall are nearby. Fishing and riding 1 mile, golf 3 miles, bicycle hire 10 miles. Shop and garage 1 mile.

At a glance

Welcome & Ambience	✓✓✓✓	Location	✓✓✓✓
Quality of Pitches	✓✓✓✓	Range of Facilities	✓✓✓✓

Directions

Capesthorne Hall is on A34, 3 miles south of Alderley Edge and 6 miles north of Congleton, just south of the crossroads with the A537. O.S.GR: SJ840730.

Charges 2004

Per unit incl. 2 persons and electricity	£ 12.00
incl. 2 children	£ 14.00

Reservations

Essential for peak season and B.Hs.
Tel: 01625 861779.

Open

1 April - 31 October.

UK5280 Abbey Farm Caravan Park

Dark Lane, Ormskirk L40 5TX (Lancashire)

This quiet, well equipped, family park beside the Abbey ruins has views over open farmland. It is an ideal base for a longer stay with plenty of interest in the local area, including Ormskirk parish church, unusual for having both a tower and a spire. Market days are on Thursday and Saturday. The park is divided into small paddocks, one of which is for 30 privately owned seasonal units, one for tents, the others for touring units, plus a rally field for special events. The 60 touring pitches, all with electricity (10/16A), are on neatly mown level grass, separated by small shrubs and colourful flower borders. Some mature trees provide shade in parts. Amenities include a farm walk and a small, free lending library with a good stock of tourist information. The owners organise two annual events – a barbecue in early June and Bonfire Night in November. They have planned plenty of routes for walkers from the park. Southport with its beach and Pleasureland is 10 miles. Wigan Pier, Aintree for the Grand National, the annual Beatles Festival or Southport Flower Show and Martin Mere Nature reserve are some of the attractions within easy reach. A member of the Countryside Discovery group.

Facilities

The main toilet block is modern, heated and spotless, providing controllable hot showers. Dual purpose family bathroom that includes facilities for disabled people. A second smaller unit has individual shower/WC/washbasin cubicles. Dishwashing sinks under cover at both units. Laundry room with washing machine, dryer, spinner, ironing board and airing cupboard. Small well stocked shop shares space with reception, with a butcher calling twice weekly. Indoor games room with table tennis and football games machine. Small adventure playground and large field for ball games. Fishing lake (£2 per rod, per day).

Open

All year.

At a glance

Welcome & Ambience	✓✓✓✓✓	Location	✓✓✓✓
Quality of Pitches	✓✓✓✓	Range of Facilities	✓✓✓✓✓

Directions

From M6 junction 27 take A5209 (Parbold) road. After 5 miles turn left (just before garage) onto B5240, and then first right into Hob Cross Lane, following signs to site. O.S.GR: SD433099.

Charges 2004

Per unit incl. 2 adults	£ 9.60 - £ 11.00
serviced pitch	£ 13.00 - £ 14.50
extra adult	£ 2.00
child (5-15 yrs)	£ 1.20
electricity	£ 1.70 - £ 2.00
Less 10% for 7 nights booked on or before arrival.	

Reservations

Essential for high season or B.Hs. Min charge 3 nights for B.Hs. + £10 deposit. Tel: 01695 572686.
Email: abbeyfarm@yahoo.com

UK5360 Willowbank Touring Park

Coastal Road, Ainsdale, Southport PR8 3ST (Mersey)

Well situated for the Sefton coast and Southport, Willowbank is a fairly new park still undergoing some development under new ownership. The touring park is on the edge of sand dunes amongst mature, wind swept trees. Entrance to the park is controlled by a barrier, with a pass-key issued at the excellent reception building which doubles as a sales office for the substantial static development that is under-way here. The new owners are very well supported on the touring side by Norman and Christine Roberts who have considerable experience in managing touring parks and have encouraged the development of the touring pitches. Already there are 40 gravel hardstanding pitches, with more planned. Eventually the park will have 93 pitches, but presently only 54 are developed, all with 10A electricity. The park does not accept motorhomes longer than 27 feet. There could be some noise from the nearby main road. This is a good area for cycling and walking and the attractions of Southport with its parks, gardens, funfair and shopping are 4 miles away.

Facilities

The purpose built, heated toilet block is of a high standard including an excellent bathroom for disabled visitors, although the showers are rather compact. Baby room. Small dishwashing room. Laundry with washing machine and dryer. Motorcaravan service point. Play area. Off site: Beach 1.5 miles. Golf and riding 0.5 miles. Fishing 4 miles. Bicycle hire 4.5 miles. Martin Mere nature reserve nearby.

Open

All year excl. 11 January - 28 February.

At a glance

Welcome & Ambience	✓✓✓✓✓	Location	✓✓✓✓
Quality of Pitches	✓✓✓✓	Range of Facilities	✓✓✓✓

Directions

Park is 4 miles south of Southport. From Ainsdale on A565 travel south for 1.5 miles to second traffic lights (Woodvale) and turn right into Coastal Road to site on right in 150 yds. From south pass RAF Woodvale and turn left at second set of lights. O.S.GR: SD308108.

Charges 2004

Per unit incl. 2 adults	£ 9.50 - £ 12.50
hardstanding	£ 1.00
extra adult	£ 2.30
child (5-16 yrs)	£ 1.75
dog (max 2)	£ 0.75
Less 5% for stays over 7 days or more.	

Reservations

Made with £5 deposit and £1 fee. Tel: 01704 571566. Email: mail@willowbankcp.co.uk

UK5330 Marton Mere Holiday Village

Mythop Road, Blackpool FY4 4NX (Lancashire)

If Blackpool is your holiday destination and your family are looking for lots to do then this Haven Holidays park may well be a suitable choice. Although mainly used for static caravan holiday homes, there are 210 touring pitches with hardstanding, of which 58 are fully serviced. All have electricity hook ups (10/16A). A few trees give a small amount of shade, but as with a lot of coastal sites, it can be a little windy. During the day buses depart every 30 minutes from the main reception area to Blackpool. On site there is plenty of entertainment including three licensed bars, discos and the Rainbow room where children are entertained. For small children (under 12s), there is the Bradley Bear Club with face painting, disco dancing, games and competitions. In the autumn months (Sept - Nov), the Blackpool illuminations are a must for young and old alike. Other places to visit include the historic towns of Lytham and St Annes, the world of Coronation Street and many fantastic golf courses.

Facilities

Two heated toilet blocks (key pad entry system) have piped music playing and although of older design are clean and well kept with large pre-set showers and hairdryers. Each block has dishwashing sinks under cover, a suite for disabled people, baby room, family bathroom and launderette. Well stocked supermarket with all day bakery, bars, fast food outlets and restaurants. New outdoor splash pool and heated indoor pool with flume, jacuzzi and sauna. Amusement arcades, multi-sports court, crazy golf and bowling. Two children's clubs with full entertainment schedule. Dogs are accepted on certain pitches. Off site: Martin Mere nature reserve. Blackpool beach, entertainment, etc.

At a glance

Welcome & Ambience	✓✓✓✓	Location	✓✓✓✓
Quality of Pitches	✓✓✓✓	Range of Facilities	✓✓✓✓

Directions

From M55 junction 4, turn right at roundabout taking A583 towards Blackpool. Pass the windmill, then right at the traffic lights by the Clifton Arms into Mythop Road. Park is on the left O.S.GR: SD344351.

Charges 2004

Per unit incl. up to 4 persons	
and electricity	£ 25.00 - £ 44.00
serviced pitch	£ 35.00 - £ 54.00
extra person	£ 2.00 - £ 3.00
Variety of special offers available.	

Reservations

Made with £25 deposit; contact park for details. Tel: 01253 767544.

Open

21 March - 31 October.

UK5300 Kneps Farm Holiday Park

River Road, Stanah, Thornton-Cleveleys FY5 5LR (Lancashire)

A well established park with top class modern facilities, Kneps Farm is still operated by the family who opened it in 1967. Next to Wyre Country Park, it makes an excellent base from which to explore the area. A card operated barrier system flanks the reception building which also houses a well stocked shop. The 70 marked and numbered touring pitches are generally on hardstandings with electricity (10A) available to most, and all are accessed from tarmac roads. There are also some grassy pitches and a separate area with 80 caravan holiday homes (most privately owned). A path leads through a gate at the back of the site into the country park. Just down the lane is a public slip-way and the Wyreside Ecology Centre. A list and map are provided of local services and amenities, including pubs, restaurants, takeaway, etc. Other local attractions include Marsh Mill Village with a restored windmill, the Freeport Shopping and Leisure village at nearby Fleetwood (discount shopping), and several bird-watching sites around the estuary and country park.

Facilities

The excellent, large, centrally heated sanitary building is warm and inviting with ten individual family bathrooms, each providing a WC, basin and bath/shower. Separate toilet facilities with electric hand-wash units for men and women. Well equipped room for disabled visitors. Dishwashing sinks. Combined baby care/first aid room. Laundry room with washing machines, dryers, spinner and ironing facility. Shop. Small, fenced children's playground. Up to two dogs are accepted per unit. Off site: Fishing 0.5 miles, golf 2.5 miles.

Open

1 March - 15 November.

At a glance

Welcome & Ambience	✓✓✓✓✓	Location	✓✓✓✓
Quality of Pitches	✓✓✓✓✓	Range of Facilities	✓✓✓✓

Directions

From M55 junction 3, take A585 towards Fleetwood. Turn right at traffic lights by Shell station (for Thornton-Cleveleys), straight across next traffic lights, then right at the next roundabout by River Wyre Hotel. After one mile (past school) turn right at mini-roundabout into Stanah Road, continue across second mini-roundabout and eventually into River Road with site entrance ahead of you. O.S.GR: SD350430.

Charges 2004

Per unit incl. 2 adults, 2 children and electricity	£ 17.50 - £ 20.00
tent incl. 2 adults and 2 children	£ 15.00 - £ 17.50
adult couple	£ 11.50 - £ 15.50
extra child	£ 1.75 - £ 2.25

Special Senior Citizen rates.

Reservations

Essential for B.Hs. and peak season and illuminations, and made with £10 deposit. Tel: 01253 823632. Email: enquiries@knepsfarm.co.uk

UK5350 Holgates Caravan Park

Middlebarrow Plain, Cove Road, Silverdale, Carnforth LA5 0SH (Lancashire)

This attractive, very high quality park is in an outstanding craggy, part-wooded, hillside location with fine views over Morecambe Bay. It takes 70 touring units, with 339 privately owned caravan holiday homes and 11 to rent located in woodland away from the touring pitches. With just 5 grassy pitches for tents, the remaining 65 large touring pitches are on gravel hardstandings, all with electricity (16A), free TV connection, individual drainage and water points. The main complex, with reception and the entrance barrier provides a well stocked supermarket, lounge bar, restaurant with good value meals and a terrace with views over the bay. There is also an indoor leisure centre. Children have a choice of two adventure playgrounds and plenty of space for ball games. Also on site is a small but challenging golf course. Everything is completed to the highest standards.

Facilities

Two modern, heated toilet buildings, built from local stone, are fully equipped with top quality fittings and including some private cubicles with WC and washbasin. Dishwashing sinks at each block. Excellent separate provision for disabled visitors with a reserved pitch and parking bay adjacent. Launderette. Shop. Gas supplies. Bar and restaurant. Indoor pool (17 x 17 m; with lifeguard) with spa pool, steam room and sauna (all free to campers, no unaccompanied under 10s). Playgrounds. Games room with pool table and video games. Golf course (£1.50 per person). Facilities are limited mid-week in January and early February. Admission restrictions include no unaccompanied under 18s or single sex groups, certain breeds of dog or commercial vehicles. Off site: Riding, cycling, walking and fishing all within 9 miles. Morecambe or Lancaster are just 12 miles and Kendal 15 miles.

At a glance

Welcome & Ambience	✓✓✓✓✓	Location	✓✓✓✓✓
Quality of Pitches	✓✓✓✓✓	Range of Facilities	✓✓✓✓✓

Directions

From traffic lights in centre of Carnforth take road to Silverdale under low bridge (12'9"). After 1 mile turn left signed Silverdale and after 2.5 miles over level crossing, carry on and turn right at T-junction. Follow Holgates sign from here watching for left then right forks (narrow roads). O.S.GR: SD460755.

Charges 2004

Per unit incl. 2 adults, 2 children	£ 23.00 - £ 27.75
extra adult	£ 7.00
extra child (5-17 yrs)	£ 4.00
awning or pup tent	£ 3.00

Minimum stays apply for all B.H. weekends.

Reservations

Essential for B.Hs and peak season; made with £15 deposit for 1 or 2 nights, £25 for longer. Tel: 01524 701508. Email: caravan@holgates.co.uk

Open

All year excl. 3 Nov - 21 Dec.

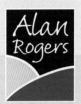

With spectacular lakes, undulating fells, impressive mountains and lush green valleys, Cumbria is ideal for those who wish to get away from it all and unwind in peaceful, natural surroundings, or for the more active who want to participate in a range of outdoor pursuits.

Cumbria is best known for the beautiful Lake District National Park, with the picturesque valleys and lakes of Windermere, Ullswater and Derwentwater, each with its own distinctive character. Windermere offers no shortage of watersports, whereas Ullswater mainly attracts peaceful sailing boats. While the Lake District is well known, there are also many quiet, undiscovered areas in the region including the wild, rugged moors of the north Pennines and the beautiful Eden Valley, an ideal place for a casual stroll along the riverside footpaths. The Western Lakes and Fells offer more tranquillity. Here the fells drop down to a long and spectacular coastline, with many undiscovered, quiet corners from Ennerdale and Esdale to the sandstone cliffs of St Bees Head, now part of a designated Heritage Coast. The Lake District Peninsulas along the southern coast of Cumbria also display beautiful scenery and are home to a cluster of ancient ruins such as Furness Abbey and the medieval castle, built by monks, on Piel Island. Rich in heritage, the historic city of Carlisle, which was sited on the Roman built Hadrian's wall, boasts an impressive castle, Cumbria's only cathedral, a superb Victorian covered market and an array of speciality shops.

Did you know?

Cumbria has the steepest road in England, called the Hardknott Pass

The Lake District was the inspiration for many poets, writers and artists, including William Wordsworth, Beatrix Potter and John Ruskin

Ulverston is the birthplace of Quakerism and pole vaulting

Bassenthwaite is the only real lake in the Lake District! All the others are either meres, (Windermere) or waters (Derwentwater, Coniston Water and Ullswater)

Cumbria is home to England's only breeding pair of Golden Eagles, nesting near the Haweswater reservoir

Stretching 73 miles, Hadrian's Wall was built by Romans in the second century

Places of interest

Barrow-in-Furness: South Lakes Wild Animal Park; Dalton Castle; Furness Abbey; Piel Island

Carlisle: 11th century castle; Birdoswald Roman fort; Lanercost Priory

Ravenglass: Muncaster Castle, an historic haunted castle and Headquarters of the World Owl Trust

Ulverston: world's only Laurel and Hardy museum

Kendal: historic riverside town situated between the Lakes and Dales, famous for its mint cake and castle ruins

Lake Derwentwater: lakeside theatre open all year hosting plays, music, dance, comedy and film

Windermere: Steamboat Centre, a collection of Windermere's nautical heritage with boats on display; World of Beatrix Potter

Grasmere: Dove Cottage and Wordsworth Museum

 tip

THE WORLD GURNING CHAMPIONSHIPS TAKE PLACE AT THE EGREMONT CRAB FAIR IN SEPT. IN A TRADITION DATING BACK TO 1267. THE FAIR ALSO FEATURES WRESTLING AND SINGING.

UK5530 Walls Caravan & Camping Park

Ravenglass CA18 1SR (Cumbria)

Once part of the large Pennington Estate in western Cumbria, Walls is a small, neat park set in five acres of woodland amongst a variety of mature trees. It has space for 25 touring units on hard standing pitches with a grass verge for awnings (plus 25 seasonal units). A circular gravel road provides access and all pitches have electrical hook-ups (10A). A small grass area at the top and back of the park provides an attractive spot for ten tents overlooking the fields. A central courtyard complex includes the owners' home, reception and the facilities. All is maintained by Keith and Stephanie Bridges, who provide a very warm welcome and having used the site since it was first developed, now own it. It is a useful site for all sorts of walking - estuary, river or fell - or to explore the Cumbrian coast with its Roman connections, the western Lake District or to enjoy the Ravenglass and Eskdale Miniature Railway. When we visited some rail noise was heard during the day but this stopped at about 10.30 pm giving an undisturbed night's sleep.

Facilities

The toilet block provides all the usual amenities, is well kept and has a fully equipped laundry room and dishwashing facilities. Motorcaravan service point. Shop (only a few basic necessities plus gas). Off site: Fishing and bicycle hire 3 miles, boat launching 1.5 miles, golf 6 miles. The small village of Ravenglass, a single, cottage lined street, is within walking distance, has a pub and holds a Charter Fair in June. Daily bus service runs from Whitehaven to Barrow calling at Ravenglass, or trains from the local station to Carlisle and Barrow.

Open

1 March - 31 October.

At a glance

Welcome & Ambience	✓✓✓	Location	✓✓✓
Quality of Pitches	✓✓✓	Range of Facilities	✓✓✓

Directions

Park is just off A595 (between Egremont and Millom) on road into village of Ravenglass. O.S.GR: SD096965.

Charges 2004

Per unit incl. 2 adults	£ 10.25
extra person	£ 2.00
child (under 16 yrs)	free
medium tent (2 persons)	£ 10.00
small tent (1 person)	£ 5.00
awning	£ 1.00

No credit cards.

Reservations

Contact park. Tel: 01229 717250.
Email: wallscaravanpark@ravenglass98.freeserve.com

UK5510 The Larches Caravan Park

Mealsgate, Wigton CA7 1LQ (Cumbria)

Mealsgate and The Larches lie on the Carlisle – Cockermouth road, a little removed from the hectic centre of the Lake District, yet with easy access to it (and good views towards it) and to other attractions nearby - the Western Borders, Northumberland, etc. It is a quality, family run park which takes 73 touring units of any type and also accommodates 100 privately owned holiday homes. Touring pitches are in different grassy areas with tall, mature trees, shrubs and accompanying wildlife. Some are sloping and irregular, others on marked hardstandings, with electricity (10A), water and drainage. Events in the surrounding district each day displayed prominently in the window of the shop. On arrival visitors are loaned very comprehensive tourist information brochures. There are bus routes to Carlisle and Keswick, walks from the park and good restaurants nearby. The Elliott family provide a warm welcome at this peaceful, well organised park which is undergoing some redevelopment. This is an ideal haven for couples – only adult visitors are accepted.

Facilities

Toilet facilities, in two purpose designed blocks, are of good quality providing en-suite facilities for both sexes. Washbasins for ladies are in cubicles, those for men set in flat surfaces. Separate unit for disabled visitors can be heated. Campers' kitchen with cooker and microwave (metered). Laundry room. Well stocked shop incl. camping accessories, gas and off licence. Small indoor heated pool. Table tennis. Wildlife pond. Caravan storage. Off site: Golf 3.5 miles. Bicycle hire 7 miles. Fishing 8 miles. Riding 10 miles.

Open

1 March - 31 October.

At a glance

Welcome & Ambience	✓✓✓✓	Location	✓✓✓✓
Quality of Pitches	✓✓✓✓	Range of Facilities	✓✓✓✓

Directions

Park entrance is south off A595 road (Carlisle - Cockermouth) just southwest of Mealsgate. O.S.GR: NY206415.

Charges 2004

Per unit incl. 2 adults	£ 9.00 - £ 12.90
incl. electricity	£ 11.90 - £ 14.90
extra person	£ 2.00 - £ 2.50
awning or extra car	£ 1.00
backpacker	£ 5.50 - £ 6.50
from to	

Discounts for senior citizens and bookings over 7 nights. No credit cards.

Reservations

Made with £1 per night deposit, balance on arrival.
Tel: 01697 371379.
Email: info@larchescaravanpark.co.uk

UK5660 Castlerigg Hall Caravan & Camping Park

Keswick CA12 4TE (Cumbria)

This well laid out park was started in the late 1950s by the Jackson family, who over the years have developed and improved the site whilst maintaining its character. Good use has been made of the traditional stone buildings to house the reception and shop, whilst another building houses a modern amenity block along with a really excellent campers' kitchen. Tarmac roads wend their way around the site to the separate tent area of 110 pitches. Gently sloping with some shelter, these pitches have fine views across Keswick, Derwentwater and the western Fells. The 45 caravan pitches tend to be on terraces, again overlooking the lake. Each terrace has a maximum of seven pitches, all on hardstanding and with 10A electricity and nearly all with a water tap and grey water drain. Places to visit include Keswick (about 20 minutes walk), Derwentwater, Ullswater, Penrith, Carlisle, Hadrian's Wall, Rhegad (the village in the hill) and, quite close to the site, Castlerigg stone circle which is believed to be some 4,000 years old, and of course as much walking as you might want. The Jacksons are committed to conservation.

Facilities

The main toilet block is beautifully fitted out, fully tiled and heated, with showers, vanity style washbasins (2 in cabins) and hair care areas. Unit for disabled visitors (key). Baby area. Fully equipped laundry and dishwashing area. Games room and campers' kitchen complete with microwave, toasters, kettle and hot plates. Two other toilet blocks are older in style but newly decorated and clean. Reception houses tourist information, internet point and a well stocked shop (with gas). Off site: Hotel/pub for meals adjacent to site. Fishing, golf, riding. bicycle hire and boat launching, all 1.5 miles.

Open

Mid March - November.

At a glance

Welcome & Ambience	✓✓✓✓✓	Location	✓✓✓✓✓
Quality of Pitches	✓✓✓✓	Range of Facilities	✓✓✓✓✓

Directions

From Penrith take A66 towards Keswick and Cockermouth. Leave at first sign for Keswick (A591) and follow to junction (A5271). Turn left on A591 signed Windermere and after 1 mile, take small road on right signed Castlerigg and Rakefoot. Park entrance is on right after 400 yards. O.S.GR: NY282227.

Charges 2004

Per unit incl. 2 persons	£ 11.30 - £ 14.95
extra person (over 4 yrs)	£ 2.10 - £ 14.00
awning (strong steel pegs required)	£ 1.00 - £ 1.50
tent camper	£ 3.90
tent, car and 2 persons	£ 9.30 - £ 11.70

Reservations

Accepted for caravans or motorcaravans only with £10 deposit. Tel: 017687 74499.
Email: info@castlerigg.co.uk

UK5560 Sykeside Camping Park

Brotherswater, Patterdale, Penrith CA11 0NZ (Cumbria)

This small touring park is located in a really beautiful, quiet spot in the northern Lakes area, just 400 yards from Brotherswater. It is surrounded by fells and ideal for active outdoor holidays with walking or climbing on the high hills. With views up the Dovedale valley, the park has 100 pitches in the valley floor, including a few hardstandings. Caravans are now permitted and the access road has been improved. Pitches are not marked and campers arrange themselves to best enjoy the views. There are 19 electrical connections (5/10A). The stone-built building, an original barn, near the entrance just 200 yards from the field, houses all the facilities. These include the Barn End bar where meals are available at busier times. The nearby Brotherswater Inn is open all day for meals and has rooms to let.

Facilities

The toilet block includes hot showers and has been refurbished, with a chemical disposal point added. Small launderette and dishwashing room. Self-service shop with camping equipment, gas and an ice-pack service, doubles as reception. Cosy, licensed bar and restaurant serving breakfast (8.15-10 am) and evening meals during peak periods (6-9 pm, bar open 5-11 pm). Bunkhouse accommodation for 30 persons in various groupings. Fishing nearby. Off site: Bicycle hire 3 miles. Riding 8 miles. Golf 10 miles.

Open

All year.

At a glance

Welcome & Ambience	✓✓✓	Location	✓✓✓✓
Quality of Pitches	✓✓✓	Range of Facilities	✓✓✓

Directions

On west side of A592 road about 2 miles south of Patterdale, which lies at the southwestern end of Ullswater - entrance is just behind the Brotherswater Inn. O.S.GR: NY396005.

Charges 2004

Per adult	£ 3.00 - £ 3.50
child (4-14 yrs)	£ 1.50
car or motorcycle	£ 2.50 - £ 3.00
electricity	£ 2.00
dog	£ 1.20

Min. charge for motorcaravan £15 per night.

Reservations

Made with £15 per pitch deposit (not possible to book electric hook-up) with balance on arrival. Easter or Spr. B.H. - min. booking, 3 and 4 days respectively. Reservation is essential in peak seasons.
Tel: 017684 82239. Email: info@skyeside.co.uk

UK5605 Woodclose Caravan Park

Kirkby Lonsdale LA6 2SE (Cumbria)

Woodclose is an established, nine-acre park with new owners. Situated in the Lune Valley and just one mile from the market town of Kirkby Lonsdale, this park offers a peaceful and secluded setting catering for walkers, tourers and people who just want to relax. Access to the park is narrow, so care should be taken. The whole park has a very well cared for appearance with well mown grass, flowering tubs and neat hedges. The upper part contains many privately owned holiday homes with neat terraces built from local stone. Screened by a hedge and placed around the perimeter are several seasonal pitches with touring units being placed in the centre. These pitches are numbered and mostly level, some on hard-standing, some on grass, with 16A electricity and digital TV hook-ups. More seasonal pitches and holiday homes on the lower part of the park, most again attractively terraced with stone walling and paths. Reception is part of the well stocked shop which includes local produce and fresh baked bread; an information room is adjoining with tables and chairs.

Facilities

Two toilet blocks, the main one central to the touring area. These facilities are all unisex in large, heated, individual rooms with toilets, washbasin and toilet or washbasin and shower, all well equipped and very clean. Indoor dishwashing, well equipped laundry and chemical disposal within the same building. The second block is in the lower part, again all unisex in cubicles together with an indoor dishwashing area. No motorcaravan service point or facilities for disabled visitors. Shop. Small adventure play area. Table tennis. American style motorhomes accepted (limited space). Gates locked 12.00 - 07.30, warden and telephone on site for emergencies. Off site: Golf 1 mile. Fishing 7 miles. Beach 20 miles.

Directions

From M6 exit 36 take A65 to Kirkby Lonsdale. Site is off the A65 in 6 miles. O.S.GR: SD620781.

Charges 2004

Per unit incl. 2 persons, electricity	£ 12.00 - £ 20.00
tent incl. 2 persons	£ 11.00 - £ 13.00
extra adult	£ 3.50
child (5-16 yrs)	£ 2.00
awning	£ 2.00
dog	£ 1.00

Reservations

Contact park. Tel: 015242 71597.
Email: info@woodclosepark.com

Open

1 March – 1 November.

At a glance

Welcome & Ambience	✓✓✓✓	Location	✓✓✓✓
Quality of Pitches	✓✓✓✓	Range of Facilities	✓✓✓✓

UK5615 Hill of Oaks Caravan Park

Tower Wood, Windermere LA23 3PJ (Cumbria)

This park on the banks of Lake Windermere lives up to its name 'Hill of Oaks'. Set on a hillside in mature woodland, the park offers families a safe natural environment with nature walks through the managed ancient woodlands, as well as six jetties for boat launching and access to watersport activities (jet skis are not allowed). The road into the park passing the farmhouse is long, winding and narrow, so care should be taken especially with long outfits, reception being about half a mile from the entrance. The entrance barrier is open from 08.00 till dusk with a security code being provided for exit. The reception and shop selling basics with a tourist information room adjacent are on the lakeside in wooden chalet-type buildings with an abundance of hanging baskets and flowers. Privately owned caravan holiday homes have been built into the hillside on terraces and are quite unobtrusive, screened by hedges and trees. Although the park is situated on Lake Windermere the touring pitches nestle within the trees, not actually by the lake. All 43 have electricity (16A), digital TV hook-up and hardstanding, most large enough to take a car and boat. Three large super pitches, all hardstanding, have 16A electricity, drain, water and digital TV. Tents are not accepted at Hill of Oaks.

Facilities

The central tiled toilet block, recently refurbished, is very clean and heated. Vanity style washbasins, controllable showers and free hair dryers. Baby changing areas. Fully equipped laundry. Dishwashing area under cover. New unit for disabled visitors (combination lock). Recycling bins. No motorcaravan service point. Shop for basics. Two fenced play areas, one for toddlers and adventure type for over 5s. Picnic areas and nature trails. Fishing (licence required). Off site: Fell Foot Park and Gardens 1 mile, with rowing boat hire or ferry rides to Lakeside or Ambleside. Aquarium of the Lakes (3.5 miles) at Newby Bridge. Golf 4 miles. Riding and bicycle hire 6 miles.

Directions

From M6 exit 36 head west on A590 towards Barrow and Newby Bridge. Follow A590 to roundabout signed Bowness and turn right on A592 for about 3 miles. Site is signed on left. O.S.GR: SD384903.

Charges 2004

Per pitch	£ 17.50
with services	£ 19.50
awning	£ 3.00
boat	£ 6.00 - £ 11.00

Reservations

Contact site. Tel: 015395 31578.
Email: enquiries@hillofoaks.co.uk

Open

1 March – 14 November.

At a glance

Welcome & Ambience	✓✓✓✓	Location	✓✓✓✓
Quality of Pitches	✓✓✓✓	Range of Facilities	✓✓✓✓✓

UK5610 Waterfoot Caravan Park

Pooley Bridge, Penrith CA11 0JF (Cumbria)

Waterfoot is a quiet family park for caravans and motorcaravans only. It is set in 22 acres of partially wooded land, developed in the fifties from a private estate. The 146 private caravan holiday homes are quite separate from the 37 touring pitches. Lake Ullswater is only about 400 yards away and a half mile stroll through bluebell woods brings you to the village of Pooley Bridge. Waterfoot's touring pitches are arranged very informally in a large clearing. Most are level, there are some hardstandings and all have 10A electricity. The park no longer accepts American RVs. There is a bar in a large, imposing mansion, in the past a family home then a golf hotel. Public footpaths lead straight from the park. The regular lake steamer service calls at Pooley Bridge, the Ullswater yacht club is only 10 minutes drive and the market town of Penrith is 5 miles. The historic house and gardens of Dalemain are a short walk.

Facilities

The heated toilet block includes washbasins and preset showers in cubicles. New facilities for disabled visitors. Large, light and airy dishwashing room and fully equipped laundry. Small shop selling basics, gas and newspapers. Bar with strictly enforced, separate family room open weekend evenings in low season and every evening in high season. Large fenced field with play equipment to suit all ages and goal posts for football. Off site: Fishing 0.5 miles. Riding 1.5 miles. Golf 5 miles. Pooley Bridge has a post office/ general store, hotels and restaurants.

At a glance

Welcome & Ambience	✓✓✓✓✓	Location	✓✓✓✓✓
Quality of Pitches	✓✓✓✓	Range of Facilities	✓✓✓✓

Directions

From M6 junction 40, take A66 signed Keswick. After 0.5 miles at roundabout take A592 signed Ullswater and site is on right after 4 miles. O.S.GR: NY460245.

Charges 2004

Per unit incl. all persons and electricity	£ 11.50 - £ 16.00

No credit cards.

Reservations

Essential for B.Hs and summer holidays.
Tel: 017684 86302.
Email: enquiries@waterfootpark.co.uk

Open

1 March - 14 November.

Waterfoot Park, Ullswater   ETC 5★

Waterfoot Caravan Park, in the grounds of a Georgian Mansion overlooking Ullswater is the ideal location for touring caravans, motor homes and static caravan holidays.

The Park enjoys a quiet family orientated character even in busier holiday periods, with 24 hour security. Toilet/shower block with disabled facilities, baby changing and laundry facilities. Large secure children's play area. Shop and bar. David Bellamy Gold Award.

Ullswater, Pooley Bridge, Penrith, Cumbria, CA11 0JF Tel: 017684 86302 email: enquiries@waterfootpark.co.uk • web: www.waterfootpark.co.uk

Hills of Oak, Windermere   ETC 5★

One of the most beautifully secluded lakeside caravan estates, Hill of Oaks touring caravans offer exclusive lake frontage for 1km onto Windermere. The site is set on a farm, nestling on the slopes of an ancient woodland. The park welcomes touring caravan, motor homes and static caravan holidays.

Own jetties and launching facilities; children's play area and licensed shop. Toilet/shower block, baby changing and laundry facilities. David Bellamy Gold Award.

Windermere, Cumbria, LA12 8NR Tel: 015395 31578 email: enquiries@hillofoaks.co.uk • web: www.hillofoaks.co.uk

Woodclose Caravan Park   ETC 5★

Woodclose Caravan Park is a private and secluded site, spreading over nine acres, in a privileged location in an area of outstanding beauty and situated only a short walk from the picturesque market town of Kirkby Lonsdale. The site welcomes tents, touring caravans and motor homes.

Children's play area and shop. Toilet/shower blocks, baby changing and laundry facilities are available on site.

Kirkby Lonsdale, Cumbria, LA6 2SE Tel: 015242 71597 email: info@woodclosepark.com • web: www.woodclosepark.com

UK5630 The Quiet Site Caravan Park

Watermillock, Penrith CA11 0LS (Cumbria)

The Quiet Site is a secluded, family run park on a hillside in the National Park with views over the fells and just 1.5 miles from Lake Ullswater. There are 84 unmarked pitches, including some with hardstanding and 60 with electricity connections. Most have been terraced to provide level surfaces, but a few are very sloping (levelling blocks are supplied). The camping area is very undulating (we noticed that some tents were pitched amongst the caravans to find flatter ground). In a separate part of the park, screened by mature trees, are 23 privately owned caravan holiday homes and one for hire. In converted old farm buildings, the amenities are centred around the reception and shop and include a first floor 'Olde-Worlde' bar with oak beams and barrel seats. Many beautiful walks start from right outside the park and the numerous activities and attractions of the Lake District are within a short drive. The owners, the Holder family, are continuing to develop this attractive, well maintained park.

Facilities

The upgraded toilet block provides pre-set showers and open style washbasins. Bathroom with facilities for disabled visitors (key from reception). Baby changing area. Dishwashing under cover. Laundry facilities. Well stocked shop at reception. Gas supplies. Bar (weekends only in low season), adult only room with pool and darts. TV and games room. Excellent adventure play area. Caravan storage. American motorhomes would find access very difficult. Off site: Fishing 1.5 miles. Riding and bicycle hire 3 miles. Golf 8 miles.

Open

1 March - 15 November.

At a glance

Welcome & Ambience ✓✓✓✓ Location ✓✓✓✓
Quality of Pitches ✓✓✓✓ Range of Facilities ✓✓✓✓

Directions

From M6, exit 40, take A66 (Keswick) for 1 mile, then A592 signed Ullswater for 4 miles. Turn right at Lake junction, still on A592 signed Windermere. After 1 mile turn right (at Brackenrigg Inn) and follow for 1.5 miles to site on right (large units should phone for an alternative route). O.S.GR: NY431236.

Charges 2004

Per unit incl. 2 persons, awning and electricity	£ 14.00 - £ 20.00
tent incl. 2 persons	£ 10.00 - £ 18.00
extra person	£ 1.00 - £ 3.00
dog	£ 1.00

Camping Cheques accepted.

Reservations

Made with deposit. Tel: 017684 86337.
Email: info@thequietsite.co.uk

UK5620 Cove Camping Park

Ullswater, Watermillock, Penrith CA11 0LS (Cumbria)

Cove Camping is a delightful small site, some of the 50 pitches having great views over Lake Ullswater. A separate area behind the camping field holds 38 privately owned caravan holiday homes, plus one for hire. The grass is well trimmed, there are ramps to keep speeds down to 5 mph and the site is well lit. At the top of the park are 17 level pitches with electric hook-ups and 13 with hardstanding suitable for touring caravans and motorcaravans. The rest of the park is quite sloping. Rubbish bins are hidden behind larch lap fencing, as are recycling bins. The park is well situated for walking, boating, fishing and pony trekking activities. The road up from the A592 is narrow, but a self imposed one way system is generally adhered to and the warden will advise on a different way to leave the site.

Facilities

The tiled toilet block is immaculate and heated in cooler months, providing adjustable showers, some washbasins in cabins and, for ladies, a hairdressing area with stool and a baby changing unit. Foyer containing a freezer (free), coffee machine and tourist information. Laundry with washing machine, dryer and an iron. Dishwashing sinks in a separate area. Gas supplies. Small, grass based play area. Off site: Shop nearby. Fishing 1.5 miles. Riding 3 miles. Golf 6 mile. Bicycle hire 7 miles (will deliver).

Open

March - 31 October.

At a glance

Welcome & Ambience ✓✓✓✓✓ Location ✓✓✓✓
Quality of Pitches ✓✓✓✓ Range of Facilities ✓✓✓✓✓

Directions

From A66 Penrith - Keswick road, take A592 south, signed Ullswater. Turn right at Brackenrigg Inn (site signed) and follow road uphill for about 1.5 miles to park on left. This road is narrow so if you have a larger unit, telephone the park for advice about an alternative route. O.S.GR: NY431236.

Charges 2004

Per unit incl. 2 persons, electricity	£ 12.00 - £ 15.00
tent incl. 2 persons	£ 10.00 - £ 12.00
extra person (over 4 yrs)	£ 3.00
dog	£ 1.00

No credit cards.

Reservations

Made with deposit (caravans or motorcaravans £10, tents £5); contact park. Tel: 017684 86549.
Email: info@cove-park.co.uk

UK5545 Park Cliffe Camping & Caravan Estate

Birks Road, Windermere LA23 3PG (Cumbria)

Set in the heart of the Lake District National Park, this attractive park has been recently acquired by the Holgates family. Sitting high in open countryside it has spectacular views over the Lakeland Fells and Lake Windermere. Well managed and maintained, the park is neat and tidy with attractive shrubs and plants in local, stone-built troughs set around the entrance. The touring pitches here have been redeveloped into numbered gravel hardstandings with electricity (10A), water and drainage services, excluding one which has been left on grass for trailer tents. There are also 24 seasonal pitches positioned high on the hillside with commanding views. Two areas have been set aside for tents, one unmarked on the hillside divided by an original stone wall and adjacent to the tourers and one across the road for tents that require electric hook-ups - these are marked and numbered but quite undulating. There is no automatic barrier, but gates closed to both campers and caravanners 23.00 - 07.30 with a warden on site for emergencies. A new development for caravan holiday homes is being constructed in a valley offset from the main park.

Facilities

The central main building includes two blocks of toilets and showers. These are tiled, heated and very clean with vanity style washbasins, hair drying areas, full facilities for disabled visitors and excellent baby room (both with combination lock). On the floors above five rooms with bath, wc and washbasin for hire (min. 3 days, £10 per day). Fully equipped laundry. Covered dishwashing area. Bar and area with pool table for over 16s. Restaurant and takeaway. Small well stocked shop. Freezer for ice packs (20p). Games room with table tennis and video games. Large outdoor adventure type play area is set secluded to one side of the tourers, not fenced as a public footpath runs through to Moor How. Off site: Fellfoot Park with boat launching (sail), Walking, climbing, cycling and many other activities possible. Cruises on the lake. Many visitor attractions.

At a glance

Welcome & Ambience	✓✓✓✓✓	Location	✓✓✓✓✓
Quality of Pitches	✓✓✓✓	Range of Facilities	✓✓✓✓✓

Directions

From M6 exit 36 take A590 to Newby Bridge. Turn right on A592 for 3.6 miles and turn right. Site is signed shortly on the right. Note: Caravans and trailers must approach Park Cliffe from the direction of Newby Bridge on the A592. O.S.GR: SD391911.

Charges 2004

Per unit incl. 2 persons, electricity	£ 14.00 - £ 17.00
tent incl. 2 persons	£ 12.00 - £ 15.20
extra adult	£ 3.00 - £ 3.80
child (2-14 yrs)	£ 1.00 - £ 2.00
awning	£ 3.00 - £ 3.80
dog	£ 3.00 - £ 3.80

Reservations

Made with 25% deposit. Tel: 015395 31344. Email: info@parkcliffe.co.uk

Open

1 March – 14 November.

UK5550 Limefitt Park

Windermere LA23 1PA (Cumbria)

Now under new ownership, Limefitt Park offers fine views and walks, and is centrally located for the southern Lake District. With various active pursuits on offer nearby and some evening entertainment, it is designed for families or couples (no organised groups of young people). Of the 145 touring pitches, 85 are on hardstanding, with electricity (10A), a fresh water tap and waste water point, and a further 38 fully serviced pitches are on grass. The ground by the beck has been developed for 45 log cabins (for private sale) in addition to some caravan holiday homes (a few for hire). Sporting activities include walking and fishing and many local facilities, including bicycle hire, can be booked from the park. Away from the camping area is a play field and adventure playground on grass by the river and a small riverside area with picnic tables. American motorhomes, dogs, boats, single persons, groups and rallies are not accepted; to quote, 'in order to preserve Limefitt's unique atmosphere and provide restful nights, we accept families and couples only.' The park is popular throughout the season so advanced reservation is recommended.

Facilities

Sanitary facilities consist of one large, central block for the tenting area and a smaller block for the caravan area, accessed by combination locks. Both are of excellent quality, well equipped with modern fittings. Part of one building is dedicated to three toddlers' rooms with half-size bath and changing facilities. Covered washing-up and vegetable preparation areas. Camper's kitchen. Launderette. Motorcaravan service point. Supermarket. Bar (real ales), bar meals and takeaway, all open all season. Weekly entertainment. Gas available. Games room with many machines. Play area. Dogs are not accepted. Off site: Riding 3 miles. Golf 5 miles.

At a glance

Welcome & Ambience	✓✓✓	Location	✓✓✓✓✓
Quality of Pitches	✓✓✓✓✓	Range of Facilities	✓✓✓✓

Directions

Limefitt Park lies 2.5 miles north up the A592 from its junction with the A591 north of Windermere. O.S.GR: NY416030.

Charges 2004

Per unit incl. 2 persons, electricity and TV hook up	£ 8.50 - £ 14.00
tent incl. 2 persons	£ 11.00 - £ 17.00
extra adult	£ 2.00 - £ 3.00
Prices are higher for stays not booked in advance.	

Reservations

Contact site. Tel: 015394 32300.

Open

1 March - 3 November.

203

UK5540 Fallbarrow Park

Rayrigg Road, Bowness, Windermere LA23 3DL (Cumbria)

Fallbarrow Park is most attractively situated alongside Lake Windermere with a lake frontage of about 600 metres; one can stroll among the lawns and gardens near the lake. The major part of the park is occupied by approximately 260 seasonal holiday homes, with about 90 for letting, the remainder privately owned. In the 'Lake' area (not actually by the lake, but some pitches have lake views), there are 38 fenced or hedged touring pitches, all with hardstanding, fresh and waste water points, electric hook-up (10/16A) and TV aerial connection. Reception is smart and comfortable, with plenty of tourist information. The Boathouse pub has a spacious and comfortable lounge with bar meals and snacks, a separate restaurant section with varied menu and table service, and an attractive outdoor terrace. TV lounge with occasional entertainment and a large games room with pool table and games machines. The site has a boat park with winter storage and two launching ramps and three jetties can cater for craft up to 18 ft in length. The centre of Bowness is only a short walk and facilities for pony trekking and numerous visitor attractions are close.

Facilities

Two excellent toilet blocks serve the touring sections (combination locks) with top quality fittings and heating when required, controllable showers, make up and hairdressing areas and a baby washroom. Dishwashing sinks. Very well equipped laundry which also houses a freezer. Motorcaravan service point. Gas is available at the well stocked supermarket. Restaurant. Bar. Fishing. Adventure play area and sports field. American motorhomes are accepted by prior arrangement. Dogs are accepted, but only one per booking (exercise area provided). Off site: Bicycle hire 1 mile. Riding 2 miles. Golf 3 miles.

At a glance

Welcome & Ambience	✓✓✓✓	Location	✓✓✓✓
Quality of Pitches	✓✓✓✓	Range of Facilities	✓✓✓✓

Directions

Park is beside the A592 road just north of Bowness town centre. O.S.GR: SD401971.

Charges 2004

Per unit incl. 2 persons	£ 17.00 - £ 24.00
extra person	£ 1.50 - £ 2.00
child	£ 1.00 - £ 1.50
awning	£ 3.00 - £ 4.00
dog	£ 2.00 - £ 3.00

Reservations

Essential for June - Sept. and B.Hs. Made for min. 3 nights (7 at Spring BH). Payment in full at time of booking. Tel: 015394 44422.
Email: enquiries@southlakeland-caravans.co.uk

Open

8 March - 9 November.

UK5590 Tebay Park Touring & Static Caravan Park

Tebay, Orton, Penrith CA10 3SB (Cumbria)

For caravans and motorcaravans only, this is the ideal stopover for anyone heading either north or south, near the M6 motorway, but far enough away for the traffic noise not to be too disturbing. There are 77 level pitches on gravel, divided into bays of about six or seven units (41 for touring units, 34 seasonal and 7 for caravan holiday homes). All touring pitches have electricity (10/16A). The bays are backed by grassy banks alive with rabbits and birds - a long list in the office describes the large variety of birds to be seen on the site. There is good site lighting and a late arrivals area.

Facilities

The heated toilet block is kept very clean. Showers are pre-set and coin operated (10p) with all other hot water free. Facilities for disabled visitors planned. Sinks for laundry and dishwashing. Laundry. Reception sells gas. Bicycle hire. Off site: Shops, restaurants and a bar five minutes walk away at the motorway service area.

Open

22 March - 28 October.

At a glance

Welcome & Ambience	✓✓✓✓	Location	✓✓✓✓
Quality of Pitches	✓✓✓✓	Range of Facilities	✓✓✓

Directions

From the M6, just north of junction 38, exit for Tebay Services (site signed). Site is accessible from the services travelling north or south. O.S.GR: NY607060.

Charges 2004

Per unit incl. 2 persons	£ 10.50 - £ 11.50
extra adult	£ 1.95 - £ 2.00
child	free
awning	£ 1.75 - £ 2.00
electricity	£ 2.50 - £ 2.40

Special rates for 3, 5 or 7 days.
Discount on hotel and café meals.

Reservations

Advised for B.Hs. and July/Aug Tel: 015397 11322.

UK5520 Skelwith Fold Caravan Park

Ambleside LA22 0HX (Cumbria)

Skelwith Fold has been developed in the extensive grounds of a country estate taking advantage of the wealth of mature trees and shrubs. The 300 privately owned caravan holiday homes and 150 touring pitches are absorbed into this unspoilt natural environment, sharing it with red squirrels and other wildlife in several discrete areas branching off the central, mile long main driveway. Touring pitches (no tents) are on gravel hardstanding and metal pegs will be necessary for awnings. Electricity hook-ups (10A) and basic amenities are available in all areas. Youngsters and indeed their parents will find endless pleasure exploring over 90 acres of wild woodland and, if early risers, it is possible to see deer, foxes, etc. taking at the almost hidden tarn deep in the woods. This is a fascinating site where you feel at home with nature at any time of the year, but it is particularly beautiful in the spring with wild daffodils, bluebells and later rhododendrons and azaleas. Only caravans, motorcaravans and trailer tents are accepted.

Facilities

Eight toilet blocks, well situated to serve all areas, have the usual facilities including laundry, drying and ironing rooms. Some blocks have facilities for disabled visitors. Well stocked, licensed shop. Battery charging, gas and caravan spares and accessories. Adventure play area. Family recreation area with picnic tables and goal posts in the Lower Glade. Bicycle hire. Off site: Ambleside village 1.5 miles. Pubs within walking distance. Fishing 200 m. Riding 3 miles.

Open

1 March - 15 November.

At a glance

Welcome & Ambience	✓✓✓	Location	✓✓✓✓
Quality of Pitches	✓✓✓✓	Range of Facilities	✓✓✓✓

Directions

From Ambleside take the A593 towards Coniston. Pass through Clappergate and on the far outskirts watch for the B5286 to Hawkshead on the left. Park is clearly signed approx. 1 mile down this road on the right. O.S.GR: NY358028.

Charges 2004

Per pitch	£ 12.00 - £ 17.00
electricity	£ 2.50
awning	£ 3.00
Discounts for weekly or monthly stays.	

Reservations

Essential for July/Aug and B.Hs. and made for min. 3 days with £10 deposit. Tel: 01539 432277. Email: info@skelwith.com

UK5670 Flusco Wood Touring Caravan Park

Flusco, Penrith CA11 0JB (Cumbria)

Flusco Wood Caravan Park is still being developed but everything is to a very high standard. Set amongst woodland with the touring pitches in bays, this park will meet the needs of those requiring a quiet holiday (with plenty of walks from the site) and also those travelling up or down the M6 looking for a quiet night's rest. There are pitches on grass and hardstanding, with an area near reception with hard-standings for motorcaravans. Recent additions here include 19 new log cabins (privately owned), with a further 11 planned. The area abounds with wildlife including deer and red squirrels, as well as many breeds of birds (we watched a woodpecker taking food from a bird feeder). For a wet day you are about 2.5 miles from Rheged, the 'village in the hill' and, if the weather improves, a short drive from Ullswater, Keswick, Penrith and Carlisle. Member of the Countryside Discovery group.

Facilities	Directions
A log cabin style building houses very clean, heated facilities including pre-set showers and vanity style washbasins (1 cubicle). Large en-suite shower rooms for families or disabled visitors, one in the ladies' and one in the men's. Dishwashing sinks under cover. Laundry, drying room and boot washing sink. Second log cabin serves as reception/shop with basic supplies, gas and daily newspapers. Play equipment on bark. Grass area for ball games. Off site: Pub and P.O. stores 2 miles. Fishing, bicycle hire and golf 4 miles. Riding 5 miles.	From M6 take A66 towards Keswick. Go straight on at first roundabout, then third right at top of hill (signed Flusco, Recycling Centre, Pottery and caravan sign). After 0.5 miles road turns right up hill (narrow, so take care in large units), site is on left at the top. Site is 4 miles from M6. O.S.GR: NY457293.

Open

Easter - end October.

At a glance

Welcome & Ambience	✓✓✓✓	Location	✓✓✓✓
Quality of Pitches	✓✓✓✓	Range of Facilities	✓✓✓✓✓

Charges 2004

Per unit incl. 2 persons, electricity	£ 15.00 - £ 18.00
extra person (over 3 yrs)	£ 2.00 - £ 2.25

Reservations

Made with deposit (£20 per week, £5 for single nights). Tel: 017684 80020.
Email: admin@fluscowood.co.uk

Planning your **next short break?**
don't forget to see our directory
ON PAGE 294

UK5600 Pennine View Caravan & Camping Park

Station Road, Kirkby Stephen CA17 4SZ (Cumbria)

Suitable for night halts or longer breaks to visit the Lake District or the Yorkshire Dales, Pennine View is a super small park, well managed and well maintained. With a very attractive rockery at the entrance, the whole site is very neat and tidy. Level, numbered pitches with gravel hardstanding are arranged around the perimeter with grass pitches in the centre. The pitches are of a good size (some being especially large) and all are supplied with electricity hook-ups (16A). Pennine View was opened in 1990 and is built on reclaimed land from a former railway goods yard. One end of the park adjoins the River Eden with steps leading down huge projecting stone slabs on the river bank (good for sunbathing). There are trout but a licence is needed for fishing.

Facilities	Directions
Built of local stone, the modern toilet block is accessed by a digital keypad and includes individual wash cubicles and deep sink for a baby bath. Both ladies and men have large en-suite units for disabled visitors. Well equipped laundry room. Dishwashing sinks under cover. Gas available. Off site: Nearby hotel offers bar meals and takeaway pizzas. Kirkby Stephen 1 mile. Bicycle hire 300 m. Golf 4 miles.	Park is on the A685 on the southerly outskirts of Kirkby Stephen (just under a mile from the town centre). Turn left at small site sign opposite the Croglin Castle hotel. Site is 50 yds on right. O.S.GR: NY772075.

Open

1 March - 31 October.

At a glance

Welcome & Ambience	✓✓✓✓✓	Location	✓✓✓✓
Quality of Pitches	✓✓✓✓✓	Range of Facilities	✓✓✓✓

Charges 2004

Per adult	£ 4.50 - £ 4.80
child (4-15 yrs)	£ 1.75 - £ 2.00
pitch	£ 1.00 - £ 2.00
electricity	£ 1.90 - £ 2.40
cyclist or backpacker	£ 4.50 - £ 4.75

Reservations

Made with £5 deposit; min. 3 days Easter and B.Hs.
Tel: 017683 71717.

UK5570 Wild Rose Park

Ormside, Appleby-in-Westmorland CA16 6EJ (Cumbria)

Set in the Eden Valley within easy reach of the Lake District and the Yorkshire Dales, Wild Rose is a well known park with an excellent reputation. The entrance is very inviting with its well mown grass, trim borders and colourful flower displays and impressive with a 'state of the art' entrance barrier and inter-com system. It is immediately apparent that this is a much loved park, and this is reflected throughout the site in the care and attention to detail. There are 170 touring pitches, two areas with their own warden to ensure that everything is always neat and tidy. The top areas have been upgraded to provide neat, level, fully serviced pitches. These are separated by hedges (plus a small fence until the hedge grows) and many have views. The lower touring area, on a slightly sloping field, caters for both tents and caravans. Next to this are six individual 'super' pitches, fenced or hedged with full services, some including patio, barbecue, picnic table, grass area and satellite TV connections. Privately owned caravan holiday homes (270) occupy their own areas and do not intrude. Wild Rose deserves its excellent reputation, which the owners strive to maintain and improve. Nothing is overlooked from recycling bins, electric dust carts to keep the noise down, 'sac-o-matic' special bags in the dog walk and cycle racks placed around the park. A member of the Best of British group.

Facilities

Three toilet blocks (two heated) are of excellent quality and kept spotlessly clean. Most washbasins are in cubicles. Hair-washing basins, baby baths and bottle warmers. Full facilities for disabled visitors. Fully equipped laundry with washing lines and drying rooms. Motorcaravan service point. Exceptionally well stocked shop (with gas). Licensed restaurant with takeaway and conservatory/coffee lounge (all 1/4-5/11), good for Sunday lunches. Outdoor pool kidney shaped pool with sunbathing area (heated mid-May - mid-Sept and open 10.00 - 22.00). Well kept, fenced play area. Indoor playroom for under fives. Games room with table tennis and video games for older children and two TV rooms, one with a cinema style screen. BMX track. Half court tennis. Field for ball games. Certain breeds of dog are not accepted. Caravan storage. Off site: Fishing 2 miles. Golf and riding 3 miles.

At a glance

Welcome & Ambience	✓✓✓✓	Location	✓✓✓✓
Quality of Pitches	✓✓✓✓✓	Range of Facilities	✓✓✓✓✓

Directions

Park is signed south off B6260 road 1.5 miles southwest of Appleby. Follow signs to park, in the direction of Ormside. O.S.GR: NY697165.

Charges 2004

Per unit incl. 2 adults	£ 10.50 - £ 17.90
'super pitch' incl. mains services and awning	£ 14.90 - £ 26.00
extra person (over 4 yrs)	£ 2.00
walker or cyclist	£ 3.80
dog	£ 0.70

Less 10% for 7 nights or more. Special winter or long-stay rates.

Reservations

Essential for B.Hs and July/Aug; made with deposit of £5 per night + £2 fee, remainder on arrival. Min. 3 nights at B.Hs. Tel: 01768 351077. Email: mail@wildrose.co.uk

Open

All year.

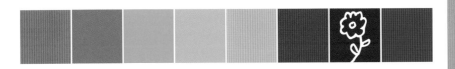

207

UK5650 The Ashes 'Exclusively Adult' Caravan Park

New Hutton, Kendal LA8 0AS (Cumbria)

The Ashes is a friendly, small, adult only park in an extremely peaceful setting in the rolling Cumbrian countryside, yet less than three miles from the M6, and only slightly further from Kendal. Thus it is not only a convenient night stop, but also a useful base from which to explore the Lake District and the Yorkshire Dales. A very tidy park, the central grass area is attractively planted with shrubs and bushes, and there is an open vista with little shade. There are 24 hardstanding gravel pitches, all with electrical connections (10A). These are neatly placed around the perimeter, with an oval access road. The whole area slopes gently down from the entrance, with some pitches fairly level and others with a little more slope. No other tents are accepted other than trailer tents.

Facilities

A small, purpose built stone building with a slate roof houses two unisex, heated shower rooms and the washing and toilet facilities. Grab rails and step-free access for disabled visitors. Laundry service. Off site: Mr and Mrs Mason have prepared a full information sheet with details of shopping, eating and many other local venues. Fishing 2 miles, golf or riding 3 miles.

Open

1 March - 15 November.

At a glance

Welcome & Ambience ✓✓✓✓✓	Location	✓✓✓✓✓
Quality of Pitches ✓✓✓✓✓	Range of Facilities	✓✓✓

Directions

From M6 junction 37 follow the A684 towards Kendal for 2 miles. Just past a white cottage turn sharp left at crossroads signed New Hutton. Site is on right in 0.75 miles at a left bend. O.S.GR: SD560908.

Charges 2005

Per unit incl. 2 adults, electricity	£ 11.00 - £ 13.00
extra person (over 18's only)	£ 3.50
awning	£ 2.00
extra car/trailer	£ 1.00

Reservations

Advised for B.Hs and peak season and made with deposit 1 night £8, 2 or more nights £16.
Tel: 01539 731 833.
Email: info@ashescaravanpark.co.uk

Need a
POWR Product?
SEE PAGE 294

UK5640 Green Acres Caravan Park

High Knells, Houghton, Carlisle CA6 4JW (Cumbria)

Green Acres is a small, family run park situated in beautiful, rural surroundings, yet only two miles from the M6/A74 - perfect for a night halt or a longer stay to enjoy Cumbria, Hadrian's Wall and the delights of Carlisle city (4 miles away). Mr and Mrs Brown have developed Green Acres over the last few years into an attractive, well maintained and level touring park. There are 30 numbered pitches arranged in a semi-circle, some on grass but most on large hardstandings. There are 19 electricity connections (10A). Divided by a long beech hedge is a large camping field including on one side 6 new hardstanding 'super' pitches for seasonal letting and, in one corner, a small play area.

Facilities

Small, very clean toilet block with open style washbasins and coin operated showers (50p for 10 minutes). No facilities for disabled people. Dishwashing sinks under cover. Laundry room in farm building. Car wash area. No shop but ices, drinks and sweets from reception. Play area. Caravan storage. Off site: Golf 3 miles. Fishing 8 miles. Riding and bicycle hire 10 miles.

Open

March - end October.

At a glance

Welcome & Ambience ✓✓✓✓✓	Location	✓✓✓✓✓
Quality of Pitches ✓✓✓✓✓	Range of Facilities	✓✓✓✓

Directions

Leave M6/A74 at junction 44 and take A689 for 1 mile. Turn left towards Scaleby (site signed) and site is 1 mile on left. O.S.GR: NY419615.

Charges 2004

Per unit incl. 2 persons	£ 7.50 - £ 8.75
extra person	£ 1.25
awning	£ 1.00
electricity	£ 2.00

Reservations

Contact park. Tel: 01228 675418.
Email: info@caravanpark--cumbria.com

The most northerly region of England, Northumbria is steeped in history, full of ancient forts and fairytale castles. The great outdoors offers limitless walking with plenty of trails stretching across moorlands and beaches, encompassing views of the beautiful scenery.

The region comprises of:
Northumberland, Durham, Tyne and Wear, and Teeside

The 400 square mile Northumberland National Park is one of the most peaceful, remote places in England. With endless walks across moorlands and hills, it stretches south from the Cheviot Hills, through the Simonside Hills, to the crags of Whin Sill, where it engulfs a section of the historic Hadrian's Wall, built by the Romans to mark the northern limit of their empire. The Pennine Way was the country's first official long-distance path and is still the longest. At 268 miles, it stretches from the Peak National Park to the border. The coastline is not to be forgotten, with miles upon miles of deserted, safe sandy beaches, with resorts that still have an old fashioned feel to them, such as Whitley Bay, South Shields and Seaton Carew. The majestic castles of Bamburgh, and Dunstanburgh can be seen for miles along the Northumberland coast. Surrounded on three sides by the river Wear, the small, historic city of Durham is dominated by England's greatest Norman Cathedral. With cobbled medieval streets and restricted car access it is a popular place with visitors. Further north is the bustling city of Newcastle. Home to an array of cosmopolitan restaurants and bars, music venues, and fabulous architecture, it also boasts a lively nightlife.

Did you know?

Alnwick Castle is used as the setting of Hogwarts in the Harry Potter films

Stretching from Wallsend in the east to Bowness-on-Solway in the west, Hadrian's Wall is 81 miles long; it is now possible to walk the entire length

Born in Northumbria in 1825, George Stephenson was the first person to design the steam engine that ran on wheels

In the past 300 years Berwick has changed hands between the Scottish and the English no less than 13 times

The Angel of The North is made up of 200 tonnes of steel and rises 20 metres from the ground

Built in 1817, HMS Trinacomalee is the oldest ship afloat in the UK

Places of interest

Northumberland: Bamburgh Castle; Alnwick Castle and gardens; Berwick-upon-Tweed; bird reserve on Farne Islands, home to large colony of grey seals; Hauxley Nature Reserve; Dunstanburgh Castle; Corbridge Roman sites at Hadrian's Wall

Durham: Durham Castle and Cathedral; Barnard Castle, a ruined castle overlooking the River Tees; Diggerland at Langley Park; Harperley POW Camp

Tyne and Wear: New Metroland, Europe's only indoor theme park within a large shopping complex; Newcastle with Life Science Centre, Discovery Museum and Castle Keep; Whitley Bay

Teeside: Kirkleatham Owl Centre; Darlington Railway Centre and Museum; Guisborough Hall; Hartlepool Historic Quay and HMS Trinacomalee; Butterfly World in Stockton-on-Tees

tip

THE ALNWICK MEDIEVAL FAIR IN JUNE IS A COSTUMED RE-ENACTMENT OF A FAIR DATING FROM THE MIDDLE AGES, WITH CRAFT STALLS, DUCKING-STOOL AND STAGED ENTERTAINMENT.

UK5740 White Water Caravan Club Park

Tees Barrage A66, Thornaby, Stockton-on-Tees TS18 2QW (Teeside)

Being part of the multi-million pound development at the Tees Barrage, this pleasantly landscaped club site caters for all tastes, especially water sports enthusiasts. The recently opened Tees Barrage has transformed eleven miles of the Tees, providing clean, non-tidal water for many activities. The adjoining White Water Course (Britain's largest purpose-built canoe course) provides facilities for both advanced and beginner canoeists, and hosts major national and international events. Close to the site are wetlands that provide a home for a variety of birds. The site itself provides 115 pitches set in bays and hedged with bushes, all with 16A electricity connections, plus 21 fully serviced pitches (fresh water and waste disposal) on hardstandings. The site is well lit, with a security barrier.

Facilities

The central, heated toilet block of high quality including washbasins in cubicles, baby changing facilities and a well appointed unit for disabled visitors. Washing up sinks. Laundry room. Motorcaravan service point. Play area on fine gravel. Club room with TV and pool table for wet weather. Off site: Supermarket 6 minutes. Hotel near the entrance. Retail and leisure park, just across barrage bridge, with 14-screen cinema, 10-pin bowling, shops and fast food outlets. North Yorkshire Moors and the Hartlepool Historic Quay within 40 minutes drive.

Open

All year.

At a glance

| Welcome & Ambience | ✓✓✓✓ | Location | ✓✓✓✓ |
| Quality of Pitches | ✓✓✓✓✓ | Range of Facilities | ✓✓✓✓ |

Directions

From A1(M1) take A66 for Darlington and follow until you pick up signs for Teeside Retail Park and the Tees Barrage. Cross railway bridge and the Barrage bridge, then first right to site on left in 400 yards. O.S.GR: NZ463194.

Charges 2004

Per adult	£ 2.30 - £ 3.50
child (5-16 yrs)	£ 1.10 - £ 1.30
pitch incl. electricity (non-member)	£ 7.50 - £ 9.00
Tent campers apply to site.	

Reservations

Contact site by phone or in writing. Made with £5 deposit. Tel: 01642 634880.

UK5720 Barnard Castle Camping & Caravanning Club Site

Dockenflatts Lane, Lartington, Barnard Castle DL12 9DG (Co. Durham)

For those readers with tents who wish to visit this area, we have added this Club site, as nearby Doe Park does not take tents. Also welcoming non-members, the Camping and Caravanning Club site at Barnard Castle was only opened in '96. Originally level farm fields, one side of the site is bordered by mature trees and 11,000 young trees and bushes have been planted, so eventually it will become an even more attractive location. With 90 pitches, most on grass but including 12 hardstanding pitches (gravel base with room for both car and caravan and space for an awning on grass), there are 56 electrical hook-ups (16A). Barnard Castle, an old town with its market cross still standing, is well worth a visit. The Bowes museum in the town is a French style chateau housing a fine art collections. Raby Castle, near Staindrop, is an impressive mediaeval castle, formerly the seat of the powerful Neville family. Durham has a castle and cathedral (both World Heritage Sites). High Force, England's highest waterfall is about 12 miles away, and the forest of Hamsterly about 16 miles. A riding centre is next to the site and a public footpath leads from the site to Barnard Castle, with a network of public footpaths in the area.

Facilities

The centrally located toilet facilities are of good quality and kept spotlessly clean. Washbasins are in cubicles and free, controllable showers are roomy. Dishwashing sinks. Baby room. Fully equipped unisex unit for visitors with disabilities. Large laundry with washing machine, dryer, iron and sink, with outside lines provided. Motorcaravan service point. Gas supplies. Central play area with rubber safety base. Caravan storage. Off site: Riding 200 m. Fishing 4 miles. Golf 2.5 miles. Bus service from end of lane.

Open

25 March - 31 October.

At a glance

| Welcome & Ambience | ✓✓✓✓✓ | Location | ✓✓✓✓✓ |
| Quality of Pitches | ✓✓✓✓ | Range of Facilities | ✓✓✓ |

Directions

Follow B6277 from Barnard Castle (towards Middleton in Teesdale) for 1 mile to Lartington. Turn left at club sign into narrow lane with passing places to site entrance on left (there is no need to go into Barnard Castle). O.S.GR: NZ025168.

Charges 2005

Per adult	£ 4.80 - £ 6.40
child (6-18 yrs)	£ 1.90
non-member pitch fee	£ 5.00

Reservations

Necessary and made with deposit; contact site or Central Reservations 0870 243 3331. Tel: 01833 630228.

UK5710 Doe Park Touring Caravan Park

Cotherstone, Barnard Castle DL12 9UQ (Co. Durham)

This is Hannah Hauxwell country and the Dales, less frequented than other upland areas, provide wonderful walking country; indeed part of the Pennine Way runs near this peaceful site. The farm and park are close to where the River Balder joins the Tees at Cotherstone and the ancient oak wood beside the river is an SSSI (Site of Special Scientific Interest) for its insects and flowers, but is also a haven for bird-watchers. The park's reception is in a log cabin at the entrance to the pitch area, although at quiet times you may be directed to the farmhouse, formerly Leadgard Hall. This is a mellow three storey, Grade II listed building with a history of its own. Mr and Mrs Lamb or son Stephen will make you very welcome and personally take you to your pitch. The camping fields have a lovely open aspect with wonderful views and the 70 pitches are spacious with well mown grass, all with 10A electricity, over 40 with hardstanding (no tents are taken). A bus service passes the park from Barnard Castle to Middleton and the village of Cotherstone is only half a mile with post office and a restaurant with bar meals, a pleasant walk by road or river bank.

Facilities

With toilet facilities at the farmhouse, two good quality blocks are closer to the pitches. Built in local stone, these are fully tiled with the newest one heated. Washbasins in cabins and metered, adjustable showers (20p). Well appointed unisex unit for disabled visitors. Dishwashing sinks. Small laundry. Eggs and milk are available from the farmhouse, plus gas supplies and battery charging. No play area but a large grass area in front of some of the pitches can be used for ball games. River fishing on site. Dogs and pets are accepted by arrangement only. Off site: Reservoirs (sailing, water skiing and fishing) 3 miles. Bicycle hire or golf 4 miles. Riding 2 miles. Local leisure centre with pool 4 miles.

At a glance

Welcome & Ambience	✓✓✓✓	Location	✓✓✓✓✓
Quality of Pitches	✓✓✓✓	Range of Facilities	✓✓✓

Directions

Follow B6277 from Barnard Castle in direction of Middleton in Teesdale. The farm is signed on the left just after Cotherstone village (there is no need to go into Barnard Castle). O.S.GR: NZ005204.

Charges 2004

Per unit incl. 2 persons	£ 7.00 - £ 9.00
with electricity (10A)	£ 9.00 - £ 11.00
extra person (over 6 yrs)	£ 1.50
full awning	£ 1.00
family rate (2 adults, 2 children)	£ 11.50 - £ 13.50

No credit cards.

Reservations

Advised for high season and made with £10 deposit (send SAE); min. 4 days at B.Hs. Tel: 01833 650302.

Open

1 March - 31 October.

DOE PARK TOURING CARAVAN SITE

ETC ★★★★

Cotherstone, Barnard Castle, Co. Durham

Quiet family run touring site set in picturesque North Pennine Dales. Pleasant walks, bird watching, private fishing, easy reach of Yorkshire Dales, Lake District & Durham City. Village ½ mile.

FOR COLOUR BROCHURE CALL/FAX 01833 650302

UK5770 Dunstan Hill Camping & Caravanning Club Site

Dunstan Hill, Dunstan, Alnwick NE66 3TQ (Northumberland)

Northumberland is not very well blessed with good campsites, so we are pleased to feature Dunstan Hill. Off a quiet lane between Embleton and Craster this is a rural site with a tree belt to shelter it from the north wind and access to the beach by a level footpath through the fields, across the golf course and past the ruins of Dunstanburgh Castle. This is just over a mile by car. With gravel access roads, the peaceful site has 150 level, well spaced pitches, 80 with 16A electricity. Reception is manned by very helpful managers and there is a large area for parking and late arrivals at the entrance. This is a wonderful area to visit, with its unspoilt beaches and the whole area is steeped in history with Holy Island, the Farne Islands, Bamburgh, Dunstanburgh, Walkworth and Alnwick castles (featured in the Harry Potter films).

Facilities

Two very clean and well maintained toilet blocks have some washbasins in cubicles, hairdryers and a washroom for children with deep sinks. Fully equipped suite for disabled visitors in one block, a laundry in the other. Small shop for gas and basic provisions. Bread and milk can be ordered and a mobile shop and the paper man visit. Tourist information room. Small play area. Torches are useful. Off site: Buses pass the site entrance and there are good eating places near. Fishing 1.5 miles. Golf 1.5 miles. Beach 1.5 miles. Riding 8 miles. Bicycle hire 10 miles.

At a glance

Welcome & Ambience	✓✓✓✓	Location	✓✓✓✓
Quality of Pitches	✓✓✓	Range of Facilities	✓✓✓

Directions

From A1 just north of Alnwick take B1340 or B6347 (further north) for Embleton. Site is signed in Embleton village - avoid signs to Dunstanburgh Castle and follow those for Craster. Site is (south) on the left after approx. 0.5 miles. O.S.GR: NU236214.

Charges 2005

Per adult	£ 4.30 - £ 6.40
child (6-18 yrs)	£ 1.90
non-member pitch fee	£ 5.00

Reservations

Advised and made with deposit; contact site or Central Reservations 0870 243 3331. Tel: 01665 576310.

Open

March - October.

(211)

UK5810 Fallowfield Dene Caravan & Camping Park

Acomb, Hexham NE46 4RP (Northumberland)

Although only 2.5 miles from Hexham, Fallowfield Dene Caravan Park is very secluded, situated in mature woodland at the end of a no-through road. Set in woodland glades, each with a Roman name (Hadrian's Wall is close), are 118 seasonal pitches and 32 touring pitches, all with 16A electricity. The park entrance, with reception and a small shop, is neat, tidy and very colourful. There is no play area or games field, but the surrounding woods are a paradise for children. Fallowfield Dene itself is a network of tracks and there are footpaths from the site entrance. The site is a haven for wildlife with red squirrels, foxes and badgers to be seen. Hadrian's Wall is only a mile away, with Roman forts such as Housteads Fort and Chesters, being great attractions. In fact the whole area abounds with well preserved Roman remains. Hexham has its Border History museum, housed in the oldest purpose-built gaol in England, where one can learn about the Border Reivers. This site has a very friendly atmosphere.

Facilities

Brick built toilet blocks (one for each sex) are central and heated in cool weather. Well tiled and kept very clean, there are washbasins in cabins and free hairdryers. Separate, fully equipped room for disabled people. Laundry room with dishwashing sinks. Motorcaravan service point. Small shop for necessities, including gas. Barrier card £5 deposit. Off site: Supermarkets and other shops at Hexham or Corbridge. Good restaurant five minutes walk. Fishing or riding 3 miles. Golf 5 miles.

Open

1 April - 2 January.

At a glance

Welcome & Ambience	✓✓✓✓	Location	✓✓✓✓
Quality of Pitches	✓✓✓	Range of Facilities	✓✓✓

Directions

From A69 Newcastle - Carlisle road, take A6079 north signed Bellingham and Rothbury. At village of Acomb, site is signed to right. Follow site signs for approx. 1.5 miles. The last 0.5 miles is single track with passing places. O.S.GR: NY938676.

Charges 2004

Per unit incl. 2 persons	£ 10.00 - £ 11.00
extra adult	£ 3.00
child (5-17 yrs)	£ 1.25
electricity	£ 2.00
dog	£ 0.50

Reservations

Made with deposit (£5 for one night, £10 for two or more); min. 3 nights at B.Hs. Tel: 01434 603553.

UK5800 Ord House Country Park

East Ord, Berwick-upon-Tweed TD15 2NS (Northumberland)

Ord House is 40-acre park for 200 privately owned holiday homes and 75 touring caravan and tent pitches. The park has a very well cared for appearance throughout with well mown grass and colourful arrays of flowering bushes. The touring pitches, all with electricity (10A), are in small sections, from the secluded, walled orchard to the more open areas nearer the toilet blocks. There are 39 hardstanding pitches, each with electricity, water and drainage, 19 in the walled garden separated by shrubs and camomile lawns. At the entrance to the park an area with a few pitches is suitable for wheelchair users and close by is a small sanitary unit with WCs and showers plus a large, unisex, well appointed unit (Radar key). The whole site is 'wheelchair friendly' with good access to the airy reception and the well stocked accessory shop. Ord House itself, an 18th century mansion, has been tastefully converted to provide a bar, lounge bar and family room. Although there are many caravan holiday homes, they are not overwhelming and their presence does mean that other amenities can remain open all season. A member of the Best of British group.

Facilities

The main, modern toilet building is of excellent quality and cleanliness, very well maintained and can be heated. Two good large family bathrooms (with two showers, a bath, WC and washbasin). Two rooms for disabled visitors. Dishwashing sinks. Large well equipped laundry. Motorcaravan service point. Gas supplies. Bar, bar food and family room (1/3-10/1). Six-hole golf practice area. Bicycle hire. Crazy golf. Table tennis. Draughts. Play area. No commercial vehicles are accepted. Dogs are only accepted by prior arrangement. Off site: Post office stores 50 yards from the entrance. Leisure centre with a pool 15 minutes walk. Fishing 1.5 miles. Riding 8 miles. Golf 2 miles. Sea fishing can be booked in Berwick. Beach 1.5 miles.

At a glance

Welcome & Ambience	✓✓✓✓	Location	✓✓✓✓
Quality of Pitches	✓✓✓✓✓	Range of Facilities	✓✓✓✓✓

Directions

From A1 Berwick bypass take East Ord exit and follow signs. O.S.GR: NT982515.

Charges 2004

Per unit incl. up to 4 persons and electricity	£ 11.00 - £ 17.40
extra person over 6 yrs	£ 2.50
awning	£ 2.50
dog	free - £ 1.50

Discounts for small tents and for longer stays.

Reservations

Advisable at all times, essential in high seasons (min. 3 nights at B.Hs) - contact park for details. Tel: 01289 305288. Email: enquiries@ordhouse.co.uk

Open

All year.

UK5780 Brown Rigg Caravan & Camping Park

Bellingham, Hexham NE48 2JY (Northumberland)

Bellingham is tucked away amidst heather clad moors in the North Tyne valley, just below the Scottish Borders on the edge of the Northumberland National Park - 'full of history, myth and legend', to quote from the Bellingham town guide. This interesting park is being developed in the grounds of an old school. It provides 70 pitches, 52 with electricity (10/16A), for all types of unit on a level grass field between the moor and the road. Reception, a games room and the toilet facilities have all been converted from the former wooden school dormitory buildings with a central courtyard area and are rather distinctive. A tea shop and plant sales area have been added. Bellingham is half a mile away and an 18 hole golf course has been opened recently. The Pennine Way passes the entrance and Kielder Water is 9 miles to the west, as is Hadrian's Wall to the south.

Facilities

Toilet facilities for ladies, finished in pine, provide washbasins in cubicles, controllable showers and a free hairdryer. Baby bath. The unit for men has been tiled. It is a good provision overall, cleverly adapted and well maintained (key system). Washing machine and dryer, free iron and board. Laundry and dishwashing sinks. Reception provides tourist information and basic food supplies, gas and battery charging. Games room with pool and table tennis. TV room. Play area. Off site: Fishing or golf within 1 mile. Bicycle hire 7 miles. Riding 10 miles.

At a glance

Welcome & Ambience	✓✓✓✓	Location	✓✓✓✓
Quality of Pitches	✓✓✓✓	Range of Facilities	✓✓✓

Directions

Park is on the B6320, 0.5 miles south of Bellingham. O.S.GR: NY835826.

Charges 2004

Per unit incl. 2 persons	£ 9.00 - £ 11.00
incl. electricity	£ 11.25 - £ 13.25
extra adult	£ 4.50 - £ 5.50
child (0-14 yrs)	£ 2.50

Reservations

Made with £10 deposit for bookings. Tel: 01434 220175. Email: enquiries@northumberlandcaravanparks.com

Open

Easter - 31 October.

UK5750 Waren Caravan Park

Waren Mill, Bamburgh, Iford NE70 7EE (Northumberland)

Developed from 100 acres of undulating private owned heath and woodland, Waren Park is a large, spacious family site with marvellous views over Northumberland's golden beaches and the sea. A large section of caravan holiday homes (for hire) is separate from a self contained four acre touring area. Enclosed by sheltering banks, this provides 170 reasonably level pitches, 100 with electrical connections (10A). As well as the spacious grounds to wander in, there is much to see nearby from historic castles, the Farne Islands to the Cheviot Hills and miles and miles of sandy beaches.

Facilities

The older toilet facilities are poor and in need of refurbishment, whilst a newer block provides good facilities for disabled visitors, baby mats, bathroom and four self-contained family rooms with shower, WC and washbasin. Laundry room. Dishwashing sinks. Motorcaravan service point. Licensed shop. Bar with terrace serving bar meals (all season). Games room. Solarium. Children's play park and playing fields. Splash pool (June - Sept). Off site: Beach 500 yds. Golf or bicycle hire 2 miles. Riding 5 miles. Birdwatching opportunities nearby.

Open

20 March - 1 November.

At a glance

Welcome & Ambience	✓✓✓	Location	✓✓✓
Quality of Pitches	✓✓✓	Range of Facilities	✓✓✓

Directions

Follow B1342 from the A1 to Waren Mill towards Bamburgh. After Budle Bay turn right and follow signs. O.S.GR: NU154342.

Charges 2004

Per unit incl. 2 persons	£ 9.00 - £ 17.00
extra person (over 5 yrs)	£ 1.70
1-man tent	£ 6.00 - £ 10.00
boat or awning	£ 2.20
dog	£ 1.30
Less 10% for bookings of 7 days or over.	

Reservations

Early reservation advisable for high season. Deposit of one night's charge plus £1 fee. Tel: 01668 214366. Email: enquiries@warencp.demon.co.uk

UK5755 South Meadows Caravan Park

South Meadows, Belford NE70 7DP (Northumberland)

South Meadows is a new park set in the north Northumberland countryside, within walking distance of the village of Belford with its market cross and old coaching inn. Covering five acres of level grass, there are 77 pitches, all with electricity (13A), water and TV aerial point. At present 40 pitches are available for touring units. The park is pleasantly landscaped and two short walks lead into the adjacent Blue Bell woods with streams, wildlife and spring flowers. Just off the A1 road, this would be a convenient stopover but Northumberland is an undiscovered county with castles and stately homes, the Farne Islands, Holy Island and long golden beaches, and you would be made most welcome here for a longer stay. This attractive, well maintained park is already popular with couples and young families and booking is advised.

Facilities

The new, fully tiled toilet block is excellent, heated in cool weather, with washbasins in cabins and roomy showers (free). Hairdryers. Full facilities for disabled visitors. Laundry with washing machines, dryers and iron plus a baby unit. Food preparation and cooking area. Coffee shop (weekends, incl. Sunday roast) and takeaway (daily until 16.00). Play area. Caravan storage and servicing. Off site: Village with pub and shops 0.5 miles. Golf 0.5 miles. Riding 3 miles. Beach 3 miles. Alnwick Castle of Harry Potter fame.

At a glance

Welcome & Ambience	✓✓✓✓	Location	✓✓✓✓
Quality of Pitches	✓✓✓✓	Range of Facilities	✓✓✓✓

Directions

Turn off A1 about 15 miles from Alnwick to Belford village and park is signed at the southern end. O.S.GR: NU115331.

Charges 2004

Per unit incl. 2 persons	£ 8.50 - £ 10.00
extra adult	£ 5.00 - £ 6.00
child (2-16 yrs)	£ 2.00 - £ 2.20

Reservations

Advised and made with deposit (£15 p/week). Tel: 01668 213326. Email: g.mcl@btinternet.com

Open

1 March - 30 November.

Land of ancient myths and Celtic legends, Wales is a small and compact country boasting a diverse landscape, from lakes and mountains, rivers and valleys to beautiful coastlines and rolling wooded countryside. It offers superb opportunities for an active holiday.

We have divided the list of campsites in Wales into North, Mid and South regions

Wales' biggest asset is undoubtedly its countryside, home to three National Parks that make up almost a quarter of the country's total area. Snowdonia National Park in the north combines dramatic mountain scenery with glacial valleys, lakes and streams, while in the south the Brecon Beacons boast mountains, moorlands, forests and wooded gorges with deep caves. The surrounding area of the Wye Valley on the borders with England is a designated Area of Outstanding Beauty; as is the Gower Peninsula, the Lleyn Peninsula, the Anglesey Coast and the Clwydian Range. The endless miles of largely unspoilt and beautiful Pembrokeshire coastline in the west has some of the finest long beaches in Europe, with pretty little bays plus the large and lively traditional seaside resorts of Tenby and Whitesand. Further inland is the secluded and pretty Gwaun Valley. The capital of Wales, Cardiff, has many attractions, including its newly developed waterfront, the Millennium Stadium and castle. In fact castles can be seen all over Wales, ranging from tiny stone keeps to huge medieval fortresses; some of the best preserved are Caernarfon, Conwy and Harlech, all built by Edward I.

Did you know?

The origins of the Red Dragon flag may date back to the Roman period, when the dragon was used by military cohorts

St David's in Pembrokeshire is Britain's smallest city by virtue of its Cathedral to the patron saint of Wales.

There are many sites in Wales linked to the legend of King Arthur: Castell Dinas Brân, near Llangollen, is reputed to be the resting-place of the Holy Grail

Towering at 1085 metres Mount Snowdon is the highest mountain in England and Wales

'The Dam Busters' was filmed on location in the Elan Valley

The Welsh language is one of Europe's oldest languages and shares its roots with Breton, Gaelic and Cornish

Places of interest

North: Isle of Anglesey; Dr Who Exhibition, Victorian School of 3R's and Motor Museum at Llangollen; Victorian seaside resort of Llandudno; Colwyn Bay; Penrhyn Castle at Bangor; Caernarfon Castle; Snowdon Mountain Railway at Llanberis

Mid: Elan Valley west of Rhayader; Dyfi National Nature Reserve at Ynyslas; Felinwynt Rainforest and Butterfly Centre; Museum of Modern Art, Wales and King Arthur's Labyrinth in Machynlleth; Powis Castle and gardens in Welshpool

South: National Showcaves Centre in Abercave; National Wetlands Centre in Llanelli; Dolaucothi Gold Mines in Llanwrda; Swansea; Manor House Wild Animal Park in Tenby; Pembroke Castle; Caerphilly Castle, the largest moated medieval castle in Wales; Oakwood Theme Park in Narberth

tip

THE LLANDRINDOD WELLS VICTORIAN FESTIVAL HAS STREET ENTERTAINMENT AND COSTUMES; THE MUD FESTIVAL IN LLANELLI INVOLVES MUD SAFARIS AND SCULPTURES (BOTH AUGUST).

UK5890 Glen Trothy Caravan & Camping Park

Mitchel Troy, Monmouth NP25 4BD (Monmouthshire)

Glen Trothy is a pretty park on the banks of the river Trothy and visitors are greeted by an array of colourful flowerbeds and tubs around the entrance and reception area. The owners, Horace and Merle Price, are working hard on their site bringing its facilities up-to-date, recently adding a new reception office. Three fields provide 40 level touring pitches. The first and largest field has a circular gravel road with seasonal pitches arranged on the outer side of the road and touring pitches on the inner side. These have slabs for vehicle wheels and electricity hook-ups. The second field, just past the toilet block, has pitches for trailer tents and tents only, whilst the camping field is for tents only (no cars allowed on this area).

Facilities

The sanitary block is old but bright and cheerful (possibly stretched at peak times). Facilities for disabled visitors. Laundry and dishwashing. Bicycle hire. Fishing in the River Trothy (WWA licence required). Dogs are permitted in motorcaravans and caravans only, not in tents. Only purpose built barbecues are allowed. Off site: Golf 2 miles. Shopping and supermarkets at Monmouth. The Wye Valley and the Forest of Dean are nearby for outings.

Open

1 March - 31 October.

At a glance

Welcome & Ambience	✓✓✓✓	Location	✓✓✓✓
Quality of Pitches	✓✓✓✓	Range of Facilities	✓✓✓

Directions

From the A40 at Monmouth, continue at roundabout. Go straight over at lights, and after 150 m. turn left just before tunnel. At T junction, turn left and follow signs for Mitchel Troy. Site is on right just past village sign. O.S.GR: SO495105.

Charges 2004

Per unit	£ 7.00 - £ 11.00
extra person	£ 1.50
electricity	£ 2.00
dog (by arrangement)	£ 2.00

Reservations

Booking advised (no single night bookings taken in July/Aug). Tel: 01600 712295.

UK5910 Saint Pierre Caravan Park

Portskewett, Chepstow NP6 4TT (Monmouthshire)

Saint Pierre Caravan Park was created in the early 1990s on fairly level grass with outstanding views over the Severn estuary with its two magnificent bridges. A wide entrance drive leads on to the site, which is well served by a wide, circular, block-paved road. The site has 50 pitches, all with electric hook-ups (6A), 22 on grass and 28 with hardstandings. Some hedging divides up the site, providing several small bays of two or three pitches, and there are some individual ones. There is no shop on-site, with the nearest supermarket in Chepstow, 4.5 miles. The site has no playground or activities for teenagers.

Facilities

A modern building which can be heated provides large controllable hot showers, dishwashing and laundry facilities with washing machine and dryer. WC and basin unit for disabled people. Small well equipped gym (free for campers). Boules court. Fenced dog walk. Calor gas. Off site: Golf 0.5 miles. Fishing on Rivers Wye and Usk.

Open

All year.

At a glance

Welcome & Ambience	✓✓✓✓	Location	✓✓✓✓
Quality of Pitches	✓✓✓✓	Range of Facilities	✓✓✓

Directions

From Chepstow take A48 south for 4 miles to roundabout, and turn left on B4245, and immediately turn left again (signed to site and Portskewett). Site is 250 yds. on left. O.S.GR: ST508901.

Charges 2004

Per unit incl. electricity	£ 14.00 - £ 15.00
2 person tent	£ 10.00
Discount (10%) for senior citizens. No credit cards.	

Reservations

Advisable for B.Hs and peak season. Tel: 01291 425114.

UK6060 Tredegar House Country Park Caravan Club Site

Coedkernen, Newport NP10 8TW (Newport)

This immaculate Caravan Club site is ideally situated for breaking a journey or for longer stays. It can accommodate 82 caravans, all with 16A electricity hook-up and 40 with gravel hardstanding. A further grass area is allocated for 30 tents, with its use limited to families and couples - no single sex groups are accepted. The site itself is set within the gardens and park of Tredegar House, a 17th century house and country park which is open to the public to discover what life was like 'above and below stairs'. Some road noise may be expected at times, but otherwise this is an excellent site.

Facilities

The sanitary block is of an excellent standard with a digital lock system. Washbasins in cubicles. Bathroom for visitors with disabilities. Baby bathroom. Dishwashing sinks. Laundry. Good motorcaravan service point. Calor gas available. Off site: Supermarket nearby. Newport 3 miles.

Open

28 March - 3 November.

At a glance

Welcome & Ambience	✓✓✓✓	Location	✓✓✓✓
Quality of Pitches	✓✓✓✓	Range of Facilities	✓✓✓✓

Directions

From M4 take exit 28 or from A48 junction with the M4 follow brown signs for Tredegar House. The caravan park is indicated to the left at the house entrance. O.S.GR: ST299855.

Charges 2004

Per adult	£ 3.30 - £ 4.80
child (5-16 yrs)	£ 1.10 - £ 1.60
pitch incl. electricity (non-member)	£ 8.00 - £ 11.00

Reservations

Advisable for peak season - contact the warden. Tel: 01633 815600.

UK5930 Cwmcarn Forest Drive Campsite

Cwmcarn, Crosskeys, Newport NP1 7FA (Newport)

Set in a narrow, sheltered valley with magnificent wooded slopes (it's hard to believe it was once the site of the Cwmcarn Colliery), this park is not only central for the many attractions of this part of Wales, but there is now also much of the natural environment to enjoy including a small fishing lake. The seven mile forest drive (open daily in season) shares its Visitor Centre with the camp reception and has much to offer - bird watching, badger seeking, the Twmbarlwm ancient hill fort to visit with its magnificent views across the Severn to Somerset, Devon and Gloucestershire. The site has a slightly wild feel, but is stunningly located and has 40 well spaced, flat pitches (30 with 15A electricity, 3 with concrete hard-standing and with tarmac for the car) spread over three small fields between the Visitor Centre and the small lake (fishing permits available). Wardens are on hand daily and the Visitor Centre and reception are open 9 am - 5 pm. (6 pm. at weekends, Oct - Easter Fridays 9 am - 4.30 pm), so arrive before then.

Facilities

The single well equipped, heated toilet block (£5 deposit for key) includes toilet facilities for disabled visitors, laundry with washing machine, dryer, iron and board, and a kitchen with two washing up sinks, small cooker and fridge (hot water free). Visitor Centre coffee shop selling refreshments and snacks. Guided walks and popular Twrch (15 km) mountain bike route are available. Numeracy trail and environmenteering routes for children. Rallies accommodated. Dogs accepted by prior arrangement. Off site: Shops, a leisure centre, pubs and takeaway food are available in the village under a mile away. Riding 2 miles, golf 6 miles.

At a glance

Welcome & Ambience	✓✓✓✓	Location	✓✓✓✓✓
Quality of Pitches	✓✓✓	Range of Facilities	✓✓✓

Directions

Cwmcarn Forest Drive is well signed from junction 28 on M4. From the Midlands and the 'Heads of the Valleys' road (A465), take A467 south to Cwmcarn. O.S.GR: ST230935.

Charges 2004

Per unit	£ 7.50 - £ 8.50
large tent	£ 6.50 - £ 7.50
small ridge tent	£ 5.00 - £ 6.00
electricity	£ 2.00

Reservations

Contact the Warden. Tel: 01495 272001. Email: cwmcarn-vc@caerphilly.gov.uk

Open

All year excl. 23 December - 2 January.

UK5925 Cardiff Caravan Park

Pontcanna Fields, Via Sophia Close, Cardiff CF11 9LB (Cardiff)

Run by the city council, this popular site is in a fairly central location, ideal for visiting the many attractions of the city of Cardiff. The County Cricket Ground, sports facilities and swimming pool, the Millennium Stadium, Cardiff Castle, museums and many other attractions are within walking distance. The recently redeveloped Cardiff Bay area is a 2.5 mile cycle ride (a good city centre cycle route map is available from reception) or there is a bus service from just outside the gate. The campsite has 73 pitches which are on a fairly open area, attractively landscaped, with 43 on grassed grid surface having electric hook-ups (16A), the remainder are on grass. The site is not fenced and there is a public right of way through the site. However, security is good with an on-site warden 24 hours a day, and security cameras (infra red) constantly scanning the whole area. Remember though that you are in a city centre environment, so lock up your valuables.

Facilities

Two heated buildings each with keycode entry systems, the one by reception has a laundry with washer and dryer, and facilities for disabled campers. Both have controllable hot showers, baby changing and dishwashing facilities. Bicycle hire - the site specialises in cycles adapted for disabled people. Riding can be arranged. Off site: The Millennium Stadium, Glamorgan County Cricket Ground, Cardiff Bay. Local shops and services within easy walking distance. Fishing 0.25 mile, golf 4 miles.

Open

All year.

At a glance

Welcome & Ambience	✓✓✓	Location	✓✓✓✓
Quality of Pitches	✓✓✓✓	Range of Facilities	✓✓✓

Directions

From the A48 turn south onto the A4119 (Cardiff Road). Follow round past church on left, following signs for Institute of Sport and at next set of traffic lights turn into Sophia Close and Sophia Gardens. Turn left at the Welsh Institute of Sport, and continue past the County Cricket Ground on your right, continue through an avenue of trees, and the site entrance is on your left. O.S.GR: ST171772.

Charges guide

Per adult	£ 3.00
child (4-14 yrs)	£ 1.50
vehicle	£ 2.50

Reservations

Essential for peak season and B.Hs. Tel: 02920 398362.

Have you
forgotten something?
see the Alan Rogers Directory
ON PAGE 294

UK5927 Acorn Camping & Caravanning

Rose Dew Farm, Ham Lane South, Llantwit Major CF61 1RP (Vale of Glamorgan)

A well appointed and friendly site in a near coastal location, you will find a warm welcome here from the resident owners. The 105 pitches are mostly on grass, with a few private and rental mobile homes at the far end of the site, leaving around 90 pitches for tourers. Four have gravel based hardstandings and there are 44 electric hook-ups (10A). Reception also houses a very well stocked shop which includes groceries and essentials, souvenirs, children's toys, camping gear, a delicatessen, and takeaway meals available on demand. Site lighting is kept to a minimum to allow guests to enjoy the night sky - a torch might be useful. The Heritage Coastal path is a short walk from the site, and St Illtud's church in Llantwit Major is also worth a visit for its wall paintings, mediaeval altar, and collection of Celtic stones.

Facilities

A warm, modern building houses all the facilities. Dishwashing sinks and laundry facilities are in the central atrium which is accessed through a double glazed foyer, where there is a drinks machine. Inside are spacious shower cubicles with washbasins, ample WCs, a family/baby room, and a suite for disabled campers (key to the block £10 deposit). Shop. Gas available. Recycling of glass, paper and metal. Adjacent to reception is a snooker room (charged), a general games room and, just outside, a good playground on rubber and grass. Off site: Glamorgan Heritage Coastal footpath. Llanerch Vineyard. Cosmeston Lakes Country Park at Penarth has a reconstructed Mediaeval Village. Fishing 1 mile (sea), 4 miles (lake). Riding 2 miles. Golf 9 miles. Boat launching 9 miles.

Open

1 February - 8 December.

At a glance

Welcome & Ambience ✓✓✓✓	Location	✓✓✓✓
Quality of Pitches ✓✓✓✓	Range of Facilities	✓✓✓

Directions

From the east from M4 exit 33 follow signs to Cardiff airport, then take B4265 for Llantwit Major. Turn left at first traffic lights, pass through Broverton and turn left into Ham Lane East (between playing fields), finally turning left into Ham Manor Park and follow signs to campsite. From the west: M4 exit 35, turn south on A473 for 3 miles, then left on A48, turning right at Pentre Meyrick towards Llantwit Major on B4268/70. Left at first roundabout on B4265, straight on at mini-roundabout, right at traffic lights into Llanmaes Road, left at mini-roundabout, continue around back of the town, left at mini-roundabout, and right into Ham Lane East and continue as above. O.S.GR: SS974678.

Charges 2004

Per unit incl. 2 persons	£ 7.00 - £ 8.00
extra adult	£ 2.25 - £ 2.75
child	£ 2.00 - £ 2.50
electricity	£ 2.75
dog	£ 0.50

Reservations

Essential for peak season and B.Hs, and made with £10.00 non-refundable deposit. Tel: 01446 794024. Email: info@acorncamping.co.uk

UK5940 Pembrey Country Park Caravan Club Site

Pembrey, Llanelli SA16 0EJ (Carmarthenshire)

This very popular Caravan Club site reopened in 2002 following major changes and refurbishment to the club's high standards. The extended 12-acre grounds provide 50 large hardstanding pitches and 80 level, grass pitches, all with 16A electricity. Tents are not accepted. Thoughtful landscaping has included the planting of many species of tree and a circular, one-way tarmac road provides easy access. Sensibly placed service points provide fresh water and waste disposal of all types. Close to reception is a late arrivals area that includes electric hook ups. RAF jets do practice in this area (generally no flying at weekends). However, the real plus for this site is its proximity to the Country Park - access to this is free on foot or cycle direct from the site, or the Club has organised a special weekly car pass for £11. Within the 520 acres of parkland are delightful walks, cycle trails, unlimited flora and fauna, bird hides, an equestrian centre, children's play area, toboggan and ski runs, pitch and putt, narrow gauge railway and picnic areas, all fronted by Cefn Sidan, an eight mile stretch of golden sands. The nearest section of beach is a 20 minute walk, whilst car parks place you close to the visitor centre, gift shop and the lifeguard patrolled bathing area. At some distance, naturists frequent the extreme northern end of the beach.

Facilities

The refurbished toilet block gives the impression of a new building with the interior to the latest design and specification including washbasins in cabins. Full facilities for disabled visitors (with key). Baby room. Fully equipped laundry room. Dishwashing room and further sinks under cover. Motorcaravan service point. Gas available. Local delivery vans visit each morning selling milk, bread and newspapers. Play area. Off site: Dogs are restricted to one end of the beach May - Sept (follow signs).

Open

All year, except 6 January - 30 March.

At a glance

Welcome & Ambience ✓✓✓✓	Location	✓✓✓✓
Quality of Pitches ✓✓✓✓	Range of Facilities	✓✓✓

Directions

Leave M4 at junction 48 onto A4138. After 4 miles turn right onto A484 at roundabout signed Carmarthen. Continue for 7 miles to Pembrey. The Country Park is signed off the A484 in Pembrey village; site entrance is on right 100 yds before park gates. O.S.GR: SN413006.

Charges 2004

Per adult	£ 3.75 - £ 5.00
child (5-16 yrs)	£ 1.00 - £ 1.60
pitch (non-members)	£ 8.50 - £ 10.00
electricity	£ 1.00 - £ 1.50

Reservations

Essential for July/Aug. and B.Hs; contact the Warden. Tel: 01554 834369.

UK5960 Abermarlais Caravan Park

Llangadog SA19 9NG (Carmarthenshire)

Apart from the attractions of south or mid Wales for a stay, this sheltered, family run park could also double as a useful transit stop close to the main holiday route for those travelling to Pembrokeshire. In a natural setting, up to 88 touring units are accommodated in one fairly flat, tapering five-acre grass field edged by mature trees and a stream. Pitches are numbered, and generously spaced around the perimeter or on either side of a central, hedged spine at the wider end, with 42 electrical hook-ups (10A) and some hardstanding. Backpackers have a small, separate area. The park is set in a sheltered valley with a range of wildlife and nine acres of woodland walks. There is also an old walled garden, with some pitches and lawns for softball games, that screens the park, both audibly and visibly, from the A40 road. However, the most sought after pitches are beside the stream, loved by children and a haven for wildlife. A torch would be useful.

Facilities

The one small toilet block is older in style, but is clean, bright, cheerful and adequate with controllable showers. Two external, covered washing-up sinks but no laundry facilities - nearest about 5 miles. Motorcaravan service point. Shop doubling as reception. Gas supplies. Play area with tennis and volleyball nets and play equipment. Winter caravan storage. Off site: Little Chef restaurant near. Pubs, etc. at Llangadog. Fishing 2 miles.

Open

14 March - 14 November.

At a glance

Welcome & Ambience	✓✓✓✓	Location	✓✓✓✓
Quality of Pitches	✓✓✓✓	Range of Facilities	✓✓✓

Directions

Park is on the A40, between the junctions with the A4069 and A482, between Llandovery and Llandeilo. O.S.GR: SN685295.

Charges 2005

Per adult	£ 1.50
child (over 5 yrs)	£ 1.00
pitch	£ 5.50
awning	£ 0.75
electricity	£ 2.00

Reservations

Any length, with £5 deposit. Tel: 01550 777868.

UK5950 Afon Lodge Caravan Park

Parciau Bach, St Clears SA33 4LG (Carmarthenshire)

This small park is personally run by the owners. There are some narrow lanes to be negotiated to get here, but it is well worth it to enjoy its quality and peaceful, rural setting. The 31 privately owned caravan holiday homes (plus 3 to rent) are hidden in the wooded slopes at the back of the park - a haven for wild flowers and squirrels. The open field for tents is sloping, but now has individual terraced places with dividing shrub hedges (10 pitches) and a lower level, terraced for 25 caravan pitches. With views across the valley, all these have electricity hook-ups (16A) and 23 have hardstanding, water and TV connections. The owner's pine chalet home, sited on the slope between the touring field and the wooded area houses reception, a tourist information room and the sanitary facilities. The park is a haven of tranquillity, even when we visited in peak season. If you tire of the rural atmosphere, Tenby is only 18 miles, with the 7 mile long Pendine Sands 6 miles away or to the north, the Preseli Mountains. Birdwatching opportunities abound. A member of the Countryside Discovery group.

Facilities

Recently extended toilet facilities also include a laundry room and facilities for dishwashing. Shop at reception (limited hours, Easter - end Oct). Children have an adventure play unit and a pets corner. Off site: Riding 0.5 miles, fishing 2 miles, golf 5 miles.

Open

All year except 9 January - 1 March.

At a glance

Welcome & Ambience	✓✓✓	Location	✓✓✓✓
Quality of Pitches	✓✓✓✓	Range of Facilities	✓✓✓

Directions

From St Clears traffic lights, take road to Llanboidy forking right after 100 yds. Follow this road for almost 2 miles and turn right. After less than a mile turn right at small crossroads and park is on left. O.S.GR: SN298184.

Charges 2005

Per unit incl. 4 persons, electricity	£ 12.00 - £ 15.00
tent incl. 3 persons (no electricity)	£ 5.00 - £ 10.00
awning	£ 1.00
dog	£ 0.50
No credit cards.	

Reservations

May be advisable for B.Hs. Tel: 01994 230647. Email: yvonne@afonlodge.f9.co.uk

UK6070 Rhandirmwyn Camping & Caravanning Club Site

Rhandirmwyn, Llandovery SA20 0NT (Carmarthenshire)

This is a popular site with those who like a peaceful life with no on-site entertainment, just fresh air and beautiful countryside. The site is only a short drive from the magnificent Llyn Brianne reservoir and close to the Dinas RSPB nature reserve, where a two mile trail runs through oak and alder woodland alongside the River Tywi and the wildlife includes many species of birds including red kites. The site is in a sheltered valley with 90 pitches on level grass, 51 electric hook-ups (16A) and 17 hardstandings. The village is within walking distance although there is a fairly steep hill (the return is much easier), and you can take a short cut through the woodland grove dedicated to John Lloyd, a former Chairman of the Club.

Facilities

The single heated sanitary block is kept very clean and tidy. Some washbasins in cubicles, dishwashing sinks and fully equipped laundry. Drive-over motorcaravan service point. Small playground with rubber base. Off site: The village has a Post Office and general store and the Royal Oak Inn serves good value meals. Fishing 6 miles. Golf 7 miles. Riding 11 miles.

Open

March - October.

At a glance

Welcome & Ambience	✓✓✓✓✓	Location	✓✓✓✓✓
Quality of Pitches	✓✓✓✓	Range of Facilities	✓✓✓

Directions

From centre of Llandovery take A483 towards Builth Wells, after a short distance turn left, signed Rhandirmwyn, continue for approx. 7 miles along country lanes. O.S.GR: SN779435.

Charges 2005

Per adult	£ 4.30 - £ 6.40
child (6-18 yrs)	£ 1.90
non-member pitch fee	£ 5.00

Reservations

Advised for high season and made with deposit; contact site or Central Reservations 0870 243 3331. Site tel: 01550 760257.

UK5880 Springwater Lakes

Harford, Llanwrda SA19 8DT (Carmarthenshire)

Set in 20 acres of Welsh countryside, Springwater offers a selection of fishing lakes to keep even the keenest of anglers occupied. However, it is not just anglers who will enjoy this site - it is a lovely base to enjoy the peace and tranquillity of this part of Wales. Springwater offers 20 spacious, flat pitches either on grass or hardstanding, all with electricity hook-ups (16A). Malcolm and Shirley Bexon are very proud of their site and welcome all visitors with a smile. This is not a site for children unless they enjoy fishing (no play areas). If you want to learn about fishing Malcolm will be happy to help.

Facilities

The modern, heated toilet block is very clean and includes facilities for disabled visitors (there is also access to the lakes for wheelchairs). Dishwashing. Baker visits daily. Tackle/bait shop. Off site: Spar shop and garage 500 yards, other shops 5 miles. Bicycle hire and riding 2 miles. Golf 5 miles.

Open

March - 31 October.

At a glance

Welcome & Ambience	✓✓✓✓	Location	✓✓✓✓✓
Quality of Pitches	✓✓✓✓	Range of Facilities	✓✓✓

Directions

From A40 at Llanwrda take A482 to Lampeter. After 6 miles go through village of Pumsaint and site is 1 mile further on the left, just before garage shop. O.S.GR:SN637431.

Charges 2004

Per person	£ 4.00
electricity	£ 2.00 - £ 2.00
dog	free - £ 1.00

Reservations

Contact site Tel: 01558 650788.

UK5990 Freshwater East Caravan Club Site

Freshwater East, Lamphey SA71 5LN (Pembrokeshire)

This Caravan Club site in the Pembrokeshire Coast National Park is open to non-members (for all units). At the bottom of a hill, it has 140 mainly level pitches bounded by trees, 128 with 16A electrical hook-ups and around half on hardstanding. There are a further 12 pitches for tents. The beach and the Pembroke Coastal Path are about a five minute walk. This is an excellent area for walking with magnificent cliff views and birdwatching. You will find St David's, the smallest cathedral city, well worth a visit. Note: TV aerial connections are available, but you will need your own extension cable.

Facilities

The two heated toilet blocks are modern and clean with washbasins in cubicles, and free hairdryers or sockets for your own. Facilities for disabled visitors. Fully equipped laundry rooms. Waste point for motorcaravans. Small play area. Gas supplies. Off site: Shop 0.5 miles. Fishing within 5 miles.

Open

26 March - 1 November.

At a glance

Welcome & Ambience	✓✓✓✓	Location	✓✓✓✓
Quality of Pitches	✓✓✓✓	Range of Facilities	✓✓✓

Directions

From east on A477, fork left 1.25 miles past Milton on A4075 Pembroke road. After 2 miles in Pembroke immediately (after railway bridge) turn sharp left at roundabout on A4139 Tenby road. In 1.75 miles in Lamphey turn right on B4584 (Freshwater East). In 1.75 miles turn right signed Stackpole and Trewent and after 400 yds at foot of hill, right into lane at Club sign. Do not tow to the beach. O.S.GR: SS015979.

Charges 2004

Per adult	£ 3.80 - £ 5.00
child (5-16 yrs)	£ 1.10 - £ 1.60
pitch incl. electricity (non-member)	£ 8.50 - £ 11.50

Reservations

Contact the Warden. Tel: 01646 672341.

UK5985 Manorbier Country Park

Station Road, Manorbier, Tenby SA70 7SN (Pembrokeshire)

This area of southwest Wales is quite attractive, with a variety of activities available, sandy beaches and an extensive coastal footpath. This campsite is relatively small, with 99 caravan holiday homes and 14 seasonal units, which leaves only around 35 pitches for tourists. From reception you pass through the area of holiday homes to the touring area which, although neat, is rather uninspiring. There are seven rows of concrete and gravel hardstanding pitches set into a level grass field; 32 pitches have electric hook-ups (16A), cable TV and a shared water tap, and 4 are multi-service pitches (electricity, water, waste water, sewage, TV). Additionally, 10 grass pitches are on the opposite side of the car park with electric hook-ups, and 4 grass pitches at the front of the main field with no services. Cars park away from the caravans on a wide tarmac parking area. A small grassy recreation area is at one end of the touring site, and a playground is behind the main complex. The complex offers a bar with family entertainment in season, a good value restaurant and an indoor pool. Large units should book in advance and motorhomes over 23 ft. are not accepted. Some noise is possible as there is a Royal Artillery range nearby, and RAF jets fly in this area.

Facilities

A single building at one end of the car parking area provides all toilet facilities, it can be heated, and has controllable hot showers (on payment), a multi-purpose room suitable for families, babies and disabled campers. Small laundry room and dishwashing sinks outside under cover. Shop. Bar and restaurant. Indoor heated swimming and paddling pools. Jacuzzi. Sauna and steam room, vertical solarium, gym and tennis (all charged). Dogs are not accepted. Off site: Bicycle hire, boat launching and beach 1.5 miles. Golf and riding 3 miles. Adjacent garden centre restaurant serves cream teas and Sunday lunches. Fish and chip bar opposite. Manorbier Castle overlooks the sandy beach. Tenby 6 miles.

At a glance

Welcome & Ambience	✓✓✓✓	Location	✓✓✓
Quality of Pitches	✓✓✓✓	Range of Facilities	✓✓✓✓

Directions

From Tenby take A4139 towards Pembroke, passing through Penally and Lydstep. At crossroads (Manorbier signed to left) continue straight on following signs to the station. Turn right by Baptist Chapel into Station Road, and continue to site entrance (do not go into Manorbier village). O.S.GR: SS068991.

Charges 2004

Per unit incl. up to 4 persons	£ 14.50 - £ 20.00
extra person	£ 1.50
awning	£ 1.50

Reservations

Essential for peak season and B.Hs. Gazebos, pup tents, dogs or single sex groups are not accepted. Tel: 01834 871952. Email: enquiries@countrypark.co.uk

Open

1 March - 31 October.

UK5980 Moreton Farm Leisure Park

Moreton, Saundersfoot SA69 9EA (Pembrokeshire)

Moreton Farm has been developed in a secluded valley, a 10-20 minute walk from Saundersfoot and four miles from Tenby. It provides 30 caravan (all with 16A electricity, and including 17 with hardstanding) and 30 tent pitches on two sloping, neatly cut grass fields, with 12 pine holiday lodges and four cottages for letting occupying another field. The site is approached under a railway bridge (height 10 ft 9 ins, width across the top 6 ft 6 ins, but with alternative access over the railway line for larger vehicles just possible). There are a few trains during the day, none at night. An attractive lake at the bottom of the valley is home to ducks, geese and chickens (fishing is no longer available) – pride of place must go to 'Missy' and her girls! Pembroke and Carew castles and a variety of visitor attractions are close. This is a quiet family site.

Facilities

The toilet blocks (which can be heated) are light and airy, providing pre-set hot showers (on payment), and a ramp to a unit for disabled visitors with toilet and washbasin, a baby bath, dishwashing sinks and laundry facilities. Fenced, outside clothes drying area. Small shop for basics and gas. Playground. No dogs or other pets are accepted. Off site: Fishing or riding 1 mile, bicycle hire 2 miles, golf 4 miles.

Open

1 March - 31 October.

At a glance

Welcome & Ambience	✓✓✓✓	Location	✓✓✓✓
Quality of Pitches	✓✓✓✓	Range of Facilities	✓✓✓

Directions

From A477 Carmarthen - Pembroke road take A478 for Tenby at Kilgelly. Park is signed on left after 1.5 miles. Watch carefully for sign and park is 0.5 miles up poorly made-up road and under bridge. O.S.GR: SN122047.

Charges 2004

Per unit incl. 2 persons	£ 10.00 - £ 12.00
tent incl. 2 persons	£ 8.00 - £ 10.00
extra adult	£ 1.00
child (2-17 yrs)	£ 0.50
awning	£ 1.50
electricity	£ 2.50
No credit cards.	

Reservations

Made with deposit (£15/20 p/week), balance 28 days before arrival. Tel: 01834 812016. Email: moretonfarm@btconnect.com

(221)

UK5995 Caerfai Bay Caravan & Tent Park

St Davids, Haverfordwest SA62 6QT (Pembrokeshire)

About as far west as one can get in Wales, St David's is Britain's smallest city, noted for its Cathedral and Bishops Palace. This cliff-top site has direct access to the Pembrokeshire Coastal Path and a magnificent sandy beach is just a few minutes away, down the path from the car park by the site entrance. The camping area is spread over three open and sloping fields, all with magnificent views over St Brides Bay. The caravan field also has a small number of holiday homes and is closest to reception. The second and third fields are for tents and motorcaravans, almost all on grass with a few hardstandings available. Main access roads are tarmac. Altogether there are 105 touring pitches and 45 electric hook-ups (10A). Caerfai Farm Shop is just across the lane (opens end of May), and other shops and services are just 1 mile. Site lighting is deliberately minimal, so a torch would be useful.

Facilities

Two main buildings house the sanitary facilities, one by reception and the second in the tent field. The first,the newest and heated, contains a facility for disabled visitors, also suitable for families, baby changing facilities, and a room with dishwashing sinks, microwave and hot drinks machine. Also in this block is a useful 'storm shelter' for inclement weather. The second, a double block between the tent fields, is older, but well maintained and includes a dishwashing room. The adjacent part provides 4 family rooms with heating. Basic motorcaravan services. Wet suit washing facility and enclosed clothes drying area. Gas stocked. Off site: Walk the Pembrokeshire coastal path, visit Ramsey Island Bird and Grey Seal Reserve. Sea fishing 0.25 miles. Indoor pool and bicycle hire 1 mile. Golf 2 miles. Riding 10 miles. Boat launching 1.5 or 3 miles.

At a glance

Welcome & Ambience	✓✓✓✓	Location	✓✓✓✓✓
Quality of Pitches	✓✓✓	Range of Facilities	✓✓✓

Directions

From Haverfordwest take the A487 to St David's. On passing the town boundary, turn left into lane immediately before the National Park Visitor Centre (site signed), and continue on for 0.75 mile to site entrance on right. O.S.GR: SM757243.

Charges 2004

Per unit incl. 2 persons	£ 8.50 - £ 13.50
tent incl. 2 persons	£ 7.00 - £ 9.50
extra person	£ 3.00
child (3-15 yrs)	£ 2.50
electricity	£ 2.25
dog	£ 0.50

Reservations

Advised for peak season and B.Hs, and made with £20 non-refundable deposit. Tel: 01437 720274. Email: info@caerfaibay.co.uk

Open

1 March - 15 November.

CAERFAI BAY CARAVAN & TENT PARK

Quiet family-run park uniquely situated in St Davids and within Pembrokeshire Coast National Park. The perfect spot to relax on the beach and explore Pembrokeshire.

• Free Hot Showers • Electric Hook-up Points • Launderette
• Dishwash Rooms • Disabled Toilet & Shower • Dogs Allowed

Call: **01437 720274** or visit: **www.caerfaibay.co.uk**

UK6010 Cenarth Falls Holiday Park

Cenarth, Newcastle Emlyn SA38 9JS (Ceredigion)

The Davies family have developed an attractively landscaped, part wooded holiday home park with 80 privately owned units and 7 for hire. However, a neat well cared for, sheltered grassy area at the top of the park provides 30 touring pitches, all with sunken grass grid hardstanding and electricity (16A). Accessed via a semi-circular tarmac road, they enjoy views across the Teifi valley. A sunken, kidney shaped outdoor pool with landscaped surrounds and sun-beds is very pleasant. Opened in October 2002, the Coracles Health and Country Club provides an indoor pool, spa, sauna and steam rooms and fitness suite (reduced rates for campers). It also provides a bar, restaurant area, adult-only lounge and a large function room where live entertainment is organised weekly all season. A footpath leads to the village and the famous Cenarth Falls (with leaping salmon). The National Coracle Centre is well worth a visit. A member of the Best of British group.

Facilities

The excellent, heated sanitary block has easy ramped access. Accessed by key, it uses a system that controls heating, lighting, water and air-freshener on entry - very efficient. Both men and ladies have a family room (doubling as provision for disabled visitors), an additional well equipped shower and also one washbasin in a private cabin. Laundry room with two washing machines, two dryers and ironing facilities (used by the whole park). No laundry sinks, but two dishwashing sinks under cover. Motorcaravan services. Gas supplies. Outdoor pool (Whitsun - mid-Sept). Health and Country Club (see above). Play area. Games room. Off site: Shop within 0.5 miles. Fishing 0.25 miles, bicycle hire 8 miles, riding 7 miles, golf 10 miles.

At a glance

Welcome & Ambience	✓✓✓✓✓	Location	✓✓✓✓✓
Quality of Pitches	✓✓✓✓	Range of Facilities	✓✓✓✓✓

Directions

Follow A484 Cardigan - Newcastle Emlyn road and park is signed before Cenarth village. O.S.GR: SN265421.

Charges 2005

Per unit incl. up to 4 people	£ 13.00 - £ 20.00
extra person	£ 2.00
awning	£ 2.00
dog	£ 2.00

Reservations

Made with 33% deposit; contact park. Tel: 01239 710345. Email: enquiries@cenarth-holipark.co.uk

Open

1 March - 9 January.

UK6290 Glan-y-Mor Leisure Park

Clarach Bay, Aberystwyth SY23 3DT (Ceredigion)

Follow the road to Clarach Bay and on the sea-front is Glan-y-Mor, a busy, holiday-style park with an enviable situation. On a wet day you may not wish to go far with the comprehensive leisure centre on site - it is open eight months of the year with reduced entry fee for campers. Although the balance of pitches is very much in favour of caravan holiday homes (3:1) which dominate the open park and bay, there are 60 touring pitches, 45 with electricity (10A) and 4 new 'super' pitches. They are rather pressed together in two small sections on the lower part of the park. In high season, tents, tourers or motorcaravans can opt for space and fine views (but maybe winds) on a ridge of higher ground above the park. The well equipped leisure centre offers a heated pool, jacuzzi, solarium, sauna, steam room and gym. This complex also includes reception, a video and amusement room, 10-pin bowling, bar, buffet bar and dance room (free entertainment nightly, Easter and May-Oct). This is an ideal site for those seeking 'all the bells and whistles'!

Facilities

The heated toilet block is on the lower touring area with dishwashing facilities and laundry room, plus a toilet for disabled people. A 'portacabin' type block (high season only) is on the ridge ground. A suite including shower for disabled people is in a block in the upper site, with further facilities at the leisure centre (RADAR key). Motorcaravan service point. Supermarket. Play area designed with younger children in mind, and a large sports field. Swimming pool. Licensed restaurant and takeaway (from Easter). Freezer pack service and gas supplies. No dogs are accepted on touring pitches during B.H. and school summer holiday periods. Off site: Reduced rates are available at local golf courses.

Open

1 March - 31 October.

At a glance

Welcome & Ambience	✓✓✓	Location	✓✓✓✓✓
Quality of Pitches	✓✓✓✓	Range of Facilities	✓✓✓✓✓

Directions

Clarach is signed west from the A487 (Aberystwyth - Machynlleth) in village of Bow Street. Follow signs over crossroads to beach and park. Access for caravans from Aberystwyth on B4572 is difficult. O.S.GR: SN580850.

Charges 2004

Per unit incl. 2 persons	£ 6.00 - £ 12.00
super pitch	£ 20.00
extra person (over 18 yrs)	£ 2.00
child	free
electricity	£ 2.00
awning	£ 3.00

Top camping area max. charge £10 plus £2 for electricity. Club membership (but not Leisure complex) included.

Reservations

Any length, with £20 deposit; balance 28 days before arrival. Tel: 01970 828900.
Email: glan-y-mor@sunbourne.co.uk

There are places to stay or there are places to enjoy a holiday.

So Much To Pack In - 60 touring pitches, 45 with electricity, 4 new 'super' pitches, heated toilet block and showers, disabled toilet, dishwashing facilities, laundry room, supermarket, kids' play areas, sports field, great views, licensed restaurant and takeaway, freezer pack service and gas supplies, heated swimming pool, jacuzzi, solarium, sauna, steam room and gym, bars, amusement room, 10-pin bowling, buffet bar and dance room and club with live entertainment.

Glan y Môr Leisure Park, Clarach Bay, Nr Aberystwyth, Ceredigion SY23 3DT.
Tel: (01970) 828900 Fax: (01970) 828890 Email: glan-y-mor@sunbourne.com

UK6280 Aeron Coast Caravan Park

North Road, Aberaeron SA46 0JF (Ceredigion)

Aeron Coast is a family park with a wide range of recreational facilities, on the west coast of Wales. Although it has a high proportion of caravan holiday homes (200 privately owned), touring units of all types are provided for in two fields separated from the beach and sea by a high bank (although the best beach is on the south side of this traditional fishing village). Pitches are on level grass with all units regularly and well spaced in lines in traditional style. The main attraction of the park is its excellent provision for families, both in and out of doors. This includes two outdoor pools (one new) and a toddlers' pool (unsupervised) in a paved, walled area good for sunbathing, a tennis court and small half-court for youngsters, football and a sand pit. The indoor leisure area provides an under-5s room with slide, etc, teenagers-only room with juke box, table tennis, pool and games machines and TV room. In high season activities are organised nightly free of charge in the large entertainment room. In low season reception is closed on Mondays and Wednesdays - choose a pitch and return to the office in the morning.

Facilities
Two modern toilet blocks offer excellent facilities (card operated entry system with £10 deposit) including large family showers. Facilities for disabled people and babies are in one block. Basic motorcaravan service point. Club house and bar (from Easter, 12-2 and from 7 pm) with family room serving bar meals and takeaway in school holiday periods. Reception keeps a wide range of tourist information. Shop at the petrol station at the entrance. Swimming pools (1/6-30/9). Only one dog per unit is accepted. Off site: Beach, fishing and boat launching 0.5 miles. A steam railway, craft centre, woollen mills and potteries can be visited locally.

At a glance
Welcome & Ambience	✓✓✓✓	Location	✓✓✓✓
Quality of Pitches	✓✓✓✓	Range of Facilities	✓✓✓✓

Directions
Park is on northern outskirts of Aberaeron village with entrance on the right beside a petrol station - not too easily seen. O.S.GR: SN461633.

Charges 2005
Per unit incl. 2 persons, electricity	£ 10.50 - £ 14.00
extra person (over 18 yrs)	£ 3.00
child (2-12 yrs)	£ 0.50 - £ 1.00

Reservations
Made with £20 deposit. Tel: 01545 570349. Email: aeroncoastcaravanpark@aberaeron.freeserve.co.uk

Open
1 March - 31 October.

UK6245 Morben Isaf Touring & Holiday Home Park

Derwenlas, Machynlleth SY20 8SR (Powys)

Machynlleth is a market town, home of Owain Glyndwr's fifteenth century Welsh Parliament building and the Celtica Centre, and is also close to the Tal-y-Llyn Steam Railway, the Centre for Alternative Technology, Corris Craft Centre and King Arthur's Labyrinth. This site is in a convenient location for an overnight halt, or a short stay whilst visiting all these attractions. It provides 26 multi-service touring pitches, all with 16A electricity, water tap, waste water drain and a satellite TV hook-up. There is further grassy space below the touring pitches which is normally used as a football pitch but can accommodate around 30 tents who do not need any services. On a lower level, behind the site manager's bungalow, and barely visible from the touring site, are 87 privately owned holiday mobile homes. Also on site is a coarse fishing lake which campers are free to use.

Facilities
A small but well equipped, heated modern toilet block includes spacious controllable showers, baby changing and child seats in both ladies' and men's, and a well equipped laundry and dishwashing facilities. There are no facilities for disabled campers. Powered motorcaravan service point suitable for American RVs. Gas available. Off site: Pub serving hot food 1.5 miles. Leisure Centre, shops and services in Machynlleth 3 miles. Centre for Alternative Technology 6 miles.

Open
Mid March - 31 October.

At a glance
Welcome & Ambience	✓✓✓✓	Location	✓✓✓✓
Quality of Pitches	✓✓✓✓	Range of Facilities	✓✓✓

Directions
Site is 2.5 miles southwest of Machynlleth beside A487. O.S.GR: SN705985.

Charges 2004
Per unit incl. 2 adults, 2 children and electricity	£ 12.50 - £ 14.00
extra person	£ 2.00
2-man tent	£ 10.50
tent on field	£ 7.50 - £ 12.50
dog	free - £ 1.00

Reservations
Essential for peak season and B.Hs. Tel: 01654 781473.

Planning your **next short break?**
don't forget to see our directory
ON PAGE 294

UK6040 Pencelli Castle Caravan & Camping Park

Pencelli, Brecon LD3 7LX (Powys)

Open all year round, this is a quality park with atmosphere and character which continues to improve. Set amidst the Brecon scenery, it offers excellent facilities in peaceful, rural tranquillity. The owners, Liz and Gerwyn Rees, have retained the country charm but have added an all embracing range of spacious, heated, luxury facilities, attractively enhanced by potted plants, etc. There are three touring fields. The 'Orchard' incorporates 15 fully serviced pitches with hardstanding, amongst shrubs, fruit trees and a stone cider mill. The 'Oaks' taking 20 caravans and tents and the 'Meadow' for 40 tents (with boot and bike wash) are bordered by majestic trees and the Monmouthshire and Brecon Canal, where gaily painted barges slip past. All the fields are level with neatly mown grass and tarmac access roads. The historic manor house, that dates back to 1583, is adjacent to arched barns that house an increasing collection of vintage farm machinery including carts and rare tractors. For mountain bikers and walkers, a path leaves the village to reach the top of the Brecon Beacons or there is an easy towpath ramble to Tal-y-Bont where there are pubs, tea rooms and a post office.

Facilities

The well designed toilet block includes some private cubicles, two large rooms for families or disabled visitors incorporating double showers, baby changing and bath facilities, all humorously decorated for the young at heart. Laundry. Drying room (a must as this is walking country). Information/planning room. Indoor dishwashing/food preparation room. Motorcaravan service point. Small shop (basics). Playground and nature trail. Bicycle hire. Dogs are not accepted. Off site: The Royal Oak Inn with meals 100 m. Golf or bicycle hire 5 miles. Riding 2 miles.

Open

All year.

At a glance

Welcome & Ambience	✓✓✓✓✓	Location	✓✓✓✓✓
Quality of Pitches	✓✓✓✓✓	Range of Facilities	✓✓✓

Directions

From A40 south after Brecon bypass take B4558 at signs for Llanfrynach and later Pencelli (narrow bridge). If travelling north on A40, approach via Tal-y-Bont. Site at south end of Pencelli. O.S.GR: SO095249.

Charges 2004

Per unit incl. 2 persons	£ 11.00 - £ 14.00
extra adult	£ 5.00
child (5-13 yrs)	£ 4.00
awning	£ 1.50
electricity	£ 2.50
tent - per adult	£ 6.00 - £ 7.00

No credit cards.

Reservations

Advised for peak season and B.Hs. Tel: 01874 665451. Email: pencelli.castle@virgin.net

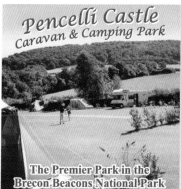

Pencelli Castle Caravan & Camping Park

The Premier Park in the Brecon Beacons National Park

Peacefully set at the foothills of the Brecon Beacons and within walking distance of the highest peaks. Adjoining Monmouth & Brecon Canal and the Taff Cycle Trail. Village pub 150 yards. Shop, hardstandings, serviced pitches and luxurious shower block. Also red deer, ducks, vintage farm machinery and children's play area. Open All Year. NO DOGS.

- 2004, 03 & 02 Practical Caravan - The Top 100 Family Park in Wales Winner
- 2003 National Tourism Awards for Wales - Best Place to Stay (self catering)
- 2003 Loo of the Year - National Winner Wales
- 2003, 02 & 01 Gold David Bellamy Conservation Award
- 2002 AA - Best Campsite in Wales
- 2001 Calor Gas - Best Park in Wales

Pencelli • Brecon • Powys • Wales • LD3 7LX • Tel: 01874 665 451
Email: pencelli.castle@virgin.net • www.pencelli-castle.co.uk

UK6250 Dolswydd Caravan Park

Dolswydd, Pen-y-Bont, Llandrindod Wells LD1 5UB (Powys)

Dolswydd is on the edge of a pretty, traditional working farm. Peaceful and tranquil, with fine views of the Welsh hills and surrounding area, it has modern facilities and 25 good spacious pitches mainly on hardstandings, all with electricity (16A). The park is within walking distance of the local pub which offers good, home cooked food. The Hughes family extend a warm and friendly welcome to their little park, surrounded by hills and wandering sheep, which is ideal as a touring base or for a one night stop, but booking is advised, especially at peak times and during the Victorian Festival (last week in August).

Facilities

Modern and clean facilities include lots of hot water, dishwashing, laundry, and a WC/washroom for disabled people. Fishing (free, but licence required). Off site: Within walking distance are the local pub, Post Office and garage. Riding 1 mile. Golf 5 miles. Bicycle hire 5 miles.

Open

Easter - end October.

At a glance

Welcome & Ambience	✓✓✓✓	Location	✓✓✓✓
Quality of Pitches	✓✓✓✓	Range of Facilities	✓✓✓

Directions

Pen-y-bont is 2 miles east of the junction of the A44 and A483 roads at Crossgates. Take A44 signed Kington. Go through village of Pen-y-bont and cross cattle grid to site on the right. O.S.GR: SO117639.

Charges 2004

Per unit with 2 adults and 2 children	£ 7.00
electricity	£ 1.50

Reservations

Advised; contact site. Tel: 01597 851267. Email: Hughes@dolswydd.freeserve.co.uk

UK6030 Brynich Caravan Park

Brecon LD3 7SH (Powys)

Brynich is a well kept, family run park with a picturesque setting and super views towards the Brecon Beacons, developed over the years by Colin and Maureen Jones to very high standards. Originally farmland near the Brecon bypass, there are now three level, hedged and neatly mown camping fields with tarmac roads and a mixture of hardwood trees and shrubs maturing nicely. These fields provide for 130 touring units of all types with hardstanding on many pitches, 108 electricity points (10/16A) and 10 multi-serviced pitches with grass or gravel hardstandings. In a sloping field leading down to a stream, is an extensive dog walk on one side of the Brynich Brook and, on the opposite side, an adventure play area. The stream is shallow and an added attraction along with the play equipment and there is a large recreation field for ball games. For smaller children there is some play equipment near reception and the Play Barn which provides extensive indoor entertainment for the under-12s (charges apply). In a beautifully converted barn adjacent to the campsite the fully licensed restaurant uses local produce in its good value menus. Being within the Brecon Beacons National Park, this is a good area for hill walking and climbing. A member of the Best of British group.

Facilities

Two modern, heated toilet blocks have well equipped showers, washbasins in cubicles, dishwashing sinks and a laundry room. Two fully equipped units for disabled visitors in one block, one providing left handed toilet facilities, the other right handed (key system). Baby unit including bath. Family room with bath, shower, toilet and handbasin. Fridge, freezer and microwave for visitors' use. Motorcaravan service point with bike wash. Reception and well stocked shop (with gas). Play areas. Restaurant and indoor Play Barn open all year. Boules court. Off site: Local pub within walking distance. Access to the towpath of the Brecon and Monmouthshire Canal is 200 yds. Market days in Brecon on Tuesday and Friday. Fishing or bicycle hire 1.5 miles. Riding 2 miles. Golf 3 miles.

At a glance

Welcome & Ambience	✓✓✓✓✓	Location	✓✓✓✓
Quality of Pitches	✓✓✓✓✓	Range of Facilities	✓✓✓✓✓

Directions

From the A40 Abergavenny road, at roundabout on the Brecon bypass (A40/A470) take A470 and park is 150 yards on right. O.S.GR: SO069278.

Charges 2005

Per unit incl. 2 persons, electricity	£ 13.00 - £ 16.00
with services	£ 15.00 - £ 18.00
tent incl. 2 persons	£ 10.00 - £ 13.00
extra adult	£ 3.00
child (4-16 yrs)	£ 2.00
dog	£ 1.00

Reservations

Advisable for hook-ups at B.Hs. and made with £ 20 deposit. Tel: 01874 623325.
Email: holidays@brynich.co.uk

Open

18 March - 30 October.

UK6330 Daisy Bank Touring Caravan Park

Snead, Montgomery SY15 6EB (Powys)

For adults only, this pretty, tranquil park in the Camlad Valley has panoramic views, and is an ideal base for walkers. Attractively landscaped with 'old English' flower beds and many different trees and shrubs, this small park has been carefully developed. The Welsh hills to the north and the Shropshire hills to the south overlook the three fields which provide a total of 55 pitches. The field nearer to the road (perhaps a little noisy) is slightly sloping but there are hardstandings for motorcaravans, while the second field is more level. All pitches have 16A electricity, water and waste water drainage and most have TV hook up. With many walks in the area, including Offa's Dyke, a series of walk leaflets is available centred on Bishop's Castle three miles away. The owners will site your caravan for you and there is a late arrivals area with hook-up. A security bar at the entrance has to be lifted for motorcaravans. Although technically in Wales, the park is 500 yards from the Shropshire border, an area rich in history.

Facilities

The well equipped, heated toilet block now incorporates modern, en-suite units (6 with shower, WC and washbasin, 2 with WC and washbasin). Dishwashing sinks at the rear of the block are covered. Washing machine, laundry sink and drying room. Gas supplies. Brick built barbecues. Small putting green (free loan of clubs and balls). Off site: Supermarket 2 miles. Many eating places near. Bicycle hire or fishing 3 miles. Golf or riding 10 miles.

At a glance

Welcome & Ambience	✓✓✓✓✓	Location	✓✓✓✓✓
Quality of Pitches	✓✓✓✓✓	Range of Facilities	✓✓✓

Directions

Site is by the A489 road 2 miles east of Churchstoke in the direction of Craven Arms. O.S.GR: SO302930.

Charges 2004

Per unit incl. 2 adults, all services	£ 13.50 - £ 17.00
extra person	£ 4.00
dog	£ 0.75

Reservations

An adult only park. Contact park. Tel: 01588 620471. Email: j.spurgeon@tesco.net

Open

All year.

UK6320 Fforest Fields Caravan & Camping Park

Hundred House, Builth Wells LD1 5RT (Powys)

This secluded 'different' park is set on a family hill farm in the heart of Radnorshire. Truly rural, there are glorious views of the surrounding hills and a distinctly family atmosphere. This is simple country camping and caravanning at its best, without man-made distractions or intrusions - a place to unwind and watch the stars. The facilities include 67 large pitches on level grass on a spacious and peaceful, carefully landscaped field by a stream. Electrical connections (mostly 16A) are available and there are 13 hardstanding pitches, also with electricity. Several additional areas without electricity are provided for tents. George and Kate, the enthusiastic owners, have opened up much of the farm for moderate or ample woodland and moorland trails which can be enjoyed with much wildlife to see. Indeed wildlife is actively encouraged with nesting boxes for owls, song-birds and bats, by leaving field margins un-mown to encourage small mammals and by yearly tree planting. George and Kate also run a para-gliding school where beginners are welcome.

Facilities

The toilet facilities are acceptable with baby bath, dishwashing and laundry facilities including washing machines and a dryer. Milk, eggs and orange juice are sold in reception and gas, otherwise there are few other on-site facilities, but the village of Hundred House, one mile away, has a pub, village stores and post office. Torches are useful. Off site: Fishing 3 miles, bicycle hire or golf 5 miles, riding 10 miles.

Open

Easter - 17 November.

At a glance

Welcome & Ambience	✓✓✓✓	Location	✓✓✓✓✓
Quality of Pitches	✓✓✓✓	Range of Facilities	✓✓✓

Directions

Park is 4 miles east of Builth Wells near the village of Hundred House on A481. Follow brown signs. O.S.GR: SO098535.

Charges 2004

Per unit incl. awning	£ 3.00
extra adult	£ 3.00
child (4-16 yrs)	£ 2.00
electricity	£ 2.00

Special senior citizen low season rate.
No credit cards.

Reservations

Contact park. Tel: 01982 570406. Email: office@fforestfields.co.uk

UK6310 Bacheldre Watermill Caravan Park

Churchstoke, Montgomery SY15 6TE (Powys)

A delightful little site, Bacheldre has just 25 pitches arranged around the perimeter of a grass meadow, with no site roads and just one lamp on the outside of the toilet block. However, there are 18 electric hook-ups (10A) and 5 hardstandings. Ideal for tenters and small units, it is not really suitable for large units and American RVs. The watermill is fully operational, producing high quality organic wheat flour, which can be purchased from reception, together with eggs and bread. The mill is not normally accessible, although guided tours can be arranged. Note: there are obvious hazards for small children – a deep partially fenced millpond, moving waterwheel and the stream.

Facilities

A portacabin provides the usual facilities including one controllable hot shower per sex with dishwashing sinks in a separate room. Calor gas stocked. Torches could be useful. Off site: Walking and cycling along Offa's Dyke 800 yards from site. Clun Castle ruins are worth a visit. Steam enthusiasts are well catered for with the Welshpool and Llanfair light railway. Supermarket at Churchstoke 2 miles.

Open

All year.

At a glance

Welcome & Ambience	✓✓✓✓	Location	✓✓✓✓
Quality of Pitches	✓✓✓✓	Range of Facilities	✓✓✓

Directions

Bacheldre is just off the A489 between Newtown and Churchstoke, 9 miles east of Newtown, 2 miles west of Churchstoke. Turn into narrow lane (signed), over bridge to site on the right. O.S.GR: SO243929.

Charges 2004

Per unit incl. 2 adults	£ 8.00 - £ 10.00
extra person	£ 2.00
No credit cards.	

Reservations

Advisable for B.Hs and peak season. Made with deposit of 50% of total fees. Tel: 01588 620489. Email: bacheldre@onetel.net.uk

UK6240 Cringoed Caravan Park

Cringoed, Llanbrynmair, Newtown SY19 7DR (Powys)

Cringoed is a pleasant, peaceful, small park with a river to one side, hills on the other and trees at either end. There are 50 spacious pitches of which 25 are in a level open touring field. Some of these have hardstanding and all have electricity (16A). Caravan holiday homes are at the far end amongst the trees. This is a relaxing base where you can sit and listen to the river and watch the wildlife, but it is also within easy reach of some of mid-Wales' best scenery and not far from the coast.

Facilities

The single toilet block is neat, modern and quite adequate. Laundry and dishwashing. Adventure play area. Small tourist information room. Off site: Shops 1 mile. Fishing 5 miles. Riding 12 miles.

Open

7 March - 7 January.

At a glance

Welcome & Ambience	✓✓✓✓✓	Location	✓✓✓✓
Quality of Pitches	✓✓✓✓	Range of Facilities	✓✓✓

Directions

From A470 between Newton and Machynlleth in the village of Llanbrynmair take B4518 signed Staylittle (caravan signs). After 1 mile just before bridge turn right, go over bridge and into site. O.S.GR: SH886014.

Charges 2004

Per unit incl. 2 persons	£ 11.00
extra person	£ 2.50
electricity	£ 2.00

Reservations

Contact site. Tel: 01650 521237.

UK6370 Hendre Mynach Touring Caravan & Camping Park

Llanaber, Barmouth LL42 1YR (Gwynedd)

A neat and tidy family park, colourful flowers and top rate facilities make an instant impression on arrival down the steep entrance to this park (help is available to get out if you are worried). The 200 pitches are allocated in various areas, with substantial tent areas identified. Forty gravel hardstandings are available and around the park there are 110 electricity hook-ups (10A). The seaside and fishing town of Barmouth is under a mile away, a 15-20 minute walk along the prom. The beach is only 100 yards away but a railway line runs between this and the park. It can be crossed by pedestrian gates which could be a worry for those with children. Snowdonia National Park and mountain railway, the Ffestiniog railway, castles and lakes everywhere provide plenty to see and do - a classic park in a classic area.

Facilities

Two toilet blocks, one modern and one traditional, both offer excellent facilities including spacious showers (free) and washbasins in cubicles in the new block. Facilities for disabled visitors. Motorcaravan services. Well stocked shop. Snack bar and takeaway (Easter - 1 Nov). Off site: Fishing, boat launching and bicycle hire within 0.5 miles. Riding 5 miles. Golf 9 miles.

Open

All year excl. 10 Jan - 28 Feb.

At a glance

Welcome & Ambience	✓✓✓✓	Location	✓✓✓✓
Quality of Pitches	✓✓✓✓	Range of Facilities	✓✓✓✓

Directions

Park is off A496 road north of Barmouth in village of Llanaber down a steep drive. O.S.GR: SH608168.

Charges 2005

Per unit incl. 2 persons, electricity	£ 8.00 - £ 20.00
2 adults and up to 3 children	£ 15.00 - £ 25.00
extra adult	£ 3.00
child (2-15 yrs)	£ 1.00
first dog free, extra dog	£ 0.50
Plus £1 per night for certain weekends.	

Reservations

Made with £20 deposit. Tel: 01341 280262. Email: mynach@lineone.net

UK6355 Woodlands Caravan Park

Harlech LL46 2UE (Gwynedd)

This delightful little site is lovingly tended by its owners and has just 15 pitches for tourists, all with gravel hardstanding and electric hook-up (10A) for caravans and motorcaravans only. Tents are not accepted. There are also 21 privately owned holiday homes, one for rent and a holiday cottage. However, the location of this site certainly makes up for its diminutive size, nestling under the massive rock topped by Harlech Castle, now a designated World Heritage Site. The narrow lane running alongside the site up to the old town above, is the steepest hill in Britain – no wonder the town is considering installing a funicular railway in the future. The coastal railway runs close to the site and the station is just 100 yards away. Railway noise should not be a problem (the small 'Sprinter' trains do not run at night). The 'Blue flag' beach is only 500 yards, and the Leisure Centre with its indoor pool is 250 yards.

Facilities

The modern stone built toilet facilities are heated, clean and tidy with controllable showers (25p), vanity style washbasins, a small laundry with a baby changing area, but with no dedicated facilities for disabled visitors (£5 deposit for the key to the facilities). Chemical disposal point but no motorcaravan service point. Off site: Harlech Castle. The town also has a theatre and cinema.. Nearby is Maes Artro Village with its Museum of Bygone Days. Portmeirion, location of the cult TV series 'The Prisoner', 8 miles. Barmouth (market Thursday & Sunday) 10 miles. Golf 0.25 mile. Fishing 3 miles. Riding 3 miles.

At a glance

Welcome & Ambience	✓✓✓✓	Location	✓✓✓✓✓
Quality of Pitches	✓✓✓✓	Range of Facilities	✓✓✓

Directions

From Barmouth take A496 to Harlech and continue downhill past Royal St David's Golf Course. Fork right immediately before railway crossing, and site is 200 yards on right. DO NOT turn towards town centre which lies on B4573, it is very narrow and congested. O.S.GR: SH583314.

Charges 2004

Per unit incl. 2 persons and electricity	£ 10.00
extra person	£ 2.00
awning	£ 1.50
No credit cards.	

Reservations

Recommended at all times. Tel: 01766 780419. Email: grace@woodlandscp.fsnet.co.uk

Open

1 March - 7 January.

UK6345 Glanllyn Lakeside Caravan & Camping Park

Llanuwchllyn, Bala LL23 7ST (Gwynedd)

This 16 acre site alongside the southern end of Bala lake has 204 pitches. With around 40 seasonal units, this leaves 164 tourist pitches, 94 of which have electric hook-ups. In this location, virtually all the pitches have wonderful views of the lake or the surrounding mountain sides. The terrain is grassy, fairly open and level, but with natural terraces. There are around ten individual hardstandings and a further hardstanding area by the beach is a favourite with motorcaravanners. The site is served by main tarmac access roads with speed bumps. Lake swimming is possible and the private beach allows easy access for windsurfing. The park is also an ideal base for some serious walking.

Facilities

A complex of three modern buildings (one can be heated and is used in low season) is located centrally at the rear of the site. All refitted in 2002 to a good standard, they provide a good supply of services including pre-set hot showers, hairdressing and shaver stations, a laundry and dishwashing room, facilities for babies and a suite for disabled people with keycode access. Motorcaravan service point. Well stocked shop at reception (Easter - Oct) and plenty of tourist information. Freezer pack service and gas supplies. Splendid, well fenced adventure style playground on bark surface. Bus stops outside site gate. Only 2 dogs per unit permitted (fenced dog walk area). Off site: Ideal for exploring the southern part of Snowdonia National Park. Bicycle hire, indoor swimming pool and golf in Bala 3 miles. Riding 18 miles.

At a glance

Welcome & Ambience	✓✓✓✓	Location	✓✓✓✓✓
Quality of Pitches	✓✓✓✓	Range of Facilities	✓✓✓✓

Directions

From Bala take A494 southwest towards Dolgellau for about 3 miles, entrance is on left, on right hand bend. O.S.GR: SH890325.

Charges 2004

Per unit incl. 2 persons	£ 10.00
1 extra adult	£ 3.00
child (9-16 yrs)	£ 2.00
child (3-8 yrs)	£ 1.00
electricity	£ 2.00
dog (max .2)	£ 1.00

Reservations

Essential for peak season and B.Hs (when min. stay is 3 nights) and made with £20 deposit. Tel: 01678 540227. Email: info@glanllyn.com

Open

Mid March (Easter) - mid October..

229

UK6340 Pen-y-Bont Touring & Camping Park

Llangynog Road, Bala LL23 7PH (Gwynedd)

This is a pretty little park with 35 pitches on level grass or hardstanding for caravans and 60 for tents on mainly sloping grass. Connected by circular gravel roads, they are intermingled with trees and tall trees edge the site. Electricity connections (16A) are available, including 11 for tents, and there are 24 new serviced pitches with hardstanding, electricity, water and drainage. The park entrance and the stone building that houses reception and the well stocked shop provide quite a smart image. With views of the Berwyn mountains, Pen-y-bont has a peaceful, attractive and useful location being the closest park to Bala town, 100 yards from Bala Lake and 3 miles from the Welsh National White Water Centre, with Snowdonia on hand.

Facilities

The toilet block includes washbasins in cubicles and spacious hot showers. Two new cubicles with washbasin and WC. Separate laundry room and an en-suite unit for disabled visitors, that doubles as a baby room, operated by key (£2 deposit). Outside covered area with fencing and concrete floor for dishwashing sinks and bins. Motorcaravan services. Shop. Caravan storage. Off site: Fishing 200 yds. Boat launching, bicycle hire, golf and riding 2 miles.

Open

1 April - 31 October.

At a glance

Welcome & Ambience	✓✓✓✓	Location	✓✓✓✓
Quality of Pitches	✓✓✓✓	Range of Facilities	✓✓✓✓

Directions

Park is 0.5 miles southeast of Bala village on the B4391. Bala is between Dolgellau and Conwen on the A494. O.S.GR: SH931349.

Charges 2004

Per unit incl. 2 persons	£ 10.10 - £ 11.10
with electricity	£ 12.30 - £ 13.30
extra person (over 5 yrs)	£ 1.00 - £ 3.00
awning	£ 2.00 - £ 2.30

Reservations

Made for exact dates for particular pitches, with deposit of £10 per pitch. Tel: 01678 520549.
Email: penybont@balalake.fsnet.co.uk

UK6350 Barcdy Caravan & Camping Park

Talsarnau, Harlech LL47 6YG (Gwynedd)

Barcdy is partly in a sheltered vale, partly on a plateau top and partly in open fields edged by woods, with fells to the rear and marvellous views across the Lleyn peninsula in one direction and towards the Snowdon range in another. The Roberts family opened to their first visitors sixty years ago, and they still welcome them today. The park provides for all tastes with level or sloping grass pitches, either secluded in the valley or enjoying the view from the plateau or the lower field. There are 108 pitches, including 38 for touring caravans and 40 for tents, with or without 10A electricity (50 electricity points), plus 30 caravan holiday homes. The grounds of the farm include 28 acres of open fields and natural oak woods (a haven for children) and further up the hills are the two Tecwyn lakes for fishing or just to relax by and enjoy the views. Harlech beach and the castle are only 4 miles, the Italianate village of Portmeirion is nearby and Snowdonia is on the doorstep. A member of the Countryside Discovery group.

Facilities

Two toilet blocks, the one at the top of the valley opened in high season only, include large, comfortable showers, that open direct to the outside. Two new family shower rooms at each block, one for each sex. Hot water is free to the washbasins and dishwashing sinks, metered to the showers (25p). Basic motorcaravan services. Shop for essentials including gas (open 8.30-11 am. and 4-7 pm. Spr. B.H, then mid July-end Aug). Dogs are not accepted. Off site: Riding 4 miles, golf 4 or 6 miles.

Open

Easter/1 April - 30 September.

At a glance

Welcome & Ambience	✓✓✓✓	Location	✓✓✓✓
Quality of Pitches	✓✓✓✓	Range of Facilities	✓✓✓

Directions

Park is just off the A496 between villages of Llandecwyn and Talsarnau, 4 miles north of Harlech. O.S.GR: SH622371.

Charges 2004

Per unit incl. 2 persons	£ 8.50 - £ 12.00
plus 2 children	£ 10.50 - £ 14.00
extra adult	£ 4.00 - £ 5.00
extra child (up to 16 yrs)	£ 1.00 - £ 1.50
electricity (10A)	£ 2.50

Reservations

Contact park. Tel: 01766 770736.
Email: anwen@barcdy.co.uk

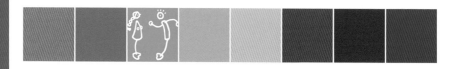

UK6580 Llanystumdwy Camping & Caravanning Club Site

Tyddyn Sianel, Llanystumdwy, Criccieth LL52 0LS (Gwynedd)

Overlooking mountains and sea, Llanystumdwy is one of the earliest Camping and Caravanning Club sites. Well maintained with good facilities, it is on sloping grass. However, the managers are very helpful and know their site and can advise on the most suitable pitch and even have a supply of chocks. There are 70 pitches in total (20 ft. spacing), 45 with 10A electricity connections, spaced over two hedged fields with mainly caravans in the top field with four hardstandings for motorcaravans, and with tents lower down. A little library with a supply of tourist information is next to the small reception. A shop and pub are in the village and a bus leaves each hour from outside the site to Pwllheli or Porthmadog. This is a good base from which to explore the Lleyn peninsula or Snowdonia National Park. Portmeirion with its Italianate village is near.

Facilities

A purpose-built toilet block to one side provides excellent, full facilities for disabled visitors including access ramp, one washbasin each in a cubicle for male and female and extra large sinks. Facilities for babies. Laundry (taps with fitting for disabled people). Gas supplies. Off site: Riding or fishing 0.5 miles, golf 2.5 miles. Beach 3 miles.

Open

March - October.

At a glance

Welcome & Ambience	✓✓✓✓	Location	✓✓✓✓
Quality of Pitches	✓✓✓	Range of Facilities	✓✓✓

Directions

Follow A497 from Criccieth west and take second right to Llanystumdwy. Site is on the right. O.S.GR: SH469384.

Charges 2005

Per adult	£ 4.30 - £ 6.40
child (6-18 yrs)	£ 1.90
non-member pitch fee	£ 5.00

Reservations

Necessary and made with deposit; contact site or Central Reservations 0870 243 3331. Site tel: 01766 522855.

For more site inspiration
see our directory ON PAGE 294

UK6590 Forestry Commission - Beddgelert Caravan & Camp Site

Caernarfon Road, Beddgelert LL55 4UU (Gwynedd)

This well equipped Forestry Commission site is in the heart of Snowdonia. Set in a marvellous, natural, wooded environment on the slopes of Snowdon there is abundant fauna and flora, tumbling streams and always something to watch from the cheeky squirrels to the smallest bird in Britain. Well equipped and well managed, the site provides 280 pitches - tents in a semi-wooded field area and caravans amongst the trees with numbered hardstandings, and 105 places with 10A electricity. Tents may pitch where they like in their areas leaving 6 metres between units or there are 6 new grass pitches with electrical hook-ups for tents. Metal tent pegs may be best (available from the shop). Free maps of the forest walks are provided in reception and orienteering and fishing are possible. A bus service stops at the top of the entrance lane (two hourly for Caernarfon and Porthmadog).

Facilities

Two fully equipped modern sanitary toilet blocks clad in natural wood provide large, free hot showers (with good dry areas). Laundry equipment is in one block. A small unit provides extra washbasins and toilets in peak season and there is a toilet and washbasin for disabled visitors. Excellent drive-through motorcaravan service point. Recycling bins. Reception is central, as is a well provisioned shop (Easter - end-Sept. approx). Well equipped adventure playground. Log cabin common room. Off site: Pub within walking distance (under a mile) and other eating places nearby. Bicycle hire within 500 m. in forest.

At a glance

Welcome & Ambience	✓✓✓✓	Location	✓✓✓✓✓
Quality of Pitches	✓✓✓✓	Range of Facilities	✓✓✓

Directions

Site is clearly signed to the left 1 mile north of Beddgelert on A4085 Caernarfon road. O.S.GR: SH578490.

Charges 2004

Per unit incl. 2 persons	£ 7.00 - £ 11.60
extra adult	£ 2.70
child (5-14 yrs)	£ 2.00
electricity	£ 2.50

Reservations

Necessary for B.Hs and peak times (min. 3 nights with £30 deposit). Contact (at all times): Forest Holidays, Forestry Commission, 231 Corstorphine Road, Edinburgh EH12 7AT. Tel: 0131 314 6505.

Open

All year except 4 November - 31 December.

231

UK6600 Bryn Gloch Caravan & Camping Park

Betws Garmon, Caernarfon LL54 7YY (Gwynedd)

Bryn Gloch is a well kept and family owned touring park in the impressive Snowdonia area - an unusual feature is the mountain railway which passes through the park. Neat and quiet, it takes some 160 units on five flat, wide meadows with some breathtaking views. With tarmac access roads and free areas allowed in the centre for play, 100 pitches have electricity connections (10A). These include 20 all weather pitches, 18 'super' pitches and 6 serviced pitches (shared), all with hardstanding. In addition, there are 12 caravan holiday homes. Fishing is possible on the river bordering the park with a barbecue and picnic area, adventure play area and field for ball games. Tourist information is provided in the complex by reception and the park is very popular with walkers and cyclists. Caernarfon with its famous castle is 5 miles.

Facilities

The two main toilet blocks (one recently refurbished) include washbasins in cabins, a family bathroom (hot water £1), baby room and complete facilities for visitors with disabilities (coded access). The far field has a 'portacabin' style unit containing all facilities, for use in peak season. Well equipped laundry and separate drying room. Motorcaravan service point and car wash. Shop (1/3-30/10). TV and games rooms with pool tables and amusement machines. Minigolf. Entrance barrier with coded access. Off site: Pub 1 mile. Riding 2.5 miles, bicycle hire or golf 5 miles.

Open

All year, limited facilities 1 Nov - 1 March.

At a glance

Welcome & Ambience	✓✓✓✓	Location	✓✓✓✓✓
Quality of Pitches	✓✓✓✓✓	Range of Facilities	✓✓✓✓

Directions

From Caernarfon take A4085 signed Beddgelert. Park is just beyond Waunfawr, 4.5 miles southeast of Caernarfon. At Betws Garmon, after crossing river bridge, watch for signs and entrance is opposite Saint Garmon church. O.S.GR: SH538578.

Charges 2004

Per unit incl. 2 persons	£ 12.00
extra adult	£ 2.00
child (3-16 yrs)	£ 1.50
electricity	£ 2.50
serviced pitch, plus	£ 4.50
awning or pup tent	£ 1.50

Reservations

Necessary for B.Hs. (min. 3 nights) with payment in full; other times with deposit of first night's fee. Tel: 01286 650216. Email: eurig@bryngloch.co.uk

UK6620 Plas Gwyn Caravan & Camping Park

Llanrug, Caernarfon LL55 2AQ (Gwynedd)

In a beautiful location, this traditional touring site is within the grounds of a house that was built in 1785 in the Georgian style with a colonial style veranda. Of historical interest, Prime Minister Lloyd George was a frequent visitor to Plas Gwyn House. The site is just 2.5 miles from the Llanberis Pass, the Snowdon Mountain Railway, the Electric Mountain Visitor Centre, and this is also good walking country. The 27 touring caravan pitches are set around the perimeter of a slightly sloping grass field, and there are four hardstandings for motorcaravans. The separate tent field has 10 pitches. There are 30 electric hook-ups (16A), and with minimal site lighting on the caravan field and none on the tent field a torch could be very useful. A further separate small field houses 18 caravan holiday homes. This site is not really suitable for American RVs. A member of the Countryside Discovery Group.

Facilities

An older style building houses the toilet facilities - although the fittings and tiling inside are modern and are kept neat and tidy. Controllable free hot showers, dishwashing sinks, a good laundry room (by reception), but no dedicated facilities for babies or disabled campers. Drive-over motorhome service point. Gas stocked. Reception stocks basic food items, etc. Off site: Llanberis and Snowdon Mountain Railway 2.5 miles, Golf 1 mile, riding, 2.5 miles, bicycle hire 3 miles, fishing 4 miles.

Open

1 March - 31 October.

At a glance

Welcome & Ambience	✓✓✓✓	Location	✓✓✓✓✓
Quality of Pitches	✓✓✓✓	Range of Facilities	✓✓✓

Directions

Site is on A4086, 3 miles from Caernarfon, and 2.5 miles from Llanberis, well signed with easy access. O.S.GR: SH522632.

Charges 2004

Per unit incl. awning and electricity	£ 6.50 - £ 10.00
tent pitch	£ 2.00 - £ 5.00
adult	£ 2.00
child (under 5 yrs)	£ 1.00
child (5 - 15 yrs)	£ 2.25

Reservations

Advised for peak season and B.Hs. Tel: 01286 672619. Email: info@plasgwyn.co.uk

UK6640 Home Farm Caravan Park

Marianglas, Anglesey LL73 8PH (Gwynedd)

A tarmac drive through an open field leads to this neatly laid out quality park, with caravan holiday homes to one side. Nestling below what was once a Celtic hill fort, later decimated as a quarry, the park is edged with mature trees and farmland. A circular, tarmac access road leads to the 61 well spaced and numbered pitches. There are 23 hardstanding pitches all with 16A electric hook-ups, including 9 larger pitches with TV hook-ups, water tanks and waste water drain, and 14 normal size pitches with water taps and waste water drain. All the remaining pitches have 10A hook-ups and are on neatly cut grass, some areas are slightly sloping, and there is a separate area for tents. The 'piece de resistance' of this park must be the children's indoor play area, large super adventure play equipment, complete with tunnels and bridges on safe rubber matting, not to mention an outside fenced play area and fields available for sports, football, etc. and walking. Various beaches, sandy or rocky, are within a mile. A member of the Best of British group.

Facilities

Two purpose built toilet blocks, one part of the reception building, are of similar design and can be heated. They include en-suite provision for people with disabilities (with key) and an excellent small bathroom for children with baby bath and curtain for privacy, a family room (with key), a laundry room and good washing up facilities. Motorcaravan service point. Reception provides basic essentials, gas and some caravan accessories. Indoor and outdoor children's play areas. TV and a pool table. Hard tennis (extra charge) with racket hire. Off site: Fishing or golf 2 miles, riding 8 miles.

Open

April - October.

At a glance

Welcome & Ambience	✓✓✓✓	Location	✓✓✓✓
Quality of Pitches	✓✓✓✓✓	Range of Facilities	✓✓✓✓

Directions

From the Britannia Bridge take second exit left signed Benllech and Amlwch on the A5025. Two miles after Benllech keep left at roundabout and park entrance is approx. 300 yards on the left beyond the church. O.S.GR: SH498850.

Charges 2004

Per unit incl. 2 persons	£ 10.25 - £ 15.75
incl. electricity and hardstanding	£ 14.50 - £ 19.00
incl. full services	£ 17.50 - £ 22.00
extra adult	£ 1.50 - £ 2.50
child (5-16 yrs)	£ 1.50 - £ 1.75
dog (max. 2)	£ 1.00 - £ 2.00

Reservations

Essential for peak season (min. 3 days at B.Hs) and made with £20 deposit. Tel: 01248 410614.
Email: enq@homefarm-anglesey.co.uk

UK6635 Fron Caravan & Camping Park

Brynsiencyn, Anglesey LL61 6TX (Isle of Anglesey)

A traditional, all touring campsite in a peaceful rural location, Fron has panoramic views over the surrounding countryside. From the entrance gate a tarmac drive passes through a two-acre level grass paddock, which is reserved for 35 large sized tent and trailer tent pitches. The drive leads up to the old farmhouse which houses reception, a well stocked shop, and plenty of tourist information. Behind the farmhouse is another two-acre sloping paddock with 40 caravan and motorcaravan pitches, 5 with hardstandings, and 37 electric hook-ups (10A). An adventure style playground is located in the tent paddock, and by the farmhouse a well fenced outdoor heated swimming pool (30 x 14 ft. and open May - Sept) is well controlled by the owners. No single sex groups are accepted. Torches would be useful. Only breathable groundsheets are permitted.

Facilities

Toilet facilities are in three units of varying ages and designs located at both sides of the farmhouse. These include a new unit for ladies with some basins in cubicles, good hot showers with dividers (20p), hairdryers, and a baby area with mat. Laundry with a twin tub washing machine and dishwashing sinks (hot water 30p). Motorcaravan service point. Outdoor heated swimming pool. Gas stocked. Recycling of glass and newspapers. Max. 2 dogs per pitch. Off site: Nearby are Anglesey Sea Zoo, Plas Newydd House, Foel Farm Park, Anglesey Transport and Agriculture Museum and the Menai Bridges. Brynsiencyn Village (0.5 mile) has a hotel and Spar shop. Anglesey Model village 0.5 mile. Fishing 1.5 miles, riding 3 miles, golf 4 miles.

At a glance

Welcome & Ambience	✓✓✓✓	Location	✓✓✓✓
Quality of Pitches	✓✓✓✓	Range of Facilities	✓✓✓✓

Directions

After crossing the Britannia Bridge, take first slip road signed Llanfairpwll A4080, then next left signed Newborough and Brynsiencyn. Continue on A4080 for 5 miles, turning right in village at the Groeslon Hotel. Continue through Brynsiencyn to site at western end of village. O.S.GR: SH475670.

Charges guide

Per unit incl. 2 adults and 2 children	£ 10.00
extra adult	£ 2.00
extra child	£ 1.00
electricity	£ 2.50
single person tent	£ 6.00
No credit cards.	

Reservations

Essential for peak season and B.Hs, and made with 25% deposit. Tel: 01248 430310.

Open

Easter - end September.

UK6690 Bron-Y-Wendon Touring Caravan Park

Wern Road, Llanddulas, Colwyn Bay LL22 8HG (Conwy)

Bron-Y-Wendon is right by the sea between Abergele and Colwyn Bay on the beautiful North Wales coast road. This is a quiet park which, by its own admission, is not really geared up for the family unit - there is no playground here, although there is a games room with table tennis and a TV room. The park is manicured to the highest standards and caters for a large number of seasonal caravans on pitches with gravel bases which are kept very tidy. There are a further 65 grass based, and 20 hardstanding touring pitches, all with electrical hook ups (16A) and tarmac access roads. All pitches have coastal views and the sea and beach are just a short walk away. Colwyn Bay, Conwy, Anglesey, Llandudno, Snowdonia and Chester are all within easy reach, so there is lots to do. Having said how peaceful and quiet everything is (particularly for a seaside park in this area), there is some road noise from the adjacent A55 and during our visit a small train passed on the tracks between the park and the sea (just a few yards) and at night with little else going on it could be just noticeable. Trailer tents are accepted, but not other tents.

Facilities
Two toilet blocks, both with heating, provide excellent facilities including men's and women's shower rooms separate from the toilets and washbasins. Good facilities for disabled visitors. Laundry with washing machines and dryers. Mobile shop visits daily. Gas supplies. Off site: Llanddulas village with shops and several good pubs is very near. Fishing 1 mile. Golf 4 miles. Riding 6 miles. Bicycle hire 15 miles.

Open
All year.

At a glance
Welcome & Ambience	✓✓✓	Location	✓✓✓
Quality of Pitches	✓✓✓✓	Range of Facilities	✓✓✓

Directions
From A55 Chester - Conwy road turn at Llanddulas interchange (A547), junction 23. Turn right opposite Shell garage and park is approx. 400 yards, signed on coast side of the road. O.S.GR: SH903785.

Charges 2004
Per unit incl. 2 persons, electricity	£ 12.00 - £ 15.00
extra person	£ 2.00
child (2 -12 yrs)	£ 1.00
awning	£ 2.00

Reservations
Made with £5 per night deposit; contact park.
Tel: 01492 512903.
Email: bron-y-wendon@northwales-holidays.co.uk

UK6650 Hunters Hamlet Caravan Park

Sirior Goch Farm, Betws-yn-Rhos, Abergele LL22 8PL (Conwy)

This small, family owned park is licensed for all units except tents (trailer tents allowed). On a gently sloping hillside providing beautiful panoramic views, one area provides 15 well spaced pitches with hardstanding and 10A electricity hook-ups, with access from a circular, hard-core road. A more recent area has been developed next to this of a similar design but with 8 fully serviced 'super pitches' (water, waste water, sewage, TV and electricity connections). Shrubs and bushes at various stages of growth enhance both areas. A natural play area incorporating rustic adventure equipment set amongst mature beech trees with a small bubbling stream is a children's paradise. Milk and papers can be ordered and the Hunters will do their best to meet your needs, even to survival rations! The park is well situated to tour Snowdonia and Anglesey and is within easy reach of Llandudno and Rhyl.

Facilities
The tiny heated toilet block has fully tiled facilities including showers en-suite with toilets for both sexes. A covered area to the rear houses laundry and dishwashing (H&C), washing machine and dryer, iron and board, freezer and fridge. Family bathroom (metered) and basic toilet and shower facilities for disabled visitors. Play area. All year caravan storage. Max. 2 dogs per pitch. Off site: Fishing or golf 2 miles, riding 10 miles.

Open
21 March - 31 October.

At a glance
Welcome & Ambience	✓✓✓✓	Location	✓✓✓✓
Quality of Pitches	✓✓✓✓	Range of Facilities	✓✓✓

Directions
From Abergele take A548 south for almost 3 miles; turn onto B5381 in direction of Betws-yn-Rhos and park is on left after 0.5 miles. To date there are no local authority caravan signs so watch carefully for the farm after turning - it can be identified by a artistically painted sign with the house and farm name: 'Sirior Goch Farm' and Hunter's Hamlet. O.S.GR: SH929736.

Charges 2005
Per unit incl. 2 adults, electricity	£ 12.00 - £ 15.00
super pitch (fully incl.)	£ 17.00 - £ 20.00
extra adult	£ 2.00
child	£ 1.00

Less £5 on weekly bookings. Aug. B.H, plus £1.00.

Reservations
Made with £20 deposit; B.H. bookings min. 4 nights.
Tel: 01745 832237. Email: huntershamlet@aol.com

UK6655 Ty Mawr Holiday Park

Towyn Road, Towyn, Abergele LL22 9HG (Conwy)

Ty Mawr is located close to the many attractions of the North Wales Coast and the Snowdonia National Park. It is an easy walk into the town of Towyn with seaside facilities and Rhyl some three miles along the coast is a busy resort with a fun fair and holiday amusements on its wide promenade. Ty Mawr is ideal for families seeking plenty of holiday park type activities, with organised children's clubs for 5-11 and 12-16 year olds. The whole family are catered for in the entertainment complex which provides mini ten-pin bowling, pool and darts. In the evening there are discos and live spectaculars. The heated indoor pool complete with flume is the venue for organised water-based activities. There are two areas for touring units, one on open meadows with facilities provided in 'portacabin' style units, the other in a more well established area near the entertainment facilities. Both areas are flat with views of open countryside. There is some traffic noise from the road adjacent to the meadow. There is a large proportion of privately owned and rental caravan holiday homes which are neatly sited on grass pitches.

Facilities

Two well maintained, functional blocks which can be heated serve the main touring area with 'portacabin' style units (unisex) on the open meadows. They are regularly cleaned. Washbasins are open style, preset showers have curtains and hooks, but no seats. Baby rooms. Facilities for disabled visitors (key). Launderette. Ice pack service. Shop. Bar with meals, cafeteria and takeaway. Indoor pool. Multi-sport courts. Excellent play areas and children's clubs. Evening family entertainment. Off site: Bicycle hire 0.5 miles. Golf, riding and boat launching 3 miles. Fishing 6 miles. Beach 0.25 miles.

At a glance

Welcome & Ambience	✓✓✓✓	Location	✓✓✓✓
Quality of Pitches	✓✓✓	Range of Facilities	✓✓✓✓

Directions

Take the A55 in a westerly direction into North Wales and take exit for Abergele. Follow signs for A548 Rhyl towards Towyn. Shortly after Towyn turn right into site. O.S.GR: SH965791

Charges 2004

Per unit incl. electricity	£ 6.00 - £ 25.00
tent	£ 3.00 - £ 25.00
dog	free - £ 3.00

Reservations

Contact site. Tel: 01745 832079.

Open

Easter - 30 October.

UK6700 Ty-Ucha Farm Caravan Park

Maesmawr Road, Llangollen LL20 7PP (Denbighshire)

Only a mile from Llangollen, world famous for the Eisteddfod, Ty Ucha has a rather dramatic setting, nestling under its own mountain and with views across the valley to craggy Dinas Bran castle. It is a neat, ordered park, providing 40 pitches (30 with 10A electrical hook-up) for caravans and motorcaravans only. They are well spaced round a large, grassy field with an open centre for play and a small paddock area. One side slopes gently and is bounded by a stream and wood in which a Nature Trail has been made. A path leads from here for various mountain walks, depending on your energy and ability. Because of overhead cables, kite flying is forbidden; no bike riding either. The paddock area provides for those who prefer to be without the company of children or dogs. Tents are not accepted.

Facilities

The single toilet block, although of 'portacabin' style, is clean and well maintained and can be heated. It includes two metered showers for each sex (a little cramped). Dishwashing sink with cold water outside. No laundry facilities but there is a launderette in Llangollen. Gas supplies. Games room with table tennis. Late arrivals area. Note: tents are not accepted. Off site: Hotel 0.5 miles with reasonably priced meals. Fishing 1 mile, golf 0.5 miles.

At a glance

Welcome & Ambience	✓✓✓✓	Location	✓✓✓✓✓
Quality of Pitches	✓✓✓✓	Range of Facilities	✓✓✓

Directions

Park is signed off A5 road, 1 mile east of Llangollen (250 yds). O.S.GR: SJ228411.

Charges 2005

Per unit incl. 2 persons	£ 7.00 - £ 8.00

No credit cards.

Reservations

Necessary for B.Hs. and Eisteddfod and made with £10 deposit; 3 days min. at B.Hs. Tel: 01978 860677.

Open

Easter - October.

(235)

UK6670 The Plassey Touring & Leisure Park

Eyton, Wrexham LL13 0SP (Wrexham)

Set in 247 acres of the Dee Valley, The Plassey offers many activities. It is not just a touring park but is also a leisure and craft centre with a friendly, busy atmosphere and pleasant environment. The Edwardian farm buildings have been tastefully converted to provide a restaurant, coffee shop, health, beauty and hair studio, a small garden centre and 16 different craft and retail units, open all year to the public. Unusually there is also a small brewery on site, producing its own unique Plassey Bitter! The park itself is spacious with pitches around the outer edges of a series of fields forming circles. There are 110 touring pitches with electrical connections (16A), including 30 new serviced pitches (with hard-standing, water, waste water, electricity, lighting). Five further areas take 120 seasonal caravans which may put pressure on the facilities at peak times. There is much to do and to look at in a rural setting at the Plassey but it is probably best enjoyed mid-week and avoiding the busy Bank Holidays. Certainly for peace and quiet, you should try and pitch away from reception, the clubhouse and arcade games.

Facilities

The original toilet facilities beside the entrance and under the clubhouse have been refurbished to a good standard. These are supplemented by a good, new heated block in the top field area with individual washbasin cubicles, a room for disabled visitors or families, dishwashing sinks and a larger laundry. Motorcaravan service point. Shop (all season) and gas. Club house with children's room (open March-Oct). Heated indoor pool with sunbed and sauna (May - Sept, limited hours mid-week, £1 per hour). Badminton court. Adventure playground with equipment for smaller children (note: bicycles, skateboards or footballs are not allowed). Nine hole golf course, fishing pools, wildlife meadow and countryside footpaths. Winter caravan storage. Red phone box. Off site: Riding 2 miles. Bicycle hire 5 miles.

At a glance

Welcome & Ambience	✓✓✓✓	Location	✓✓✓✓
Quality of Pitches	✓✓✓✓	Range of Facilities	✓✓✓✓✓

Directions

Follow brown and cream signs for The Plassey from the A483 Chester - Oswestry bypass onto the B5426 and park is 2.5 miles. Also signed from the A528 Marchwiel - Overton road. O.S.GR: SJ349452.

Charges 2004

Per unit incl. 2 adults, electricity	£ 12.50 - £ 15.50
serviced pitch	£ 4.00
extra person, dog or awning	£ 2.00

Includes club membership, coarse fishing, badminton and table tennis (own racquets and bats required). B.H. supplement £4 per weekend. Discount for weekly booking.

Reservations

Necessary for weekends, B.Hs and July/Aug. and made with £30 deposit. Tel: 01978 780277.
Email: enquiries@theplassey.co.uk

Open

March - October.

UK6680 James' Caravan Park

Ruabon, Wrexham LL14 6DW (Wrexham)

Open all year, this park has a heated toilet block and attractive, park-like surroundings with mature trees and neat, short grass. However, edged by two main roads it is subject to some road noise. The old farm buildings and owner's collection of original farm machinery, carefully restored and maintained, add interest. The park has over 40 pitches, some level and some on a slope, with informal siting giving either a view or shade. Electricity (6/10A) is available all over, although a long lead may be useful. Tourist information and a free freezer for ice packs are in the foyer of the toilet block. This is a useful park with easy access from the A483 Wrexham - Oswestry road.

Facilities

The heated toilet block offers roomy showers with a useful rail to help those of advancing age with feet washing. En-suite facilities for visitors with disabilities complete with special 'clos o mat' toilet! Motorcaravan service point. Gas available. Off site: The village is a 10 minute walk with a Spar shop, fish and chips, a restaurant, launderette and four pubs. Golf 3 miles.

Open

All year.

At a glance

Welcome & Ambience	✓✓✓✓	Location	✓✓✓
Quality of Pitches	✓✓✓	Range of Facilities	✓✓✓

Directions

Park is at junction of A483/A539 Llangollen road and is accessible from the west-bound A539. O.S.GR: SJ302434.

Charges 2005

Per unit incl. 2 persons and electricity	£ 10.00
extra person	£ 2.00
awning	£ 2.00
gazebo	£ 5.00
dog	£ 1.00

No credit cards.

Reservations

Contact park for details. Tel: 01978 820148.
Email: ray@carastay.demon.co.uk

From gentle rolling hills and rugged coastlines, to dramatic peaks, punctuated with beautiful lochs, Scotland is a land steeped in history that provides superb opportunities to enjoy wild, untamed and spectacular scenery.

We have divided the campsites in Scotland into the following regions:
Lowlands, Heart of Scotland, Grampians, and Highlands and Islands

Probably the most striking thing about Scotland is the vast areas of uninhabited landscape. Southern Scotland boasts beautiful fertile plains, woodlands and wild sea coasts, with many fantastic walking trails. It also has a rich heritage with ancient castles, abbeys and grand houses. Further north are the Trossachs with their heather-clad hills, home of Rob Roy, the folk hero. The Highlands and Islands, including Skye, Mull and Islay, have some of the most dramatic landscapes in Europe, dominated by breathtaking mountain ranges, such as Ben Nevis and the Grampians, plus deep glistening lochs: the largest being Loch Ness, where the monster reputedly lives. And lying at the very edge of Europe, the islands of the Inner and Outer Hebrides share a rugged natural beauty, with unspoilt beaches and an abundance of wildlife. The two largest cities in Scotland, Edinburgh and Glasgow, have their own unique attractions. The capital, Edinburgh, boasts magnificent architecture comprised of the medieval Old Town and the Georgian New Town, with the ancient castle standing proud in the middle; while a short distance to the west, Glasgow has more parks and over 20 museums and galleries, with numerous works by Charles Rennie Mackintosh scattered around the city.

Did you know?

Dunfermline Abbey is the final resting place of 22 kings, queens, princes and princesses of Scotland, including Robert the Bruce

Whales can be seen off the west coast of the Highlands, and the Moray Firth is home to bottle-nosed dolphins

Arbroath Abbey is the site where Scotland's nobles swore independence from England in 1320

Since 1861, every day (except on Sundays), the one o'clock gun has boomed out from Edinburgh castle

Charles Rennie Mackintosh, famous architect and designer, was born in Glasgow in 1868

Eas Coul Aulin near Kylesku in west Sutherland is Britain's highest waterfall at 200 metres – four times the height of Niagara

Ben Nevis is the highest mountain in the UK

Places of interest

Lowlands: Floors Castle near Kelso; Scottish Seabird Centre in North Berwick; Museum of Scotland and Balmoral Castle in Edinburgh; People's Palace, Burrell Collection in Pollock Park, Glasgow; Sweetheart Abbey near Dumfries; New Lanark World Heritage Site; Melrose Abbey

Heart of Scotland: fishing town of Oban; Stirling Castle and Wallace Monument; Loch Lomond; Pitlochry; university town of St Andrews; Aberdeen; Dunfermline Abbey; fishing villages of Crail and Anstruther; Famous Grouse Experience in Crieff

Highlands and Islands: Fort William; Eilean Donan Castle near Dornie; the Cairngorms; Highland Wildlife Part at Kingussie; Inverness; Aviemore; Urquhart Castle near Drumnadrochit; Jacobite Steam Train, operates between Fort William and Mallaig; Dunvegan Castle on the Isle of Skye

 tip

THE EDINBURGH FESTIVAL FRINGE, IN AUGUST, IS THE WORLDS LARGEST ARTS CELEBRATION, WITH ALL MANNER OF STREET PERFORMERS AND THEATRE PRODUCTIONS.

237

UK6950 Brighouse Bay Holiday Park

Brighouse Bay, Borgue, Kirkcudbright DG6 4TS (Dumfries and Galloway)

Hidden away within 1,200 exclusive acres, on a quiet, unspoilt peninsula, this spacious family park is only some 200 yards through bluebell woods from a lovely sheltered bay. It has exceptional all weather facilities, as well as golf and pony trekking. Over 90% of the 210 touring caravan pitches have electricity (10/16A), some with hardstanding and some with water, drainage and TV aerial. The three tent areas are on fairly flat, undulating ground and some pitches have electricity. There are 120 self-contained holiday caravans and lodges of which about 30 are let, the rest privately owned. On site leisure facilities include a golf and leisure club with 16.5 m. pool, water features, jacuzzi, steam room, fitness room, games room (all on payment), golf driving range and clubhouse bar and bistro. The 18 hole golf course extends onto the headland with superb views over the Irish Sea to the Isle of Man and Cumbria. A nine-hole family golf course is a popular attraction. Like the park, these facilities are open all year. The BHS approved pony trekking centre (April - Oct) offers treks for complete beginners, slow hacks for the nervous or inexperienced or gallops on the beach for the more experienced. This is a well run park of high standards and a member of the Best of British group.

Facilities

The large, well maintained main toilet block includes 10 unisex cabins with shower, basin and WC, and 12 with washbasin and WC, a launderette and covered dishwashing sinks. A second, excellent block next to the tent areas has en-suite shower rooms (one for disabled people) and bathroom, separate washing cubicles, showers, baby room, laundry sinks, and covered dishwashing sinks. One section is heated in winter. Motorcaravan service point. Gas supplies. Licensed supermarket. Bar, restaurant and takeaway (all year). Golf and Leisure Club with indoor pool (all year). Play area. Riding centre. Mountain bike hire. Quad bikes, boating pond, 10 pin bowling, playgrounds, putting. Nature trails. Coarse fishing ponds plus sea angling and an all-tide slipway for boating enthusiasts. Caravan storage.

At a glance

Welcome & Ambience	✓✓✓✓✓	Location	✓✓✓✓✓
Quality of Pitches	✓✓✓✓✓	Range of Facilities	✓✓✓✓

Directions

In Kirkcudbright turn onto A755 and cross river bridge. In 400 yards turn left onto B727 at international camping sign. Or follow Brighouse Bay signs off A75 just east of Gatehouse of Fleet. O.S.GR: NX630455.

Charges 2004

Per unit incl. 2 persons	£ 10.60 - £ 14.35
extra adult	£ 2.10
child (4-15 yrs)	£ 1.35
electricity	£ 3.00
fully serviced pitch	£ 4.00 - £ 4.50
awning	£ 1.10 - £ 2.10

Contact site for full tarrif. Low season golf packages. Camping Cheques accepted.

Reservations

Advance booking is advised and made with £30 deposit. Tel: 01557 870267. Email: info@gillespie-leisure.co.uk

Open

All year.

UK6900 Seaward Caravan Park

Dhoon Bay, Kirkcudbright DG6 4TJ (Dumfries and Galloway)

Seaward Caravan Park is little sister to the much larger Brighouse Bay Holiday Park, 3.5 miles away. Set in an idyllic location overlooking the bay, this park is suitable for all units. The terrain is slightly undulating, but most of the numbered pitches are flat and of a good size. There are 35 pitches (18 hardstandings) designated for caravans and motorcaravans, a further 14 for tents, plus 43 caravan holiday homes (6 for hire). Electric hook-ups (16A) are on 32 of the touring pitches and 12 are also serviced with water, drain and TV socket. Visitors can play golf on the park's nine-hole course (£3 per round) or watch others play while walking the dog around its perimeter. Facilities at the larger Brighouse Bay Holiday Park are available to all campers at discounted rates. This is a quiet park with excellent views ideally suited for that relaxing holiday or for touring the region.

Facilities

The principal, fully equipped toilet block is to the rear of the park. Four rooms with en-suite facilities are also suitable for disabled campers. Well equipped baby room. Laundry and dishwashing room. No motorcaravan service point but the manager can lift a manhole cover to empty waste water tanks. The reception/shop stocks basic provisions, books, gifts, gas, and tourist information. TV/family room. Unsupervised heated outdoor swimming pool with sunbathing area (15/5-15/9). Central play area with bark surface, outdoor chess, rocking horse, table tennis and picnic tables. Excellent games room. Golf. Off site: Beach and sea angling nearby. Riding or bicycle hire 3.5 miles. Kirkcudbright 2.5 miles.

Open

1 March - 31 October.

At a glance

Welcome & Ambience	✓✓✓✓✓	Location	✓✓✓✓
Quality of Pitches	✓✓✓✓	Range of Facilities	✓✓✓✓

Directions

In Kirkcudbright turn onto A755 signed Borgue. Go over river bridge and after 400 yards turn left onto B727 at international camping sign. Proceed with caution when turning right into site entrance as the turn is tight. O.S.GR: NX680510.

Charges 2004

Per unit incl. 2 persons	£ 9.30 - £ 12.65
extra adult	£ 1.70
child (4-15 yrs)	£ 1.30
electricity	£ 3.00
awning	£ 1.10 - £ 1.90
dog	£ 1.10

Less 5-10% for bookings (not valid with some other discount schemes).

Reservations

Made with deposit of £25 per week booked, balance on arrival. Tel: 01557 331079. Email: info@seaward-park.co.uk

238

Scotland

UK6880 Sandyhills Bay Leisure Park

Sandyhills, Dalbeattie DG5 4NY (Dumfries and Galloway)

Sandyhills Bay is a small, quiet park beside a sheltered, sandy beach. Reception is on the left through a car park used by visitors either walking the hills or enjoying the beach. Beyond is a large flat camping area, above which, divided by a tree lined hedge, are 60 pitches, half taken by mobile homes situated around the perimeter. The 30 touring pitches, 28 with electrical connection (16A) are in the centre of the all grassed flat area. This is an excellent family park, with the beach and a children's play area at the site, whilst up the hill next to the park is an 18 hole golf course where you can enjoy a bar meal in the club-house and within walking distance at Barend is an approved riding centre suitable for all the family. There is a well stocked licensed shop and a takeaway with table and chairs outside from where you can enjoy the well kept garden and splendid views across the Solway.

Facilities

The sanitary facilities are of traditional design, situated in one central block to the side of the touring area. Laundry room (tokens from reception). Shop and small takeaway. New adventure play area by the beach. Visitors can also use the facilities at Brighouse Bay the largest park in the Gillespie Group. Off site: Cliff top walk from Sandyhills to Rockcliffe approx. 10 miles. Pleasant drive to Rockcliffe and Kippford a well known sailing centre.

Open

23 March - 31 October.

Directions

From Dumfries take A710 Solway coast road (approx. 16 miles). Site is on left just after signs for Sandyhills. O.S.GR: NX890549.

Charges 2004

Per unit incl. 2 persons	£ 8.50 - £ 12.35
extra adult	£ 1.70
child (4-15 yrs)	£ 1.10
electricity	£ 3.00 - £ 2.30
awning	£ 1.10 - £ 1.80
dog	£ 1.10

Reservations

Made with £25 deposit. Tel: 01387 780257. Email: info@sandyhills-bay.co.uk

At a glance

Welcome & Ambience	✓✓✓✓	Location	✓✓✓✓
Quality of Pitches	✓✓✓✓	Range of Facilities	✓✓✓✓

UK6945 Barlochan Caravan Park

Palnackie, Castle Douglas DG7 1PF (Dumfries and Galloway)

Barlochan Caravan Park is situated on a hillside overlooking the Urr Estuary on the Solway Coast close to Dalbeattie and Castle Douglas, with the small village of Palnackie being a short walk away. Set on terraces, level, marked and numbered, most of the touring and tent pitches are on grass with a limited number of hardstandings available. There are 12 with electrical connections (16A). In addition, 55 mobile homes (5 for rent) are positioned on terraces high above the touring areas and screened by mature shrubs and trees. Just to the left of the entrance there is a minigolf course and an adventure play area screened from the park with mature trees. Through the village, under a mile from the park, there is a course fishing lake which is free for visitors to the park. Castle Douglas is just 9 miles away and gardeners will enjoy an afternoon at the well known Threave Gardens.

Facilities

The toilet block is of traditional design with pine ceiling and walls, kept spotlessly clean. Shower cubicles have recently been made larger suitable for wheelchair entry, but if required there is also a separate unit with WC and basin. Fully equipped laundry with outside drying area. Dishwashing under cover. Reception and well stocked shop. Heated outdoor swimming pool with large sunbathing area but parents must supervise, (mid May - mid Sept). Large games/TV room. Off site: Fishing 400 yds. Bicycle hire 6 miles. Golf 7 miles. Riding 10 miles. Beach 10 miles.

Directions

From Dumfries take A711 west to Dalbeattie. Continue through Dalbeattie for 0.5 miles and bear left at T-junction signd Auchencairn. Site is 2 miles on the right. O.S.GR: NX819571

Charges 2004

Per unit incl. 2 persons	£ 8.50 - £ 11.50
extra adult	£ 1.60
child (4-15 yrs)	£ 1.10
electricity	£ 3.00
dog	£ 1.10

Reservations

Contact site. Tel: 01556 600256.

Open

Easter - end October.

At a glance

Welcome & Ambience	✓✓✓✓✓	Location	✓✓✓✓✓
Quality of Pitches	✓✓✓✓	Range of Facilities	✓✓✓✓

UK6910 Hoddom Castle Caravan Park

Hoddom, Lockerbie DG11 1AS (Dumfries and Galloway)

The oldest part of Hoddom Castle itself is a 16th century Borders Pele Tower, or fortified Keep. This was extended to form a residence for a Lancashire cotton magnate, became a youth hostel and was then taken over by the army during WW2. Since then parts have been demolished but the original 'Border Keep' still survives, unfortunately in a semi-derelict state. The site's bar and restaurant have been developed in the courtyard area from the coach houses, and the main ladies' toilet block was the stables. The park is landscaped and spacious, well laid out on mainly sloping ground with many mature and beautiful trees, originally part of an arboretum. The drive to the site is just under a mile long, with a one way system. Many of the 120 numbered pitches have good views of the castle and have gravel hard-standings with grass for awnings, most with electrical connections (16A). In front of the castle are flat fields for tents and caravans not needing electricity. Amenities include a comfortable bar lounge with a family room and TV. The park's nine hole golf course is in an attractive setting alongside the Annan river, where fishing is possible for salmon and trout (tickets available). Coarse fishing is also possible elsewhere on the estate. This is a peaceful base from which to explore historic southwest Scotland.

Facilities

The main toilet block can be heated and is very well appointed, with washbasins in cubicles and an en-suite shower unit for disabled visitors. Two further tiled blocks, kept very clean, provide washbasins and WCs only. Each block has dishwashing sinks. Well equipped laundry room at the castle. Motorcaravan service point. Licensed shop at reception (gas available). Bar, restaurant and takeaway (restricted opening outside high season). Games room with pool tables, table tennis and video games. Large, grass play area. Crazy golf. Bicycle hire and mountain bike trail. Fishing. Golf. Guided walks organised in high season. Caravan storage. Off site: Tennis nearby.

At a glance

Welcome & Ambience	✓✓✓✓	Location	✓✓✓✓
Quality of Pitches	✓✓✓✓	Range of Facilities	✓✓✓✓✓

Directions

Leave A74M at junction 19 (Ecclefechan) and follow signs to park. Leave A75 at Annan junction (west end of Annan by-pass) and follow signs. O.S.GR: NY155725.

Charges 2005

Per unit incl. 2 persons	£ 7.00 - £ 12.00
small tent	£ 6.00 - £ 9.50
extra adult	£ 2.00
child (7-16 yrs)	£ 1.00
electricity (10A)	£ 2.50

Reservations

Necessary for July/Aug and B.Hs. Any length with deductible £10 deposit. Tel: 01576 300251. Email: hoddomcastle@aol.com

Open

1 April - 25 October.

- Fishing
- Walking
- Golf
- Cycle Hire

ENQUIRIES: The Warden, Hoddom Castle, Hoddom, Lockerbie DG11 1AS
Tel: 01576 300251 • www.hoddomcastle.co.uk • Email: hoddomcastle@aol.com

UK6870 Glenearly Caravan Park

Dalbeattie DG5 4NE (Dumfries and Galloway)

Glenearly is a new park (opened in 2000), owned and managed by Mr and Mrs Jardine. Rurally located, it has been tastefully developed from farmland into a touring and mobile home, all year park. There are 39 marked, open pitches, all with 16A electrical connections (and TV), mostly on level grass areas with 14 hardstandings available. Seasonal units use some pitches. Walls and shrubs divide the touring section from the caravan holiday homes (two for rent), with mature trees around the perimeter. There are attractive views over the hills and forest of Barhill and buzzards, yellow wagtails, woodpeckers and goldfinch are some of the birds that can be seen, along with the park's own donkeys, ponies and sheep. The large games room, converted from an old barn, is excellent - heated and with plenty of chairs and tables for parents to supervise the activities. A super play area suitable for all ages is conveniently situated behind the touring area. A ten minute stroll brings you into the small town of Dalbeattie.

Facilities

Situated in the centre of the touring area, the toilets and showers are fitted out to a high standard. Unit for disabled visitors or families. Laundry room with washing machines and dryer and an outside drying area. Large games room. Play area. Off site: Shops, pubs, restaurants, etc. at Dalbeattie. Bicycle hire at Mabie Forest just 3 miles from Dumfries on the A710.

At a glance

Welcome & Ambience	✓✓✓✓✓	Location	✓✓✓✓
Quality of Pitches	✓✓✓✓	Range of Facilities	✓✓✓✓

Directions

From Dumfries take A711 towards Dalbeattie and after 6 miles and beyond Beeswing pass sign for Edingham Farm, park is signed with entrance on right (beside a bungalow). O.S.GR: NX834626.

Charges 2004

Per unit incl. 2 persons	£ 8.50 - £ 10.00
electricity	£ 2.00 - £ 2.50

Reservations

Made with £10 deposit. Tel: 01556 611393.

Open

All year.

241

UK6930 Park of Brandedleys

Crocketford, Dumfries DG2 8RG (Dumfries and Galloway)

Brandedleys is a first class park providing pitches for some 75 caravans and a limited number of tents, plus 60 self-contained caravan holiday homes in three or four flat and variably sloping fields with tarmac access roads. It has excellent facilities and amenities. Caravan pitches are on lawns or terraced hard-standings, many with a pleasant outlook across a loch. There are 80 electrical connections (10A), 21 pitches with water and drainage, plus some 'premier' pitches with TV connections and a picnic bench. Improvements continue with more serviced pitches and a new fishing lake. A small, heated outdoor swimming pool is open when the weather is suitable and the heated indoor pool adjacent to the bar/restaurant is open all season with changing room and a sauna (both pools free). The bar and licensed restaurant are open for lunch and dinner with full menus at reasonable prices and a patio area over-looking Auchenreoch Loch. Walks on the open moors or forest and beautiful sandy beaches 12 miles away. A popular, quality park and a member of the Best of British group.

Facilities
The main heated toilet block has been extensively modernised with clean, well appointed shower cubicles with toilet and washbasin (just one for men), in addition to the normal provision. Bathroom for disabled visitors. Laundry room, baby and hair care room. Covered dishwashing sinks. A second block of equal size and standard is in the lower field, also with laundry and dishwashing facilities. Bar and restaurant. Takeaway food to order (18.00-21.30 hrs). Swimming pools. All-weather tennis courts, outdoor badminton court and draught board. Play area. Games room with TV. Table tennis, pool table and air-hockey table. Football pitch. Putting course and golf driving net. Fishing lake. Off site: Riding 5 miles. Golf 6 miles. Bicycle hire 9 miles. Beach 12 miles.

At a glance
Welcome & Ambience	✓✓✓✓✓	Location	✓✓✓✓✓
Quality of Pitches	✓✓✓✓	Range of Facilities	✓✓✓✓✓

Directions
Park is 9 miles from Dumfries on the south side of the A75 Dumfries - Stranraer road, just west of the village of Crocketford. O.S.GR: NX830725.

Charges 2004
Per unit incl. 2 persons, electricity	£ 12.50 - £ 18.00
family unit (5)	£ 15.50 - £ 21.00
serviced pitch	£ 2.00
awning	£ 2.00
pup tent	£ 3.00
No single sex groups.	

Reservations
Advised for peak dates and made with £20 deposit per pitch. Tel: 0845 4561759.
Email: brandedleys@holgates.com

Open
All year.

UK6890 Mossyard Caravan Park

Gatehouse of Fleet, Castle Douglas DG7 2ET (Dumfries and Galloway)

Mossyard is a family run park set within a working farm right beside the sea in a sheltered bay. The park and farmhouse appear together suddenly over the horizon and in the distance as you approach, with some breathtaking views across the Solway where the Galloway Hills and the waters of Wigtown Bay meet. On arrival you pass through the farm buildings into the park which is divided into two sections by stone walls. Around the perimeter are several new wooden chalets and holiday homes and self catering holiday cottages. There are 30 grass pitches (15 for tourers), some flat but most on an elevated sloping area, plus 20 for tents or motorhomes on a level camping field which adjoins the beach but is a little way from the sanitary facilities. Electrical connections (10A) are available for the caravans and some tent pitches. This is a wonderful park for outdoor activities such as watersports and fishing where small craft can be launched from site. Although some of the beaches and tides around the Solway Coast are dangerous, the one around this bay is very safe.

Facilities
Some of the farm buildings around the main farmhouse have been utilised for the toilet facilities, which are of traditional design. Showers are coin operated (20p). Facilities for disabled visitors are planned for 2005. Dishwashing area covered, with plenty of hot water. Airy laundry room with washing machine, dryer and spin dryer (coin operated). No shop on site but milk can be obtained from the farmhouse. Off site: Gatehouse of Fleet with shops, pubs and restaurants, 4 miles.

Open
Easter - October.

At a glance
Welcome & Ambience	✓✓✓✓	Location	✓✓✓✓✓
Quality of Pitches	✓✓✓✓	Range of Facilities	✓✓✓✓

Directions
Take A75 road from Dumfries towards Stranraer and park is signed to the left, 4 miles west of Gatehouse of Fleet, approx. 1 mile down a single track farm road. O.S.GR: NX547518.

Charges 2004
Per caravan	£ 9.00 - £ 10.00
motorcaravan	£ 8.00 - £ 9.00
tent	£ 8.00 - £ 10.00
electricity	£ 2.00
awing	free - £ 1.00

Reservations
Contact park. Tel: 01557 840226.
Email: enquiry@mossyard.co.uk

UK7020 Aird Donald Caravan Park

London Road, Stranraer DG9 8RN (Dumfries and Galloway)

Aird Donald is a good stopping off place when travelling to and from the Irish ferries, but it is also useful for seeing the sights around Stranraer. This tidy park comprises 12 acres surrounded by conifers, flowering trees and shrubs and the 300 yard drive is lit and lined with well trimmed conifers. There are grass areas for caravans or tents and hardstandings with electricity hook-up (these very handy for hardy winter tourers). A small play area caters for young children, but the local leisure centre is only a walk away and provides for swimming, table tennis, gym, etc, and a theatre that hosts everything from country and western to opera. It also has bar facilities. The area has three world famous gardens to visit, numerous golf courses, fishing, riding and watersports.

Facilities

Two toilet blocks, the new block modern and heated. Kept very clean with excellent, tiled facilities, this one is kept locked with a key deposit of £5. There are two types of shower, an electric one which is metered (20p) and two others which are free (strange, because they are all excellent). Washbasins in vanity units, ladies having one in a cubicle. Unit for visitors with disabilities has a washbasin and WC. The original block is being renovated but is more basic with free showers and open all the time. Dishwashing sinks and a small laundry with sinks, dryer, washing machine, an old fashioned mangle and clothes lines. Motorcaravan services. Play area.

At a glance

Welcome & Ambience	✓✓✓✓✓	Location	✓✓✓✓
Quality of Pitches	✓✓✓✓	Range of Facilities	✓✓✓✓

Directions

Enter Stranraer on A75 road. Watch for narrow site entrance on left entering town, opposite school. O.S.GR: NX075605.

Charges 2004

Per unit incl. 2 persons	£ 10.00
extra person (over 2 yrs)	£ 1.00
electricity	£ 1.80
awning	£ 1.00

No credit cards.

Reservations

Contact park. Tel: 01776 702025.
Email: aird@mimman.u-net.com

Open

All year.

UK7015 The Ranch Holiday Park

Culzean Road, Maybole KA19 8DU (South Ayrshire)

This holiday park is situated in the Ayrshire countryside, four miles from the small town of Maybole. The Ranch, a Caravan Club Affiliated Site, is managed by the McAuley family who moved here in November 2003. The park is beautifully set out with 55 spacious touring pitches, all with 10-16A electricity connections and including 8 super pitches. Most are on level hardstanding with a few level, all grass pitches arranged open plan facing a huge playing field. There are also 65 caravan holiday homes, 2 for rent. The superb facilities include a private Leisure Centre with an indoor heated pool, sauna, solarium and well equipped gym, complete with changing room, toilets, shower and free hair dryers. To the rear is a small unfenced play park adjacent to the small camping area which has undercover seating for those rainy days. A 'Wee Honesty Shop' offers exchange books and magazines and a kiddies corner for the under 5s. This is an excellent park for relaxing and enjoying the amenities or for touring the area with nearby sandy beaches at Maybole Shore and Croy Bay plus the wonderful freak of nature, where the laws of gravity are turned upside down at the Electric Brae, where you can see water run uphill.

Facilities

The sanitary facilities are away from the touring area and older in style, but kept spotlessly clean. Washbasins in vanity units, four in cubicles with WCs for ladies. Large showers operated individually by gas geysers. Individual unit with WC and basin for disabled visitors. Purpose built wooden building housing well equipped laundry with dishwashing area on the end. No shop on site but reception has a good information area. Off site: Golf courses at Turnberry and fishing at Mochram Loch.

At a glance

Welcome & Ambience	✓✓✓✓	Location	✓✓✓✓
Quality of Pitches	✓✓✓✓	Range of Facilities	✓✓✓✓

Directions

From Maybole turn onto B7023 (signed Culzean Maidens) for 1 mile and site is signed on left. O.S.GR: NS286102

Charges 2004

Per unit incl. 2 persons	£ 9.60 - £ 15.60
extra person	£ 3.30 - £ 4.80
child	£ 1.10 - £ 1.60

Reservations

Advised for summer season. Tel: 01655 882446.

Open

March - October.

UK7010 Culzean Castle Camping & Caravanning Club Site

Maybole KA19 8JJ (South Ayrshire)

With wonderful views of the Firth of Clyde and over to the Isle of Arran, this quiet Camping and Caravanning Club site is next door to Culzean Castle (pronounced Kullayne). Visitors are given a pass to walk in the grounds (when open) with their 17 miles of footpaths as many times as they wish. The 18th century, cliff top castle is built on the site of a former ancient castle and its armoury exhibition is superb. Besides the woodland walks, deer park and aviary, there are three miles of rocky shore and small sandy beaches. A full programme of events is staged at the castle over the season, including special children's weeks, sheepdog trials, bands, battle re-enactments, ranger walks and craft fairs. The campsite has 90 pitches, some level others slightly sloping, and 60 have electrical hook-ups (10A). A few level pitches are suitable for motorcaravans and 20 pitches have hardstanding. American style motorhomes (more than 27 ft.) must contact the site prior to arrival as large pitches are limited. Should you have your fill of the castle and its grounds, Maybole is only four miles and the area has a wealth of places to visit.

Facilities

The toilet blocks, kept very clean, can be heated and include some washbasins in cubicles. Unit for disabled visitors has a WC, washbasin and shower - an excellent facility. Dishwashing sinks. Well equipped laundry with clothes lines. Small shop with very basic provisions opens for short periods morning and evening. Adventure playground. Units over 25 ft long only accepted by prior arrangement. Off site: Golf or bicycle hire 4 miles, fishing 8 miles. Buses pass the gate.

Open

March - November.

At a glance

Welcome & Ambience	✓✓✓✓	Location	✓✓✓✓
Quality of Pitches	✓✓✓✓	Range of Facilities	✓✓✓✓

Directions

From Maybole follow signs for Culzean Castle and Country Park, turning in the town on B7023 which runs into the A719. Country Park entrance is clearly signed on right after 3.75 miles; entrance to caravan park is on the right in Country Park drive. O.S.GR: NS247103.

Charges 2005

Per adult	£ 4.30 - £ 6.40
child (6-18 yrs)	£ 1.90
non-member pitch fee	£ 5.00
services	£ 2.40

Reservations

Advised for high season and made with deposit; contact site or Central Reservations 0870 243 3331. Site tel: 01655 760627.

UK6960 Crossburn Caravan Park

Edinburgh Road, Peebles EH45 8ED (Borders)

A peaceful, friendly small park, suitable as a night stop, Crossburn is on the south side of the A703 road, half a mile north of the town centre. The entrance has a fairly steep slope down to reception and the shop which sells basic food items (as the town is so close) and a very large selection of caravan and camping accessories. Passing the caravans for sale and the holiday homes you might think that this is not the site for you, but persevere as the touring area is very pleasant, with attractive trees and bushes. Of the 50 pitches, 46 have electricity (16A), 20 have hardstanding and 8 are fully serviced. There is also a sheltered area for tents. The field behind the resident donkey has a nine hole putting green. If you decide to stay longer, the area has many places to visit and things to do. From historic homes, abbeys, woodland walks, fishing, horse riding, golf and canoeing - it's all there. Edinburgh is only 40 minutes drive. Perhaps the night halt may turn into a longer visit.

Facilities

There are two toilet blocks, the smaller one (which can be heated) with fairly basic facilities, the other more modern with washbasins in cubicles, free hairdryers and spacious, controllable free showers. Campers' kitchen (key at reception) with free use of an electric hot plate, kettle and fridge. Shop. Adjacent is a large games room with table tennis and games machines. Good play area on bark chippings. Riverside dog walk.

Open

Easter/1 April - end October.

At a glance

Welcome & Ambience	✓✓✓✓	Location	✓✓✓✓
Quality of Pitches	✓✓✓✓	Range of Facilities	✓✓✓✓

Directions

Park is by the A703 road, about 0.5 miles north of Peebles. O.S.GR: NT248417.

Charges 2004

Per unit incl. 2 persons	£ 10.00 - £ 11.00
with services	£ 12.00 - £ 15.00
extra person (5 yrs and over)	£ 1.00
awning	£ 2.00
hiker or cyclist plus tent	£ 5.00

Reservations

Advised for July/Aug. and made with £14 deposit including £2 fee. Tel: 01721 720501. Email: enquiries@crossburncaravans.co.uk

UK7030 Gibson Park Caravan Club Site

High Street, Melrose TD6 9RY (Borders)

This is an ideal transit park, being so close to the A68, but is also a perfect base for exploring this Southern Scotland area or indeed a trip to Edinburgh, as this is only 35 miles away by car or one of the regular buses which run from the park entrance. This small, three acre park has only 60 touring pitches plus, unusually, an extra 12 tent pitches (summer only) next to the adjacent rugby pitch. All touring pitches have electricity (16A) and TV connections (otherwise it is a bad signal here), 57 have hardstanding and 10 are serviced with water and drainage. A one-way system on the tarmac roads is in operation. This is Sir Walter Scott country - visit Abbotsford House, his romantic mansion on the banks of the River Tweed. Melrose's Abbey ruins are believed to be the final resting place of Robert The Bruce and the starting place of St Cuthbert's Way. A 62 mile, cross border trail leads to Northumberland's Lindisfarne.

Facilities

First rate toilet facilities are in a new building with spacious showers, washbasins in cabins, centrally heated and all fitted out with purpose made faced boarding giving a very pleasing finish. Laundry facilities. Separate room with shower and WC for disabled visitors. Motorcaravan service point. Gas is available. Off site: Situated on the edge of the little town of Melrose, a five minute walk, shops, pubs and restaurants are all in easy reach. Play area next to site.

Open

All year.

At a glance

| Welcome & Ambience | ✓✓✓✓ | Location | ✓✓✓✓ |
| Quality of Pitches | ✓✓✓✓ | Range of Facilities | ✓✓✓ |

Directions

Turn left off A68 Jedburgh - Lauder road at roundabout about 2.5 miles past Newton St Boswell onto A6091 Galashiels road. In about 3.25 miles at roundabout turn right onto B6374 to Melrose. Site is on right at filling station opposite Melrose Rugby Club, just before entering town centre. O.S.GR: NT545340.

Charges 2004

Per adult	£ 3.80 - £ 5.00
child (5-16 yrs)	£ 1.10 - £ 1.60
pitch incl. electricity (non-members)	£ 8.50 - £ 11.50

For tent pitches apply to site.

Reservations

Recommended at all times and made with £5 per night deposit. Tel: 01896 822969.

UK7050 Edinburgh Caravan Club Site

Marine Drive, Edinburgh EH4 5EN (Edinburgh)

Situated as it is on the northern outskirts and within easy reach of the city of Edinburgh, this large, busy Caravan Club site (open to non-members) provides an ideal base for touring. A bus (numbers 8A and 28A stop just outside the gates) takes you right into the centre of the city and within walking distance of many of its attractions. Enter the site through rather grand gates to find the visitors' car park and reception to the left. There are 147 large flat pitches (103 hardstandings, 12 with water tap and waste water disposal) with electric hook-ups (16A) and TV aerial and provision for 50 tents in a separate field (hook-ups available) with a covered cooking shelter and bicycle stands close by. As the bushes planted around the site mature, there will be shade. The nearest hotel/restaurant is about half a mile, Royal Yacht Britannia and many other attractions in the city, Firth of Forth bridge about 2 miles.

Facilities

Two heated, well kept toilet blocks provide washbasins in cubicles, hair and hand dryers, an en-suite room for campers with disabilities, plus a baby and toddler room with child-size facilities. Each block houses a dishwashing and vegetable preparation area, and a laundry. Drying room. No shop, but milk, bread, and newspapers can be ordered. You can purchase ice cream and exchange gas cylinders at reception. Fenced play area. Dog walk in the only natural wood in Edinburgh (part of the site).

At a glance

| Welcome & Ambience | ✓✓✓✓ | Location | ✓✓✓✓✓ |
| Quality of Pitches | ✓✓✓✓✓ | Range of Facilities | ✓✓✓ |

Directions

From A720 (signed City Bypass North), turn right at Gogar roundabout onto A8 and follow international camping signs. O.S.GR: NT212768.

Charges 2004

Per adult	£ 3.80 - £ 5.00
child (5-16 yrs)	£ 1.10 - £ 1.60
pitch incl. electricity (non-member)	£ 8.50 - £ 11.50

Tent campers apply to site.

Reservations

Made with £5 deposit, balance on arrival. Tel: 0131 312 6874.

Open

All year.

Planning your
next short break?

don't forget to see our directory
ON PAGE 294

UK6990 Mortonhall Caravan Park

38 Mortonhall Gate, Frogston Road East, Edinburgh EH16 6TJ (East Lothian)

The Mortonhall park makes a good base to see the historic city of Edinburgh and buses to the City leave from the park entrance every ten minutes (parking in Edinburgh is not easy). Although only four miles from the city centre, Mortonhall is in quiet mature parkland, in the grounds of Mortonhall mansion, and easy to find with access off the ring road. There is room for 250 units mostly on numbered pitches on a slight slope with nothing to separate them, but marked by jockey wheel points. Over 180 places have electricity (10/16A), several with hardstanding, water and drainage as well, and there are many places for tents. The park is very popular but only part is reserved and tourists arriving early may find space. An attractive courtyard development houses a lounge bar and restaurant, open all year and to all, with good value meals in pleasant surroundings.

Facilities

Two modern toilet blocks with outside, but covered dishwashing sinks, but the only cabins are in the third excellent facility at the top of the park, which has eight unisex units incorporating shower, washbasin and WC. The courtyard area provides further standard facilities and 'portacabin' type units are added for the high season to serve the large number of tents. Facilities for disabled visitors. Laundry room with washing machines and dryer. Bar/restaurant. Self-service shop. Games and TV rooms. Table tennis. Play area. Late arrivals area with hook-ups. Torches useful in early and late season. Security lockers, environmentally friendly recycling and a new motorcaravan service point have been added. Off site: Golf courses and driving range 2 miles. Riding 2 miles. Bicycle hire 4 miles.

At a glance

Welcome & Ambience	✓✓✓✓	Location	✓✓✓✓
Quality of Pitches	✓✓✓✓	Range of Facilities	✓✓✓✓

Directions

Park is well signed south of the city, 5 minutes from A720 city by-pass. Take Mortonhall exit from Straiton junction and follow camping signs. Entrance is beside Klondyke Garden Centre. O.S.GR: NT262686.

Charges 2005

Per unit incl. 2 persons	£ 10.00 - £ 16.00
with electricity	£ 12.00 - £ 18.00
extra person (5 yrs and over)	£ 1.50
awning	£ 2.50 - £ 5.00
dog	£ 1.50

Reservations

Made with 1 night's charge plus £1.50 fee. Tel: 0131 664 1533. Email: mortonhall@meadowhead.co.uk

Open

12 March - 4 January.

UK7060 Tantallon Caravan Park

Dunbar Road, North Berwick EH39 5NJ (East Lothian)

Tantallon is a large park with views over the Firth of Forth and the Bass Rock, which is a popular venue for bird-watchers with its world famous gannet colony. Tantallon and Dirleton Castles are also nearby. Access to the beach is through the golf course and then down the road or via cliff paths. The park has 147 quite large, grass touring pitches in two lower, more sheltered areas (Law Park), with the rest having good views at the top (Bass Park). Many have some degree of slope. There are 75 electrical connections (15A) and 10 pitches with water and drainage. Each area has its own toilet facilities. About 55 caravan holiday homes are in their own areas. This a mature, well managed park with good facilities.

Facilities

Bass Park has 8 unisex units with shower, washbasin and toilet. The other areas have open washbasins. Two heated units for disabled visitors. Dishwashing sinks. Good launderette with spin dryer and free iron. Motorcaravan service point. Small shop. Games room with pool table and TV. Good playground and better than average putting green. Dogs are only accepted by prior arrangement. Off site: Golf next door, sea fishing, safe sandy beaches in walking distance. Riding 5 miles. Bicycle hire 1 mile.

At a glance

Welcome & Ambience	✓✓✓	Location	✓✓✓✓
Quality of Pitches	✓✓✓✓	Range of Facilities	✓✓✓

Directions

Park is beside the A198 just east of North Berwick, between Edinburgh and Dunbar. O.S.GR: NT567850.

Charges 2004

Per unit	£ 8.00 - £ 15.00
with electricity	£ 10.00 - £ 17.00
dog	£ 1.00

Reservations

Advisable in July and August. Tel: 01620 893348. Email: tantallon@meadowhead.co.uk

Open

20 March - 31 October.

UK6980 Drum Mohr Caravan Park

Levenhall, Musselburgh EH21 8JS (East Lothian)

This family owned, attractively laid out touring park is on the east side of Edinburgh. It is a secluded, well kept modern park, conveniently situated for visits to Edinburgh, the Lothian and Borders regions. It has been carefully landscaped and there are many attractive plants, flowers and hedging. There are 120 individual pitches, 40 with hardstanding, for touring units of any type, well spaced out on gently sloping grass in groups of 12 or more, marked with white posts. Most have electric hook-ups and 13 are fully serviced with water and waste water connections. Free space is left for play and recreation. Five chalets to rent were added in 2002. Musselburgh centre is 1.5 miles, Edinburgh 7, with a frequent bus service to the latter. Managed personally by the owner, Mr Melville, this is a well run park and is a member of the Best of British group.

Facilities

The two toilet blocks are clean, attractive, of ample size and can be heated. Free hot water to washbasins (one cabin for men, two for ladies in each block) and to four external washing-up sinks, but hot water is on payment for the showers (outside the cubicle) and laundry sinks. Laundry facilities in each block. Motorcaravan service point. Well stocked, licensed shop (gas available, bread and papers to order). Playground on sand. Excellent dog walk. Off site: Golf course adjacent.

Open

1 March - 31 October.

At a glance

Welcome & Ambience	✓✓✓✓	Location	✓✓✓✓
Quality of Pitches	✓✓✓✓✓	Range of Facilities	✓✓✓✓

Directions

From Edinburgh follow A1 signs for Berwick on Tweed for 6-7 miles. Turn off for Wallyford and follow camp and Mining Museum signs. From south follow the A1 taking junction after Trenent village (A199 Musselburgh) and follow signs. O.S.GR: NT371732.

Charges 2004

Per unit incl. 2 persons	£ 12.00 - £ 14.50
extra person (over 5 yrs)	£ 1.50 - £ 2.00
awning	£ 1.50
extra pup tent	£ 2.00
service pitch incl. electricity	£ 4.00
dog	£ 0.50

Reservations

Made for any length with deposit of one night's charge plus £1 fee. Tel: 0131 665 6867. Email: bookings@drummohr.org

UK7040 Slatebarns Caravan Park

Slatebarns, Roslin EH25 9PU (Mid Lothian)

Slatebarns is a recently developed, well groomed park, perfectly located for that trip to Edinburgh, a nightstop on the way north or for local walks, including the nearby Pentland Hills. It has only 30 pitches, all with electricity hook-ups (10A), some with hardstanding (with grass for awnings) and some on grass (steel awning pegs useful). Buses run from the village (five minutes walk) regularly into Edinburgh (30 minute journey, 6 miles), although they are less frequent in the evening. Slatebarns is a small park with little on site for children or teenagers. Managed under contract for the Caravan Club, non-members are also very welcome. An ideal base to get away from the bustle after a full day in Edinburgh, or equally attractive as a touring base or country hideaway, it can unsurprisingly get busy.

Facilities

Small purpose built toilet block with washbasins in cubicles for ladies and excellent separate provision for those with disabilities. Good launderette. Very practical motorcaravan service point. Gas supplies. Off site: Village shops, pubs and hotels.

Open

Easter - 31 October.

At a glance

Welcome & Ambience	✓✓✓✓	Location	✓✓✓✓
Quality of Pitches	✓✓✓✓	Range of Facilities	✓✓✓✓

Directions

From Straiton junction on A720 (Edinburgh bypass) go south on A701 signed Bilston, Penicuik. At roundabout in Bilston turn left on B7006 signed Roslin. After 1 mile, in Roslin continue over crossroads signed Rosslyn Chapel. Site entrance is immediately past Chapel. O.S.GR: NT275632.

Charges 2004

Per pitch incl. electricity	£ 9.50 - £ 11.00
adult	£ 3.50 - £ 4.00
child	£ 1.20

No credit cards.

Reservations

Contact park for details. Tel: 0131 440 2192.

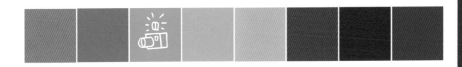

UK7230 Trossachs Holiday Park

Aberfoyle FK8 3SA (Perth and Kinross)

Nestling on the side of a hill, three miles south of Aberfoyle, this is an excellent base for touring this famously beautiful area. Lochs Lomond, Ard, Venachar and others are within easy reach, as are the Queen Elizabeth Forest Park and, of course, the Trossachs. This park specialises in the sale and hire of top class mountain bikes. Very neat and tidy, there are 45 well laid out and marked pitches arranged on terraces with hardstanding. All have electricity and TV connections and most also have water and drainage. There is also a large area for tents. There are trees between the terraces and lovely views across the valley. The adjoining oak and bluebell woods are a haven for wildlife, with wonderful walks. You will receive a warm welcome from Joe and Hazel Norman at this well run, family park. A member of the Best of British group.

Facilities

A modern wooden building houses sanitary facilities providing a satisfactory supply of toilets, showers and washbasins, the ladies' area being rather larger, with two private cabins. Laundry room. Well stocked shop (all season) and bike shop. Games room with TV. Play equipment (on gravel). Off site: Nearby are opportunities for golf, boat launching and fishing (3 miles). A passport scheme arranged with a local leisure centre (10 miles, 8 passes) provides facilities for swimming, sauna, solarium, badminton, tennis, windsurfing, etc.

At a glance

| Welcome & Ambience | ✓✓✓✓ | Location | ✓✓✓✓✓ |
| Quality of Pitches | ✓✓✓✓ | Range of Facilities | ✓✓✓✓ |

Directions

Park is 3 miles south of Aberfoyle on the A81 road, well signed. O.S.GR: NS544976.

Charges 2004

Per unit incl. 2 persons, electricity	£ 12.00 - £ 15.50
with all services	£ 14.50 - £ 18.00
tent pitch incl. 2 persons	£ 10.00 - £ 13.50
extra adult	£ 2.00

Reservations

Advisable and made for min. 3 days with £25 deposit. Tel: 01877 382614.
Email: info@trossachsholidays.co.uk

Open

1 March - 31 October.

UK7240 Lomond Woods Holiday Park

Tullichewan, Old Luss Road, Balloch G83 8QP (West Dunbartonshire)

A series of improvements over the last few years has made this one of the top parks in Scotland. Almost, but not quite, on the banks of Loch Lomond, this landscaped, well planned park is suitable for both transit or longer stays. Formerly known as Tullichewan Holiday Park, it takes 120 touring units, including 30 tents, on well spaced, numbered pitches on flat or gently sloping grass. Most have hardstanding, 106 have electrical connections (10A) and 8 have water and waste water too. Watersport activities and boat trips are possible on Loch Lomond, with a visitor attraction, 'Lomond Shores' opened nearby. This is a well run park, open all year, with very helpful wardens and reception staff. A member of the Best of British group.

Facilities

The single large heated, well kept toilet block includes some showers with WCs, baths for ladies, a shower room for disabled visitors and two baby baths. Covered dishwashing sinks. Launderette. Motorcaravan service points. Well stocked shop at reception. Games room with TV, table tennis and pool table. Playground. Leisure suite providing a sauna, sun-bed and spa-bath (on payment). Bicycle hire. Caravan storage. American motorhomes accepted with prior notice. Off site: Fishing and boat launching 400 yards, riding 4 miles, golf 5 miles. Rail and road connections to Glasgow. Restaurants and bar meals in Balloch (5 mins).

At a glance

| Welcome & Ambience | ✓✓✓✓✓ | Location | ✓✓✓✓ |
| Quality of Pitches | ✓✓✓✓✓ | Range of Facilities | ✓✓✓✓ |

Directions

Turn off A82 road 17 miles northwest of Glasgow on A811 Stirling road. Site is in Balloch at southern end of Loch Lomond and is well signed. O.S.GR: NS389816.

Charges 2004

Per unit incl. 1 or 2 persons	
and electricity	£ 13.00 - £ 18.00
incl. mains services and awning	£ 15.00 - £ 20.00
extra person	£ 2.00
dog	£ 0.50

Reservations

Made for any length with deposit of first night's charge and £2 fee. Tel: 01389 755000.
Email: lomondwoods@holiday-parks.co.uk

Open

All year.

Have you
forgotten something?
see the Alan Rogers directory
ON PAGE 294

UK7860 Glendaruel Caravan Park

Glendaruel PA22 3AB (Argyll and Bute)

Glendaruel is in South Argyll, in the area of Scotland bounded by the Kyles of Bute and Loch Fyne, yet is less than two hours by road from Glasgow and serviced by ferries from Gourock and the Isle of Bute. There is also a service between Tarbert and Portavadie. Set in the peaceful wooded gardens of the former Glendaruel House in a secluded glen surrounded by the Cowal hills, it makes an ideal centre for touring this beautiful area. The park takes 35 units on numbered hardstandings with electricity connections (10A), plus 15 tents, on flat oval meadows bordered by over 50 different varieties of mature trees. In a separate area are 28 privately owned holiday homes. The converted stables of the original house provide an attractive little shop selling basics, local produce, venison, salmon, wines (some Scottish!) and tourist gifts. Glendaruel is a park for families with young children or for older couples to relax and to enjoy the beautiful views across the Sound of Bute from Tighnabruaich or the botanical gardens which flourish in the climate. The owners, Quin and Anne Craig, provide a warm welcome and will advise you where to eat and what to do - they are justifiably proud of their park and its beautiful environment. A member of the Best of British group.

Facilities

The toilet block is ageing but it is kept very neat and tidy and can be heated. Washing machine and dryer. A covered area has picnic tables for use in bad weather and dishwashing sinks. Shop (hours may be limited in low season). Gas available. Games room with pool table, table tennis and video games. Behind the laundry is a children's play centre for under 12s and additional play field. Fishing. Torches advised. Off site: Sea fishing and boat slipway 5 miles, adventure centre (assault courses, abseiling and rafting) and sailing school close. Golf 12 miles.

Open

28 March - 26 October.

At a glance

Welcome & Ambience	✓✓✓✓	Location	✓✓✓✓✓
Quality of Pitches	✓✓✓✓	Range of Facilities	✓✓✓✓

Directions

Entrance is off A886 road 13 miles south of Strachur. Alternatively there are two ferry services from Gourock to Dunoon, then on B836 which joins the A886 about 4 miles south of the park - this route not advised for touring caravans. Note: the park has discount arrangements with Western Ferries so contact the park before making arrangements (allow 7 days for postage of tickets). O.S.GR: NS001865.

Charges 2004

Per unit incl. 2 persons	£ 10.00 - £ 13.00
extra adult	£ 2.00
child (3-15 yrs)	£ 1.50
electricity (10A)	£ 2.00

Special weekly rates and senior citizen discount outside July/Aug.

Reservations

Any length, with £10 deposit and £2 fee.
Tel: 01369 820267.
Email: enquiries@glendaruelcaravanpark.co.uk

UK7260 Ardgartan Forestry Commission Campsite

Ardgartan, Arrochar G83 7AR (Argyll and Bute)

Ardgartan is a rugged Forestry Commission site in the Argyll Forest Park. Splendidly situated with mountains all around and lovely views of Loch Long, there are lots of sightseeing and activity opportunities. At the northern end of the Cowal Peninsula, the site is on a promontory on the shores of Loch Long, with good sea fishing and facilities for launching small boats. The 160 touring pitches are in sections which are well divided by grass giving an uncrowded air. Most with hardstanding and marked by numbered posts, they are accessed from hard surfaced roads and 46 have electrical hook-ups. There are additional grass areas for tents. Walking and climbing, as well as sea and river fishing (permits obtainable locally), are all possible nearby. The site gate is locked 10.30 pm. - 7.30 am.

Facilities

The main toilet block is opposite the reception and shop with two small others (one for each sex) close by for the busiest periods. It is a basic, but clean provision with facilities for disabled visitors and a launderette. These facilities may be quite stretched when the park is busy. Play equipment is provided (bark surfaces). Raised barbecues are allowed. Off site: Arrochar village (2 miles) has fuel, general stores and a restaurant.

Open

21 March - 24 October.

At a glance

Welcome & Ambience	✓✓✓✓	Location	✓✓✓✓✓
Quality of Pitches	✓✓✓	Range of Facilities	✓✓✓

Directions

From A82 (Glasgow - Crianlarich) take A83 at Tarbet signed Arrochar and Cambletown. Site is 2 miles past Arrochar, the entrance on a bend. O.S.GR: NN275030.

Charges 2004

Per unit incl. 2 persons	£ 7.00 - £ 10.20
extra adult	£ 2.50
child (5-14 yrs)	£ 2.00
electricity	£ 2.50
'select' pitch incl. electricity	£ 3.60

Less 20% all year for disabled guests and outside 7/7-28/8 for senior citizens.

Reservations

Necessary for B.Hs and peak times (min. 3 nights with £30 deposit); contact site. Brochure requests: Forest Holidays, Forestry Commission, 231 Corstorphine Road, Edinburgh EH12 7AT. Tel: (0131) 314 6505. Tel: 01301 702293.
Email: fe.holidays@forestry.gsi.gov.uk

UK7310 Twenty Shilling Wood Caravan Park

Comrie PH6 2JY (Perth and Kinross)

Everyone gets a warm welcome from the Lowe family when they arrive at Twenty Shilling Wood. Set amongst 10.5 acres of wooded hillside, this unusual park has a few touring pitches for caravans and motorcaravans (no tents), plus a number of owner occupied caravan holiday homes. However, with terracing and landscaping, not many of these are visible and flowering trees and shrubs help to hide them. The lowest level is the entrance where there is a late arrivals area and visitor car park. The just 16 level touring pitches are on gravel with grass bays between them. All have 10A electricity hook-ups and because of poor TV reception, a free TV aerial hook up with lead provided. You will be escorted to your pitch. There are many walks in the area from strenuous Munros to a gentle stroll to the Devil's Cauldron waterfall.

Facilities

The clean and spacious toilet blocks have some washbasins in cubicles for both men and women. Dishwashing area and laundry. No shop but rolls, milk and papers can be ordered at reception. Games room with pool table, table tennis (both free) and lounge area with comfortable seating and well stocked library. Fenced adventure playground for all ages. Automatic entrance barrier; £10 deposit for card. Only two dogs per pitch are accepted. Off site: Buses pass the gate. Comrie is 1 mile where most things can be purchased. Golf or fishing within 1 mile, riding or bicycle hire 6 miles. Glen Turret, Scotland's oldest distillery is at Crieff, 7 miles away, Auchingarrich Wildlife centre is 2.5 miles, there are watersports at Loch Earn, 11 miles.

At a glance

Welcome & Ambience	√√√√√	Location	√√√√
Quality of Pitches	√√√√	Range of Facilities	√√√√

Directions

Park is on north side of A85 Crieff - Lochearmead road, about 0.75 miles west of B827 junction, 0.5 miles west of Comrie. O.S.GR: NN762222.

Charges 2004

Per unit incl. 2 adults, electricity and TV hook-up	£ 14.00
extra person (over 2 yrs)	£ 1.50
awning (rock pegs required)	£ 1.00

Reservations

Advised for B.Hs and July/Aug; made with £10 deposit. Tel: 01764 670411. Email: alowe20@aol.com

Open

23 March - 23 October.

UK7270 Auchterarder Caravan Park

Nether Coul, Auchterarder PH3 1ET (Perth and Kinross)

This is a charming small park, purpose designed and landscaped by the owners Stuart and Susie Robertson. In a sheltered position, it is conveniently situated for exploring central Scotland and the Highlands with many leisure activities close at hand (particularly golf) and within walking distance of the village (1 mile). The 21 original pitches, all with electricity (6A) and hardstanding, 12 with drainage, are well spaced around the edge of the elongated, level grass park. Marked pitches with grass frontage back on to raised banks which are planted with trees. Further pitches have been developed to one side of the site, along with a trout fishing pond (exclusively for campers) and a woodland walk. A tarmac area at the entrance for late arrivals (with electricity) ensures that no one is disturbed. Also at the entrance, a modern pine chalet blending with the environment houses reception and a small library. There is easy access from the nearby A9 road which does create some background road noise, although it is peaceful at night.

Facilities

Excellent toilet facilities with key system and piped music include controllable, well equipped hot showers. A toilet for disabled people is provided in both the male and female units. Laundry room with sink and washing machine; an iron can be provided. Dishwashing is under cover. Caravan storage. Off site: Golf 1 mile, bicycle hire or riding 6 miles. The historic cities of Perth and Stirling are less than half an hour's drive away.

Open

All year.

At a glance

Welcome & Ambience	√√√√√	Location	√√√√
Quality of Pitches	√√√√	Range of Facilities	√√√

Directions

Park is between the A9 and A824 roads east of Auchterarder village, only 0.5 miles from the main road. It is reached by turning on to the B8062 (Dunning) road from the A824. O.S.GR: NN964138.

Charges 2004

Per unit incl. up to 4 adults	£ 10.00
extra person (over 5 yrs)	. £ 1.00
awning	£ 1.00
electricity and drainage	£ 1.50 - £ 2.50
No credit cards.	

Reservations

Advisable July/Aug. and made with deposit of one night's charge and booking fee (£1). Bookings held until 5 pm. on day reserved. Tel: 01764 663119. Email: info@prestonpark.co.uk

UK7300 Blair Castle Caravan Park

Blair Atholl, Pitlochry PH18 5SR (Perth and Kinross)
This attractive, well kept park is set in the grounds of Blair Castle, the traditional home of the Dukes of Atholl. The castle is open to the public, its 32 fully furnished rooms showing a picture of Scottish life from the 16th century to the present day, while the beautiful grounds and gardens are free to those staying on site. The caravan park has a wonderful feeling of spaciousness with a large central area left free for children's play or for general use. There is space for 283 touring units with 196 electricity connections (10/16A), 144 hardstandings and 42 fully serviced pitches with water and waste water facilities also. Caravan holiday homes, 85 privately owned and 28 for hire, are in separate areas. The castle grounds provide many walking trails and the village is within walking distance with hotels, shops, a water mill craft centre and folk museum. A quality park, quiet at night and well managed. A member of the Best of British group.

Facilities
The five toilet blocks can be heated and are of excellent quality with very high standards of cleanliness. Large hot showers are free, some also incorporating WC and washbasin, and further cubicles with WC and washbasin. Four blocks have facilities for disabled visitors, two with bath, two with shower, all with WC and washbasins. Baby changing mats. Dishwashing. Motorcaravan service point. A new central development incorporates reception, a shop, games room, laundry and internet gallery. Gas supplies. American motorhomes are accepted (max. 30 ft or 5 tons). Off site: Mountain bike hire, riding, golf and fishing within 1 mile.

At a glance

Welcome & Ambience	✓✓✓✓✓	Location	✓✓✓✓✓
Quality of Pitches	✓✓✓✓✓	Range of Facilities	✓✓✓✓

Directions
From A9 just north of Pitlochry take B8079 into Blair Atholl. Park is in grounds of Blair Castle, well signed. O.S.GR: NN868659.

Charges 2004

Per unit incl. 2 persons	£ 10.00 - £ 13.00
tent (no car)	£ 8.00 - £ 11.00
child (5-12 yrs)	£ 0.50
electricity	£ 2.50
dog (max 2)	£ 0.50

Reservations
Made for any length with deposit of 1 night's charge.
Tel: 01796 481263.
Email: mail@blaircastlecaravanpark.co.uk

Open
1 March - 30 November.

BLAIR CASTLE CARAVAN PARK
BLAIR ATHOLL, PERTHSHIRE PH18 5SR   TEL: 01796 481263 FAX: 01796 481587
www.blaircastlecaravanpark.co.uk

★ 32 Acre Park set amidst spectacular mountain scenery
★ Grass and hard-standing mains serviced pitches
★ Spacious park and recreation areas
★ Extensive woodland, hill and riverside walks
★ Heated amenity blocks
★ Indoor Games Room and Television Lounge
★ Scottish Tourist Board rated Excellent
★ Holder of Thistle Award for our hire caravan holiday homes
★ Situated in the grounds of the historic and elegant Blair Castle (open to public)
★ Pony trekking, golf, fishing, bowling, mountain bikes all available from the village of Blair Atholl (100 yards)

PLEASE WRITE OR TELEPHONE FOR OUR FREE COLOUR BROCHURE

UK7292 Tayport Links Caravan Park

Tayport DD6 9ES (Fife)
Tayport Links Caravan Park is located on the seashore in the small fishing village of Tayport, overlooking the Firth of Tay. It is just a 10 minute drive from the city of Dundee, with its excellent shops and leisure facilities. The park is well laid out and attractively landscaped with 70 holiday homes (2 for rent) and a small secluded touring park. This currently provides 34 level touring pitches, some with hardstanding and some on grass, all with 10A electricity hook-ups. We are told, however, that touring units will not be taken after the 2005 season. There is no shop on site, but the village is just 10 minutes away.

Facilities
Traditional style sanitary block with WCs, open style washbasins and showers. Fully equipped laundry with washing machine, dryer and two laundry sinks. Covered dishwashing area. Telephone and information room. Torches may be useful. Off site: Sailing, boating and fishing on the Tay estuary. Good golf courses nearby.

Open
26 March - 31 October.

At a glance

Welcome & Ambience	✓✓✓✓	Location	✓✓✓✓✓
Quality of Pitches	✓✓✓✓	Range of Facilities	✓✓✓

Directions
Entering Tayport from north or south proceed on B945 and follow caravan park signs to left or right respectively. The park is by the sea, behind the recreation ground and is about 400 yards from the main road. O.S.GR: NO464283.

Charges 2004

Per pitch	£ 10.00 - £ 15.00
2-man tent	£ 8.00 - £ 12.00

Reservations
Necessary for July/Aug; contact park.
Tel: 01382 552334.

UK7320 Witches Craig Caravan Park

Blairlogie, Stirling FK9 5PX (Stirling)

Witches Craig is a neat and tidy park, nestling under the Ochil Hills and the friendly Stephen family take each visitor to their pitch to make sure that they are happy. All 60 pitches have 10A electrical hook-ups and 14 have hardstanding, 7 of these being large (taking American style motorhomes easily). Reasonably level, the park covers five well maintained acres with the grass beautifully manicured. Seven residential park homes are well kept and surrounded by flowering shrubs. The area has a wealth of historic attractions, starting with the Wallace Monument which practically overlooks the park. Its 220 ft. tower dominates the surrounding area and the climb up its 246 steps gives spectacular views. Stirling is known as the 'Gateway to the Highlands' and its magnificent castle is world renowned. Being by the A91, there is some day-time road noise. Trees have been planted to try to minimise this but the further back onto the park you go, the less the traffic is heard, although the main touring section with the sanitary facilities is at the front.

Facilities

The modern, heated toilet block is well maintained, and includes one cubicle with washbasin and WC each for ladies and men. Showers are on payment. Baby bath and mat. Good unit for disabled campers. Dishwashing sinks. Laundry, with free fridge/freezer facilities. Bread, milk, drinks and papers are available daily (supermarket 2.5 miles). Large fenced play area. Field for team games. Off site: Riding or bicycle hire 2 miles, fishing 3 miles, golf 1 mile. Buses stop at the park entrance. Within 10 miles there are castles, museums, cathedrals and parks. There are many walks from the site into the Ochil Hills

At a glance

Welcome & Ambience	✓✓✓✓	Location	✓✓✓✓
Quality of Pitches	✓✓✓✓	Range of Facilities	✓✓✓

Directions

Park is on the A91, 2 miles northeast of Stirling. O.S.GR: NS822968

Charges 2004

Per unit incl. 2 adults	£ 11.00 - £ 14.00
extra adult	£ 2.00
child (2-13 yrs)	£ 1.00
awning (no groundsheet)	£ 2.00

£5 deposit for key to facilities. No credit cards.

Reservations

Made without deposit. Tel: 01786 474947. Email: info@witchescraig.co.uk

Open

1 April - 31 October.

UK7290 Craigtoun Meadows Holiday Park

Mount Melville, St Andrews KY16 8PQ (Fife)

This attractively laid out, quality park has individual pitches and good facilities. Although outnumbered by caravan holiday homes, the touring section here is an important subsidiary. Its facilities are both well designed and comprehensive. With 67 units taken on gently sloping land, caravans go on individual hardstandings with grass alongside for awnings on most pitches. All caravan pitches are large (130 sq.m) and are equipped with electricity (16A), water and drainage. There are 15 larger 'patio pitches' with summer house, barbecue patio, picnic table and chairs, partially screened. Tents are taken on a grassy meadow at one end, also with electricity available. The 157 caravan holiday homes stand round the outer parts of the site; 27 are owned and let by the park. Buses pass the entrance and Craigtoun park with boating pond and miniature railway, etc. is within walking distance. This is a well run park, two miles from St Andrews with its golf courses and long, sandy beaches, from where there is a picturesque view of St Andrews and its ruined Abbey and Castle.

Facilities

An excellent, de-luxe, centrally heated sanitary building serves the touring area. All washbasins are in cabins and each toilet has its own basin. Showers are unisex, as are two bathrooms, with hand and hair dryers, facilities for disabled people and babies. Dishwashing room. Launderette. Shop and attractive licensed restaurant (both restricted hours in low seasons), also providing takeaway. Games room. Well equipped playground, play field and 8 acres of woodland. Barbecue area. All weather tennis court. Small information room. Dogs and other pets are not accepted. Off site: Fishing 5 miles. Golf or bicycle hire 1.5 miles. Riding 6 miles.

Open

1 March - 31 October.

At a glance

Welcome & Ambience	✓✓✓✓✓	Location	✓✓✓✓✓
Quality of Pitches	✓✓✓✓✓	Range of Facilities	✓✓✓✓

Directions

From M90 junction 8 take A91 to St. Andrews. Just after sign for Guardbridge (to left, A919), turn right at site sign and sign for Strathkinness. Go through village, over crossroads at end of village, left at next crossroads, then 0.75 miles to park. O.S.GR: NO482151.

Charges 2005

Per unit incl. 3-6 persons and electricity	£ 16.50 - £ 23.00
tent incl. 2 persons	£ 15.50 - £ 22.00
backpacker's tent (1 person)	£ 13.50

Only 'breathable' type groundsheets may be used in awnings.

Reservations

Advised for main season; any length with full payment at time of booking. Tel: 01334 475959. Email: craigtoun@aol.com.

UK7280 Nether Craig Caravan Park

By Alyth, Blairgowrie PH11 8HN (Perth and Kinross)

Nether Craig is a family run touring park, attractively designed and beautifully landscaped, with views across the Strathmore valley to the long range of the Sidlaw hills. The 40 large pitches are accessed from a circular, gravel road; 26 have hardstanding (for awnings too) and 10A electrical connections. The majority are level and there are 9 large tent pitches on flat grass. There is a personal welcome for all visitors at the attractive wooden chalet beside the entrance (with a slope for wheelchairs) which doubles as reception and shop providing the necessary essentials, gas and tourist information. A one mile circular woodland walk from the park has picnic benches and a leaflet guide is provided. Otherwise you can just enjoy the peace of the Angus Glens by hill walking, birdwatching, fishing or pony trekking. Alyth with its Arthurian connections is only 4 miles away and Glamis Castle, the childhood home of the Queen Mother, is nearby, as is the beautiful Glenshee and Braemar with its castle.

Facilities

The central, purpose built toilet block is modern, well equipped and maintained, and can be heated. Unit for disabled visitors (entry by key). Separate sinks for dishwashing and clothes are in the laundry room (metered hot water), plus a washing machine, dryer and iron, and a rotary clothes line outside. Shop. Play area. Small football field. Bicycle hire. Caravan storage. Off site: Fishing 2 miles. Riding 4 miles. Three golf courses within 4 miles. Boat launching 6 miles.

At a glance

Welcome & Ambience	✓✓✓✓✓	Location		✓✓✓✓
Quality of Pitches	✓✓✓✓✓	Range of Facilities		✓✓✓

Directions

From A926 Blairgowrie - Kirriemuir road, at roundabout south of Alyth join B954 signed Glenisla. Follow caravan signs for 4 miles and turn right onto unclassified road signed Nether Craig. Park is on left after 0.5 miles. O.S.GR: NO265528.

Charges 2005

Per unit incl. 2 persons, electricity	£ 13.50 - £ 15.50
tent per person	£ 4.50
extra person	£ 1.50 - £ 2.50

Reservations

Advisable for main season. Tel: 01575 560204. Email: nethercraig@lineone.net

Open

15 March - November.

UK7400 Lochlands Caravan Park

Dundee Road, Forfar DD8 1XF (Angus)

Lochlands Caravan Park is situated just off the A90 road, near the town of Forfar. The entrance to the park is past the coffee shop and garden centre following the caravan sign. Mr and Mrs Delft moved to this garden centre and caravan park three years ago and during that time have created an excellent, well maintained park suitable for a night visit or a long stay to visit the east coast towns of Arbroath and Montrose. Attached to the large shop, which has various gifts for home and garden, there is a most unusual and attractive coffee shop which was originally a horse mill used in the 1800s. Homemade food is served at reasonable prices and for the gardening enthusiasts - a show of camellias during March and April. The park is level with 40 marked pitches, several with hardstanding and all with 10A electricity. Dividing the park is a mature hedge with a large grass area which could be used for recreation or camping and there is a well equipped play area.

Facilities

Toilets and showers are in two 'portacabin' style buildings near the entrance but are excellent and spotlessly clean. Dishwashing area divides units. No laundry. Shop and coffee shop/café (Thursday, Friday and Saturday, all year). Play area. Off site: Fishing 5 miles. Golf 3 miles. Riding 10 miles.

Open

All year.

At a glance

Welcome & Ambience	✓✓✓✓	Location		✓✓✓✓
Quality of Pitches	✓✓✓✓	Range of Facilities		✓✓✓✓

Directions

From Dundee take A90 north for 7 miles, turning right at Forfar sign (A932). Site is immediately on right at rear of garden centre. O.S.GR: NO444478.

Charges 2004

Per adult	£ 3.50 - £ 4.50
child (5-16 yrs)	£ 1.25
pitch & 2 people	£ 7.00
with electricity	£ 13.00

Reservations

Made with £10 deposit. Tel: 01307 463621. Email: vandelft@btinternet.com

UK7550 Huntly Castle Caravan Park

The Meadow, Huntly AB54 4UJ (Aberdeenshire)

Huntly Caravan Park was opened in '95 and its hard-working owners, the Ballantynes, are justly proud of their neat, well landscaped 15 acre site that is managed under contract for the Caravan Club (non-members welcome). The 76 level grass and 41 hardstanding, numbered touring pitches are separated, with everyone shown to their pitch. Arranged in three bays with banks of heathers and flowering shrubs separating them, 66 pitches have electric hook-ups (16A) and 15 are fully serviced with water and waste water. Two bays have central play areas and all three have easy access to a toilet block, as has the camping area. Campers are provided with a covered cooking shelter (with work tops) should the weather turn inclement. The park also has 33 privately owned caravan holiday homes (3 to hire). An Activity Centre near the entrance contains two indoor safe play areas (one for up to 2 yrs old, the other up to height 1.37 metres). There are snooker and pool tables, table tennis, badminton and short tennis. The area abounds with things to do, from forest trails to walk or cycle, a falconry centre, malt whisky distilleries and an all year Nordic ski track. A member of the Best of British group.

Facilities

The three heated toilet blocks are well designed and maintained, with washbasins (in cubicles for ladies) and large, free showers. Each block also has a family shower room (even larger), dishwashing sinks with free hot water and a good room for disabled visitors. Well equipped laundry room. No shop but milk and papers may be ordered at reception. Activity centre (there is a charge and the facilities are also open to the public, with tea, coffee and ices sold; open weekends and all local school holidays). Off site: The town of Huntly is only 10 minutes walk with shops and pubs and castle. Fishing, golf or bicycle hire within 1 mile, riding 5 miles

At a glance

Welcome & Ambience	✓✓✓✓✓	Location	✓✓✓✓✓
Quality of Pitches	✓✓✓✓✓	Range of Facilities	✓✓✓✓

Directions

Site is well signed from A96 Keith - Aberdeen road. O.S.GR: NJ526402.

Charges 2004

Per unit incl. 2 persons, electricity	£ 12.30 - £ 15.50
extra adult	£ 2.50
child (5-16 yrs)	£ 1.30 - £ 1.70
awning	£ 1.00 - £ 1.75
pup tent	£ 1.75

Reservations

Contact park. Tel: 01466 794999.
Email: enquiries@huntlycastle.co.uk

Open

24 March - 29 October.

UK7530 Aden Country Park Caravan Park

Station Road, Mintlaw AB42 8FQ (Aberdeenshire)

Aden Country Park is owned by the local authority and is open to the public offering several attractions for visitors including an Agricultural Heritage Centre, Wildlife Centre, Nature Trail and restaurant, as well as open and woodland areas with a lake, for walking and recreation. The caravan and camping site is on one side of the park. Beautifully landscaped and well laid out with trees, bushes and hedges, it is kept very neat and tidy. It provides 48 numbered pitches for touring units, with varying degrees of slope (some level) and all with electrical hook-ups (16A), plus an area for tents. There are also 12 caravan holiday homes in a row on the left as you enter. The park is in a most attractive area and one could spend plenty of time enjoying all it has to offer.

Facilities

The modern, fully tiled toilet block, with good facilities for disabled visitors, was very clean when we visited. It can be heated and provides free, pre-set hot showers, hairdryer for ladies, and a baby bath, but no private cabins. Dishwashing and laundry facilities are together, with washing machines, tumble and spin dryers and an iron - all metered. Small shop (sweets and ice-creams) in the reception area. Restaurant in the Heritage Centre. Two games areas and items of play equipment (with safety surfaces). Large dog exercise area. Off site: Mintlaw half a mile for shopping. Fishing 1 mile, riding 2 miles.

At a glance

Welcome & Ambience	✓✓✓✓	Location	✓✓✓✓
Quality of Pitches	✓✓✓✓	Range of Facilities	✓✓✓✓

Directions

Approaching Mintlaw from the west on A950 road, park is shortly after sign for Mintlaw station. From the east, go to the western outskirts of the village and entrance is on left - 'Aden Country Park and Farm Heritage Centre'. O.S.GR: NJ985484.

Charges 2004

Per unit incl. electricity	£ 12.40 - £ 13.90
small tent per person	£ 3.70 - £ 4.70
awning	£ 1.05 - £ 1.15

Reservations

Advisable for weekends; write for details.
Tel: 01771 623460.

Open

Easter - 25 October.

UK7540 Aberlour Gardens Caravan & Camping Park

Aberlour-on-Spey AB38 9LD (Moray)

This pleasant park is within the large walled garden of the Aberlour Estate on Speyside. Mr and Mrs Moss, the owners, have made many improvements to the sheltered, five acre, family run park which provides a very natural setting amidst spruce and Scots pine. Of the 64 level pitches, 35 are for touring units leaving the remainder for holiday homes (1 for rent) and seasonal units. All pitches have electrical connections (10A) and 9 are 'all-weather' pitches. This is an ideal area for walking, birdwatching, salmon fishing and pony trekking or for following the only 'Malt Whisky Trail' in the world, while Aberlour has a fascinating old village shop - a 'time capsule'.

Facilities

The toilet block can be heated and has four large unisex showers on payment and facilities for disabled visitors (can be used as family or baby changing room). Laundry facilities. Motorcaravan service point. Small licensed shop stocking basics and with an information area. Play area. Caravan storage. Off site: Fishing 1 or 5 miles, golf 4 miles, riding 0.5 miles, swimming or bicycle hire 1 mile.

Open

1 April - 31 October.

At a glance

Welcome & Ambience	✓✓✓✓✓	Location	✓✓✓✓✓
Quality of Pitches	✓✓✓✓✓	Range of Facilities	✓✓✓

Directions

Turn off A95 midway between Aberlour and Craigellachie onto unclassified road and site is signed in 500 yds. Vehicles over 10'6" high should use A941 Dufftown road (site signed). O.S.GR: NJ282432.

Charges 2004

Per caravan, motorcaravan, trailer tent incl. 2 persons	£ 11.50 - £ 14.50
tent incl. 2 persons	£ 7.50 - £ 9.00
extra person (over 5 yrs)	£ 2.00
backpacker and tent (per person)	£ 5.00 - £ 6.00

Reservations

Advised for July/Aug; made with deposit (1 nights fee). Tel: 01340 871586. Email: Aberlourgardens@aol.com

UK7670 Grantown-on-Spey Caravan Park

Seafield Avenue, Grantown-on-Spey PH26 3JQ (Highland)

John Fleming takes care of this excellent park which is managed under contract for the Caravan Club (non-members are welcome). Peacefully situated on the outskirts of the town, with views of the mountains in the distance, the park consists of well-tended gravel (raked so that it is perfect for each occupant) and grass pitches. Trees and flowers are a feature of this landscaped location. There are 100 pitches for caravans or motorcaravans, of which 15 offer fresh and waste water facilities and 16 have individual fresh water taps. A further 20 pitches are used for seasonal occupation, and there is space for 50 or more tents. More than 80 pitches have 10A electrical hook-ups. The wardens escort visitors to their pitch and will help to site caravans if necessary. Caravan holiday homes are located in a separate area of the park. Grantown is a pleasant touring base for the Cairngorms and for the Malt Whisky Trail. A peaceful park with a warden on site at all times.

Facilities

A new toilet and shower block is planned, complete with laundry and drying room. A further block provides good, clean toilet facilities, with new wash-cabins for ladies. Dishwashing sinks under cover. Laundry room. New motorcaravan service point planned. No shop because the town is just a short distance, however gas cylinders, ice creams, cold drinks and camping accessories can be purchased at reception. Games room with table tennis and pool table. Winter caravan storage. Off site: Fishing, golf and mountain bike hire within 1 mile, riding 3 miles.

At a glance

Welcome & Ambience	✓✓✓✓✓	Location	✓✓✓✓
Quality of Pitches	✓✓✓✓	Range of Facilities	✓✓✓

Directions

Park is signed from the town centre. O.S.GR: NJ028283.

Charges 2004

Per pitch incl. 2 persons and 10A electricity	£ 13.00 - £ 15.00
small 2-man tent	£ 7.00 - £ 9.00
extra person	£ 1.50 - £ 2.50

Reservations

Advised for peak periods and made with £10 deposit. Tel: 01479 872474. Email: team@caravanscotland.com

Open

28 March - 31 October.

Grantown-on-Spey
In the heart of the Highlands......a warm welcome awaits!
01479 872474 www.caravanscotland.com
e-mail: team@caravanscotland.com
Seafield Avenue, Grantown-on-Spey Ph26 3JQ

UK7680 Forestry Commission - Glenmore Caravan & Camping Site

Aviemore PH22 1QU (Highland)

The site managers here have made tremendous improvements to this site, which had been neglected for a while. The Glenmore Forest Park lies close to the sandy shore of Loch Morlich amidst conifer woods and surrounded on three sides by the impressive Cairngorm mountains. It is conveniently situated for a range of activities, including skiing (extensive lift system), orienteering, hill and mountain walking (way-marked walks), fishing (trout and pike) and non-motorized watersports on the Loch. The campsite itself is attractively laid out in a fairly informal style in several adjoining areas connected by narrow part gravel, part tarmac roads, with access to the lochside. One of these areas, the Pinewood Area, is very popular and has 32 hardstandings (some distance from the toilet block). Of the 220 marked pitches on fairly level, firm grass, 137 have electricity (10A). This site with something for everyone would be great for family holidays.

Facilities

We understand that there are to be improvements to the sanitary facilities during the winter of 2004/5. We will report on these following our next visit. Next to the site is a range of amenities including a well stocked shop (open all year), a café serving a variety of meals and snacks, and a Forestry Commission visitor centre and souvenir shop. Barbecues are not permitted in dry weather. Off site: The Aviemore centre with a wide range of indoor and outdoor recreations 7 miles. Several golf courses within 15 miles. Fishing and boat trips.

Open

All year except 1 November - 19 December.

At a glance

Welcome & Ambience	✓✓✓✓✓	Location	✓✓✓✓
Quality of Pitches	✓✓✓✓	Range of Facilities	✓✓✓

Directions

Immediately south of Aviemore on B9152 (not A9 bypass) take B970 then follow sign for Cairngorm and Loch Morlich. Site entrance is on right past the loch. O.S.GR: NH976097.

Charges 2004

Per unit incl. up to 4 persons	£ 7.80 - £ 12.90
extra person (over 5 yrs)	£ 2.00
electricity	£ 2.60
'select' pitch incl. electricity	£ 11.80 - £ 16.90

Less 20% all year for disabled guests and outside 7/7-28/8 for senior citizens.

Reservations

Made with £30 deposit (min. 2 days or 3 at B.Hs). Contact. Forest Holidays, Forestry Commission, 231 Corstorphine Road, Edinburgh EH12 7AT. Tel: 0131 314 6505. Site tel: 01479 861271. Email: fe.holidays@forestry-gsi.gov.uk

UK7690 Torvean Caravan Park

Glenurquhart Road, Inverness IV3 6JL (Highland)

Torvean is a small and neat, select touring park for caravans and motorhomes only. It is situated on the outskirts of Inverness beside the Caledonian Canal and is within easy reach of the town's amenities which include an ice rink, theatre and leisure sports centre. Excursions to the coast and Highlands, including Loch Ness, are possible in several directions. The pitches on level grass are clearly marked with a tarmac access road and street lighting giving a very neat appearance. There are 47 touring pitches (27 with 10A electricity connections, 18 fully serviced with fresh water tap, waste water disposal and electricity).

Facilities

Two heated toilet blocks are of good quality - ladies have two cubicles with washbasin and toilet and a hair washing cubicle. Controllable hot showers on payment. Suite for disabled people with toilet and shower. Launderette. Motorcaravan service point. Gas available. Play area. Only one dog per unit is accepted. Off site: Golf adjacent, bicycle hire or fishing 3 miles.

Open

Easter - end-October.

At a glance

Welcome & Ambience	✓✓✓✓	Location	✓✓✓✓
Quality of Pitches	✓✓✓✓	Range of Facilities	✓✓✓

Directions

Park is off the main A82 road on the southwest outskirts of the town by the Tomnahurich Canal Bridge. O.S.GR: NH638438.

Charges guide

Per unit incl. 2 adults	£ 9.00 - £ 9.50
extra adult	£ 2.00
child (under 16 yrs)	£ 1.00
electricity	£ 2.50
de-luxe pitch incl. electricity	£ 12.50 - £ 13.00
awning	£ 2.00 - £ 3.00

No credit cards.

Reservations

Necessary for July/Aug. and made with first night's charge and £1 fee. Tel: 01463 220582.

UK7700 Pitgrudy Caravan Park

Poles Road, Dornoch IV25 3HY (Highland)

In a rural situation, Pitgrudy has superb views over the Dornoch Firth and the surrounding Ross-shire hills. There are 40 touring pitches for caravans, motorcaravans or tents, mostly on slightly sloping grass and with electrical connections (10A). A few have hardstanding (unfortunately still on a slope) and six are fully serviced (drinking water, waste water disposal point and electricity). Located at the top of the park are 35 caravan holiday homes, of which 25 are privately owned. The whole park is on immaculately tended grass with tarmac roads. The pleasant little town of Dornoch is less than a mile away with shops, restaurants, plus the cathedral. A member of the Best of British group.

Facilities

Sanitary facilities are in a modern, superior 'portacabin' style unit which is very clean and well equipped. Laundry with washing machine, dryer and iron. Dishwashing sinks. Gas supplies. Off site: Safe sandy beach 1 mile. The area is good for walking and golf (there are 7 courses within 15 miles of the park). Fishing 1 mile, bicycle hire or boat launching 3 miles, riding 5 miles.

Open

25 April - 30 September.

At a glance

Welcome & Ambience	✓✓✓✓	Location	✓✓✓✓✓
Quality of Pitches	✓✓✓✓	Range of Facilities	✓✓✓

Directions

At the war memorial in Dornoch, turn north (park signed) on the B9168. Park is 0.5 miles on the right (45 miles north of Inverness). O.S.GR: NH795911.

Charges guide

Per unit incl. 2 persons	£ 7.50 - £ 12.00
extra person	£ 0.75 - £ 1.50
electricity	£ 2.50

No credit cards.

Reservations

Made with deposit (1st night's rent) and £1 fee. Contact: GNR Sutherland, Caravan Sales, Edderton, Tain, Ross-shire IV19 1JY. Tel: 01862 821253.

UK7720 Woodend Camping & Caravan Park

Achnairn, Lairg IV27 4DN (Highland)

Woodend is a delightful, small park overlooking Loch Shin and perfect for hill walkers and backpackers. Peaceful and simple, it is owned and run single-handedly by Mrs Cathie Ross, who provides a wonderfully warm Scottish welcome to visitors. On a hill with open, panoramic views across the Loch to the hills beyond and all around, the large camping field is undulating and gently sloping with some reasonably flat areas. The park is licensed to take 55 units and most of the 22 electrical hook-ups (16A) are in a line near the top of the field, close to the large, fenced play area. There are opportunities for fishing and hill walking. The famous Falls of Shin is an ideal place to see the salmon leap (about 10 miles).

Facilities

The sanitary facilities are of old design but kept very clean and are quite satisfactory. Laundry with two machines and a dryer. Kitchen with dishwashing sinks and eating room for tent campers. Reception is at the house, Sunday papers, daily milk and bread may be ordered. Fishing licences for the Loch (your catch will be frozen for you).

Open

1 April - 30 September.

At a glance

Welcome & Ambience	✓✓✓✓✓	Location	✓✓✓✓
Quality of Pitches	✓✓✓	Range of Facilities	✓✓✓

Directions

Achnairn is near the southern end of Loch Shin. Turn off the A838 single track road at signs for Woodend. From the A9 coming north take the A836 at Bonar Bridge, 11 miles northwest of Tain. O.S.GR: NC558127.

Charges 2005

Per unit incl. electricity	£ 8.00 - £ 9.00
tent	£ 7.00 - £ 8.00

No credit cards.

Reservations

Not considered necessary Tel: 01549 402248.

UK7710 Ardmair Point Caravan Park

Ardmair Point, Ullapool IV26 2TN (Highland)

This spectacularly situated park, overlooking the little Loch Kanaird, just round the corner from Loch Broom, has splendid views. The 68 touring pitches are arranged mainly on grass around the edge of the bay, in front of the shingle beach. Electrical hook-ups (10A) are available and some gravel hardstandings are on the other side of the access road, just past the second toilet block. Tent pitches, together with cheaper pitches for some tourers are in a large field behind the other sanitary facilities. Scuba diving is popular at Loch Kanaird because the water is so clear. Seals and otters are regularly seen in the bay and the area is full of interest, including visits to Inverewe Gardens and the Isle Martin bird and seal colonies.

Facilities

Two toilet blocks, both with good facilities. One block has views from the large windows in the launderette and dishwashing rooms, plus large en-suite rooms for disabled people. Motorcaravan service point. Limited shop. Play area. Off site: Ullapool 3 miles. Golf or bicycle hire 3 miles.

Open

1 May - late September, depending on the weather.

At a glance

Welcome & Ambience	✓✓✓✓	Location	✓✓✓✓✓
Quality of Pitches	✓✓✓✓	Range of Facilities	✓✓✓

Directions

Park is off the A835 road, 3 miles north of Ullapool. O.S.GR: NH109983.

Charges 2004

Per unit incl. 2 persons	£ 9.50 - £ 13.00
extra adult	£ 2.00 - £ 3.00
child (over 5 yrs)	£ 1.00 - £ 1.50

Reservations

Recommended for July/Aug. (min. 2 nights). Tel: 01854 612054. Email: sales@ardmair.com

UK7730 Scourie Caravan & Camping Park

Harbour Road, Scourie IV27 4TG (Highland)

Mr Mackenzie has carefully nurtured this park over many years, developing a number of firm terraces with 60 pitches which gives it an attractive layout – there is nothing regimented here. Perched on the edge of the bay in an elevated position, practically everyone has a view of the sea and a short walk along the shore footpath leads to a small sandy beach. Access roads are tarmac and gravel, with well drained grass pitches and some hard-core hardstandings with electricity. A few are on an area which is unfenced from the rocks (children would need to be supervised here). There are very good facilities for disabled visitors, although the ramps leading to them are a little steep. Mr Mackenzie says that this is the only caravan park in the world from where, depending on the season, you can see palm trees, Highland cattle and Great Northern divers from your pitch. The clear water makes this area ideal for diving.

Facilities

Toilet facilities can be heated. Showers have no divider or seat. Fully equipped laundry and dishwashing sinks. Motorcaravan services. The 'Anchorage' restaurant (used as reception at quiet times) is large and well appointed with meals cooked to order (I/4-30/9). Boat launching. Fishing permits (brown trout) can be arranged. Off site: The village has a well stocked shop with post office, gas is available from the local petrol station and mobile banks visit.

Directions

Park is by Scourie village on A894 road in northwest Sutherland. O.S.GR: NC153446.

Charges 2004

Per unit incl. 1-2 adults	£ 10.00
electricity	£ 2.00
No credit cards.	

Reservations

Not made. Tel: 01971 502060.

Open

1 April - 30 September, but phone first to check.

At a glance

Welcome & Ambience	✓✓✓	Location	✓✓✓✓✓
Quality of Pitches	✓✓✓✓	Range of Facilities	✓✓✓✓

UK7740 Loch Greshornish Camping Site

Arnisort, Edinbane IV51 9PS (Isle of Skye)

This spacious site with simple facilities is a beautiful, peaceful setting with views over the loch to the low hills to the northwest of Skye. There are 30 level grass pitches for motorcaravans and caravans, 28 with 10A electric hook-ups. There are also places for up to 100 tents (but numbers never reach that level). A new building houses reception and a small shop selling basic essentials and including an off-licence. The owners offer bicycle hire (with safety helmets) and canoe hire, with plans including a play area.

Facilities

The refurbished toilet facilities are light, airy and spotlessly clean. A new block and laundry is planned. Showers are a little cramped. Dishwashing sink in the ladies' and another in the men's. Laundry service. Camper's shelter with seating, cooking and eating area. Small shop. Bicycle hire. Canoe hire. Off site: The village has two hotels for drinks and meals; Portree, the nearest town, 15 miles. Riding 2 miles. Golf 5 miles.

Directions

Site is 15 miles west of Portree on the A850 Dunvegan road by Edinbane. O.S.GR: NG343524.

Charges 2004

Per person	£ 1.25 - £ 3.50
tent	£ 1.00 - £ 1.50
electricity	£ 1.75

Reservations

Advised for high season. Tel: 01470 582230. Email: info@skyecamp.com

Open

Easter - 15 October.

At a glance

Welcome & Ambience	✓✓✓✓✓	Location	✓✓✓✓✓
Quality of Pitches	✓✓✓✓	Range of Facilities	✓✓✓

UK7750 Staffin Caravan & Camping Site

Staffin IV51 9JX (Isle of Skye)

This simple camping site is on the side of a hill just outside Staffin, where the broad sweep of the bay is dotted with working crofts running down to the sea. A marked walk from the site leads to the seashore and slipway (good for walking dogs but too far to be taking a boat). With 50 pitches, the site is quite sloping but there are 18 reasonably level pitches with irregular hardstanding, all with electrical hook-ups (16A). Skye has many activities to offer and for the truly dedicated walker the Cuillins are the big attraction. However, the road from Portree is not suitable for caravans and large motorhomes.

Facilities

The sanitary block includes large, controllable showers. Washing up sinks are not under cover and have only cold water. An older block is only opened at very busy times. Large hardstanding area has a motorcaravan service point. Gas. Off site: Fishing or boat launching 1 mile, bicycle hire 5 miles, riding 9 miles. Staffin village is 400 yards and has a large shop (open six days a week), a restaurant, launderette.

Open

1 April - 30 September.

Directions

Site is 15 miles north of Portree on A855 (2 miles of single track at the start), just before 40 mph signs on the right. O.S.GR: NG496668.

Charges 2004

Per unit incl. 2 persons		£ 7.50 £ 9.50
extra person		£ 1.00 - £ 3.00
electricity		£ 1.50
No credit cards.		

Reservations

Maybe necessary for peak periods (made with £10 deposit), but will always try to fit you in. Tel: 01470 562213. Email: staffin@namacleod.freeserve.co.uk

At a glance

Welcome & Ambience	✓✓✓✓	Location	✓✓✓
Quality of Pitches	✓✓✓	Range of Facilities	✓✓✓

UK7760 Reraig Caravan Site

Balmacara, Kyle of Lochalsh IV40 8DH (Highland)

This is a small, level park close to Loch Alsh with views over to Skye and a wooded hillside behind (criss-crossed with woodland walks). Set mainly on well cut grass, it is sheltered from the prevailing winds by the hill and provides just 45 numbered pitches, 36 with electrical connections (10A) and some hard-standings. Large tents and trailer tents are not accepted at all. Small tents are permitted at the discretion of the owner, so it would be advisable to telephone first if this affects you. Awnings are not permitted during July and August in order to protect the grass. The ground can be stony so there could be a problem with tent pegs. Reraig makes a good base from which to explore the Isle of Skye and the pretty village of Plockton with its palm trees (remember Hamish Macbeth on TV?) Reservations are not necessary but it may be best to arrive before late afternoon in July and August.

Facilities

The single sanitary block has been extensively refurbished and is kept immaculately clean. Children have their own low basins, controllable hot showers are on payment (10p for 2 minutes). Sinks for clothes and dishwashing. Use of a spin dryer is free. Motorcaravan drainage point. Off site: Adjacent to the park is the Balmacara Hotel (with bar), shop (selling gas), sub-post office and off licence.

Open

1 May - 30 September.

At a glance

Welcome & Ambience	✓✓✓✓	Location	✓✓✓✓✓
Quality of Pitches	✓✓✓✓	Range of Facilities	✓✓✓

Directions

Take A87 towards Kyle of Lochalsh. Park is signed very soon after sign for Balmacara, on the right just before Balmacara hotel. O.S.GR: NG815272.

Charges 2004

Per unit incl. 2 persons	£ 9.30
extra person (13 yrs or over)	£ 2.00
awning (May, June, Sept only)	£ 2.00
electricity (10A)	£ 1.20
backpackers/cyclists per 2 person tent	£ 7.80

Reservations

Not necessary so not accepted by phone; if considered essential, by letter enclosing cheque/PO for first night's fee (non-returnable). Tel: 01599 566215.

UK7780 Faichem Park

Ardgarry Farm, Faichem, Invergarry PH35 4HG (Highland)

Small and unsophisticated, and under new ownership, Faichem Park is situated on a hillside in a beautiful setting with glorious views over Ben Tee (2,955 ft) near Loch Ness. The road up to the site is now tarmaced and accessible to all except American motorhomes. For children there is the attraction of helping to feed the animals - sheep and lambs, chickens, many types of ducks and strange marvellous looking types of pheasants, and the pony and the white 'runner' ducks which march like soldiers around the park and farm. There are 30 pitches with plenty of space, including 15 with electrical connections and 10 with level concrete hardstanding. There are also four wood chalets to rent, terraced on the hillside. Four barbecues are positioned around the camping area for visitors to use. Dogs are accepted (but care is needed with the livestock) and there is an excellent area above the site for walks. A flexible system for night-time road illumination allows campers to turn off lights close to their pitch if necessary. There are numerous places to fish in the area, golf in Fort Augustus and Fort William, pony trekking, a pleasure cruiser on Loch Ness (you might see Nessie) and the Great Glen water park (2 miles).

Facilities

A log type cabin houses the toilet facilities which are older in style but very clean (key, £1 deposit). Hot water to the showers is metered but is free to washbasins and dishwashing sinks. Washing machine and dryer. Hair and hand dryers. Gas is available and free range eggs are sold at the farm but there is no shop (closest 2 miles towards Fort William). Bicycle hire. Off site: Boat slipway 2 miles, golf 7 miles. The village is 0.5 miles with a hotel.

Open

15 March - 15 October.

At a glance

Welcome & Ambience	✓✓✓✓✓	Location	✓✓✓✓✓
Quality of Pitches	✓✓✓✓✓	Range of Facilities	✓✓✓

Directions

From A82 at Invergarry take A87 (in direction of Kyle of Lochalsh) and continue for 1 mile. Turn right at Faichem sign and bear left up hill, farmhouse and reception is the first entrance on the right, the site is second. From opposite direction on A87, turn left at Faichem sign, take third entrance on left for reception, second left for park. O.S.GR: NH285023.

Charges 2004

Per unit incl. 2 persons	£ 7.80 - £ 8.00
tent incl. 2 persons	£ 7.00 - £ 7.50
extra adult	£ 1.00
child	£ 0.50
electricity	£ 1.50
No credit cards.	

Reservations

Advised in main season and made with small deposit. Tel: 01809 501226. Email: enquiries@ardgarry.farm

UK7850 Linnhe Lochside Holidays

Corpach, Fort William PH33 7NL (Highland)

This quiet well run park has a very peaceful situation overlooking Loch Eil, and it is beautifully land-scaped with wonderful views. There are individual pitches with hardstanding for 65 touring units (12 seasonal) on terraces leading down to the water's edge. They include 32 with electricity connection (16A), water and drainaway, plus 30 with electricity only (10A). A separate area on the lochside takes 15 small tents (no reservation). There are also 64 caravan holiday homes and 11 centrally heated pine chalets for hire. Fishing is free on Loch Eil and you are welcome to fish from the park's private beach or bring your own boat and use the slipway and dinghy park. About five miles from Fort William on 'The Road to the Isles', the park is conveniently placed for touring the Western Highlands. Easily accessible are Ben Nevis and the Nevis range (cable car to 2,000 ft.), geological, Jacobite and Commando museums, distillery visits, seal island trips, the Mallaig steam railway and the Caledonian Canal.

Facilities

Toilet facilities are excellent, heated in the cooler months and include baths (£1). Dishwashing room. First class laundry and separate outdoor clothing drying room (charged per night). Self-service, licensed shop (end May - end Sept). Gas supplies. Barbecue area. Toddlers' play room and two well equipped play areas on safe standing. Large motorhomes are accepted but it is best to book first. Caravan storage. Up to two dogs per pitch are accepted. Off site: Bicycle hire 2.5 miles, riding or golf 5 miles.

Open

20 March - 31 October.

At a glance

Welcome & Ambience	✓✓✓✓	Location	✓✓✓✓✓
Quality of Pitches	✓✓✓✓✓	Range of Facilities	✓✓✓✓

Directions

Park entrance is off A830 Fort William - Mallaig road, 1 mile west of Corpach. O.S.GR: NN072772.

Charges 2004

Per unit	£ 11.00 - £ 13.00
with services	£ 11.50 - £ 14.00
tent pitch	£ 8.00 - £ 10.00
person	£ 1.00
awning, extra tent or car	£ 1.50
dog (max 2, not on tent pitches)	£ 0.50

Seasonal rates available.

Reservations

Made with £30 deposit for min. 3 nights.
Tel: 01397 772376.
Email: holidays@linnhe.demon.co.uk

UK7800 Resipole Farm Caravan & Camping Park

Loch Sunart, Acharacle PH36 4HX (Argyll and Bute)

This quiet, open park is marvellously set on the banks of Loch Sunart, 8 miles from Strontian, on the Ardnamurchan peninsula. It is a must for anyone seeking peace and tranquility and really worth the journey. With views across the water and regularly visited by wild deer, Resipole Farm offers a good base for exploring the whole of this scenic area or, more locally, for fishing, boating (launching from the site's own slipway) and walking in the unspoilt countryside. There are 60 touring pitches here, more than half with hardstanding and electric hook-ups (10/16A), and 4 with all services. Tents are sited by the hedges. This is a good location for day trips to Mull via the Lochaline ferry.

Facilities

The central, modern sanitary block can be heated and is kept very clean. Good dishwashing facilities. Excellent provision for visitors with disabilities. Laundry facilities. Adjoining the farmhouse is a well equipped bar and restaurant offering reasonably priced home made food in the evenings (vegetarians catered for). Caravan storage. Art gallery and studios. Off site: Riding 5 miles.

Open

1 April - 31 October.

At a glance

Welcome & Ambience	✓✓✓✓✓	Location	✓✓✓✓✓
Quality of Pitches	✓✓✓✓✓	Range of Facilities	✓✓✓✓

Directions

From A82 Fort William road, take the Corran ferry located 5 miles north of Ballachulish and 8 miles south of Fort William. On leaving ferry, turn south along the A861. Park is on the north bank of Loch Sunart, 8 miles west of Strontian. The road is single track for 8 miles approaching Resipole and care is needed, but it is well worth it. O.S.GR: NM676740.

Charges 2004

Per unit incl. 2 persons	£ 9.00 - £ 10.50
extra adult	£ 3.00
child (5-16 yrs)	£ 1.00
serviced pitch incl. electricity (10A)	£ 2.00
backpacker or cyclist tent	£ 7.50 - £ 8.00

Reservations

Advisable for hook-ups and made for any period with one night's fee. Tel: 01967 431235.
Email: info@resipole.co.uk

UK7830 Glen Nevis Caravan & Camping Park

Glen Nevis, Fort William PH33 6SX (Highland)

Just outside Fort William in a most attractive and quiet situation with views of Ben Nevis, this spacious park is used by those on active pursuits as well as sightseeing tourists. It comprises eight quite spacious fields, divided between caravans, motorcaravans and tents (steel pegs required). It is licensed for 250 touring caravans but with no specific tent limits. The large touring pitches, many with hardstanding, are marked with wooden fences, 200 with electricity (13A) and 100 also have water and drainage. The park becomes full in the peak months but there are vacancies each day. If reception is closed (possible in low season) you site yourself. There are regular security patrols at night in busy periods. The park's own modern restaurant and bar with good value bar meals is a short stroll from the park, open to all. This is a well managed park with a bustling, but pleasing ambience, watched over by Ben Nevis. Around 1,000 acres of the Glen Nevis estate are open to campers to see the wildlife and explore this lovely area.

Facilities

The four modern toilet blocks make a good provision with free hot showers (extra showers in two blocks); and units for visitors with disabilities. An excellent block in Nevis Park (one of the eight camping fields) has some washbasins in cubicles, showers, further facilities for disabled visitors, a second large laundry room and dishwashing sinks. Motorcaravan service point. Self-service shop (Easter - mid Oct), barbecue area and snack bar (May - mid-Sept). Play area on bark. Off site: Pony trekking, golf and fishing near.

At a glance

Welcome & Ambience	✓✓✓✓	Location	✓✓✓✓✓
Quality of Pitches	✓✓✓✓✓	Range of Facilities	✓✓✓✓

Directions

Turn off A82 to east at roundabout just north of Fort William following camp sign. O.S.GR: NN124723.

Charges 2004

Per person	£ 1.60 - £ 2.20
child (5-15 yrs)	£ 0.80 - £ 1.10
pitch incl. awning	£ 5.20 - £ 8.80
serviced pitch plus	£ 1.60 - £ 2.20

Reservations

Made with £13 deposit and fee (£2).
Tel: 01397 702191. Email: camping@glen-nevis.co.uk

Open

15 March - 31 October.

Glen Nevis Caravan & Camping Park

Glen Nevis
Fort William PH33 6SX
Tel: 01397 702191
camping@glen-nevis.co.uk

This award-winning environmental park - **Calor 1998 Best Park in Scotland -
David Bellamy Gold Conservation Award** - situated at the foot of Ben Nevis, Britain's highest mountain, offers modern, clean and well-equipped facilities including Motor caravan service point.
Many pitches are fully serviced with electricity, water and drainage
Showers, scullery, laundry. licensed shop, gas and play areas are all on park
with our own spacious restaurant and lounge only a few minutes walk.
Holiday Caravans, Cottages, Lodges on adjacent park. Colour brochures available.

UK7790 Invercoe Caravan & Camping Park

Invercoe, Glencoe PH49 4HP (Argyll and Bute)

On the edge of Loch Leven, surrounded by mountains and forest, Iain and Lynn Brown are continually developing this attractively located park in its magnificent historical setting. It provides 60 pitches on level grass with gravel access roads (some hardstandings). You choose your own numbered pitch, those at the loch side being very popular. The only rules imposed are necessary for safety because the owners prefer their guests to feel free and enjoy themselves. There is much to do for the active visitor with hill walking, climbing, boating, pony riding and sea loch or fresh water fishing in this area of outstanding natural beauty. This is a park you will want to return to again and again.

Facilities

The well refurbished toilet block can be heated. Dishwashing under cover, excellent laundry facilities with a drying room. New large under-cover eating area. Motorcaravan service point comprising multi-drainage point, fresh water, dustbins, and chemical disposal point. Shop (Easter - end Sept). Play area with swings. Fishing. Off site: The village with pub and restaurant is within walking distance. Visitor's Centre at Glencoe 2 miles. Golf 3 miles. Bicycle hire 2 miles.

Open

All year excl. November.

At a glance

Welcome & Ambience	✓✓✓✓	Location	✓✓✓✓✓
Quality of Pitches	✓✓✓✓	Range of Facilities	✓✓✓

Directions

Follow A82 Crianlarich - Fort William road to Glencoe village and turn onto the B863; park is 0.5 miles along, well signed. O.S.GR: NN098594.

Charges 2004

Per unit incl. 2 persons and electricity	£ 14.00
extra adult	£ 2.00
child (3-15 yrs)	£ 1.00
awning	£ 1.50
Senior citizens less £1 per person outside July/Aug.	

Reservations

Advised for electricity for peak season; made with £17 deposit and £3 fee. Tel: 01855 811210.
Email: invercoe@sol.co.uk

UK7810 Oban Camping & Caravanning Club Site

Barcaldine, By Connel PA37 1SG (Argyll and Bute)

Owned by the Camping and Caravanning Club, this site at Barcaldine, 12 miles north of Oban, is a small, intimate site taking 75 units. Arranged within the old walled garden of Barcaldine House, the walls give it some protection from the wind and make it quite a sun trap. There are 23 level, fairly small pitches with hardstanding and 52 electrical hook-ups (16A). Being a small site, it has a very cosy feel to it, due no doubt to the friendly welcome new arrivals receive. Through the garden gate, one is immediately in the Barcaldine forest with its miles of forest tracks, absolutely perfect for both dog walking and mountain biking. Unusually for a club site there is a lounge bar selling very reasonably priced meals most evenings. This is a very comfortable area, only open until 10.30 pm. (no children after 8 pm) with bar meals served 6-8 pm. The loch across the road is handy for sea fishing and a 20 minute walk takes you to a freshwater lake for fishing.

Facilities

The central toilet block can be heated and is kept very clean with free hot showers, hair dryers and plenty of washbasins and WCs. Excellent unit for disabled visitors. Laundry. Motorcaravan service point. Small shop open a few hours each day for basic provisions and gas. Bar serving bar meals. Small play area with effective safety base. Off site: Sea Life Centre 2 miles. A not too frequent bus passes the gate.

At a glance

| Welcome & Ambience | ✓✓✓✓ | Location | ✓✓✓✓ |
| Quality of Pitches | ✓✓✓✓ | Range of Facilities | ✓✓✓✓ |

Directions

Entrance is off the A828 road on south side of Loch Creran, 6 miles north of Connel Bridge. O.S.GR: NM966420.

Charges 2005

Per adult	£ 3.70 - £ 5.15
child (6-18 yrs)	£ 1.65
non-member pitch fee	£ 4.60

Reservations

Necessary for high season; contact site or Central Reservations 0870 243 3331. Tel: 01631 720348.

Open

April - end October.

UK7840 North Ledaig Caravan Park

Connel, Oban PA37 1RU (Argyll and Bute)

The views over the Sound of Mull here are magnificent and Mr and Mrs Weir have tried to ensure good views by staggering the pitches and not planting many trees. The park provides 260 pitches for caravans, motorcaravans and trailer tents only, all with electricity (10A) and 228 with hardstanding. A dog walk follows the disused railway track that runs through the park. An award winning 30 acre nature reserve with ponds and walks (strictly no dogs) to attract wildlife has been developed on land across the road. Being well organised and run, this is a quiet park which makes a good base for exploring the area, visiting the islands from Oban or simply relaxing on the shores of the loch. Fishing and sailing are possible from the site (there is a slipway for small boats), hill walking or pony trekking are close. A member of the Caravan Club's 'managed under contract' scheme, non-members are also very welcome.

Facilities

The main sanitary block is central - a bit of a walk depending on your pitch but a new, semi-underground block is planned. The current amenities are excellent and include full facilities for disabled visitors and for babies (access by key). Washbasins in cabins for ladies (one for men). Well equipped laundry with irons for hire, and dishwashing. Motorcaravan service area. Further, well renovated sanitary facilities are behind the reception block. Well stocked, licensed shop. Play area. Caravan storage. Off site: Bicycle hire and golf 6 km. Buses pass the gate five or six times a day.

At a glance

| Welcome & Ambience | ✓✓✓✓✓ | Location | ✓✓✓✓✓ |
| Quality of Pitches | ✓✓✓✓✓ | Range of Facilities | ✓✓✓✓ |

Directions

Park is about 1 mile north of Connel Bridge, on the A828 Oban - Fort William road, 7 miles from Oban. O.S.GR: NM913456.

Charges guide

Per adult	£ 3.25 - £ 4.50
child (5-17 yrs)	£ 1.00 - £ 1.50
pitch incl. electricity	£ 4.00 - £ 6.00

Reservations

Any length, with £10 deposit incl. £1 non-returnable fee. Tel: 01631 710291.

Open

27 March - 31 October.

With a diversity of unspoilt landscapes, ranging from wild coastlines to green valleys, rugged mountains and shimmering lakes, to the natural phenomenon of the Giant's Causeway, Northern Ireland, though small, is crammed full of sights offering something for everyone.

Northern Ireland is comprised of the following counties:
Antrim, Armagh, Down, Fermanagh, Londonderry and Tyrone

The rugged coastline of the Causeway Coast and the nine Glens of Antrim, in the north, is an area of outstanding natural beauty, with white sandy shores and little bays, tranquil forests and romantic ruins and castles, full of tales of the ancient Irish Giants and other myths and legends. At over 60 million years old, with a mass of 4,000 tightly packed basalt columns, each a polygon shape, the Giant's Causeway is a popular attraction. One of the most beautiful regions is in the west around Londonderry, a delightful walled city set on a hill on the banks of the Foyle estuary. Further south is the beautiful region of Fermanagh, with glistening lakes and little islands all surrounded by lush green fields, hillsides and forests. The large lake of Lough Erne is to be found here: made up of two channels, the lower and upper Loughs, the meeting point of these channels is Enniskillen, a town steeped in history, boasting numerous preserved buildings including a castle. Across to the eastern shores lies the ancient Kingdom of Down, with its endless miles of spectacular coastline, little fishing villages, country parks and the Mountains of Mourne. And ringed by hills, sea lough and river valley is Belfast, a bustling city full of theatres, concert halls, art galleries and restaurants.

Did you know?

Northern Ireland measures 85 miles from north to south and is about 110 miles wide

The world's most famous ship the Titanic, was built in Belfast

Legend has it that the rugged Giant's Causeway was built by Finn McCool, the legendary Irish Giant, when he travelled across to Scotland to bring back his sweetheart

At 2,240 yards an Irish Mile is 480 yards longer than a standard English mile

Mountsandel near Coleraine is where Ireland's first known house was built 9,000 years ago

Nothern Ireland is the birthplace of John Boyd Dunlop, who developed and patented the pneumatic tyre

Places of interest

Antrim: Antrim Lough Shore Park; Rathlin Island Giant's Causeway; Dunluce Castle near Portrush

Belfast & environs: Belfast zoo and castle; Irish Linen Centre in Lisburn; Carrickfergus Castle

Armagh: Gosford Forest Park near Markethill; Lough Neagh Discovery Centre on Oxford Island

Down: County Museum and Downpatrick Cathedral; Mourne Mountains; Castlewellan forest park; Ballycopeland Windmill near Millisle

Fermanagh: Enniskillen Castle and Castle Coole; village of Belleek; Marble Arch Caves, near Lough Macnean; Devenish Island on Lough Erne

Londonderry: St Columb's Cathedral, Harbour Museum, Foyle Valley Railway Centre in Derry

Tyrone: Omagh; Beaghmore stone circles near Cookstown; Dungannon; Sperrin Mountains

tip

THE OLD LAMMAS FAIR, HELD AT BALLYCASTLE IN AUGUST, IS IRELAND'S OLDEST TRADITIONAL MARKET FAIR. IT FEATURES HORSE TRADING, MARKET STALLS AND STREET ENTERTAINMENT.

UK8320 Curran Court Caravan Park

131 Curran Road, Larne BT40 1XB (Co. Antrim)

Formerly run by the local borough council, this park is now managed by the Curran Court Hotel (opposite the park). Attractive garden areas add to the charm of this small, neat site which is very conveniently situated for the ferry terminal and only a few minutes walk from the sea. The 29 pitches, all with hardstanding and electricity connections (14A), give reasonable space off the tarmac road and there is a separate tent area of 1.5 acres. Larne market is on Wednesdays. You may consider using this site as a short term base for discovering the area as well as an ideal overnight stop. The warden can usually find room for tourists so reservations are not normally necessary.

Facilities

The toilet block is clean and adequate without being luxurious. Laundry room with dishwashing facilities. Play area with good equipment and safety surfaces. Bowls and putting on site. Late arrivals can call at the hotel. Off site: Bicycle hire 1 km. Golf 3 km. Boat launching 500 yds. Many other amenities are very close including a shop (100 yds), the hotel for food and drink, tennis and a leisure centre with swimming pool (300 yds).

At a glance

Welcome & Ambience	✓✓✓✓	Location	✓✓✓
Quality of Pitches	✓✓✓✓	Range of Facilities	✓✓✓

Directions

Immediately after leaving the ferry terminal, turn right and follow camp signs. Site is 400 yards on the left.

Charges 2004

Per caravan, motorcaravan or large tent	£ 10.00
tent	£ 5.00
electricity	free

Reservations

Not normally necessary. Tel: 028 2827 3797.
Email: curran.court-hotel@virgin.net

Open

Easter - 30 September.

UK8310 Carnfunnock Country Park Caravan Site

Coast Road, Drain's Bay, Larne BT40 2QG (Co. Antrim)

In a magnificent parkland setting overlooking the sea, what makes this touring site popular is its scenic surroundings and convenient location. It is 3.5 miles north of the market town of Larne on the famed Antrim Coast Road and offers 28 level 'super' pitches, all with hardstanding, water, 15A electricity, drainage, individual pitch lighting and ample space for an awning. The site has a neat appearance with a tarmac road following through to the rear where a number of pitches are placed in a circular position with allocated space for tents. Run by the Borough Council and supervised by a manager, the surrounding Country Park is immaculately kept. The Visitor Centre includes a gift shop and information about local attractions and the restaurant/coffee shop is pleasant and looks towards the sea. Spending time around the parkland, you find a walled time garden with historic sundials, a maze, forest walk, children's adventure playground, putting green, 9 hole golf course, wildlife garden and miniature railway. There is also a summer events programme.

Facilities

A small building beside the entrance gates houses sanitary toilet facilities (entry by key) which are kept clean, but now starting to show signs of wear. There are shower units, facilities for disabled people and dishwashing. Motorcaravan service point. Off site: Fishing and boat launching 400 m.

Open

Easter - 30 September.

At a glance

Welcome & Ambience	✓✓✓✓	Location	✓✓✓✓
Quality of Pitches	✓✓✓✓	Range of Facilities	✓✓✓

Directions

From ferry terminal in Larne, follow signs for Coast Road and Carnfunnock Country Park; well signed 3.5 miles on A2 coast road.

Charges 2004

Per caravan or motorcaravan	£ 11.50
serviced hardstanding	£ 13.00
tent (2 persons)	£ 7.00
5-7 nights (incl. electricity)	£ 59.00 - £ 80.00
tent (3 or more persons)	£ 11.50

Reservations

Advisable for weekends; peak periods and B.Hs. Tel: 028 2827 0541.

UK8340 Drumaheglis Caravan Park

36 Glenstall Road, Ballymoney BT53 7QN (Co. Antrim)

A caravan park which continually maintains high standards, Drumaheglis is popular throughout the season. Situated on the banks of the lower River Bann, approximately four miles from the town of Ballymoney, it appeals to watersports enthusiasts or makes an ideal base for exploring this scenic corner of Northern Ireland. The marina offers superb facilities for boat launching, water-skiing, cruising, canoeing or fishing, whilst getting out and about can take you to the Giant's Causeway, seaside resorts such as Portrush or Portstewart, the sands of Whitepark Bay, the Glens of Antrim or the picturesque villages of the Antrim coast road. For tourers only, this site instantly appeals, for it is well laid out with trees, shrubs, flower beds and tarmac roads. There are now 53 serviced pitches with hardstanding, electricity (5/10A) and water points. Ballymoney is a popular shopping town and the Joey Dunlop Leisure Centre provides a high-tech fitness studio, sports hall, etc. There is much to see and do within this Borough and of interest is the Ballymoney museum in Charlotte Street.

Facilities
Modern toilet blocks, spotlessly clean when we visited, include individual wash cubicles and facilities for disabled visitors, plus four family shower rooms. Dishwashing sinks. Washing machine and dryer. Children's play area. Volleyball and table tennis. Barbecue and picnic areas. Off site: Bicycle hire and golf 4 miles, riding 0.5 miles.

Open

Easter - 1 October.

At a glance

Welcome & Ambience	✓✓✓✓	Location	✓✓✓✓
Quality of Pitches	✓✓✓✓✓	Range of Facilities	✓✓✓✓

Directions

From A26/B62 Portrush - Ballymoney roundabout continue for approx. 1 mile on the A26 towards Coleraine. Site is clearly signed - follow International camping signs.

Charges guide

Per unit incl. electricity	£ 13.50
for 7 days	£ 81.00
pitch without services	£ 10.50
for 7 days	£ 63.00

Reservations

Essential for peak periods and weekends.
Tel: 028 2766 6466. Email: info@ballymoney.gov.uk

UK8350 Bush Caravan Park

95 Priestland Road, Bushmills BT57 8UJ (Co. Antrim)

An ideal base for touring the North Antrim Coast, this family run, recently extended park is only minutes away from two renowned attractions, the Giant's Causeway and the Old Bushmills Distillery. This fact alone makes Bush a popular location, but its fast growing reputation for friendliness and top class facilities makes it equally appealing. Conveniently located just off the main Ballymoney-Portrush Road (B62), it is approached by a short drive. The site itself is partly surrounded by mature trees and hedging, but views across the countryside can still be appreciated. Tarmac roads around the site lead to 43 well laid out and spacious pitches, with hardstanding and electric hook-up (16A), or to a grass area for tents. Unique features on site are murals depicting the famed scenery, sight and legends of the Causeway Coast. The enthusiastic owners organise tours to the Distillery and coastal trips - a musical evening cannot be ruled out.

Facilities
The toilet block (opened by key-pad) is modern, clean and equipped to a high standard. Facilities include controllable showers with excellent provision for people with disabilities. Washing machine, dryer and dishwashing sinks. Central children's play area. Recreation room for all ages.

Open

Easter - 31 October.

At a glance

Welcome & Ambience	✓✓✓✓	Location	✓✓✓✓
Quality of Pitches	✓✓✓	Range of Facilities	✓✓✓

Directions

From Ballymoney A26/B62 roundabout proceed north on B62 towards Portrush for 6.5 miles. Turn right onto B17 and site is 350 yds on the left.

Charges guide

Per unit incl. all persons, electricity	£ 12.00
tent	£ 6.00 - £ 10.00
awning	£ 1.00

Reservations

Advised for high season or weekends.
Tel: 028 2073 1678.

UK8360 Ballyness Caravan Park

40 Castlecatt Road, Bushmills BT57 8TN (Co. Antrim)

Ballyness is immaculately cared for and is designed with conservation in mind. In keeping with the surrounding countryside, it is extensively planted with native trees and shrubs which attract local wildlife and birds. The overall appearance of this site, with its entrance gate, white stone pillars and broad tarmac drive are appealing. The drive leads to 30 hardstanding pitches with electric hook-ups, water and drainage. There is a dedicated area for tents and several caravan holiday homes, but these are placed away from the touring pitches. From the site you can enjoy a relaxing walk by way of the meadow ponds and winding pathway alongside the stream known as St Columb's Rill.

Facilities

One clean and well decorated, cottage style heated sanitary block (key coded) includes facilities for disabled visitors (toilet and shower), a bathroom and baby unit, laundry room and dishwashing. Play area. Football field. Nature trail.

Open

17 March - 31 October.

At a glance

Welcome & Ambience	✓✓✓✓✓	Location	✓✓✓✓
Quality of Pitches	✓✓✓✓	Range of Facilities	✓✓✓

Directions

From M2 follow A26 N. At Ballymoney turn right on B66 towards Dervock and turn left. Stay on B66 and site is 5.5 miles on right.

Charges 2004

Per unit incl. 2 persons, electricity	£ 13.00
extra person over 5 yrs	£ 0.50
2 person tent	£ 9.00

Reservations

Contact site. Tel: 028 2073 2393.
Email: info@ballynesscaravanpark.com

UK8600 Bellemont Caravan Park

10 Islandtasserty Road, Coleraine BT52 2PN (Co. Londonderry)

Close to Coleraine and Portstewart, this well kept park makes an immediately favourable impression with its white concrete roads, its perfect grass areas and well laid out appearance. The gently sloping ground rises at the far right of the park to give views over Portstewart and towards the sea. To the left of the entrance and security gate are five privately owned caravan holiday homes. There are 30 spacious touring pitches, all with hardstanding, electric hook-up and water (tents are not accepted). These are well distributed around this open, parkland style setting. In a central position stands a gleaming white building, with flower tubs decorating the forecourt, which houses reception and heated sanitary facilities. Bellemont makes a good base for visiting the university town of Coleraine, the resorts and beaches of Portstewart and Portrush, or famous sights such as Dunluce Castle and Carrick-a-Rede rope bridge.

Facilities

Toilet facilities with good sized showers (token operated). En-suite unit for disabled visitors. Laundry room with two washing machines, two dryers and iron (token operated), plus dishwashing sink and drainer to the outside. Play area for children with swings and slide on a bark surface. Dogs are not accepted.

Open

Easter - 30 September.

At a glance

Welcome & Ambience	✓✓✓✓	Location	✓✓✓
Quality of Pitches	✓✓✓✓	Range of Facilities	✓✓✓

Directions

From Lodge Road roundabout on eastern outskirts of Coleraine follow A29 north to fourth roundabout. Continue towards Portrush and site is clearly signed on left after 400 yards.

Charges 2004

Per unit incl. all persons (no tents)	£ 10.50
with electricity	£ 12.50
awning	£ 2.00
No credit cards.	

Reservations

Contact site. Tel: 028 7082 3872.

UK8590 Tullans Farm Caravan Park

46 Newmills Road, Coleraine BT52 2JB (Co. Londonderry)

A quality, well run family park convenient for the Causeway coast, Tullans Farm is one of the most popular in the area. It has a quiet, heart of the country feel, yet the University town of Coleraine is within a mile, the seaside resort Portrush and Portstewart five miles and a shopping centre a five minute drive. Tullans Farm has earned a reputation for its very clean toilet block, attractive flower displays and its well cared for appearance. In a central position, fronted by a parking area, stands a long white building housing the toilet facilities and reception. The park roads are gravel and the 32 pitches are on hardstanding; all with electricity (10A). In season the owners organise barbecues and barn dances in aid of charity.

Facilities

The toilet and shower rooms, including a family shower unit, are spacious, modern and include facilities for people with disabilities. Laundry and washing up room with sinks, washing machine, dryers and a large fridge. Play area. TV lounge and barn used for indoor recreation.

Open

March - 30 September.

At a glance

Welcome & Ambience	✓✓✓✓	Location	✓✓✓
Quality of Pitches	✓✓✓	Range of Facilities	✓✓✓

Directions

From Lodge Road roundabout (south end of Coleraine) turn east on A29 Portrush ring road and proceed for 0.5 miles. Turn right at sign for park and Windy Hall.

Charges 2005

Per unit incl. all persons, electricity	£ 14.00
tent	£ 8.00 - £ 10.00
No credit cards.	

Reservations

Advised for peak times. Tel: 028 7034 2309.
Email: tullansfarm@hotmail.com

UK8430 Banbridge Touring Caravan & Camping Park

200 Newry Road, Banbridge BT32 3NB (Co. Down)

This conveniently situated touring park on the main A1 Belfast - Newry road is an ideal place for a stopover if travelling between Southern and Northern Ireland. It is within easy towing distance of the main ports or would make an ideal base for discovering many tourist attractions such as the Bronte Homeland or Scarva Visitor Centre. A tiny site, with 8 hardstanding pitches and electrical connections (6A), it is part of the Banbridge Gateway Tourist Information Centre complex. The centre is an attractive building of modern design surrounded by a well maintained garden area and car park. Housed inside, apart from the offices of the centre and a bureau de change, is a display area for Irish crafts. The restaurant and coffee shop within the complex (10.00-17.00 hrs daily) serves lunchtime specials, scones, cakes, etc. The touring park, located in the far left hand corner of the complex, is enclosed with ranch fencing, plus a security gate and barrier. The town of Banbridge is 1 mile.

Facilities

Excellent, ultra-modern toilet facilities, spotlessly clean and key operated, include two showers, good facilities for disabled people and an outside, covered dishwashing area. Extensive children's play area with safety base. Off site: Shops, restaurants, pubs and all services within 1 mile. Fishing, bicycle hire or golf within 3 miles.

Open

All year, but closed Sundays October - May inclusive.

At a glance

Welcome & Ambience	✓✓✓✓	Location	✓✓✓
Quality of Pitches	✓✓✓✓	Range of Facilities	✓✓✓

Directions

Follow signs to Tourist Information Centre off the A1 Belfast - Newry dual carriageway, 1 mile south of Banbridge.

Charges 2004

Per unit incl. electricity	£ 10.00
tent	£ 5.00

Max. stay 5 consecutive nights. Refundable key deposit (gate, WCs and showers) £20.

Reservations

Contact centre during office hours (summer: Mon-Sat 09.00-19.00, Sun. 14.00-18.00; winter: Mon-Sat 10.00-17.00, Sun. closed). It is essential to arrive during opening hours to obtain keys.
Tel: 028 4062 3322. Email: tic@banbridgedc.gov.uk

UK8420 Tollymore Forest Caravan Park

178 Tullybrannigan Road, Newcastle BT33 6PW (Co. Down)

This popular park, for tourers only, is located within the parkland of Tollymore Forest. It is discreetly situated away from the public footpaths and is noted for its scenic surroundings. The forest park, which is approached by way of an ornate gateway and majestic avenue of Himalayan cedars, covers an area of almost 500 hectares. It is backed by the Mourne mountains and situated two miles from the beaches and resort of Newcastle. The site is attractively laid out with hardstanding pitches, 72 of which have electricity (6A). The Head Ranger at Tollymore is helpful and ensures that the caravan site is efficiently run and quiet, even when full. Exploring the forest park is part of the pleasure of staying here, and of note are the stone follies, bridges and entrance gates. The Shimna and Spinkwee rivers flow through the park adding a refreshing touch and tree lovers appreciate the arboretum with its many rare species.

Facilities

Toilet blocks, timbered in keeping with the setting, are clean and modern with wash cubicles, facilities for disabled people, dishwashing and laundry area. Off site: Confectionery shop and tea room nearby. Small grocery shop a few yards from the exit gate of the park with gas available.

Open

All year.

At a glance

Welcome & Ambience	✓✓✓✓	Location		✓✓✓✓✓
Quality of Pitches	✓✓✓✓	Range of Facilities		✓✓✓

Directions

Approach Newcastle on the A24. Before entering the town, at roundabout, turn right on to A50 signed Castlewellan and follow signs for Tollymore Forest Park.

Charges 2004

Per unit incl. car and occupants	£ 9.00 - £ 13.00
electricity	£ 1.50

Low season mid-week special rates.

Reservations

Advisable in high season and for B.Hs. and made with £10 deposit. Contact: Tollymore Forest Park (Administration). Tel: 028 4372 2428.

UK8405 Cranfield Caravan Park

123 Cranfield Road, Cranfield West, Kilkeel BT34 4LJ (Co. Down)

On the shores of Carlingford Lough with direct access to a blue flag beach, this friendly family run park immediately impresses with its well cared for flower beds, neat hedging, cordyline trees and the elegant building which incorporates the family home and the reception. Situated at Northern Ireland's most southerly point, the surrounding scenery of the Mourne Mountains, the Lough and distant vistas is stunning. A focal point is the Haulbowline lighthouse, built in the 1800s, which sits in the middle of the sea. Despite the many privately owned caravan holiday homes on site, touring pitches are kept separate and situated towards the park entrance. Each pitch has a sea view, has hardstanding and all have tower units providing an electricity hook up (16A), water, waste water point and TV outlet; 19 have a main sewerage connection.

Facilities

A modern, heated toilet block (entrance by key) is well maintained with tiled walls/floors, pre-set showers (50p token) and open style washbasins. Excellent suite for disabled visitors doubles as a family room, also a night WC (by key). Dishwashing sinks and well equipped laundry in a separate building. Play area (outside park). Sea fishing, boat launching and beach (with lifeguard). Off site: Kilkeel town (3.5 miles). Golf, hill walking in the Mournes, Anglo Norman castle.

Open

17 March - 31 October.

At a glance

Welcome & Ambience	✓✓✓✓✓	Location	✓✓✓✓
Quality of Pitches	✓✓✓✓	Range of Facilities	✓✓✓

Directions

Travelling southeast on A2 Newry/Kilkeel Road turn right approx. 5.5 miles after passing through Rostrevor onto local road, signed Cranfield/Greencastle. Site is signed at the end of the road.

Charges guide

Per unit incl. all persons and electricity	£ 12.00
awning	£ 1.50

Reservations

Contact park. Tel: 028 417 62572.
Email: jimchestnut@btconnect.com

For more **site inspiration**
see our directory ON PAGE 294

UK8510 Mullynascarthy Caravan Park

Lisnaskea BT92 0NZ (Co. Fermanagh)

This is a well kept touring site situated on the banks of the Colebrooke River. It has instant appeal, for the setting at Mullynascarthy is more like a mature garden. The pitches to the right of reception, which are grass on hardstanding, are mostly angled between the many tree varieties, also separated by low hedging and flowering shrubs. To the left of the facility block additional pitches are spread over meadow-like terrain and all have electric hook-ups. Sanitary facilities, although not ultra modern, are kept very clean and housed alongside reception, which doubles up as a sub post office. The attention and care this site obviously receives is due to the warden who also extends a friendly warm welcome to her guests. Lisnaskea makes an ideal base for exploring this lakeland county which abounds in historic treasures and stately homes. The Marble Arch caves are an experience not to be missed.

Facilities	Directions
The toilet block (key operated) includes open washbasins, facilities for people with disabilities (washbasin/WC), laundry room and dishwashing sinks. Games and sports area. Play area. River fishing (licences and permits available).	From Enniskillen take A4 towards Dungannon for 8 miles, then turn right on A34 signed Lisnaskea. Continue on A34 for 3.5 miles and turn right onto B514 where site is signed Mullynascarthy.

Open	Charges guide	
17 March - 31 October.	Per unit incl. 2 persons and electricity	£ 13.00
	Reservations	
	Contact site. Tel: 028 6772 1040.	

At a glance

Welcome & Ambience	✓✓✓✓	Location	✓✓✓
Quality of Pitches	✓✓✓✓	Range of Facilities	✓✓✓

UK8550 Dungannon Park

Moy Road, Dungannon BT71 6DY (Co. Tyrone)

This small touring park nestles in the midst of a 70-acre park with a multitude of tree varieties, brightly coloured flower beds and a 12 acre fishing lake. The 12 pitches, which are discreetly sited, some with lake views, are on hardstanding with water, waste and 16A electricity connections. Run by Dungannon Council the park, which also incorporates tennis courts and football/cricket pitches lies about a mile south of Dungannon town. Walkers can enjoy parkland walks which command views of the surrounding countryside and Lough Neagh. A Visitor Centre houses reception and the sanitary facilities.

Facilities	Directions
Sanitary facilities which include showers (by token), washbasins, baby mat and spacious unit for disabled visitors are to the rear of the Amenity Centre. Laundry room with washing machine and dryer, dishwashing area and chemical disposal unit. Night watchman (until 6 am). Excellent play area. Tennis, fishing and walking. Off site: Shop at main entrance to park. Restaurants, shops, leisure facilities in Dungannon. Tyrone Crystal (guided tours), walking/cycling in Clogher Valley, local markets.	Leave M1 at exit 15 to join A29 towards Dungannon. Turn left at second traffic lights to Dungannon Park.

	Charges 2004	
	Per pitch	£ 10.00
	with electricity	£ 12.00
	tent	£ 8.00
	Reservations	
	Contact park. Tel: 028 8772 7327. Email: dungannonpark@utvinternet.com	
	Open	
	1 March - 31 October.	

At a glance

Welcome & Ambience	✓✓✓✓	Location	✓✓✓✓
Quality of Pitches	✓✓✓✓✓	Range of Facilities	✓✓✓

UK8460 Delamont Country Park Camping & Caravanning Club Site

Delamont Country Park, Downpatrick Road, Killyleagh BT30 9TZ (Co. Down)

This is Northern Ireland's first Camping and Caravanning Club site located within Delamont Country Park. It is an idyllic location for those seeking an away from it all feel, yet wanting to be within easy reach of attractions. The country park is a designated area of outstanding natural beauty and commands from its highest point, breathtaking vistas of Strangford Lough and surrounding countryside. Facilities on the campsite itself are excellent and it has an orderly, neat and tidy appearance. Reception stands to the fore of the site and the sanitary block towards the rear. The 64 all weather pitches on level terrain all have electricity, plus water and waste hook-ups. Although the site is surrounded by trees and the rich vegetation of the country park, the young shrubs and trees around the pitches will take time to mature.

Facilities	Directions
The single modern toilet block, with heating, has wash cubicles and a baby bath. En-suite facilities for disabled visitors. Laundry sinks, washing machine and dryer; dishwashing inside. Small shop area selling basics. Adventure playground and miniature railway in country park. Free admittance to park for campers. Off site: Tyrella beach 7 miles. Fishing and riding 1 mile. Golf 4 miles.	From Belfast take A22 southeast to Killyleagh. Pass through village and site entrance is on left after 1 mile.

	Charges 2005	
	Per adult	£ 4.30 - £ 6.40
	non-member pitch fee	£ 5.00
	Reservations	
	Contact site or Central Reservations 0870 243 3331. Tel: 028 4482 1833.	
	Open	
	March - October.	

At a glance

Welcome & Ambience	✓✓✓✓✓	Location	✓✓✓✓✓
Quality of Pitches	✓✓✓✓✓	Range of Facilities	✓✓✓✓

269

Famed for its folklore, traditional music, and friendly, hospitable people, the Republic of Ireland offers spectacular scenery contained within a relatively compact area. With plenty of beautiful areas to discover, and a decidedly relaxed pace of life, it is an idea place to unwind.

Ireland is made up of four provinces: Connaught, Leinster, Munster and Ulster, comprised of 32 counties, 26 of which fall in the Republic of Ireland

Ireland is the perfect place to indulge in a variety of outdoor pursuits while taking in the glorious scenery. There are plenty of way-marked foot and bridle paths, which lead you through woodlands, across cliffs, past historical monuments and over rolling hills. The dramatic coastline, with its rocky headlands, secluded coves and sandy beaches, is a fantastic place for watersports enthusiasts: from sailing to windsurfing, scuba diving and swimming; or for those who just simply want to relax and watch the variety of seabirds that nest on the shores. The Cliffs of Moher, in particular, is a prime location for birdwatching and Goat Island, just offshore, is where Puffins make their nesting burrows. Fishing is another popular activity; the country is full of pretty streams, rivers, hidden lakes and canals, which can all be explored by hiring a boat. In the south the beautiful Ring of Kerry is one of the most visited regions. This 110-mile route encircles the Inveragh Peninsula, and is surrounded by mountains and lakes. Other sights include: the Aran Islands, home to some of the most ancient Christian and pre-Christian remains in Ireland, and the Rock of Cashel, with its spectacular group of medieval buildings; not to mention the bustling cities of Dublin, Galway and Cork.

Did you know?

The official currency of the Republic of Ireland is the Euro

The Blarney Stone was reputedly cast with a spell, made by a witch to reward a king who saved her from drowning, and is said to bestow the gift of eloquence on all those who kiss it

The harp is a symbol of the Irish people's love of music: since mediaeval times it has been the official emblem for Ireland

Hurling is the oldest native sport

Doctors once prescribed Guinness as a cure for debility, anaemia and to help patients through their convalescence, including nursing mothers

On display in Trinity College, the Book of Kells is one of the oldest books in the world, written around the year 800 AD

Places of interest

Connaught: Boyle Abbey; Connemara National Park; Céide Fields at Ballycastle; Kylemore Abbey; Aran Islands; Galway city; Westport; Sligo Abbey; megalithic tombs of Carrowmore

Leinster: Wicklow Mountains National Park; Rock of Cashel; Killkenny Castle; Guinness brewery, Trinity College and National Museum in Dublin; Dunmore Cave at Ballyfoyle; Wexford Wildfowl Reserve

Munster: harbour towns of Kinsale and Clonakilty; Blarney Castle in Cork; historical city of Limerick with 13th century castle fortress and old town; Ring of Kerry; Bunratty Castle; Cliffs of Moher; Killarney National Park

Ulster: Glenveagh National Park; Slieve League, the highest sea cliffs in Europe; Donegal Castle; Newmills Corn and Flax Mills in Letterkenny

tip

PUCK FAIR IS TRADITIONAL HORSE FAIR, WHICH INCLUDES OPEN AIR CONCERTS, PARADES AND FIREWORKS. HELD IN AUGUST, IN CO. KERRY, IT IS ONE OF IRELAND'S OLDEST FESTIVALS.

IR8640 Knockalla Caravan & Camping Park

Magherawarden, Portsalon (Co. Donegal)

What adds to the popularity of this site is its location, nestling between the slopes of the Knockalla Mountains and Ballymastocker Bay amidst the breathtaking scenery of County Donegal. The fact that the beach here has been named 'the second most beautiful beach in the world' is not surprising. Approached by an unclassified but short road, Knockalla's elevated situation commands a panoramic view of the famed Bay, Lough Swilly, Inishowen Peninsula and Dunree Head. The family run park is partly terraced giving an attractive, orderly layout with reception, shop and restaurant in a central position and the touring area sited to the left of reception. All 50 touring pitches have electrical hook-ups and hard-standing, offering a choice of tarmac only or with adjoining grass to allow for awnings. Tents are pitched on a lower level facing reception and to the far left of the tourers, with caravan holiday homes placed around the right hand perimeter and to the rear of the park. Specialities at the shop and café are home made scones, apple cakes, jams, etc. with a takeaway or table service. Full Irish breakfasts are served.

Facilities

The main toilet block, tastefully refurbished and kept clean and fresh, can be heated. Showers (€ 1 token). Dishwashing area and campers' kitchen with hot water. Laundry service operated by staff. Motorcaravan service points. Gas available. Play area. TV/games room. Shop and café (both July/Aug, plus B.H. w/ends). Off site: Golf 3 miles, fishing, riding and bicycle hire within 10 miles.

Open

15 March - 19 September.

At a glance

| Welcome & Ambience | ✓✓✓✓ | Location | ✓✓✓✓✓ |
| Quality of Pitches | ✓✓✓✓ | Range of Facilities | ✓✓✓✓ |

Directions

From Letterkenny take R245 to Rathmelton. Continue on R245 to Milford. Turn right on R246 to Kerrykeel. In village turn left towards Portsalon and at second crossroads turn right onto Portsalon/Knockalla coast road. Turn right at sign to park.

Charges 2004

Per unit incl. 2 adults, 2 children	€ 17,00
extra adult	€ 4,00
electricity (5A)	€ 2,00
awning	€ 2,00
small tent	€ 12,00

No credit cards.

Reservations

Advisable for July/Aug and B.H. w/ends.
Tel: 074 915 9108.

knockalla caravan & camping park

MAGHERAWARDEN, PORTSALON, CO. DONEGAL

Nestling between the slopes of the Knockalla Mountains and Ballymastocker Bay amidst the breathtaking scenery of County Donegal. Play area. TV/games room. Shop - try our home made scones, apple cakes and jams.

for further information call: 074 9159108

IR8690 Greenlands Caravan & Camping Park

Rosses Point (Co. Sligo)

Just off the N15 road and 8 km. from Sligo town, this is a well run park at Rosses Point, in the sand hills adjoining a championship golf course. It is thoughtfully laid out with small tents placed to the front of reception and the hardstanding touring pitches separated from the trailer tent pitches which occupy the rear. The ground is undulating and adds interest to the overall appearance. Your view depends on where you are pitched - look towards Coney Island and the Blackrock lighthouse which guards the bay, take in the sight of Benbulben Mountain or appreciate the seascape and the water lapping the resort's two bathing beaches. Electricity hook-ups (10A) are available for touring units. This is an excellent base from which to explore the 'Yeats Country' and discover the beauty spots immortalised in his poems, such places as Lissadell, Dooney Rock, the Isle of Innis free and the poet's burial place at Drumcliffe.

Facilities

Modern toilet facilities, recently extended and refitted, are kept exceptionally clean, with hot showers (€ 1 token) dishwashing and laundry sinks, washing machine, dryer and iron. Motorcaravan service point. New campers' kitchen. Information point and TV room beside reception. Play area, sand pit for children and outdoor chess and draughts sets. Night security. Off site: Mini-market, restaurant and evening entertainment in the village. Fishing and boat launching 100 m. Golf 50 m. Bicycle hire 8 km. Riding 14 km.

At a glance

| Welcome & Ambience | ✓✓✓✓ | Location | ✓✓✓✓ |
| Quality of Pitches | ✓✓✓ | Range of Facilities | ✓✓✓ |

Directions

From Sligo city travel approx. 800 m. north on N15 road, turn left onto R291 signed Rosses Point. Continue for 6.5 km. and park is on right after village.

Charges 2004

Per person	€ 1,00
pitch	€ 15,00
awning or pup tent	€ 2,00
electricity (10A)	€ 3,00
hiker/cyclist incl. small tent	€ 9,00

Weekly rates available.

Reservations

Contact park. Tel: 071 917 7113.

Open

Easter - 30 September.

(271)

IR8740 Cong Caravan and Camping Park

Lisloughrey, Quay Road, Cong (Co. Mayo)

It would be difficult to find a more idyllic and famous spot for a caravan park than Cong. Situated close to the shores of Lough Corrib, Cong's scenic beauty was immortalised in the film 'The Quiet Man'. This well kept park is 1.6 km. from the village of Cong, near the grounds of the magnificent and renowned Ashford Castle. The owner's house that incorporates reception, shop and the hostel, stands to the fore of the site. Toilet facilities and the holiday hostel accommodation are entered from the courtyard area. The 40 grass pitches, 36 with electricity, are placed at a higher level to the rear, with the tent areas below and to the side. The park can be crowded and busy in high season. When not spending time around the village of Cong with its picturesque river setting and Monastic relics, there is much to keep the active camper happy. Watersports, cycling, walking, climbing, caving and scenic drives can all be pursued. Not least of the attractions at this park is a mini cinema showing 'The Quiet Man' film nightly all season.

Facilities
Toilet facilities are tastefully decorated, kept clean and are heated when necessary. Hot showers with curtains (€ 1 charge), hairdryers, soap and hand towels. Dishwashing area (charge for hot water). Campers' kitchen. Launderette service. Central bin depot. Barbecue, games room and extensive play area. Shop. Catering is a feature - full Irish or continental breakfast, dinner or packed lunch may be ordered, or home baked bread and scones purchased in the shop. Bicycle hire. Off site: Riding or golf within 2 km. Fishing and boat slipway 500 m.

Open
All year.

At a glance
Welcome & Ambience ✓✓✓✓ Location ✓✓✓✓
Quality of Pitches ✓✓✓ Range of Facilities ✓✓✓✓

Directions
Leave N84 road at Ballinrobe to join R334/345 signed Cong. Turn left at end of the R345 (opposite entrance to Ashford Castle), take next road on right (approx. 300 m) and the park is on right (200 m).

Charges 2004
Per adult	€ 2,50
child	€ 2,00
pitch	€ 12,00
awning	€ 4,00
electricity (16A)	€ 4,00
hiker/cyclist incl. tent and 1 person	€ 10,00

Reservations
Contact park. Tel: 094 954 6089.
Email: quiet.man.cong@iol.ie

IR8750 Belleek Caravan & Camping Park

Ballina (Co. Mayo)

Belleek has a quiet woodland setting, only minutes from Ballina, a famed salmon fishing centre. With excellent pitches and toilet block, the family owners are committed to ensuring that it is immaculate at all times. From the entrance gate, the park is approached by a drive that passes reception and leads to 58 well spaced pitches. With a very neat overall appearance, 32 pitches have hardstanding, 45 have electricity hook-ups, and you may choose your pitch. Sports facilities within a short distance of the park include a swimming pool, tennis and bicycle hire. Other local attractions are the Blue Flag beach at Ross, Ceide Fields (Neolithic farm), Down Patrick Head, Mayo North Heritage Centre or a seaweed bath at Kilcullen's Bath House, Enniscrone.

Facilities
Spotlessly clean, tastefully decorated toilet block providing showers (€ 0.80 token), baby sink and facilities for disabled people. Laundry sink, two washing machines and two dryers. TV room and games room with table tennis and football game. Campers' kitchen and emergency accommodation with beds provided. Play area, ball game area, basketball and tennis courts. Barbecue area. Reception includes a shop (June-Sept) and a tea room that also serves breakfasts. Off site: Fishing 1 km. Bicycle hire 3 km.

Open
15 March - 8 October; by arrangement all year.

At a glance
Welcome & Ambience ✓✓✓✓✓ Location ✓✓✓✓
Quality of Pitches ✓✓✓✓✓ Range of Facilities ✓✓✓✓

Directions
Take R314 Ballina - Killala road. Park is signed on right after approx. 1.75 miles.

Charges 2004
Per unit incl. 2 persons	€ 14,00 - € 16,00
extra adult	€ 4,00
child	€ 2,00
electricity (10A)	€ 2,50
hiker/cyclist and tent	€ 7,00
No credit cards.	

Reservations
Contact park. Tel: 096 71533.
Email: lenahan@indigo.ie

Don't forget!
the international dialling code for the Republic of Ireland is **00 353**

IR8790 Carra Caravan & Camping Park

Belcarra, Castlebar (Co. Mayo)

This is an ideal location for those seeking a real Irish village experience in a 'value for money' park. Small, unpretentious and family run, it is located in Belcarra, a regular winner of the 'Tidiest Mayo Village' award. Nestling at the foot of a wooded drumlin, it is surrounded by rolling hills and quiet roads which offer an away from it all feeling, yet Castlebar the county's largest town is only an 8 km. drive. On the pleasant 1.5 acre park, the 20 unmarked touring pitches, 14 with electric hook-up (13A), are on flat ground enclosed by ranch fencing and shaded in parts by trees. An additional novel idea at Carra are eight horse-drawn caravans for hire. Also of interest are the talks that the owner Sean and daughter Deirdre give on the area. There are recommended walks and maps provided. New to the area is the National Museum of Country Life at Turlough (8 km) which is now a super attraction.

Facilities

The basic toilet block has adequate, well equipped showers (€ 0.40). Combined kitchen, dishwashing, laundry area with fridge/freezer, sink, table, chairs, washing machine and dryer. Comfortable lounge with TV, books and magazines located at reception. Off site: Village shops, a post office and 'Flukies' cosy bar which serves Irish breakfast and where Irish stew is a speciality. Leisure centre and tennis courts. Free fishing area and special walkway to the river. Golf 8 km.

At a glance

Welcome & Ambience	✓✓✓✓	Location	✓✓✓
Quality of Pitches	✓✓✓	Range of Facilities	✓✓✓

Directions

From Castlebar take N60 Claremorris road for 8.5 km. southeast and turn right at sign for Belcarra. Continue for 4.5 km. to village and site on left at end of village.

Charges 2004

Per unit incl. all persons	€ 8,00
electricity	€ 2,00
No credit cards.	

Reservations

Contact park. Tel: 094 903 2059.
Email: post@mayoholidays.com

Open

5 June - 18 September.

CARRA CARAVAN & CAMPING PARK
Mayo HORSE DRAWN CARAVAN HOLIDAYS
HOLIDAY COTTAGES, MOBILE HOMES AND HORSE DRAWN CARAVANS,
Cycling • Fishing • Walking • Golfing
Pubs • Restaurants • Irish Music Sessions
Belcarra, Castlebar, Co. Mayo. Tel + 353 (0) 94 32054 ★ www.horsedrawn.mayonet.com

IR8730 Keel Sandybanks Caravan & Camping Park

Keel, Achill Island (Co. Mayo)

This is a park offering a taste of island life and the opportunity to relax in dramatic, scenic surroundings. Achill, Ireland's largest island, is 15 miles long and 12 miles wide and is connected to the mainland by a bridge. The site is situated beside Keel village and approached by the R319 from the swivel bridge at Achill Sound. Although there are static holiday caravans on this site, the 42 pitches for caravans and 42 for tents are kept separate. Some with hardstanding are located at the perimeter fence overlooking the beach. Although sand based, the ground is firm and level. Roads are tarmac and there is direct access to the beach which is supervised by lifeguards. Occasionally a traditional music evening is organised on the site. Whilst a treat in store is the natural beauty of Achill, worth seeing are Kildownet Castle, the Slievemore deserted village and the Seal Caves.

Facilities

Two modern toilet blocks serve the site, one at the entrance gate beside reception and the other in a central position. Heated facilities include WCs (one for disabled visitors), washbasins and hot showers (on payment). Hair and hand dryers. Dishwashing and laundry sinks. Chemical disposal facilities. Play area with safety base. TV room. Watersports enthusiasts can enjoy surfing, canoeing and board sailing on Keel Strand and Lough. Fishing trips can be arranged. Off site: Bicycle hire and golf 200 m. Riding 10 km. In the village there is a food shop, takeaway, restaurants and music at night in the pubs.

At a glance

Welcome & Ambience	✓✓✓✓	Location	✓✓✓✓
Quality of Pitches	✓✓✓✓	Range of Facilities	✓✓✓✓

Directions

From Achill Sound follow the R319 for 10 miles. Site is on the left before Keel village.

Charges 2004

Per pitch	€ 10,00 - € 16,00
hiker/cyclist and tent	€ 8,00 - € 10,00
electricity (6A)	€ 2,00
No credit cards.	

Reservations

Contact site. Tel: 098 43211.
E-mail: post@mayoholidays.com

Open

27 May - 4 September.

IR8770 Parkland Caravan & Camping Park

Westport House Country Park, Westport (Co. Mayo)

Located in the grounds of an elegant country estate, this popular park offers the choice of a 'pitch only' booking, or a 'special deal' (min. stay three nights). This includes free admission to Westport House and children's animal and bird park, plus other activities, such as boating and fishing on the lake and river, pitch and putt, 'slippery dip', ball pond and 'supabounce', new play adventure world, hillside train rides and a flume ride. Stay one week or more and all the above are free, plus tennis, a par-3 golf course and 20% discount on bar food in the Horse and Wagon bar on the site. From Westport Quay, you enter the grounds of the estate by way of a tree lined road that crosses the river and leads to the site. In an attractive, sheltered area of the parkland, set in the trees, are 155 pitches. There are 65 with hard-standing and 76 electric hook-ups. The gate is closed 11.30 pm.- 9 am. with good lighting around the site. If late, vehicles must be parked in the car park. Early in the season the site may not be fully prepared, and only minimal facilities may be available. Westport is an attractive town with splendid Georgian houses and traditional shop fronts. There are many good restaurants and pubs.

Facilities
Toilet facilities are provided at various points on the site, plus a 'super-loo' located in the farmyard buildings. Facilities for disabled people. Dishwashing and laundry sinks, washing machines and dryers plus free ironing facilities. Fifties style function room and bar with food and musical entertainment (all 1/6-31/8). Dogs are not accepted. Off site: Within 5 km. of the estate are an 18 hole golf course and deep sea angling on Clew Bay.

Open
14 May - 5 September.

At a glance
Welcome & Ambience	✓✓✓✓	Location	✓✓✓✓✓
Quality of Pitches	✓✓✓	Range of Facilities	✓✓✓✓

Directions
Take R335 Westport - Louisburgh road and follow signs for Westport Quay, then turn right into Westport House.

Charges 2004
Per unit excl. free facilities,	
pitch only	€ 23,00 - € 25,00
hiker or cyclist incl. 2 persons	€ 20,00 - € 22,00
Electricity incl. No credit cards.	

Reservations
Contact park. Tel: 098 27766.
Email: camping@westporthouse.ie

IR8810 Lough Lannagh Caravan Park

Castlebar (Co. Mayo)

Lough Lannagh is an attractive holiday village on the lake shore which comprises quality accommodation, self catering cottages and a caravan park. It is within walking distance of Castlebar with its many restaurant, pubs and shops. County Mayo's main attractions are also within a short drive. The caravan park has 20 touring pitches, well laid out in a separate dedicated corner of the village, all on hard-standing with electric connections. One reception area serves all and is situated to the right of the security barrier. When not out and about, there are many on site activities for all the family. The main attraction is the fitness suite, sauna and steam room, plus reflexology and therapies available (over 18s only admitted to the gym). Popular with the young is the three times weekly club held in July/August. Anglers need only travel 500 metres, or if you prefer cycling, bicycles can be hired.

Facilities
One modern heated sanitary block provides washbasins and well equipped, pre-set showers. En-suite unit for disabled people. Laundry room with sink, washing machines and dryers; dishwashing area. Café (serving breakfast). Fitness suite. Tennis. Table tennis. Bicycle hire.

Open
All year, excl. 22 Dec - 2 Jan.

At a glance
Welcome & Ambience	✓✓✓✓	Location	✓✓✓✓
Quality of Pitches	✓✓✓✓	Range of Facilities	✓✓✓✓

Directions
To get to Castlebar take the N5, N60 or N84. At Castlebar ring road follow directions for Westport. Site is signed on all approach roads to the Westport roundabout.

Charges 2004
Per unit incl. all persons,	
electricity and hardstanding	€ 20,00 - € 26,00
tent incl. 2 persons	€ 18,00 - € 24,00

Reservations
Advised for high season; contact site.
Tel: 094 902 7111. Email: llv@eircom.net

IR8780 Knock Caravan & Camping Park

Claremorris Road, Knock (Co. Mayo)

This park is immediately south of the world famous shrine that receives many visitors. Comfortable and clean, the square shaped campsite is kept very neat with tarmac roads and surrounded by clipped trees. The pitches are of a decent size accommodating 50 caravans or motorcaravans, 20 tents and 18 caravan holiday homes (for rent). All pitches have hardstanding (5 doubles) and there are 52 electrical connections (13A), with an adequate number of water points. There is also an overflow field. Because of the religious connections of the area, the site is very busy in August and indeed there are unlikely to be any vacancies at all for 14-16 August. Besides visiting the shrine and Knock Folk Museum, it is also a good centre for exploring scenic Co. Mayo.

Facilities

Two heated toilet blocks have good facilities for disabled visitors and a nice sized rest room attached, hot showers (on payment) and adequate washing and toilet facilities. Laundry and dishwashing room. Gas supplies. Playground. Off site: Fishing 4.5 km. Golf or riding 11 km.

Open

1 March - 31 October.

At a glance

Welcome & Ambience	✓✓✓✓	Location	✓✓✓✓
Quality of Pitches	✓✓✓✓✓	Range of Facilities	✓✓✓✓

Directions

Exit from N17 at Knock bypass and from roundabout follow signs to site which is just south of the village.

Charges 2004

Per person	€ 1,00 - € 2,00
pitch	€ 13,00 - € 14,00
electricity (13A)	€ 2,00
hiker or cyclist incl. tent	€ 6,50 - € 7,50

No credit cards.

Reservations

Made for any length, no deposit. Tel: 094 938 8100. Email: info@knock-shrine.ie

---

IR8960 Lough Ree (East) Caravan & Camping Park

Ballykeeran, Athlone (Co. Westmeath)

This touring park is alongside the river, screened by trees but reaching the water's edge. Drive into the small village of Ballykeeran and the park is discreetly located behind the main street. The top half of the site is in a woodland situation and after the reception and sanitary block, Lough Ree comes into view and the remaining pitches run down to the shoreline. There are 60 pitches, 20 with hardstanding and 52 with electricity. With fishing right on the doorstep there are boats for hire and the site has its own private mooring buoys, plus a dinghy slip and harbour. A restaurant and 'singing' pub are close.

Facilities

The toilet block is clean without being luxurious. Hot showers (€ 0.50). Dishwashing sinks outside. Laundry room. A wooden chalet houses a pool room and campers' kitchen. Off site: Golf or riding 4 km.

Open

1 April - 30 September.

At a glance

Welcome & Ambience	✓✓✓✓	Location	✓✓✓✓
Quality of Pitches	✓✓✓	Range of Facilities	✓✓✓

Directions

From Athlone take N55 towards Longford for 4.8 km. Park is in the village of Ballykeeran, clearly signed.

Charges 2004

Per adult	€ 4,00
pitch	€ 4,00 - € 6,00
electricity	€ 3,00

No credit cards.

Reservations

Contact park for details. Tel: 090 6478561. Email: athlonecamping@eircom.net

---

IR9140 Valley Stopover & Caravan Park

Killough, Kilmacanogue (Co. Wicklow)

In a quiet, idyllic setting in the picturesque Rocky Valley, this small, neat, family run park is convenient for the Dublin ferries. Situated in the grounds of the family home, covering under an acre, it can be used either as a transit site or for a longer stay. It will appeal to those who prefer the more basic 'CL' type site. There are 15 grassy pitches, 11 with electricity hook-ups, 3 hardstandings, 2 water points, night lighting and a security gate. Staying put here you are only minutes from Enniskerry which lies in the glen of the Glencullen river. Here you can enjoy a delight of forest walks, or visit Powerscourt, one of the loveliest gardens in Ireland. Bray is 6 km. and is one of the oldest seaside resorts in the country.

Facilities

Toilet facilities, clean when we visited, are housed in one unit and consist of two WCs with washbasins, mirrors, etc. and a shower. Dishwashing and laundry sink, a spin dryer and a campers' kitchen. Full cooked Irish breakfast is available in the family guest house. Off site: Fishing 16 km. Riding 3 km. Golf 7 km.

Open

Easter - 31 October.

At a glance

Welcome & Ambience	✓✓✓✓	Location	✓✓✓
Quality of Pitches	✓✓✓	Range of Facilities	✓✓✓

Directions

Turn off N11 Dublin - Wexford road at Kilmacanogue, following signs for Glendalough. Continue for 1.6 km. and take right fork signed 'Waterfall'. Park is first opening on the left in approx. 200 m.

Charges 2004

Per unit with car	€ 11,00
electricity	€ 1,50
awning	€ 1,50

Reservations

Advised for July/Aug. Tel: 01 282 9565. Email: rowanbb@eircom.net

275

IR9130 Roundwood Caravan & Camping Park

Roundwood (Co. Wicklow)

In the heart of the Wicklow mountains, this park is under new management, but still maintains high standards. It is neatly laid out with rows of trees dividing the different areas and giving an attractive appearance. There are 31 hardstanding pitches for caravans and 8 motorcaravans, all with electricity (6A), plus 40 pitches for tents, arranged off tarmac access roads. There are excellent walks around the Varty Lakes and a daily bus service to Dublin city. Close by are the Wicklow and Sally Gap, Glendalough, Powerscourt Gardens, plus many other places of natural beauty. Apart from its scenic location, this site is well placed for the ferry ports.

Facilities

The renovated sanitary block is kept clean, with adequate washing and toilet facilities, plus spacious showers on payment (€ 1). The block also houses two dishwashing sinks and good laundry facilities, but ask at reception as machines are not self-service. Motorcaravan service point. Campers' kitchen and dining room. TV room. Adventure playground. Bicycle hire. Off site: Roundwood village has shops, pubs, restaurants, takeaway food, and a Sunday market. Fishing or golf 1 km.

Open

29 April - 26 September.

At a glance

Welcome & Ambience	✓✓✓✓	Location	✓✓✓✓
Quality of Pitches	✓✓✓✓	Range of Facilities	✓✓✓

Directions

Turn off N11 Dublin - Wexford road at Kilmacanogue towards Glendalough and then 15 km. to Roundwood.

Charges 2004

Per adult	€ 6,00
child (under 14 yrs)	€ 3,00
pitch	€ 6,00 - € 8,00
electricity (5A)	€ 2,00
No credit cards.	

Reservations

Accepted without deposit and advisable for July/Aug. Tel: 01 281 8163.
Email: info@dublinwicklowcamping.com

IR9150 River Valley Caravan & Camping Park

Redcross Village (Co. Wicklow)

In the small country village of Redcross, in the heart of County Wicklow, you will find this popular, family run park. Based here you are within easy reach of beauty spots such as the Vale of Avoca (Ballykissangel), Glendalough and Powerscourt, plus the safe beach of Brittas Bay. The 95 touring pitches at River Valley are mostly together in a dedicated area, all have electricity connections (6A) and offer a choice of hard-standing or grass - you select your pitch. Within this 16-acre site children can find day long amusement, whether it be Fort Apache, the adventure playground, the tiny tots playground, or at the natural mountain stream where it is safe to paddle. There is also a pets corner with a 'fat belly pig'. An attractive wine and coffee bar with a conservatory is inviting, or an alternative may be the restaurant where home made, traditional dishes are on the menu (1/6-31/8). The late arrivals area has electricity hook-ups, water and night lighting.

Facilities

A luxurious new sanitary block has a modern, well designed appearance. Facilities for disabled visitors are excellent. Showers are on payment (€ 0.50). Laundry area. Campers' kitchen. Motorcaravan service points. Gas available. Wine/coffee bar and restaurant. TV and games room. Three tennis courts. Par 3 golf course. Bowling green. Sports complex with badminton courts and indoor football and basketball. Adventure and tiny tots playgrounds. Area allocated for rallies. Caravan storage. Dogs are not accepted in July/Aug.

Open

12 March - 26 September.

At a glance

Welcome & Ambience	✓✓✓✓✓	Location	✓✓✓✓
Quality of Pitches	✓✓✓✓	Range of Facilities	✓✓✓✓

Directions

From Dublin follow N11 Wexford road. Turn right in Rathnew and left under railway bridge onto the Wexford-Arklow road. Continue for 11 km. and turn right at Doyle's Pub. Park is in Redcross village, under 5 km.

Charges 2004

Per unit incl. 2 adults	€ 15,00 - € 17,00
extra adult	€ 5,00
child (2-15 yrs)	€ 3,00
small tent incl. 2 persons	€ 13,00 - € 14,00
electricity	€ 2,00

Reservations

Made with deposit. Tel: 0404 41647.

IR9160 Moat Farm Caravan and Camping Park

Donard (Co. Wicklow)

Providing a true feel of the countryside, this park is part of a working sheep farm. It offers incredible vistas across a scenic landscape, yet is within driving distance of Dublin and Rosslare. Driving into the village of Donard you little suspect that alongside the main street lies a pleasant, well cared for and tranquil five-acre campsite. The entrance is approached by way of a short road where the ruins of a Medieval church sit high overlooking the forecourt and reception. There are 40 pitches for caravans and tents. Spacious pitches with hardstanding line both sides of a broad avenue, incorporating ample space for awning and all with electricity and drainage points. A large field takes tents and further caravans. The site makes a good base for touring or going on foot, for this area is a walker's paradise with a 30 minute circular walk around the perimeter of the site.

Facilities

The toilet block is kept very clean and includes spacious showers, facilities for visitors with disabilities, and a well equipped laundry room. Good quality campers' kitchen and large recreation/entertainment room with an open fire. Three large barbecues and a patio area. Caravan storage. Off site: Mountain climbing or sites of archaeological interest nearby. Fishing 3 km, bicycle hire 15 km, golf 13 km.

Open

1 March – 30 September.

At a glance

Welcome & Ambience	✓✓✓✓	Location	✓✓✓✓
Quality of Pitches	✓✓✓✓	Range of Facilities	✓✓✓

Directions

Park is 16.5 km. south of Blessington. Leave M50 Dublin ring motorway at exit 10 to join N81 southwest for 19 km. to Blessington. Continue on N81 for a further 16.5 km. and turn left at Old Toll House pub onto local road and follow signs to park in Donard village (3.5 km).

Charges 2004

Per adult	€ 5,00
child (0-14 yrs)	€ 3,00
caravan, motorcaravan or family tent	€ 8,00
electricity (10A)	€ 2,50
motorcyclist, cyclist or hiker incl. tent	€ 10,00

No credit cards.

Reservations

Contact site. Tel: 045 404727.
Email: moatfarm@ireland.com

IR9100 Camac Valley Tourist Caravan & Camping Park

Naas Road, Clondalkin Dublin 22 (Co. Dublin)

Opened in 1996, this campsite is not only well placed for Dublin, but also offers a welcome stopover if travelling to the more southern counties from the north of the country, or vice versa. Despite its close proximity to the city, being located in the 300 acre Corkagh Park gives it a 'heart of the country' atmosphere. The site entrance and sign are distinctive and can be spotted in adequate time when approaching on the busy N7. Beyond the entrance gate and forecourt stands an attractive timber fronted building. Its design includes various roof levels and spacious interior layout, with large windows offering a view of the site. Housed here is reception, information, reading, TV and locker rooms plus shop and sanitary facilities. There are 163 pitches, 48 for tents placed to the fore and the hardstandings for caravans laid out in bays and avenues with electrical connections, drainage and water points. Young trees separate pitches and roads are of tarmac. After a day of sightseeing in Dublin, which can be reached by bus from the site, Camac Valley offers an evening of relaxation with woodland and river walks in the park or a number of first class restaurants and pubs nearby.

Facilities

Heated sanitary facilities include good sized showers (token), facilities for disabled people, baby changing room, laundry and washing up. Playground with wooden play frames and safety base. Shop and coffee bar (open June, July and August). Electronic gate controlled from reception and 24 hour security. Dogs are not accepted in July/Aug. Off site: Bicycle hire 1.5 km. Golf 6 km. Fishing 8 km. Riding 9 km.

Open

All year.

At a glance

Welcome & Ambience	✓✓✓✓✓	Location	✓✓✓✓
Quality of Pitches	✓✓✓✓✓	Range of Facilities	✓✓✓

Directions

From north follow signs for West Link and M50 motorway. Exit M50 at junction 9 onto N7 Cork road. Site is on right of dual carriageway (beside Green Isle Hotel) after 2 km. and is clearly signed. At City West business park, cross over bridge and return on dual-carriageway following camp signs - site is on left after 800 m.

Charges 2004

Per unit incl. 2 adults	€ 16,00 - € 20,00
incl. 2 adults and up to 4 children	€ 17,00 - € 22,00
extra adult	€ 4,00
1 child	€ 3,00
electricity (10A)	€ 3,00
motorcyclist, cyclist or hiker and tent (per person)	€ 8,00 - € 9,00

Reservations

Advance bookings necessary (max. stay operates at certain times). Tel: 01 464 0644.
Email: reservations@camacvalley.com

IR9080 Forest Farm Caravan and Camping Park

Dublin Road, Athy (Co. Kildare)

This site makes an excellent stopover if travelling from Dublin to the southeast counties. It is signed on the N78 and approached by a 500 m. avenue of tall pines. Part of a working farm, the campsite spreads to the right of the modern farmhouse, which also provides B&B. The owners have cleverly utilised their land to create a site which offers 64 unmarked touring pitches on level ground. Of these, 32 are for caravans, all with electricity connections and 10 with hardstanding, and 32 places are available for tents. Full Irish breakfasts are served at the farmhouse and farm tours are arranged on request.

Facilities	Directions
The centrally located, red brick toilet block is heated and double glazed, providing quality amenities including a spacious shower unit for disabled visitors, a family room with shower and WC. It also houses a laundry room, a campers' kitchen with dishwashing sinks, a fridge/freezer, cooker, table and chairs and a comfortable lounge/games room (a TV can be provided). Basketball net, sand pit and picnic tables. Off site: Golf courses nearby. Course and game fishing 4 km.	Site is 4.8 km. northeast of Athy town off the main N78 Athy - Kilcullen road.

Charges 2004

Per adult	€ 1,50
child	€ 0,50
pitch	€ 10,00
1 or 2 person tent per person	€ 5,00
hiker, cyclist or motorcyclist incl. tent	€ 5,00
electricity (16A)	€ 2,00

Reservations

Contact site. Tel: 05986 31231.
Email: forestfarm@eircom.net

Open

All year.

At a glance

Welcome & Ambience	✓✓✓✓	Location	✓✓✓
Quality of Pitches	✓✓✓	Range of Facilities	✓✓✓

IR9240 Tree Grove Caravan & Camping Park

Danville House, Kilkenny (Co. Kilkenny)

The entrance gate to this small family run site is easily spotted off the R700 road. Tree Grove is within walking distance of medieval Kilkenny, known for its elegance and famed for its beer and cats. An orderly, neat park, it has instant appeal because its young owners are friendly and have insisted on a logical layout to suit both the terrain and campers needs. It is terraced with the lower terrace to the right of the wide sweeping driveway laid out with 11 hardstanding pitches for caravans. All 30 pitches have electrical hook-ups (10A) and plenty of water points are to be found. On a higher level, is a grass area for hikers and cyclists with further caravan and tent pitches sited near the elevated sanitary block. If needed more grass pitches face reception, which is housed in a modern wooden chalet. Whilst there are mature trees at the entrance and around the site perimeter, many shrubs have been effectively placed together with flower troughs. On the patio there are bench seats with tables and umbrellas. There is much to see and do around the ancient city of Kilkenny (1.5 km) with its cobbled streets and castle. County Touring Routes are worth following.

Facilities	Directions
House plants add decoration inside the toilet block giving a cared for look to this modern building which includes a family room with shower, WC and washbasin which can be used by disabled people. Laundry room. Open, covered kitchen for campers with fridge, work-top, sink and electric kettle adjoins a comfortable games/TV room with pool table, and easy chairs. Bicycle hire. Tents to rent on site. Off site: Fishing 500 m, riding 1 km. Golf 2 or 15 km.	Travelling north on the N10 Waterford/Kilkenny Road turn right at roundabout on ring road. Continue to 2nd roundabout and turn right onto R700. Site is 150 m. on right.

Open

1 March - 15 November.

Charges 2004

Per caravan or motorcaravan incl. 2 persons	€ 11,50
family tent	€ 10,50
extra adult or child	€ 1,50
awning	€ 1,00
electricity (10A)	€ 2,00
1 man tent	€ 5,50
No credit cards.	

Reservations

Contact site Tel: 05677 70302. Email: treecc@iol.ie

At a glance

Welcome & Ambience	✓✓✓✓✓	Location	✓✓✓✓
Quality of Pitches	✓✓✓✓	Range of Facilities	✓✓✓✓

IR9230 Nore Valley Park

Annamult, Bennettsbridge (Co. Kilkenny)

This lovely site is set on a grassy hillock overlooking the valley and the river Nore, with a woodland setting behind. Situated on a working farm, it offers 70 pitches, 40 with hardstanding and 6A electricity for caravans and motorcaravans, and 30 for tents. The owners pride themselves on their home baking and farm produce and during high season cooked breakfasts are available in the small café. An attractive courtyard houses several unusual facilities including a sand pit, pedal go-karts, tractor rides and a straw loft play area for wet weather. This is an ideal park for families, offering children and adults alike the opportunity to feed the animals (goats, lambs, ducks, chickens and donkey). It is 11 km. from Kilkenny, renowned for its castle, history and crafts, and 3 km. from the village of Bennettsbridge, where there are shops and eating places. Note: the tractor rides, go-karts and the café are closed on Sundays.

Facilities
The modern toilet block is kept spotlessly clean and can be heated. Two units suitable for disabled visitors. Dishwashing sinks. Laundry room with washing machine and dryer. Motorcaravan services. The original block in the courtyard is used mainly in the low season. New reception, shop (basic items such as milk, bread and camping gaz) and café (June-Aug). Comfortable lounge. Games room with pool table. Fenced children's play area. Crazy golf. Bicycle hire. Off site: Outdoor pursuits nearby such as canoeing, walking or fishing (4 km). Riding 6 km. Golf 10 km.

At a glance
Welcome & Ambience	✓✓✓✓	Location	✓✓✓✓
Quality of Pitches	✓✓✓✓	Range of Facilities	✓✓✓✓

Directions
From Kilkenny take R700 to Bennettsbridge. Just before the bridge turn right at sign for Stoneyford and after approx. 3 km. site is signed Nore Valley Park.

Charges 2004
Per person over 2 yrs	€ 2,50
caravan	€ 10,50
motorcaravan	€ 9,50
tent	€ 7,00 - € 10,00

Reservations
Contact park. Tel: 05677 27229.
Email: norevalleypark@eircom.net

Open
1 March - 31 October.

IR9330 Casey's Caravan Park

Clonea, Dungarvan (Co. Waterford)

Set on 20 acres of flat grass, edged by mature trees, this family run park offers 284 pitches which include 154 touring pitches, 118 with electrical hook-ups and 30 with hardstanding. The remainder are occupied by caravan holiday homes. There is direct access from the park to a sandy, 'Blue Flag' beach with a resident lifeguard during July and August. A highly recommended leisure centre is adjacent should the weather be inclement. The park is 5.5 km. from Dungarvan, a popular town for deep sea angling, from which charter boats can be hired and three 18 hole golf courses are within easy distance. Suggested drives include the scenic Vee, the Comeragh Drive and the coast road to Tramore.

Facilities
The central toilet block (key system), has good facilities kept spotlessly clean, with showers on payment (€1), washing up sinks and small laundry with machine and dryer. A further luxurious and modern block provides an excellent campers' kitchen, laundry room and toilet for disabled visitors. Large adventure play area with bark surface in its own field (not supervised). Games room with pool table, table tennis and amusements. TV lounge. Crazy golf. Gas supplies. Full time security staff in high season. Off site: Two village stores near the beach. Golf.

At a glance
Welcome & Ambience	✓✓✓✓	Location	✓✓✓✓
Quality of Pitches	✓✓✓✓	Range of Facilities	✓✓✓✓

Directions
From Dungarvan centre follow R675 east for 3.5 km. Look for signs on the right to Clonea Bay and site. Site is approx. 1.5 km.

Charges 2004
Per unit incl. all persons	€ 17,00
hiker, cyclist or m/cyclist incl. tent	€ 10,00
electricity 10A	€ 3,00
No credit cards.	

Reservations
Are made in low season, but not between 10 July - 15 Aug; contact park. Tel: 058 41919.

Open
26 April - 7 September.

IR9340 Newtown Cove Camping & Caravan Park

Tramore (Co. Waterford)

Well run and friendly, this small park is only five minutes walk from the beautiful Newton Cove. It offers views of the famous Metal Man and is 2.5 km. from Tramore beach and 11 km. from Waterford. Neatly set out on gently sloping grass with an abundance of shrubs and bushes, there are 40 pitches. All have electrical connections (10A), some with hardstanding also, with access by well lit, tarmac roads. There are around 50 privately owned caravan holiday homes. A modern building at the entrance houses reception, the amenities and further sanitary facilities. The village of Tramore, with a wide range of shops and eating houses, is close and there is a choice of many delightful cliff walks in the immediate vicinity.

Facilities
The main sanitary block at the bottom end of the site is not very modern but provides good facilities including a bathroom. Showers on payment. Campers' kitchen with cooking facilities, lounge, dishwashing and small laundry. Small shop (1/7- 30/8). TV room. Games room. Small play area. Off site: Golf 800 m. Fishing 400 m, riding 3 km.

Open
15 April - 2 October.

At a glance
Welcome & Ambience	✓✓✓✓	Location	✓✓✓✓
Quality of Pitches	✓✓✓✓	Range of Facilities	✓✓✓

Directions
From Tramore on R675 coast road to Dungarvan. Turn left 2 km. from town centre, following signs.

Charges 2005
Per unit	€ 6,00 - € 16,00
person	€ 5,00
child	€ 2,00
electricity (10A)	€ 3,00

No credit cards. No single sex groups.

Reservations
Not needed or accepted; for information contact park.
Tel: 051 381979. Email: info@newtow1.ncove.com

IR9420 Streamstown Caravan & Camping Park

Streamstown, Roscrea (Co. Tipperary)

This family run site, set on a dairy farm in the centre of Ireland, is conveniently situated off the N7 Dublin - Limerick road. It makes a good overnight halt or for a longer stay if you are seeking a quiet, restful location with little to disturb the peace. This is a working farm and the owners, who are friendly and welcoming, are in the process of improving and developing their site. What impresses most here is the tidy overall appearance with neatly trimmed hedging, tables placed around the grass areas and with flower baskets a special feature. There are 27 touring pitches, 10 with hardstanding and separated by low hedges. The remainder are on grass and more suitable for units with awnings.

Facilities
The sanitary facilities, clean when we visited, are in a modern block, although showers, toilets and washbasins are of the older type and slightly out of keeping with the outside appearance. Good campers' kitchen with fridge/freezer and electric cooker. Good play area. TV and pool room. Off site: Fishing 1.8 km. Golf 5 km. Riding 8 km.

Open
7 April - 1 November.

At a glance
Welcome & Ambience	✓✓✓✓	Location	✓✓✓
Quality of Pitches	✓✓✓✓	Range of Facilities	✓✓✓

Directions
From Roscrea centre follow signs for R491 Shirone. Continue towards Shirone following camp signs for approx. 2.5 km and site entrance is on left.

Charges 2004
Per adult	€ 3,50
child (under 12 yrs)	€ 2,00
pitch	€ 10,00
electricity (10A)	€ 3,00

Reservations
Contact site. Tel: 0505 21519.
Email: streamstowncaravanpark@eircom.net

IR9380 Parsons Green Caravan and Camping Park

Clogheen (Co. Tipperary)

In a tranquil and scenic location, this small, family run park commands panoramic views toward the Vee Gap and Knockmealdown Mountains. In open style, surrounded by low ranch fencing, it offers 34 pitches with hardstanding for caravans and motorcaravans and 10 on grass, all with 6A electrical connections, plus 20 pitches for tents. There is a range of things to do and see including a garden area, river walks, picnic area, an extensive farm museum, a pet field with selection of domestic and rare animals and birds, pony and trap rides, boating on the small lake and trout fishing river. If not sitting back enjoying the scenic surroundings or participating in the many activities, there is much to see and do in this area.

Facilities
Toilet facilities are near the top of the site and are kept clean. Good facilities for disabled people (shower and toilet). Laundry. Coffee shop and takeaway. Playground. Minigolf. Fishing. TV/games room. Campers' kitchen. Off site: Village within 500 m. Riding and golf 8 km.

Open
All year.

At a glance
Welcome & Ambience	✓✓✓✓	Location	✓✓✓✓
Quality of Pitches	✓✓✓✓	Range of Facilities	✓✓✓✓

Directions
Site is in the village of Clogheen, 200 m. off the R665, 24 km. west of Clonmel, 19 km. east of Mitchelstown.

Charges 2004
Per adult	€ 3,00
child	€ 2,00
caravan, family tent or motorcaravan	€ 7,00
small tent	€ 6,00
electricity (6A)	€ 2,00

Reservations
Contact site. Tel: 052 65290. Email: pjkn@eircom.net

IR9410 The Apple Camping & Caravan Park

Moorstown, Cahir (Co. Tipperary)

This fruit farm and campsite combination offers an idyllic country holiday venue in one of the most delightful situations imaginable. For tourers only, it is located off the N24, midway between Clonmel and Cahir. Entrance is by way of a 300 m. drive which follows straight through the heart of the farm. Apple trees guard the route, as do various non-fruit tree species, which are named and of interest to guests who are free to spend time walking the paths around the farm. When we visited, strawberries were being gathered – the best we had tasted all season – and apple juice, jams, etc. are also sold on the farm. Reception is housed with the other site facilities in a large farmyard barn. Although a rather unusual arrangement, it is very effective. The 32 pitches are in a secluded situation behind the barns and are mostly grass with a few hardstandings, with electricity connections to 25. The towns of Cahir and Clonmel are of historic interest and the countryside around boasts rivers, mountains, Celtic culture and scenic drives.

Facilities

Toilet facilities, kept very clean, quite modern in design and with heating, comprise showers, washbasins with mirrors, electric points, etc. in functional units occupying two corners of the large floor space. Facilities for disabled visitors. Also in the barn are dishwashing sinks, washing machine and a fridge/freezer for campers to use. Motorcaravan service point. Tennis court, basketball/football pitch and play area. Dogs are not accepted. Off site: Fishing, golf, bicycle hire and riding within 6 km.

At a glance

| Welcome & Ambience | ✓✓✓✓ | Location | ✓✓✓✓ |
| Quality of Pitches | ✓✓✓✓ | Range of Facilities | ✓✓✓ |

Directions

Park is 300 m. off main N24, 9.6 km. west of Clonmel, 6.4 km. east of Cahir.

Charges 2005

Per person	€ 5,00 - € 5,50
child (0-12 yrs)	€ 3,00
electricity (13A)	€ 2,00
Less 20% for groups of 4 or more.	

Reservations

Contact site. Tel: 052 41459.
Email: con@theapplefarm.com

Open

1 May - 30 September.

IR9390 Carrick-on-Suir Camping and Caravan Park

Carrick-on-Suir (Co. Tipperary)

This memorable site is not only conveniently situated off the main N24 between Waterford and Clonmel, it also makes an ideal first stop from the port of Rosslare. On this quiet, family run site campers are guaranteed the finest example of 'Cead Mile Failte' is possible to encounter - personal attention and advice on where to go and what to see in the area is all part of the service given by its owner, Frank O'Dwyer. The entrance to the park is immediately past the O'Dwyers' shop, through a gate which is closed at 11 pm. The tarmac drive leads past tall hedges and well kept shrubs to the right and several caravan holiday homes (for hire) to the left. The touring park lies to the rear with scenic views to the wooded hills. At present there are 30 level pitches, 33 with electricity hook-ups (6/10A) and several with hardstanding, but this number is to be extended. What makes this site distinctive is its excellent, well designed sanitary block which has a sparkling clean freshness. Within a short drive is the 'magic road', the Mahon Falls, a slate quarry or a romantic river walk. Carrick is well placed en-route to the west, only 90 minutes from Rosslare.

Facilities

Toilet facilities are kept clean and fresh with plenty of hot water. Showers cost € 0.50. Laundry room with washing machine. Campers' kitchen with dishwashing area and TV (no cooker). Motorcaravan service point. Good grocery shop with hot snacks to take away and a selection of fine wines. Gas supplies. Good night lighting. Off site: Fishing 1 km, riding 6 km, golf 3 km. Carrick town centre is five minutes walk for shops, pubs, restaurants, etc. plus a castle which is open to the public.

Open

1 March - 1 November.

At a glance

| Welcome & Ambience | ✓✓✓✓✓ | Location | ✓✓✓✓ |
| Quality of Pitches | ✓✓✓✓ | Range of Facilities | ✓✓✓ |

Directions

Approaching town on N24 road, follow signs for R690 in the direction of Kilkenny. Site is north of town, clearly signed at junction with R697.

Charges 2004

Per adult	€ 3,00
child	€ 2,50
pitch	€ 16,00
electricity	€ 2,50
hiker /cyclist incl. tent	€ 10,00

Reservations

Contact site. Tel: 051 640461.
Email: coscamping@eircom.net

www.alanrogers.com for latest campsite news

IR9455 Adare Camping & Caravan Park

Adare (Co. Limerick)

This attractive, family run park is popular because of its location three kilometres from Adare, which is claimed to be Ireland's prettiest village. It also makes an ideal overnight halt en-route to the southwest of the country. A small park, set back from the busy N21 Tralee – Limerick road, it has an open layout with young maturing shrubs and is screened by mature trees. There are 28 unnumbered, level pitches, of about 80-100 sq.m. Of these, 15 have hardstanding with 16A electricity hook-ups, whilst the remainder are on grass and used mainly for tents. An added facility for campers is a number of picnic tables.

Facilities	Directions
The heated toilet block is well tiled and houses spacious showers, washbasins, baby room and facilities for disabled visitors (washbasin and WC); covered dishwashing sinks. Fridges. Laundry room with sink, washing machine, dryer, iron/ironing board. A campers' kitchen is almost completed. Games room, hot tub and a play area for children. Night lighting: Off site: Fishing 2 km. Golf 3 km. Riding 3 km.	Travelling north on the N21 Tralee - Limerick road turn right onto R519 (signed Ballingarry) 1 km. before Adare Village and follow camp signs.

Charges 2004	
Per unit incl. 2 persons	€ 19,00
small tent incl. 2 persons	€ 17,00
extra adult	€ 4,00
child	€ 2,00
electricity (16A)	€ 3,00

Open

12 March - 30 September.

Reservations

Contact site. Tel: 061 395376.
Email: dohertycampingadare@eircom.net

At a glance

Welcome & Ambience	✓✓✓✓	Location	✓✓✓
Quality of Pitches	✓✓✓✓	Range of Facilities	✓✓✓

IR9480 Blarney Caravan & Camping Park

Stone View, Blarney (Co. Cork)

There is a heart of the country feel about this 'on the farm' site, yet the city of Cork is only an 8 km. drive. What makes this friendly, family run park so appealing is its secluded location and neatly laid out, open appearance. The terrain on the three acre park is elevated and gently sloping, commanding views towards Blarney Castle and the surrounding mountainous countryside. The 40 pitches, 30 of which have hardstanding and 10A electrical connections, are with caravans sited to the centre and left and tents pitched to the right. There are gravel roads, well tended young shrubs and a screen of mature trees and hedging marks the park's perimeter. In the Blarney area, apart from the castle, house and gardens, there are shops, restaurants, pubs with traditional music and an abundance of outdoor pursuits such as walking, riding and fishing.

Facilities	Directions
Well kept toilet areas, one new, are housed in converted farm buildings with reception and small shop. Facilities for disabled visitors. Laundry room with sinks, washing machine, dryer and ironing. Dishwashing area in the large campers' kitchen. Motorcaravan service point. Shop (1/6-31/8). TV lounge. 18 hole golf and pitch and putt course. Night lighting. Off site: Public bar and restaurant 100 m. serving food all day. Within easy reach of the ports of Cork and Rosslare.	Site is 8 km. northwest of Cork, just off the N20. Take N20 from Cork for approx. 6 km. and then left on R617 to Blarney. Site clearly signed at Esso station in village, in approx. 2 km.

Charges 2004	
Per adult	€ 4,50
child	€ 2,00
caravan, family tent, motorcaravan	€ 6,50 - € 8,00
small tent and car	€ 5,50 - € 6,50
electricity (10A)	€ 3,00
awning	€ 1,50 - € 2,00

Open

1 March - 31 October.

Reservations

Contact park. Tel: 021 451 6519.
Email: con.quill@camping-ireland.ie

At a glance

Welcome & Ambience	✓✓✓✓✓	Location	✓✓✓✓
Quality of Pitches	✓✓✓✓	Range of Facilities	✓✓✓✓

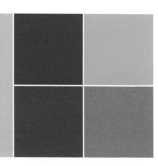

Don't forget!

the international dialling code for the Republic of Ireland is **00 353**

(then drop the first '0' of the number)

IR9500 The Meadow Camping Park

Glandore (Co. Cork)

The stretch of coast from Cork to Skibbereen reminds British visitors of Devon before the era of mass tourism. This is rich dairy country, the green of the meadows matching the emerald colours of the travel posters. The Meadows is best described as a one acre garden surrounded by lush meadows. It lies 1.5 km. east of the fishing village of Glandore. A further 5 km. west is the regional centre, Skibbereen, beyond which the landscape moves from unspoilt Devon to unspoilt Cornwall. The owners, who live on the park, have cunningly arranged accommodation for 19 pitches among the flower beds and shrubberies of their extended garden. Space is rather tight and only small caravans are encouraged. There are 10 hard-standings for motorcaravans with 6A electric hook-ups. Among the homely features are a sitting room and a well equipped kitchen. Note: tents, small caravans and motorcaravans only.

Facilities

Facilities are limited but well designed and immaculately maintained. Showers on payment. Washing machine and dryer. American motorhomes accepted with charge according to length. Off site: Fishing or riding 2 km, fishing, swimming, boat launching and sailing at Glandore (2 km).

Open

15 March - 30 September.

At a glance

| Welcome & Ambience | ✓✓✓✓ | Location | ✓✓✓ |
| Quality of Pitches | ✓✓✓ | Range of Facilities | ✓✓✓ |

Directions

Park is 1.5 km. east of Glandore, off N71 road, on R597 mid-way between Leap and Rosscarbery.

Charges 2005

Per unit incl. 2 persons	€ 15,00
electricity (6A)	€ 2,00
hiker or cyclist incl. tent (per person)	€ 7,00

No credit cards.

Reservations

Please phone site for details. Tel: 028 33280.
Email: the_meadow@oceanfree.net

IR9505 The Hideaway Camping & Caravan Park

Skibbereen (Co. Cork)

A sister park to The Meadow at Glandore, the Hideaway is ideally situated as a touring base for the southwest of Ireland. It is a well run site under the constant supervision of the owners and although it enjoys tranquil surroundings, including preserved marshland, it is within a ten minute walk from the busy market town of Skibbereen. A touring only park, it has 60 pitches which include 45 with hard-standing and 6A electric hook-up. The remainder for tents and caravans are on grass. Shrubs and low hedges divide the park giving an open feel overall and with commanding views across the fields and hills. One long building houses reception, the toilet facilities and a games room.

Facilities

The modern toilet block has .well equipped showers (on payment). Baby room. En-suite unit for disabled visitors. Dishwashing sinks. Laundry machines. Campers' dining room. Motorcaravan services. Adventure play area. Off site: Fishing 1.6 km. Golf 2 km. Riding 4 km. Bicycle hire 1 km.

Open

28 April – 21 September.

At a glance

| Welcome & Ambience | ✓✓✓✓ | Location | ✓✓✓✓ |
| Quality of Pitches | ✓✓✓✓ | Range of Facilities | ✓✓✓ |

Directions

From Skibbereen town centre take R596 (signed Casteltownsend). Site is on the left after approx.1 km.

Charges 2005

Per unit incl. 2 adults	€ 15,00 - € 16,00
hiker, cyclist or m/cyclist and tent, per person	€ 7,00
electricity	€ 2,00

Reservations

Contact site. Tel: 028 33280.
Email: the_hideaway@oceanfree.net

IR9510 Eagle Point Caravan & Camping Park

Ballylickey, Bantry (Co. Cork)

Midway between the towns of Bantry and Glengarriff, the spectacular peninsula of Eagle Point juts into Bantry Bay. The first impression is of a spacious country park rather than a campsite. As far as the eye can see this 20 acre, landscaped, part-terraced park, with its vast manicured grass areas separated by mature trees, shrubs and hedges, runs parallel with the shoreline. Suitable for all ages, this is a well run park devoted to tourers, with campers pitched mostly towards the shore. It provides 125 pitches (for 60 caravans and 65 tents), and electric hook-ups. Eagle Point makes an excellent base for watersports enthusiasts – swimming is safe and there is a slipway for small craft.

Facilities

Three well maintained, well designed toilet blocks are above expected standards. Laundry and dishwashing. Motorcaravan services. Play area. Tennis courts. Football field to the far right, well away from the pitches. Fishing. Supermarket at park entrance. Dogs are not accepted. Off site: Bicycle hire 6 km, riding 10 km, golf 2 km.

Open

25 April - 30 September.

At a glance

| Welcome & Ambience | ✓✓✓✓ | Location | ✓✓✓✓ |
| Quality of Pitches | ✓✓✓✓✓ | Range of Facilities | ✓✓✓✓ |

Directions

Take N71 to Bandon, then R586 Bandon to Bantry. From Bantry take N71 to Glengarriif. 6.4 km. from Bantry; park entrance is opposite EMO petrol station.

Charges 2004

Per unit	€ 19,00 - € 24,00
extra adult	€ 6,50
motorcyclist, hiker or cyclist (per person)	€ 8,00
electricity (5A)	€ 2,00

Reservations

Bookings not essential. Tel: 027 50630.
Email: eaglepointcamping@eircom.net

IR9560 Wave Crest Caravan & Camping Park

Caherdaniel (Co. Kerry)

It would be difficult to imagine a more dramatic location than Wave Crest's on the Ring of Kerry coast. Huge boulders and rocky outcrops tumble from the park entrance on the N70 down to the seashore which forms the most southern promontory on the Ring of Kerry. There are spectacular southward views from the park across Kenmare Bay to the Beara peninsula. Sheltering on grass patches in small coves that nestle between the rocks and shrubbery, are 65 hardstanding pitches and 20 on grass offering seclusion. Electricity connections are available (13A). A unique feature is the TV room, an old stone farm building with a thatched roof. Its comfortable interior includes a stone fireplace heated by a converted cast iron marker buoy. Caherdaniel is known for its cheerful little pubs and distinguished restaurant. The Derrynane National Park Nature Reserve is only a few kilometres away, as is Derrynane Cove and Bay. This park would suit older people looking for a quiet, relaxed atmosphere.

Facilities
Two blocks house the sanitary facilities and include hot showers on payment (€ 1), toilet for disabled people and dishwashing sinks. Laundry service. Small shop and takeaway service (May - Sept). Play area. Fishing and boat launching. Off site: Riding 1 km, bicycle hire or golf 10 km. Small beach near. Derrynane Hotel with bar and restaurant.

Open
All year.

At a glance			
Welcome & Ambience	✓✓✓✓	Location	✓✓✓✓
Quality of Pitches	✓✓✓✓	Range of Facilities	✓✓✓✓

Directions
On the N70 (Ring of Kerry), 1.5 km. east of Caherdaniel.

Charges 2004	
Per adult	€ 2,00
child	€ 1,00
pitch	€ 13,00
small tent	€ 12,00
awning	€ 4,00
electricity (13A)	€ 2,00

Reservations
Write for details. Tel: 066 947 5188.

IR9590 Fossa Caravan & Camping Park

Killarney (Co. Kerry)

This mature, well equipped park is in a scenic location, ten minutes drive from the town centre. Fossa Caravan Park is recognisable by its forecourt on which stands a distinctive building housing a roof top restaurant, reception area, shop and petrol pumps. The well laid out park is divided in two - the touring area lies to the right, tucked behind the main building and to the left is an open grass area mainly for campers. Touring pitches, with electricity and drainage, have hardstanding and are angled between shrubs and trees in a tranquil, well cared for garden setting. To the rear at a higher level and discreetly placed are 50 caravan holiday homes. Sheltered by the thick foliage of the wooded slopes which climb high behind the park, these are unobtrusive. Not only is Fossa convenient for Killarney (5.5 km), it is also en-route for the famed 'Ring of Kerry', and makes an ideal base for walkers and golfers.

Facilities
Modern toilet facilities kept spotlessly clean include showers on payment. Laundry room, washing up area. Campers' kitchen. Shop (April - Sept). Restaurant (1 June - end Aug) and takeaway (July/Aug). TV lounge. Play area. Picnic area. Games room. Bicycle hire. Night lighting and security patrol. Off site: Fishing or golf 2 km, riding 3 km.

Open
25 March - 30 September.

At a glance			
Welcome & Ambience	✓✓✓✓✓	Location	✓✓✓✓
Quality of Pitches	✓✓✓✓	Range of Facilities	✓✓✓✓

Directions
Approaching Killarney from all directions, follow signs for N72 Ring of Kerry/Killorglin. At last roundabout join R562/N72. Continue for 5.5 km. and Fossa is the second park to the right.

Charges 2004	
Per adult	€ 4,50
child (under 14 yrs)	€ 1,50
pitch	€ 5,00 - € 6,50
awning	€ 3,00
electricity (10/15A)	€ 3,00
motorcycle and tent, per person	€ 6,75 - € 7,50

Reservations
Advisable in high season and made for min. 3 nights with £20 deposit. Tel: 064 31497. Email: fossaholidays@eircom.net

IR9570 Creveen Lodge Caravan & Camping Park

Healy Pass, Lauragh (Co. Kerry)

The address of this park is rather confusing, but Healy Pass is the well known scenic summit of the road (R574) crossing the Beara Peninsula, which lies between Kenmare Bay to the north and Bantry Bay to the south. Several kilometres inland from the north coast road (R571), the R574 starts to climb steeply southward towards the Healy Pass. Here, on the mountain foothills, is Creveen Lodge, a working hill farm with a quiet, homely atmosphere. Although not so famed as the Iveragh Peninsula, around which runs the Ring of Kerry, the northern Beara is a scenically striking area of County Kerry. Creveen Lodge, commanding views across Kenmare Bay, is divided among three gently sloping fields separated by trees. To allow easy access, the steep farm track is divided into a simple one-way system. There are 20 pitches, 16 for tents, 4 for caravans, with an area of hardstanding for motorcaravans, and electrical connections are available. The park is carefully tended with neat rubbish bins and rustic picnic tables informally placed. This is walking and climbing countryside or, of interest close by, is Derreen Gardens.

Facilities

Well appointed and immaculately maintained, the small toilet block provides showers on payment (€ 0.65), plus a communal room with a fridge, freezer, TV, ironing board, fireplace, tables and chairs. Reception is in the farmhouse. Play area. Off site: Water sports, riding, 'Seafare' cruises, shops and a restaurant nearby. Fishing 2 km, bicycle hire 9 km, boat launching 9 km.

Open

Easter - 31 October.

At a glance

Welcome & Ambience	✓✓✓✓✓	Location	✓✓✓✓
Quality of Pitches	✓✓✓	Range of Facilities	✓✓✓✓

Directions

Park is on the Healy Pass road (R574) 1.5 km. southeast of Lauragh.

Charges 2005

Per adult	€ 2,00
child	€ 1,00
pitch	€ 10,00
motorcyclist incl. tent	€ 5,50
electricity (5A)	€ 2,00

No credit cards.

Reservations

Write to site with an S.A.E. Tel: 064 83131. Email: info@creveenlodge.com

IR9550 Anchor Caravan Park

Castlegregory (Co. Kerry)

Of County Kerry's three long, finger like peninsulas which jut into the sea, Dingle is the most northerly. Tralee is the main town and Anchor Caravan Park is 20 km. west of this famed town and under 4 km. south of Castlegregory on Tralee Bay. A secluded and mature, five acre park, it is enclosed by shrubs and trees, with a gateway leading to a beautiful, sandy beach which is safe for bathing, boating and shore fishing. There are 30 pitches, all with electric hook-ups and some also with drainage and water points. Although there are holiday homes for hire, these are well apart from the touring pitches. In this area of great beauty, miles of sand abounds and taking in the panorama of mountain scenery from the top of the Conor Pass is a wonderful experience.

Facilities

Toilet facilities (entry by key) are kept clean (three or four times daily in busy periods) providing showers on payment (€ 0,50), two private cabins, toilet with handrail, dishwashing and laundry facilities (incl. clothes lines). Motorcaravan services. Two play areas. Games/TV room. Night lighting. Off site: Beautiful sandy beach 2 minutes. Fishing 2 km. Riding or bicycle hire 3 km. Golf 4 km.

Open

Easter - 30 September.

At a glance

Welcome & Ambience	✓✓✓✓	Location	✓✓✓
Quality of Pitches	✓✓✓	Range of Facilities	✓✓✓

Directions

From Tralee follow the Dingle coast road for 19 km. Park is signed from Camp junction.

Charges 2004

Per unit incl. all persons	€ 17,00 - € 18,00
small tent incl. 1 or 2 persons	€ 12,00 - € 13,00
motorcyclist, hiker or cyclist, tent	€ 10,00 - € 11,00
electricity	€ 2,00
awning	€ 2,50

No credit cards.

Reservations

Contact site. Tel: 066 7139157. Email: anchorcaravanpark@eircom.net

IR9630 Donoghues White Villa Farm Caravan & Camping Park

Cork Road (N22), Killarney (Co. Kerry)

This is a very pleasing small touring park in scenic surroundings on the N22 Killarney-Cork road. It is set on a 100 acre family operated dairy farm which stretches as far as the River Flesk, yet is only five minutes away from Killarney town. Trees and shrubs surround the park but dominant is a magnificent view of the MacGillicuddy's Reeks. There are 24 pitches for caravans and tents, 15 with hardstanding and a grass area for awnings, electricity (10A), water points and night lighting. An unusual novelty is old school desks placed around the site, plus an antique green telephone box. One can also enjoy walking through the oak wood, fishing on the Flesk or visiting the site's own National Farm Museum.

Facilities

The toilet block, a sandstone coloured building to the rear of the park, is kept spotlessly clean and houses showers on payment, a good toilet/shower room for disabled visitors, laundry room, clothes lines and dishwashing sinks. Motorcaravan service area. Campers' kitchen with TV. Play area. Basketball. Bicycle hire. Max. 2 dogs per pitch are accepted (not certain breeds). Off site: Riding, golf and boat launching 5 km. Killarney town 5 minutes, the National Park is 10 minutes away.

Open

1 April - 3 October.

At a glance

Welcome & Ambience	✓✓✓✓	Location	✓✓✓✓
Quality of Pitches	✓✓✓✓	Range of Facilities	✓✓✓

Directions

Park is 3 km. east from Killarney town on N22 Cork road. Park entrance is 500 m. east of N22/N72 junction. From Killarney follow N22 Cork road signs and 'White Villa Farm' finger signs from Park Road roundabout. From Kenmare take R569 via Kilgarvan to the N22, then as above.

Charges 2005

Per adult	€ 4,75
child according to age	€ 1,50 - € 3,00
pitch	€ 3,00 - € 4,50
hiker or cyclist incl. tent	€ 6,00 - € 6,25
electricity	€ 3,00

No credit cards. Seven nights for the price of six.

Reservations

Made with deposit (€ 15 or UK £10). Tel: 064 20671. Email: killarneycamping@eircom.net

IR9620 Fleming's White Bridge Caravan Park

Ballycasheen Road, Killarney (Co. Kerry)

Once past the county border, the main road from Cork to Killarney (N22) runs down the valley of the Flesk river. On the final approach to Killarney off the N22 Cork road, the river veers away from the road to enter the Lower Lake. On this prime rural position, between the road and the river, and within comfortable walking distance of the town, is Fleming's White Bridge, a nine acre woodland park. The ground is flat, landscaped and generously adorned with flowers, shrubs and trees. There are now 92 pitches (46 caravans and 46 tents) that extend beyond a wooden bridge to an area surrounded by mature trees and where a new toilet block, one of three, is sited. This is obviously a park of which the owners are very proud, and the family personally supervise the reception and grounds, maintaining high standards of hygiene, cleanliness and tidiness. The park's location so close to Ireland's premier tourism centre makes this park an ideal base to explore Killarney and the southwest.

Facilities

Three toilet blocks are maintained to high standards. Dishwashing sinks. Motorcaravan service point. Campers' drying room and two laundries. Shop (1/6-1/9). Two TV rooms and a games room. Fishing (advice and permits provided). Canoeing (own canoes). Bicycle hire. Woodland walks. Off site: Riding 3 km, golf 2 km.

Open

15 March - 31 October.

Reservations

Advised for high season; write with € 5 non-refundable reservation fee. Tel: 064 31590. Email: fwbcamping@eircom.net

At a glance

Welcome & Ambience	✓✓✓✓✓	Location	✓✓✓✓
Quality of Pitches	✓✓✓✓	Range of Facilities	✓✓✓✓

Directions

From Cork and Mallow: at N72/N22 junction continue towards Killarney and take first turn left (signed Ballycasheen Road). Proceed for 300 m. to archway entrance on left. From Limerick: follow N22 Cork road. After passing Super Valu and Killarney Heights Hotel take first right (signed Ballycasheen Road) and continue as above. From Kenmare: On N71, pass Gleneagles Hotel and Flesk Bridge. Turn right before Shell filling station into Woodlawn Road and Ballycasheen Road, continue 2 km. to archway.

Charges 2004

Per person	€ 6,00
child (under 14 yrs)	€ 2,00
pitch	€ 5,00 - € 6,00
hiker or cyclist incl. tent	€ 7,50 - € 8,00
electricity (10A)	€ 3,50

No credit cards.

IR9600 Glenross Caravan & Camping Park

Glenbeigh (Co. Kerry)

Its situation on the spectacular Ring of Kerry and the Kerry Way gives Glenross an immediate advantage, and scenic grandeur around every bend of the road is guaranteed as Glenbeigh is approached. Quietly located before entering the village, the park commands a fine view of Rossbeigh Strand, which is within walking distance. On arrival, a good impression is created with the park well screened from the road and with new stone entrance and gates. There are 30 touring pitches including hardstanding pitches with electricity and, although there are six caravan holiday homes, the park is attractively laid out. There is no catering on site but the Glenbeigh Hotel next door is popular and village shops are near. Not least is the Kerry Bog Village where you can go back in time in this reconstructed pre-famine village.

Facilities

Well maintained modern toilet block includes facilities for laundry and dishwashing. Motorcaravan service point. Games room. Bicycle hire. Shelter for campers. Sun lounge and barbecue patio. Off site: Watersports and tennis near. Riding and fishing 200 m. Golf 500 m.

Open

2 May - 15 September.

At a glance

Welcome & Ambience	✓✓✓✓	Location	✓✓✓✓
Quality of Pitches	✓✓✓✓	Range of Facilities	✓✓✓

Directions

Park is on the N70 Killorglin - Glenbeigh road, on the right just before entering the village.

Charges 2004

Per person	€ 6,00
child (under 14 yrs)	€ 2,00
pitch	€ 5,50 - € 6,50
electricity (10A)	€ 3,50
awning	€ 2,00 - € 2,50
motorcyclist and tent	€ 8,00 - € 8,50

No credit cards.

Reservations

Write to site for details Tel: 066 97 68451.
Email: fwbcamping@eircom.net

IR9610 Mannix Point Camping & Caravan Park

Cahirciveen (Co. Kerry)

A quiet and peaceful, beautifully located seashore park, it is no exaggeration to describe Mannix Point as a nature lovers' paradise. Situated in one of the most spectacular parts of the Ring of Kerry, over-looking the Portmagee Channel towards Valentia Island, the park commands splendid views in all directions. It is flat and open being right on marshland which teems with wildlife (a two acre nature reserve) with direct access to the beach and seashore. The owner has planted around 500 plants with plans for around 1,000 more trees and shrubs. There are 42 pitches, 15 for tourers and 27 for tents, with electrical connections (6A) available. A charming old fisherman's cottage has been converted to provide reception, there is a cosy sitting room with turf fire, and an 'emergency' dormitory for campers is a feature. There is no television, but compensation comes in the form of a knowledgeable, hospitable owner who is a Bord Fáilte registered local tour guide. This park retains a wonderful air of Irish charm aided by occasional impromptu musical evenings. Watersports, bird watching, walking and photography can all be pursued. Local cruises to Skelligs Rock with free transport to and from the port for walkers and cyclists. This is also an ideal resting place for people walking the Kerry Way.

Facilities

Toilet facilities, now upgraded and immaculate, have well designed showers (on €0.80 payment). Modern campers' kitchen. Laundry facilities with washing machines and dryer. Motorcaravan service facilities. Dogs are not accepted in July and August. Off site: Bicycle hire 800 m. riding 3 km, golf 14 km. Pubs, restaurants and shops 15 minutes walk.

Open

15 March - 1 October.

At a glance

Welcome & Ambience	✓✓✓✓✓	Location	✓✓✓✓
Quality of Pitches	✓✓✓	Range of Facilities	✓✓✓

Directions

Park is 250 m. off the N70 Ring of Kerry road, 800 m. southwest of Cahirciveen (or Cahersiveen) on the road towards Waterville.

Charges 2004

Per adult	€ 6,50
child (1 or 2 children)	€ 2,00

Book 7 nights, pay 6. Reductions for groups if pre-paid. No credit cards.

Reservations

Made with deposit (1 one night's fee).
Tel: 066 9472806.
Email: mortimer@campinginkerry.com

IR9640 The Killarney Flesk Caravan & Camping Park

Muckross Road, Killarney (Co. Kerry)

At the gateway to the National Park and Lakes, near Killarney town, this family run, seven acre park has undergone extensive development and offers high quality standards. Pitches are well spaced and have electricity (10A), water, and drainage connections; 21 also have hardstanding with a grass area for awnings. The grounds have been well cultivated with further shrubs, plants and an attractive barbecue and patio area. This is to the left of the sanitary block and is paved and sunk beneath the level roadway. Surrounded by a garden border, it has tables and chairs, making a pleasant communal meeting place commanding excellent views of Killarney's mountains.

Facilities

Modern, clean toilet blocks are well designed and equipped. Baby bath/changing room. Laundry room. Campers' kitchen with dishwashing sinks. Comfortable games room. Other on site facilities include petrol pumps, supermarket (all year), delicatessen and café (March - Oct) with extra seating on the sun terrace. Night lighting and night time security checks. Winter caravan storage. Off site: Fishing 300 m, boat launching 2 km.

Open

17 April - 30 September.

At a glance

Welcome & Ambience	✓✓✓✓	Location	✓✓✓✓
Quality of Pitches	✓✓✓✓	Range of Facilities	✓✓✓✓

Directions

From Killarney town centre follow the N71 and signs for Killarney National Park. Site is 1.5 km. on the left beside the Gleneagle Hotel.

Charges 2004

Per adult	€ 5,75
child (under 14 yrs)	€ 1,50
pitch	€ 6,00 - € 6,50
small tent	€ 5,50 - € 5,50
awning	€ 2,00
electricity (10A)	€ 3,50

Reservations

Advisable in peak periods, write to park.
Tel: 064 31704. Email: killarneylakes@eircom.net

IR9650 Woodlands Park Touring Caravan & Camping Park

Dan Spring Road, Tralee (Co. Kerry)

Tralee is not only the Capital of County Kerry and gateway to the Dingle Peninsula, it is also Ireland's fastest growing visitor destination, with Woodlands its newest touring caravan park. Although only a ten minute walk from the town centre, this park is located on a 16 acre elevated site approached by a short roadway and bridge that straddles the River Lee. Once on site the town seems far removed, with a countryside environment taking over. Hedging, trees, grazing fields and the distant Slieve Mish Mountain create the setting. The owners of Woodlands have designed and equipped their park to a high standard. A distinctive feature is its impressive yellow coloured building which houses an 'on top' family dwelling and ground floor services. There are 85 pitches with hardstanding, electricity, water and drainage plus night light, to the left and centre behind the main building, and a grass area for 40 tents is to the right. Young shrubs, cordyline trees and flower beds have been planted around the park and a security barrier is in operation. Interesting is the award winning 'Kerry the Kingdom' museum with its incredible time car trip through the Middle Ages. Evening entertainment in Tralee means a selection of singing pubs, restaurants and the National Folk Theatre.

Facilities

Heated sanitary facilities include sizeable showers (€1 token) and provision for disabled guests. Campers' kitchen and dishwashing sinks. Laundry room with washing machines and dryer. Café/snack bar. Shop. Games room. TV and adult room. Fenced adventure play area. Off site: The nearby Aqua Dome offers half price admission after 6 pm. Golf 6 km, riding 2 km. Blue flag beaches on the Dingle Peninsula.

Open

Easter - 30 September.

At a glance

Welcome & Ambience	✓✓✓✓	Location	✓✓✓✓
Quality of Pitches	✓✓✓✓	Range of Facilities	✓✓✓✓

Directions

Site is 1 km. southwest of Tralee town centre. From N21/N69/N86 junction south of Tralee follow camp signs for 2.4 km. to park, 200 m. off the N86 Tralee - Dingle road. Site is 300 m. east of the Aqua Dome

Charges 2005

Per unit incl. 2 adults	€ 15,50 - € 17,00
incl. 2 adults and 2 children	€ 18,50 - € 20,00
extra adult	€ 5,50
child (under 16 yrs)	€ 1,50
electricity (10A)	€ 3,50

Reservations

Advisable for high season. Tel: 066 7121235.
Email: wdlands@fircroft.net

A visit to the Channel Islands offers a holiday in part of the British Isles, yet in an area which has a definite continental flavour. All the islands have beautiful beaches and coves, pretty scenery and fascinating histories.

The Channel Islands is comprised of the islands of:

Jersey, Guernsey, Sark, Herm and Alderney

The largest of the Channel Islands is Jersey, which is also the most commercial with more entertainment on offer. It has long stretches of beaches that are safe for bathing, and ideal for water-based activities such as windsurfing and banana rides. Caravans and motor caravans are now allowed on Jersey, but with a number of limitations (for example, length of stay, width and length of the unit). A permit is required which is obtained as part of the booking procedure with the campsite of your choice. You must book in advance but the campsite owner will advise you on all aspects of your visit.

Guernsey will suit those who prefer a quieter, more peaceful holiday. Caravans and motor caravans are not allowed here. Guernsey too has wide, sandy beaches plus sheltered coves. The historical, harbour town of St Peter Port has steep and winding cobbled streets, with plenty of shops, cafes and restaurants.

For those who want total relaxation, one of the smaller islands – Sark or Herm, would be ideal. No cars are permitted on either of these islands. Sark, the larger of the two, has over 40 miles of coastline; cycling is the best way to explore the island, or you could opt for a guided trip by horse drawn carriage. Herm is tiny, with beautiful quiet golden beaches and a tiny harbour village. Shopping in all the islands has the advantage of no mainland VAT – particularly useful when buying cameras, watches and alcohol.

Did you know?

Jersey has been associated with knitting for nearly 400 years

The Channel Islands were the only part of the British Isles to be occupied by the Germans during the Second World War

The first road side letterboxes in the British Isles were erected in St Helier on 23rd November 1852

Herm island is just one and a half miles long and only half a mile wide

Le Jerriais is the native language of Jersey, a blend of Norse and Norman French

Places of interest

Jersey: St Helier; Jersey Zoo; Jersey War tunnels; Elizabeth Castle;German Underground Hospital in St Lawrence; Samarès Manor in St Clement; Shell Garden at St Aubin; Battle of Flowers Museum in St Ouen

Guernsey: Castle Cornet at St Peter Port Harbour; Victor Hugo's House; Guernsey Folk Museum; German Occupation Museum; Fort Grey Shipwreck Museum; Saumarez Park

Sark: La Coupée; La Seigneurie, with old dovecote and gardens; Gouliet and Boutique Caves; Le Pot on Little Sark; Venus Pool; Little Sark Village

tip

THE JERSEY BATTLE OF THE FLOWERS TAKES PLACE IN MID AUGUST: A CARNIVAL PROCESSION OF LORRIES AND TRACTORS DECKED OUT IN FLOWERS COMPETE TO BE THE WINNER.

UK9710 Rozel Camping Park

Rozel, St Martin, Jersey JE3 6AX (Jersey)

This family owned park is within walking distance of the famous Jersey Zoo and the pretty harbour and fishing village of Rozel, where the north coast cliff path commences. The surrounding countryside is quieter than many areas of the island. A car is probably necessary to reach the main island beaches, although a bus service does run to St Helier from close by. The park itself is quietly situated at the top of a valley (the French coast can be seen on a clear day) and is surrounded by trees providing shelter. There are two main camping areas providing 130 pitches of which 45 have electric hook ups (10/16A) and 20 are used for fully equipped tents to hire. Some pitches, mainly for smaller tents are arranged on terraced areas. The remainder are on a higher, flat field where pitches are arranged in bays with hedges growing to separate them into groups. Caravans and motorcaravans are now accepted and the site has provided easy access, plus chemical and grey waste disposal facilities. In addition to package deals for tent hire and travel, the site offers a good range of camping equipment for hire on a daily basis. Boats are accepted by prior arrangement.

Facilities

Two first rate, heated sanitary buildings include a bathroom for disabled people with a shower, toilet and washbasin with an access ramp (in the lower block). Family shower room (upper block) with small heater for cooler weather. Dishwashing under cover. Fully equipped laundry. Shop. Attractive, sheltered swimming pool (June-Sept) with children's pool and sunbathing areas. Play area. Crazy golf. Games room, reading and TV room. Torches useful. Dogs are not accepted. Off site: Beach 2 miles. Fishing 1 mile. Riding 3 miles. Golf 4 miles.

Open

23 May - 10 September.

At a glance

Welcome & Ambience	✓✓✓	Location	✓✓✓✓
Quality of Pitches	✓✓✓	Range of Facilities	✓✓✓✓

Directions

Leave harbour by Route du Port Elizabeth, take A1 east through the tunnel and the A17. At fourth set of lights turn left on A6. Keep in the middle lane. Continue to Five Oaks and on to St Martin's church. Turn right, then immediately left at the 'Royal' pub on B38 to Rozel, continue to end of road, turn right and park is on the right.

Charges 2005

Per person	£ 6.80 - £ 8.20
child (4-11 yrs)	£ 2.70 - £ 3.90
electricity	£ 1.50
Tent hire and travel packages.	

Reservations

Made for any length with £40 deposit; balance due 14 days before arrival. Tel: 01534 855 200. Email: rozelcampingpark@jerseymail.co.uk

UK9720 Beuvelande Camp Site

St Martin, Jersey JE3 6EZ (Jersey)

What a pleasant surprise we had when we called here - the outstanding sanitary building gives campers facilities often associated with top class hotels. A licensed restaurant with covered terrace area is also situated in this building, open morning and evening all season, but perhaps a few less hours at quiet times. There are 150 pitches, 60 with fully equipped tents for hire, but with plenty of space for those with their own tents. Sixty of the pitches have electric hook ups (5/10A) and cars may be parked next to your tent. Torches would be useful. Car hire can be arranged and bicycle hire is possible from the site. This family run park prides itself on quality, cleanliness and hospitality.

Facilities

The toilet block is tiled top to bottom and spotlessly clean, with controllable showers, two fully equipped bathrooms for disabled people, and a baby room. Plenty of dishwashing facilities and a laundry can now be found in the original sanitary building. Games room with arcade games and pool. TV room. Well stocked shop open 8 am. - 7 pm. during peak times and stocks gas. Licensed restaurant. Ice pack and battery charging services for a small charge. Outdoor heated swimming pool (41 x 17 ft) with a sun terrace and small waterslide. Play area and large playing field. Off site: Fishing, golf or riding within 3 km.

Open

1 May - 15 September.

At a glance

Welcome & Ambience	✓✓✓✓	Location	✓✓✓✓
Quality of Pitches	✓✓✓✓	Range of Facilities	✓✓✓

Directions

On leaving the harbour by Route du Port Elizabeth, take A1 east through the tunnel and the A17. At the fourth set of traffic lights turn left on A6. Continue to Five Oaks and on to St Martin's RC church, then right into La Longue Rue, right again Rue de L'Orme then left to site.

Charges guide

Per adult	£ 6.00 - £ 8.00
child (2-8 yrs)	£ 3.50
child (8-14 yrs)	£ 4.50
dog	£ 2.00
Single sex groups not accepted.	

Reservations

Made with £30 deposit; contact park for details. Tel: 01534 853 575.

UK9780 Fauxquets Valley Farm Campsite

Castel, Guernsey GY5 7QA (Guernsey)

Situated in the rural centre of the island, Fauxquets is in a pretty sheltered valley, hidden down narrow lanes away from busy roads and is run by the Guille family. A car would be useful here to reach the beaches, St Peter Port and other attractions, although there is a bus service each day (20 minutes walk). It was once a dairy farm, but the valley side has now been developed into an attractive camp site, with the old farm buildings as its centre. Plenty of trees, bushes and flowers have been planted to separate pitches and to provide shelter around the various fields which are well terraced. The 86 touring pitches are of a good size, most marked, numbered and with electricity, and there is lots of open space. There are also 15 smaller places for backpackers. The site has 23 fully equipped tents for hire, but there are no tour operators. The Haybarn licensed restaurant and bar provides breakfast, morning coffee and cake and evening meals. There is plenty of room to sit around the heated swimming pool, including a large grassy terrace with sun-beds provided.

Facilities

Good toilet facilities have controllable showers, some washbasins in private cabins with a shower, baby bath and changing unit. Dishwashing facilities under cover and a tap for free hot water. Laundry room with free irons, boards and hairdryers. Swimming pool (20 x 45 ft.) with paddling pool, heated from 31/5. Restaurant and bar (25/6-7/9). Small shop with ice-pack hire and gas. TV room and table tennis. Small play area and play field. Bicycle hire. Torches useful. Off site: Fishing and boat launching 3 miles, riding and golf 2 miles.

Open

Easter - 15 September.

At a glance

Welcome & Ambience	✓✓✓✓	Location	✓✓✓✓
Quality of Pitches	✓✓✓✓	Range of Facilities	✓✓✓✓

Directions

From harbour take second exit from roundabout. At top of hill, turn left at 'filter in turn' into Queens Road, then right at next filter. Follow straight through traffic lights and down hill past hospital, through pedestrian lights and straight on at next lights at top of hill. Continue for 0.75 miles, then turn right opposite sign for German Hospital. Fourth left is pedestrian entrance, cars carry on for 400 yds to gravel entrance on left.

Charges 2004

Per adult	£ 5.00 - £ 5.90
electricity	£ 2.50
children (at school)	£ 2.50 - £ 2.95

Child (at school) half price.
Fully equipped tents with fridge for hire.

Reservations

Made for independent campers for any length, with £50 deposit. Tent hire details from site.
Tel: 01481 255 460. Email: info@fauxquets.co.uk

UK9770 Vaugrat Camping

St Sampson's, Guernsey GY2 4TA (Guernsey)

Vaugrat Camping is a neat, well tended site, close to the beach in the northwest of the island. Owned and run by the Laine family, it is centred around attractive and interesting old granite farm buildings dating back to the 15th century, with a gravel courtyard and attractive flower beds. It provides 150 pitches on flat grassy meadows, that are mostly surrounded by trees, banks and hedges to provide shelter. Tents are arranged around the edges of the fields, giving open space in the centre, and while pitches are not marked, there is sufficient room and cars may be parked next to tents. Only couples and families are accepted and the site is well run and welcoming. It also offers 30 fully equipped tents for hire. Housed in the old farmhouse, now a listed building, are the reception area, and shop where fresh croissants are baked every morning. Upstairs is the Coffee Barn, with views to the sea, where breakfast is served; one can also sit here in the evenings. A cider room complete with the ancient presses is now the games/TV room.

Facilities

Well kept sanitary facilities are in two buildings. The first block is in the courtyard, with hot showers on payment. Unit for disabled visitors with shower, basin and toilet (although there is a 6 inch step into the building). Laundry room with washing machine, dryer and iron. Second block near the camping fields provides toilets, washbasins and dishwashing facilities. Shop with ice pack hire and gas (main season only). Café serving breakfast only. Dogs are not accepted. Torches useful. Off site: Bus service within easy reach. Car or bicycle hire can be arranged. Fishing, riding and golf within 1.5 miles. Hotel and bar nearby.

Open

1 May - 30 September.

At a glance

Welcome & Ambience	✓✓✓✓	Location	✓✓✓✓
Quality of Pitches	✓✓✓	Range of Facilities	✓✓✓

Directions

On leaving St Peter Port, turn right onto coast road for 1.5 miles. At filter turn left into Vale Road. Straight over at two sets of lights then first left turn by church. Follow to crossroads (garage opposite) turn right. Carry on past Peninsula Hotel, then second left, signed for site. Site on left after high stone wall (400 yds) with concealed entrance.

Charges guide

Per adult	£ 5.95
child (under 14 yrs)	£ 4.75
car or boat	£ 1.10

Families and couples only.
Fully equipped tents to hire (details from site).

Reservations

Made for independent campers for any length, with £10 deposit and balance on arrival. Tel: 01481 257468. Email: enquiries@vaugratcampsite.com

UK9830 Seagull Campsite

The Administration Office, Herm Island GY1 3HR (Herm)

This tiny site, and indeed the island of Herm, will appeal to those who are looking for complete tranquillity and calm. Reached by boat (20 minutes and approx. £7.50 return fare for adults, £3.75 for children) from Guernsey, the 500 acre island allows no cars only tractors on its narrow roads and paths (no bicycles either). One is free to stroll around the many paths, through farmland, heath and around the coast, where there are beautiful beaches. The campsite is a 20 minute uphill walk from the harbour, but your luggage will be transported for you by tractor. It consists of several terraced areas offering a total of 40 pitches, and 22 fully equipped tents for hire on flat grass areas. There are no electricity hook-ups. One may bring one's own tent and equipment or hire both (but not bedding, crockery and lighting) from the site. Herm is definitely not for those who like entertainment and plenty of facilities, but for total relaxation, with the absence of any bustle and noise it takes some beating! Due to the stony footpaths on Herm, sensible walking shoes are advised.

Facilities

Small, modern, but open, toilet block on site. Hot showers (£1 payment - there is a shortage of water on Herm). Freezer for ice-packs. The harbour village is about ten minutes walk down the hill where there is a small shop for provisions, gas, a post office, pub, restaurants and café. Fishing on the island. No dogs or pets are allowed. Torches useful.

Open

14 May - first w/end in September.

At a glance

Welcome & Ambience	✓✓✓	Location	✓✓✓✓
Quality of Pitches	✓✓✓	Range of Facilities	✓✓✓

Directions

Reached by boat from St Peter Port - report to Administration Office on arrival. Do not take your car as it is unlikely you will be able to park long term in St Peter Port.

Charges 2004

Per adult	£ 5.00
child (under 14 yrs)	£ 2.50
transportation of luggage	£ 6.50
Equipped tents for hire.	
Groups of single people not accepted.	

Reservations

Made for any length with £20 deposit. Details of hire tents from above address. Tel: 01481 722 377.
Email: camping@herm-island.com

UK9870 Pomme de Chien Campsite

Sark (Sark)

'The island where time stands still' is an apt description of Sark, one of the smallest inhabited Channel Islands, some 45 minutes from Guernsey by boat. There is no airport, no cars or motorcycles and (apart from a tractor-drawn 'train' up Harbour Hill) the only transport is by bicycle (which must be hired on the island) or horse-drawn carriage. However, all you are likely to need for a tranquil holiday is provided with several small shops, pubs, hotels, restaurants, a Tourist Office and even two banks! Situated five minutes from the shops and ten from the beach, the Pomme de Chien campsite is small with only 50 pitches, of which 8 are occupied by fully equipped tents for rent. The remainder are for campers with their own tents (no caravans, motorcaravans or trailer tents of course). The pitches are large, on fairly level ground, but none have electricity hook-ups. There is a warm welcome from the owners Chris and Jill Rang with the famous charm of Sark. Although you cannot take your car to the island, the Condor service via Guernsey means you can get there in a little over three hours either with your own small tent or of course you could hire one of the site's own (equipment includes everything you're likely to need except bedding and a torch).

Facilities

Modern sanitary block was added in 1999 with free hot showers (large, with bench and hook), toilets and washbasins. Dishwashing sinks are outside. Outside washing line. Dogs are not accepted and torches are necessary. Baggage can be transferred from the harbour right to the site by tractor trailer, at a cost of 80p per item. Off site: Fishing 10 mins. walk, bicycle hire 5 mins. Beach 10 mins.

Open

All year - incl. campers; June - September for hire tents.

At a glance

Welcome & Ambience	✓✓✓	Location	✓✓✓✓✓
Quality of Pitches	✓✓✓	Range of Facilities	✓✓✓

Directions

Take the tractor drawn 'train' up Harbour Hill (80p; you can walk but it is a ten minute hike). Once at the top take road leading off left, then second right, and follow the lane to the site entrance. Reception is at the house with white gates.

Charges guide

Per adult	£ 5.50
child	£ 3.50
hire tent (per week)	£ 160.00
No credit cards.	

Reservations

Write to site. Tel: 01481 832 316.

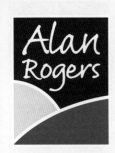

NEW for 2005
The Directory

Your essential directory for camping and caravanning products and services.

Going on holiday is just the final part of the fun – planning and preparation for the trip is all part of the experience.

Many readers have asked for more information on useful suppliers and contacts, relevant to their holiday preparations; and so we have added this new section, designed to complement the campsite information we provide and assist you in finding reliable, quality suppliers and products. We hope you find it useful.

When contacting them, please be sure to mention the Alan Rogers guide.

Happy Travelling!

Apply today and receive 2 FREE Club Site Nights

All the signs are looking good for The Caravan Club VISA Card. Exclusive to Caravan Club members, we'll give you 2 FREE Club Site Nights when you've made your first transaction, which is just one of a great range of benefits we offer...

- Just 14.9% APR (variable)
- Earn FREE nights on Club Sites when you spend on the card
- Take up to 50 days interest free credit
- Pay off your balance every month by Direct Debit
- Internet fraud guarantee
- No commission on purchases in the EU*
- No annual fee
- FREE Purchase Protection (min. claim £30; max. £500 per item)

> **"**Not only is Frizzell one of the very few UK finance houses that add no charges abroad, but it gives you that day's 'Bank rate' exchange and not the lesser 'tourist rate'... why pay any other way?**"**
>
> David Parry-Jones, Wrexham.

Call us FREE on 0800 373 191

Quoting exclusive member code WABQ
Lines open 8am-8pm Mon to Fri, and 8am-4pm Sat. Textphone for the hearing impaired 0800 169 3391

NEW! Apply online at www.frizzell.co.uk/cara

FRIZZELL

THE CARAVAN CLUB

3 ISSUES FOR £1

Practical Caravan is the UK's biggest and best selling caravan magazine. Written by enthusiasts for enthusiasts, each issue is packed full with holiday tips, technical advice, reader reviews, superb photography, reader offers... and much more!

Try the next 3 issues for just

Then, if you like what you see - just sit back and relax! Your subscription will continue at the discounted rate of £7.80 every 3 issues for Practical Caravan or £7.15 for Practical Motorhome. That's **20% off** the shop price.

We and thousands of subscribers guarantee you will love it!

This offer is also valid on

Practical Motorhome

NOW EVEN BIGGER AND BETTER!

3 FREE ISSUES!

THE UK'S FAVOURITE MOTORHOME MAGAZINES...

The UK's best selling motorhome magazine for 38 years, MMM is considered to be the only place to look for the latest news from the motorcaravanning world.

The UK's leading magazine for motorhome buyers, Which Motorcaravan has more hot news of new models and in-depth vehicle tests than any rival publication.

Reply now and you will get the next **3 issues of MMM for just £1 each** or the next **3 issues of Which Motorcaravan FREE!**

Then, if you like what you see - do nothing! Your subscription will continue at the LOW RATE of just £8 every 3 months for MMM, or £5 every 3 months for Which Motorcaravan, giving you a saving of up to 44% off the shop price!

100% RISK FREE OFFER
If you feel that the magazine is not for you simply write to us within 10 days of receiving your third issue and you won't pay a penny more! Additionally, you may cancel your subscription at any time and we will refund in full the cost of all unmailed copies.

Call our Hotline today on 01778 391180
(Please have your bank details ready & quote ref: ALANROGERS05)

Offer is open to UK residents and is a Direct Debit offer only. Your subscription will start with the next available issue. Please note, only one trial offer per magazine will be processed per household during a 12 month period.

Belle
FRANCE

Walking & Cycling Holidays

& NOW BOATING

Discover the easy going
alternative

Belle France offers leisurely holidays through the most beautiful and interesting parts of France.

On our walking and cycling holidays your luggage is moved for you whilst you find your own way, at your own pace with our detailed maps and notes.

Relax in the evening in charming family run hotels, offering a good standard of accommodation and a warm and friendly welcome.

Our boating holidays allow you to wander along France's beautiful, slow moving waterways.

Follow suggested routes, stopping where you choose and enjoy complete freedom.

Walking, Cycling & Boating 2003

Call now for a
FREE brochure
0870 405 4056

www.**bellefrance**.co.uk

The best magazines, whatever your lifestyle

For buying information, top tips and technical help, Caravan, Motor Caravan Magazine and Park Home & Holiday Caravan are all you need — every month!

Subscribe and save 25%

Just call our special hotline number below

+44 (0)845 676 7778

SAVE
UP TO 55%
OFF YOUR HOLIDAY

_ooking for **the best sites in the UK**?

_ooking for **low season value**?

_ooking for **flexibility**?

Camping Cheque ©

Wooda Farm Park - Bude

Pentewan Sands - Cornwall

Cofton Farm - Devon

Camping Cheque offers a choice of 511 of Europe's finest sites, including Britain and Ireland, all at an incredible fixed price of just **£9.95** per night for pitch, 2 adults and electric hook-up.

That's a saving of up to **55%** off normal site tariffs.

www.campingcheque.co.uk

2005

Holiday Savings guide

Amazing Ferry Deals

Camping Cheque

For a **FREE** guide to saving up to 55% on your holiday call

0870 405 4057

The following parks are understood to accept caravanners and campers all year round, although the list also includes some parks that are open for at least ten months. These parks are marked with a star (*) – please refer to the park's individual entry for details. It is always wise to phone the park to check as the facilities available, for example, ma be reduced.

England

UK0030	Ayr
UK0180	Carnon Downs
UK0310	Trekenning
UK0350	Whitsand Bay
UK0440	Dolbeare
UK0460	Croft *
UK0530	Trethiggey *
UK0710	Hidden Valley
UK0800	Higher Longford
UK0910	Ross Park *
UK1075	Golden Coast *
UK1130	Hoburne Torbay *
UK1306	Mill Farm
UK1350	Quantock Orchard
UK1400	The Isle of Avalon
UK1420	Southfork
UK1440	Baltic Wharf
UK1450	Bath Marina
UK1460	Newton Mill
UK1480	Home Farm *
UK1500	Long Hazel *
UK1510	Bath Chew Valley
UK1520	Waterrow
UK1550	Bucklegrove *
UK1630	Brokerswood
UK1640	Greenhill Farm
UK1650	Coombe
UK1670	Alderbury
UK1700	Devizes
UK1810	Newlands
UK2020	Ulwell Cottage *
UK2030	Wareham Forest
UK2080	Merley Court *
UK2100	Sandford Park *
UK2270	Oakdene Forest *
UK2280	Lytton Lawn *
UK2290	Sandy Balls
UK2360	Hill Cottage Farm *
UK2450	The Orchards *
UK2600	Barnstones
UK2620	Wysdom
UK2750	Highclere Farm *
UK2810	Chertsey
UK2890	White Rose *
UK2930	Sheepcote Valley
UK2940	Honeybridge
UK2950	Washington
UK3030	Tanner Farm
UK3040	Broadhembury
UK3050	Pine Lodge
UK3070	Canterbury
UK3090	Black Horse Farm
UK3230	Lee Valley *
UK3260	Abbey Wood
UK3270	Crystal Palace
UK3310	Low House
UK3330	Moat Barn *
UK3340	Polstead
UK3382	Rose Farm
UK3400	Old Brick Kilns
UK3420	Two Mills *
UK3470	Breckland *
UK3550	Old Manor
UK3575	Stroud Hill
UK3580	Ferry Meadows
UK3690	Bainland
UK3730	Skegness Sands
UK3760	Tallington Lakes *
UK3850	Rivendale *
UK3910	Shardaroba
UK3920	Riverside
UK3940	Smeaton's Lakes
UK4070	Somers Wood *
UK4075	Hollyfast
UK4130	Moreton-in-Marsh
UK4140	Winchcombe *
UK4150	Croft Farm *
UK4170	Tudor
UK4210	Lickhill Manor
UK4300	Poston Mill
UK4345	Townsend *
UK4390	Westbrook Park
UK4400	Stanmore Hall
UK4410	Beaconsfield Farm
UK4420	Severn Gorge
UK4430	Oxon Hall
UK4540	St Helens *
UK4550	Cayton Village *
UK4640	Goose Wood *
UK4650	Fangfoss *
UK4710	Rudding *
UK4740	Jasmine Park
UK5280	Abbey Farm
UK5350	Holgates *
UK5360	Willowbank *
UK5560	Sykeside
UK5570	Wild Rose
UK5740	White Water
UK5755	South Meadows *
UK5800	Ord House

Wales

UK5910	Saint Pierre
UK5925	Cardiff
UK5927	Acorn *
UK5930	Cwmcarn *
UK5940	Pembrey
UK5950	Afon Lodge *
UK6010	Cenarth Falls *
UK6040	Pencelli Castle
UK6240	Cringoed *
UK6310	Bacheldre
UK6330	Daisy Bank
UK6355	Woodlands
UK6370	Hendre Mynach
UK6590	Beddgelert *
UK6600	Bryn Gloch *
UK6680	James'
UK6690	Bron-Y-Wendo

Scotland

UK6870	Glenearly
UK6930	Brandedleys
UK6950	Brighouse Bay
UK6990	Mortonhall *
UK7020	Aird Donald
UK7030	Gibson Park
UK7050	Edinburgh
UK7240	Lomond Wood
UK7270	Auchterarder
UK7400	Lochlands
UK7680	Glenmore *
UK7790	Invercoe *

Northern Ireland

UK8420	Tollymore Fore
UK8430	Banbridge *

Republic of Ireland

IR8740	Cong
IR8750	Belleek *
IR8810	Lough Lannag
IR9080	Forest Farm
IR9100	Camac Valley
IR9380	Parsons Green

Channel Islands

UK9870	Pomme de Chi

INSPECTE CAMPSIT & SELECTE

DOGS

For the benefit of those who want to take their dogs with them or for people who do not like dogs at the parks they visit, we list here the sites that have indicated to us that they do not accept dogs. If you are, however, planning to take your dog we do advise you to phone the park first to check – there my be limits on numbers, breeds, etc. or times of the year when they are excluded.

Never – these parks do not accept dogs at any time:

UK0200	Newquay	UK4220	Riverside	IR8770	Parkland
UK0250	Pentewan Sands	UK4100	Hoburne Cotswold	IR8890	The Tain
UK1130	Hoburne Torbay	UK4160	Christchurch	IR9410	The Apple
UK0870	Beverley Park	UK4530	Northcliffe	IR9500	The Meadow
UK1380	Blue Anchor	UK5550	Limefitt Park	IR9510	Eagle Point
UK1490	Greenacres	UK5980	Moreton Farm	UK9710	Rozel
UK2130	Grove Farm	UK6040	Pencelli Castle	UK9770	Vaugrat
UK2160	Harrow Wood	UK6350	Barcdy	UK9830	Seagull
UK2300	Ashurst	UK7290	Craigtoun Meadows	UK9870	Pomme de Chien
UK3120	Gate House Wood	UK7820	Oban Divers		
UK3050	Pine Lodge	UK8600	Bellemont		
UK3060	Yew Tree	IR8810	Lough Lannagh		

Sometimes – these parks do not accept dogs at certain times of the year:

UK0015	Rose Hill	not July/Aug	UK2510	Whitecliff Bay	not high season
UK0850	Galmpton	not mid July/Aug	UK6010	Cenarth Falls	not high season
UK1550	Bucklegrove	not high season	IR9100	Camac Valley	not July/Aug
UK2080	Merley Court	not 17/07-03/09	IR9150	River Valley	not July/Aug
UK2100	Sandford	not high season			

Maybe – accepted at any time but with certain restrictions:

UK0010	Chacewater	by arrangement	UK4200	The Boyce	by arrangement
UK0030	Ayr	1 only	UK4210	Lickhill Manor	by arrangement
UK0155	Tregarton	max 2	UK4300	Poston Mill	max 2
UK0490	Mullion	max 1	UK4400	Stanmore Hall	max 2
UK0690	Stowford Farm	max 2	UK4410	Beaconsfield	max 2
UK0710	Hidden Valley	max 2	UK4420	Severn Gorge	max 2
UK0760	Barley Meadow	max 2	UK4430	Oxon Hall	max 2
UK0950	River Dart	max 2	UK4520	Flower of May	by arrangement
UK1520	Waterrow	max 2	UK4630	Ripley	by arrangement
UK1540	Batcombe Vale	max 1	UK4640	Goose Wood	max 2
UK1575	Unity	max 2	UK4790	Bronte	max 2
UK1680	Plough Lane	max 2	UK5240	Lamb Cottage	max 2
UK1810	Newlands	max 2	UK5300	Kneps Farm	max 2
UK2100	Sandford	max 1	UK5330	Marton Mere	by arrangement
UK2250	Hoburne Bashley	max 1	UK5350	Holgates	by arrangement
UK2290	Sandy Balls	max 2	UK5360	Willowbank	max 2
UK2470	Southland	by arrangement	UK5710	Doe Park	by arrangement
UK2530	Waverley	max 2	UK5750	Waren	by arrangement
UK2620	Wysdom	max 2	UK5800	Ord House	by arrangement
UK2900	Horam Manor	max 2	UK5960	Abermarlais	max 2
UK3095	Little Satmar	max 1	UK6280	Aeron Coast	max 1
UK3110	Quex	max 1	UK6340	Pen-y-Bont	max 2
UK3420	Two Mills	max 2	UK6640	Home Farm	max 2
UK3430	Kelling Heath	max 2	UK6650	Hunters Hamlet	max 2
UK3485	Clippesby	max 1	UK6930	Brandedleys	max 2
UK3520	Searles	not all breeds	UK6960	Crossburn	max 2
UK3550	Old Manor	max 2	UK6990	Mortonhall	by arrangement
UK3650	Cherry Tree	max 3	UK7300	Blair Castle	max 2
UK3760	Tallington Lakes	max 2	UK7310	Twenty Shilling	max 2
UK3970	Glencote	max 2	UK7850	Linnhe Lochside	max 2
UK3980	Longnor Woods	max 2	IR9630	White Villa	max 2

FISHING

We are pleased to include details of parks which provide facilities for fishing on the site. Many other parks, particularly in Scotland and Ireland, are in popular fishing areas and have facilities within easy reach. Where we have been given details, we have included this information in the site reports. It is always best to contact parks to check that they provide for your individual requirements.

England

UK0060	River Valley
UK0170	Trevella
UK0220	Trevornick
UK0250	Pentewan Sands
UK0315	White Acres
UK0380	Wooda Farm
UK0530	Trethiggey
UK0750	Minnows
UK0790	Harford Bridge
UK0950	River Dart
UK0970	Cofton
UK1020	Oakdown
UK1060	Yeatheridge
UK1075	Golden Coast
UK1090	Peppermint Park
UK1390	Old Oaks
UK1420	Southfork
UK1460	Newton Mill
UK1480	Home Farm
UK1520	Waterrow
UK1540	Batcombe Vale
UK1570	Northam Farm
UK1575	Unity
UK1580	Warren Farm
UK1590	Exe Valley
UK1630	Brokerswood
UK1640	Greenhill Farm
UK1740	Golden Cap
UK1760	Wood Farm
UK1780	Freshwater Beach
UK2130	Grove Farm
UK2150	Woolsbridge
UK2290	Sandy Balls
UK2450	The Orchards
UK2510	Whitecliff Bay
UK2520	Thorness Bay
UK2530	Waverley
UK2700	Hurley
UK2810	Chertsey
UK2820	Horsley
UK2900	Horam Manor

UK2920	Bay View
UK2965	Brakes Coppice
UK3030	Tanner Farm
UK3210	Lee Valley
UK3290	Fen Farm
UK3300	Homestead Lake
UK3430	Kelling Heath
UK3440	Gatton Waters
UK3520	Searles
UK3760	Tallington Lakes
UK3940	Smeaton`s Lakes
UK3970	Glencote
UK4080	Riverside
UK4090	Island Meadow
UK4140	Winchcombe
UK4150	Croft Farm
UK4170	Tudor
UK4190	Kingsgreen
UK4200	The Boyce
UK4210	Lickhill Manor
UK4220	Riverside
UK4300	Poston Mill
UK4310	Luck's All
UK4320	Broadmeadow
UK4330	The Millpond
UK4380	Fernwood
UK4390	Westbrook
UK4410	Beaconsfield
UK4440	The Green
UK4500	Burton Constable
UK4510	Thorpe Hall
UK4610	Moorside
UK4640	Goose Wood
UK4790	Bronte
UK5280	Abbey Farm
UK5540	Fallbarrow
UK5600	Pennine View
UK5615	Hill of Oaks
UK5710	Doe Park

Wales

UK5880	Springwater
UK6040	Pencelli Castle
UK6250	Dolswydd
UK6345	Glanlynn
UK6670	The Plassey

Scotland

UK6890	Mossyard
UK6910	Hoddom Castle
UK6930	Brandedleys
UK6950	Brighouse Bay
UK7270	Auchterarder
UK7710	Ardmair Point
UK7720	Woodend
UK7740	Loch Greshornish
UK7800	Resipole
UK7850	Linnhe Lochside

Northern Ireland

UK8340	Drumaheglis
UK8550	Dungannon

Republic of Ireland

IR8770	Parkland
IR8960	Lough Ree
IR9630	White Villa

We understand that the following parks have bicycles to hire on site or can arrange for bicycles to be delivered. However, we would recommend that you contact the park to check as the situation can change.

England

UK0140	Penrose
UK0220	Trevornick
UK0250	Pentewan Sands
UK0360	Lakefield
UK0450	Pennance
UK0690	Stowford Farm
UK0750	Minnows
UK1075	Golden Coast
UK1390	Old Oaks
UK1400	Avalon
UK1490	Greenacres
UK1550	Bucklegrove
UK1575	Unity
UK2100	Sandford
UK2130	Grove Farm
UK2290	Sandy Balls
UK2350	Red Shoot
UK3330	Moat Barn
UK3370	Kessingland
UK3390	Dower House
UK3430	Kelling Heath
UK3560	Highfield Farm
UK4410	Beaconsfield
UK4560	Golden Square
UK4620	Upper Carr
UK5520	Skelwith Fold
UK5590	Westmorland
UK5800	Ord House

Wales

UK6040	Pencelli Castle

Scotland

UK6950	Brighouse Bay
UK7230	Trossachs
UK7240	Lomond Woods
UK7280	Nether Craig
UK7740	Loch Greshornish
UK7780	Faichem

Republic of Ireland

IR8740	Cong
IR8790	Carra
IR8810	Lough Lanagh
IR9130	Roundwood
IR9230	Nore Valley
IR9455	Adare
IR9590	Fossa
IR9630	White Villa

Channel Islands

UK9780	Fauxquets

GOLF

We understand that the following parks have facilities for playing golf on site. Where facilities are within easy reach and we have been given details, we have included this information in the individual site reports. However, we recommend that you contact the park to check that they meet your requirements.

UK0200	Newquay	UK2250	Hoburne Bashley	UK6670	The Plassey
UK0220	Trevornick	UK3230	Lee Valley	UK6900	Seaward
UK0380	Wooda Farm	UK3520	Searles Leisure	UK6910	Hoddom Castle
UK0690	Stowford Farm	UK4070	Somers Wood	UK6950	Brighouse Bay
UK1010	Lady's Mile	UK4300	Poston Mill		
UK1020	Oakdown	UK4520	Flower of May	IR9150	River Valley
UK1070	Woolacombe Bay	UK4710	Rudding Park		
UK1575	Holiday Unity	UK6330	Daisy Bank		

HORSE RIDING

We understand that the following parks have horse riding stables on site. Where facilities are within easy reach and we have been given details, we have included this information in the individual site reports. However, we recommend that you contact the park to check that they meet your requirements.

UK0360	Lakefield	UK1780	Freshwater Beach	UK2950	Washington
UK0690	Stowford Farm	UK2100	Sandford	UK6950	Brighouse Bay
UK1060	Yeatheridge	UK2290	Sandy Balls		
UK1370	Burrowhayes	UK2520	Thorness Bay	IR9160	Moat Farm
UK1575	Unity	UK2900	Horam Manor		

BOAT LAUNCHING

We understand that the following parks have boat slipways on site. Where facilities are within easy reach and we have been given details, we have included this information in the individual site reports. However, we recommend that you contact the park to check that they meet your requirements.

UK0250	Pentewan Sands	UK4080	Riverside	UK6950	Brighouse Bay
UK0750	Minnows	UK4150	Croft Farm	UK7710	Ardmair Point
UK1530	Slimeridge	UK4210	Lickhill Manor	UK7740	Loch Greshornish
UK1540	Batcombe Vale	UK4310	Luck's All	UK7800	Resipole
UK2510	Whitecliff Bay	UK4500	Burton Constable	UK7850	Linnhe Lochside
UK2520	Thorness Bay	UK5540	Fallbarrow	UK8340	Drumaheglis
UK2700	Hurley	UK5615	Hill of Oaks	IR8960	Lough Ree
UK3290	Fen Farm	UK6345	Glanlynn		
UK3760	Tallington Lakes	UK6890	Mossyard		

We list here the sites that have indicated to us that they do not accept children at any time during the year, at certain times, or in certain areas of their site.

The following parks have made the decision not to accept children:

UK0010	Chacewater (30 yrs+)	UK3440	Gatton Waters (18 yrs+)
UK0820	Moor View	UK3450	Little Haven
UK1390	The Old Oaks (18 yrs+)	UK3650	Cherry Tree
UK1510	Chew Valley	UK3980	Longnor Wood (18 yrs+)
UK1520	Waterrow (18 yrs+)	UK4070	Somers Wood
UK1590	Exe Valley (18 yrs+)	UK4410	Beaconsfield (21 yrs+)
UK1640	Greenhill Farm (18 yrs+)	UK4610	Moorside 16 yrs+)
UK1680	Plough Lane (21 yrs+)	UK4790	Bronte
UK1770	Binghams Farm	UK5510	The Larches
UK2620	Wysdom	UK5650	The Ashes (18 yrs+)
UK3420	Two Mills	UK6330	Daisy Bank

The following parks also do not accept children at certain times or in certain areas of their site:

UK0280	Powderham	UK4400	Stanmore Hall
UK3800	Highfields	UK4430	Oxon Hall
UK4380	Fernwood		

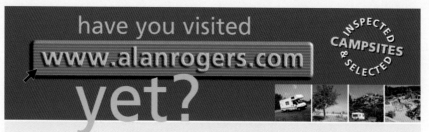
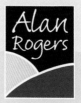

REPORTS BY READERS

We always welcome reports from readers concerning sites which they have visited. Generally reports provide us with invaluable feedback on parks already included in the Guide or, in the case of those not featured in our Guide, they provide information which we can follow up with a view to adding them in future editions. However, if you have a complaint about a site, this should be addressed to the campsite owner, preferably in person before you leave.

Please make your comments either on this form or on plain paper. It would be appreciated if you would indicate the approximate dates when you visited the park and, in the case of potential new parks, provide the correct name and address and, if possible, include a park brochure. Send your reports to:

Alan Rogers Guides, Spelmonden Old Oast, Goudhurst, Kent TN17 1HE

Name of Park and Ref. No. (or address for new recommendations)

_____

_____

Dates of visit: _____

Comments:

Reader's Name and Address: _____

_____

_____

_____

GERRY AND CHRIS BULLOCK'S PAGE

Who are they and why give them a page?

Gerry and Chris are both disabled. Chris has been a wheelchair user for many years and Gerry has, as he puts it, a bionic leg and wrist! For many years they have been involved with many aspects of camping and motor caravanning for the disabled with various publications – they were the original authors of the MMM Mobility Guide. They also assist people such as the National Trust regarding access difficulties and problems that arise. They visit cities around the country and assist local tourist boards regarding access reports.

Over the years Gerry and Chris have become 'experts' in finding parks that offer good facilities for the wheelchair users which are truly useable.

They have also looked very carefully at the Disabled Discrimination Act, which came into force this year, and have noted points that may be of relevance to site owners and of which they should be aware. Site owners need to be aware that from 2004 any services they offer to the general public, must also be accessible to the disabled, or at least the owner must offer an alternative – 'make reasonable adjustment to the service offered'.

For example:

A park with steps up to the shop – if a person in a wheelchair comes to the site the shop assistant will come out to greet the wheelchair user and get whatever they require and bring it to the customer. This is reasonable.

A park has an upstairs restaurant below which is the reception – if persons staying on the site using a wheelchair want a meal and a table and chairs are available in the reception and the site owner allows this to be used and food and drinks are brought down to them. Again, reasonable adjustment...

Here are some of the things they look for when inspecting sites:

- Access to the facilities block.
- Are there special facilities either for wheelchair users or walking disabled?
- The shower and its access for users?
- Handrails – are they adequate?
- Is there an emergency cord?

- En-suite or separate or just a W.C.?
- What does the room offer and is it suitable?
- What facilities are on offer?
- Sink – its height and the type of taps?
- Height of mirrors and other accessories?

They also look at the site from the wheelchair user's (non powered) point of view.

- Kerbs and paths
- Grass and general condition of the pitches

- Roads and their surfaces
- Access to other areas

Of course they look at all parks with the attitude that you cannot expect a small (say 20-30 pitch, private park) to offer the same quality or range of equipment as a large commercial or club-owned site. They recommend that disabled campers join one of the larger clubs, as their disabled rooms are usually of a very high standard. They also try to make disabled campers aware of one point – that "camping is still sleeping in a field", whether you are in a tent, a caravan or a motorhome; you will not find the same facilities as in your converted home, nor will not be all concrete and tarmac, with all rooms and areas accessible. These are things that may only be found in a specialist hotel. What Gerry and Chris try to do is offer a list of sites that have been inspected and that readers can rely on.

Please note: To ensure suitable pitching when you visit a campsite chosen to suit your needs, we would advise booking. Giving information of your requirements to the site means that they can place you as best as possible (but please be patient as it is hard to please everyone no matter how hard they try).

If readers require any further information, or have any suggestions, or any site owners need any assistance, Gerry and Chris would like to hear from you. Their address is:

97 Stalham Road, Hoveton, Norwich, Norfolk NR12 8EF Telephone: 01603 784152

NOTE. They are not looking at facilities for persons with special needs. They leave this to the such people as the Sue Ryder Foundation, etc. which cater very well in this field.

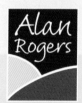

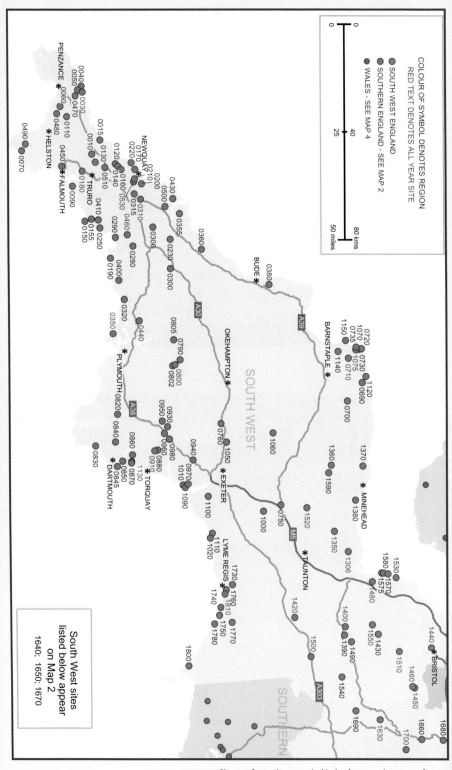

COLOUR OF SYMBOL DENOTES REGION
RED TEXT DENOTES ALL YEAR SITE

- SOUTH WEST ENGLAND
- SOUTHERN ENGLAND - SEE MAP 2
- WALES - SEE MAP 4

SOUTH WEST

SOUTHERN

South West sites
listed below appear
on Map 2
1640; 1650; 1670

Please refer to the numerical index for campsite page reference

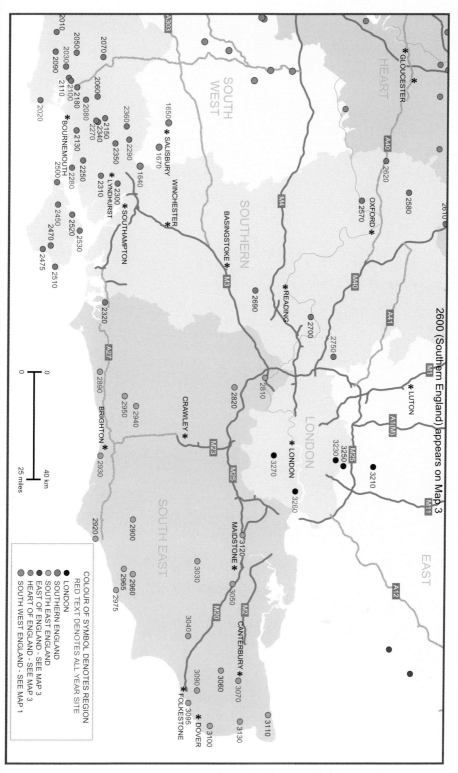

2600 (Southern England) appears on Map 3

*GLOUCESTER
*

A303

HEART

SOUTH
WEST

SOUTHERN

A40

2620

OXFORD *
2570

2580

2610

LONDON

EAST

A41

*LUTON

A1(M)

M1

M25

3230
3250
3220

3210

M11

A12

2010
2030
2090
2110
2050
2100
2070
2060
2180
2080
2040
2130
2340
2270
2150
2350
2290
2310
2280
2250
2180
2360
2020

*BOURNEMOUTH

2500

2260

2450
2520
2530
2470
2475
2510

1650
1670
1640

*SALISBURY

*WINCHESTER
*

2320

A27

BASINGSTOKE *

M3

2690

M4

*READING

2700

2750

2890

BRIGHTON *
2930

2950
2940

CRAWLEY
*

M23

2820
2810

3270

*LONDON
3260

M25

2920

2900
2960
2965
2975

3030

3040

MAIDSTONE *
3120
3050

CANTERBURY *
3070
3095
3090
3060

3100
3130
3110

*DOVER
*FOLKESTONE

M20

M2

SOUTH
EAST

A303
SOUTHAMPTON
LYNDHURST
0

0   40 km

25 miles

COLOUR OF SYMBOL DENOTES REGION
RED TEXT DENOTES ALL YEAR SITE

● LONDON
● SOUTHERN ENGLAND
● SOUTH EAST ENGLAND
● EAST OF ENGLAND - SEE MAP 3
● HEART OF ENGLAND - SEE MAP 3
● SOUTH WEST ENGLAND - SEE MAP 1

Please refer to the numerical index for campsite page reference

317

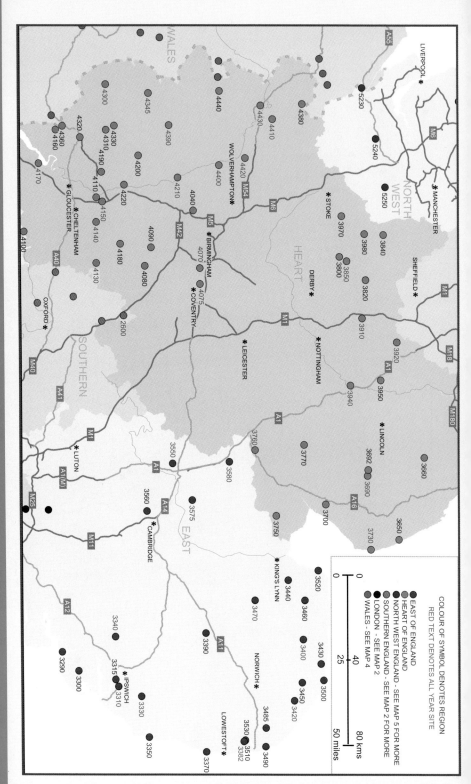

Please refer to the numerical index for campsite page reference

COLOUR OF SYMBOL DENOTES REGION
RED TEXT DENOTES ALL YEAR SITE

- EAST OF ENGLAND
- HEART OF ENGLAND
- NORTH WEST ENGLAND - SEE MAP 5 FOR MORE
- SOUTHERN ENGLAND - SEE MAP 2 FOR MORE
- LONDON - SEE MAP 2
- WALES - SEE MAP 4

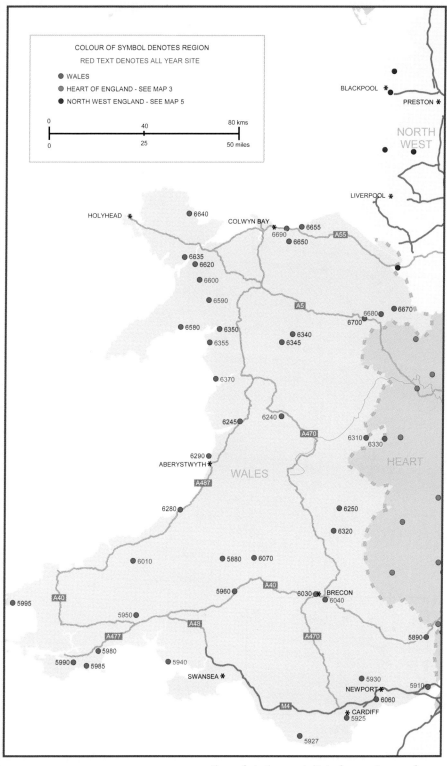

Please refer to the numerical index for campsite page reference

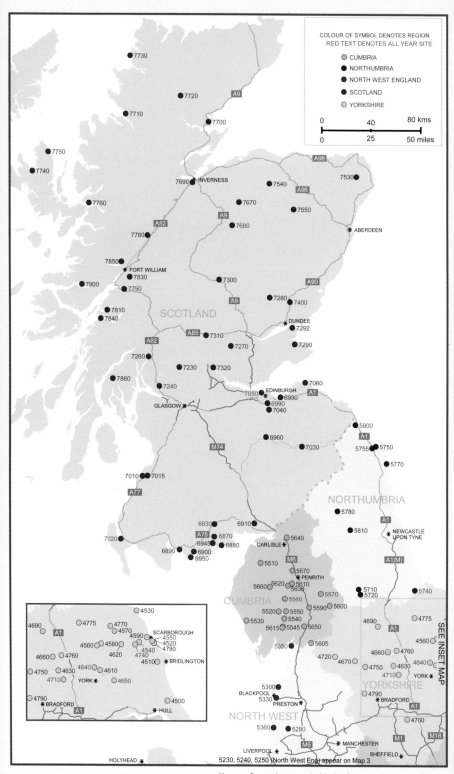

COLOUR OF SYMBOL DENOTES REGION
RED TEXT DENOTES ALL YEAR SITE

- CUMBRIA
- NORTHUMBRIA
- NORTH WEST ENGLAND
- SCOTLAND
- YORKSHIRE

0   40   80 kms
0   25   50 miles

7730
7720
7710
7700
A9
7750
7740
7760
7690 INVERNESS   7540   7530
A98
A96
7670
7550
A82   7680   A9
7780   ABERDEEN
7850
FORT WILLIAM   7830
7800   7790
7810   7300   A90
7840   7280 7400
SCOTLAND   A9
A82   A85 7310   DUNDEE   7292
7260   7270   7290
7230   7320
7860   7240
7060
7050 EDINBURGH   A1
6980
GLASGOW   6990
7040
5800
A1
6960   5755 5750
7030   5770
7010 7015
A77
NORTHUMBRIA
5780
6930   6910   5810
7020   A75   6870   NEWCASTLE
6945   6880   CARLISLE   5640   UPON TYNE
6890   6900   A1(M)
6950   5510   M6
5670
PENRITH   5710
5660   5620   5610   5720   5740
CUMBRIA   5630
5560   5570
5520   5550   5590   5600
5530   5540
5615   5545 5650
5350   5605
4720   4670
BLACKPOOL   5300
5330   PRESTON
NORTH WEST
5360   5280
LIVERPOOL   MANCHESTER
SHEFFIELD
5230, 5240, 5250 (North West Eng) appear on Map 3

4530
4690   4775   4770
A1   4570
4560   4580   4590   SCARBOROUGH
4540   4520
4620   4740   4780
4660   4760   4510   BRIDLINGTON
4750   4630   4640   4610
47110   YORK   4650
4790   BRADFORD
A1
4500
HULL
HOLYHEAD

4690   A1   4775
4560
4660   4760
4750   4630   4640
4710   YORK
4790
BRADFORD
A1
4700
YORKSHIRE
SEE INSET MAP
M1
M18

Please refer to the numerical index for campsite page reference

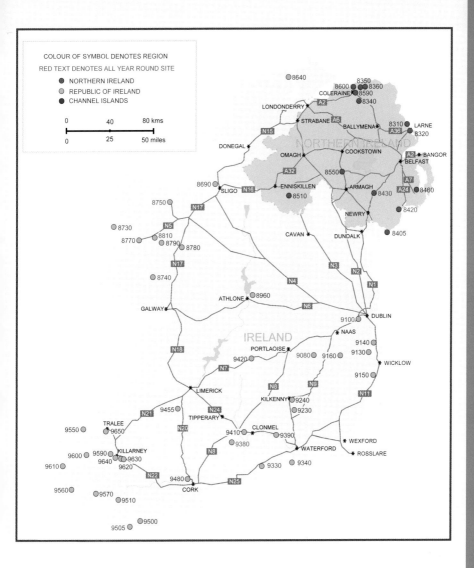

COLOUR OF SYMBOL DENOTES REGION

RED TEXT DENOTES ALL YEAR ROUND SITE

● NORTHERN IRELAND
○ REPUBLIC OF IRELAND
● CHANNEL ISLANDS

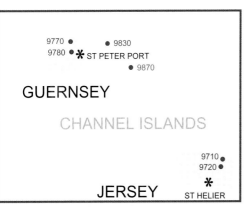

9770 ●   ● 9830
9780 ●✱ ST PETER PORT
            ● 9870

GUERNSEY

CHANNEL ISLANDS

9710 ●
9720 ●

JERSEY   ✱ ST HELIER

Please refer to the numerical index for campsite page reference

Wales

Scotland

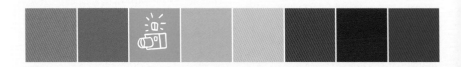

England

South West England

Cornwall

Devon

Somerset

INSPECTED CAMPSITES SELECTED

East of England

Essex

Suffolk

Norfolk

Cambridgeshire

Heart of England

Lincolnshire

Nottinghamshire

Derbyshire

Staffordshire

Warwickshire

West Midlands

Worcestershire

Gloucestershire

Herefordshire

Shropshire

Yorkshire

IMAGES We would like to thank the following Tourist Boards for supplying images for this guide:

Somerset Tourist Board	North West Tourist Board
South West Tourist Board	Cumbria Tourist Board
Southern Tourist Board	Northumbria Tourist Board
Southeast Tourist Board	Wales Tourist Board
London Tourist Board	Scotland Tourist Board
East of England Tourist Board	Ireland Tourist Board
Heart of England Tourist Board	Jersey Tourism
Yorkshire Tourist Board	British Tourist Authority

Tell Us About the Alan Rogers Guides!

We're keen to constantly improve our service to you and the key to this is information. If we don't know what makes our readers 'tick' then it's difficult to offer you more of what you want.

WIN A COMPLETE SET OF ALAN ROGERS GUIDES

Return this completed questionnaire and you could win a complete set of 2006 Alan Rogers Guides. Why not complete an on-line version of this? Go to www.alanrogers.com/feedback

About the Alan Rogers Guides

1 For how many years have you used the Alan Rogers Guides?

Never	1-2 yrs	3-6 yrs	7-10 yrs	Over 10 yrs

2 How frequently do you refer to it?

Never	Each year	Every 2 yrs	Every 3 yrs

3 How frequently do you buy a new copy?

Never	Each year	Every 2 yrs	Every 3 yrs

4 If you lend it to friends, how many others might refer to it?

1	2	3	4	Over 4

5 Please rate the Alan Rogers Guides on a scale of 1–10 where 10 is excellent and 1 is extremely poor

1	2	3	4	5	6	7	8	9	10

6 Do you have any comments about the Alan Rogers Guides?

....

....

7 What do you consider to be the best thing about the guides?

Independent reviews	Honest descriptions	Accurate information	Range of sites	Depth of information

Other ....

8 What do you consider to be the worst thing about the guides?

....

9 How many sites featured in the guides have you visited in the past? *(best estimate)* ....

10 Can you comment on any other campsite guides?

Title .... Your opinion ....

About Your Holidays

11 a) Do you own any of the following?

Caravan	Motorhome	Trailer Tent	Tent

Other *(please specify)* ....

b) How many times a year do you use it?

1	2-3	4-6	7-10	More than 10

12 When on holiday, do you participate in any of the following?

Fishing	Golf	Cycling	Sailing/Boating	Walking	Bird Watching

Other *(please specify)* ....

13 How many years have you been camping / caravanning?

3 yrs or less	4 – 7 yrs	8 – 12 yrs	13 – 15 yrs	16 – 20 yrs	Over 20 yrs

About You

Mr/Mrs/Ms, etc.   Initial   Surname

Address

                                                  Post code

e-mail address   @   Telephone

14 **Your age**   30 and under   31-50   51-65   Over 65

15 **Do you have children – if so, how old is the youngest?**
                                          6 and under   7-12   Over 12

16 **Do you work (full or part time)?**   Yes   No

17 **Are you retired?**   Yes   No

About Your Leisure Time

18 **Are you a member of any caravan/motorhome clubs?**
The Caravan Club   The Camping & Caravanning Club   The Motor Caravanners Club

Other *(please specify)*

19 **Are you a member of the following?**
          National Trust   English Heritage   RSPB   CSMA   Ramblers

20 **Which (if any) camping/caravanning magazines do you read regularly?**
          MMM   Practical   Practical   Caravan   Which   Motor-   Caravan
                   Motorhome   Caravan   Life   Motorcaravan   caravan

21 **Which other magazines do you read regularly?**

22 **Which newspapers do you read regularly?**
          Express   Mail   Telegraph   Times   Guardian   Observer   Sun

Other (please specify)

23 **Do you enjoy any particular hobbies?** *(please specify)*

24 **Do you have regular access to the internet?**   Yes   No

   If yes, which camping/caravanning websites do you visit regularly?

And Finally

25 **Do you have any useful camping/caravanning tips?**

26 **If you could change one thing about camping/caravanning holidays what would it be?**

We may wish to publish your comments, please tick this box if you would prefer us not to.

Might you be interested in becoming an Alan Rogers site inspector?
If so, please tick the box and we will send you further information

Camping Cheque and Alan Rogers may use this data to send you information and Special Offers.
Please tick here if you do not wish to receive such information

Thank you very much for your time and trouble in completing this questionnaire
Please return to: Alan Rogers Travel Service, FREEPOST NAT17734, Cranbrook, TN17 1BR